A New Understanding o

M.R. Haberfeld · Agostino von Hassell
Editors

A New Understanding of Terrorism

Case Studies, Trajectories
and Lessons Learned

 Springer

Editors
M.R. Haberfeld
City University of New York
John Jay College of Criminal
   Justice
899 Tenth Ave.
New York NY 10019
USA
mhaberfeld@jjay.cuny.edu

Agostino von Hassell
399 Park Ave., 26th Floor
New York NY 10022
The Repton Group LLC
USA
avonhassell@thereptongroup.com

ISBN 978-1-4419-0114-9 (hardcover)   e-ISBN 978-1-4419-0115-6
ISBN 978-1-4419-8374-9 (softcover)
DOI 10.1007/978-1-4419-0115-6
Springer Dordrecht Heidelberg London New York

Library of Congress Control Number: 2009928507

Printed on acid-free paper

Springer is part of Springer Science+Business Media (www.springer.com)

To my daughters, Nellie and Mia, for whom I will always strive to contribute to the creation of a less violent world.

Maria (Maki) R. Haberfeld

To the U.S. Marines KIA 23 October 1983 in Beirut

And the French Foreign Legionnaires, Nos Frères

Agostino von Hassell

Preface

Through the review of numerous terrorist events and scenarios, some in distant places and times, this book presents the reader with a unique perspective of looking at terrorist incidents that took place in many countries and were perpetrated by individuals who had just one thing in common – they were the minority in a majority world. A grieved minority, whose claims and motivation are understood by some and rejected by others yet, in the grand scheme of things, they managed to change the way we should be thinking about and react to the phenomenon of terrorism.

The chapters of this volume represent a wide range of time lines and situations that brought about the actions of the actors involved in the attacks. It is not our aim or goal to judge their causes and motivations but it is our goal to enable the reader to gain a much broader perspective on the understanding of terrorism, one that is not rooted in or focused on one particular religion, geographic location, or time line. It was Fredrick Hacker who divided the terrorist's motivation into three, very broad, categories: criminals, crusaders, or crazies. Although the definitions are very helpful while dealing with terrorist involved in various hostage situations, on a daily level they do not further our understanding or who and why we are dealing with. Hopefully, this volume will provide the reader with a more comprehensive understanding of the Have Nots – the ones who have some sort of grievances against the Haves and yet the only way that appears plausible to them to resolve these grievance is through the path of violence that more frequently than not is covered with bodies of innocent victims. Furthermore, at the end of the day, in the overwhelming majority of the cases, the grievances remain still unresolved. We do not presume that through the analysis of what happened we will be able to resolve the grievances but, if we are able to prepare and react in a way that will minimize the intended damage then the creation of this book will be well justified.

The idea of looking at the terrorist events and through their analysis arrive at a generic template of response is rooted in our background, both distant and more recent. We both looked at the ugly face of terrorism in an up closed and personal manner, from Lebanon to Israel we saw the carnage, the victims, and the pain. We both carry the scars of the images that will forever stay with us and define our way of thinking about and understanding of terrorism.

This was the past that influenced our more recent present, when we taught the New York Police Department's (NYPD) officers at John Jay College in New York

City in the counter-terrorism class and learned as much from their insights and perceptions as much as they learned from us. In a way it was our way of giving back and trying to cope with the images imprinted in our hearts and minds.

Egon Bittner, a renowned scholar in the field of policing, in his attempt to explain the nature of police work stated that policing is needed when "Something – ought-not- to – be- happening- about- which – something- ought- to – be- done – NOW!"

We wish you, the reader, an insightful journey throughout many places where things happened – that ought not to be happening about which something ought to be done right now! We hope that this intellectual journey will be translated into a practical implementation where the root causes of the problems will be treated and responded to with words and not with guns or explosives.

New York, NY, USA

Maria (Maki) R. Haberfeld
Agostino von Hassell

Acknowledgments

It is probably the most gratifying stage in the creation of a book, when the authors or editors can finally put together a few words of gratitude to all those who helped us make our visions come true.

We would like to start with thanking one of the original three editors, Dr. Heath Grant who, for personal reasons, needed to withdraw from this project. As always, Heath was a partner in thinking and outlining the ideas presented in this book and we missed his input and contributions during the years of struggle to complete the volume that was first conceptualized almost 5 years ago.

To the many reviewers of the manuscript, in its various stages of incompletion, our entire gratitude is extended, as usual, the ones who help in shaping the final product are always in the shadow but, we would like to acknowledge the fact that without the many helpful comments this book would have not reached its production stage.

Needless to say, that all this would not have been possible without the amazing vision of the Senior Editor Welmoed Spahr and her wonderful Editorial Assistant Theresa Culver and the entire editorial and production team of Springer. We are forever grateful for affording us the opportunity to see our ideas in a format that will allow us to spread them around the world.

It goes without saying that the volume contributors deserve all the appreciations for their diligence and patience over the years it took us to finalize this project. Our chief gratitude goes to one of the contributors, Dr. Charles Lieberman, who offered much of his time and effort to shape the final product.

The concluding words of the acknowledgment go to the ones who shape our way of thinking and acting on a daily basis, and who enable us to make a miniscule dent in our struggle to make a difference.

Contents

Contributors

Book Editors

Maria (Maki) R. Haberfeld is a professor of Police Science, in the Department of Law, Police Science and Criminal Justice Administration at John Jay College of Criminal Justice in New York City. She was born in Poland and immigrated to Israel as a teenager. During her army service in the Israeli Defense Force, she was assigned to a special counter-terrorist unit that was created to prevent terrorist attacks in Israel. She left the army at the rank of a Sergeant.

Prior to coming to John Jay she served in the Israel National Police, and left the force at the rank of Lieutenant. She also worked for the U.S. Drug Enforcement Administration, in the New York Field Office, as a special consultant.

She holds two Bachelor or Art degrees, two Master degrees, and a Ph.D. in Criminal Justice. Her research interests and publications are in the areas of private and public law enforcement, training, police integrity, and comparative policing. She has also done some research in the area of white-collar crime, specifically organizational and individual corruption during the Communist era in Eastern Europe. For 4 years, 1997 through 2001, she has been a member of the research team, sponsored by the National Institute of Justice, studying police integrity in three major police departments in the United States.

Between the years 1999 and 2003 she was also a principal investigator of the National Institute of Justice sponsored research project in Poland, where she studied the Polish National Police and its transformation to community-oriented policing. Her recent publications include a book on police training, titled *Critical Issues in Police Training* (2002), her co-edited book, titled *Contours of Police Integrity* (2004) features an overview of police misconduct in 14 countries, an edited volume of an *Encyclopedia of Law Enforcement*, the International Volume (2005) covers entries on police forces from over 120 countries, a book on 17 prominent police chiefs in the United States titled *Police Leadership* (2005), co-authored, book *Enhancing Police Integrity* (2006) depicts three case studies of police departments that are characterized by high levels of professional integrity, a co-edited book on *Comparative Policing: The Struggle for Democratization* (2007) and a co-authored book *Counter-terrorism in Comparative and International Context* (forthcoming,

Fall 2009). In addition, she is an author or co-author of numerous book chapters, journal articles, and research reports in the areas of her expertise.

For the last 8 years (2001–2009) she has been involved in developing, coordinating, and teaching in a special training program for the New York City Police Department. Professor Haberfeld has developed a graduate course, titled "Counterterrorism policies for law enforcement" which is taught by her at John Jay, to the ranking officers of the New York Police Department. Between the years 2004 and 2008 she was also an academic coordinator of the Law Enforcement Executive Police Institute for the State of New York, where she oversaw the delivery of the training modules and taught leadership courses. She is involved in two major research studies, one on Use of Force by the Police in 10 different countries, and the other Counter-Terrorism police training response post 9/11, which also involves comparative studies of a number of countries around the world. mhaberfeld@jjay.cuny.edu

Agostino von Hassell spent his formative years in the United States, studying European History at Columbia University graduating with a B.A. in 1974. He then attended Columbia Journalism School, graduating with awards in 1975. After Columbia he worked for a trade magazine in New York. In addition he freelanced for *Newsweek* in 1976 and was published in *The Marine Corps Gazette, Die Zeit* (Germany), *Naval Proceedings, Defense News, The Navy Times,* and others.

He is the author of three military histories (published by Howell Press, Inc., Charlottesville, Virginia): *Warriors: The United States Marine Corps* (published first in 1988); *Strike Force: Marine Corps Special Operations* (1990). In 2003 he published along with Herm Dillon a book on the bicentennial of the United States Military Academy under the title *West Point: The Bicentennial Book.* In 2004 he published in *Honor of America,* a small photo book.

In September 2006, he published *Military High Life:* an illustrated book on elegant military food through the ages. On November 14, 2006, St. Martin's Press in New York released *Alliance of Enemies: The Untold Story of the Secret American and German Collaboration to End World War II,* a book on the secret contacts between the OSS and Germany's Abwehr in World War II.

Hassell is a life member of the United States Marine Corps Combat Correspondents, the National Defense Industry Association, the American Society of Magazine Photographers, the Marine Corps Law Enforcement Foundation, and the Authors Guild.

He is now the president of The Repton Group LLC, a New York City consulting group that deals mostly with national security issues. Hassell has been an adjunct professor in the NYPD Program at John Jay College, teaching subjects as diverse as leadership and counter-terrorism for law enforcement. avonhassell@thereptongroup.com

Chapter Contributors

Rebecca Bucht is currently in the final year of her Ph.D. in Criminal Justice with a specialization in Forensic Science at the Graduate Center of CUNY. Her research interests lie in the integration of forensic science data into investigative and intelligence applications. She has been teaching in the Science Department of John Jay College of Criminal Justice since 2004. Prior to moving to New York, she completed B.Sc in Forensic Science at the University of Glamorgan in Wales, UK. rbuch@jjay.cuny.edu

Serguei Cheloukhine is an assistant professor of the Department of Law, Police Science and Criminal Justice Administration at John Jay College of Criminal Justice. He holds degrees in Comparative Politics from York University, Canada, and the Russian President Academy of Public Administrations. Cheloukhine worked as a police officer in Caucasus and Chechnya and professor at Rostov-on-Don Law School (former Police Academy) from 1987 to 1995. From 1998 to 2001, he was the first Russian police officer working at the Nathanson Center for the Study of Organized Crime and Corruption (Canada) where, as a researcher, Cheloukhine participated in projects that studied Russian organized crime, corruption, money laundering, and terrorism. scheloukhine@jjay.cuny.edu

Kirsten Christiansen is a doctoral student in Criminal Justice at The Graduate Center of the City University of New York. She holds a B.A. in Psychology and Social Work from the University of Wisconsin-Madison and an M.A. in Criminal Justice from John Jay College of Criminal Justice. Her research interests include legal and constitutional issues surrounding the policing of protest activity and the use of public space. She is currently working on her dissertation on policing and the anti-war movement in New York City. kjaysi@yahoo.com

Tonya M. DeSa is a doctoral student in Criminal Justice at The Graduate Center of the City University of New York. She holds B.A. degrees in Psychology and Recreational Leadership from Alderson-Broaddus College, Philippi, WV, a J.D. from West Virginia University College of Law, Morgantown, WV, and a M.A. from John Jay College of Criminal Justice, New York, NY. Her dissertation research examines child abductors who have killed their victims. She has spent the last 12 years as a special agent with the Federal Bureau of Investigation (FBI) and continues to serve in that capacity. She is currently assigned to the Newark Division of the FBI as the Training Coordinator and also serves the New Jersey law enforcement community as the Primary Coordinator for the National Center for the Analysis of Violent Crime, based in Quantico, VA. tdesa555@yahoo.com

Albert Gamarra was born in Brooklyn, New York. His various work experiences range from law firms to high-profile government agencies such as the U.S. Marshals. He graduated with a B.A. in International Criminal Justice from the City University of New York-John Jay College of Criminal Justice. He also received a Masters degree in Criminal Justice from CUNY-John Jay College. Currently he is a fifth year student in the Doctoral program in Criminal Justice at the Graduate Center of the City University of New York. tito1183@hotmail.com

Courtney Hougham is a Ph.D. student in Criminal Justice at CUNY Graduate Center/John Jay College of Criminal Justice in New York City. Her research focus is primarily on the juror's ability to disregard inadmissible evidence. She has a B.A. in Psychology from Grinnell College in Iowa and an M.A. in Psychology from New York University. She is an adjunct lecturer in Undergraduate Statistics at John Jay College. She also works for the Jury Research Division of the New York State Unified Court System. cah254@nyu.edu

Ji Hyon Kang received her Ph.D. in Criminal Justice from John Jay College/CUNY Center, CUNY. Her dissertation research examines the impact of crime victimization on residents' involvement in social control considering the effects of neighborhood conditions. Her research agenda presently centers on crime and community, family violence/elder abuse, victims' reporting behavior, and quantitative analysis. jihyonkang@yahoo.com

William LaRaia is an adjunct professor in the Department of Law, Police Science, and Criminal Justice at John Jay College of Criminal Justice in New York City. He received his Masters degree in Administrative Science from Fairleigh Dickinson University and his Bachelor of Science in Police Studies from John Jay College of Criminal Justice. A 23 year veteran of the Englewood Cliffs Police Department (NJ), he serves as Lieutenant and is assigned to Patrol and heads the Training Division. Lt. LaRaia is a police academy instructor and a graduate of the West Point Command & Leadership Program and an instructor in this program. He teaches at the undergraduate level for the NYPD Leadership Certificate Program. His theoretical interests include police administration and organization, police leadership and supervision, police ethics, and police training. wlaria@jjay.cuny.edu

Charles A. Lieberman is a faculty member at John Jay College of Criminal Justice in the Department of Law, Police Science and Criminal Justice Administration. Prior to joining academia, he served with the NYPD, from 1990 to 2005, and was involved with investigative duties for 12 of his 15 years. His main research interests include crime prevention, policing, and terrorism. Charles recently completed a research project that examines the feasibility of employing community policing as a counter-terrorism tactic. He also recently completed work on a grant from the

National Institute of Justice and has published in the fields of policing and terrorism. clieberman@jjay.cuny.edu

Jon R. Lindsay is a doctoral candidate in the Massachusetts Institute of Technology Department Political Science, Security Studies Program. His research focus is on the evolution of military technology and institutions and secondarily on counterinsurgency and civil war. He has served as an intelligence officer with the U.S. Navy for 12 years in Europe, Latin America, and the Middle East, recently completing a tour in Iraq's Anbar Province. lindsayj@mit.edu

Brian A. Maule is an adjunct lecturer of Sociology at John Jay College of Criminal Justice in New York City. He was born in Saint Vincent and the Grenadines and immigrated to the United States as a teenager. He holds an M.B.A. from Baruch College, an M.A. in Criminal Justice from John Jay College and is in the Ph.D. program at City University of New York's Graduate Center. Maule has taught at the Intermediate High School in Saint Vincent and at John Jay College in New York. His research interests and publications are in the areas of terrorism and policing in the United States and the Caribbean. bmaule@law.nyc.gov

Kevin E. McCarthy received his A.B. from Harvard, J.D. from Fordham, and M.A. from John Jay College of Criminal Justice, and he continues studies in the doctoral program in Criminal Justice at the City University of New York while teaching at John Jay. He spent over 20 years as a criminal prosecutor, first at the New York County District Attorney's Office, then at the United States Attorney's Office in New Jersey where he served as Chief of the Organized Crime Strike Force Division. kmccarthy@jjay.cuny.edu

Meredith L. Patten background includes working as an assistant research professor/applied criminologist, on site in Trinidad and Tobago, evaluating reform initiatives with the Police Service, a Guggenheim Graduate Fellowship assisting journalists with understanding crime statistics, and research on a variety of issues including the criminal backgrounds of the domestic far right, the Catholic Church abuse scandal, and death penalty research for Human Rights Watch. She holds an AB in Politics/International Relations from Occidental College, an MS in Justice, Law, and Society from The American University, and an M.Phil. from The Graduate Center, City University of New York. merepatten@gmail.com

Jon M. Shane is an assistant professor in the Department of Law and Police Science at John Jay College of Criminal Justice in New York City. Dr. Shane received his Ph.D. in criminal justice from Rutgers University, School of Criminal Justice. His research interests include violent crime, police policy and practice, and environmental criminology. His theoretical interests include situational crime prevention, routine activities, and social disorganization. jmsnpd@comcast.net

Staci Strobl is an assistant professor in the Department of Law, Police Science and Criminal Justice Administration at John Jay College of Criminal Justice. Her areas of specialization are policing in the Middle East and comic book portrayals of crime in the United States. She was the recipient of a Fulbright grant to Bahrain where she completed an ethnographic study of policewomen. Earlier in her career, she worked as a U.S. Probation Officer and a crime journalist. Dr. Strobl completed her doctorate in Criminal Justice at the City University of New York's Graduate Center, received her M.A. in Criminal Justice at John Jay, and her B.A. in Near Eastern Studies at Cornell University. strobl@jjay.cuny.edu

Amanda S. Twilliger (Wu) is a criminologist pursuing her degree at The Graduate Center, City University of New York. Her interests include crime and deviance and forensic psychology. She holds a B.A. from Trinity College and is currently living in London, England. awu1@hotmail.com

Michael C. Walker is the former police director of the Paterson (New Jersey) Police Department, where he oversaw a force of 500 sworn and 100 civilian personnel and a budget of approximately $49 million. He had retired from that Department with the rank of Police Captain. He is a graduate of the 170th Session of the F.B.I. National Academy. He has earned a Bachelor of Science degree in Criminal Justice Administration from the William Paterson University of New Jersey and a Master degree in Public Administration, with a concentration in Criminal Justice Policy, from the City University of New York, John Jay College of Criminal Justice. Michael is an assistant professor of Criminal Justice at the Passaic County Community College in Paterson and is an adjunct professor at the John Jay College of Criminal Justice in New York City. He has lectured both internationally and throughout the United States on topics related to Police Leadership and Police Training. His current research includes policing in emerging democracies, police use of force, and international comparisons of crime. mwalker@pccc.edu

Scott G. White is a librarian for the City University of New York (CUNY), LaGuardia Community College and a Ph.D. student in Criminal Justice at John Jay College, CUNY. In addition to the chapter included in this volume, he has written about the USA Patriot Act and Fourth Amendment issues surrounding the surveillance of Internet communications. swhite@lagcc.cuny.edu

Chapter 1
Today's Terrorism – Introduction and Analysis: The Have Nots Versus the Haves

M.R. Haberfeld

The Have Nots Versus the Haves

The multiple definitions of terrorism as a phenomenon, or terrorists as actors involved in the way this phenomenon is perceived and reacted to by populations of many countries around the Globe, do not appear to be conducive to our understanding of what is happening, who is responsible for it, and how to counter and prevent or, in general, respond to what many perceive as an existential threat to the world we know. Over the past couple of decades, but more intensively since the events of September 11, 2001, scholars, politicians, military leaders, and practically every informed or interested party came out with some sort of "final" and "comprehensive" definition as to what constitutes an act of terror or what kind of activities one needs to be engaged in to be labeled as a terrorist or a freedom fighter for that matter. This abundance of verbiage is not very helpful in our individual or collective understanding of terrorism or terrorists and one may claim that it is counterproductive to us ever coming even close to the understanding what and who we are dealing with.

Being a pragmatist in nature, this author chose to address the issue through the prism of effective countermeasures, policies, and responses. In order to prevent, prepare, and respond effectively, there is a clear need to understand what exactly we need to prevent, prepare for, and respond to once it happens. No current definition offers this encompassing understanding, hence the proposed clarification of concepts that may, hopefully, proved to be more user friendly for those in charge of prevention, preparedness and response. At the risk of being criticized by those who are more academically oriented and will not find in this characterization enough research oriented depth the following is being proposed:

> Terrorist can be defined as individuals who have some sort of a grievance against the larger society in which they live, either physically or identify with conceptually. They represent a

M.R. Haberfeld (✉)
Department of Law, Police Science and Criminal Justice Administration, John Jay College of Criminal Justice, New York, NY, USA
e-mail: mhaberfeld@jjay.cuny.edu

M.R. Haberfeld, A. von Hassell (eds.), *A New Understanding of Terrorism*,
DOI 10.1007/978-1-4419-0115-6_1, © Springer Science+Business Media, LLC 2009

minority in the majority world dominated by those who have or claim to have this that the minority do not have or claim not to have. These **Have Nots (the minority)** seek to acquire what the majority (**The Haves**) claim to have or/and the Have Nots also seek to disrupt or destroy whatever it is that The Haves claim to have and enjoy. It is a battle of the Have Nots versus Haves and their weapon is Fear.

If we accept the above definition, we will have to acknowledge that the range of responses, in terms of prevention and preparedness, becomes much wider than we would like to accept or admit. However, this asymmetric approach to understanding the phenomenon of terrorism is very much in sync with what others have already written about and addressed from the conceptual standpoint; however, their thoughts and ideas were never really translated into operational realities. Rosenau (2003) compared the phenomenon of terrorism to a cascade, a term derived from physics and other sciences, where the cascade represents a water fall that flows in a way that is very much unpredictable in terms of its scope, duration, and intensity. Comparing terrorism to a water cascade gives it a lot of justice since we do react to any given terrorist act in a way that is truly unpredictable, generates reaction and overreactions that last for years if not for decades; these reactions penetrate into various systems and sub-systems and the consequences are truly beyond and above what makes sense and is required. Although each terrorist event is different in its nature, scope, and intensity, we tend to prevent and respond in a way that is uniformed and predefined, almost a generic template for all and everything while we are dealing, each time, with different actors and different situations that have only one thing in common – The Have Nots acting against the Haves.

As the author of the Locus of Error Theory (Sahni, 2003) pointed out, we have the tendency to focus and iconize specific terrorist groups or actors, and as a result of this we customize our response based on these images that were created by us and have very little to do with reality. This Locus of Error Theory prompts us to respond in a distorted way, on an operational but possibly also on a conceptual level, to events and individuals that require a totally different response technique. The misdirected initiatives and clumsy responses in which we involve ourselves from the law enforcement, military, and policy-making angles do not produce what we hope for and frequently claim that they produce. One should not wait till the London bombings incident to start paying attention to the grievances of the locally born population or till the carnage in Mumbai to devise a contingency training and plan to respond to an operation of that scope and intensity. We should not assume that what happened in the past will repeat itself in the future in the identical manner nor we should ignore the vital signs of discontent displayed by the Have Nots. As Antoine de Saint-Exupery (1943) noted that it is not up to us to predict the future but it is our duty to enable it, we must start looking at the phenomenon of terrorism and the actors involved in various incidents from the prism of Have Nots acting against the Haves and prepare our responses accordingly. As the Locus of Error Theory imposes on many governments and its military and law enforcement agencies a particular theory and pattern of response, Sahni (2003) very insightfully stresses that it also predefines the stage of appropriate counter-terrorism response, at a point that occurs well after a particular terrorist activity and operational planning has crystallized and secured a high level of lethality, while often ignoring the problem until an exceptionally outrageous terrorist attack makes it impossible to disregard the threat.

In order to move away from the errors of judgments we engage in while, following the principles of the Locus of Error Theory, we need to look at a sample of activities perpetrated by the Have Nots and through the analysis of their motivations, the attacks, and finally the governmental response, devise a way in which we can prevent as much as possible, react as effectively as needed, and respond with an eye toward the future rather than toward the past. We are, after all – The Haves.

The Conceptual Themes Through A Pragmatic Lens

Haberfeld and von Hassell introduce the readers to the new conceptual framework of understanding the acts, the actors, and the responders. In their chapter on the Proper Response to Counter – Terrorism in Urban Environments, the authors build upon the notions of the threat being very amorphous and lacking proper definition, which, by default, renders it very difficult to prevent, plan for, and respond. Without going into the specific characteristics of any individual group or terrorist, the two argue that in order to enhance the quality of the law enforcement response in urban environment, there is a dire need to change the way local law enforcement forces are training or rather not trained to prevent and respond. The currently employed preventive response to terrorist attacks, at least from the perspective of the training that law enforcement officers go through around the country, resembles more what can be referred to as "post hoc training," much more reactive than proactive approach, with a heavy emphasis on one-dimensional look at the phenomenon of terrorism, viewed primarily at the threat that will be perpetrated by the members of the Al-Qaeda organization. This narrowly defined and rather myopic view of the threat prevents the true first responders, the patrol officers on the streets, from being aware of their surroundings and preventive during their patrol shifts. Furthermore, the training offered to the majority of the officers does not include the contingency planning element, which even further hampers their ability to respond to the aftermath of the future attacks. The authors argue that only through a very thorough and much more inclusive training, with a changed focus of orientation, we can provide a much more effective response to the terrorist threat in urban environment. Their chapter provides a generic transition into the reminder of this volume, which is organized by three themes: cases that happened in the United States, Chapters 3–7, cases that deal with thematic themes like Aviation or Maritime Security, Chapters 8–11, and finally Chapters 12–17, which overview various terrorist attacks around the world, prior to concluding with Chapter 18, where the editors of this book attempt to draw upon some lessons learned from responses to terrorist attacks described by the volume's contributors. It is important to note that the chapters are organized on the thematic scale and not time line, therefore there is no real importance attached to the order they are presented in the book – the readers should look for the themes and not the time line.

Patten and Wu open the first thematic part of the book, one that covers the events that occurred in the past on the soil of the United States, with their chapter depicting the events that took place in Texas in 1993, during the violent interaction between the members of the Branch Davidians cult and the Federal Bureau of Investigations that culminated with many of the cult members being killed as an outcome of the FBI's response. Although many would argue the incident in Texas does not fall within the definition of an encounter between a terrorist group and a law enforcement agency, it is precisely this locus of error that we try to correct by introducing this specific event to the reader and including it within the definition of the Have Nots versus Haves. The readers are encouraged to analyze the root causes of this event, the history of the cult, the event itself and the law enforcement response, and make their own decision with regard to applicability of the event to the definition of terrorism, as offered in this chapter. There is no doubt, however, that the act and the actors involved carry a lot of characteristics that appear in other, more acceptable definitions of terrorist activities, like the one offered in the chapter itself, a definition offered by the Federal Bureau of Investigations in 1993.

DeSa and McCarthy follow with the Solo Crusader, introduce two individual Have Nots or solo crusaders Ted Kaczynski and Timothy McVeigh. Although their grievances were of very different nature, they definitely fall within the operationalization of the terrorism phenomenon and its actors, as offered in this chapter. Two distinctly different individuals offer a rather frightful insight into their motivations and, despite the limited resources available to them, were able to perpetrate carnage and damage that generated fear and cascading reaction of the public and the law enforcement agencies dedicated to the investigative process and response. It is without doubt the most bothersome type of terrorist activity when one individual is capable of generating terror and overreaction on the part of the larger population and numerous law enforcement agencies. It is also the hardest one to prepare for and respond. Nevertheless, the analysis of their motivation and actions provides for a useful template for awareness and customized response.

White, in his chapter, which depicts some cases of biological terrorism in the United States, touches upon one of our most sacred fears. We tend to dismiss, on a regular basis, the feasibility of a biological terrorist act actually happening here, on our soil. However, as White poignantly outlines in the title of his chapter, it already happened here – in the United States. His portrayal of the food poisoning and the anthrax cases is a rude awakening to many in the policy-making arenas as well as law enforcement agencies. One does not have to be a member of a highly organized, well–structured, and funded group in order to generate one of the most disastrous terrorist attacks. It is sufficient to have the motivation and a little bit of an imagination. His chapter provides the readers with a rare insight into the world of Have Nots who feel that generating fear at random with Weapons of Mass Destruction is the best possible way to achieve and/or to destroy what the Haves cherish – the freedom of walking in the streets, going to work, and dinning outside without a concern for being killed or otherwise injured or hurt.

Then, there are the ones thoroughly concerned with various causes, the radical Environmentalist. Christiansen provides a rare insight into the world of those who are willing to kill and destroy in the name of an environmental cause. The problems with the sympathetic nature of the cause, be it clean air, the fight against the global warming, or against the animal cruelty, are further complicated by the lack of proper legal definitions as to what actually constitutes an eco-terrorist act. The response tends to be either inadequate or nonexistent and the actors viewed themselves more a semi deranged saboteurs rather than terrorists. Despite the diverge perspective, they do fit into the category of Have Nots and as such their actions need to be treated as acts of terrorism and the response to their act needs to be devoid of the ambiguity it currently exhibits.

September 11, 2001 needs not much of an introduction. There is hardly a person above the elementary school age in the United States and in many countries around the world who have not heard about the tragic events of this otherwise good weather day of the early fall season. However, despite the numerous depictions of what happened prior to this event, who was involved, what happened on the day itself, and in the aftermath of the attack, Shane provides a fresh perspective on the time line of the events and the errors of judgments that accompanied all the stages. One cannot understand the phenomenon of terrorism without understanding the events of 9/11 and maybe not so much the events on the day itself but the background of the people involved, the actors on both sides of the scene – the terrorists and the by standers – and also the law enforcement response. If there is one chapter that exemplifies the Locus of Error Theory in a much more detailed manner than the others, it is the chapter about the events of 9/11. Unfortunately, as Haberfeld and von Hassell point to, lessons are yet to be learned.

The next part of the book centers around thematic approach, which emphasizes more heavily the theme of the threat rather than a specific event, although the themes are defined and analyzed based on a number of specific events. Hougham addresses the problems of Aviation Security through the analysis of the Pan Am flight 103 in 1981 and the events that led up to the bombing of the flight. Although many lessons have been learned over the past few decades in the area of Aviation Security, there is still much to be implemented and much to be understood. Some countries responded in a more comprehensive manner than others to the various possible threats against its flying machines, others despite the rather misleading and sometimes overwhelming resource allocations are still nowhere near where they should be. Jurisdictional and legal impediments are frequently cited as partial explanations in the proactive planning and reactive response. Not always such impediments can and will be overcome but there are always valuable lessons to be learned from those who apply a wider and more comprehensive approach to the way they secure their planes and the passengers onboard.

Maritime security connotes some romantic notion of pirates and the search for hidden treasures. Maule, in his chapter on Maritime Security, could not have been any further from such thoughts. His depiction of the USS Cole incident and other threats to port and maritime security sends some real chills about the state of our preparedness and response to the Have Nots who chose to attack this specific type of our transportation. Considering the fact that United States is heavily dependent upon the security of its vessels, be it Navy or cargo, it is imperative to give additional attention to the threat analysis and assessment as they are applied or rather not applied to the various vessels shipping under our flag or that of any other country, as long as their destinations are our shore lines.

Time has passed since trains used to be considered our primary modes of transportation. Still, both in the United States and around the world, the railroad security and its paramount importance to the economies of many countries cannot be ignored. Beyond being yet another mode of transportation for people and cargo, it is also a symbolic carrier of potential threat from one place to another with very limited security measures to prevent any type of possible terrorist attack. Lieberman and Bucht, through the analysis of two specific terrorist attacks, one in Angola and the other in Spain, portray a threat that is as real nowadays as it was decades ago and potentially more lethal today than ever before. It appears that what we tend to overlook or relate to as a lesser of a problem might potentially create a snowballing reaction, above and beyond the original event. Analyzing the events in Angola and in Spain provides yet another dimension in understanding the power of the Have Nots versus Haves while utilizing this particular mode of transportation.

The Olympic Games represent the one and only event that should connote peace, cooperation, harmony and, maybe, some hope for a better future. Not according to Gamarra's depiction of the Olympic events, when in his chapter he analyzes the tragic events of the Munich Olympics and the terrorist attempts during the Atlanta 1996 Games. While looking at one of the most likeable events in the history of the human kind, Gammara provides us with an insight into a very powerful environment that was, and probably will be once again, exploited by those who feel that this platform of exposure for their causes and grievance is the most powerful and appropriate one. Although the most recent Olympic Games in China were saved, through a tremendous effort on the part of the Chinese government, from any terrorist attacks, it is hard to envision any other host country in the near future being able to afford to invest the vast amounts of money that the Chinese government was willing to allocate to this event and a thorough analysis of what happened and what could be done in the future is certainly a valuable lesson to be learned.

From air, through maritime and ground transportation, the book moves to its final theme depicting the various specific events around the world that appear to represent some interesting examples for human's undying desire to destroy in the name of rebuilding and creating anew. Hyon Kang, in her chapter on the Tokyo subway attack, portrays the lack of awareness on the part of the local law enforcement regarding the very serious threat brewing underneath the ground – both literally and figuratively. The Shinrikyo sect in Japan had no qualms in introducing the poisonous gas in the subway cars of the Tokyo underground metro system. Although the authorities were aware of the existence of the movement, there was not enough recognition about the nature of their criminal activities. The law enforcement and other first responder's reaction was inadequate; if it happens again, will it be properly customized? The answer to this question can and should be found in this chapter.

Lieberman and Cheloukhine introduce the readers to one of the more prominent terrorist attacks in the recent years, the events referred to in general terms as the London Bombings, which occurred originally on July 7, 2005 in the capital city of the United Kingdom. The magnitude of the events in the United Kingdom was not the most dominant feature of these terrorist attacks, what made the difference was the origins of the actors involved in the brutal and bloody attacks that were perpetrated not by foreign-born or -bred individuals but by actually homegrown young men who did not think much of planting explosive devises on various modes of public transportation, with full recognition of the consequences. It is probably safe to say that nothing hit harder than the betrayal of your own children. In a way the failure of the British law enforcement to gather any intelligence on the various stages of these attacks is a very critical point in understanding what the proper preparedness to terrorist attacks should be and where our tendency for self-deception and the ignorance of the obvious is.

From England to Russia, where the same authors, Cheloukhine and Lieberman discuss the events that led to the hostage takeover in Beslan by the Chechen terrorist and the tragically erroneous response of the Russian military and law enforcement forces. As much as one cannot always deploy its resources in the fight against the terrorists in a way that is totally and completely operationally focused and devoid much of other consideration; while analyzing the Beslan event and its aftermath, it is tempting to arrive at some rather far reaching conclusions that will be further depicted in the last chapter of this book. While the overreaction to incidents of such intensity can be easily justified, the overall response of the Russian authorities appears to be disproportionate and rather dysfunction vis-à-vis the actual threat of the Have Nots. One would like to hope that the death of so many children in the Beslan's school would, at minimum, produce some long-lasting and relevant lessons in the area of counter-terrorist response.

Although the attack on the US Marines in Beirut in 1983 was primarily associated with a failed military preparedness and response to the event, it is an important chapter in our understanding of what the proper, proactive response to terrorist activities in urban environment should be, as a blend of military and law enforcement intelligence and response that should have taken place but did not. Von Hassell, in his depictions of the events that led to the 1983 bombings and the aftermath response, points out to what was ignored, what was misunderstood and what needs to be done in the future to prevent a similar occurrence. Although many reports have been written and many lessons were offered to be learned, it is still an open question if and when we will learn.

Strobl and Lindsay pick up from the 1983 events in their chapter on the Khobar Towers attack and the ambiguities of terrorism in the 1990s. The events of 1996 are portrayed, during which a fuel truck packed with explosives detonated on the perimeter of Khobar Towers, a residential complex housing US Air Force personnel in an Air Base in Dhahran, Saudi Arabia, killing 19 American airmen and injuring over 500 other Americans, Saudis, and Bangladeshis. The bombing, as well as the official investigations in its wake, prompted the military services to adopt more robust force-protection measures and various official investigations that led to the broader counter-terrorism policy measures pursued by the US government in response. This chapter's importance cannot be overemphasized as it underscores the fact that despite what we know, we still refuse to implement this knowledge, in its full-fledged potential, in our struggles against the Have Nots.

The final thematic chapter of the book depicts the siege in Mumbai, which for the first time in the history of the fight against terrorism in urban environment actually already generated a response, on the part of some local law enforcement agencies, which appears to be a sort of rapid learning mode to an event that was long predicted by some researchers, among them Haberfeld and von Hassell. Walker and Laraia in their overview of the carnage in India spare no details to familiarize the reader with the overall context of what happened prior, during, and in the aftermath of the attacks. Their sources of information are the most detailed and chilling in their realistic depictions. While it is always hard to choose the chapter that will naturally lead the reader to the final conclusion of the book, Walker and LaRaia's work provide for a perfect transition to the final writings in this volume and the answer to the title of its final chapter – A New Understanding of Counter-Terrorist/m Response?

While the editors of this book do not claim to have all the insights into the understanding of the phenomenon of terrorism and the actors involved in the interactions, they offer yet another perspective on a topic that has been explored by many and claimed to be understood by even more; however, this knowledge remains underutilized and the ultimate goal of this book is to shed some light on what we know and how we can use it to the benefits of the Haves.

References

Rosenau, J. N. (2003). *Distant proximities: Dynamics beyond globalization*. Princeton: Princeton University Press.
Sahni, A. (2003). "The locus of error: Has the gravity of terrorism shifted" in Asia? In R. Gunaratna (Ed.), *Terrorism in the Asia Pacific – threat and response*. Singapore: Eastern University Press.
Saint-Exupery, A. d. (1943). *The little prince*. New York: Harcourt, Brace & World.

Chapter 2
Proper Proactive Training to Terrorist Presence and Operations in Friendly Urban Environments

M.R. Haberfeld and Agostino von Hassell

Introduction

As police organizations in democratic countries struggle to mount a proper reactive and proactive approach to the internal and external terrorist threats, the variety of responses in counter-terrorism (C-T) range from innovative to inadequate or simply misguided.

This chapter examines various attempts of law enforcement agencies around the world to rapidly reorganize their infrastructure to provide, at minimum, a feeling of safety and security to the public, which does not always translate into effective tactics and strategies. Suggestions for change of directions and new training modules together with reorganization of certain field units will constitute the backbone of a proper proactive response in the friendly urban environments.

Reacting to Terrorism

Only four major countries' police forces in democratic society have had in place a sustained package of training, awareness, and investigative actions vis-à-vis terrorist activities prior to September 11, 2001.

- Spain (democratic only since the death of El Caudillo General Francisco Franco in November 1975) had been faced with sustained attacks in urban centers (mostly Madrid) of the Basques (*Euskadi Ta Askatasuna* or ETA). When ETA declared a cease fire in the Spring of 2006, 31 years of law enforcement response came to an end only to be replaced with strong law enforcement responses needed

M.R. Haberfeld (✉)
Department of Law, Police Science and Criminal Justice Administration, John Jay College of Criminal Justice, New York, NY, USA
e-mail: mhaberfeld@jjay.cuny.edu

Reprinted with permission from: *Understanding and Responding to the Terrorism Phenomenon – A Multi-Dimensional Perspective.* NATO Security through Science Series: Human and Societal Dynamics (vol. 21)

M.R. Haberfeld, A. von Hassell (eds.), *A New Understanding of Terrorism,*
DOI 10.1007/978-1-4419-0115-6_2, © Springer Science+Business Media, LLC 2009

against Islamic Fundamentalist terrorists that killed over 200 people in simultaneous commuter train bombings in 2004. However, based on the information gathered during the field research trip to Spain in 2005, the local law enforcement will concentrate on more of a militaristic – storm the building approach to training – rather than the much broader in scope proactive training that will be introduced and discussed further down in this chapter. In addition the response will differ based on the specific force as standardized training for police forces in Spain is nonexistent and is basically regional and force specific; therefore, by default, it hampers the effectiveness of a unified response, so much needed in the case of an effective and comprehensive C-T training.

- Italy faced during the 1970–1985 period the violence and murderous spree of the Maoist-inspired Red Brigades (*Brigate Rosse*). The Red Brigades were credited with 14,000 acts of violence in the 1970s alone and in 1978 kidnapped and murdered former Italian Prime Minister Aldo Moro. In addition, Italy's highly diverse police forces faced the actions of the various organized crime gangs (*Cosa Nostra* and others) who fought against prosecution with terror-like killings of police officers, politicians, and prosecutor. Same as in Spain, the C-T response is in the hands of multiple forces that are not subjected to any uniformed standard of training.

- Germany – which has a form of democracy that can only be defined as imposed from the outside and followed as a dictate (in the writers' view, democracy is not truly inherent to the Germans) – faced a wave of terrorism in the 1970s that started with the extremely violent Bader-Meinhoff Gang. In addition, Germany's police forces have attempted to combat the latent terror tendencies of the extreme right wing or Neo-Nazis as well as imported terrorism from Armenians, Turks, and gangsters from countries of the former Yugoslavia. Same as Spain and Italy, police forces are trained in 16 federal training centers that do not have a uniformed module for the C-T training.

- The United Kingdom had a highly refined terror response, honed in over 50 years of combat against the Irish Republic Army (IRA) and its various offshoots. Lately, the police forces of Her Majesty have tried to apply those lessons to the present terror threat of primarily homegrown Islamic fundamentalism. The situation in the United Kingdom is much better than in Spain, Italy, and Germany since its 43 police forces are exposed to national standards – with exception for C-T training, where regional constraints, chief among them the budgetary considerations, do not allow for uniformity of training in this area, therefore, again, hampering the effective and proactive response. Recent report published by the British authorities identified such weaknesses and recommended consolidation of the forces, especially the smaller forces, and putting the total number of police forces in Britain at 12; however, nothing final has been decided in this regard and the deliberations will, probably, continue into the more distant future. In addition, British C-T efforts have almost always been in close coordination with regular police and military forces (Haberfeld, 2004/2006).

Other nations have faced terrorism and evolved their own unique counterterrorism stance. One is the State of Israel, which has confronted terrorism in some form or other since 1948. Yet for the purposes of this chapter, Israel's experience – while ultra useful for other police forces – must be seen in the stark light that Israel has almost been permanently at war since 1948. It is this "war stance" that has shaped Israel's counter-terrorism response. In addition, Israel has adapted the somewhat questionable British methods (such as the destruction of houses of actual and suspected terrorists) that would not work in North America or Europe. Day-to-day tactics learned from Israel do, however, have a major lesson value, particularly with the United States now essentially on a war footing (which when observing shoppers at Bloomingdales in New York City is hard to believe).

We also have to distinguish between the ways Israelis deal with the C-T training in the occupied territories and the response in Israel itself, which differs in a significant way from the one used in the occupied territories. The issues related to the friction between the ideas of democratic policing vis-à-vis effective C-T training can be easily demonstrated while observing the two, distinctively different, approaches.

Japan has been faced with a few incidents of terrorism. Most notable is the 1995 Sarin gas attack by Aum Shinrikyo, a religious cult. Beyond that Japan has been relatively free of terrorism. The well-known Japanese Red Army has operated almost exclusively outside of the borders of this island nation. As a highly homogenous population, subject to extreme traditional discipline, few proactive steps by the well-trained Japanese police forces are required. Nonetheless, the revelations of North Korean kidnappings of Japanese from Japanese shores over many decades and North Korean missile firings are yet to be fully understood effects on the Japanese views of terrorism and national defense.

However, Japan has a strong history of modeling its police forces after certain European countries and it is only a matter of time before they can be expected to adopt one of the C-T modules of the European forces and, again, the thin line between democracy and effective policing will be put to a test.

In terms of counter-terrorism actions in democratic societies, the recent experiences in Russia cannot be included here. That country operates on a level of democracy that is not recognizable by "western standards" and is slipping back into a dictatorship-like climate.

Proactive Law Enforcement Response

One of the most complex problems in developing proper counter-terrorism stances in democratic police forces is the traditional police mindset. Police forces are – by training and culture – more inclined to react to a crime rather than take proactive steps to prevent a crime.

On a micro level, the typical police force will respond to reports of a crime. For instance, in the case of a burglary, the police will respond and then investigate. Only if there are multiple burglaries in a certain neighborhood and a pattern emerges will police forces attempt to take proactive steps to prevent future burglaries and get to the root cause of the societal problem.

Initiatives such as various forms of community policing and extensive data tracking as evolved by New York City Police Commissioner William

Bratton – COMPSTAT (Computer Comparison Statistics) – were supposed to "fix" some of these problems. In some cities this has worked. For instance, the "impact squads" of the New York Police Department, which target specific high-crime incidents, are such a positive development. Yet is this all applicable to terrorism and is this the proper response?

We must not ignore the fact that aggressive street policing is always a threat to democratic values, especially in countries where one person's problem is another person's constitutional right.

Definition is one root cause of the lack of effective response to terrorism. The general public as well as most democratic police forces see terrorism as a phenomenon *sui generis*. However, treating terrorism as a crime would and should help rapidly reshape the law enforcement response.

For instance, the at time high-intensity war against narcotics in major urban centers such as Amsterdam, London, Paris, Rome, New York, Los Angeles, and Atlanta (among others) is an action quite similar to the stance, we believe, law enforcement should take vis-à-vis terrorism. The actions of drug dealers – operating often in highly trained, well-financed, and quite sophisticated gangs – do parallel actions by terrorists. Additionally two other factors could help guide police response:

- Narcotics are probably the second largest source of funding for Islamic fundamentalists, apart from the various "charities." The poppy cultivation in Afghanistan, as one example, means that the drug consumer on Manhattan's Upper West Side or in the elegant streets of Paris essentially makes a "donation" to various Islamic extremists. Note further that in the United States the bulk of the true successes against terrorism came from the US Drug Enforcement Agency, which managed to interdict numerous times since September 11, 2001 the flow of drugs and money that would have been of benefit to terror groups.
- Traditional terror groups such as Columbia's FARC (Fuerzas Armadas Revolucionarias de Colombia) have emerged as major drug dealers on the own. With estimated annual sales just below US$1 billion, FARC does rely on the drug trade to sustain traditional terrorist operations (von Hassell and Haberfeld, 2005/2006, Personal communication).

Responses that Fail

Using the old military maxim that superior firepower will defeat the enemy, democratic police forces have resorted to response mechanisms that do little in terms of actual counter-terrorism and are, at times, downright ridiculous.

It has become the almost automatic reaction of big-city and small-town police forces to react to terror incidents as follows: flood the streets with police officers, often heavily armed with submachine guns or military-quality carbines; police officers in heavy armor patrol airports, bridges, public spaces, transportation systems (such as subways and commuter rails), inspect bags at random, and create a very visible presence on urban streets. This reaction is common now in Europe and in the United States.

While this *may* help reassure the public – and a study on this would be a worth-while academic undertaking – such efforts do next to nothing in reducing terror threats. They are costly – NYPD's Hercules and Atlas units consume substantial portions of limited budgets – and are often put in place for just a few days or maybe weeks. Possibly the most extreme (and patently ridiculous) such deployment was the multiyear stationing of heavily armored military vehicles equipped with 50-caliber machine guns on the major highways leading toward the Pentagon in Washington, DC. Apart from utterly demoralizing the soldiers assigned to this meaningless bor-ing duty, it would have had – even in extreme cases – no real impact on any terrorist attack planning.

Similarly the annual security effort that surround the United Nationals General Session opening session in September in New York has evolved into an extremely expensive and highly questionable form of use of law enforcement power to protect against terrorism. It would be highly unlikely that New York – headquarters of the United Nations (an unlikely target to begin with) – would be attacked during this time period when world leaders, including representative from nations who are well-known sponsors of state terrorism (i.e., Iran), assemble in New York. Yet still, over 10,000 law enforcement officers blockade the streets.

Why?

Terrorists have no known record of attacking into an alert. Counter-measures are analyzed by terrorists and their tactics will be adjusted. For instance, the first attempt at New York City's World Trade Center in 1993 used a car bomb in a garage below the center. Since that attack, the trade center incorporated sophisticated counter-measures against future bomb-laden track entering the garage. Yet the terrorists, fully aware of this, worked around this and developed a new method: using airplanes as giant bombs.

In some countries – mostly Saudi Arabia – Al-Qaeda and related groups will issue warnings of impending attacks. Typically and inside of 2 weeks, such a warn-ing will be followed by an actual attack. Yet the warnings are sufficiently vague to prevent any effective counter-measures in terms of physical security. Globally, Islamic terror groups will issue routine threats, often highly vague. The only result of such threats is to instill a "feeling of terror" in the general populace and a scur-rying about by intelligence services and law enforcement looking for what this vague threat could mean. Alert levels are routinely increased (and then lowered a few weeks later).

Suggested Mechanism for Effective Law Enforcement Counter-Terrorism

A careful study of counter-terrorism programs in England, Northern Ireland, Spain, Ireland, Sweden, Turkey, Poland, and the Netherlands, as well as actual work with the New York City Police Department, suggests a series of measures that may help in this current time of crisis (Haberfeld, 2005–2006).

Do note that the proactive stance of the London Metropolitan Police that led to the arrest of two dozen suspected bombers this past August was based in part on this approach.

- Police officers require solid training

  ○ History of terrorism and terrorists groups: just like cops study the background and M.O. of criminals, terror groups must be subjected to the same analysis. This requires training or more adequately college level educational modules, with all the nuances and biases carefully examined and surgically addressed.
  ○ Exposure to how past terrorist attacks evolved and what their root causes are will help develop a deeper understanding that can, if done right, translate into improved day-to-day policing.
  ○ Simulation: we believe police officers should boost training levels by (a) simulating possible attacks and (b) learn to get into the mindset of the "terrorist criminal" by studying a group and then planning an attack themselves.
  ○ However, training cannot be overdone: an excessively intensive exposure to terror issue will translate into mental overload.
  ○ Training on how terrorists operate will help street cops in community policing to spot developments that could assist in the overall intelligence gathering effort.

- Intelligence gathering is critical yet not emphasized enough

  ○ Few police departments do a good job in collecting intelligence. Major exemptions are both the London Metropolitan Police and the New York Police Department. The latter has a multilingual and well-trained intelligence unit in place that works these issued and present a "must follow" example for other urban centers. However, New York's intelligence unit is hampered by the lack of proper coordination with federal sources as well as the lack of sufficient police officers with high-enough security clearances to actually see the stream of information collected.

- Interagency cooperation must finally reach the levels mandated by the US Congress as well as by the appalling lack of such cooperation prior to the September 11, 2001 attacks.

  ○ The culture war between the various law enforcement agencies and intelligence gathering units in the United States continues. None of the Congressional mandates have been able to overcome decades of resentment. This problem has been identified some time ago with regard to nonterrorist-related activities, just the "plain" 101 traditional crime activities and is referred to in the police literature as "linkage blindness." We simply became blind to the importance of cooperation and sharing that is the vital and most essential link to effective enforcement.

- For instance, computer systems between the FBI and the CIA are virtually incompatible. Free exchange of information between the FBI and the CIA remains an occasional activity.
- Key units in the front lines in the Global War on Terror – such as the US Drug Enforcement Administration – are not even included in the national intelligence sharing network.

Definitions

It is very hard to create any type of effective C-T training or any other training for that matter without having a clearly defined and operationalized target, against which we want to train our forces.

With regard to various C-T definitions, it is impossible to adopt one or even a few of the myriad of the definitions existing out there and customize any effective training module/s that will address all the complexities involved in multiple definitions and approaches.

After scanning and surveying the infinite number of such definitions, the authors opt to propose one of their own – a definition that is broad enough in its scope and overreaches other definitions. This definition will enable us to create a training response that is not myopic and skewed toward particular political goal or orientation. It will allow for a much more comprehensive approach to C-T training.

The concept of *Haves versus Have Nots* has been popularized in social sciences for many, many decades. It goes back to the Marxist theories of power and control that led to defining and labeling certain groups and individuals and their behaviors as criminals and crimes. The "Haves" were the ones with the means and the power and the "Have Nots" the ones without.

Borrowing from this concept but reversing its order, we propose to define the terrorist phenomenon as a struggle between the Have Nots and the Haves. The Have Nots will encompass a very broad number of individuals of various ethnic, racial, religious backgrounds who harbor various grievances against the Haves.

There are two recent examples that support the validity of this definition:

- Northern Ireland has started to boom economically in the past decade: this removed one key element from the traditional war between the IRA and London, a war that was often based on claims of economic discrimination. The improvements in the economy of Northern Ireland (in part a spillover of the economic miracle of the Irish Republic) had, in the authors' view, much to do with the cease fire declared by the IRA. In a sense the IRA as a fighter for economic justice became irrelevant and lost its popular support.
- Similarly, in Spain the massive economic buildup in the Basque region – paid for in part with generous grants of the European Union – robbed the ETA of its *raison d'être* and led to the cease fire in 2006.

There is always something that one of the Have Nots is missing from his/her life that the Haves possess – be it a separatist movement that wants its own piece of land, separate from the mainland, a religious fanatic who wants his/her religion to be the one that guides and restricts the behaviors and freedoms of the Haves, or the cause-oriented mercenary who will perform any heinous act for the cause – and this cause will be to get the money that he himself does not have – but the Haves definitely do.

Borrowing another concept from the social sciences – "the paradox of the dispossession" – which basically spells out that the less one has to lose the less one is threatened by the authority. If you feel that you have nothing to lose, nothing will deter you – not your own death and certainly not the death of the others (Muir, 1977).

It would be opportune for C-T police officers to fully understand Mao Tse Tung's concept of insurgent warfare – which is based on more than 3,000 years of military thinking in China. Mao basically said that guerillas (or in modern parlance, insurgents or terrorists) must swim like fish in the sea: they must be embraced by the general (impoverished) population – and use that as a place to hide and sustain themselves (Mao, 1963). The economic booms in Northern Ireland and in the Basque regions essentially led to "the sea" (i.e., the aggrieved population) to reject "the fish" (i.e., the insurgents or terrorists). This, in all likelihood, may be one useful concept for the situation in Iraq: note here that the economically sound Kurdish region has little or no problems with insurgency.

In other words, we need to look for those many different individuals and groups whose claim to fail is some real or perceived injury caused by the Haves or those who the Haves represent. Such an approach will allow us to step back and away from the misguided preoccupation with one religion and one or two groups who are defined as the major threat to any given law enforcement agency. This broadening of the scope of our academic inquiries into a somewhat amorphous and esoteric definition of the phenomenon of terrorism will allow the practitioners to focus on the following – very pragmatic approach to C-T training.

What Can We Do? – A Two-Prong Approach

The authors propose – based on having studied C-T efforts of police forces around the globe and trained between them well over 1,500 police officers in C-T tactics – a two-prong approach to C-T training.

The first "prong" is *Programmatic/Strategic*:

(a) What is the next stage in training? – "the paradox of the dispossession" – and
(b) What are the new criteria for deployment?

The second "prong" is *Operational/Tactical*. This involves multiple steps:

(a) Who are the new partners? (i.e., local law enforcement coordinates efforts with national assets and the military as well as the national intelligence community).
(b) Who will continue with the traditional law enforcement? – Care must be taken that standard police work does not suffer from the additional burden of C-T efforts.

(c) Who will gather and disseminate the information? This is probably the most sensitive and complex issue: who controls intelligence and who is allowed to gather it.

To lead police forces in C-T – without degrading standard police work – police leaders must proactively engage in increasing C-T awareness (i.e., communicate); decreasing overreaction (i.e., extreme "flooding" of the streets with cops), and customizing a police department's response to local needs, risks, and capabilities.

The final or maybe the opening statements that epitomize the importance of proper proactive training will have to deal with the implementation of an effective C-T training in a country that refers to its form of government as a democratic one. Police scholars have argued over the years that policing is hard on democracy or in reverse, democracy is hard on policing. Police after all is about use of force – and the basic principles of a democratic government are not grounded in coercion. C-T training, by default, connotes the ideas of use of force – by the police (the arm of the Haves) against certain minority members (the Have Nots) who reside amongst larger communities (of the Haves).

There is a very thin line and a very delicate balance that needs to be maintained in order to prevent the larger passive sympathizers of the Have Nots from crossing the line of passive into active. The more civilized we become as a society, the more we resent the idea of use of force against us – even when such use of force is authorized by the legitimately elected governments.

C-T training *must* balance the softer – more academic approach with the best of the police street operational work. In order to achieve this mix, we must carefully design the training modules, the ones created for the generalists and the ones for the specialized unit. This careful design cannot be properly achieved without cross-pollination between the academics and the practitioners. This approach has been already utilized in a number of countries but the key to a successful training scenario is not just the amalgamation of the academics with the practitioners but the proper blend of the right academics with the right practitioners. As enigmatic as this last statement might sound, it has a very simple translation – not everybody who is a member of a given profession knows what he/she is doing.

Being a college professor who specializes in a given field does not automatically makes one a good match with any practitioner whose major qualifications are the number of years spent on the force. Without getting into any specific details – we have seen this happen, both in the United States and in other countries. Matching the two right individuals – the academic and the practitioner – is a science in itself.

Proper Proactive Training to Terrorist Presence and Operations in Friendly Urban Environments

This could and should be addressed as a two-prong approach:

1. A proactive training devised for each and every law enforcement officer as they are not only the first respondents but the true eyes and ears of any police organization.

2. Focus on devising proper proactive training for specialized units that deal with counter-terrorism and Intel gathering as their primary specialization.

What we are seeing around the world is a strong focus on the training of the specialized units with almost peripheral or nonexistent allocation of resources to the street officers or all the other officers in a given department.

Why is this preoccupation with the specialized units and the allocation of the majority of resources toward their training priorities? To understand this misguided approach (at least in the eyes of the authors of this chapter), one needs to understand that our response to the terrorism phenomenon is grounded in the history of training and organizational structures of police departments.

O.W. Wilson studied the relationship between effective organizational structure of police agency and specialization. While he did not find much of a benefit in specialized units for smaller police departments, since their patrol officers appear to be jacks of all trades, he identified a number of advantages for large police agencies:

- placement of responsibility
- development of expertise
- promotion of group esprit de corps
- increased efficiency and effectiveness (Wilson & McLaren, 1972)

However, most police departments in the United States are small, and these are the ones who according to the above would not benefit from a specialized training. In addition, the idea of a generalist training, one that will create a well-rounded officer who is equally knowledgeable in Community-Oriented Policing, Conflict Resolution, Parking Ordinances, Protection of Wild Animals, and the local terrorist cells, gained a lot of popularity in the local law enforcement.

Proponents of the idea of generalist point to a number of problems associated with specialization; it appears to

- create increased friction and conflict between the units;
- create loyalty to the specialized unit instead of the department;
- contribute to a decrease in overall job performance due to job factionalism; and
- hamper the development of a well-rounded police program (Swanson, Territo, & Taylor, 2001).

Based on the above history of two extreme approaches to police training, we either will continue to follow the controversy by creating only specialized C-T units and providing training modules that are very narrowly defined or will go with the generalist approach and create modules that are so general and reactive in nature that will render most, if not all, of this training as a CYA concept rather than something truly proactive and effective.

Unfortunately, if on the one han, the idea of a "generalist" approach to C-T training will prevail in American policing and furthermore, gain some momentum, especially for the small departments and on the other hand, the idea of specialized units will take over the role of fighting the phenomenon of terrorism in urban environments and only leftover resources will be allocated to the generalists, we predict a very troublesome future.

We do not give our officers the necessary tools to perform their profession, as the basic academy training cannot and will not offer them these tools (if it continues to offer modules of training that are inadequate both in length and content), and the so-called specialized and developmental training creates an impression, in many instances, of a further deterioration of the idea of professionalism for law enforcement.

The length of the training, in itself, is seldom a fully inclusive indicator of the quality of a given training module. However, coupled with the six answers to the following questions the picture is quite clear.

The basic questions to be answered about the quality of specialized, counter-terrorist training are the following:

1. What?
2. When?
3. Where?
4. Who?
5. By whom?
6. How much?

The multitude of topics and themes that needs to be covered during truly proactive counter-terrorism training points to the complexity of a proper police response. This complexity necessitates a serious and structured approach. An old and well-known adage says: with force you can be successful against a specific terrorist but you will not win the war against terrorism.

One of the more prominent events that highlighted the need for specialized training can be traced to the early 1960s. In August 1966, an incident occurred in Austin, Texas, that contrary to other incidents pushed law enforcement toward assessment of their capabilities in handling high-risk situations. After killing his wife and mother, Charles Whitman went to the rooftop of the University of Texas and began a shooting spree, killing 15 people and wounding 30 others. This event contributed to the establishment of special police teams to handle high-risk situations (Haberfeld, 2002).

9/11 was a similar catalyst in the area of counter-terrorist/intelligence training. However, when one analyzes the themes of police specialized training in the above areas, it appears that the inter-relations between history, religion, social justice and real or perceived injustice, economic trends, migration trends paired with the increase in violent crimes, high-technology crimes, the increased number of high-risk repeat offenders (an outcome of prison overcrowding), the overall sophistication of criminal element, diversity-related issues and a host of additional problems which create the need for a very carefully designed specialized and developmental training approach generate, at best, what these authors would call a "post hoc training" approach.

Police scholars, when describing police subcultures, refer to the concept of "post hoc morality" when dealing with explanations for unethical or questionable behaviors. The post hoc morality provides an alibi, an explanation, or/and a justification for officer's behavior, after the fact (Crank, 1998).

The quality and the quantity of various approaches to C-T and intelligence training, both during the academy and later on in-service in the form of specialized and developmental training courses, seem to be providing the similar outlet for police agency as the adoption of post hoc morality. There is, indeed, an element of alibi, explanation, and justification in the various specialized and developmental courses offered to law enforcement officer; there is, however, no trace of an element of a true expertise.

A two-day course dealing with the history of terrorism or the phenomenon of suicide bombers or the more "in-depth" approach to the study of the Islam (like if it was the only terrorist-related religion) certainly serves as an alibi for a department that needs to enhance its officers people skills or prepare for accusations of indifference toward a certain group of victims or profiling of certain communities; however, it will not provide the adequate tools to deal with these problems, not even in a semi-effective manner.

The authors of this chapter (both college professors) realize quite too well that after 15 weeks of instruction, with two and half hours a week, which amounts to about 38 h (38–40 h of instructions are considered to be an average length of a course in any college environment), the knowledge of counter-terrorism response and policies for law enforcement is, at best, comparable to scratching a tip of an iceberg. However, 40 h of instructions allocated to C-T training for the generalists in the field is rarely in existence in police departments around the country or the world for that matter.

But, any and all that is delivered to police officers in these areas provides an alibi for a given police organization and a false sense of security for the officers in the field. We must and actually have an obligation to look at the history of specialized training in this country and learn from our mistakes. Gould (1997) conducted a research study to evaluate the experiences of police officers exposed to a specialized Community-Oriented Training offered in-service to officers with some level of seniority in the field. The experienced officers felt that the course was a waste of time, and their criticism was summarized in five points:

1. a feeling that the community did not understand or appreciate what the officers were trying to accomplish;
2. a feeling that most police administrators and many supervisors had lost touch with the reality of policing as the officers face it today;
3. a feeling that many police administrators and community politicians were looking for a quick-and-dirty scapegoat, therefore often blaming police officers for things over which they have no control;
4. that the "rules of the street" far too often weighted against the police;
5. that there is a divergence between what is being taught in the course and what society actually asks a police officer to do (Gould, 1997, p. 351).

Gould's finding could be probably directly replicated if somebody had surveyed the C-T training offered to l/e officers today in the America and around the world. Gould suggested some policies to be considered, based on the findings of his study. Some of his suggestions about the venues to improve community-oriented training were customized by these authors for the benefit of improvement of the C-T training. Following are the points that should be taken into profound consideration when a given agency puts together C-T modules that will be looked upon as proactive and not post hoc:

1. It should be remembered that teaching C-T concepts also means the "unteaching" of some already existing culturally intensive attitudes, prejudice, biases, and behaviors.
2. A change in behavior of a given police officer will not generally result from sitting through one C-T course, no matter how extensive in scope and intensity.
3. For the training to have its greatest effect, it should be tailored to meet the needs of the officers as well as the community. In other words, it is not enough to train officers in understanding the problems, grievances, and other issues related to a particular community that might be perceived as "the assailant community" without having a real input from this community. For example, the authors spoke to a number of minority members in England. Some of them expressed a certain degree of satisfaction with the way police treated them, the others were vocally militant in their hatred toward the police.
4. The training of experienced officers should include the training of administrators in the same classroom setting. Decision making still takes place on the top and the decision makers who do not walk the streets not always understand what is happening on the streets and how the realities of life changed since they stood in the rain. For example, an officer in Madrid told one of the authors that his bosses have no clue with regard to what is happening in this area in terms of possible counter-terrorism threat and that only those who patrol this neighborhoods realize in what direction things are deteriorating; however, they are not the ones who have any influence over training or policy making of the department.
5. C-T training should begin early in an officer's career, during the basic academy, and should include basic modules on intelligence gathering. When the authors spoke to police officers in England and asked them how come they had no clue about the July (2005) bombers and their activities in the respective communities, they were told that this is not the police business but rather the Security Service's. The authors cannot disagree more.
6. The training should be reinforced throughout the officer's career and especially given the almost daily developments in the C-T area – it is almost mandatory to bring it above the level of the roll-call FYI routine into a more specialized and periodically offered in-service modules.

American society is still preoccupied with race, ethnicity, and diverse cultural orientations. The 9/11 events and the explosion of the C-T militaristic orientation within the local law enforcement will continue to divide and define our society. Law enforcement, in its essence, can be complex, painful, and problematic regardless of the multicultural dimensions. The goal of the C-T training modules should be to analyze the concepts of racial, ethnic, and cultural stereotypes and evaluate the impact of prejudice on police professionalism.

References

Crank, J. P. (1998). *Understanding police culture*. Cincinnati, OH: Anderson.

Gould, L. A. (1997). Can an old dog be taught new tricks? Teaching cultural diversity to police officers. *Policing, 20*, 339–356.

Haberfeld, M. R. (2002). *Critical issues in police training*. Upper Saddle River, NJ: Prentice Hall.

Haberfeld, M. R. (2005–2006). Field notes. Germany, Ireland, Northern Ireland Spain, Italy, Turkey, United Kingdom.

Mao, Z. (1963). *Selected military writings of Mao Tse-tung*. Peking: Foreign Language Press.

Muir, W. K. (1977). *Police streetcorner politicians*. Chicago, IL: University of Chicago Press.

Swanson, C. R., Territo, L., & Taylor, R. W. (2001). *Police administration: Structures, processes, and behavior* (5th ed.). Upper Saddle River, NJ: Prentice Hall.

Wilson, O. W., & McLaren, R. C. (1972). *Police administration*. New York, NY: McGraw-Hill Book Company.

Chapter 3
Waco: A Review of the Response by Law Enforcement

Meredith L. Patten and Amanda S. Twilliger

> *When the cause of the movement are everything, and the self is nothing, giving ones own life may be a small price for what one has had, or for what may be achieved by the gesture. When individual identity is so thoroughly tied to a collected identity and subordinated to the will and authority of a leader personifying that collective identity, and threat to the leader or the community is a threat to the self. Life is far less important than protection of the leader, defence of the movement's ideal, or indictment of its enemies (Dawson, 1998, p. 49).*

Introduction

The organization Cult Awareness Network (CAN) states that there are seven qualities to a destructive cult. These seven qualities are mind control, deception, self-destruction, exclusivity, alienation, charismatic leadership, exploitation, and a totalitarian world view (Tabor & Gallagher, 1995). The Branch Davidians, a millennial religious sect located in Mt. Carmel, Texas, near Waco, are commonly seen as a destructive cult. Until April 19, 1993, the religious "cult" was under the leadership of David Koresh, once known as Vernon Wayne Howell. Under Koresh's power, the Branch Davidians, like similar millennial groups, believed that they had a unique role to play in the history of the world. Koresh led the group with the belief that he could open the Seven Seals from the Bible. The opening of the seals was said to be a trigger for the end of the world (Officials Simply Fail, 1993, p. A1). Some have referred to the Branch Davidian compound in Mt. Carmel as "Ranch Apocalypse" (Leiby, 1999, p. F.01). The FBI defines a terrorist incident as "a violent act or an act dangerous to human life, in violation of the criminal laws of the United States or of any state, to intimidate or coerce a government, the civilian population, or any segment thereof, in furtherance of political or social goals" (Federal Bureau of

M.L. Patten (✉)
Research Administration of Justice, Occidental College, The American University, New York, NY, USA
e-mail: merepatten@gmail.com

M.R. Haberfeld, A. von Hassell (eds.), *A New Understanding of Terrorism*,
DOI 10.1007/978-1-4419-0115-6_3, © Springer Science+Business Media, LLC 2009

Investigation, Terrorism in the United States, 1993, p. 28). In the spring of 1993, the federal government sought to eradicate the Branch Davidians and a terrorist incident ensued. This chapter will give a general overview of cults, in particular the Branch Davidians, give an overview of the terrorist incident near Waco, Texas, from February to April 1993 and an analysis of the law enforcement response to the 51-day siege.

History and Description of Cults

When one thinks of cult violence, images often arise of the conflagration at the Waco compound or the mass suicide by ingestion of cyanide-laced Kool-aid in Jonestown. Although cult activity can turn violent, as proved to be the case in the two instances mentioned above, such acts are rare considering the number of cults or new religious movements throughout the world today (Dawson, 1998). Using the term "cult" in association with religious groups brings a negative connotation of control and violence (Dawson, 1998). The question that arises then is, what are the characteristics of a cult or a new religious movement that propel such groups to participate in violent activity?

There are three often sited common characteristics of cults. First, cults are always organized around a group leader who is often charismatic, self-appointed, and usually believed to have been chosen by God as a modern day prophet who can bring his (group leaders have been found to be predominantly male) followers to another level of existence (Fennell & Branswell, 1997). Second, cults operate around a belief system established by the leader. Cultic groups often have a "written tome" that serves as the basis of their belief system and is used for recruiting, creating values, and identifying the practices of the group (Galanter, 1989a). These groups are often authoritarian and "appear to be innovative and exclusive" in their structure, in that they offer services or promises that cannot be gained anywhere else (Singer, 2003, p. 9). And finally, cults foster an environment of unequivocal acceptance of their members, which provides unity of the group, unified against the outside world, practicing honesty within the group and dishonesty and mistrust of nonmembers. Cults expect total devotion from their members, which often includes a change in lifestyle as members become increasingly immersed in the group (Singer, 2003, p. 9). Conformity is gained through a shared belief system, and dependence is gained through the social structure of the group (Galanter, 1989b).

The majority of cult members are normal, middle-class, well-educated individuals from functional families, demonstrating that anyone can become involved in a cult (Singer, 2003, p. 17). Cults offer solace in a world of choice and ambiguity, they provide structure to those unable to make their own decisions or those disturbed by the state of the world, and they can provide focus and meaning to those searching for purpose. Group norms and rules provide structure and stability for members, as well as an instant family, safety, organization, and protection (Schwartz, 1999). So then what is wrong with cults, and what causes these groups to turn violent?

The history of cults in America dates as far back as colonization when "Roger Williams...fled Puritan New England...and established his own cultic commune (the Baptists) in Rhode Island" (Galanter, 1989a, p. 57). Cults initially arose as offshoots of mainstream religion. Apocalyptic cults first started to appear in the period between 1776 and 1865 with examples such as the Shakers, Mormons, and Millerites (Galanter, 1989a, p. 59). The most recent upsurge in apocalyptic cultic activity has been attributed to the counter culture of the 1960s and the disillusioning events that occurred in this era, focusing society on bettering the world, which some did by turning from politics to religion in an attempt to give meaning to the world (Dawson, 1998, pp. 73–74). Dawson has termed these groups "world rejecting movements," in which the predominant view is that the world has strayed from "God's prescriptions and plan" by focusing too highly on the pursuit of material goods and in turn has filled the world with pollution, crime, and hatred (Dawson, 1998, p. 40). World rejecting movements see the coming of the millennium as a chance to wipe the slate clean and "recover the world for God" in order to create a utopian ideal (Dawson, 1998, p. 42). These groups carry apocalyptic beliefs of "last days" and "end times"; beliefs that often foster violence because of the belief that violence will precede the last days. Apocalyptic beliefs can work to both draw a group closer together in expectation of the last days and hopes for salvation and also to create an environment of paranoia with feelings of persecution from the outside world (Dawson, 1998, p. 347). The primary task of these groups is to "prepare for the messianic end they envision" (Galanter, 1989b, p. 99). These groups propagate a doomsday prediction, offering salvation only to their members (Singer, 2003; Schwartz, 1999).

The charismatic leader adds to the volatility of these apocalyptic beliefs by responding to threats or perceived threats to his authority by becoming more authoritarian, which he does by imposing tests of loyalty, which in turn prepare the group for acts of violence through fear and discipline. These leaders do not ascribe to normal societal rules and are therefore able to practice ultimate authority over a group. Without outside societal controls, members of the group become habituated to accept "increasingly bizarre behavior on the part of the leader" (Dawson, 1998, pp. 351–352). The authoritarian nature of these groups is compounded by the social structure that many religious cults adopt. These groups function as total institutions, which are extremely organized and tightly controlled, in which members live, work, and socialize with little contact with the outside world (Dawson, 1998). In addition to being physically confining in their structure, these groups practice "boundary control" of members by dictating the diet, "dress, customs, or ideology," psychologically breaking down the members, and fostering an environment of dependence, fear, and paranoia (Galanter, 1989a, p. 35).

Cultic relationships are characterized by a buildup of dependence by members on their leader and the organization for all major decisions (Singer, 2003). Ultimately the individuals' sense of self is broken down, and their world view is altered to adopt the view that the leader has prescribed (Singer, 2003). Because these groups are highly structured and the beliefs of the group are continuously reinforced, members eventually adopt these group beliefs, altering their previous belief systems and affecting their judgment (Galanter, 1989b, p. 64). As membership is voluntary, groups rely on either fear or love to persuade members to stay. Sexual promiscuity within the group is often used as a means to maintain members and enforce communal not individual bonds (Dawson, 1998). "The life of the world rejecting movement tends to require considerable subordination of individual interest, will, and autonomy in order to maximize collective solidarity and to eliminate disruptive dissent" (Dawson, 1998, p. 48).

Cults of today are more organized, focused, and violent than cults of the 1960s and 1970s. The focus has turned from raising money and protesting a cause to attending to the grievances of the cult leader (Schwartz, 1999). As these grievances grow more extravagant, so does the threat of violence.

Description of the Branch Davidians

The Branch Davidians are a millennial religious group with deep ties to the Seventh-Day Adventists. The group's roots began in 1831 when William Miller began studying the prophecies of the bible and concluded that the world would end sometime between 1843 and 1844. His movement came to be known as the "Millerites." These types of groups became known as apocalyptic cults or millennialists because of their world ending views. When the world did not end in 1844 as predicted, the Millerites referred to the nonevent as "the great disappointment" and the group began to disintegrate (Wright, 1995). It was then that a woman named Ellen White influenced the group now commonly referred to as the Seventh-Day Adventist Church. After Ellen White died, the church did not have a leader until Victor Houteff, a Bulgarian immigrant, joined the church believing he was a prophet from God. Houteff's erratic behavior eventually led him to be excommunicated from the Church and he began his own subgroup in 1935. He named the group the Davidian Seventh-Day Adventists. Trying to avoid fighting in World War II, Houteff attached the group's name to the Adventists, believing that the religious affiliation would preclude him and his followers from having to serve in the war (Wright, 1995). He moved his followers to Mt. Carmel, Texas. The Davidians believed they were the "true remnant called to proclaim divine judgment" (Wright, 1995, p. 25). In an attempt to show strength and independence from the outside world, the Davidians even maintained their own form of currency for use while at the Mt. Carmel compound (Wright, 1995). Houteff continued to lead the Davidians until his death in 1955 at which time his wife, Flo, took over. Benjamin Roden, a member of the church, attempted to claim leadership and when he failed, he formed another sect named the Branch Davidian Seventh-Day Adventists. "Branch" was added to the Davidian name to distinguish the group from other sects of the Davidians. It refers to Jesus, as interpreted from the Bible (Wright, 1995).

In 1962, Roden acquired Victor Houteff's property in Mt. Carmel, Texas, after Flo Houteff fled to California with much of the Davidian's money. Roden died in 1978 and his wife, Lois, gained ownership of the church. In 1981, Vernon Wayne

Howell, later known as David Koresh, joined the Branch Davidians and began receiving messages from God stating that he was the "Antitypical Cyrus." Lois Roden, seeing Howell as a prophet, began to mentor him as a potential leader of the Branch Davidians (Wright, 1995). *But just who was David Koresh?* David Koresh was born as Vernon Wayne Howell in 1959. He was born in Houston, Texas, and raised by his grandparents. Howell had a very lonely childhood and spent a great deal of time playing musical instruments and developed a strong interest in the Bible (Tabor & Gallagher, 1995). "By the age of 12, he had memorized and interpreted the New Testament. This would later become an obsessive interest of his" (Sumpter & Burroughs, 1994). Throughout his history with the Seventh-Day Adventist Church, Koresh was viewed as overbearing and obsessive about the religion, attempting to convert all members to ascribing to his interpretation of the religion (Sumpter & Burroughs, 1994). He was just 20 years when he left the Seventh-Day Adventists and joined the Branch Davidians. After a dispute with Lois Roden's son, George, over whom would lead the church, Howell succeeded and eventually changed his name to David Koresh, David for King David and Koresh for Cyrus (Tabor & Gallagher, 1995). Between 1989 and 1993, Koresh exerted his power over Branch Davidian followers, leading them to believe that the end of the world was approaching (United States Department of Justice, 1993). He began to interpret the "Seven Seals," which comes from the Book of Revelations and predicted the end of the world (United States Department of Justice, 1993). The Branch Davidians interpreted the opening of the Seven Seals to accomplish two things: "God's plan of salvation through Koresh, the second Christ figure, and the final events of the end of history" (Tabor & Gallagher, 1995, p. 54).

The Davidians have been described as a group of "desperate religious fanatics expecting an apocalyptic ending, in which they were destined to die defending their sacred ground and destined to achieve salvation" (Stone, 1994). Not only did the Davidians follow a credo of an apocalyptic ending, they additionally viewed the government as their enemy, referring to the government as "the Beasts," and a belief that they were living in their last days, which would be characterized by a "cataclysmic confrontation between themselves and the government, and that they would thereafter be resurrected" (Gotschall, 1994; Barkun, 1994). Confrontation with the government was viewed by the group to be a "means to religious salvations" (Danforth, 2000, p. 125).

By the spring of 1993, approximately 130 Branch Davidians were living at the compound in Mt. Carmel, Texas. It has been said that the "Waco cult is the product of an apocalyptic theology, refined over decades by a succession of zealous but nonviolent splinter groups, that was seized at last by a charismatic and combustible leader" (Lacayo, 1993). The 131 people living at Mt. Carmel were composed of 46 women, 42 men, and 43 children under the age of 16 (Tabor & Gallagher, 1995). Most of those living at Mt. Carmel were recruited in the late 1980s by Koresh and came from various countries including the Philippines and New Zealand. Koresh prided himself on promoting diversity among his followers and the racial makeup of the Branch Davidians reflected that ideal. Koresh used his authority so extensively as to persuade those who accepted his teachings to take the surname Koresh (Tabor

& Gallagher, 1995). Koresh was extremely authoritarian and used various forms of mind control and psychological persuasion to ensure that his followers remained under his reign. He often had them repeatedly watch violent movies and had all members maintain a strict and rationed vegetarian diet. Television was generally forbidden, as were birthdays and sex, and days were mixed with hard work and long hours of bible study (Lacayo, 1993). Koresh allowed only himself to have sexual relations and took it upon himself to do so with all female cult members, regardless of age. He had multiple wives and his ultimate goal was to procreate to carry on his name and the teachings of the Branch Davidians. It has been said, however, that Koresh feared outside authority so much that he arranged for other male members to marry his "wives" in an attempt to prevent the government from taking his children away from him (Tabor & Gallagher, 1995).

Political and Historical Context

Two days prior to the initial raid by the Bureau of Alcohol, Tobacco, and Firearms (ATF) on the Mt. Carmel compound of the Branch Davidians, the World Trade Center had experienced a terrorist attack when a bomb exploded in the parking structure. Critics of the ATF believe that this event detracted from the preparation of the ATF for the Waco raid, as the ATF's attention was not sufficiently focused on the events at Waco (Barkun, 1994). Regardless of the distraction of the World Trade Center attack, the ATF and the FBI had prior experience with isolated religious groups involving firearms violations. In 1985 the ATF assaulted the Zarephath-Horeb commune of the Covenant, Sword and Arm of the Lord (CSA) cult after they learned that the group, in preparation for the "end times," had stockpiled massive amounts of firearms and explosive devices (Barkun, 1994). The FBI negotiation team along with 80 federal agents was called in, and after 2 days of negotiation, the incident ended with the surrender of the cult avoiding any fatalities. Unfortunately, in the 2 days of negotiating, the ATF believe that the CSA were able to destroy most of the evidence that would have allowed a case to be brought against them (Barkun, 1994). Although the ATF and the FBI were able to end this event without fatalities, the religious nature of the group was not addressed in the course of negotiations, and the objective of the raid was thought to have been compromised as the sought after evidence was destroyed. Then in August 1992, US Marshals attempted to serve a warrant to Randy Weaver, a Christian Identity survivalist accused of attempting to sell firearms to undercover ATF agents (Barkun, 1994). Although the FBI hostage negotiation team was called in, this event did not end peacefully, with fatalities to both sides. The 11-day standoff was "eventually ended through the mediation of James "Bo" Gritz, a right-wing political figure and fringe presidential candidate" (Barkun, 1994). In both cases the ATF and the FBI relied on massive shows of force in order to intimidate their opponents into surrendering, but in the later case, this show of force did not end the conflict. Instead, an outside party was called in, a party that Weaver was able to identify with his cause, as Gritz was affiliated with the Christian Identity movement. In this case the ATF and the FBI did address the religious nature of the group in order to foster surrender. Both of these events shared important characteristics with the nature of the Waco raid. All three cases involved fringe religious groups in isolated locations, accused of firearms violations, and known to possess massive amounts of firearms. In the first two cases, federal agents were able to secure the perimeter of the compounds, avoid mass media attention, and confront their opposition without them being forewarned. The Waco situation differed in at least one major regard, the element of surprise had been compromised when both the media and David Koresh had been tipped of the impending raid (Church, 1995). Speculation exists that the media were tipped off by members of ATF's public relations in an attempt to gain publicity to "showcase its costly Special Response Team (SRT)" (Gotschall, 1994).

Description of the Incident

There has been a significant amount of literature written on the events that occurred at the Branch Davidians compound in Mt. Carmel, Texas, between February 28, 1993 and April 19, 1993. The literature reflects the various views of what occurred during the standoff that is commonly known as "Waco." There is much in dispute over who fired first. However, what is not in dispute are the basic facts of how the Bureau of Alcohol, Tobacco, and Firearms (ATF) arrived at the Branch Davidian compound and the major events which occurred thereafter.

While attempting to execute an arrest warrant for David Koresh, leader of the "Branch Davidians", at his compound near Waco, Texas, on February 28, 1993, numerous Bureau of Alcohol, Tobacco, and Firearms agents came under fire. The warrant was issued by a federal judge and agents were to arrest Koresh and search his compound on suspicion of federal firearms and explosives violations. The government was led to believe that Koresh and his followers were converting rifles into automatic weapons (Tabor & Gallagher, 1995). During the initial gunfire, 4 ATF agents were killed, 16 were wounded and 2 of Koresh's followers were killed and 5 wounded (Danforth, 2000). Refusing to emerge from his compound or negotiate and not permitting any followers including children to leave, the Federal Bureau of Investigation's hostage negotiation team was called in to assist. During the next 51 days, hundreds of law enforcement personnel attempted to negotiate with Koresh to have him release the hostages. The standoff finally ended on April 19, 1993, when fires engulfed the Branch Davidian compound, killing dozens of children and adults. Below is a chronology of the events at the Mt. Carmel compound between February 28, 1993 and April 19, 1993.

In June 1992, the Bureau of Alcohol, Tobacco, and Firearms began an investigation into the religious group known as the Branch Davidians. The ATF's interest in the Branch Davidians and the property in Mt. Carmel, Texas, began after they received a tip that members of the group were participating in the manufacturing of illegal firearms on the compound in late May 1992. In June 1992, the ATF had investigated the claims and found them to be true (Danforth, 2000). By July 1992, the

ATF interviewed a firearms dealer about his business with David Koresh. The dealer shared information with Koresh and acted as a go-between relaying to ATF agents that Koresh had invited them to inspect all of his weapons and paperwork. At that time, the ATF declined to take him up on his offer (Lynch, 2001). During the initial investigation, the ATF also learned of the Branch Davidians anti-government views. In December 1992, the ATF's undercover operation began and the Department of Defense offered the bureau aerial reconnaissance support (Danforth, 2000). Two surveillance flights were flown in January and four in February of 1993 (Danforth, 2000). Using ATF agents posing as college students, the ATF began surveillance on the Mt. Carmel property in January 1993 (Chua-Eoan, 1993). The continuing investigation led ATF agents to believe that they had probable cause that Koresh was in violation of federal firearms regulations. A warrant claiming "unlawful possession of a destructive device" was issued on February 25, 1993, in preparation to arrest Koresh and search the Branch Davidian Compound (Danforth, 2000).

The investigation continued until February 1993 when the ATF requested an arrest and search warrant for David Koresh and the group's compound. After rehearsals, the ATF prepared to deliver the warrant with over 70 armed agents. Before the warrant was served on February 28, 1993, ATF agents went through minimal training for the raid on Mt. Carmel and no real plan of attack was formulated. Koresh was tipped off and the ATF lost the element of surprise, and perhaps their only semblance of a plan. At that time, gunfire ensued. The origin of such gunfire remains in dispute with the ATF claiming that they were fired upon and refrained from returning fire, while members of the Branch Davidians stating that they were fired upon first. A number of Branch Davidians and numerous ATF agents were killed on the first day and David Koresh was seriously wounded. The casualties led to the worst day in the US law enforcement history (Lynch, 2001).

With the standoff continuing, the ATF turned all negotiation efforts over to the Federal Bureau of Investigation's Hostage Rescue Team (HRT). The first major negotiation came a day later when on March 2, Koresh agreed to surrender as long as officials nationally broadcast one of his messages. Law enforcement officials agreed to this request, but Koresh did not surrender. Also on March 2, the FBI called in renowned psychiatrist Dr. Park Dietz to develop an assessment of Koresh and to ascertain exactly whom the government was up against. Over the course of the next couple of days, Dietz was given hundreds of pages of documents from the government and the anti-cult organization, Cult Awareness Network (CAN). Dietz determined that Koresh was a psychopath and that negotiations would inevitably fail (Tabor & Gallagher, 1995). However, over the course of the next week, 23 Koresh followers left the compound to safety. The standoff continued while dozens of adults and children remained confined in the compound. The FBI concluded that the Mt. Carmel compound was stocked with enough food and meals ready to eat for approximately 1 year and Koresh, on March 28, 1993, said he had "no intention to die and he was waiting for word from God" (Frontline Online, retrieved October 19, 2004, http://www.pbs.org/wgbh/pages/frontline/waco/timeline3.html). On March 30, 1993, FBI agents allowed defense attorney Dick DeGuerin to enter the compound to discuss a peaceful surrender with Koresh. All attempts at such a negotiation failed. On April 15, 1993, the HRT advised that "negotiations were at an impasse" (Danforth, 2000). After a total of 41 demands of which 26 were met throughout the standoff, the FBI and attorney general Janet Reno agreed to try and draw the Branch Davidians out of the compound. The action took place on April 19, 1993.

Using tanks, the FBI approached the compound and smashed into the structured walls. While doing this, the tanks emitted a CS, orthochlorobenzylidenemalononi-trile, gas. The idea was to have the gas draw the followers out of the compound but would not be harmful to children. However, Koresh and his followers were equipped with gas masks and appeared to be unaffected by the insertion of the CS gas, and hence no one emerged from the compound. In response, the FBI then shot three pyrotechnic rounds which emitted more tear gas into the compound. Hours later, a fire broke out in the compound and only nine Davidians survived. In total, 80 Branch Davidians died, including 21 children. Five men and one woman died on the first day of the siege. Thirty-five people left the compound before the fire on April 19 and 32 women, 21 men, and 21 children died on April 19, 1993. Although the majority who died on April 19 died from smoke inhalation, it was found that many had suffered from gunshot wounds as a result of gunfire from within the compound. Koresh's body was identified weeks later and the coroner concluded that a gunshot wound to the forehead was the likely cause of death. The FBI, along with the ATF, then began to analyze their handling of the incident on April 19, 1993, along with what occurred 50 days prior (Danforth, 2000).

Controversy Surrounding the Waco Standoff

There are numerous criticisms of the government's handling of the raid on the Mt. Carmel compound, the most pronounced of which are the use of CS gas and pyrotechnic devices, the conception of the Branch Davidians as cult members and lack of emphasis on the religious and millenarian nature of the group, and the lack of coherent communication between government officials and offices. The number one criticism that resonates throughout the literature on Waco is the appropriateness of the use of CS gas and pyrotechnic rounds on the compound, especially considering the large number of children known to be housed in the complex.

One thing that the literature agrees upon is attorney general Janet Reno's concern and apprehension over the use of CS gas in the course of the April 19 raid on the Waco compound. The plan by the FBI for using tear gas began to take place in March 1993, and was eventually presented to Janet Reno on April 12 (Reavis, 1995b). The intentions of the plan were to gradually inject tear gas throughout the compound over the course of a 2-day period in hopes of flushing out those remaining inside. If this plan failed to draw out the Davidians, the contingency plan was to use tanks to gradually tear down the walls of the structure until the innards of the building were exposed and there was nowhere else for the Davidians to hide (Reavis, 1995b). At this time Janet Reno expressed concern over the use of CS tear gas, as she feared its effects on the pregnant women and children inside the compound. Although no conclusive empirical evidence exists that CS gas does not harm children, Janet Reno was given assurance that the use of CS gas was nonlethal and any damage done would be nonpermanent (Reavis, 1995b; Danforth, 2000). Additionally, Janet Reno gave explicit directions prohibiting the use of pyrotechnics in the course of the raid after having been advised by military experts that there was a possibility of a fire as a result of a tear gas assault (Danforth, 2000). This latter requirement would later become the focus of intense debate over the semantics of the instructions as CS gas exists in two forms, both pyrotechnic and nonpyrotechnic, the former requiring a charge in order to disperse the gas. Reno authorized the use of only the latter form of the gas on the compound (Danforth, 2000). "CS is the common name for orthochlorobenzylidenemalononitrile, a white power that manufacturers and vendors classify as a 'lachrymator irritant' – a substance that causes tearing" (Reavis, 1995b). However, unlike this benign description of the effects, the use of such gas has been banned for use in warfare, and the US Army and manufacturers of the gas have warned that the effects of the gas may make those exposed to it too disoriented to find legitimate escape, and if burned, the gas may "give off lethal fumes" (Reavis, 1995b). After receiving much assurance from multiple forces that the tear gas was nonlethal, Janet Reno approved the plan and the use of nonpyrotechnic tear gas on April 17, 1993.

The question then becomes, how and why were three rounds of pyrotechnic tear gas used on the compound, and did they contribute to the start of the fire that eventually engulfed and destroyed the compound and almost all of its inhabitants? There is evidence of two prior raids by the FBI using tear gas that ended in massive fires, one in 1974 against the Symbionese Liberation Army in Los Angeles and the second in 1984 against "right-wing fugitive" Robert Matthews in Washington (Reavis, 1995b). Despite this evidence, at some point in the raid the FBI chose to fire three pyrotechnic devices at the concrete structure attached to the compound. Not in dispute is the fact that the first nonpyrotechnic tear gas rounds were fired into the complex at 6:05 a.m., this assault continued throughout the morning until a total of 389 rounds of tear gas had been fired into the compound, all failed to draw anyone out, which researches have used as evidence that the levels of CS gas administered into the compound never reached levels of lethal proportions (Danforth, 2000). Then at 7:48 a.m., permission was given to fire military or pyrotechnic rounds from tanks at the concrete construction pit attached to the compound. This is the point in the raid where communication really starts to break down. Apparently the FBI felt that it was not violating Janet Reno's implicit instructions not to use pyrotechnic devices because they felt that the concrete construction pit was not flammable and not part of the living quarters of the compound. The next stage of the assault was the use of tanks to smash walls and doors, but in the course of this action, it has been postulated that the stairwells connecting the first and second floor were destroyed, and exits were blocked (Reavis, 1995b). At about this time, FBI recording devices picked up discussion among the Davidians of spreading fuel throughout the compound and discussion of starting a fire. Finally, at 12:07 p.m., FBI surveillance tape show records of the first fire starting on the second floor, followed by two additional fires and the sound of gunshots from within the compound (Danforth, 2000). Evidence of the first fire did not occur until some 4 h after the pyrotechnic devices were fired, indicating that these rounds were not the cause of the ignition of the fire; however, it was not until August 1999 before the Department of Justice admitted that pyrotechnic devices had been used by the FBI. Was this a deliberate cover-up, a total breakdown of communication, or truly a problem of terminology? Much speculation exists that the FBI deliberately hid this information from investigators, a claim that is bolstered by the fact that, although in the early days of the case all three casings and two shells of the pyrotechnic devices were reportedly witnessed, only one shell ever made it into evidence. The remaining shells and casings are still missing to this day (Danforth, 2000). Additionally, evidence exists that the criminal prosecution team was aware of the use of pyrotechnic devices as early as November 1993 but failed to disclose this information to the defense team (Danforth, 2000). Compounding the criticism of the handling of the event is the fact that the FBI had decided that in the event of a fire, the arrival of the fire department would be delayed, purportedly for their own safety due to the risk of Davidians opening fire. This may have been a costly decision, as the first fire was reported at 12:10 p.m., but it was 12:34 p.m. before fire trucks were allowed on the scene (Danforth, 2000).

Throughout the course of the raid, the Davidians in the compound were handled as hostages, with negotiations handled through the FBI's hostage negotiation team, references to the group as a cult, implying blind obedience to their leader, and implications of their irrational beliefs. There is much criticism that the FBI's conception of the Waco situation was faulty in that the FBI chose to look at Waco as a hostage situation instead of looking at the group as a new religious movement, sincere in their beliefs and prepared to die for their cause (Barkun, 1994). The FBI did not seek to consult any experts in millenialism or new religious movements and therefore did not give enough credence to the group's millenarian views (Barkun, 1994). The FBI's behavioral scientists warned that a massive show of force was exactly what the Davidians were expecting and "played into Koresh's hands" (Barkun, 1994, p. 91). By surrounding the compound in a massive show of force, and alerting the media, the FBI demonstrated that they did not understand the mindset of the Davidians and perhaps should have given more credence to the advice of their own behavioral scientists (Church, 1995). The FBI played down the religious nature and apocalyptic visions of the group, and were unprepared to understand the language and behavior of Koresh and his followers, referring to Koresh's negotiation conversations as "Bible babble" (Barkun, 1994). The FBI's view of the Davidians as irrational cult members made them less focused on negotiations and more focused on their tactical responses (Barkun, 1994). "The FBI's behavioral-science unit realized that Koresh and his followers were in a desperate kill-or-be-killed mode" and willing to die defending their ideals, making them unlikely to submit to tactical pressures (Stone, 1994). However, the tactical response was prioritized over continuing negotiations. Toward the end of the standoff, Koresh was focused on his interpretation of the Seven Seals. He believed that by interpreting the Seven Seals, the inevitable Last Days would be delayed (Barkun, 1994). On April 14, 1993, Koresh sent a letter to negotiators saying that he would surrender after he finished interpreting the Seven

Seals. Lawyers projected that it would take between 10 and 14 days to complete the interpretations, the FBI projected it would take 20 days, yet the raid occurred only 5 days later (Church, 1995). Did the FBI place enough importance on this request from Koresh? Did their lack of understanding of the religious nature of the group prevent them from grasping the gravity of the situation and Koresh's demands? In Janet Reno's testimony, she defended her decision to endorse the raid by stating that Koresh had broken multiple surrender promises before. Reno stated that federal agents had obtained information from Waco that the Davidians were planning to strap explosive devices to their waist and exit the compound in a suicide/murder spree (Walker, 1995). Then on April 16 and 17, Davidians in the compound displayed signs reading "The flames await Isaiah 13" and conversations were recorded, indicating that a fire would ensue, prompting the raid 2 days later (Danforth, 2000). All evidence indicates that the Davidians were a violent group prepared to fight to their death, particularly if their demands were not met. But after a 51-day standoff, why was the FBI so determined to end the standoff on April 19?

Perhaps the explanation lies in the number of agencies involved in the standoff and the relationship between these agencies. Waco had been the home of the Branch Davidians for more than 50 years, and in that time the local law enforcement had developed a peaceful accepting relationship with the group and all of its leaders. However, when the ATF began their surveillance of the compound, they chose to bypass the local law enforcement who were the most familiar with this group and their practices, and chose to go undercover to collect their evidence (Gotschall, 1994). Although the ATF decided to bypass the local law enforcement, they did not attempt to handle the situation on their own. Throughout the course of the 51-day standoff and the collection of evidence, the Texas Rangers, the US Military, the FBI, the "Tarrant County Medical Examiner's Office, the Houston Fire Department's Arson Division, the United States Attorney's Office for the Western District of Texas, the Texas Department of Public Safety Crime Laboratory, the Texas Highway Patrol, the ATF, and the Smithsonian Institution" were all involved in the investigation (Danforth, 2000, p. 86). Although the FBI took prime responsibility for the negotiations, "the FBI had a poor relationship with other law enforcement agencies involved in the incident" (Danforth, 2000, p. 86). In addition to having strained relations between agencies involved, strained relations existed between the tactical and negotiation teams, with the former pushing for the use of force, not negotiation to end the standoff (Barkun, 1994). The two teams led different and conflicting operations, likely leading to some of the confusion on the day of the raid. The communications breakdowns began before the first round of tear gas was ever thrown. The FBI and Janet Reno are still unable to agree on what plan was agreed upon for the raid, and the Texas governor first learned of the attack when he witnessed it on television (Danforth, 2000). After the fire, the authority was turned back to the Texas Rangers for evidence collection. Although it is speculated that the FBI had reason to want to hide the evidence of pyrotechnic devices, the Rangers were in charge of evidence collection. The two agencies in conjunction with a "line search" found and photographed the third missing projectile, but this projectile failed to be logged into evidence by either agency (Danforth, 2000). The 17-day search involved more than

200 law enforcement members from various agencies, and on May 17 the chain of command was turned back to the FBI. Throughout the course of the confrontation at the Mt. Carmel complex and the ensuing investigation, the chain of command changed hands from the ATF to the FBI to the Texas Rangers and back to the FBI. Tactical and negotiation initiatives were frequently inconsistent, the formal plan for the raid was blatantly breached, and communication lapses abounded.

Implications and Conclusion

All in all, the raid on the Branch Davidian compound in Mt. Carmel, Texas, is not seen as a successful venture. Only nine Davidians survived the raid, and any evidence from inside the compound was lost in the conflagration. Although the use of CS gas is not believed to have been the cause of death to any of the Davidians, given the evidence that Office of Special Counsel has collected from this case, the implication is that the possibility for the future use of CS gas in similar raids is not positive. Future use of such gas must be scrutinized on a situational basis, keeping in mind the negative effects the use of the gas had in this instance (Danforth, 2000). Although the fire team, assisted by accelerant detection dogs, determined that the "fire was caused by the intentional act(s) of a person or persons inside the compound;" the "fires were set in three separate areas of the complex;" and "flammable liquids were used to accelerate the spread and intensity of the fire," the destruction of the stairwells and blockage of exits in the compound did little to better the situation for this trapped inside (Danforth, 2000). The ability to deal with similar situations in the future depends on the understanding of the beliefs that these groups are acting under (Barkun, 1994). In order to understand the likelihood of surrender, the religious nature of the groups must be addressed. As has been exhibited throughout history, religious cults harboring apocalyptic endings are unlikely to fall to massive shows of force, and in many instances, these shows of force serve only to enforce and validate their apocalyptic visions. As a result of Waco, "when confronted with complex hostage situations like that in Waco," the ATF practices more dialogue and enforced perimeter control, making communication a much higher priority (Thurman, 1998). Hopefully, improved communication, a better understanding of apocalyptic cults and their potential for violence, and a greater understanding of the effects of CS gas on hostages in enclosed spaces will help to prevent future standoffs from ending with the mass casualties that resulted from the raid on Waco.

In the post-9/11 world, incidents such as Waco and groups similar to the Branch Davidians will not be tolerated. The events of 9/11 have made the United States and US law enforcement sensitive to anti-government sentiments. Our mission is to protect our nation from terrorists, whether from abroad or home grown. The stance taken by the government at Waco was, at the time, seen by many as hardnosed, is a stance that may not be questioned with so much intensity if it were to occur today.

References

Barkun, M. (1994). Millenarian groups and law enforcement agencies: The lessons of Waco. *Terrorism and Political Violence, 6*(1), 75–95.

Chua-Eoan, H., (1993, October 11). Tripped up by lies. *Time Magazine.*

Church, E. (1995, July 29). Waco probes focuses on wisdom, not legality, of FBI action. *Congressional Quarterly Weekly Report, 53*(30), 2278–2279.

Danforth, J. C. (2000). Final report to the deputy attorney general concerning the 1993 confrontation at the Mt. Carmel complex, Waco, Texas. November 8, 2000.

Dawson, L. (Ed.). (1998). *Cults in our midst: Readings in the study of new religious movements.* New Brunswick: Transaction Publishers.

Federal Bureau of Investigation (1993). Terrorism in the United States.

Fennell, T., & Branswell, B. (1997, April 7). Doom sects. *Maclean's, 119*(14), 48.

Frontline Online, retrieved October 19, 2004, http://www.pbs.org/wgbh/pages/frontline/waco/timeline3.html

Galanter, M. (Ed.). (1989a). *Cults and new religious movements.* Washington, D.C.: The American Psychiatric Association.

Galanter, M. (1989b). *Cults: Faith, healing, and coercion.* New York: Oxford University Press.

Gotschall, M. (1994, April 4). A marriage made in hell. *National Review, 46*(6), 57–60.

Lacayo, R. (1993, March 15). Cult of death. *Time Magazine.*

Leiby, R. (1999, September 26). Sex, God and rock-and-roll. *The Washington Post.*

Lynch, T. (2001). No confidence: An unofficial account of the Waco incident. No. 395, April 9, 2001.

Officials simply fail to grasp resolve of millennial cults. (1993, April 21). *The Salt Lake Tribune,* p. A1.

Reavis, D. (1995a). *The ashes of Waco: An investigation.* New York: Simon & Schuster.

Reavis, D. (1995b, July). What really happened at Waco. *Texas Monthly, 23*(7), 88–95.

Schwartz, L. (1999). Cults: Predisposed to communal violence? In H. Hall & L. Whitaker (Eds.), *Collective violence: Effective strategies for assessing and interviewing in fatal group and institutional aggression* (pp. 239–254). Boca Raton: CRC Press.

Singer, M. (2003). *Cults in our midst: The continuing fight against their hidden menace.* San Francisco: Jossey-Bass.

Stone, A. (1994, February). How the FBI helped fuel the Waco fire. *Harper's Magazine, 288*(1725), 15–18.

Sumpter, R., & Burroughs, R. (1994, Summer). Dysfunctional gifted students and counseling: Jim Jones and David Koresh. *Education, 114*(4), 542–546.

Tabor, J., & Gallagher, E. (1995). *Why Waco? Cults and the battle for religious freedom in America.* Berkeley: University of California Press.

Thurman, J. (1998, April, 17). Criticism leads ATF to soften 'thug' image. *Christian Science Monitor, 90*(99), 5.

United States Department of Justice (1993). Report on the events at Waco, Texas: February 28–April 19, 1993.

Walker, S. (1995, August 2). Reno stands by Waco decision. *Christian Science Monitor, 87*(173), 3.

Wright, S. (1995). *Armageddon in Waco.* Chicago: University of Chicago Press.

Chapter 4
The Solo Crusader: Theodore Kaczynski and Timothy McVeigh

Tonya M. DeSa and Kevin E. McCarthy

Introduction

Hacker (1976) categorized terrorists as criminals, crusaders, or crazies. Two of America's most infamous homegrown terrorists, Theodore Kaczynski and Timothy McVeigh, occupied Hacker's crusader category because they believed that their actions were for the greater good of their respective causes. Both were loners. McVeigh largely plotted and conducted his single bombing on his own, and Kaczynski lived in a hermit's isolation during his long bombing campaign. Both espoused radical political philosophies – McVeigh described himself as being on the "far right" and Kaczynski as being on the "far left" ("McVeigh Vents," 2001). This chapter examines their backgrounds and their terrorist acts. Law enforcement responses will be reviewed, along with the prosecutions that yielded very different results. The chapter ends with analysis and suggested countermeasures.

Kaczynski's History: The Progressive Deterioration

Born in 1942, Theodore "Ted" Kaczynski was raised by his Polish immigrant parents in a working-class suburb of Chicago. He had one sibling, a circumstance that would eventually lead investigators to solve the case. After attending public schools and excelling academically, the 16-year-old Kaczynski entered Harvard, where he kept to himself in his math studies and left few impressions with those who knew him beyond some of his odd personal habits. Postgraduate schooling took Kaczynski to the University of Michigan, where he worked and taught with considerable success. Several of his papers were published in academic journals, and his 1967 doctoral dissertation that solved an obscure mathematical problem received his department's top prize. His next career move was to accept a tenure-track professorship at the University of California, Berkeley (Chase, 2003).

T.M. DeSa (✉)
City University of New York, New York, NY, USA
e-mail: tdesa555@yahoo.com

M.R. Haberfeld, A. von Hassell (eds.), *A New Understanding of Terrorism*,
DOI 10.1007/978-1-4419-0115-6_4, © Springer Science+Business Media, LLC 2009

At Berkeley, Kaczynski stepped into an intense scene of college protests and counterculture extremism. Later, Kaczynski used markings on his bombs and issued communications that suggested his association with a fictitious radical organization. A "manifesto" that Kaczynski finally forced into publication advocated positions that were topical in radical circles of the late 1960s and early 1970s (Johnston, 1995). In fact, Kaczynski continued his pattern of having limited contact with others at Berkeley, and the coat-and-tie wearing professor displayed no outward signs of being influenced by persons or organizations operating in that area at that time. His superiors were surprised when he tendered his resignation in the spring of 1969 (Graysmith, 1997).

Kaczynski left behind more than academia. He turned away from mathematics, which had been the focus of his intellectual life since high school. Years later, the manifesto convinced some that the bomber's background was in the social sciences, not mathematics. Kaczynski returned to the family home in the Chicago area and also looked for land in Canada. With no job and without school to occupy his time, Kaczynski stayed at home and wrote letters to publications voicing his complaints about matters ranging from advertising to motorcycles. The Canadian land never materialized, so he followed his brother David to Montana, where David took a job after college. In June 1971, Kaczynski purchased 1.4 acres of land outside of the town of Lincoln. There he built the 10" × 12" cabin that would become his home and bomb factory.

Contrary to some reports, Kaczynski's cabin was not in an extremely remote location. It was close to an access road and had postal service through a mailbox on the main road. Approximately four miles away, Lincoln was a small town to which Kaczynski would travel by bicycle to buy supplies or use its public library. The town also offered easy bus connections to Helena or Missoula from which Kaczynski could begin his trips to plant or mail bombs. In 1978, he returned to his family's home and briefly took a job in a factory, but he had a serious falling out with his brother, and one of the few attempts in his life to date a woman ended badly. Kaczynski's first bomb exploded during that time, in May 1978, at Northwestern University outside of Chicago.

The Long Crusade

Kaczynski planted or mailed 16 bombs from 1978 to 1995. The public was not even aware that a serial bomber was at work until Kaczynski was more than halfway through his bombings. Three victims died, and some two dozen suffered injuries ranging from minor smoke inhalation to serious maiming. Property damage was minimal. While Kaczynski's tally of death and destruction did not equal that of many other killers, his methods caused grave public concern and, to that point, the most extensive manhunt in US history.

Part of the concern created by the so-called "Unabomber" was that the severity of the bombings acts escalated over the years. Kaczynski used explosive devices that tended to become more powerful and sophisticated as he gained experience. Two of the three deaths of victims occurred in the final two bombings. Perhaps more significant was the manner in which he struck. His bombings ranged from coast to coast and usually involved devices being left in commonplace locations – parking lots, offices, and classrooms – or delivered by US mail carriers to the privacy of victims' homes.

Kaczynski's bombings can be chronologically divided into three periods, based on extended gaps between the periods.

I. Kaczynski delivered seven bombs from May 1978 to July 1982. The first bomb used materials of explosive powder and match heads in a crude pipe bomb packaged in a carefully crafted wood box. Kaczynski left the package in a Chicago parking lot, addressed to a University of Illinois professor. When it was found, however, it was delivered to the return address at Northwestern University, where it exploded and injured a security guard. One year later, in May 1979, Kaczynski placed a bomb in a building at Northwestern. It exploded, injuring a random student who tried to open it.

The third bomb involved Kaczynski's first use of the mail as a delivery system. The bomb was mailed from Chicago in November 1979 and detonated by an altimeter device in the cargo hold of an American Airlines flight. Twelve passengers suffered from smoke inhalation, and the plane made a safe emergency landing. In June 1980, the president of United Airlines was injured in his home in Lake Forest, Illinois, when he opened a bomb mailed by Kaczynski. This early targeting of universities and the airline industry led to the investigative title of UNABOM.

In October 1981, Kaczynski left a bomb in a classroom at the University of Utah in Salt Lake City. It was defused without injuring anyone. He returned to the postal service as his delivery method in May 1982 with a bomb mailed to a professor at Vanderbilt University in Nashville which seriously injured a secretary who opened it. The seventh and last incident in the first group of bombings occurred when Kaczynski left a device in a fourth floor room in a college building at Berkeley near where he had studied and taught in his earlier life. A professor was seriously injured when he moved the device.

Although this first group of bombings killed no one, the incidents had escalated in severity. From the first bomb that used a triggering device of a nail held in tension by rubber bands, Kaczynski moved into electronic switches. He also progressed from wood to metal plugs to seal the ends of his pipe bombs, thereby increasing their destructiveness. The Salt Lake City (fifth) and Berkeley (seventh) bombs that were left in academic buildings had gasoline canisters that were to ignite with the explosion, but both failed. Kaczynski had not yet communicated any supposed motives for the bombings, but with the Lake Forest (fourth) bombing he began to include a metal component etched with the initials "FC" which was designed to survive the blast.

II. After no activity for nearly 3 years, Kaczynski struck five more times from May 1985 to February 1987. Kaczynski's eighth bomb seriously injured a Berkeley graduate student. The device was left in the same building that was the site of the previous bombing; the prior victim was one of the first persons to give aid to the new victim. At about the same time, Kaczynski made his final attack on the airline industry by mailing a package from Oakland, California, to the Boeing company in Auburn, Washington. By the middle of June, the package had arrived at Boeing and aroused the suspicions of a mailroom clerk. Police were called, and the bomb was defused.

In November 1985, Kaczynski mailed a package from Salt Lake City to the home of a prominent professor at the University of Michigan. A letter taped to the outside of the package suggested that it contained a book from a student at the University of Utah. The professor and his assistant were injured when the package was opened.

Efforts turned deadly for the first time in December 1985 with the 11th bombing. Kaczynski left a bomb concealed within nail-studded blocks of wood in the parking lot of a computer store in Sacramento, California. The owner of the store, who had studied at Berkeley when Kaczynski was there, tried to pick it up and was killed by the explosion. About 14 months later, Kaczynski left his 12th bomb disguised as a road hazard in another computer store parking lot, this time in Salt Lake City. Kaczynski was seen by a secretary as he placed the item on the ground, which was the basis for a sketch of the suspect. The explosion badly injured the store owner when he tried to pick it up.

Kaczynski continued his improvements in his bomb-making techniques. The first group of bombs involved types of smokeless powders and match heads. The second group advanced to stronger chemical combinations including aluminum powder, ammonium nitrate, and potassium sulfate. His triggering mechanisms were more dependable, and pipes were sealed more securely. He continued the pattern by which approximately half of the bombs were left at locations and half were mailed, and all of the bombs had the identifying "FC" marking.

III. Kaczynski's terror campaign was dormant for over 6 years, and then he delivered his final four bombs between June 1993 and April 1995. He returned bolder than ever, with his 13th and 14th bombs mailed on the same day from Sacramento. The first caused serious injuries to a geneticist when it exploded in his hands at his home in Timburon, California. The second was delivered to the office of a computer scientist at Yale University in New Haven, Connecticut. He suffered grave injuries when he tried to open the package.

A letter postmarked from Sacramento and delivered to the *New York Times* shortly after the Yale bombing claimed to be from "the anarchist group calling ourselves FC" and suggested that more communications would occur using a nine digit number for identification. More than 15 years after the start of the bombings, this was Kaczynski's first statement of purported motive or responsibility.

Kaczynski was quiet again until December 1994 when a bomb mailed from San Francisco killed an advertising executive in his home in North Caldwell, New Jersey. A few months later, in April 1995, Kaczynski mailed his most powerful bomb to the California Forestry Association in Sacramento addressed to a man who had been its president. The bomb killed his successor. At the same time, Kaczynski sent another letter to the New York Times. This letter was several pages long, attempted to explain the anarchist and antitechnology goals of the supposed terrorist group FC, and asserted that the bombings would cease if a long article were published. Two months later, in June 1995, Kaczynski sent a letter to a San Francisco newspaper stating that the group FC planned to blow up an airliner out of Los Angeles in the next week. Nothing came of it, outside of the concerned reactions by law enforcement authorities and the airlines, but it seemed clear that the bomber's discipline was breaking down.

In this final group of bombings, Kaczynski's devices continued to become more powerful. It was fortuitous that only the last two bombings in this group, and not all four, were fatal. All of the bombs were delivered by mail, perhaps because Kaczynski feared another eyewitness sighting.

After the 16th and last bombing in June 1995, Kaczynski mailed copies of what became known as his manifesto to the *New York Times* and the *Washington Post*. Titled "Industrial Society and Its Future," the 35,000-word manifesto meandered through complaints about society with the overarching theme of scorn for modern technology. Kaczynski used the first person plural "we" to attempt to continue the charade that the stated views belonged to an organization. Most importantly, with his new penchant for attention and communication, Kaczynski set the stage for his arrest.

Pursuit of the Unabomber

Kaczynski's first two bombs at Northwestern University were relatively minor and produced little public concern outside of the Chicago area. The Bureau of Alcohol, Tobacco and Firearms (ATF) assessed them routinely and without fanfare. The Federal Bureau of Investigation (FBI) joined the investigation only after the American Airlines incident, which also precipitated the involvement of the United States Postal Service because the bomb had been mailed. While Kaczynski did not use the FC tag until the next incident, authorities already suspected that they were dealing with a single person or group. The three federal agencies of the FBI, the ATF and the Postal Service would form the nucleus of the UNABOM task force as it ebbed and flowed until Kaczynski's arrest in 1996.

Kaczynski's modus operandi frustrated investigators. His bombs were homemade and constructed largely from parts that he made himself or scrap pieces that were untraceable. When he mailed items, he attached stamps purchased from vending machines and used mailboxes, so there was little chance of a postal clerk identifying him. He left no fingerprints on the packages or saliva traces on the stamps. The locations where he set bombs himself were widely scattered, as were the locations from which he mailed the others. Many of the victims were random – whoever happened to pick up the device – and those that were targeted were not persons that had discernable connections with Kaczynski. All of the elaborate steps that Kaczynski took in the construction and delivery of the bombs were extraordinarily time consuming, but his reclusive existence placed no constraints on his time and allowed few opportunities for others to observe his suspicious activities.

For the first several years of the bombings, federal investigators did not announce to the public that a serial bomber was being sought. The arguments in favor of this tactic included not wanting to reveal to the bomber how much investigators knew, discouraging copycat bombers, and avoiding public panic. The counterarguments were that the public might better protect itself with warning about the bombings, and disclosure could encourage witnesses or tipsters to step forward. The debate over disclosure continued until the first fatal bombing in December 1985 in Sacramento. Finally, the magnitude of that crime and risk of investigative leaks overcame objections. Just over a week after the crime, investigators held a press conference in Sacramento to announce the link to the 10 earlier incidents, suggest that the bomber could be a "fired academician," and post a $25,000 reward (Sanchez & Brank, 1985).

The next incident in Salt Lake City in February 1987 included the eyewitness sighting, so authorities had a description and sketch that needed to be disseminated. The woman who saw Kaczynski was an observant and provided what might have been case-breaking information. The wanted poster sketch of the hooded, sunglasses-wearing suspect included a description with an age estimate of 25–30. With the unfair benefit of hindsight, two questions can be seen. First, would more publicity about the investigation at an earlier stage have increased the chances that this witness might have called the police or that other potential witnesses might have noted suspicious actions by Kaczynski? Second, did the age estimate of the bomber possibly cause investigators to overlook Kaczynski? At the time of the Salt Lake City sighting, Kaczynski was 44.

Just as the investigation heated up with the death of a victim and the description by a witness, it cooled off with the ensuing inactivity by Kaczynski. Databases for criminals and motor vehicle records were checked for persons meeting the rough description of the bomber, while the FBI's profile depicted an educated, unmarried, childless loner. With Kaczynski unheard from for over 6 years, speculation grew that he was incarcerated, hospitalized, injured, or killed by one of his own devices, or had simply given up bombing (Gibbs, Lacayo, Morrow, Smolowe, & Van Biema, 1996). In any event, the investigation seemed to come nowhere near Kaczynski.

After Kaczynski reemerged in June 1993 with two mailed bombs and the letter to the *New York Times*, unprecedented investigative steps were taken. On June 28, 1993, Attorney General Janet Reno announced a reorganization of the UNABOM task force. The task force would be permanently based in the San Francisco FBI office, with all evidence from all bombings gathered at that location. The FBI, the ATF and the Postal Service would assign agents on a long-term basis, rather than using shorter rotations that hindered continuity in the investigation. The reward jumped to $1 million (Graysmith, 1997).

The task force was organized to deal with both the old and the new in the investigation. Agents were assigned to individual bombing incidents to achieve greater mastery of the details of each case. Past leads were reexamined and many persons were reinterviewed. In a change from standard procedure in federal agencies, agents from nearby field offices did not conduct important interviews. Instead, the agents most familiar with the particular case summoned persons for more in-depth interviews at the task force offices in San Francisco. The task force relied heavily on computer systems to store and cross-reference all investigative matters. New leads poured in by the thousands and were systematically prioritized, pursued, and entered into the computer system, and the FBI used the new technology of the Internet to create a web site providing information and requesting assistance (Gibbs et al., 1996; Hubert & Adams, 1994).

A task force approach can sometimes be an unsuccessful attempt to paper over interagency rivalries, either between federal agencies or between federal, state, and local agencies. Few such problems were evident in the well-managed, reconstituted UNABOM task force. Nevertheless, the new task force did encounter two unavoidable difficulties. First, whatever its configuration, the task force lacked promising leads. Every lengthy criminal investigation includes pursuing leads that prove fruitless, but the scale of the UNABOM investigation magnified the frustration. For instance, a paper impression of "Call Nathan R Wed 7 p.m." on the first letter to the *New York Times* caused agents to contact thousands of persons with the first name Nathan and a last name starting with R, all to no avail. The second difficulty was familiar as well. The investigative attention span waned as Kaczynski sent no bombs in the next $1\frac{1}{2}$ years. Again, the task force shrunk in size (Markoff, 1994).

While the December 1994 bombing in New Jersey quickened the task force's efforts with a new murder to investigate, the breakthrough investigative decision did not come until after Kaczynski's last threatened bombing in June 1995. Amidst a flurry of communications, Kaczynski mailed copies of his manifesto to the *New York Times* and the *Washington Post*. The crucial decision was whether to encourage its publication. Although Kaczynski held out publication as a way to end his bombings, law enforcement officials who favored publication did not rely on that justification. Instead, they felt that the 35,000-word manifesto might give a member of the public an opportunity to identify the bomber. Those who opposed publication wanted to avoid the precedent of acceding to terrorist demands and feared that the writer might be emboldened to commit new crimes (Johnston, 1998). Agents poured over the manifesto looking for clues that might reveal the bomber's identity. In the end, Attorney General Reno and FBI Director Louis Freeh approved of the publication. The *Washington Post* published the manifesto as a supplement in its September 19, 1995 issue. A fruitless FBI stakeout of a San Francisco newsstand that sold the paper on that day was a small addition to the frustrating investigation (Johnston, 1998).

After a deep soul searching and his own inquiry, Kaczynski's younger brother David gave the FBI the information necessary to set the arrest process in motion. David had recognized similarities in thoughts and phraseology between the manifesto and his brother's writings from the early 1970s. The elder Kaczynski was arrested on April 24, 1996. Insurmountable proof of his involvement was found in the books, papers, and typewriter seized under a search warrant in his Montana cabin. Extensive bomb-making equipments and chemicals were recovered, suggesting that Kaczynski did not intend to cease his activities with the manifesto publication.

A somewhat cynical adage about criminal investigations states, "Look busy until someone tells you who did it." It is impossible to say whether the elaborate UNABOM task force could have solved the case without someone coming forward to tell them. Kaczynski did appear among the tens of thousands of names of persons on the task force databases through his connections to the Chicago area and northern California. Any scrutiny of Kaczynski may have been delayed because he was considerably older than the bomber's profile (Johnston, 1998). Locating the right suspect in those databases was like finding a needle in a haystack, made all the more difficult if the task force looked in different haystacks than the one that contained Kaczynski. It is clear, nonetheless, that the task force set the stage for someone to come forward, whether David or someone else. Fielding a suggestion about a possible suspect, often from a family member, was nothing new for the task force. When David's concerns were heard, the task force pursued the information quickly and flawlessly. Writings were compared by experts, Kaczynski's comings and goings for nearly two decades were compared to those of the bomber, and Kaczynski's cabin was placed under observation without arousing his suspicions. He was arrested without incident.

From Cabin to Courtroom

Kaczynski was found competent to stand trial, although a court psychiatrist provided a primary diagnosis of paranoid schizophrenia (Johnson, 1998). Prosecutors filed notice of intent to seek the death penalty. Jury selection in federal court in Sacramento began on November 12, 1997 and lasted for 6 weeks, but issues related to a potential insanity defense threatened to derail the start of trial. Kaczynski argued with his attorneys and advised the court that he did not want an insanity defense presented to the jury. The defense attorneys agreed not to present expert testimony of Kaczynski's mental state, and the trial was set to commence on January 5, 1998 (United States v. Kaczynski, 2001).

On the day that opening statements were to begin, however, Kaczynski resumed his complaints to the court. He protested that his attorneys still intended to present nonexpert testimony concerning his mental condition to the jury, and he asked that a new attorney be appointed to represent him. Proceedings sputtered through hearings and Kaczynski's shifting requests, along with a possible suicide attempt by Kaczynski, all while the selected jury awaited the start of the trial. Kaczynski asked permission to represent himself, which the court denied, and then he decided to plead guilty to his involvement in all 16 bombings after prosecutors agreed not to pursue the death penalty. On May 4, 1998, Kaczynski was sentenced to life incarceration (United States v. Kaczynski, 2001). He is serving his sentence at the "Supermax" federal prison in Florence, Colorado. For a time, one of his neighbors in the prison was Timothy McVeigh.

McVeigh's Journeys and the Militia Movement

Timothy McVeigh grew up in a working-class family in upstate New York. He graduated from high school in 1986 and then worked as a security guard while he developed an increasing fascination with firearms. He enlisted in the United States

Army in 1988, received training as a tank gunner at Ft. Riley, Kansas, and successfully rose through the ranks to become a sergeant. After reenlisting, he saw action in the Gulf War in 1991. He passed tests to qualify for the Army's elite Special Forces (Green Berets) but dropped out after early difficulties with the physical demands of training. By 1992, McVeigh was back in upstate New York with a security guard job. In 1993, though, he left New York and began his wanderings across the country that would ultimately lead to Oklahoma City (Michel & Herbeck, 2001a).

Although there is some doubt as to whether McVeigh was a formal militia member, the militia movement provided a forum for his antigovernment sentiments. Beginning in the late 1980s, the modern day militia movement had its roots in the northwest United States, led by an adherent of both the Christian Identity and the Aryan Nation philosophies (Swomley, 1995). Due to its strong connection to far-right, super conservative ideology, it is sometimes called the "patriot movement" (Kelly & Villaire, 2002).

The majority of militia members live in small, rural communities. Militia members tend to be non-college educated white males from the rural working class. Many of these men have been left behind by society due to the structural transformation of the economy from a manufacturing base to communication and service jobs. In addition to the geographical isolation, many rural communities suffered economic difficulties in the late 1980s and the early 1990s, particularly if their outdated economies did not allow them to take part in the jobs created by new technologies (Kelly & Villaire, 2002).

The military aspect of militia membership is of vital importance. The historical institution of the military provides honor and status in society. Membership in the militia evokes a traditional conception of masculinity in the form of the soldier, specifically the guerrilla-commando (Kelly & Villaire, 2002).

Militias argue that they are necessary because government is corrupt. Without a militia, agents of the New World Order could violate individuals' rights with impunity. By exposing the conspiracies of what they called the Shadow Government, challenging illegal actions like Ruby Ridge and Waco, and violently resisting abuses of federal power, militia members serve to protect, preserve, and defend the Constitution of the United States (Crothers, 2002).

Militia members contend that United States Code 10 § 311 provides legitimacy to the militias by establishing that all 17–45-year-old men are militia members. The militia is thus composed of an organized militia – the National Guard – and an unorganized component. The unorganized component is entitled to the same rights under the Second Amendment as the organized militia, especially the right to bear arms. Guns, training, and exposure to the enemy are the only chance ordinary Americans have to confront and defeat the manipulations of the Shadow Government. There is no difference between guns, freedom, and individual rights in militia thought (Crothers, 2002).

Norman Olson and others formed the Michigan Militia Corps in April 29, 1994 (Duffy & Witkin, 1995). In 1995, the Michigan Militia operated in at least nine states (Nemeth, 1995) and claimed to have more than 10,000 members (Duffy & Witkin, 1995). Both McVeigh and Terry Nichols, an army buddy of McVeigh, attended militia meetings and militia material was later found during the execution of a search warrant at the Michigan farm owned by Nichols, where McVeigh occasionally stayed (Snow, 1995). Although there is some dispute as to whether McVeigh and Nichols were formal militia members, the militia movement gave the conspiracy theories and antigovernment rhetoric espoused by McVeigh and Nichols a sense of legitimacy. The militias, and McVeigh, blamed the FBI and the ATF for the militia movement's twin tragedies: the deaths of white supremacist Randy Weaver's wife and son in a 1992 confrontation at Weaver's home in Ruby Ridge, Idaho, and the 1993 siege of the Branch Davidians' compound in Waco, Texas, that resulted in the deaths of 82 cult members, including their leader David Koresh (Gleick & Barnes, 1995).

The thousands of supporters of Weaver, McVeigh included, believed that Weaver had been tricked into selling a gun to a government informant and was only defending his family and his home when federal marshals came for him. On the first day of the 11-day standoff between the United States Marshals Service and Weaver, the Weaver dog barked and howled as the marshals approached the house. Weaver, his son Sam, and their friend Kevin Harris all come out of the house armed. A government agent shot at the dog, followed by Sam shooting at the marshals. The gunfight that ensued claimed the life of Marshal William Degan and Sam Weaver, who was shot in the back as he ran toward the house. FBI agents, including members of the Hostage Rescue Team (HRT), joined the marshals. FBI Special Agent Lon Horiuchi shot and killed Randy Weaver's wife, Vicki, who was inside the cabin holding her baby, with a shot that was intended for Kevin Harris. Weaver refused to surrender for days. To the supporters of Weaver, three people were dead because the government invaded the privacy of one of its own citizens and the government forgave itself for killing Weaver's son and wife by saying the federal agents were justified in their actions (Stickney, 1996).

While it can be said that the incident at Ruby Ridge was the impetus that started the modern militia movement, it was the federal government's blunders the following year at Waco, Texas, that solidified the concept for these angry, bitter militia members. ATF followed up on complaints that David Koresh, leader of the Branch Davidians, and his followers were acquiring large amounts of illegal firearms and explosives at their Mount Carmel compound in order to survive the apocalyptic end to civilization that they believed was approaching. ATF agents obtained warrants against Koresh for various criminal violations involving these illegal firearms and explosives. A complex plan, which relied heavily upon the element of surprise, was devised for service of these warrants. However, an unfortunate incident occurred in which a television news cameraman told a postal worker, who happened to be a Branch Davidian, about the imminent raid and the element of surprise was lost. Although the ATF supervisors learned that their secret raid had been compromised, they allowed the service of the warrants to go forward. The Branch Davidians were armed and ready for the raid, which resulted in the deaths of four ATF agents and six Branch Davidians (Snow, 1995).

ATF then pulled back and the FBI's HRT, the same group involved in the Ruby Ridge situation, took over the incident scene. The standoff between the federal authorities and the Branch Davidians continued for the next 51 days. HRT succeeded in persuading a small number of people to come out of the compound through negotiation and psychological pressure but could not convince the majority of the people still inside. During this standoff, McVeigh traveled to Waco, where he sold right-wing literature. Finally, on April 19, 1993, with approval from Attorney General Janet Reno, HRT stopped negotiating and began using force to induce the surrender of Koresh and the remainder of the Branch Davidians. A fire erupted inside the Mount Carmel compound, eventually burning down the compound and killing all of the people inside, including 25 children. The Branch Davidians reportedly started the fire. However, some vehemently oppose this conclusion, claiming the fire was the result of the tear gas used by HRT in order to force the surrender of those still inside (Snow, 1995).

McVeigh became infuriated that no one in the federal government was held responsible for what he saw as mass murder. Authorities believe that soon after the Waco incident, McVeigh formulated his plan of retaliation against the federal government for their actions against the Branch Davidians (Snow, 1995).

McVeigh's plan eerily resembled the fictional story of Earl Turner in *The Turner Diaries*. Turner was a gun enthusiast who reacted to tighter firearms laws by making a truck bomb and destroying the FBI headquarters in Washington, DC. McVeigh had read *The Turner Diaries* several years earlier and was known to distribute and sell copies of the book to persons like himself who feared that the federal government would someday take away individual liberties, such as the right of law-abiding citizens to own guns (Michel & Herbeck, 2001a).

The Bombing: April 19, 1995

McVeigh reportedly selected Oklahoma City as the site of his bombing for several reasons. No one would believe that such an act could occur in America's heartland. Additionally, the federal building had low security, which meant the truck loaded with explosives could be parked right in front of the building. More importantly, McVeigh believed that the federal agents responsible for the Waco incident had come from the Oklahoma City office (Snow, 1995).

Shortly after the Waco incident, McVeigh recruited his old army buddy, Terry Nichols, into his plan of retaliation. Nichols had a long-standing history of sympathy with right-wing causes, as well as a life of failed endeavors. The actual work on the bombing plot began when McVeigh purchased a book on bomb making. McVeigh and Nichols then traveled around the country purchasing and stealing all the necessary materials, including almost 5,000 pounds of ammonium nitrate (Snow, 1995).

On the morning of Wednesday, April 12, 1995, one week before his target date, McVeigh began his journey east from Arizona, where he had been staying. The journey included a trip to Oklahoma City to confirm that there had been no new road construction since his last check a few months ago. He spent Thursday and

Friday, April 13 and April 14, in Kansas obtaining and preparing a getaway car he intended to stash in Oklahoma City prior to the target date. On Saturday morning, April 15, McVeigh finalized the rental of a 20-ft truck from Elliot's Body Shop in Junction City, Kansas (Michel & Herbeck, 2001a).

On Easter Sunday, April 16, 1995, McVeigh planned to drive to Oklahoma City and stash the getaway car. However, Nichols failed to show at the arranged time and place to follow McVeigh from Kansas to Oklahoma City. Following a heated phone call, Nichols agreed to leave his family on Easter Sunday for the 10-h round trip from Kansas to Oklahoma City and back. They arrived in Oklahoma City on Sunday evening and parked the getaway car several blocks from the Murrah Building, returning to Kansas at approximately 2:00 a.m. on Monday morning, April 17 (Michel & Herbeck, 2001a).

By 6:00 p.m. Monday, April 17, 1995, McVeigh retired to his room at the Dreamland Motel with the Ryder truck parked outside. He laid out his clothes for the next day and packed before turning in for the night (Michel & Herbeck, 2001a).

At 4:30 a.m., Tuesday, April 18, 1995, McVeigh looked the Ryder truck over and drove 25 miles south to a rented storage unit in Herington, Kansas. Over the next few hours, McVeigh and Nichols loaded the materials for the bomb into the truck (Michel & Herbeck, 2001a).

By 7:30 a.m., McVeigh and Nichols arrived at Geary Lake in Geary State Park, the site McVeigh had chosen to mix the bomb. After more than 3 hours, the bomb was complete. McVeigh wiped down the interior of the truck's cab for fingerprints, washed up in the lake, changed into a fresh set of clothes (he later dumped the bomb-sullied clothes on the way to Oklahoma), put on a pair of gloves, and climbed back into the cab. McVeigh drove south crossing from Kansas to Oklahoma and spent the night in a small gravel lot near a roadside motel in northern Oklahoma (Michel & Herbeck, 2001a).

About 8:50 a.m. on Wednesday, April 19, 1995, McVeigh entered Oklahoma City, driving the yellow Ryder rental truck packed with explosives. The weather was warm and sunny, and the sky was a brilliant blue. McVeigh drove with special care: with seven thousand pounds of explosives in the truck, he could hardly afford an accident. Perhaps more importantly, McVeigh did not want to arrive at the Alfred P. Murrah Federal Building too early (Michel & Herbeck, 2001a). McVeigh knew the occupancy of the building would be at a peak around 9:00 a.m. (Snow, 1995). A serious loss of human life was the only way to emphasize his message to the American government (Michel & Herbeck, 2001a).

McVeigh lit the five-minute fuse, and then the two-minute fuse, while approaching his target. McVeigh parked right below the tinted windows of the America's Kids Day Care Center on the second floor, with the back end of the truck facing the building. He grabbed an envelope full of antigovernment articles, locked the truck, and walked away. He was wearing a nondescript blue windbreaker over a T-shirt, a black baseball cap, army boots, and faded black jeans (Michel & Herbeck, 2001a).

The T-shirt was McVeigh's favorite patriot T-shirt. On the front was a drawing of Abraham Lincoln and the phrase SIC SEMPER TYRANIS – "Thus ever to tyrants." John Wilkes Booth had shouted this statement as he interrupted a performance at

Ford's Theatre and shot President Lincoln. On the back of the T-shirt was an image of a tree with droplets of red blood dripping off the branches, and superimposed on the tree was one of McVeigh's favorite quotes from Thomas Jefferson: THE TREE OF LIBERTY MUST BE REFRESHED FROM TIME TO TIME WITH THE BLOOD OF PATRIOTS AND TYRANTS (Michel & Herbeck, 2001a, p. 226).

At 9:02 a.m., the detonation source fired and caused the ammonium nitrate/fuel oil (ANFO) bomb to explode with such tremendous energy that most of the front of the Murrah Building was destroyed and many of the nine floors crashed down onto one another. In total, 168 people died in the federal building and other nearby buildings. Included in the death toll were 19 children, 15 of whom were crushed to death in the America's Kids Day Care Center, and 4 who happened to be elsewhere in the federal building (Snow, 1995).

The date McVeigh chose for the bombing was significant in two ways. It was the 2-year anniversary of the end of the siege at Waco. Additionally, on April 19, 1775, the beginning of the Revolutionary War between the American patriots and their British oppressors took place with the commencement of the Battle of Lexington (Gleick & Barnes, 1995). The attack on the Murrah Building McVeigh believed would instigate a nationwide insurgency for freedom from federal tyranny (Parachini, 2001). McVeigh later described the bombing as being "for the larger good" (Michel & Herbeck, 2001b, p. 13).

The Response

The Oklahoma City Fire Department (OCFD) was on the scene within minutes. Initial commands were established, units were assigned to search each of the buildings, fire lines were laid to extinguish car fires, and triage centers were setup. The Emergency Services Authority (EMSA) ambulances, police cars, and private vehicles transported over 200 injured people to hospitals within the first few hours (City of Oklahoma, 1996b).

An Incident Command System (ICS) structure was used to manage the incoming resources. All operations involved in the rescue and recovery efforts over the next 16 days were under the command of the OCFD. A Multi-Agency Coordination Center (MACC) was established where representatives from a number of agencies were brought together under the OCFD Incident Commander (City of Oklahoma, 1996b).

Although members of the Oklahoma City Police Department (OCPD) initially assisted in the immediate recovery of survivors and victims, primary responsibility of the OCPD was scene and perimeter security. A critical contribution of the OCPD was the controlling of the perimeters surrounding the Murrah Building: keeping traffic lanes open for rescue vehicles (City of Oklahoma, 1996a). The OCPD Command coordinated all law enforcement activities for scene and perimeter security, utilizing a daily average of 238 OCPD personnel and 258 officers from 73 municipal agencies, 33 sheriffs' department, 8 different state agencies, and the National Guard (City of Oklahoma, 1996c).

An invaluable experience in the coordination of the interagency response, specifically for the City of Oklahoma, occurred in July 1994. Representatives from all components of the community attended a course at the Emergency Management Institute (EMI) in Emmitsburg, Maryland, that dealt with handling large-scale disasters. Key personnel of all city departments, volunteer agencies, and utility companies attended. Following the bombing, plans were implemented quickly and efficiently because of the training and the relationships formed during this training (City of Oklahoma, 1996a).

Immediately following the bombing of the Murrah Federal Building, the FBI and the Department of Justice established a task force to investigate the crime and assumed primary jurisdiction for the criminal investigation of the bombing (City of Oklahoma, 1996a). At its peak, the OKBOMB Task Force, as it was dubbed, consisted of over 200 investigators, prosecutors, and support personnel. In addition to the personnel assigned to OKBOMB, thousands of other investigators from the FBI's 56 field offices, its foreign offices, and other law enforcement agencies also participated in the OKBOMB investigation (US Department of Justice, 2002).

It was not the work of the OKBOMB Task Force, however, that resulted in the identification of McVeigh as the suspect in the Oklahoma City bombing. An Oklahoma Highway Patrol trooper, aware of the bombing but carrying out his normal duties, was responsible for the first link in the chain of events that ultimately identified McVeigh as the prime suspect in the bombing of the Murrah Building. McVeigh was stopped 78 min after the bombing for failure to have a license plate on his vehicle, just 80 miles north of the bombing near Perry, Oklahoma. During the routine traffic stop, the Oklahoma Highway Patrol trooper noticed that McVeigh carried a concealed Glock semiautomatic handgun. McVeigh was booked on four misdemeanor charges and had a good chance of obtaining a quick release, as he had no prior criminal history (Michel & Herbeck, 2001a).

Back at the Murrah Building, rescue efforts as well as an extraordinary evidence recovery process were underway. Within hours of the bombing, law enforcement officials recovered valuable physical evidence: the 250-pound rear axle of the Ryder truck with a confidential vehicle identification number and the rear bumper with its license plate intact. A series of computer checks revealed that the vehicle had been rented at a body shop in Junction City, Kansas. Composite sketches of John Doe No. 1 and John Doe No. 2 were drawn from information obtained from the body shop workers. Door-to-door canvasses around Junction City with the sketches resulted in John Doe No. 1 being recognized as Timothy McVeigh by the manager of the Dreamland Motel at which he had stayed under his true name. A check with the National Crime Information Center revealed that an Oklahoma trooper had run a computer check on McVeigh less than 2 hours after the bombing. The Noble County Sheriff's Office still had McVeigh in their custody and was instructed to hold him (Michel & Herbeck, 2001a).

At the time of the attack, the obvious assumption for the identity of the individual(s) responsible for the bombing of the Murrah Building was that of foreign terrorists, most likely Arab. However, Special Agent Clinton R. Van Zandt of the FBI's Behavioral Science Center (now known as the National Center for the

Analysis of Violent Crime) in Quantico, Virginia, who had served as the lead FBI negotiator at Waco during the weeks before the tragedy, put together a psychological profile of the Oklahoma City bomber. Special Agent Van Zandt's profile was that of a white male, acting alone or with one other person, mid-twenties, with military experience and a fringe member of some militia group. Additionally, the bomber would be angry at the government for what happened at Ruby Ridge and Waco (Michel & Herbeck, 2001a). Timothy McVeigh fit this profile.

Upon learning that McVeigh listed the Nichols family farm in Michigan as his home address at the Dreamland Motel in Junction City, Kansas, the FBI began checking into McVeigh's ties to Terry Nichols and his older brother James, who still lived at the Michigan farm. Terry Nichols turned himself into the Herington Police Station in Herington, Kansas, on April 21, 2 days following the blast, after he heard a radio news broadcast mentioning him as a possible suspect in the bombing. Nichols was arrested on a material witness warrant and taken into custody. More substantial charges would be filed later (Michel & Herbeck, 2001a).

FBI Director Louis Freeh deployed approximately half of his 10,000-plus special agents, with a price tag into the millions (Duffy, 1995). The OKBOMB Task Force conducted over 28,000 interviews, followed more than 43,000 investigative leads, including the review of 13.2 million hotel registration records and 3.1 million Ryder truck rental records, and collected nearly $3\frac{1}{2}$ tons of evidence (*FBI File Management*, 2001).

The Prosecution: US v. McVeigh

The trial of *United States v. Timothy J. McVeigh* began on April 24, 1997. The McVeigh trial was unique: it was the largest mass murder trial to date in American history with more surviving victims and family members of deceased victims to accommodate than any previous trial. Two special acts were passed by Congress and signed into law by President Bill Clinton. One of the acts permitted victims who appeared as witnesses to watch the trial from the spectators' area on days when they were not testifying. The federal courts as a rule do not permit witnesses to watch trials, out of concern that something they see or hear could influence their testimony. The other act allowed victims and their families in Oklahoma to monitor the proceedings in an Oklahoma City auditorium via closed-circuit television since the trial had been moved to Denver, Colorado. McVeigh's trial was the first in federal court history to be shown via closed-circuit television (Michel & Herbeck, 2001a).

McVeigh was convicted on 11 counts of murder and conspiracy, after just 11 h of deliberation (Annin & Morganthau, 1997). On Friday, June 13, 1997, jurors sentenced McVeigh to death. Almost 4 years later, on June 11, 2001, he was executed for his crimes.

Approximately 6 months after the verdict in McVeigh's trial, on December 23, 1997, a federal jury convicted Nichols of one count of conspiracy and eight counts of involuntary manslaughter. The jury acquitted Nichols of first-degree murder charges and of using a weapon of mass destruction. The jurors believed that Nichols played a part in the bombing but were not convinced that he intentionally took part in the killings and injuries at the Murrah Building. On June 4, 1998, Nichols was sentenced to life in prison without parole (Michel & Herbeck, 2001a).

Until his death, McVeigh maintained his position of no regrets for his actions. However, McVeigh admitted to feeling sorry for Nichols, as McVeigh had miscalculated the power and breadth of federal conspiracy laws. McVeigh acted under the naïve assumption that as long as he delivered and detonated the bomb himself, no one else could be held responsible. McVeigh also maintained that Nichols' assistance in mixing the bomb components came under duress, only after McVeigh threatened Nichols and his family (Michel & Herbeck, 2001a). Thus, to himself, McVeigh was a solo crusader in bringing terror to the heartland of America.

Countermeasures and Analysis

Kaczynski's simple delivery methods for his bombs were to either leave them somewhere or to mail them. By the end of his spree, he appeared to prefer the mailing method. Public awareness of the dangers posed by unidentified packages can reduce the likelihood of a bomber's success. The Postal Service has become more careful in processing items and more selective in what items will be accepted. Today, the Postal Service will not allow packages weighing over 13 ounces to be sent from mailboxes. Such packages must be either brought to a post office counter or handed to a postal carrier. Even for mailing items weighing less than 13 ounces, the public has a more difficult time due to security measures because the Postal Service has removed thousands of street level mailboxes (Sharp, 2002).

When a serial bomber is at work, law enforcement must make the difficult decision of when to bring the matter to the public's attention. Although one does not want to unnecessarily alarm the public nor encourage copycats, the investigation of the Unabomber may have demonstrated that earlier disclosure would have been the wiser course. With public awareness comes vigilance.

If the public awareness produces reports about suspicious packages or activities, local police must have the capability to respond. Local police need close working relationships with state and federal authorities for the sharing of intelligence about individuals or groups. Local police also need access to bomb detection techniques when they are called to respond to reports of suspicious packages.

Some security advocates recommend legislation that would require buyers of certain fertilizers known to have high explosive potential to present identification and stores to keep a record of such purchases. In March 2007, a bill was introduced in the House of Representatives, H.R.1680, which would regulate the purchase and sale of ammonium nitrate to prevent its misappropriation or use in a terrorist act (THOMAS, 2007a). This bill was passed by the House of Representatives on October 23, 2007, and referred to the Senate Committee on Homeland Security and Government Affairs on October 24, 2007 (THOMAS, 2007a). A companion bill has also been introduced in the Senate, S.1463 (THOMAS, 2007b).

Although federal legislation is lacking more than 10 years after the Oklahoma City bombing, at least six states (New York, California, Nevada, South Carolina, Michigan, and Oklahoma) have passed laws regulating the sale of ammonium nitrate, a major component of the bomb used by McVeigh (Hall, 2006).

It is unlikely that regulations such as these would deter the small bomb maker, like Kaczynski. However, McVeigh may have had difficulty acquiring the desired amount of ammonium nitrate for his tremendous truck bomb. Although it is entirely possible for terrorists to acquire the tools of their trade using aliases and fictitious identification, law enforcement would at least have a starting point by analyzing the sales records should a fertilizer bomb be the weapon of choice for a future terrorist attack.

As with most law enforcement investigations, the arrest and conviction of Timothy McVeigh was the result of a lot of hard work and a little luck. Many pieces of the puzzle fell into place, such as the recovery of the axle that contained the confidential vehicle identification number, McVeigh registering at the Dreamland Motel under his true name, and the traffic stop for which McVeigh was still being held in custody. As McVeigh revealed to Lou Michel (2001a) during interviews for *American Terrorist: Timothy McVeigh and the Oklahoma City Bombing*, he was ambivalent about being caught. McVeigh believed that he would launch a nationwide revolt from federal tyranny and reverting back to his army days, in traditional military form, was comfortable with the thought of laying down his life for what he believed.

The death penalty raised controversy in its application to both Kaczynski and McVeigh. Kaczynski faced the possibility of the death penalty until the start of his trial, when the certainty of a plea to life imprisonment seemed a reasonable alternative disposition. McVeigh was given no such alternative and received the ultimate sanction. For terrorist crusaders such as Kaczynski and McVeigh, the possibility of a death sentence likely has little value for deterrence. Now the regrettable possibilities exist that McVeigh will be seen as a martyr for his cause and Kaczynski will communicate and lend some support to those who follow his cause. Nevertheless, the majority of the American public sees the death penalty as appropriate punishment for terrorists who kill. For both Kaczynski and McVeigh, the availability of the death penalty was an important part of how justice was served in each case.

Since the Oklahoma City bombing, security around federal buildings, and other symbolic targets, has tightened. Many such potential targets have "setbacks" for ordinary traffic and conduct thorough examinations of all delivery trucks entering the premises.

In response to the public outcry that an event such as the Oklahoma City bombing could occur, the United States Congress responded by enacting The Antiterrorism and Effective Death Penalty Act of 1996. Although it was the product of legislative efforts stretching back over a decade, a major impetus to the legislation was the Oklahoma City tragedy. Its intention was to limit stays of execution and speed up the appeal process for death penalty cases (Michel & Herbeck, 2001a). More specifically, Title I of the Act substantially amended federal habeas corpus law (a writ requesting release from unlawful imprisonment) for both state and federal prisoners, whether on death row or imprisoned for a term of years. Title II addressed, among other things, assistance and compensation available to the victims of terrorism. Titles III and IV were concerned with international and immigration-related terrorism issues. Titles V and VI addressed materials, including plastic explosives, capable of producing catastrophic damage (Doyle, 1996).

In the years immediately following the Oklahoma City bombing, militia activity reached an all-time high. By 2001, however, the number of active militias plummeted to 194 from a high of 858 in 1996. Coordinated law enforcement efforts increased resources to combat domestic terrorism, as well as lawsuits against some of the more extreme groups likely all played a part (McCarthy, Dawson, Marotz, Roarke, and Szczesny, 2001). Additionally, as with most terrorist ideology, once the idealistic pursuit of change breaks down, activity slows or even ceases. McVeigh may have believed his act was the "shot heard round the world" to bring an end to federal tyranny, but the anticipated war against the federal government did not occur.

On a scale larger than just the response to the bombing of the Murrah Federal Building, US counterterrorism strategies must address the role of communication and information in deterring future acts of domestic terrorism, preparing for the possibility of future acts of terrorism and responding to and mitigating the effects of a terrorist attack in the event deterrence fails. The media are vital partners in the response to any act of terrorism on US soil. Despite their crucial role in providing information to the public, the media's full participation in ongoing counterterrorism planning and preparedness activities has fallen short. A case study of critical information flows in the Alfred P. Murrah Building Bombing raised several critical issues and questions regarding the role of communication and information in the US counterterrorism strategies. These include, but are not limited to, the following:

- The 24-h news cycle. Coverage of any domestic terrorism incident will begin immediately. The relationship between the government and the media before an incident begins will be of considerable importance, particularly during the initial hours following the incident.
- Is complete openness with the media appropriate for all terrorism scenarios? How should policy makers draw the line between information shared with the public and information that is withheld? A general guideline may be to be completely open and cooperative with the media's inquiries, unless it compromises either the criminal investigation or the privacy of the victims and their families. But who is the decision maker? And what are the methods for controlling public information flows?
- Pre-incident and post-incident information flows are critical components of national preparedness efforts. Disseminating lessons learned from the response to the bombing of the Murrah Building has contributed to improving national capacities for responding to domestic terrorism incidents. (Manzi, Powers, and Zetterlund, 2002).

One mechanism to assist in the sharing of lessons learned from Oklahoma City is the Memorial Institute for the Prevention of Terrorism (MIPT). MIPT is a nonpartisan, not-for-profit organization dedicated to countering terrorism with knowledge. MIPT was established after the bombing of the Murrah Federal Building (http://www.mipt.org).

Another such mechanism is *Lessons Learned Information Sharing (LLIS)*. *LLIS* is a national network of Lessons Learned and Best Practices for emergency response providers and homeland security officials. *LLIS* seeks to improve preparedness by allowing homeland security and response professionals to share frontline expertise on the most effective planning, training, equipping, and operational practices for preventing, preparing for, responding to, and recovering from acts of terrorism (https://www.llis.dhs.gov).

Conclusion

With the arrests of McVeigh and Kaczynski in 1995 and 1996, law enforcement stopped two of America's most dangerous domestic terrorists. Although countermeasures for federal buildings and for postal services increased as a result of the actions of McVeigh and Kaczynski, America may have fallen into a false sense of security in the late 1990s. The attacks of September 11, 2001, taught the painful lesson that terrorist attacks could be even more horrific than McVeigh's, and the subsequent anthrax mailings showed that more danger could lurk in our postal system.

After spending time with Kaczynski in prison, McVeigh righteously contended that "we were much alike in that ... all we wanted out of life was the freedom to live our own lives however we chose to" (McVeigh Vents, 2001). Whatever they thought they wanted, Kaczynski and McVeigh had twisted minds that distorted their view of America. Each felt that his country had taken a wrong turn, that it was his duty to change the nation's direction, and that the bombings would advance his goals. Kaczynski and McVeigh serve as reminders that, with the exception of September 11, the most dangerous terrorists who have struck in America have been homegrown.

References

Annin, P., & Morganthau, T. (1997, June 23). The verdict: Death. *Newsweek.*

Chase, A. (2003). *Harvard and the Unabomber: The education of an American terrorist.* New York: Norton.

City of Oklahoma. (1996a). *Alfred P. Murrah Federal Building bombing April 19, 1995: Final report.* Stillwater, OK: Fire Protection Publications. Retrieved October 7, 2007, from the Memorial Institute for the Prevention of Terrorism Web site: http://www.terrorisminfo.mipt.org/murrahfinalrpt.asp

City of Oklahoma. (1996b). *The Oklahoma City bombing: Report and analysis Oklahoma City fire department.* Stillwater, OK: Fire Protections Publications. Retrieved October 7, 2007, from the Memorial Institute for the Prevention of Terrorism Web site: http://www.terrorisminfo.mipt.org/pdf/okcfr_App_B.pdf

City of Oklahoma. (1996c). *Oklahoma City police department Alfred P. Murrah building bombing after action report.* Stillwater, OK: Fire Protection Publications. Retrieved October 7, 2007, from the Memorial Institute for the Prevention of Terrorism Web site: http://www.terrorisminfo.mipt.org/pdf/okcfr_App_C.pdf

Crothers, L. (2002). The cultural foundations of the modern militia movement. *New Political Science, 24*(2), 221–234.

Doyle, C. (1996, June 3). Antiterrorism and effective death penalty act of 1996: A summary. Retrieved November 8, 2004, from http://www.fas.org.irp/crs/96-499.htm

Duffy, B. (1995, August 14). Where the finger points. *U.S. News & World Report.*

Duffy, B., & Witkin, G. (1995, May 1). The end of innocence. *U.S. News & World Report.*

FBI File Management: Hearing before the Subcommittee on Appropriations, House of Representatives, 110d Cong., (May 16, 2001). Retrieved October 7, 2007, from Federal Bureau of Investigation Web site: http://www.fbi.gov/congress/congress01/freeh051601.htm

Gibbs, N., Lacayo, R., Morrow, L., Smolowe, J., & Van Biema, D. (1996). *Mad genius: The odyssey, pursuit, and capture of the Unabomber suspect.* New York: Warner Books.

Gleick, E., & Barnes, E. (1995, May 1). Who are they? *Time.*

Graysmith, R. (1997). *Unabomber: A desire to kill.* Washington, DC: Regnery.

Hacker, F. (1976). *Crusaders, criminals, crazies: Terror and terrorism in our time.* New York: Norton.

Hall, M. (2006, October 3). Law sought on explosive fertilizer. *USA Today.* Retrieved October 8, 2007, from USA Today Web site: http://www.usatoday.com/news/Washington/2006-10-03-fertilizer-law_x.htm

Hubert, C., & Adams, J. M. (1994, December 13). Serial killer may live in north state, FBI says. *The Sacramento Bee,* p. 1.

Johnson, S. (1998). Psychiatric competency report. *United States v. Kaczynski,* CR-S-96 GEB (E.D. Cal.).

Johnston, D. (1995, November 6). Bomber is called killer who is not on political mission. *The New York Times,* p. B8.

Johnston, D. (1998, May 5). Seventeen year search, an emotional discovery and terror ends. *The New York Times,* p. A24.

Kelly, M., & Villaire, K. (2002, Summer). The Michigan militia and Emerson's ideal of self-reliance. *Journal of Social Philosophy, 33*(2), 282–296.

Manzi, C., Powers, M. J., & Zetterlund, K. (2002). *Critical information flows in the Alfred P. Murrah Building bombing: A case study.* Washington, D.C.: Chemical and Biological Arms Control Institute. Retrieved October 7, 2007, from Memorial Institute for the Prevention of Terrorism Web site: http://www.terrorisminfo.mipt.org/pdf/murrahcasestudy.pdf

Markoff, J. (1994, December 13). Bombing in New Jersey: The investigation: A task force comes alive once more. *The New York Times,* p. B8.

McCarthy, T., Dawson, P., Marotz, H., Roarke, M., & Szczesny, J. (2001, May 14). Tired of training for the apocalypse. *Time.*

McVeigh vents on 60 Minutes. (2001, May 12). *CBS News.* Retrieved January 3, 2008, from the CBS News web site: http://www.cbsnews.com/stories/2000/03/13/national/main171231.shtml.

Michel, L., & Herbeck, D. (2001a). *American terrorist: Timothy McVeigh & the Oklahoma City bombing.* New York: HarperCollins.

Michel, L., & Herbeck, D. (2001b, April 9). Live from death row. *Newsweek.* Retrieved January 8, 2008, from http: www.newsweek.com/id/79759/page/1

Nemeth, M. (1995, May 1). Why Oklahoma City? *Maclean's, 108*(18), 20–24.

Parachini, J. (2001). Comparing motives and outcomes of mass casualty terrorism involving conventional and unconventional weapons. *Studies in Conflict & Terrorism, 24,* 389–406.

Sanchez, E., & Brank, G. (1985, December 20). Sacramento case linked to ten others. *The Sacramento Bee,* p. 1.

Sharp, D. (2002, March 21). Last pickup for the corner mailbox? *USA Today,* p. 3A.

Snow, R. L. (1995). *The militia threat: Terrorists among us.* New York: Plenum Trade.

Stickney, B. M. (1996). *"All-American monster": The unauthorized biography of Timothy McVeigh*. New York: Prometheus Books.

Swomley, J. (1995, Nov/Dec). Armed and dangerous. *Humanist, 55*(6), 8–11.

THOMAS. Library of Congress. (2007). Retrieved January 13, 2008, from the Library of Congress Web site: http://thomas.loc.gov/cgi-bin/bdquery/z?d110:h1680

THOMAS. Library of Congress. (2007b). Retrieved January 13, 2008, from the Library of Congress Web site: http://thomas.loc.gov/cgi-bin/bdquery/z?d110:SN01463

U.S. Department of Justice. Office of the Inspector General. (2002). *An investigation of the belated production of documents in the Oklahoma City bombing case*. Washington, D.C. Retrieved October 7, 2007, from the U.S. Department of Justice Web site: http://www.usdoj.gov/oig/special/0203/exec.htm

United States v. Kaczynski, 239 F.3d 1108 (9th Cir., 2001).

Chapter 5
It Happened Here: Biological Terrorism in the United States

Scott G. White

Introduction

The use of biological weapons by terrorist groups, or non-state actors, vexes counter-terrorist officials. While various treaties, such as the Geneva Protocol of 1925, ban the use of biological weapons, as well as other types of weapons of mass destruction (WMDs), they have been used in conflicts throughout the 20th century. During World War I, German troops used anthrax to make horses and cattle sick, and various chemical agents such as mustard gas were used against troops on both sides (Kuhr & Hauer, 2001). Preceding World War II, Japan's infamous Unit 731, housed in occupied Manchuria, tested biological weapons on Chinese prisoners of war, dropped bombs with plague-infested insects, and served contaminated food to spread disease in Chinese cities (Tucker, 2002). The atomic bombings of the Japanese cities of Hiroshima and Nagasaki in 1945 killed tens of thousands of people. In 1979, anthrax was accidentally released from a Russian weapons manufacturing plant in Sverdlovsk, killing over 60 people (Amato, 1993; Garmon, 1980; Meselson & Guillemin, 1994). Saddam Hussein was widely reported to have used various outlawed chemical weapons during the Iran/Iraq war, and in 1988, to suppress Kurdish rebellions in northern Iraq (Cowell, 1988).

Most scholars agree that the probability of future use of WMDs is high, and the possibilities of attack should not be ignored (Kuhr & Hauer, 2001; McInnes & Lee, 2006). Many see potential threats to the food (Hope, 2004; Leviten & Alexa, 2003) and water (Burrows & Renner, 1999) supplies. Some see risks in the open environment in which scientists operate, where information, material, and specimens are freely shared between researchers (Enserink, 2003; Publish & Perish, 2003; Reppy, 2003). Such fears have escalated globally since the September 11 attacks and the subsequent anthrax attacks 1 month later.

Of most concern is that an affluent, well-trained, hostile group not tied to a state can perpetrate biological weapons attacks. Using their own money and professional

S.G. White (✉)
City University of New York, New York, NY, USA
e-mail: swhite@lagcc.cuny.edu

M.R. Haberfeld, A. von Hassell (eds.), *A New Understanding of Terrorism*,
DOI 10.1007/978-1-4419-0115-6_5, © Springer Science+Business Media, LLC 2009

expertise, such groups can gain access to harmful biological material and use it as a weapon (Koblentz, 2003/2004). Attacks perpetrated by non-state actors are more difficult to prepare for, as the usual diplomacy and negotiation strategies do not apply. Such groups do not adhere to protocols or treaties agreed to by the state. Often their mission is to disrupt the state, or attempt to create their own where there is no outside interference.

While the anthrax attacks in 2001 caused widespread fear and confusion throughout America, it was not the first biological weapons attack successfully perpetrated on American soil. In September 1985, Bhagwan Shree Rajneesh, an Indian mystic and leader of the Rajneesh movement, gave a press conference after his top aides fled first their compound in Wasco County, Oregon, and subsequently, the country. He discussed an outlandish plot hatched by Sheela and Puja, the de facto leaders of the commune in Oregon, to poison local salad bars with salmonella that was cultivated in a lab located on the grounds of the commune. He also claimed that they planned the assassination of several county officials by poisoning and other means (Trippett, 1985).

At that time, Rajneesh was discredited by county officials and law enforcement authorities. The guru had been arrested for immigration violations, and was being investigated for other crimes (Miller, Engelberg, & Broad, 2001), so law enforcement personnel thought he was trying to deflect blame from himself. Further investigation of the group, however, led to the confiscation of murder manuals, vials of pathogens, documentation of illegal immigration practices, including the arrangement of sham marriages, schemes for voting violations to rig county elections and other assorted crimes. In April, 1986, two members of the commune pleaded guilty to charges of "conspiring to tamper with consumer products by poisoning food in violation of the federal anti-tampering act" (Torok et al., 1997, p. 393). They were sentenced to 4.5 years in prison. Rajneesh was deported and moved back to India (Fitzgerald, 1986).

The salmonella attacks were designed to incapacitate members of the Wasco County community so that they would be incapable of voting in a local election. The cult, in their attempts to independently control their property, was struggling with local government regulations concerning zoning laws, voter registration, and water-use restrictions (Fitzgerald, 1986; Tucker, 2002). Planning to make native town residents sick, they targeted the area food supply using salmonella cultivated by a registered nurse and lab technician. Drawing from the vast resources garnered from member donations, the cult constructed a lab on their property that the pair used as a makeshift biological weapons plant. Members of the commune spread the salmonella throughout the Wasco County community using various methods. The group's affluence and training, combined with access to professional credentials, made it easy to exploit legal loopholes to obtain biological materials, build necessary facilities, grow harmful pathogens, and eventually weaponize them (Tucker, 2002).

At its height in the mid-1980s, the Rajneesh movement was thought to have anywhere from 150,000 to 200,000 members worldwide (Fitzgerald, 1986), although most figures are not reliable. Rajneesh's personal charisma and demands for control and obedience played a significant role in the movement, but in retrospect the cult was more than a religious counter-culture phenomenon controlled by the whims of one man. The group attempted to exert their political will over a geographic area using both legitimate and illegitimate methods, eventually committing a terrorist act to help attain their goals. For the disciples who lived there, Rajneeshpuram was as important as any individual state, transcending commonly accepted political lines of demarcation and becoming an amorphous spiritual entity that exerted control over the entire Rajneesh empire (Guest, 2005; Fitzgerald, 1986). For residents of the commune, gaining control of the space they were using meant life or death for the group.

Since the group was labeled and considered a cult, the law enforcement and government response to news of the poisonings was not as strong as if a group like Al-Qaeda would have committed the same crimes. If the attacks were to occur today, there would be a much stronger response to the cult's actions. At the time, the immediate threat the Rajneeshees posed to general society did not seem dangerous. However, if their history is examined, there is a pronounced pattern of violence toward the Wasco County community that increases as the group was dealt blow after legal blow in their battle for control of their commune (Fitzgerald, 1986). Violence committed in support of ideological goals can be confusing and shocking to general society. For those who are committing the acts, violence is a tool used to gain advantage in their struggle, however they define it. If the group's goals are important enough to them, then extraordinary means of violence are potentially possible.

The 1984 salmonella salad bar poisonings in Oregon will be reviewed in this chapter. A description of events, including characteristics of the perpetrators of the attacks will be discussed. A review of law enforcement responses to these crimes will inform suggestions for counter-terror measures, including strategies to help prepare for and mitigate a bioterrorist attack. In addition, the case of the 2001 anthrax attacks will be explored. No one has been formally charged with the crime, but it is helpful to understand what happened during the attacks, who was involved, and how law enforcement officials responded. It is hoped that patterns of understanding will emerge that can inform current counter-terrorism theory and strategy.

The Rajneeshees

The Rajneeshees originated in India, where Bhagwan Shree Rajneesh, the founder and leader of the group, proclaimed himself enlightened at the age of 23. Much of Bhagwan Rajneesh's life was shrouded in mystery, and many of the myths about him were first recorded in a biography written by Vasant Joshi (1982), an initial disciple of Rajneesh. Joshi's accounts were cryptically written to help followers find various interpretations for events in Rajneesh's life (Carter, 1990). Early followers believed that Bhagwan was their spiritual superior. As Rajneesh's legend grew, more extreme interpretations emerged, and Rajneesh was considered a deity on earth by many of his followers. Rajneesh would claim that he was not a god, but a person who could help people become higher spiritual beings. His messages were often inconsistent, however, as he would also declare, as he did when he arrived in the United States, that "I am the Messiah America has been waiting for (Carter, 1990, p. 37)."

Rajneesh's image was carefully cultivated by members who helped him manage the communes he established. The first was located in Pune, India, with more following in various parts of the world, including Australia, Europe, and America (Milne, 1986). People would come from all over the world to Pune to hear Rajneesh speak, and were reportedly so amazed at his ability to provide new meaning for their lives that they would immediately become followers, eschewing their former existence (Milne, 1986). New converts were instructed to establish communes in places where they were from (Guest, 2005). The leaders of the group were handpicked by Rajneesh, and they often served spokespersons for the group in his stead. Much of the organization's hierarchy was dominated by women recruited from England in the mid-1970s during a period of European expansion for the movement (Carter, 1990; Fitzgerald, 1986; Guest, 2005). Many of these women would play central roles in the later poisoning plot in Oregon.

In general, Rajneesh was painted as a heroic figure by his followers. He would often take vows of silence to help create spiritual and mythic interpretations of his previous words and actions. Even though he was not speaking to them, the members of the commune were reminded of his presence daily (Carter, 1990; Fitzgerald, 1986). To maintain contact with his followers, Rajneesh would drive through the Oregon compound in one of his 20 Rolls-Royces (Fitzgerald, 1986). Inhabitants of the commune would line up on the side of the road as he passed, extending greetings to him and praying. In his entrepreneurial role as leader of the commune, Bhagwan Rajneesh would only speak to large donors or address crowds when the commune was in dire need of money (Carter, 1990; Fitzgerald, 1986). Often these occasions were well publicized and well attended. His lack of public speaking created a robust market for tapes and pamphlets purported to contain his words and his voice. The proceeds from the sales of tapes helped finance the commune's activities.

The Rajneesh members were expected to dress in a certain manner, wearing orange, maroon, or red, considered the colors of the sun (Guest, 2005), live in isolated communes, and practice tantric sex therapies, ostensibly to assist them in receiving enlightenment (Carter, 1990). The Rajneeshees believed that present day society was at the root of all ills in human suffering, and its imprint needed to be stripped away from the individual (Carter, 1990; Guest, 2005). The only way to enlightenment was to work toward it. They called their work, whether toiling cleaning latrines, doing laundry, or designing buildings, "worship" (Fitzgerald, 1986; Carter, 1990). The path to enlightenment included the performance of mundane duties meant to help sanyassins, or disciples, rid themselves of destructive ego tendencies and understand the meaning of service and selflessness. It mattered little if someone outside the sect did not understand the concept. Outsiders were the "others." This is an important concept because it would later help foment an "us against them" attitude when dealing with local government officials and neighbors in Wasco County.

Rajneesh often called perceived enemies of the cult fascists, a word whose connotations are political and emotional (Guest, 2005). A clear demarcation between members and nonmembers was drawn, as demonstrated by the way disciples dressed, what they ate, and how they conducted their lives. The potential for conflict with outside groups existed before the group moved to the ranch in Oregon, because living in a commune and working together is in direct opposition to notions of self and individuality that dominates much of American culture. In addition, the area they moved in was populated with people whose religious affiliation was predominantly fundamentalist Christian (Fitzgerald, 1986). Accepting their exotic new neighbors would not be easy.

Cults and the State

The Rajneesh group is considered a cult. Defining a group as a cult is sometimes difficult because of various interpretations of cult status. Margaret Thaler Singer's definition, from her 2003 book, *Cults in Our Midst*, is based on three factors:

1. The origin of the group and role of the leader:
   a. Cult leaders are self-appointed, persuasive persons who have a special mission or special knowledge.
   b. Cult leaders tend to be determined and domineering and are often described as charismatic.
   c. Cult leaders center veneration on themselves.

2. The power structure or relationship between the leader (or leaders) and the followers:
   a. Cults are authoritarian in structure.
   b. Cults appear to be innovative and exclusive.
   c. Cults tend to have a double set of ethics.

3. The use of a coordinated program of persuasion (which is called thought reform, or more commonly, brainwashing):
   a. Cults tend to be totalistic in controlling their members' behavior and also ideologically totalistic exhibiting zealotry and extremism in their world view.
   b. Cults tend to require members to undergo a major disruption or change in lifestyle.
                                                                      (Singer, 2003, p. 7)

In the last half century, secularization and the waning of membership in traditional religions has helped give rise to "alternative" religions, many of which are considered cults according to Singer's definition (Demerath & Williams, 1984; Robbins, 1985). Cults or alternative religions are able to thrive in liberal plural democracies, especially in America because of the sharp separation of church and state (Grafstein, 1984). At the same time, there are potential conflicts between cults, organized religion, and government entities.

In my view, the increasing proliferation of church autonomy conflicts in the United States is related to two clashing trends. 1) The steady expansion throughout the twentieth century of the scope of public authority and its regulatory mandate over organizations; and 2) The recent diversification of the activities and functions of churches and the religious movements.

(Robbins, 1985, p. 239)

In most cases, these conflicts are settled peacefully. However, the consequences can be dire if they are not.

In November 1978, a mass suicide occurred in the Jonestown cult, located in Guyana, resulting in the deaths of over 900 people. That event became a touchstone in people's perceptions of cults and the levels of control they can exert over followers (Barker, 1986). The mass suicide was prompted by the murder of United States Congressman Leo Ryan and four of his colleagues, shot to death in the jungles of Guyana when visiting the cult (Barker, 1986). The congressman was investigating allegations of abuse and mistreatment lodged against the cult by relatives of members.

Several members of the cult were reportedly shot on the outskirts of the jungle as they were trying to escape the suicide ritual. Babies were given the infamous cyanide laced Kool-Aid mix in syringes (Barker, 1986). During the mass suicide, the paranoid leader of the cult, Jim Jones, implored his followers to take the drink without complaint, indicating that they were all doomed anyway because of Ryan's murder (Smith, 1982). As members protested the action, and asked about alternatives, they were shouted down, or subdued. Jones himself was shot in the head by one of his disciples (Smith, 1982).

These instances of suicide and murder demonstrated extreme levels of coercion or control exerted over the cultists in Jonestown. While it was commonly believed that some form of control was present in most cults (Galanter, 1999; Robbins, 1984; Robbins & Anthony, 1980), the extent it was taken to in Jonestown had never been imagined. At the time of the tragedy, the only plausible assumption was that leaders of the cult used mind control mechanisms to maintain control. There were few other rational explanations for such radical behavior.

The Jonestown suicide occurred at a time when religious scholars were debating the role secularization was playing in society and its particular affect on religions. The major organized religions, particularly the larger Protestant sects, were experiencing membership declines (Robbins, 1985). Alternative churches, cults, and other spiritual movements were gaining wider acceptance and experiencing growing membership (Barker, 1986; Robbins, 1985). Many of the larger new religions, such as Moon's Unification Church, the Church of Scientology, and the International Society for Krishna Consciousness were well funded and managed. They were also enjoying economic benefits the United States extends to religious organizations (Grafstein, 1984; Robbins, 1985). They did not have to pay taxes, and were exempt from providing financial records about their respective organizations.

In some cases, cults can become capitalistic and exploitive in nature (Grafstein, 1984). Each cult generally has a guru, or figurehead, who is basically an entrepreneur. As an example of the inequity between cult leaders and cult follow-ers, the leader of the Rajneeshees, Bhagwan Shree Rajneesh, was chauffeured in Rolls-Royces, acquiring over 20 of the automobiles between 1980 and 1985, while members of the cult toiled on the Antelope, Oregon ranch to help fulfill the utopian dreams of Rajneesh and create a self-sustaining community. This amounted to slav-ery, as cult members, not just in Rajneesheepuram, but other religious movements as well, were not paid for their work and were forced or coerced into giving the cult their money (Grafstein, 1984). "The entrepreneurs also benefit from a captive work force dedicated to the goals of the cult-making converts and making money, not necessarily in that order (Grafstein, 1984, p. 15)."

The Jonestown massacre helped propel cults into the political arena. The sovereignty of alternative religious movements was called into question. This is not easily done in the United States. The separation of church and state powers are important on many levels. The fear of mind control practices, coupled with the exotic, nontraditional teachings of various sects created suspicions about cults. Politicians, cult family members, and even ex-members of the groups called for fur-ther examination, focusing on whether the new religious movements needed to be more tightly controlled.

> Church/state conflicts involving the defense of "church autonomy" can be seen as conflicts involving rational-legal vs. charismatic spiritual authority, as the state attempts to advance rational criteria such as financial accountability as a standard for evaluating and reviewing the affairs of churches.
>
> (Robbins, 1985, p. 238)

The fear of "destructive" cults and their ability to inflict harm on members helped justify investigation of cult practices by the state. "If the diversified activities of churches are legitimated in terms of religious liberty and sacred individual con-science, then the state is encouraged to pose as the defender of religious freedom against exploitative, authoritarian sects (Robbins, 1985, p. 238)." This was one reason why Congressman Ryan was in Guyana.

Uncivil Movements

Labeling various group cults or terrorists creates various methods of study and contextualizing of events. Importantly, the use of various labels can cloud the under-standing of group or movement dynamics. It is possible to miss or even dismiss warning signs emanating from a group's behavior or public expression because of what we consider them to be. We have concrete understandings about what a ter-rorist and a cultist may look like, even though there are dual natures of politics and religion in both of them. By studying such groups using different concepts defined by various disciplines and using different language, examination of the underlying structures of supposedly disparate groups and their actions may initially seem incor-rect. Upon closer examination, patterns of group behavior emerge that are actually similar.

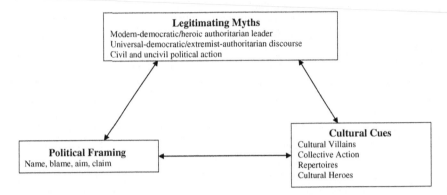

Fig. 5.1 Payne's Analytical Framework to help Explain Successful Uncivil Movements

Payne discusses the emergence of uncivil movements as the "interaction between movement agency and context: the capacity of movements to exploit political and cultural contexts to their advantage (Payne, 2000, p. 36)." In Fig. 5.1, Payne summarizes successful strategies uncivil movements use to help mobilize individuals to support their causes.

There are similarities to Singer's definition of cults and Payne's framework. The role of an authoritarian leader, the use of both legitimate and illegitimate methods to gain political advantage, mythmaking, and ideas about culture and society are prevalent in both definitions. Reported data about the Rajneeshee cult contained in accounts by Carter (1990) and Fitzgerald (1986) will help to analyze them as an uncivil movement and help understand their resorting to violence to gain political power.

An important aspect of uncivil movements is their dual political nature. They use legitimate political means to attain power, but also use illegitimate means to attack institutions they see as adversarial (Payne, 2000). This has different consequences for whether state or civil responses are designed to control a group's violent actions, and whether political sanctions can be employed or not. If the group attains power on par with other civil authorities, as the Rajneeshee did for a short time, legitimate state response becomes problematic because the Rajneeshee played a role in the state. At the same time, this dual nature causes a split in the group or organization, causing internal conflict about the role of violence in attaining group goals (Payne, 2000). If a violent, fundamentalist group takes control of the organization, then the group as a whole may be doomed to failure because violent actions will engender a stronger state rebuke. Any respect engendered through legitimate political means is lost if the group commits violent, criminal acts. This was apparent in the Rajneeshee commune.

Uncivil movement's dual political nature is supported by the dynamic interaction between a group's ability to legitimate myths, frame political situations in distinct ways, and use cultural cues to help sustain levels of activity among the "hard core" movement supporter, with the hope that such measures lead to some acceptance in the general population. The ability of a charismatic leader to frame arguments in ways that help gain support and create a potential movement of like-minded individuals is key (Payne, 2000). Their identification of threats, their ability to provide contexts and frameworks that can help people filter information through a wide variety of prisms and their mixed messages about their own authority (Payne, 2000) help potential group members develop desired conclusions about the movement.

> Movement entrepreneurs play a key role in creating these myths, but potential constituents "make sense" of them. Cohen brilliantly describes the process thus: People can find common currency in behavior whilst still tailoring it subjectively (and interpretively) to their own needs.
>
> (Payne, 2000, p. 36)

The Rajneeshees in America

In 1979, 2 years after the mass suicide at Jonestown, the Rajneeshees purchased 64,000 acres of land in Wasco County, Oregon, in the town of Antelope. The purchase was the brainchild of one of Bhagwan's trusted advisors, Ma Sheela, who would become a central figure in the group over the next several years. The commune moved there because it had been forced to move from its original base in Pune, India, due to legal trouble. Initially, relationships between the native inhabitants of the Oregon town and the members of the commune were positive because the new group spent money, with some estimates as high as $20 million (UPI, 1982), and were building and farming on land that was not being fully utilized. Eventually, the group would attempt to create a separate city within the ranch's borders, called Rajneeshpuram. The purchase of the land in Wasco County is an example of the Rajneeshees' ability to use legitimate civil and political means to pursue their agenda. Needing a place to develop their commune, but knowing that most localities would probably resist their presence, the managers of the Rajneeshee movement knew that they needed to identify a place that was isolated, but large (Carter, 1990; Fitzgerald, 1986). During their purchase of the land, the Rajneeshees indicated that they would be using the land solely for farming, and they had asked for dispensation to allow up to 40 people to stay on the "Big Muddy" ranch, as it was known, to help tend it. The town and county land use agencies granted their request (Carter, 1990; Fitzgerald, 1986). The Rajneeshees actually intended to build their commune there, and some plans indicated that they would eventually house up to 25,000 residents in the town (Carter, 1990; Fitzgerald, 1986).

Knowing that Wasco County officials would not grant them permits to buy or use the land for such purposes, the Rajneeshees lied about the application, and as soon as they were able, began to build temporary A-frame houses on the land, and complexes to house Bhagwan, the Rajneeshee managers, and other important individuals who financed or provided vital services to the cult (Carter, 1990; Fitzgerald, 1986; Guest, 2005). This is indicative of the group's ability to create collective action that is potentially illegal to help support cultural and social needs of the group, and politically "claiming" what was felt to be their land. The Rajneeshee described

the ranch as a Buddhafield, which held a special spiritual power that only followers, or sanyassin, could tap. This is also an example of mythmaking. We can see
that the Rajneeshee employed the triangular model as described by Payne, which is
represented above (2000).

The new city was incorporated in 1982, resulting in the creation of new zoning
regulations, laws, and their own police force. The group attempted to populate the
city by busing in homeless people from various cities around the country (Miller et
al., 2001). In 1982, Ma Prem Karuna, a Rajneesh sanyassin, was elected mayor of
the town of Antelope. The election was contested by members of the community
based on various voting eligibility laws, and over the next 2 years, the relationship
between the Rajneeshees, and the state, town, and county continued to deteriorate
(UPI, 1982).

The ability of the Rajneeshee group to take over the town using a semblance of
legitimate political means is interesting, but deceiving. The cult was able to win the
town election because they had moved people there illegally, against land use regulation laws that were important to the inhabitants of Wasco and Jefferson County
in that part of Oregon. One of the reasons the group moved to the area was because
it was arid, and Rajneesh and his handlers hoped it would help his many illnesses,
including asthma and diabetes (Carter, 1990; Fitzgerald, 1986). Since the area was
arid, there was a short supply of water, which led to strict land-use regulations.
There was not enough water to support such a large city. Members of the community in Wasco and Jefferson County tried to help placate both parties in the
arguments concerning water use. While continuing to pursue legitimate political
means to help solve problems of land use, the Rajneeshees embarked on a campaign to harass members of the town of Antelope, who were mostly retirees (Carter,
1990). They would follow them in their cars, take pictures of them, and ask what
they were doing. These actions forced residents to move, basically deserting the
town and removing legitimate political obstacles due to lack of resident interest and
ability to fight back against such tactics. The Rajneeshee also created cultural villains out of the local residents, calling them ignorant and "rednecks." These actions
helped make sanyassin afraid of the townspeople, and suspicious of outsiders, helping Rajneeshpuram town managers name villains and blame them for the problems
of the commune (Carter, 1990; Fitzgerald, 1986). Since members of the commune
were living in squalid conditions, it was easy to influence their thinking in this way.

The Rajneeshees attempted to win the mayoralty of the town so they could
change school zoning, state tax, and finance laws (Fitzgerald, 1986). Much of what
they accomplished by taking legitimate control of the county and school government bodies was destroyed by their inability to continue to use legitimate means
to attain what they wanted. Their intransigence on issues such as school taxes and
their threats to levy exorbitant taxes on area residents to help start a school in the
city of Rajneeshpuram were met with resistance (Carter, 1990; Fitzgerald, 1986). In
most forms, the resistance was legalistic and officious. Since most of the Rajneeshee
claims were built on illegitimate foundations, starting with inhabiting and constructing an illegally chartered city, they realized that most of what they had built could be
taken away by legitimate political and legal systems. This fact forced them to again

explore the use of illegitimate methods to maintain and continue planning future goals.

In 1984, legal challenges from the state of Oregon concerning the constitutionality of the new city of Rajneeshepuram were launched. In June, the Oregon Court of Appeals ruled in favor of the State Land Use Board of Appeals and overturned the incorporation of the town (Tension Building, 1984). Lawmakers felt that there was not proper separation of church and state in the town. The group had applied for tax-exempt status as a religion, putting the legality of their new city into question.

At the time, there were about 4,000 sanyassins living in the commune. It was obvious to the leaders of the commune that they did not have enough votes to take control of Wasco County's commission, as over 23,000 people lived in the county. Ma Anand Sheela has been identified as the mastermind behind the plot to poison residents of the area to make them too sick to vote on election day. This plan was one of several strategies employed by the group to attempt to gain control of the city. Another plan involved the bussing in of homeless people from various American cities to take part in local elections. The Rajneeshees portrayed the program as one that offered to share the life of the commune with indigent people (Tucker, 2000). Some in Wasco County, including commissioner William Hulse, a self-professed victim of a poisoning at the ranch in 1983, believed it was the cult's attempts to inflate voter registration rolls. Oregon voting law was liberal at the time, allowing registration after 20 days residence, and allowing a qualified person to register and vote on the same day (Tension building, 1984; Miller et al., 2001).

As trouble swirled around the commune, members became more withdrawn and combative. Reports about Rajneeshpuram police abuse against town residents and the presence of illegally obtained weapons (Tucker, 2000) made their way to county commissioners, causing further strain in the community. The cult was well financed and had a team of lawyers available to sue the town and state. After a series of victorious legal challenges, they began to suffer a number of legal setbacks in 1984 (Tucker, 2000). This led Sheela, who now represented Rajneesh to the members because he had taken a vow of silence, to brainstorm ways to control the November 1984 election. According to testimony of a member of the group, schemes were developed to have voters register under assumed names, rent apartments under aliases to increase voter registration rolls, and have homeless people bussed into the compound vote in the elections (Tucker, 2000). Legal challenges to homeless voter registration were filed in the Wasco County Clerk's office. Sue Profitt, the County Clerk, turned away followers of the cult when they attempted to register, under the grounds that each person was to have a hearing concerning their eligibility and mental ability to vote (Judge refuses, 1984). Many of the homeless were mentally ill and incapable of understanding what they were doing.

In the "Share-A-Home" program, the cult demonstrated an ability to coerce collective action in a scheme that was ambitious, but exploitive of homeless people. They were able to convince sanyassins to help recruit and house homeless people from all over America (Carter, 1990; Guest, 2005; Fitzgerald, 1986). They described the program to the local community as a way to help share their enlightening experience in the "Buddhafield," creating myths and legends about why they were doing something that was seemingly ill conceived. They were able to convince homeless people to leave their residences, as temporary as their residences may have been, and move to an obscure part of Oregon, literally sight unseen (Carter, 1990; Fitzgerald, 1986). Their mythmaking strategies used to convince sanyassins were infused with indirect references to what "Bhagwan" wanted. This, in turn, helped convince sanyassins to recruit homeless people to join them. While infused in imagery of brotherhood and goodwill, the scheme was designed to help inflate voter registration rolls. The hope was that the group could gain access to legitimate political power in Wasco County's government using illegal practices (Carter, 1990; Fitzgerald, 1986).

The Attack

It is in these circumstances that the plot to poison the townspeople was born. Sheela and a group of individuals in the commune, including Ma Anand Puja, nicknamed Rajneeshepuram's Dr. Mengele (Tucker, 2000), obtained samples of salmonella from labs to culture them for introduction to the area's restaurants and water supply (Tucker, 2000). Daily poisoning "missions" were conducted by various members of the cult. Puja was a licensed registered nurse in California and had access to live cultures from area labs because she was the nominal head of the Rajneesh Medical Corporation (RMC) (Miller et al., 2001). Puja had previously tried to control behavior in the commune when she experimented with drugs and chemicals by mixing Haldol, a tranquilizer, in the food of some of the unruly homeless residents present (Carter, 1990; Fitzgerald, 1986). When she was questioned about her large Haldol purchases by Oregon state medical officials, she had her staff cover up why the drug was being used (Miller et al., 2001). She was also able to order various pathogens from companies in the United States, including salmonella. The salmonella samples were cultured and weaponized by the RMC medical technician, Parambodhi.

Once Puja cultured the specimens, she produced vials of what was described as a brown liquid that were given to various members of the sect. By most accounts, including sworn testimony, eyewitness recall and written records, only about a dozen members of the Rajneeshees took part in the attack (Tucker, 2000). K.D., the mayor of Antelope and member of the commune, testified against the others in the plot after entering the eyewitness protection program (Tucker, 2000). He described individuals going to salad bars and dumping the contents of the vials in salad dressing, on food, in drink dispensers, and in the water supply. Another member of the cult described putting the bacteria mix on her hand and shaking or holding hands at a town political rally (Tucker, 2000).

The first case of food poisoning was reported to the Health Department of Wasco–Sherman County on September 17, 1984. The lone hospital in the area was inundated with patients (Tucker, 2000). On September 21, 1984, health officials were able to identify the pathogen responsible, *Salmonella* Typhimurium. The number of cases continued to expand at an alarming rate. Officials estimated that 751 people were sickened, although it is believed that number was higher because the area in Wasco County was heavily traveled, and the number of people stopping at the restaurants and traveling through was high (Tucker, 2000).

At first, officials attributed the outbreak to sick food handlers (Ill Handlers, 1984). Investigators initially considered that the outbreak was intentional because there was no apparent commonality to all of the cases (Torok et al., 1997). They quickly decided that the outbreak could not have been intentional due to a number of factors. There was no apparent motive, no information or demand from any group claiming responsibility and there was no historical precedent for such an attack (Torok et al., 1997). Although there was obvious concern about the Rajneesh group because of the amount of recent litigation, there was no connection made. Other reasons that intentional poisoning was ruled out included the fact that there were two waves of illness, no disgruntled or suspect employees were identified, no apparent unusual behavior by employees or patrons was noticed and sometimes, "even in thoroughly investigated outbreaks, the source sometimes remains occult, and, of all the reasons considered for failing to identify a source, this would be the most common (Torok et al., 1997, p. 394)."

Law Enforcement Response

Often biological weapons are lumped together with chemical and nuclear weapons and considered WMDs. This is a potential mistake, in terms of preparedness, mitigation, and preventive procedures. Emergency preparedness remains standard for many different disastrous scenarios. In most cases, an emergency event has physical cues to indicate that it is occurring, such as an earthquake or large storm. The clandestine nature of bioterrorist attacks makes identification much harder. For this reason, the response to bioterror attacks usually starts with emergency medical teams investigating and treating the source of illness. The lead agency responding to a bioterrorist incident is the Center for Disease Control (CDC) in Atlanta. Multiple hospitals in a geographic area may be involved caring for attack victims. Teams of doctors, working with state and federal health officials, usually comprise the medical response team in most emergencies. There may be doctors who have never seen smallpox or anthrax bacteria under a microscope or trained to recognize the pathogen (Cole, 2003). It is important that doctors are able to recognize symptoms and have access to quick testing and results.

In the salmonella attack, officials did not immediately understand that an attack was occurring because of the silent nature of biological weapons. Emergency responders did not recognize the salmonella outbreak until beds filled up in the local hospital (Miller et al., 2001). In contrast, attacks using other types of weapons of mass destruction usually come with some physical cues to alert people nearby that something has happened. Explosions from bombs come with sound cues, and chemical attacks may come with sound, odor or sight cues, depending on the properties of the agents and the means of deployment (Blewett, 2004). Warning properties are included in chemical agents to alert people in the area that there is danger. The smell of gas in a home, the odor that some chemicals have, and the sight of some gases being released can all provide cues to individuals to move out of the area and seek help (Blewett, 2004). For odorless gases, such as carbon monoxide, there are detectors that warn people by emitting light or sound cues.

Biological attacks are difficult for law enforcement personnel to respond to because of the expertise needed to mitigate and understand the attack. The nature of a biological weapons attack is one of stealth and includes an inherent time delay as biological agents take time to incubate. In the case of the anthrax attacks in 2001, it took over 2 weeks for symptoms to occur in victims. It took days for the salmonella poisonings to surface, but because salmonella is a naturally occurring pathogen common in the United States, the episode was not considered abnormal from a law enforcement standpoint (Tucker, 2002). Because biological agents need time to incubate, evidence of an attack may be lost (Atlas, 2002). If there is no initial evidence to suspect wrongdoing, then law enforcement involvement may never happen. For example, the initial package that poisoned Bob Stevens at AMI, Inc., during the anthrax attacks in 2001 were discarded and never found. The sources of anthrax that killed Kathy Nguyen and Ottilie Lundgren, two later victims of the attack, also were never identified. While anthrax is not a contagious pathogen, other bacteria, like smallpox and plague, are highly contagious. If these were used in an attack, people themselves would become the instruments that delivered the biological agent, and the initial specimen or case would be hard to identify.

Law enforcement reaction to the salmonella poisonings in Oregon was muted because it took over 1 year to realize that the salmonella outbreak was intentional, for a variety of reasons (Torok et al., 1997). However, medical response to the outbreak was rapid, and within days, the Center for Disease Control and Oregon state health officials were able to identify the pathogen and proscribe treatment (Torok et al., 1997). The ability to quickly recognize an attack, identify the pathogen, and administer antidotes to mitigate the effect is tantamount in the response to a biological attack. In the Rajneeshee case, it was apparent that something extraordinary was happening because it was the first time all of the beds, 125, at Mid Columbia Medical Center in the Wasco County area were full. Testing supplies began to run short, and in some cases, labs ran out of testing equipment altogether (Miller et al., 2001).

In the case of a bioterrorist incident, the work of health care employees would take precedence over law enforcement investigations. Law enforcement teams provide support, both in investigative support and logistics, such as transport, crowd control, and public communication duties. Most of the literature discussing law enforcement response to a bioterrorist incident focuses on preparedness and response (Katz, 2002; Caffey & Gold, 2001; Falkenrath, 2001). Preparedness to respond to biological attacks is different than trying to prevent them. Some steps have been taken to make it more difficult to obtain pathogens from labs, as the Rajneeshees did so easily. A 1996 law was passed to make it more difficult for people to obtain dangerous pathogens to study (Cole, 2003).

There are consequences, however, when creating a system that controls the transfer or ordering of pathogens between scientists.

Risk analysts have long observed a tendency for policymakers to respond rapidly to visible crises, even if the baseline rate of danger has not changed. . .This tendency to respond quickly encourages reactive "risk of the month" policies crafted in the wake of visible or highly publicized events, resulting in ad hoc policymaking with little regard to competing interests. . .

(Stern, 2002/2003, p. 90)

The point of research is to share ideas and understanding. This often requires the sharing of confidential or privileged information. Controlling access to dangerous pathogens is quite prudent. Not just anybody should have access to smallpox or anthrax. It is important to understand, however, that with a greater level of control, there comes the potential of more suspicion. Scientists who may be interested in studying anthrax spores will see the process of obtaining permission to receive such pathogens as daunting. Besides facilities and equipment necessary to handle such dangerous germs, one now needs to navigate a complex series of controls in order to get the germ (Cole, 2003).

Rajneeshees as Terrorists

As far as is known, the terrorist act perpetrated by the Rajneeshees was not deadly. It is also not known if they intended to kill anyone with their mass-poisoning attempt. Legitimate questions arise about whether this was indeed a terrorist act, as the group tried to conceal its operations, did not publicize it and denied it when accused. The clandestine nature of the operation demonstrates that the Rajneeshees did not think of themselves as a terrorist group. Even today, as talk of terrorism and potential terrorist acts continues to grip America, one hears little about the poisonings.

The Rajneeshees were trying to influence a political, economic, and geographic area central to their operation. They did not want to leave it, so it would not be in their best interest to destroy it. However, their actions are not inconsistent with that of a terrorist organization. In many ways, they had spent years terrorizing the community using various tactics. They manipulated the legal system in Wasco County, circumventing zoning laws to build in their new town, eschewing residency requirements for voters, and developing a police force that was not properly trained or equipped, leading to charges of abuse. Observing their body of work, the plot to poison Wasco County residents was not an isolated incident, even if it was the most sensational, violent, and criminal.

The group's acceptance and use of violence was not a new phenomenon. In Pune, India, where they were based in an ashram before moving to Oregon, there were many reports of violence in therapy sessions (Carter, 1990; Fitzgerald, 1986; Guest, 2005). As spokeswoman for the commune in Oregon, Ma Anand Sheela was becoming increasingly belligerent in interviews, threatening county officials and neighbors. Members of the Rajneeshee commune harassed residents of Antelope (Carter, 1990; Fitzgerald, 1986; Guest, 2005). Some members of the commune were specially trained in martial arts to help defend the commune from attackers. The official reason given for the training was that members practiced martial arts as a form of contact therapy.

The group brought increased scrutiny on its operations when they sought religious status, attempting to circumvent state and federal tax laws. This put their new town in jeopardy because of the separation of church and state as spelled out in the United States Constitution (Tucker, 2000). At that point, their ability to control their situation began to unravel, and in the swirling chaos at the time, a far-fetched plan was hatched. Again, however, there were signs pointing to the group's activities and their potential for violence. In 1983, as mentioned above, two county commissioners became gravely ill after visiting the compound, and they believed they were poisoned, although it was never proven (Miller et al., 2001). There was also the investigation into the amount of Haldol being ordered at the compound. These warning signs were never pursued by law enforcement or county officials, although there was suspicion of the group from the time of their arrival in the area.

There are similarities to the Rajneesh group and terrorist organizations. Margaret Singer discusses the labeling of cults in this way:

> What is labeled a cult by one researcher may not be identified as such by another. For example, some researchers count only religion-based groups, discounting the myriad cults formed around a variety of doctrines, theories and practices. Using the three factors of leader, structure, and thought reform allows us to assess the cultic nature of a particular group or situation regardless of its belief system.
>
> (Singer, 2003, p. 7).

The structure and control present in Al-Qaeda and other terrorist groups are similar to cults. September 11, 2001 is a defining moment, but it was not the initial contact American authorities had with Al-Qaeda. Throughout the 1990s, beginning with the 1993 World Trade Center bombings, Al-Qaeda perpetrated a number of attacks on American interests, often with little response. These terrorist incidents, though far more deadly, were similar to warning signals emanating from the Rajneeshee commune. When the acts are viewed as individual, stand-alone events, a stronger response may not seem warranted.

A move toward more violent methods is sometimes triggered when setbacks to group goals occur. This can result in extreme responses against the outside world. The Rajneeshee's suffered a number of legal setbacks during 1984. They felt that the county elections were the last hope they had of fulfilling their goals for their new town. Initially, the Rajneeshees were able to coexist in the secular world. When they arrived, the Rajneeshees added to the economy of Antelope, and with their money, brought a new vibrancy to a town that had suffered economically. As the Rajneesh group started to get "attacked" by legal entities in Oregon, Rajneesh took a vow of silence, and let Sheela speak for him. He also acceded power to her, a move that would later result in the poisoning plot.

In isolation, groups are able to create a schism between practicing members and the "outside" society. In cultures where normal checks and balances do not occur, the ideas of mass poisonings, or suicide bombings, become more palatable, especially when one group is pitted against another. The perceived societal persecutions against the group result in a need to strike back, sometimes aggressively. By the fall of 1984, Rajneeshee commune members were becoming more hostile, and there was an incident where Sheela and other members were demonstrating on television, vowing revenge on the "United States of Aggression" (Miller et al., 2001). Depriving members of family, having them live in primitive, squalid conditions and denying them other pleasantries makes it easier to create a schism between members of the group and society at large. Constructing myths about how society is denying them the ability to have access to what they need, it becomes easier for men such as Rajneesh to get people to bend to their will.

In Rajneeshpuram, individuals were told how to dress, walk, speak, and chant and had little to do with the outside world. Parents were encouraged to have sex with multiple partners, leaving children to fend for themselves, creating a need for people to rely on the cult for direction and sustenance (Guest, 2005; Milne, 1986; Tucker, 2000). Isolationism potentially breeds the warped response to societal "threats" as constructed by the entrepreneurial leader of the group. Aggression against the outside world increased as their respective situations seemingly became more desperate. Rajneeshees demanded allegiance to the group collective. Those who did not adhere to the group's way of life were expelled (Carter, 1990; Milne, 1986).

Without an ethical framework to resist inappropriate and destructive responses, plans such as mass poisonings or suicide attacks take on legitimate connotations. In an environment where control, fear, hatred, and isolationism exist, drastic plans will offer a power that many group members do not feel otherwise. Indeed, it seems that those who gravitate toward such groups are on the fringe of society, no matter their professional or educational background. Such persons are seeking higher truths, different meanings, or acceptance. Cults thrive in times of political, economic, or cultural turmoil (Singer, 2003). The reason to exist needs an outlet, or the group will die. The demise of such organizations is demonstrated with the Rajneeshees, because once they lost their legal challenges, and were forced to obey the laws in Oregon, their attempts to remake their society failed. When the leaders fled, the group was left to fend for itself. Although Bhagwan's teachings still inform people today, the group has morphed into something not as formal, not as powerful and not as cohesive. This has decreased the threat they pose against others.

Anthrax Attacks – Fall 2001

The Fall of 2001 was a difficult time in America. Following the terrorist attacks of September 11, 2001, people were scared and angry. The nation prepared to go to war in Afghanistan, the country harboring the terrorist group thought to be responsible for the attacks on the World Trade Center and the Pentagon. The following briefly summarizes the events of the anthrax attacks during the months of October and November, 2001.

Robert Stevens, a photo editor at American Media, Inc., the publisher that printed some of America's top tabloids, such as *The National Enquirer, The Sun*, and *The Globe*, was the first person diagnosed with inhalation anthrax, and the first person to die from it. He began feeling symptoms on September 30, 2001, and was diagnosed with anthrax on October 4, 2001. It is believed he contracted the disease from a package that was mailed to the offices of American Media, Inc., addressed to the pop superstar, Jennifer Lopez. However, no one was able to recover the original package (Cole, 2003). When Mr. Stevens was admitted to the JFK Medical Center in Atlantis, Florida, he was treated by Dr. Larry Bush, an infectious disease specialist. Dr. Bush's training led him to question conventional wisdom, and although he was unable to save Mr. Stevens' life, he probably saved the lives of countless others with his diagnosis (Cole, 2003).

Similar to the salad bar poisonings case, officials did not initially make a connection to terrorism, attributing Mr. Stevens' to a natural contraction of inhalation anthrax (Keen, 2001; Watson & Whitworth, 2001). After Mr. Stevens' death, investigations started, but law enforcement and CDC officials were hopeful that Mr. Stevens' illness was an isolated event (Cole, 2003). When Mr. Stevens died on October 5, 2001, it was reported for the first time that officials considered the possibility it was a terrorist action (Canedy & Wade, 2001). On October 9, 2001, Ernesto Blanco, a coworker of Bob Stevens, and the mailroom supervisor at American Media, Inc., also was diagnosed with inhalation anthrax. In addition, tests conducted on Bob Stevens work computer showed traces of anthrax (Cole, 2003; Canedy & Kuczynski, 2001).

Stephanie Dailey, a mailroom employee at American Media, tested positive for the presence of anthrax, but never contracted the disease. By the time the results of her test were completed, she, along with most American Media employees, was already on antibiotics (Cole, 2003; Canedy & Yardley, 2001). Hers was the last case of anthrax diagnosed at American Media. At this point, investigators were treating this as a deliberate act and opened a criminal investigation (Canedy & Yardley, 2001). Hoping that the outbreak was over, officials in Florida did not realize that the attack was already almost a month old.

It is believed that letters to television networks NBC, CBS, and ABC, as well as letters mailed to the *New York Post* and American Media, Inc., were mailed on September 18, 2001, from Trenton, New Jersey. The FBI was notified about the letters sent to NBC on September 25, 2001, but the letters were not tested for anthrax until 2 weeks later, when an assistant to Tom Brokaw, the NBC News anchor at the time, developed cutaneous anthrax (Steinhauer & Dwyer, 2001; Cole, 2003). Three other people in the New York City area who worked for companies that received anthrax letters also developed cutaneous anthrax, including a 7-month-old child of an ABC News employee, Claire Fletcher, an employee of CBS News, and Joanna Huden, a journalist at the *New York Post* (Cole, 2003).

When news of the New York City poisonings became public, there was panic in the nation. Worried citizens, in an attempt to protect themselves, created huge demands for various antibiotics used to fight inhalation anthrax, most notably Ciprofloxacin, or Cipro. It was impossible for pharmacies across America to keep the drug in stock (Andrews, 2001; Peterson & Pear, 2001). Amidst this panic, a second batch of anthrax letters was mailed from Trenton, New Jersey on October 9, 2001. One was addressed to Senator Tom Daschle and the other addressed to Senator Patrick Leahy. The anthrax contained in these letters was very potent and potentially deadly. Because of the heightened awareness of anthrax and the delivery method, staffers in Daschle's office immediately recognized that an attack was occurring. Staff offices for Daschle and Russ Feingold, Wisconsin were evacuated immediately. Even though the offices were cleared quickly, 31 people tested positive for the presence of anthrax (Purdum & Mitchell, 2001). All of the people who worked in the Hart building began taking antibiotics. The high amount of people who showed signs of exposure attests to the potent form of the anthrax sent to the Senate offices.

At this point, the CDC and the FBI were testing the strains of anthrax to see what they were and how they were delivered. The quality of the anthrax in the first batch of mailings was inferior to those that came later. Officials believe this explains why more people contracted cutaneous anthrax rather than inhalation anthrax during the first wave of attacks. The spores of anthrax were not milled finely enough to enter someone's lungs (Cole, 2003; Matsumoto, 2003). Even now, investigators are divided as to the quality and origin of the anthrax mailed in 2001 (Matsumoto, 2003; Cole, 2003). However, the fine quality of the anthrax contained in the letters sent to Senators Daschle and Leahy would claim other victims. On October 22, 2001, two US Post Office employees from Washington, D.C., Joseph P. Curseen, 47, and Thomas L. Morris Jr., 55, died of inhalation anthrax. Anthrax spores were detected in the mailroom of the Capital. The focus of the investigation quickly shifted to the post office that handled mail in the Capital building (Cole, 2003). A third employee at the Brentwood facility, Leroy Richmond, was also diagnosed with inhalation anthrax.

In most scenarios about how bioterrorist attacks would occur, it was rarely envisioned that the method of delivery would be through the mail. Although there were a number of anthrax hoaxes perpetrated against abortion clinics from 1998 to 2001 (Cole, 2003), the method of delivery usually imagined in different scenarios included some sort of aerosol spray, a bomb that would project the toxin over a wide area, or a plane, such as a crop duster, distributing pathogens in the air above densely populated areas. The mail delivery system, so vital to the country and the conduct of routine business transactions, had now been used to kill people. The most frightening part of the attack was that cross-contamintaion was so easy. Mail handlers in Boca Raton, Washington, D.C., and New York had become sick from mail that had not even been opened. The fact that it killed two postal employees in Washington now confirmed the worst fears of counter-terrorism officials. The mail facility in Brentwood, when it was tested for the presence of anthrax spores, was found to have enough anthrax in it to infect hundreds of people. Even though the envelopes were sealed with tape, the anthrax was able to pass through microscopic holes in the envelopes (Cole, 2003). When pushed through the machines that stamped and postmarked letters, the spores were strewn throughout the facility, becoming airborne and settling on equipment, clothing, and in people's nostrils and lungs.

As investigations continued in New York, Boca Raton, and Washington, another person contracted inhalation anthrax. Kathy Nguyen, an employee of New York's Eye, Ear, and Nose Hospital on New York's Upper East Side, was admitted to

Lennox Hill Hospital in New York City on October 28, 2001. On October 31, 2001, she died of inhalation anthrax, suffering cardiac arrest. There was no obvious connection to any of the previous cases (Cole, 2003). Ms. Nguyen did not work in a mailroom, although she worked close to one. There was no suspicious mail sent to the hospital, and police had no record of there being any investigations at the site. Ms. Nguyen had no obvious connections to postal employees, or to any of the networks or newspapers that had received anthrax letters. It is possible she contracted anthrax from mail cross-contamination, or she got it from something that may have been dumped in the trash that contained spores (Cole, 2003; Steinhauer, 2001).

Another perplexing anthrax case occurred in November, 2001. Ottillie Lundgren, 94, from Oxford, Connecticut, entered Griffin Hospital in Derby, Connecticut on November 16, 2001. As doctors received the results of her tests, they realized that they were dealing with a potential anthrax case, although at first they thought it could be a routine infection. (Cole, 2003). She died on November 21, 2001. The case baffled and frightened authorities. Mrs. Lundgren rarely went outside her home, never traveled and could not remember receiving any letters in the mail that contained powder (Cole, 2003). The possibility of cross-contamination in the mail made the anthrax attacks much more serious. Mrs. Lundgren's case happened about a month after most of the other cases had occurred, and testing in mail facilities, offices and homes demonstrated a path anthrax spores took after being deposited in the mail. Evidence recovered in her home all tested negative for the presence of anthrax spores. The implications of this concerned officials (Cole, 2003).

After further testing, it was found that a mail sorter in the Wallingford, CT., mail center "was heavily contaminated [with] approximately 3 million spores, roughly translated into 600 infectious doses (Cole, 2003, p. 109)." It was determined that a letter sent through the Wallingford facility had been processed at the Hamilton Center in New Jersey about 15 days after the contaminated Leahy letter had been processed on the same machine (Cole, 2003). That letter was found and contained traces of anthrax. No one had become infected in the household that received the letter (Cole, 2003). It is also possible that another letter had been sent and never recovered. Of course, there are a myriad of ways that Mrs. Lundgren could have been infected. It is reasonable to think that cross-contamination of the mail was responsible for Ms. Lundgren's contraction of anthrax. It is now incumbent on law enforcement officials, working with epidemiologists, CDC officials, and others to figure out how it happened.

Profile of the Anthrax Killer

There were several theories about who may have been responsible for the anthrax attack. The FBI initially believed that the attacker was a lone person, probably male, employed in a laboratory of some kind. The attacker probably had a professional scientific background (Critical Incident, 2001). The major component of the profile was that the person responsible was a domestic terrorist, probably American, and tied in some way to a lab that researches or maintains a source of anthrax (Cole, 2003).

Barbara Hatch Rosenberg, a molecular biologist and professor at the State University of New York (SUNY), Purchase Campus, believed that the attacker was an American who studies biological agents at Federal labs. Her examination of the strain of anthrax used in the attacks led her to conclude that it came from the US Army Medical Research Institute of Infectious Diseases (USAMRIID) at Fort Detrick, Maryland (Couzin, 2002). She also conjectured that the killer did not mean to hurt anyone because they sealed the envelopes with tape, included a message about what was contained and advised on what antibiotic to take (Couzin, 2002). This profile was similar to the FBI's, and informed FBI thinking about the attack and subsequent investigations.

Authorities investigated scientists that had worked on a study discussing hypothetical terrorist attacks, including sending anthrax through the mail (Goldstein & Shannon, 2002). They also investigated government personnel who had been administered the anthrax vaccine (Goldstein & Shannon, 2002). This would explain how the pathogen was handled without resulting in any illness to the perpetrator. One potential suspect named early in the investigation sued the government for violating his constitutional rights (Locy, 2003). There were several missteps as agencies searched for the anthrax killer.

On August 6, 2008, the FBI released documents, including search warrants and affidavits that supported an investigation of Dr. Bruce Ivins, a Fort Detrick researcher who worked with deadly pathogens (Anthrax Investigation, 2008). Dr. Ivins was about to be indicted as the anthrax killer, but took his own life, on July 29, 2008, before he could be arrested (Abbruzzese & Lipton, 2008). The government took an unprecedented step and released documents concerning the investigation after Dr. Ivins' suicide, even though there is no presumption of guilt until proven in court (Anthrax Investigations, 2008). Over time, investigators began to theorize that a scientist who wanted to highlight biodefense issues, or who was disgruntled about preparedness was responsible for the attacks.

Two puzzles have haunted investigators from the beginning: the motive of the perpetrator and his skills. Because the notes in some of the letters mailed to news media organizations and two senators included radical Islamist rhetoric, investigators initially believed the letters might have been sent by Al Qaeda.

But the F.B.I. quickly settled on a different profile: a disgruntled American scientist or technician, perhaps one specializing in biodefense, who wanted to raise an alarm about the bioterrorism threat. That theory accounted for the letters' taped seams and the notes' use of the word anthrax, a warning that allowed antibiotic treatment – not to be expected from a Qaeda attack intended mainly to kill.

(Shane & Lichtbau, 2008a)

Even though Dr. Ivins is believed to have been the perpetrator of the attacks, many are still skeptical of the FBI's conclusions in this case. In September, 2008, members of Congress, including Senator Patrick Leahy, a lawmaker to whom one of the original anthrax letters was sent, called for an independent review of the investigation (Lichtblau, 2008; Shane, 2008a, 2008b; Shane & Lichtblau, 2008b). At the time of this writing, skepticism about the case remained high.

There are others who believe the attackers were members of an Islamic militant group. The messages contained in the letter discussed Allah and vowed death to Israel and America. Following is the text of the letter sent to Senator Daschle's office (Fig. 5.2).

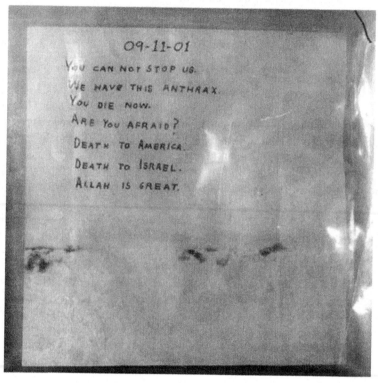

Fig. 5.2 Letter containing anthrax sent to Senator Tom Daschle's office, received October 15, 2001

The messages contained in the letter coincide with the attacks of September 11. Many of the letters were mailed exactly 1 week later, on Tuesday, September 18, 2001. There have also been reports of some of the September 11 hijackers being treated for cutaneous anthrax in a Miami, Florida hospital (Cole, 2003). Several hijackers lived within miles of the American Media offices, and two of the hijackers had rented apartments through a real estate agent who was the wife of the *National Enquirer's* editor-in-chief, Mike Irish (Cole, 2003). It was reported that two of the hijackers had subscriptions to tabloid newspapers published by American Media, Inc. (Cole, 2003; Kidwell, Garcia, & Lebowitz, 2001). In addition, American Media may have been targeted because the publishing group was running articles that were negative toward Osama bin Laden. In the words of Martha Moffett, librarian at

American Media, Inc., when responding to a question about whether Osama Bin Laden reads the tabloids, said, "I don't know, but we've been real hard on him, and you never know (Cole, 2003)."

These "coincidences" add up to a link between Islamic militants and the September 11 hijackers. Of course, since all of the hijackers died in the attacks, it is believed that someone else must have mailed the letters. There has never been any link found between the hijackers and the potential anthrax killer. There are other discrepancies that cast doubt on the September 11 hijackers somehow being involved in the anthrax letters attack. The letters contained a warning, were sealed with tape and addressed to specific people. Why would individuals responsible for the deaths of thousands of people care about the potential safety of anyone who came in contact with the letter? The letters were mailed from Trenton, New Jersey, far away from their home base in Florida. Why not just mail the letters from Florida, if you know that you are going to die in a matter of days? If one had access to such a volatile, highly weaponized form of anthrax, why not use it to kill more people? We may never know who the anthrax killer is, but it is reasonable to think that the person may still have some anthrax left and be waiting for another opportunity to use it.

Analysis

Devastating epidemics dot human history. Scourges like polio, small pox, malaria, tuberculosis, and plague have been beaten back, and in some cases, into submission. Anthrax is a naturally occurring pathogen, as is salmonella. Many believe one of the described biblical plagues that afflicted Egyptians resembled anthrax poisoning (Cole, 2003; Tucker, 2002). Flu epidemics in the early part of the 20th century killed millions of people throughout the world. Current scourges in the world include various hemorrhagic fevers, avian "super-flus," AIDS, and of course, the potential for biological terrorism. Epidemiologists, along with countless numbers of aid and health-care workers, have been at the front line battling these deadly pathogens. Some succumbed to the scourges themselves and died heroes. Some got lucky in the battles, finding weaknesses, identifying remedies, and destroying the pathogens. The fight against smallpox has been so successful that its effect as a weapon has been exponentially heightened, because a whole generation of doctors have not had to treat it.

Dr. Margaret Humphreys, an historian of epidemic disease, sees our recent experience with anthrax as one that has given "complacent Americans some exposure to the fear that disease can engender (Humphrey, 2002)." Perhaps other disciplines, like history and literature, can inform our response to the threat of biological terrorism. We have the experience of thousands before us to call upon. It will be prudent to look back to see how we respond in the future. The intentional use of biological agents to inflict disease is incredulous, and all the more ironic given that biological agents cause so much suffering now, naturally. That is what makes them effective terrorist weapons. We fear what could happen because we have already witnessed the potential destruction.

We also must not underestimate the power of advances in technology with regard to the development of superpathogens resistant to current treatments methods. If we look back at many of the technological advances over the last 150 years, several of them have been remarkably efficient at killing people when used as weapons. The invention of the aerodynamically shaped bullet made shooting more accurate, resulting in the killing of hundreds of thousands during conflicts starting in the mid-19th century through today. During the Civil War, the Franco-Prussian War and World War I, fighting tactics left soldiers at the mercy of the more accurate, more deadly, bullets. The invention of the automobile, and the airplane, while wonderful for most, also resulted in the ability to travel greater distances with munitions, and allowed attackers to be more removed from the immediacy of battle. The dropping of bombs from planes killed tens of thousands during World War II, in epic struggles such as the Battle of Britain, the Japanese attacks on Pearl Harbor, and the firebombing of Dresden, Germany. Tanks swept through northern Europe and Africa, destroying buildings, homes, and people. Beneficial technological advances made such killing possible.

We now face similar technological advances in science. The decoding of the genome has made it possible for scientists to manipulate strands of DNA to fight terrible diseases like cancer, diabetes, Alzheimer's, and other genetic disorders responsible for the deaths of hundreds of thousands of people worldwide per year. These technological advances have also given rise to the fear that super pathogens, resistant to current antibiotics, and natural immune systems, can be developed and used as a weapon, killing millions in the process. While doomsday scenarios are often far fetched, we must remember history as we move forward with technical advances in the biological sciences. Strong control in the biological community, along with government oversight and international treaties are prudent to retard the development of such weapons. At the same time, research about how to stop such potential weapons must be pursued. These competing forces will make biological research difficult over the next several years, as the greater community struggles with the results of groundbreaking research and attempts to come to terms with the legal, ethical, and moral conundrums that emerge.

Conclusion

The threat of bioterror attacks is real. As in the two incidents described above, it is possible to successfully develop and deploy biological weapons, whether the technology used is primitive, as in the case of the salmonella poisonings, or highly sophisticated, as in the anthrax attacks. In Oregon, the isolation, fervor, and control exhibited by the cult cultivated an environment where such an attack became palatable to carry out. This is similar to behavior exhibited by terrorist groups. Such groups prey on those who seek acceptance, who are aimless and who, even though potentially successful professionals, or highly educated, seek an alternative higher truth or meaning to their lives. They often find it in the messages of charismatic speakers and leaders such as Osama Bin Laden or Bhagwan Shree Rajneesh. In some cases, the messages condone violence and become deadly. It is important to focus on the human element that makes up such groups. Counter-terrorist strategy is militaristic in nature, so tactical and practical solutions take precedence over theory and academic research. It is important to inform counter-terrorist methods with a more multidisciplinary approach, because there may be more viable solutions to terrorist problems. In the case of the Rajneeshees, civil legal actions drained the cult of money, time, and intellectual resources. The use of civil law is also proving to be an effective tool in denying terrorist groups funds to operate. Research concerning how such responses can affect such groups should continue.

In the anthrax case, results of the investigation have been frustrating. It is apparent in these two cases that such attacks can be carried out anonymously, and unless there is a lucky break in the investigation, it is possible for offenders to remain anonymous. The lack of progress in the investigations should not deter people from understanding that health officials met the attacks successfully, and the mitigation of the two events resulted in few casualties. Health officials, no matter the protocol as set out, lead the response to biological weapons attacks. This makes biological weapons attacks problematic from a law enforcement standpoint, because vital information must be shared with the public. Such information could compromise investigations, allowing attackers to remain free and attack again.

Future research about characteristics of individuals who join terrorist groups or cults should merge. In addition, group histories should be researched to discover information about recruitment methods, indoctrination, and control of members. This information could make it easier to infiltrate groups to develop human intelligence that will better inform counter-terror policy. Also, on the continuum of violence, groups tend to start out benign, and progressively become more violent. At what point can this turn be recognized? Is there a point where a group's actions will indicate a potential path of violence? Studies of group dynamics, rhetoric, and action may help inform this research. It is hoped that such future studies can take the mysticism and imagery away from terrorism and lead to a better understanding of what leads to such egregious action against society.

References

Abbruzzese, S., & Lipton, E. (2008, August 2). Anthrax Suspect's Death Is Dark End for a Family Man. *New York Times*. Retrieved January 22, 2009, from http://www.nytimes.com/2008/08/02/us/02scientist.html

Amato, I. (1993). New evidence in 1979 Soviet anthrax deaths. *Science, 258*(5102), 1698.

Andrews, E. (2001). A nation challenged: The Pills; Bayer is a bit taken aback by the frenzy to get its drug. *The New York Times*, p. 8B. Retrieved December 10, 2004, from Lexis/Nexis Academic.

Anthrax investigations: Closing A chapter (2008). *Headline Archives: Federal Bureau of Investigation.* Retrieved January 22, 2009, from http://www.fbi.gov/page2/august08/amerithrax080608.html

Atlas, R. (2002). Bioterrorism: From threat to reality. *Annual Review of Microbiology, 56*, 167–185.

Barker, E. (1986). Religious movements: Cult and anticult since Jonestown. *Annual Review of Sociology, 12*, 329–346.

Blewett, W. K. (2004). Chemical and biological threats: the nature and the risk. *HPAC Engineering, 76*(9), 57.

Burrows, W. D., & Renner, S. E. (1999). Biological warfare agents as threats to potable water. *Environmental Health Perspectives, 107*, 975–985.

Caffey, A., & Gold, R. (2001, October 15). The high cost of public safety. *Wall Street Journal (Eastern Edition)*, p. B1.

Canedy, D., & Kuczynski, A. (2001, October 9). A nation challenged: A medical mystery; Second Case of Anthrax Leads F.B.I. into inquiry. *New York Times*, p. 1. Retrieved November 29, 2004, from Lexis/Nexis Academic Universe.

Canedy, D., & Wade, N. (2001, October 6). Florida man dies of rare form of Anthrax. *New York Times*, p. 9A. Retrieved November 29, 2004, from Lexis/Nexis Academic Universe.

Canedy, D., & Yardley, J. (2001, October 11). A nation challenged: A medical mystery; Florida inquiry finds anthrax in third person. *New York Times*, p. 1A. Retrieved November 29, 2004, from Lexis/Nexis Academic Universe.

Carter, L. (1990). *Charisma and control in Rajneeshpuram*. New York: Cambridge University Press.

Cole, L. (2003). *The anthrax letters: A medical detective story*. Washington, D.C.: Joseph Henry Press.

Couzin, J. (2002). Unconventional detective bears down on a killer. *Science, 297*(5585), 1264.

Cowell, A. (1988, September 5). Fleeing assault by Iraqis, Kurds tell of poison gas and lives lost. *New York Times*, p. A1. Retrieved November 2, 2004, from Lexis/Nexis Academic Universe.

Critical Incident Response Group, National Center for the Analysis of Violent Crime. (2001, November 9). *Amerithrax press briefing: Linguistic/behavioral analysis of anthrax letters*. Retrieved November 28, 2004, from Amerithrax Links website: http://www.fbi.gov/anthrax/amerithrax.htm.

Demerath, N. J., & Williams, R. (1984). A mythical past and uncertain future. *Society, 21*, 3–10.

Enserink, M. (2003). Panel seeks to balance science and security. *Science, 302*(5643), 206.

Falkenrath, R. A. (2001). Problems of preparedness: U.S. readiness for a domestic terrorist attack. *International Security, 25*(4), 147–186.

Fitzgerald, F. (1986). *Cities on a Hill*. New York: Touchstone Books.

Galanter, M. (1999). *Cults, Faith, Healing, and Coercion* (2nd ed.). New York: Oxford University Press.

Garmon, L. (1980). What happened at Sverdlovsk? *Science News, 188*(5), 73. Retrieved November 3, 2004, from EBSCOHost Academic Search Premier.

Goldstein, A., & Shannon, E. (2002). The FBI pursues an anthrax lead. *Time, 160*(7), 17.

Grafstein, L. (1984). Messianic capitalism: The invisible hand that feeds the cults. *The New Republic, 190*, 14.

Guest, T. (2005). *My life in orange: growing up with the guru*. Orlando: Harcourt, Inc.

Hope, B. K. (2004). Using fault tree analysis to assess bioterrorist risks to the U.S. food supply. *Human and Ecological Risk Assessment, 10*, 327–347.

Humphrey, M. (2002). No safe place: Disease and panic in American history. *American Literary History, 14*(4), 845–857.

Ill handlers suspected in Oregon food poisonings. (1984, October, 21). *New York Times*, Section 1, p. 33. Retrieved October 1, 2004, from LexisNexis Academic.

Joshi, V. (1982). *The awakened one: The life and work of Bhagwan Shree Rajneesh*. San Francisco: Harper and Row.

Judge refuses to back sect's voter drive. (1984, October 18). *New York Times, Section A*, p. 18. Retrieved October 2, 2004, from LexisNexis Academic.

Katz, R. (2002). Public health preparedness: The best defense against biological weapons. *The Washington Quarterly, 25*(3), 69–82.

Keen, J. (2001, October 5). Fla. Anthrax case is not seen as terrorism. *USA Today,* p. 9A. Retrieved November 26, 2004, from Lexis/Nexis Academic Universe.

Kidwell, D., Garcia, M., & Lebowitz, L. (2001, October 10). Possible anthrax match found: Fatal strain may be tied to source from 1950s. *Miami Herald* (online version). Text of article retrieved December 17, 2004, from FreeRepublic.com website: http://www.freerepublic.com/focus/f-news/544279/posts.

Koblentz, G. (2003/2004). Pathogens as weapons: The international security implications of biological warfare. *International Security, 28*(3), 84–122.

Kuhr, S., & Hauer, J. (2001). The threat of biological terrorism in the new millennium. *American Behavioral Scientist, 44,* 1032–1041.

Leviten, A., & Alexa, M. T. (2003). 9/11 and agricultural safety. *Florida Law Journal, 77*(10), 64.

Lichtblau, E. (2008, September 17). Independent review set on F.B.I. Anthrax inquiry. *New York Times,* p. A19.

Locy, T. (2003, August 27). Scientist in anthrax probe sues Ashcroft, FBI; says rights violated. *USA Today.* Retrieved December 8, 2004, from EBSCOHost Academic Search Premier.

Matsumoto, G. (2003). Bioterrorism: The anthrax powder: State of the art? *Science, 28,* 1492.

McInnes, C., & Lee, K. (2006). Health, security and foreign policy. *Review of International Studies, 32,* 5–23.

Meselson, M., & Guillemin, J. (1994). The Sverdlovsk anthrax outbreak of 1979. *Science, 266*(5188), 1202.

Miller, J., Engelberg, S., & Broad, W. (2001). *Germs: Biological weapons and America's secret war.* New York: Simon & Schuster.

Milne, H. (1986). *Bhagwan: The god that failed.* New York: St. Martin's Press.

Payne, L. A. (2000). *Uncivil movements: The armed right wing and democracy in Latin America.* Baltimore: The Johns Hopkins University Press.

Peterson, L. & Pear, R. (2001). A nation challenged: Cipro; Anthrax fears send demand for a drug far beyond output. *The New York Times,* p. 1A. Retrieved December 10, 2004, from Lexis/Nexis Academic.

Publish and perish. (2003). *Economist, 367*(8322), 74.

Purdum, T. S., & Mitchell, A. (2001, October 18). A nation challenged: the Anthrax threat; tests show anthrax exposure in at least 30 capital workers. *The New York Times,* p. A1.

Reppy, J. (2003). Regulating Biotechnology in the Age of Homeland Security. *Science Studies, 16*(2), 38–54. Retrieved October 23, 2004, from EBSCOHost Academic Search Premier.

Robbins, T. (1984). Constructing cultist "mind control". *Sociological Analysis, 45*(3), 241–256.

Robbins, T. (1985). Government regulatory powers and church autonomy: Deviants groups as test cases. *Journal for the Scientific Study of Religion, 24,* 237–252.

Robbins, T., & Anthony, D. (1980). Brainwashing and the persecution of cults. *Journal of Religion and Health, 19,* 66–69.

Shane, S. (2008a, September 18). Senator, target of Anthrax letter, challenges F.B.I. finding. *New York Times,* p. A30.

Shane, S. (2008b, September 24). Critics of Anthrax inquiry seek and independent review. *New York Times,* p. A17.

Shane, S., & Lichtblau, E. (2008a, August 2). Scientist's suicide linked to Anthrax inquiry. *New York Times,* p. A1. Retrieved January 22, 2009, from http://www.nytimes.com/2008/08/02/washington/02anthrax.html?pagewanted=1

Shane, S., & Lichtblau, E. (2008b, September 7). Seeking details, lawmakers cite Anthrax doubts. *New York Times,* p. A1.

Singer, M. T. (2003). *Cults in our midst: The continuing fight against their hidden menace.* California: Jossey Bass.

Smith, J. Z. (1982). *Imagining religion: From Babylon to Jonestown.* Chicago: University of Chicago Press.

Steinhauer, J. (2001). A nation challenged: The new case; Hospital worker's illness suggests widening threat; security tightens over U.S. *New York Times*, p. 1A. Retrieved December 6, 2004, from Lexis/Nexis Academic Universe.

Steinhauer, J., & Dwyer, J. (2001). A nation challenged: The response; FBI did not test letters to NBC or immediately notify city hall. *New York Times*, p. 1A. Retrieved December 6, 2004, from Lexis/Nexis Academic Universe.

Stern, J. (2002/2003). Dreaded risks and the control of biological weapons. *International Security, 27*(3), 89–123. Retrieved November 28, 2004, from Project MUSE database.

Tension building over Oregon Sect (1984, September 16). *The New York Times,* Section 1, p. 38. Retrieved October 2, 2004, from Lexis/Nexis Academic Universe.

Torok, T. J., Tauxe, R. V., Wise, R. P., Livengood, J. R., Sokolow, R., Mauvais, S., et al. (1997). A large community outbreak of Salmonellosis caused by intentional contamination of restaurant salad bars. *JAMA, 278,* 389–395.

Trippett, F. (1985, September 30). Blown bliss; a guru calls the police (Rajneeshuram in Oregon). *Time, 126,* 32.

Tucker, J. B. (2000). *Toxic terror: Assessing terrorist use of chemical and biological weapons.* Cambridge: MIT Press.

Tucker, J. B. (2002). A Farewell to Germs: The U.S. Renunciation of Biological and Toxin Warfare 1969–1970. *International Security, 27*(1) 107–148.

UPI. (1982, December 19). Guru's disciples taking over in Oregon town. *The New York Times,* Section 1, p. 1.

Watson, R., & Whitwirth, D. (2001, October 5). Alarm over US anthrax case. *The Times* (London).

Chapter 6
When Radical Becomes Terrorist: Law Enforcement and Eco-Sabotage

Kirsten Christiansen

> *If you would convince a man that he does wrong, do right. But do not care to convince him. Men will believe what they see. Let them see.*
>
> – Henry David Thoreau (1817–1862)

Introduction

Early on the morning of Monday, October 19, 1998, seven fires broke out at a ski lodge on Vail Mountain in Colorado. By the time the fires were put out, three buildings were destroyed, including Ski Patrol Headquarters and Two Elk Restaurant and Lodge, and four chairlifts were damaged; total damage was estimated at $12 million. Within days of the fires, a shadowy group called the Earth Liberation Front (ELF) claimed responsibility in a letter to local media outlets (Glick, 2001). The ELF stated that the arson was designed to stop Vail Associates, just beginning an 885-acre expansion, from ruining "the nation's last threatened Lynx habitat."[1] At the time, this incident represented the largest and most damaging attack ever committed in the name of environmental protection in the United States[2] and was considered by many to be proof that radical environmental groups were escalating the level of violence in their attacks (Paulson, 1998). This chapter will analyze the threats posed

K. Christiansen (✉)
The Graduate Center, City University of New York and John Jay College of Criminal Justice, New York, NY, USA
e-mail: kjaysi@yahoo.com

[1] Earth Liberation Front web site. http://www.earthliberationfront.com . Accessed November 2004.

[2] This damage amount has since been surpassed by the August 1, 2003 arson of a San Diego condominium project which caused $50 million in damage. Source: http://www.signonsandiego.com/news/metro/20030803-9999_1m3firefolo.html. Accessed 11/06/04. At the site, a banner was found that read "If you build it – we will burn it. The ELFs are mad" (Knickerbocker and Dotinga, 2003).

M.R. Haberfeld, A. von Hassell (eds.), *A New Understanding of Terrorism*,
DOI 10.1007/978-1-4419-0115-6_6, © Springer Science+Business Media, LLC 2009

by groups referred to as eco-terrorists and the law enforcement action and/or inaction response toward their activities, including the problems with legal definitions and thus proper enforcement or lack of enforcement of the relevant laws.

The Environmental Movement

The conservation of natural spaces has been a concern in the United States since the 19th century when John James Audobon brought the natural world to a wider American audience and George Bird Grinnell originated the idea of creating a society for protecting birds – a group that eventually became the Audobon Society (Shabecoff, 1993).

Much of the activities of the environmental movement, past and present, have been motivated not just by a concern for nature but by a desire for social improvement – protecting the environment also protects the human race (Marangudakis, 2001). This is particularly true of today's environmental justice movement, which highlights the connection between environmental degradation and social inequality (Moberg, 2001).

The contemporary environmental movement in the United States has grown from its origins in the social movements of the 1960s and 1970s to become a political force in the United States. In just a few short decades, concern for the environment has gone from a grassroot movement born out of the changing demands of post-World War II Americans and the social upheavals of the 1970s (Shabecoff, 1993) to a quasi-coalition of highly organized and politically sophisticated professional organizations. As with any form of political behavior, the environmental movement is not a uniform entity but rather exists on a continuum. The majority of the most prominent and well-known groups work within the system, attempting to use educational efforts, financial resources[3] and political lobbying to change the attitudes and policies of the American people and government. These groups had managed to make environmentalism a prominent issue in the minds of the public and thus an issue in governmental decision making and politicking – a massive achievement for an interest group that was considered part of the fringe or counter-culture not that long ago.[4] Current concerns about global warming have also helped to increase the visibility of environmental organizations in the public eye. But while mainstream and environmental justice groups have seen some successes in their quest to balance the protection of nature with other human interests, these groups are sometimes criticized by others within the movement for a perceived conformity to the demands

---

[3]For example, many groups locally purchase land to keep it from being developed. A list of charities involved in direct purchase of land can be found at http://www.charitynavigator.org/index.cfm?bay=search.results&cgid=4&cuid=11. Accessed February 10, 2009.

[4]Many people have argued that the creation and existence of a radical fringe has helped propel other, more moderate environmental groups into the mainstream – when the extreme end of the continuum extends, what was initially considered extreme appears less so in comparison to the new standard. See Manes (1990), Foreman (1991), and Vanderheiden (2008).

of government and industry; critics charge that mainstream environmental groups compromise the fundamental goals of environmentalism in order to maintain their position in the mainstream (Foreman, 1991). Some of these critics propose a more radical vision of environmental conservation and protection.

A key difference between mainstream and radical environmental thinking is the advocacy of violent direct action, or eco-sabotage,[5] to strike against man-made forces of environmental degradation – in particular, companies and organizations that benefit economically from practices that exploit and/or damage natural resources (Manes, 1990; Vanderheiden, 2008). These direct actions are distinct from tactics of civil disobedience endorsed by some mainstream groups such as sit-ins, blocking roads, or street theater. Eco-sabotage involves violent tactics directed at the property and equipment of targeted companies or organizations. Among groups which support the use of eco-sabotage, the ELF is one of the most active and most secretive.

The Earth Liberation Front (ELF) formed in Brighton, England, in 1992. Made up of former members of the radical group Earth First!, the ELF was a reaction to what some saw as a shift in Earth First!'s philosophy towards the conservative and away from the use of eco-sabotage in defense of the earth.[6] Many came to the radical environmental movement out of frustration with the lack of progress achieved by following the rules (Manes, 1990; Foreman, 1991) and out of a deep conviction that extreme action was necessary to address the immediate and urgent threat posed by environmental destruction.

The radical environmental movement is grounded in the philosophy of eco-centrism, which places nature at the center and humans as just one part of the greater whole.[7] In particular, the movement draws upon the tenets of deep ecology, developed by Norwegian philosopher Arne Naess. Deep ecology states that nonhuman life forms have value independent of their value to humans and that ecological diversity helps sustain and nourish both human and nonhuman life. Deep ecologists believe that humans have a far greater impact on the world than is their right and that this is only getting worse. They believe that this creates an obligation to work toward change, including a decrease in the human population growth as well as changing economic, technological, and ideological policies, particularly those policies which value standard of living over quality of life (Naess, 1998). This philosophy and the eco-centric view of the world it fosters have been described as akin to a religious movement in its connection of humans to a bigger picture (Nature

---

[5]This type of activity is referred to by different names depending on who is doing the naming; I have chosen the term "eco-sabotage" as a neutral label reflecting the subversive and criminal nature of the activity without the more emotionally charged effects of other common terms.

[6]Created in 1979 by a group of frustrated environmental activists, many from more mainstream organizations, Earth First! initially advocated nonviolent direct action, including acts of civil disobedience, and acts of eco-sabotage. Earth First! has since moved away from advocating eco-sabotage toward a more educational focus.

[7]As opposed to the more anthropocentric view of modern Western societies which sets humans at the center and all other life as resources for human use (Soper, 1995).

instead of nature) and its imposition of questions of morality on human use of natural resources (Marangudakis, 2001). It also, because it brings humans into this bigger picture as a part rather than the center, can lead to a belief that an attack on any part of Nature is an attack on all and therefore fighting back becomes a form of self-defense (Manes, 1990).

The Earth Liberation Front

The first known incident committed by the ELF on American soil was an arson attack on a US Forest Service truck in Willamette National Forest in Oregon in 1997.[8] In the period from 1990 to 2004, groups such as the ELF and its older sister the Animal Liberation Front (ALF) have committed an estimated 1,100 acts of sabotage, causing more than $110 million in damage [Committee on Environment and Public Works (109th Congress), 2005]. Targets have included lumber and paper companies, fast food restaurants, agricultural laboratories, SUV dealerships, housing developments, and laboratories engaged in animal experimentation and/or genetic research, among others.[9]

The ELF announced its presence in 1997 in an anonymous communiqué titled "Beltane,"[10] describing themselves as "the burning rage of this dying planet" (quoted in Rosebraugh, 2004). They also stated their use of anonymity as a strategy: "Authorities can't see us because they don't believe in elves. We are practically invisible. We have no command structure, no spokespersons,[11] no office, just many small groups working separately, seeking vulnerable targets and practicing our craft" (ibid.).

In the wake of the events on September 11, 2001 and the continuing threat of terrorism in this country and against American interests abroad, the threat posed by radical environmental groups appears small compared to that posed by international extremist groups. Acts of eco-sabotage by radical environmental activists and/or groups predominately result in economic and property damage alone and only very rarely in physical injury or death to persons. Indeed, of the 1,100 incidents listed by the Federal Bureau of Investigation (FBI), none involved a single human injury or death [Committee on Environment and Public Works (109th Congress), 2005]. But while most

---

[8]ELF FAQ, Animal Liberation Front website. http://www.animalliberationfront.com. Accessed November 2004.

[9]Earth Liberation Front web site. Accessed November 2004.

[10]Beltane (traditionally May 1) is one of the major pagan holidays (Pennick, 1992). The environmental and neo-pagan movements have frequently overlapped during their histories, with the strongest overlap occurring in the 1970s (Castells, 1997).

[11]Specific people have claimed to act as spokespeople for the ELF or for affiliated organizations over time, most notably Craig Rosebraugh. More recently, Dr. Jerry Vlasak has acted in this capacity. Dr. Vlasak is a controversial figure who has made statements implying advocacy of physical violence directed at humans [Committee on Environment and Public Works (109th Congress), 2005].

US attention to terrorism has been focused on foreign threats, both in the actions of our federal legislators and in the reports presented by the media, the FBI considers radical environmental groups to be one of the biggest current threats for domestic terrorism in the United States (ibid.) and some researchers, and many in law enforcement and government, believe that these groups are ripe for escalation into actions that do not just threaten property but in fact, specifically target human beings.

Investigating and Prosecuting the Eco-Sabotage

Although the FBI and the Bureau of Alcohol, Tobacco and Fire (BATF) quickly responded to the attack on Vail Mountain, finding the perpetrators proved difficult. Investigators believed that the attack was carried out by a person or persons familiar with the area, acclimatized to high altitude, and with a sophisticated level of expertise in arson. There were many suspects. The expansion had been the subject of intense protest and legal challenges by environmental activists[12] and community members since it had been proposed. Virtually everyone in town had a problem with Vail Associates, from local business owners to former and current employees, from environmentalists (both local and out-of-state) to local community leaders in surrounding towns. There was even some speculation that Vail Associates itself was responsible for the arson.[13] But the fire had destroyed most of the evidence and the site of the attack itself was remote enough to ensure there were few witnesses. Ultimately, there was little to link any one person or group to the fire. Sixth months later, on April 20, 1999, the shootings at Columbine High School diverted law enforcement resources from Vail to Littleton, Colorado (Glick, 2001).

Adding to the difficulties were interagency conflicts. Although the Eagle County Sheriff's Department quickly took charge of the investigation with the assistance of the BATF, problems arose between the Sheriff's Department, the FBI, and the Vail Police Department. Accusations flew between the sides, with the FBI accusing the Sheriff of mishandling the investigation and the Sheriff accusing the FBI of withholding information (Glick, 2001).

Eventually, although it took nearly 8 years, on May 19, 2006, each of the four people were indicted for the attack on eight charges of arson[14] by a grand jury in Denver, Colorado (Richardson, 2006). All four were already facing charges related to other incidents committed in the Pacific Northwest from 1996 to 2001,[15] along

---

[12]The failure of the more conventional protests may have led to the arson attack as a perceived last-ditch effort to halt the expansion (Rosebraugh, 2004).

[13]Vail Associates went on with the proposed expansion after the fire, ultimately building a bigger and better resort. Vail Associates also benefited from the fire in another way; afterward, the resort became perceived as a victim, effectively derailing the protests (particularly because of fears by local environmentalists that they would be seen as the perpetrators) and rallying the community around the expansion (Glick, 2001; Rosebraugh, 2004).

[14]One for each building damaged in the attack.

[15]Two of the four remain at large at the time of this writing.

with other members of a radical group given the name "the Family" (Janofsky, 2006). These indictments were achieved largely through the use of informants and included 17 incidents which caused $23 million in damages. Twelve of those indicted eventually entered guilty pleas (Bernton, 2006). At sentencing, federal prosecutors sought terrorism enhancements,[16] arguing that, although these enhancements had never been used in property crime cases,[17] the incidents in question constituted attempts to intimidate, coerce, and retaliate against government conduct and therefore met the federal definition under 18 USC § 2331 (5) (Knickerbocker, 2007). In sentencing the two persons in federal custody for the Vail and other attacks, the judge agreed handing out 9- and 13-year sentences, respectively (Yardley, 2007).

Law enforcement in Vail, Colorado, faced the same difficulty encountered by any investigative agency looking into the activities of eco-saboteurs. Successful prosecutions have been, until recently, few and far between. The ELF, like its counterpart for animal rights, the ALF, is not a group in the ordinarily understood definition of the term. There is no way to join the ELF. There is no clearly defined leadership, no membership lists, no dues, and no consistent direct communication between activists. The ELF web site has in the past provided links to how-to guides on everything from making an incendiary device to subverting building security. It has provided information on how activists can report actions taken in the ELF's name, including tips on how to securely and anonymously send mail and e-mail to avoid apprehension by law enforcement; it has not, however, provided direct orders to engage in any activity.[18] So, while the ELF has a public web presence, claims responsibility for actions,[19] and may seem like a natural place for law enforcement to start, the links between the ELF and the elves[20] are limited at best. The ELF, ultimately, is more an ideology than an organization.

Due to this anonymity and lack of connection, law enforcement has had a poor history of success at apprehending eco-saboteurs, a situation admitted to by Deputy Assistant Director John Lewis of the FBI in Senate testimony [Committee on Environment and Public Works (109th Congress), 2005]. Given that most of the activity appears to be committed by individuals or small groups working on their own, following the basic principles of the ELF but having no communication with other

---

[16]See US Federal Sentencing Guidelines, Section 3A1.4.

[17]According to Lauren Regan of the Eugene, OR, Civil Liberties Defense Center, quoted in Knickerbocker (2007).

[18]More recently, the ELF web site has changed to predominantly serve a news-gathering function. When accessed most recently in February 2009, the site no longer offers links to informational material such as that described here. A subsequent search of the ALF web site also came up empty.

[19]It is important to recognize that, owing to the obvious desire for anonymity of the perpetrators of these acts, the ELF can also claim responsibility for acts whether the true motive was in keeping with their goals or not; it is also true that individuals with no sympathies toward the goals of the ELF can invoke the name of the group to divert attention from their true motive.

[20]"Elves" is a term used in ELF communications to describe those who act in its name.

members besides anonymous communiqués after an action has taken place, infiltration by officers or agents is virtually impossible (Westneat, 2001). In addition, many members of the radical environmentalist community, drawing on lessons learned by predecessors in the social movements of the 1960s, are suspicious of law enforcement – any person infiltrating a group and advocating violence as a tactic is often immediately suspected of being an undercover officer (Glick, 2001). In the Vail case (as well as the other cases charged in the indictments), authorities used informants to great effect. However, although officials claimed the indictments (and subsequent convictions) as a "significant dent in the movement",[21] it is hard to assess the impact of the indictment, arrest, and prosecution of less than 20 individuals on the radical movement as a whole when even those working in opposition to environmental groups believe that most of these types of attacks are perpetrated by individuals with, at best, weak links to each other (Savage, 2006). Individuals who have been publicly associated with the ELF have come under intense scrutiny (Rosebraugh, 2004) but, although the rhetoric used in anonymous communiqués or on the web site may encourage violence or at the very least not condemn it, saying the earth must be protected "by any means necessary" is not the same thing as actually using violent means. Such statements are generally protected under the First Amendment; prosecution of people for what they say raises troubling questions about the status of civil liberties in a democratic society. Posting information on how to create incendiary devices has also generally been allowed, although a federal statute (18 USC § 842 (p)(2)(A)) does make it a crime

> . . .to teach or demonstrate to any person the making or use of an explosive, a destructive device, or a weapon of mass destruction, or to distribute to any person, by any means, information pertaining to, in whole or in part, the manufacture or use of an explosive, destructive device, or weapon of mass destruction, knowing that such person intends to use the teaching, demonstration, or information for, or in furtherance of, an activity that constitutes a Federal crime of violence.[22]

Ultimately, law enforcement is faced with investigating individual crimes committed by members of a very loosely connected community where most people do not personally know each other (or at least do not know what each other is doing); what connections that do exist spring from shared beliefs and anonymously shared information but little else. While successful prosecutions can and do occasionally result, they are generally directed at individuals or small groups and may have no long-term impact on the movement as a whole nor will they necessarily lead to other eco-saboteurs. A shared ideology is not the same thing as a criminal conspiracy.

---

[21] US attorney Karin J. Immergut, quoted in Harden (2006).

[22] A recent prosecution of an environmental activist under the statute ended in a mistrial in 2007 and ultimately ended with a plea deal (Moran, 2008). The legal theory behind the statute, according to a Department of Justice report, rests on the assumption that the First Amendment does not protect against "speech acts" that are "an integral part of a transaction involving conduct the government otherwise is empowered to prohibit". See http://www.usdoj.gov/criminal/cybercrime/bombmakinginfo.html

Analysis – What Should be the Adequate Response?

As law enforcement authorities investigate these individual incidents, jurisdictional issues must be resolved. Who should bear primary responsibility for investigation – local authorities investigating the specific incident or federal authorities investigating any incident as part of a larger pattern? While those convicted in the Vail case were from out of state, they were also indicted and convicted for several other crimes committed in their residential home state of Oregon, suggesting that while radical activists might travel across state lines on occasion, many of the crimes they commit will be locally situated. Because of this, state and local law enforcement agencies have to be primary in any investigation. A large proportion of actions take place in small towns or rural locations (where the battle between development and conservation is thrown into sharp relief). Local authorities have a greater depth of knowledge of the people in their communities and thus have a greater ability to narrow the field of suspects. They are also more likely to be aware of activities and movements by both locals and visitors in the days prior to any act of eco-sabotage. However, because the activities of individuals generally follow the trends of the national radical environmental movement as a whole, and because activists do, if less often, cross state lines, federal law enforcement and their associated resources are necessary for any large-scale investigation.

Because investigation must be conducted simultaneously on both local and federal levels and can involve multiple types of agencies, better interagency cooperation is critical, not just between local and federal agencies but also between different local authorities (police, sheriff, and fire departments) and between different federal organizations (FBI, BATF, etc.). This is no small task – recent attempts to improve interagency cooperation in the investigation and prevention of terrorist activity indicate that it will require a change in the very culture of law enforcement to eliminate the inevitable turf battles that will emerge.

A final issue is the legal definition of eco-sabotage. The colloquial labeling of eco-saboteurs as "terrorists" predates the attacks of September 11, 2001 (Vanderheiden, 2008)[23] but the impact of those attacks on the legal liability of eco-sabotage has been significant. The 2001 USA PATRIOT Act broadened the legal definition of terrorism to include inanimate objects, particularly the use of fire or explosives to damage or destroy property. In 2003, then-Rep. Chris Chocola, R-IN, introduced the Stop Terrorism of Property Act in the US House of Representatives, designating "eco-terrorism" as a federal crime (HR 3307 IH). The Act died in committee but 3 years later, Congress passed the Animal Enterprise Terrorism Act which defines as terrorism the intentional damage or loss of "any real or personal property (including animals or records)" related to "the operations of an animal enterprise" [S.3880 (109th)]. In addition, several states are debating or have debated legislation that could label particular groups in the animal rights and environmental movements as terrorist groups (Otis, 2003).

---

[23]Vanderheiden points out that the Oxford English Dictionary first included the word "eco-terrorism" in 1997.

Professor Steve Vanderheiden (2005) of University of Colorado at Boulder argues that acts of eco-sabotage do not meet the definition of terrorism. He states that any act of terrorism has two targets – those who are the victims of the violence and those who witness the violence and thus fear becoming victims of violence in the future; "the unique wrong of terrorism concerns not the primary target but the secondary one" (p. 428). While the federal definition of terrorism has been broadened to include attacks on inanimate objects, Vanderheiden cautions against including attacks on inanimate objects that do not ultimately create a fear for physical safety,[24] warning that todo so would "trivialize the morally relevant distinction between persons and mere objects" (p. 431).

Vanderheiden (2008) points out that "the allegation of terrorism invokes heightened law enforcement powers, fewer procedural limits on such powers to protect those suspected of supporting terrorism, and significantly increased sentences from 'terrorism enhancement' penalties" for eco-saboteurs (p. 300). It can also serve to discredit the larger movement through guilt by association or weaken it through intimidation and thus may serve interests beyond those of justice.

Within the radical environmental movement, great stress is often placed on not targeting or endangering both human and animal life. Critics point to the very high financial costs involved and the fact that while great care may be taken to harm no human or animal, accidents can happen (The green threat?, 2001). However, even this risk is historically that of unintentional harm to persons (Manes, 1990), which is qualitatively different from the intentionality implied in the definition of an act as terrorist.

And not all in government agree that these acts exist on the same level as those of extremist groups like Al-Qaeda or domestic white supremacist groups. At a hearing of the Committee on Environment and Public Works, senator Frank Lautenberg (D – New Jersey) and former senators James Jeffords (I – Vermont) and Barack Obama (D – Illinois) objected to designating the ALF and the ELF as terrorist groups [Committee on Environment and Public Works (109th Congress), 2005]. Then-senator Obama stated "[w]hile I want these crimes stopped, I do not want people to think that the threat from these organizations is equivalent to other crimes faced by Americans every day" (p. 37), pointing to the FBI's own report of the incidence of hate crimes and the number of pending cases against companies that have endangered the health or the safety of their employees or the communities in which they are situated.

What is clear is that, particularly in today's world, the term "terrorism" has an immensely pejorative effect such that labeling an act "terrorist" automatically increases its impact, both in the emotional reaction of the general public and the legislative and judicial reactions of government and the criminal justice system. The use of the terrorist label "implies a moral claim for . . . aggressive pursuit and prosecution unconstrained by the conventional limits set upon military and law enforcement action" (Vanderheiden, 2005, p. 425). The danger lies in exaggerating the actual level of harm and threat that a group or a movement poses by labeling it "terrorist"

---

[24]Examples include destruction of whole cities or destruction of infrastructure necessary for human life.

and in doing so, both disguising the true nature of the threat of a particular group or movement and blunting the very real danger of events like those that occurred on September 11, 2001.

The designation of radical environmental groups like the ELF and the ALF as among the top threats to domestic security in the United States and the massive law enforcement response to acts of eco-sabotage[25] show the strong impact of the label "terrorist." And ultimately, the broadening of the legal definition has turned the charge of terrorism into one "that can be made to silence opposition [and] intimidate potential critics" (Vanderheiden, 2008, p. 303).

Conclusions

As the radical environmental movement has taken on more and more of an anarchist element, there has been an increase in the level of violent rhetoric coming from people within the movement (Taylor, 1998). Some have begun to talk about a time when it may become necessary to escalate the violence and a time when human targets become not just feasible but imperative, in order to convey the message that humans are not the most important members of the ecosystem (Ackerman, 2003). But violent words, while frightening and potential indications of future action, are not themselves violent action. Negating this sense of impending doom are the lack of concrete evidence to suggest that radical environmentalists are, as a movement, beginning to target human life and the fact that the bedrock ideology of radical environmentalism remains the reverence for *all* life, including human.

There is no way to guarantee that individual radical environmentalists will not escalate their level of violence to the point where their actions become a continuous threat to human life. Most evidence suggests that the risk to human life from these groups is very small and comes mostly from the potential for "lone-wolf" individuals to carry out violent activities to advance a personal environmentalist agenda. Environmentalists from all points on the continuum expressed alarm and increasing frustration over the past 8 years under the environmental policies of the Bush Administration.[26] With the election of Barack Obama as President of the United States, environmentalists in general have begun to express a tentative hope of once again being able to meaningfully work toward achieving their goals.[27] While

---

[25] The investigation that ended in the indictments of the "Family" was a 9-year investment by the FBI.

[26] Multiple mass e-mail communications received by author from various environmental organizations, including the Union for Concerned Scientists and the Natural Resources Defense Council, among others.

[27] The subject line of an e-mail received by the author on November 5, 2008, from one environmental organization read "Obama wins. . .and not a moment too soon for the environment".

the new President is unlikely to meet many of the demands of those on the more radical fringe, and while the political climate under any administration is unlikely to affect the activities of "true believers" within the movement, the potential for greater opportunity for negotiation on environmental issues may reduce the perceived need for large-scale violent acts as a means to advance the environmentalist cause.

References

Ackerman, G. A. (2003). Beyond Arson? A threat assessment of the earth liberation front. *Terrorism and Political Violence, 15*(4), 143–170.

Bernton, H. (2006, November 10). 4 more plead guilty in ecosabotage cases; trial may be avoided. *Seattle Times*.

Castells, M. (1997). *The power of identity*. Malden, Massachusetts: Blackwell Publishing.

Committee on environment and public works (109th Congress). (2005). *Eco-terrorism specifically examining the earth liberation front and the animal liberation front*. Washington, D.C.: U.S. Government Printing Office.

Foreman, D. (1991). *Confessions of an Eco-warrior*. New York: Crown Publishers, Inc.

Glick, D. (2001). *Powder burn: Arson, money, and mystery on Vail Mountain*. New York: Public Affairs, a member of the Perseus Books Group.

Harden, B. (2006). 11 Indicted in 'eco-terrorism' case; 17 attacks claimed by activist groups caused $23 million in damage. *Washington Post*, p. A03.

Janofsky, M. (2006). 11 indicted in 17 cases of sabotage in west. *New York Times*, p. 9.

Knickerbocker, B. and Dotinga, R. (2003). Firebrands of 'ecoterrorism' set sights on urban sprawl. *Christian Science Monitor, 95*(176), 1.

Knickerbocker, B. (2007). 'Ecoterrorism' case stirs debate in US. *Christian Science Monitor*, USA, p. 2.

Manes, C. (1990). *Green rage: Radical environmentalism and the unmaking of civilization*. Boston: Little, Brown and Company.

Marangudakis, M. (2001). Rationalism and irrationalism in the environmental movement – the case of earth first! *Democracy & Nature, 7*(3), 457–467.

Moberg, M. (2001). Co-opting justice: Transformation of a multiracial environmental coalition in southern Alabama. *Human Organization, 60*(2), 166–177.

Moran, G. (2008, March 28). "Animal rights activist tells of regret before sentencing." *San Diego Union Tribune*, accessed online at http://www.signonsandiego.com/news/metro/20080328-9999-1m28bomb.html.

Naess, A. (1998). *Ecology, community and lifestyle*. Cambridge: Cambridge University Press.

Otis, G. A. (2003, November 11). "Terrorist tactics." *The Village Voice*, Features, p. 40.

Paulson, S. K. (1998). Vail ski lodge blaze, fires said higher of level eco-terrorism. *Laredo Morning Times*, p. 13A.

Pennick, N. (1992). *The pagan book of days*. Rochester, Vermont: Destiny Books.

Richardson, V. (2006, May 20). Four indicted in Vail ecoterrorism; 1998 firebombing at Colorado ski resort once appeared unsolvable. *Washington Times*, p. A04.

Rosebraugh, C. (2004). *Burning rage of a dying planet*. New York: Lantern Books.

Savage, C. (2006, January 21). Justice Dept. Accuses 11 of US Eco-Terrorism. *Boston Globe*, National/Foreign, p. A3.

Shabecoff, P. (1993). *A fierce green fire*. New York: Hill and Wang, a division of Farrar, Strauss and Giroux.

Soper, K. (1995). *What is Nature?* Oxford, UK: Blackwell Publishers Ltd.

Taylor, B. (1998). Religion, violence and radical environmentalism: From earth first! to the unabomber to the earth liberation front. *Terrorism and Political Violence, 10*(4), 1–42.

The green threat? (2001, December 1). *The Economist, 361*(8250), 31–32.

Vanderheiden, S. (2005). Eco-terrorism or justified resistance? Radical environmentalism and the "War on Terror". *Politics & Society, 33*(3), 425–447.

Vanderheiden, S. (2008). Radical environmentalism in an age of antiterrorism. *Environmental Politics, 17*(2), 299–318.

Westneat, D. (2001, June 4). Terrorists Go Green. *U.S. News & World Report, 130*(22), 28.

Yardley, W. (2007, May 26). Radical environmentalist gets 9-year term for actions called 'Terrorist'. *New York Times*, Section A; Column 1; National Desk, p. 9.

Chapter 7
September 11 Terrorist Attacks Against the United States and the Law Enforcement Response

J.M. Shane

Introduction

The terror attacks on the United States that occurred on September 11, 2001 are defining events in US history. The oceans separating the North American continent from the tumultuous Middle East no longer seemed such a protective barrier. The long-held belief that such things only happened *over there* showed the United States just how vulnerable she was to a highly determined enemy. By asking *How could this happen on our soil?* the nation uncovered its weaknesses in border security and law enforcement, and highlighted the competing interests of security and liberty in an open society: As one increases, the other decreases. This is the timeless art of balancing the coercive power of government with the reality of the threat so faced. Perhaps, most importantly, September 11 highlighted the centuries-old clash between religious establishments and cultures, as well as contemporary US foreign policy; that policy is at the root of Al Qaeda's animosity for the United States. Worldwide, Western power and influence is declining; Asian civilizations are expanding their power base; and Islam is experiencing dramatic growth that is impinging on traditional Muslim nations and other non-Western cultures and there is a general reaffirmation of the value of the Islamic culture (Huntington, 1996).

The challenge to an open society like the United States is balancing liberty *and* security to ensure the fundamental tenets of democracy are shored up and coexist with the highest degree of homeland security. This becomes a major undertaking in the United States with more than 17,000 law enforcement agencies at the local, county, state and federal level, complicated by the supremacy of *home rule*.[1] It is further obscured by an amalgam of professional and volunteer public safety assets (police, fire, and emergency medical technicians) and an infrastructure of disparate

---

J.M. Shane (✉)
Department of Law and Police Science, John Jay College of Criminal Justice, New York, NY, USA
e-mail: jmsnpd@comcast.net

[1] Home rule refers to the concept of self-governance with limited interference from higher units of government, thus granting the political unit increased means of local control. Increasing urbanization and the complexity of society triggered the creation of home rule.

M.R. Haberfeld, A. von Hassell (eds.), *A New Understanding of Terrorism*,
DOI 10.1007/978-1-4419-0115-6_7, © Springer Science+Business Media, LLC 2009

government bureaucracies that may not understand how their role intersects with law enforcement in protecting the homeland. Preventing another terrorist attack may depend as much on improving domestic and international law enforcement as it does on a foreign policy that emphasizes democracy and education as well as respects the unique aspects of individual cultures across the globe through an acculturation process that offers alternatives to radical Islam in the world's developing nations.

Overview of the Group Behind September 11

Terrorism is as old as recorded civilization. Frightening the enemy into submission is a timeless tactic and one that is still used as part of modern warfare (i.e., the "shock and awe" campaign; air dropping leaflets encouraging the enemy to surrender or face "the consequences;" psychological operations—PSYOPS) During the French Revolution as part of Robespierre's "Reign of Terror" from 1793 to 1794, the word "terror" recorded its first use (Miller, 2006). Since then, terrorism has been used by small resistance groups and freedom fighters who are no match for conventional military forces. These groups must necessarily resort to an alternative fear campaign to induce political will rather than confront the enemy and wage armed conflict. Terrorism as a fear generator is typically accomplished by striking a small segment of the larger population that symbolizes the oppressor. The essence of terrorism was conveyed by Sun Tzu, the ancient Chinese war strategist, with the proverb "kill one, frighten ten thousand" and Mao Zedong when he spoke of "killing one to move a thousand" (Bolz, Dudonis, & Schultz, 1996).

The group that struck the United States on September 11 was no match for the conventional military forces of the United States and her allies. So, what is this group to do about the perceived ills of US foreign policy supporting Israel as well as the desecration of holy land by US military forces in Muslim countries?

The Rise of a New Extremist Group: Al Qaeda

Al Qaeda (also spelled al-Qaida or al-Qa'ida, meaning the "foundation," the "basis," or "the base") is an international Sunni Islamist movement founded by Osama Bin Laden (UBL, also spelled Osama bin Laden) in 1988 (Atwan, 2006; Bergen, 2006). UBL is the son of a wealthy Saudi Arabian construction magnate, Mohammed bin Awdah bin Laden, who is of Yemeni descent. The US Central Intelligence Agency (CIA) characterizes UBL as an Islamic extremist financier (*The Man Who Knew,* PBS FrontLine, 2002) and the US State Department has designated Al Qaeda a foreign terrorist organization.[2] Al Qaeda has its roots in the radical Islamist[3] movement of the late 20th century that Muslims should take affirmative military

---

[2]US Department of State, Office of Counterterrorism, *Foreign Terrorist Organizations List.* Retrieved from http://www.state.gov/s/ct/rls/fs/2002/12535.htm on January 18, 2009.

[3]The term "Islamist" is used to denote anyone who seeks to return Islam to centrality, to make faith the determining component of identity and behavior, and to structure society in accordance

action to repel foreign invaders, a doctrine inspired by select Islamic principles. This radical interpretation of *jihad* (the doctrine of Holy War or a spiritual crusade against infidels—nonbelievers) provides the authority and legitimacy for a "just war" including the doctrine of "emergency defense," which gives extremists the ability to challenge established central government authority (Johnson, 2002, p. 12).

UBL became entrenched in this radical Islamist ideology because it suggested that *Sharia* law was lacking, thus reducing the stature of the Muslim world to *jahiliyyah* ("ignorance of divine guidance" or the "state of ignorance from God," see Qutb, 1981, pp. 11, 19). Muslims are cast as throwbacks to pre-Islamic Arabia, a time prior to the rise of Islam in the 630s and prior to the revelations of the Qur'an. Those who fail to live by the teachings of Islam and submit to the word of the Qur'an are said to be in a state of *jahiliyyah*. Modernization (e.g., scientific advances, technology, inductive reasoning, intellectualism and personal empowerment through individual freedom, human rights, and religious pursuits), material influences, secular lifestyle, capitalism, and Western excesses—epitomized by the United States—are the core threat to Islamic ideology (Gibbs, 2005).

UBL's driving ideology was a pure Islamic caliphate, one he viewed with great potential but unable to flourish due to foreign policy oppression by the United States and her allies (The infidels). Exposure to conservative Islamic scholars in Saudi Arabia and his association with Arab militants in Afghanistan provided the "theological and ideological" foundation for his pure Salafist Islamic state, as well as "armed resistance in the face of perceived aggression" (Blanchard, 2007, p. 2).

Al Qaeda's Roots. The forerunner to Al Qaeda was the *"Afghan Arabs,"* a group of Middle Eastern Muslims who traveled to Afghanistan in the 1980s to fight the Soviet Union during their invasion of Afghanistan in December 1979. The US government helped fund the Afghans in their fight against the Soviets by passing funds through Pakistan's Inter-Services Intelligence Agency (ISI). UBL was a central figure in the Afghan Arabs who used his personal network, finances, and influence to help supply a steady stream of fighters to the Afghan Arabs' cause. To ensure operations were cohesive, UBL established the *Maktab al Khidmat* ("Bureau of Services," also known as *Al Khifah,* "Services Office") to supply potential fighters with funding for travel and housing accommodations as they made their way to the *jihad* in Afghanistan. UBL was admired by Afghan warlords who were inspired by his belief in their cause and who benefited from his financial generosity. After the Soviets were defeated and withdrew, UBL established Al Qaeda, where he envisioned building a global Islamic army. In 1992, UBL moved to Sudan after the Saudi government exiled him. He accepted an invitation from the National Islamic Front, an Islamist extremist organization, where he continued to sharpen his ire for the United States.

---

with Islamic principles. It encompasses a range of religious movements from a number of different countries, including Afghanistan and Saudi Arabia (House of Commons Library Report, 2001, p. 33).

In Sudan, UBL began various entrepreneurial ventures to support his terrorism agenda, which was primarily focused on the United States. He began forging alliances with leaders of other militant Islamist groups that resulted in a new organization named the *World Front for Jihad Against Jews and Crusaders*. He was motivated by a deep-seated animosity toward US foreign policy supporting Israel over Palestine, which he believed was a Christian–Jewish conspiracy intent on destroying Islam and allowing oppressive Arabic regimes to remain in power. As he saw it, such an alliance between the United States and Israel frustrated his vision of a pure Islamic state, which he regarded as an attack on his faith and on his God. UBL was not particularly critical of US culture but of its political and military policy in the Islamic world. UBL specifically points to the sustained military presence in Saudi Arabia following the US-led Gulf War in February 1991 and US troop movement into Somalia in 1992. He considered this a personal affront to "the sanctity of the birthplace of Islam and a betrayal of the global Islamic community" (Blanchard, 2007, p. 3; see also Fisk, 1996).

Osama bin Laden used religious rhetoric to fuel his anti-US sentiment in the Arab world and to appeal to Muslims' faith to carry out "defensive Jihad"—an Islamic tradition where "every Muslim is obligated, as an individual duty, to take up arms against invaders" (Johnson, 2002, p. 12; see also Blanchard, 2007). In 1996, UBL issued his first *fatwa*—a declaration of war—condemning the American military presence in Saudi Arabia and demanding American soldiers stationed in Saudi Arabia leave.[4] He began to fortify Al Qaeda by developing an organizational framework, ostensibly grounded in Islamic law (*Sharia*), which gave him the rationale for its operating philosophy and existence (Fig. 7.1).

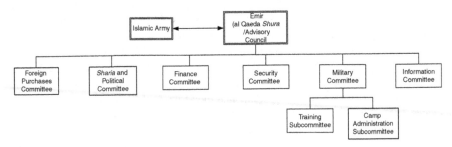

Fig. 7.1 Al Qaeda organizational structure

1. The *Shura* is UBL's inner circle of associates who serve in an advisory capacity.
2. The *Foreign Purchases Committee* is responsible for acquiring weapons, explosives, and technical equipment.

---

[4]The text of the original *fatwa* issued by Osama bin Laden was first published in *Al Quds Al Arabi*, a London-based newspaper, in August 1996. The fatwa is entitled "Declaration of War against the Americans Occupying the Land of the Two Holy Places." Retrieved on December 23, 2008 from http://www.pbs.org/newshour/terrorism/international/fatwa_1996.html

3. The *Political Committee* is responsible for issuing *fatwas*—edicts purportedly grounded in Islamic law authoring various actions, including deadly attacks.
4. The *Finance Committee* is responsible for fund-raising activities and budgetary support for training camps, housing costs, living expenses, travel, and the movement of money to sustain operations.
5. The *Security Committee* is responsible for physical protection, intelligence collection, and counterintelligence.
6. The *Military Committee* is responsible for proposing targets, gathering ideas for, and supporting operations and managing training camps.
7. The *Information Committee* is responsible for propaganda (National Commission on Terrorist Attacks Upon the United States, 2002a, pp. 2–3).

The organizational structure shown in Fig. 7.1 is a necessary prerequisite for the US Department of Justice to build a prosecution under the Racketeer Influenced Corrupt Organization (RICO) statute—the same law used to dismantle organized crime syndicates such as the Mafia, gangs, and now terror groups. However, the loose-knit confederation of Al Qaeda associates across the world is elusive, clandestine, and invisible[5] in many ways and difficult to strike, unlike hard conventional military targets (e.g., government facilities, military installations, communications, and power supply stations).

By declaring "war" on terrorism, the United States and her allies are essentially fighting a social network. It is a war against an ideology—a social movement of sorts—one defined by mental and attitudinal borders instead of physical ones, exacerbated by the enemy's ease of movement, undefined chain of command,[6] and ability to spread their radical message. Ideology is the "collection of beliefs, values, principles, and objectives by which a group defines its distinctive political identity and aims" (Rosenbaum, 1975, p. 120). It acts as a guardian of personal and cultural identity insofar as it is something that cannot be taken away, regardless of how much or how little one has. Terrorism is directly tied to religious and cultural ideology. Consequently, "war" on terrorism is a poor metaphor since "unlike most wars, it has neither a fixed enemy nor the prospect of coming to closure, be it through a win or some other denouement...If there is a 'war' against terrorism, it is a war that cannot be won...terrorism cannot be defeated—only reduced, attenuated and to some degree controlled" (Schultz & Vogt, 2003, pp. 3, 5; citing Pillar, 2001).

---

[5]That terrorists or terror groups are *invisible* is illustrated by the term "sleeper cell," where the operatives live, work, and train surreptitiously in a given community—right alongside ordinary citizens—until it is time to execute their plan. They often assume the cultural norms of the community within which they live so as not to arouse any suspicion or garner any unwanted attention. Because they appear friendly, are conversational, partake in conventional activities (i.e., patronizing bars, night clubs, and restaurants), wear culturally correct attire, and shed the "image" of a terrorist, they are able to *blend into the crowd* or *hide in plain sight*.

[6]The Earth Liberation Front (ELF), commonly defined as a domestic eco-terrorism group, operates with a similar decentralized structure, where actions are carried out by autonomous individuals who do so in the name of ELF but do not report through a chain of command to a higher authority.

One of UBL's top Al Qaeda leaders in Iraq, a Jordanian named Abu Musab al-Zarqawi, also embraced radical Islam after spending a term in a Jordanian prison. Zarqawi too was vehemently opposed to the US and Western military presence in the Islamic world, as well as Western support for Israel. Zarqawi joined Al Qaeda in 2004 and pledged *bayat* (an oath of allegiance) to UBL, who bestowed upon him the title *Emir of Al Qaeda in the Country of Two Rivers* (Chehab, 2006, p. 8). Together with UBL they began a campaign of propaganda using the Internet[7] to spread the message of *jihad* to a massive audience. Zarqawi's first major undertaking was to bomb the Jordanian Embassy in Baghdad, Iraq. He made Al Qaeda's intention clear during a video post to the Internet, where he discussed the wider purpose of his *jihad:* "We are not fighting our jihad in the name of nationalism. Our jihad is purer and higher. We fight so that Allah's word becomes the highest" (*The Insurgency,* PBS FrontLine, 2006). Then, Zarqawi bombed the United Nations building in Baghdad and released another Internet video, one of many designed to convince skeptics of his "savage determination:"

> We destroyed the UN building, the protectors of Jews, the friends of the oppressors and aggressors. The UN has recognized the Americans as the masters of Iraq. Before that they gave Palestine as a gift to the Jews, so they can rape the land and humiliate our people. Do not forget Bosnia, Kashmir, Afghanistan and Chechnya (*The Insurgency,* PBS FrontLine, 2006).

The United States, indeed the world, would soon learn that confronting and dismantling the Al Qaeda structure would be very different from confronting and dismantling a conventional wartime enemy who is bound by the international laws of war (Greig, 1976), where targets and boundaries are well defined. The acceptable practices relating to conventional warfare do not exist with Al Qaeda, which is exemplified by UBL's *fatwa*[8] issued on February 23, 1998 encouraging Muslims worldwide to attack and kill American civilians. Although terrorizing civilian populations to induce political will is not new, the unequivocal intention to commit mass murder of noncombatants (Civilians), to pursue civilian targets[9] (World Trade Center), and to use unconventional weapons (Civilian aircraft) are not accepted tactics of modern warfare (Borch, 2003; White, 2002). The 1998 *fatwa* reads, in pertinent part:

> On that basis, and in compliance with God's order, we issue the following *fatwa* to all Muslims: The ruling to kill the Americans and their allies—civilians and military—is an individual duty for every Muslim who can do it in any country in which it is possible to do

---

[7]For more on how technology is being used by the modern terrorist, see *Technology and Terror: The New Modus Operandi,* Al Qaeda's New Front, PBS FrontLine. Retrieved on January 11, 2009 from http://www.pbs.org/wgbh/pages/frontline/shows/front/special/tech.html

[8]According to Wright (2006, p. 259), the 1998 *fatwa* was jointly issued by UBL and Ayman al-Zawahiri, UBL's second in command of Al Qaeda. Zawahiri would go on to be a formidable leader in Al Qaeda and produce several pieces of propaganda taunting the United States in general and President George Bush specifically.

[9]As Borch (2003, p. 859) notes, the Pentagon is a legitimate military target; however, terrorists are not lawful combatants using legitimate weapons. Thus, Al Qaeda's attack was completely illegal in terms of accepted military engagement.

it, in order to liberate the al-Aqsa Mosque and the holy mosque [Mecca] from their grip, and in order for their armies to move out of all the lands of Islam, defeated and unable to threaten any Muslim. This is in accordance with the words of Almighty God, 'and fight the pagans all together as they fight you all together,' and 'fight them until there is no more tumult or oppression, and there prevail justice and faith in God.'[10]

This marked a turning point for Al Qaeda, for they emerged as a primary global terrorist threat by revealing their intent to attack the United States (Gunarathna, 2002, pp. 61–62).

The Motivation to Join Al Qaeda

As new *jihadists* join various terrorist elements in the name of Al Qaeda, they do so with the knowledge they are in a long-term campaign against Western values, culture, and identity that may lead to a "clash of civilizations" (Huntington, 1996). That clash may require them to sacrifice their life for the greater good (a *Shaheed* for Islam), an act of altruism they willingly accept in the name of Islam, a greater noble cause (Becker, 1973, 1975). Many new *jihadists* come from society's fringes, where they have been marginalized because legitimate avenues for success are all but closed and they fail to assimilate to the dominant culture. They do not see themselves as fully integrated members of a multicultural Western society; physically they are living in the West but mentally they are living in the land of the infidels and have very little sense of belonging. They fail to read, write, and speak the dominant language for fear of losing their primary means of communication with others in their community who are similarly situated. They furnish their homes with the décor of their ancestry and adhere to the manner of dress their heritage prescribes. They bestow their children with ethnic names as a matter of pride but unwittingly place a cultural obstacle in the second generation's path to assimilation. Their language, conversations, and daily musings are punctuated with references and remembrances of the days in their homeland with statements prefaced by *In my home town...* and *In my country...*, forever clinging to the remnants of a time and place that once defined them.

Marginalization is brought about by the convergence of various social phenomena such as poverty, unemployment, academic failure, racial and ethnic enmity, mistrust of or mistreatment by authorities, language barriers, and poor housing opportunities among the many. These conditions generate social rejection, political and economic disaffection and a growing identity complex—particularly in young adult[11] populations who cannot envision legitimate social, material, and financial success because of the persistent strain and frustration. Continued exposure to these

---

[10]Retrieved on December 23, 2008 from http://www.pbs.org/newshour/terrorism/international/fatwa_1998.html

[11]The President's Daily Briefing (PDB) of August 6, 2001 warned: "A clandestine source said in 1998 that a Bin Laden cell in New York was recruiting Muslim–American youth for attacks" (The 9/11 Commission Report, 2002, p. 262). *Youth* is the operative word in this briefing.

elements threatens personal identity, security, and dignity. Gradually, a cumulative sense of injustice wears on a person's psyche, leading to a proclivity for aggression and hostility (Kelman, 1990). The pattern of discrimination and exclusion from mainstream society creates a sense of hopelessness that overrides legitimate aspirations, eventually providing the motivation for the terrorist's deviant behavior (Agnew, 1992; Anderson, 1999; Cloward, 1959; Cloward & Ohlin, 1960; Crenshaw, 2001; Ezekiel, 1995; Gibbs, 2005; Merton, 1968; Staub, 2003).

The mindset of a terrorist willing to carry out political murder is described by Novarro's (2005) comorbidity of five phenomenon: (1) "an *uncompromising ideology* that identifies a group and a cause in which individuals can find meaning for life and continuity after death; (2) a perceived threat to this group elicits an *irreconcilable fear* stronger than the fear of death itself; (3) a *passionate hatred* for the threatening enemy, which reflects love of the in-group; (4) *prescribed violence* against the enemy is not only permitted but also advocated to save loved ones from destruction; and (5) *functional isolation*, which separates the terrorist from other groups—family, friends, coworkers—who might pull against terrorist ideology."[12] This enabling mindset gives terrorists the rationale and justification for carrying out acts of violence as they appeal to higher loyalties.

Borum (2003, pp. 7–10) identifies a four-stage process that terrorists use to establish the ideological basis for aggression as they neutralize their mindset (Agnew, 1994; Sykes & Matza, 1957). The process begins when the prevailing conditions—poverty, unemployment, discrimination, or other anomic conditions—present unpleasant or distressing feelings. This raises individual personal ire because things are not as they "should be," *It's not right.* When something is not right, *It's not fair.* This implies a comparison between social strata that not only is our situation bad but others are much better off—why can't I have a piece of that? This produces a great deal of resentment. That resentment is projected, usually onto the perceived oppressors, and blame is cast: *It's your fault.* Casting blame condemns the oppressor who is often generalized into a "single explanation for the in-group's travail: The White supremacists' problem is the Blacks; the Palestinians' problem is the Zionists; the Chechens' problem is the Russians; the Northern Irish's problem is the British; the Muslim fundamentalists' problem is the whole Western world" (Miller, 2006, p. 127). Finally, once blame is ascribed, then dehumanizing the oppressor sets in, *You're evil.* The oppressors are publicly castigated, which provides the justification for using force or intimidation; only total annihilation will bring satisfaction.

In many ways there is a direct comparison between the circumstances facing the *jihadists* of today and deviant groups of the 1960s and 1970s (e.g., Black Panthers, Symbionese Liberation Army, Weathermen—also known as the Weather Underground) who faced persistent confrontation with mainstream America and were

---

[12]From the book review by Clark R. McCauley (2007), *Hunting Terrorists: A Look at the Psychopathology of Terror.* Retrieved on January 13, 2009 from http://cjr.sagepub.com.ez.lib. jjay.cuny.edu/cgi/reprint/32/1/70

consigned to urban ghettos. Violent engagement between these groups and law enforcement is widely reported (Austin, 2006; Berger, 2006; Bryan, 1975; Harris, 2000).[13] Similarly, contemporary urban gangs (e.g., Bloods, Crips, MS-13) cite many of the same social phenomena that draw them into gang life, where the message they receive from the gang is that by joining they become part of an extended family that cares for them, respects them, and protects them from the harsh influences of mainstream society. By joining they acquire a sense of identity, respect, and social acceptance that was once absent. They shed the cloak of moral society and ascribe to a deviant (or in the case of the *jihadists,* radical) subsystem, a counterculture that permits—often advocates—using force or violence as a means of retribution, thus making things fair—leveling the playing field of sorts (Bandura, Barbaranelli, Capara, & Pastorelli, 1990, 1996). This is the message of radical *Salafism* (a radical religious offshoot of *Salafi*)—the means justify the ends—and that it is the duty of every Muslim to go anywhere in the world and bring the fight to those who oppose the will of their God. Indeed, Al Qaeda's professed goal of the September 11 attacks was to retaliate against the United States for its perceived aggression toward the Islamic world and "to signal and support the 'emergence of a new virtuous leadership' dedicated to opposing 'the Zionist-Anglo-Saxon-Protestant coalition' that Al Qaeda blames for a litany of social and political ills in the Islamic world" (Blanchard, 2007, p. 5).

The New Al Qaeda

The post-September 11 Al Qaeda structure is a product of the 1990s expansion of globalization. The group is sophisticated, decentralized, and dispersed across the world, which complicates infiltration. They are united by a common ideology, typically *Salafism,* and inspired by deeply religious local Imams in disenfranchised, isolated, and alienated Muslim communities, such as the established Moroccan community of Spain's North African population, Mombasa, Kenya,[14] and the impoverished East African nation Comoros.[15] There are no direct connections with

---

[13] See http://www.pbs.org/wgbh/amex/guerrilla/index.html for *Guerrilla: The Taking of Patty Hearst* and the Symbionese Liberation Army. Retrieved on January 25, 2009.

[14] See PBS FrontLine WORLD, *Extraordinary Rendition,* November 6, 2007 for a brief profile of a local preacher who encourages youth to prepare for jihad. The preacher Abu Drogha cites the Qur'an as inspiration for jihad: "The Koran says go into the world and spread the Islamic law. And you can't spread Islamic law by talking alone. You have to use weapons. The Americans are looking for trouble. When the Americans are slaughtered, I am happy." Retrieved on January 22, 2009 from http://www.pbs.org/wgbh/pages/frontline/view/

[15] The Union of Comoros, in the Indian Ocean between Africa and Madagascar, is an impoverished, politically unstable former French colony that is in the middle of a civil war. Terrorists are active in Comoros. Fazul Abdullah Mohammed (AKA/Haroun Fazul) was raised in Comoros and became one of Osama bin Laden's operatives. US authorities believe Fazul drove the truck responsible for the embassy bombing in Nairobi in August 1998. At age 16, Fazul became entrenched in radical Islam while growing up in the poverty and squalor that pervades this island nation. Six of the twelve terrorists indicted in Nairobi bombings were from poor East African

the new Al Qaeda as there were prior to September 11; rather, there are a series of amorphous, asymmetrical, and self-mutating loose connections among similar radical elements throughout the world. Collectively, they are anonymous and autonomous "nonstate actors" that carry out their operations under the Al Qaeda banner. The operations they engage in are classified as fourth-generation warfare (Echevarria, 2005; Lind, Nightengale, Schmitt, Sutton, & Wilson, 1989; van Creveld, 1991, p. 224).

In this decentralized environment there is no hierarchy and no centralized leadership. Indeed, it is quite the opposite. It is a bottom-up structure with a series of affinity groups—small groups of militants who are bound by a common ideology or who share a common interest in an issue—working together to mount direct political action and who may be self-funded. The House of Commons Library Report (2001, p. 109) perhaps best describes the new Al Qaeda structure and the challenges that lay ahead for dismantling it:

> Bin Laden has built an organisation difficult to disrupt, degrade and destroy. The intelligence community is unfamiliar with the network's fluid and dynamic structure and the past offers little guidance. The time-tested strategy to destroy a politically motivated armed group is to target the core and penultimate leadership, but in Bin Laden's case, this is a difficult proposition. [...]

> If Bin Laden is eliminated, he is likely to be replaced by another Islamist, although none in the second tier [of leadership] possess his charisma. The penultimate leadership is operationally significant, and so Al-Qaeda is likely to remain operational even if Bin Laden is captured or killed (Citing Gunarathna, 2001, p. 45).

With the advent of the Internet and the versatility of its decentralized structure such as searching, chatting, emailing, video conferencing, and collaborating, terrorists groups command a wider global reach and much more flexibility to carry out operations from the largest cities like New York, London, and Hong Kong to the most remote corners of the world without having to meet face-to-face for planning sessions.[16] The organizational structure shown in Fig. 7.1 must not be viewed as a rigid, hierarchical bureaucracy; rather, it constitutes the nimble constituent parts of a dynamic organizational concept, a blueprint for others to follows as they take action

---

countries like Comoros. Al Qaeda exploits the social conditions in these countries, particularly because they are rife with corruption and brutal oppression. Retrieved on January 18, 2009 from http://www.pbs.org/wgbh/pages/frontline/shows/binladen/upclose/

[16] Al-Qaeda is believed to have a presence in Algeria, Egypt, Morocco, Turkey, Jordan, Tajikistan, Uzbekistan, Syria, Xinjiang province in western China, Pakistan, Bangladesh, Malaysia, Myanmar, Indonesia, Mindanao in the Philippines, Lebanon, Iraq, Saudi Arabia, Kuwait, Bahrain, Yemen, Libya, Tunisia, Bosnia, Kosovo, Chechnya and Dagestan in the Russian North Caucasus, Kashmir, Sudan, Somalia, Kenya, Tanzania, Azerbaijan, Eritrea, Uganda, Ethiopia, and in the Palestinian Territories (House of Commons Library Report, 2001, p. 34, note 85, citing Rohan Gunarathna, Blowback, *Jane's Intelligence Review*, August 2001, pp. 42–45). Al Qaeda is also believed to have formal and informal alliances with several Middle Eastern and Asian radical Islamist groups, including the Islamic Group and Islamic Jihad of Egypt; the Armed Islamic Group (GIA) and the Salafist Group for Preaching and Combat (GSPC) in Algeria; Jaish Aden Abin al Islami in Yemen; Moro Islamic Liberation Front (MILF) and the Abu Sayyaf Group (ASG) in the Philippines (Schultz & Vogt, 2003, pp. 12–13).

in the name of Al Qaeda. This gives the Al Qaeda brand name the flexibility and efficiency to be a greater globalized threat that is intensely local with intimate ties to local communities that can recruit without raising domestic or international suspicion. Al Qaeda's propensity for violence toward Western countries—the United States in particular—seems universally accepted by many terrorism experts; however, experts do not necessarily agree on the extent of Al Qaeda's global reach and their post-September 11 capabilities to carry out attacks of similar dimension as those on September 11 (Katzman, 2005).

Al Qaeda's evolving global threat is painfully evident from attacks launched in Istanbul, Turkey (November 15, 2003 and November 20, 2003), Bali, Indonesia (October 1, 2005), London (July 7, 2005), and Madrid, Spain (March 11, 2004). If the intent of terrorism is to influence political will, perhaps Al Qaeda can claim a small victory in Madrid: Following the railway bombing at the Atocha train station, the conservative government that was allied with the United States in the war in Iraq was voted out of office.

Homegrown Terrorists

The new Al Qaeda phenomenon gives rise to the prospect that the *real* threat may not come from established international terror organizations who are working their way toward Western countries but from *homegrown* organizations. These are locally derived groups from marginal communities composed of individuals born and raised in their homeland that are informal, who embrace the Al Qaeda ideology, and who construct their operations without the formal assistance of the Al Qaeda organization that existed before September 11. Therefore, the threat may already be inside a country's homeland and ordinary citizens are, in effect, *sleeping with the enemy.* This is best illustrated by the London underground transit bombings on July 7, 2005 and the alleged sleeper cell uncovered by the FBI in the Pakistani community of Lodi, California, in 2003. Both operated under the Al Qaeda ideology.[17] US officials later retracted their original position and admitted the Lodi case *was not* an example of homegrown terrorism after it was learned that the FBI relied on a series of investigative mistakes and erroneous uncorroborated information. However, first impressions were just that.

Overview of the Events of September 11

Political and Historical Context

As the new millennium began and President William J. Clinton's presidency was coming to a close, terrorism remained a national priority, but not a top priority. There

---

[17]See *The Enemy Within* PBS FrontLine. Retrieved on December 28, 2008 from http://www.pbs.org/wgbh/pages/frontline/enemywithin/. For an analysis of the ideological content and political tone of Al Qaeda's public statements, see Blanchard, 2007, retrieved on December 21, 2008 from http://fas.org/sgp/crs/terror/RL32759.pdf

were other issues to contend with, including the Y2K[18] bug, whose risk to computer systems worldwide seemed real as well as the transition to a new president. To some degree, the past terrorist attacks appeared to be the cost of doing business in an international arena. Al Qaeda was seen as pesky. Yes, there was energy devoted to capturing the responsible parties, but that was not the first priority for the US government. International terrorism was not considered an act of war. Instead, it was viewed as a crime that was to be investigated and prosecuted, not repressed with military action.

The United States was keenly aware of the previous attacks on US interests abroad and diplomacy continued to be the primary strategy. President Clinton and his cabinet worked with officials in Afghanistan and Pakistan to deliver UBL diplomatically, but to no avail. Saudi Arabia and the United Arab Emirates (UAE), both US allies, were indifferent and selectively cooperative in terror investigations. When the United States asked Saudi Arabia for permission to interrogate senior Al Qaeda operatives in Saudi Arabia's custody, their request was denied and terrorism intelligence from Saudi officials was limited at best (The 9/11 Commission Report, 2002, p. 122). When the United States approached Saudi officials on narrowly defined issues concerning UBL's finances, they were met with "mixed results" and a general sense of apathy about Al Qaeda's financing overall (Roth, Greenburg, & Wille, no date, p. 3). The 9/11 Commission did not find a connection between Al Qaeda and the Saudi Kingdom; however, Saudi Arabia was a fertile fund-raising ground for Al Qaeda since charitable giving is embedded in the culture and subject to few restrictions. The Saudis would frequently say one thing and do another, take belated action, or simply shy away to be accommodating. As an ally of the United States, it was more convenient for US officials to believe the Saudis were cooperative instead of being obstructionists (Jehl, 2001).

Although some subsequent covert action from Clinton's administration was successful at killing or capturing suspected terrorists, many covert operations were paralyzed by legal wrangling and policy debates (Coll, 2004), and by late 1999, according to Under Secretary of State Thomas Pickering, diplomacy had "borne little fruit" (The 9/11 Commission Report, 2002, p. 126; see also National Commission on Terrorist Attacks Upon the United States, 2002e). Notwithstanding the diplomatic shortcomings of Clinton's administration, diplomacy continued into the new presidency, including building an international support coalition as well as engendering domestic support.[19] Diplomacy would soon yield to military action.

On January 20, 2001, George W. Bush was sworn into office as the 43rd President of the United States. He assembled a group of leaders to serve in his administration

---

[18]Y2K refers to the year 2000. More broadly, when stated as the "Y2K problem," the "millennium bug," or the "Y2K bug," it refers to an anticipated problem with computers not being able to understand or process the last two digits of the new millennium (00). The problem dates to early computer programming and was a significant worldwide priority for many governments because of the potential shutdown.

[19]See White House Press Release, September 20, 2001.

that had extensive federal-level experience; some had previous military or wartime backgrounds:

1. Richard B. Cheney, Vice President of the United States
2. Condoleezza Rice, National Security Advisor
3. Colin L. Powell, Secretary of Defense
4. George J. Tenet, Director of Central Intelligence Agency
5. Donald H. Rumsfeld, Secretary of Defense
6. Richard A. Clarke, National Counterterrorism Coordinator

There was no shortage of senior government officials who believed the attacks of September 11 bore the Al Qaeda signature. John McLaughlin, Deputy Director of Central Intelligence Agency (2001–2004), commented that the United States had been engaged with Al Qaeda for some time, that September 11 was a huge victory for Al Qaeda and a huge defeat for the United States.[20] Although many felt Al Qaeda was behind the attack, it was George Tenet, Director of the CIA, who confirmed Al Qaeda was responsible. Late in the afternoon of September 11, in discussions with officials in the United Kingdom, the United States corroborated Tenet's sentiment about the Al Qaeda signature. Then, they extended the discussion to the implications for state-sponsored supporters of terrorism such as Iraq and Afghanistan.

Richard Pearle, Chairman, Department of Defense Policy Board (2000–2004), set the stage for retaliatory action against Iraq and Afghanistan by noting that it would not be possible to effectively deal with global terrorism unless state sponsors were dealt with in the same manner. That is, the United States should not distinguish between the terrorists who carried out the event and the states that support or harbor them. Donald Rumsfeld, Secretary of Defense, and Colin Powell, Secretary of State—two of the Neo-conservatives in the Bush cabinet who advise on foreign policy—supported the idea of invading Iraq and Afghanistan, where UBL and his supporters were living. The idea also found support with George Tenet, whose agency was first to deliver a plan to President Bush.

The United States and her interests had been the target of terrorists' provocation for almost two decades before the attacks, events that, in retrospect, seemed to be a harbinger of September 11 and linked to either UBL or Al Qaeda (Table 7.1).[21] The US intelligence community failed to interpret the meaning of previous attacks. Indeed, they failed to understand the implications of fourth-generation warfare that they had been lured into (Schultz & Vogt, 2003, p. 21).

The United States avenged previous incidents with limited response, but nothing to the scale that was later brought to Afghanistan and Iraq in the "war on terror." President Bush, speaking before the Joint Session of Congress on September

---

[20]From *Bush's War*, PBS FrontLine. Retrieved on December 23, 2008 from http://www.pbs.org/wgbh/pages/frontline/bushswar/

[21]For a similar chronology of successful and unsuccessful terror plots by Islamic extremists in Europe, see *Chronology: The Plots, Al Qaeda's New Front*, PBS FrontLine. Retrieved on January 11, 2009 from http://www.pbs.org/wgbh/pages/frontline/shows/front/special/cron.html

Table 7.1 Terrorist episodes foreshadowing the evolving Islamist threat to the United States and her interests

Site	Date	Synopsis	Outcome
US Embassy, Beirut Lebanon	April 18, 1983	Members of the Islamic Jihad drove a stolen delivery truck on to embassy grounds and detonated the onboard bomb. Sixty-three people were killed including 32 Lebanese employees, 17 Americans, and 14 visitors and passersby. This marked one of the earliest realizations that terrorist organizations had the capability to cause widespread destruction using explosives and is regarded by some as the beginning of anti-US attacks by radical Islamist groups	Successful
Marine Barracks, Beirut, Lebanon	October 23, 1983	Members of the Islamic Jihad drove two truck bombs into the barracks occupied by US and French military forces, killing 241 American military personnel and 61 French military personnel. After the attack, international peacekeeping forces stationed in Lebanon since 1982 withdrew	Successful
Aden, Yemen	December 1992	An explosion outside two hotels in Aden, Yemen, killed one Australian tourist but no Americans. Four years after the episode, the United States learned that a Yemeni terrorist group connected to Osama Bin Laden was responsible	Partially successful
World Trade Center (WTC), New York City	February 26, 1993	Radical Islamist terrorists detonated a truck bomb beneath the WTC, killing 6 and injuring over 1,000. Abdul Basit Mahmoud Abdul Karim (Alias, Ramzi Ahmed Yousef) and some of his coconspirators were convicted in US federal court	Successful
Mogadishu, Somalia	October 1993	Two US Black Hawk helicopters were shot down by rocket-propelled grenades, killing 18 US military personnel. The United States learned that Osama Bin Laden's organization influenced Somali warlords who initiated the attack on the helicopters. Bin Laden later boasted of the incident calling it a victory for *mujahidin* and declared the United States could be forced to retreat	Successful
Various landmarks, New York City	Late year 1993	The plot was to blow up several landmarks including the Lincoln and Holland Tunnels, the George Washington Bridge, the United Nations and the New York field office of the FBI. The FBI disrupted the plot by using a source to penetrate the active terrorist cell	Disrupted by the FBI

Table 7.1 (continued)

Site	Date	Synopsis	Outcome
Manila Airlines, Manila, Philippines	January 1995	The Philippine police disrupted a plot to blow up 12 US commercial aircraft over the Pacific ocean bound for the United States from Manila (also known as the "Bojinka" plot). Ramzi Ahmed Yousef was involved in this plot as was Khalid Sheikh Mohammed, who eventually planned the September 11, 2001 attack	Disrupted by Philippine police authorities
Riyadh, Saudi Arabia	November 13, 1995	A car bomb was detonated outside the offices of the US-trained Saudi Arabian National Guard, killing five Americans and two officials from India. The perpetrators confessed claiming that they influenced were by Osama Bin Laden. The perpetrators were convicted and beheaded in Saudi Arabia	Successful
Khobar Towers, Dhahran, Saudi Arabia	June 25, 1996	Terrorists detonated a bomb killing 19 US military personnel and injuring several hundred more. The ensuing investigation resulted in the indictment of 13 individuals in June 2001	Successful
East African Embassies in Nairobi, Kenya, and Dar es Salaam, Tanzania	August 7, 1998	Al Qaeda operatives detonated near simultaneous bombs at US Embassies in Kenya and Tanzania. Twelve Americans and more than 200 Kenyans and Tanzanians were killed, and more than 4,000 were injured. Osama Bin Laden and 22 affiliates were indicted; four of the affiliates were apprehended and convicted	Successful
Various *millennium* targets in Los Angeles, California	December 14, 1999	Ahmed Ressam, an Algerian jihadist, was detained by US Customs in Port Angeles, Washington, while trying to enter the United States from Victoria, British Columbia, Canada. Ressam later acknowledged he was planning to attack the Los Angeles International Airport (LAX)	Disrupted by US Customs
USS Sullivans, Aden, Yemen	January 3, 2000	While moored in the Port of Aden, Yemen, Al Qaeda operatives attempted to sail a small vessel laden with explosives alongside the ship and detonate it. The plan failed when the vessel sank because it was too heavy with explosives. Al Qaeda made a second attempt with the same delivery system and successfully bombed the USS Cole	Unsuccessful
USS Cole, Aden, Yemen	October 12, 2000	Al Qaeda operatives successfully detonated a suicide bomb against the *USS Cole*, a US naval warship moored in the Port of Aden, Yemen. The bomb killed 17 sailors and injured 39	Successful

20, 2001, delivered an ultimatum to the Taliban leaders in Afghanistan—a rogue movement that emerged in 1994, whose fighters were drawn from Islamic theology schools (*Madrassahs*) in an effort to stabilize the government in post-Soviet Afghanistan: Deliver to US authorities all the leaders of Al Qaeda who were hiding in their country, "or share in their fate" (CNN, September 21, 2001). This was one of a few public messages President Bush delivered in the weeks following September 11 as he readied the nation for the "stress and sacrifice" that inevitably accompanies a sustained military campaign (Apple, 2001; see also White House press release, 2001). When the Taliban failed to comply, the United States launched Operation Enduring Freedom on October 7, 2001 with the stated purpose to capture UBL, destroy Al Qaeda, and remove the Taliban regime that harbored Al Qaeda members.

The Attacks

By 1999, the United States was well aware that Al Qaeda was a formidable enemy. Al Qaeda demonstrated their international travel capabilities and their ability to gather *jihadists* from around the world who were dedicated and willing to subordinate themselves to the cause, including martyrdom. UBL assembled a leadership team for the September 11 attacks that included *Khalid Sheikh Mohammed* (KSM), the chief design engineer of the plot and the principle financier of the first World Trade Center bombing in 1993; *Hambali*, the principle coordinator of the September 11 attacks under KSM; and *Abd al Rahim al Nashiri*, the chief design engineer of the attack on the *USS Cole* and leader of Al Qaeda on the Arabian Peninsula.

The synergy of the team was in their entrepreneurial spirit, past terror experience, and the varied skills they brought to bear on the September 11 plot. Like UBL, KSM was primarily motivated by a deep-seated animosity toward the United States for their foreign policy favoring Israel (The 9/11 Commission Report, 2002, p. 147), something UBL found appealing given his personal long-standing resentment toward the United States. As the chief architect of the September 11 plot, KSM knew such a plan would require financial support, logistical support, and personnel. KSM knew UBL could provide those resources, so he continued to impress UBL by demonstrating his technical usefulness and loyalty in helping other Al Qaeda members. Eventually, around late 1998 or early 1999, UBL gave KSM the go-ahead for the September 11 operation, providing him the resources and autonomy to develop the plan; around that same time, KSM formally joined Al Qaeda.

Planning the Operation. During the spring of 2001, intelligence reports about a possible terrorist attack spiked. By the summer, US intelligence services had presented numerous warnings to the White House that Al Qaeda was planning a major attack against the United States, but whether it would take place inside or outside the United States could not be confirmed (Elliot, 2002; National Commission on Terrorist Attacks Upon the United States, 2002f). Richard Clarke, National Counterterrorism Coordinator, speculated terrorist cells were already operating inside the United States and they might launch an attack from within. At the same time there was a great deal of internal dissention at the FBI that hampered follow-up investigations into two critical indicators that suggested Al Qaeda might use aircraft in an upcoming attack: (1) a July 2001 memo from the Phoenix (AZ) office that named sources who said Al Qaeda operatives were training at US flight schools and aviation colleges and (2) an August 2001 investigation by the Minnesota office into the alleged 20th hijacker Zacarias Moussaoui. Moussaoui was eventually indicted and convicted in federal court of conspiracy to kill US citizens, but Al Qaeda's plan to use aircraft was never investigated.

KSM had an interest in using aircraft to carry out the September 11 attacks after the first World Trade Center bombing in 1993, something he contemplated for quite a while. Some aircraft plans were dismissed by UBL because they were too ambitious or too complex; others were dismissed because they did not suit Al Qaeda's ends, such as hijacking an aircraft and then negotiating the release of "political prisoners" as well as the onboard hostages, then blowing up the airplane. UBL approved KSM's plan to hijack civilian aircraft and crash them into various symbols of US power: The US Capitol represented a symbol of foreign policy oppression supporting Israel; the White House was a political symbol that appealed to UBL; the Pentagon was a symbol of US military might and national defense; and the World Trade Center— one of America's ubiquitous symbols—represented economic prowess.

The idea of using aircraft was much more novel than previous projects and brought with it maximum propaganda appeal; there was a captive audience of virtually helpless civilians inside the plane and the plane itself was a long-range missile that could be maneuvered precisely where the terrorists wanted to strike and little could be done to stop it, including military intercession. It was also much "cleaner" in the sense that the component parts did not have to be purchased, then assembled, then moved from one location to another, then activated. In a conventional bombing, if the device fails to initiate, then the operatives run the risk of being captured through the investigation as well as delaying the ultimate aim of Al Qaeda.

Planning the "planes operation," as it came to be known within Al Qaeda (The 9/11 Commission Report, 2002, p. 153), began with a series of meetings between KSM and other Al Qaeda operatives, who first proposed a list of targets that had high media value (those mentioned above, which they eventually selected). A few iterations of the plan went back and forth between KSM and UBL before they settled on the final draft.

Recruiting and Training. As the plan underwent its changes, KSM began recruiting operatives that would serve as martyrs. Once selected, they received training at the *Mes Aynak* camp—an Afghan training camp—near Kabul, Afghanistan, one of many camps used for terrorist training (Bindra, 2001; Rhode & Chivers, 2002). The camp provided a full range of urban warfare capabilities including weapons, explosives, night operations, simulated shooting exercises, physical and mental conditioning. From Kabul, the participants were moved to Karachi, Pakistan, for about a week, where they received instructions on "Western culture and travel" including "basic English words and phrases. . .how to read a phone book, interpret airline time tables, use the Internet, use code words in communications, make travel reservations, rent an apartment and use video game software to increase their familiarity with aircraft models and function, and to highlight gaps in cabin security" (The 9/11 Commission Report, 2002, pp. 157–158; see also Rhode & Gall, 2005).

Following the training in Pakistan, the operatives went to Kuala Lumpur, Malaysia, for additional training in airport security and surveillance. Part of their training was to board US flights—one was to Hong Kong—and take a dry run for observation purposes. These were test flights, so the operatives could observe airport security and flight crew behavior, particularly the diligence in pre-boarding security screening, the flight crew's movements about the cabin, their timing of certain activities (food and beverage service and attentiveness), and whether or not they entered the cockpit. While in the air to Hong Kong during a dry run, one of the operatives removed a box cutter from his luggage as a test of in-flight security. No one noticed (The 9/11 Commission Report, 2002, p. 159).

These training patterns would continue for several months as a new group of *jihadists* emerged from Hamburg, Germany. Mohamed Atta, Ramzi Binalshibh, Marwan al Shehi, and Ziad Jarrah shared great zeal for *jihad,* which was made easier by their anti-US sentiment. They also came with a distinct advantage over existing Al Qaeda operatives: they were fluent in English and Western customs because they had spent a great deal of time as students in Germany. These four principle 9/11 players eventually formed a cell that became known as the "Hamburg Cell" or the "Hamburg Contingent." During this time in Hamburg, the principles recruited others who would assist in the 9/11 plot:

1. Said Bahaji, a Moroccan immigrant, was used to conduct Internet research.
2. Zakariya Essabar, a Moroccan citizen, traveled to Afghanistan to communicate the final date for the 9/11 plot to Al Qaeda leaders.
3. Mounir el Motassadeq, a Moroccan citizen, was used to conceal trips to Afghanistan.
4. Abdelghani Mzoudi, a Moroccan citizen, whose role is not explicitly clear but seems to have been more passive than active (The 9/11 Commission Report, 2002, pp. 164–165).

During their stay in Hamburg, Atta, Binalshibh, al Shehi, and Jarrah assumed more extremist views that witnesses characterized as clearly exhibiting anti-US animus foreshadowing the events to come; one witness recalled that a cell member referred to Atta as "our pilot" as early as 1999.[22] As the plan gained intensity, two key indicators that were vital to the plan's success emerged: travel documents and funding.

Traveling. Moving between countries is, by definition, necessary to carry out an international incident, like the events of September 11. Getting into the United States was not as easy as many believe. On more than one occasion, US visas were denied to operatives who sought them for different reasons including as students and tourists, some of the easiest visas to obtain; at least one operative was subsequently

---

[22]National Commission on Terrorist Attacks Upon the United States (2002a), note number 88, p. 496 for statements from prosecution witnesses who testified to comments Hamburg cell members made that portend the events of 9/11.

arrested by Yemeni authorities after he tried to secure a US visa.[23] However, US authorities missed several opportunities during the planning stage to interrupt their travel through established means. Whether US officials were lackadaisical, overburdened, under resourced, untrained, or some combination of all four, what is patently evident is that Al Qaeda operatives made several trips in and out of the United States via different airports with only momentary inconvenience.

A separate investigation into the terrorists' travel by Eldridge and colleagues (2004) suggests that there was ample evidence the hijackers could have been detained for further investigation during their movement, which might have revealed their intentions. And if their intentions were not uncovered, then at a minimum, their entry could have been dealt with as a common illegal border crossing, which might have disrupted the plot or led to watch listing:

1. "Three hijackers carried passports with indicators of Islamic extremism linked to al Qaeda.
2. Two others carried passports manipulated in a fraudulent manner. It is likely that several more hijackers carried passports with similar fraudulent manipulation.
3. Two hijackers lied on their visa applications. Once in the United States, two hijackers violated the terms of their visas. One overstayed his visa. And all but one obtained some form of state identification.
4. Six of the hijackers used these state-issued identifications to check in for their flights on September 11. Three of them were fraudulently obtained.
5. In all, they had 25 contacts with consular officers and 43 contacts with immigration and customs authorities.
6. They successfully entered the United States 33 times over 21 months, through nine airports of entry, most of which were on the East Coast" (Eldridge et al., 2004, preface).

Al Qaeda's security committee (Fig. 7.1) was responsible for securing altered documents and recycling genuine passports if an operative was killed.[24] Since a

---

[23] For an in-depth discussion of the hijackers' visa acquisition process and state-level credentials, see Eldridge et al. (2004, pp. 8–33). For a discussion on the US Visa Waiver Program and similar national security risks, see *Cross-Border Security: The Visa Loophole, Al Qaeda's New Front,* PBS FrontLine. Retrieved on January 11, 2009 from http://www.pbs.org/wgbh/pages/frontline/shows/front/special/visa.html

[24] "For more than a decade before the 2001 attacks, terrorists exploited travel in and out of the US in many ways, as well as travel in and out of Afghanistan and Pakistan, then disguising their travel history; Pakistan was the customary travel point on the way to Afghanistan. The tactics used by the terrorist have been corroborated by independent sources during several separate investigations. The tactics include:

1. Traveling on fake passports and often using more than one passport;
2. Using photo-substituted passports;
3. Training in passport forgery, including erasing and adding visas;
4. Using altered, stolen, or borrowed passports;

number of Middle East countries are vigorously monitored for illegal immigration as well as terrorism, altered documents are key because genuine documents are not easily obtained. Beginning in the 1980s, the CIA studied fraudulent documents in a project named Redbook and produced training materials for border inspectors to help identify altered documents. However, in the early 1990s, around the time of the first World Trade Center bombing in 1993, Redbook was abandoned—in fact, "no government agency would systematically analyze terrorists' travel patterns until after 9/11, thus missing critical opportunities to disrupt their plans" (Eldridge et al., 2004, preface).

On January 15, 2000, Nawaf al Hazmi and Khalid al Mihdhar became the first two Al Qaeda operatives to enter the United States in Los Angeles. Mihdhar would leave the United States abruptly and without permission from KSM to return to his family in Yemen, perhaps in a moment of wavering motivation. UBL convinced Mihdhar to continue with the project, which he did and ultimately returned to the United States Within the next couple of months, members of the Hamburg cell would enter the United States; by the summer of 2000, Marwan al Shehhi, Mohamed Atta, and Ziad Samir Jarrah were in the United States and training at flight schools. Meanwhile, back in Afghanistan, KSM came to know another potential pilot named Hani Hanjour. Hanjour was already a pilot having completed flight training in Arizona in April 1999 during several intermittent trips to the United States over the years. Hanjour arrived in the United States on December 8, 2000 and traveled to San Diego to rendezvous with Hazmi. Both men would leave San Diego for Mesa, Arizona, where Hanjour refreshed his flight skills on a Boeing aviation simulator, like the one he eventually piloted on September 11.

In January 2001, Atta met with Ramzi Binalshibh and explained all of the pilots had completed their training and were awaiting further instructions from Al Qaeda leaders. In May, 2001, two more Al Qaeda operatives—Ahmed al Ghamdi and Majed Moqed—entered the United States and took an apartment in Paterson, New Jersey; 13 months later, Mihdhar, returned to the United States and joined the others

---

5. Obtaining blank visas;

6. Buying genuine blank passports and visas and filling in personal data;

7. Keeping evidence of travel to and from Pakistan out of their passports;

8. Reporting their passports lost, stolen, or damaged in order to acquire new, "clean" new passports and to avoid revealing previous travel indicated in the old passport;

9. Using passports that contained fake travel cachets;

10. Relying on corrupt government officials to facilitate travel at border points;

11. Acquiring sophisticated graphics software to assist them in forging documents;

12. Committing serial immigration fraud;

13. Overstaying their visas;

14. Requesting political asylum;

15. Studying in the United States;

16. Traveling under aliases;

17. Entering the United States without an immigration inspection" (Eldridge et al., 2004, p. 54).

in Paterson to resume his role. Following the pilots were the "muscle hijackers," so named because they underwent intense physical training in Afghanistan specifically to provide security for the hijack pilots aboard the planes and to overcome any resistance from passengers. Most of the muscle hijackers fit the marginalized profile described earlier—young, unemployed, and undereducated. A few had undertaken university studies and while better educated, they resented the United States not for its perceived excess but for its clash of values that imperils the religious and cultural ideology of Islam (Gibbs, 2005).

During the summer months of 2001, the hijacking team made several dry runs aboard US flights to refine their observations as well as conduct some additional flight training, while the muscle hijackers trained at local gyms. Atta again communicated the progress of the plot to Ramzi Binalshibh toward the end of the summer. Among the most important details he relayed were that during the dry runs they were able to bring box cutters aboard the flights and approximately 10–15 min into the flight, the cockpit door opened for the first time.

In the final preparation, the hijackers bought their airline tickets approximately 2 weeks before September 11 and returned the excess funds from the operation to Al Qaeda. The final detail was to head to the respective staging areas, which were Laurel, Maryland (Flight 77), Newark, New Jersey (Flight 93), and Boston, Massachusetts (Flight 11 and Flight 175) (National Commission on Terrorist Attacks Upon the United States, 2002c, pp. 3, 6–10).

Funding. Originally, there was speculation that UBL financed the plot from his personal fortune. However, the 9/11 Commission determined that was not the case; rather, funding for the plot was primarily through donations acquired from fundraising activities, corrupt charities, and charities sympathetic to Al Qaeda's cause. Charities were a good source of revenue and provided an excuse for Al Qaeda members to travel freely under the guise of working for a nonprofit group with a social utilitarian purpose. The 9/11 Commission did not uncover any evidence that Al Qaeda received state-sponsored financing; however, Al Qaeda does have ties to the governments in Afghanistan, Sudan, and Pakistan (Schultz & Vogt, 2003, p. 14).

Although Saudi Arabia was a point of interest for US investigators, authorities did not make a connection between Saudi officials and Al Qaeda operatives. If there was a connection, then it might explain Saudi Arabia's reluctance to cooperate with US officials when they sought to interrogate Al Qaeda detainees. Speculation about the original cost for the 9/11 plot was a few million dollars; however, the investigation unfolded that estimate gave way to much lower figures of between $400,000 and $500,000. Most of the funds were spent in the United States for flight training, travel, housing, and incidentals, as well as flight training for the alleged 20th hijacker Zacarias Moussaoui, who was training in Minneapolis, Minnesota, something the FBI investigated and eventually disrupted.[25]

---

[25]The FBI eventually had Moussaoui indicted; he was subsequently convicted and sent to federal prison in the United States The full indictment is accessible at http://www.usdoj.gov/ag/moussaouiindictment.htm

Funding the hijackers and moving money into the United States was not something that attracted much suspicion. There were some visible transactions between Al Qaeda operatives abroad and the operatives in the United States including several legitimate wire transfers to major international banks in the United States as well as some regional banks in the United States The small amount of money moving through Al Qaeda's control was paltry considering the millions moved daily for routine commerce and banking. The transactions did not raise any suspicions nor did the operatives who opened legitimate US bank accounts.

However, Al Qaeda also moved money through an invisible system known as a *hawala,* an underground money transfer system similar to Western Union, except wire transfers do not occur and paper records are not maintained (Perkel, 2004). Hawala is an ancient trust-based money transfer system and with limited exceptions, money does not actually exchange hands. Rather, a system of trusted players—brokers known as *hawaladars*—around the globe accept a sum of money from someone wishing to transfer the money to someone else in another country. Then, the hawaladar calls another hawaladar in the receiving country and has them extend the money to the recipient, minus a commission or transaction fee. The originating hawaladar then promises to settle the account with the other hawaladar at a later time.

This system goes back and forth, where hawaladars simply keep a running sum of the funds owed on scraps of paper as clients come and go and the transactions are based entirely on the honor and good word of each hawaladar. Settling the debts does not necessarily involve exchanging cash; often, the account is settled by simply extending payment to someone else referred by another hawaladar.[26] These transactions are invisible to the legitimate banking system and to law enforcement authorities who may be looking for trends in cash flow because no promissory notes or negotiable instruments are exchanged. Funds are just a phone call away and since nothing actually changes hands, there is no paper trail.

Consequently, "conventional criminal investigations" involving financial crimes such as robbery, credit card fraud and money laundering, and document fraud such as passport counterfeiting, identity theft, and fictitious motor vehicle credentials are among the most important terrorism precursors law enforcement agencies can target (Hamm, 2005, p. vi).

Executing the Operation.[27] Tuesday, September 11, 2001, began as most other business days and a perfect day for air travel. The terrorists completed everything

---

[26] According to Roth, Greenburg, and Wille (n.d., p. 25), the Hawala was frequently combined with other means of moving money. For a single transaction, the hawaladars sometimes used both hawala and the formal banking system or money remitters; the senders and receivers of the funds also often used couriers to transfer the funds to and from their respective hawaladars. Hawala also enabled operatives to access the banking system without having to open an account. Additionally, a good discussion of hawala is found in US Department of Treasury, *A Report to Congress in Accordance with Section 359 of the USA PATRIOT Act,* December 31, 2008. Retrieved on December 23, 2008 from http://www.fincen.gov/news_room/rp/files/hawalarptfinal11222002.pdf

[27] Much of the detail in this section is summarized from The 9/11 Commission Report (2002), pages. 1–14.

in the planning stage; the only thing left was to put the operation into effect, which would happen from Boston's Logan International Airport (American Airlines flight 11 and United Airlines flight 175), Washington Dulles International Airport (American Airlines flight 77), and Newark International Airport (United flight 93) (Table 7.2).

Table 7.2   9/11 hijacking teams

Name	Role	Flight	Target
Mohamed Atta	*Team leader, hijacker and pilot*	American Airlines flight 11	North Tower, World Trade Center
Abdul Aziz al Omari	Muscle hijacker		
Waleed al Shehri	Muscle hijacker		
Satam al Suqami	Muscle hijacker		
Wail al Shehri	Muscle hijacker		
Hani Hanjour	*Hijacker and pilot*	American Airlines flight 77	Pentagon
Khalid al Mihdhar	Muscle hijacker		
Majed Moqed	Muscle hijacker		
Nawaf al Hazmi	Muscle hijacker		
Salem al Hazmi	Muscle hijacker		
Ziad Samir Jarrah	*Hijacker and pilot*	United Airlines flight 93	(Intentionally grounded) Shanksville, PA
Saeed al Ghamdi	Muscle hijacker		
Ahmed al Nami	Muscle hijacker		
Ahmad al Haznawi	Muscle hijacker		
Marwan al Shehhi	*Hijacker and pilot*	United Airlines flight 175	South Tower, World Trade Center
Hamza al Ghamdi	Muscle hijacker		
Fayez Banihammad	Muscle hijacker		
Ahmed al Ghamdi	Muscle hijacker		

Modified from Eldridge et al., 2004, p. 6.

Part of the plan included synchronizing the takeoffs, so timing had to be coordinated. All of the departures were scheduled to take off within 30 min of each other; only flight 93 was delayed due to heavy air traffic at Newark. Flight 11 was scheduled to depart at 7:45 a.m.; flight 175 at 8:00 a.m.; flight 77 at 8:10 a.m.; and flight 93 at 8:00 a.m., all destined for California with nonstop service; a nonstop transcontinental flight requires several thousand pounds of jet fuel estimated at upwards of 11,400 gallons (9/11 Commission Report, 2002, p. 4). Each of the hijackers passed through routine security screening including walk-through metal detectors and X-ray luggage screening; the weapons of choice—small knives and box cutters—were not specifically prohibited on the flights prior to September 11. Although some of the hijackers were identified for additional screening—a perfunctory security measure by all accounts—the only consequence was their luggage would not be loaded until they were approved for boarding by the security checkpoint. The additional screening did not delay the flight or disrupt the hijackers' plans in any manner (National Commission on Terrorist Attacks Upon the United States, 2002d).

Team leader, pilot, and hijacker Mohammad Atta boarded American flight 11 along with the "muscle hijackers" and assumed their seats in business class, a forward section of the aircraft behind first class, giving them a tactical edge to assault the crew and cockpit; each of the hijacking crews adopted a similar tactical position. Marwan al Shehhi and his team of coconspirators boarded United flight 175 and assumed similar seating assignments in the forward portion of the cabin. At Washington Dulles, pilot Hani Hanjour and his team boarded American flight 77, where he and some of his team sat in first class, the forward most section of the aircraft. At Newark, pilot Ziad Samir Jarrah and his crew boarded United flight 93 and also assumed seats in the first-class cabin. As the flights taxied to the runway, all 19 hijackers had kept their methods one step above America's last line of defense against a hijacking.

The Hijacking of American Flight 11.[28] American flight 11 was airborne at 7:59 a.m.. Approximately 15 min into the flight, the "Fasten Seatbelt" sign would have been turned off allowing passengers to move about the cabin. After this point, the flight crew did not have any further communication with air traffic controllers. It is believed the initial assault "began at 8:14 or shortly thereafter" (9/11 Commission Report, 2002, p. 4). Two flight attendants—Betty Ong and Madeline "Amy" Sweeny—contacted the American Airlines Southeastern Reservations Office in Cary, North Carolina, via onboard telephones and relayed the details of the incident. They told colleagues at the control center that hijackers gained control of the plane, stabbing two flight attendants that were preparing for food and beverage service. Shortly thereafter, a passenger in first class was stabbed. The hijackers sprayed some type of aerosol irritant, probably mace or pepper spray, forcing first-class passengers to the rear of the plane. Then, the hijackers claimed they had a bomb onboard.

Authorities at Boston's air traffic control center were already aware of the problem; at 8:25 a.m., one of the hijackers, probably Mohammad Atta, unwittingly broadcasts over the cockpit radio: "Nobody move. Everything will be okay. If you try to make any moves, you'll endanger yourself and the airplane. Just stay quiet" (9/11 Commission Report, 2002, p. 6). The flight attendants reported the plane was "flying erratically," and their altitude was extremely low; American flight 11 crashed into the north tower of the World Trade Center in New York City at 8:46:40 a.m., there were no survivors (9/11 Commission Report, 2002, pp. 6–7).

The Hijacking of United Flight 175. United flight 175 was airborne at 8:14 a.m.. At approximately 8:33 a.m., food and beverage service began. The hijackers' initial assault began between 8:42 and 8:46 a.m. in a similar manner: knives were used to stab the flight crew and to kill both pilots; an aerosol irritant was released; they claimed to have a bomb onboard. At approximately 8:47 a.m., the aircraft changed

---

[28]The accounts of the hijackings were pieced together from in-flight telephone calls placed by the passengers and flight crew to family members and authorities on the ground, as well as records from navigational instruments (Radar, transponders, flight data recorder), air traffic controllers, and other eyewitnesses.

beacon codes—a radar system used to monitor and separate in-flight aircraft—then the plane deviated from its altitude. Air traffic controllers in New York tried to contact the airplane with negative results. At 8:58 a.m., the plane began heading for New York City. At 9:03 a.m., United flight 11 crashed into the South Tower of the World Trade Center, killing everyone onboard (9/11 Commission Report, 2002, p. 7).

The Hijacking of American Flight 77. American flight 77 was airborne at 8:20 a.m. At approximately 8:46 a.m., cabin service should have begun. Consistent with the other attacks, there were reports of knives and movement of the passengers to the rear of the plane. There was also a report of a box cutter that had not been reported on the other flights. However, there was no report of any stabbings, Mace, or the presence of bomb like the others. At 8:54 a.m., the airplane deviated from its flight path and began heading south. About 2 min later, the plane's transponder was turned off and primary radar contact with the plane was completely lost. At 9:00 a.m., the American airlines corporation ordered all American flights that were not airborne to remain on the ground. At 9:34 a.m., the Ronald Reagan Washington National Airport notified the US Secret Service there was an unidentified aircraft heading toward the White House. At 9:37:46 a.m., American flight 77 crashed into the Pentagon, killing all onboard and several civilian and military personnel inside the building (9/11 Commission Report, 2002, pp. 9–10).

The Hijacking of United Flight 93. United flight 93 was airborne at 8:42 a.m., which was about 25 min delayed from its original departure time due to air traffic. By now, with three other airplanes having been hijacked, there was still no industry-wide warning of the hijackings to other airlines. A painful reality at this moment seems that the magnitude of the terrorists' plan was colliding with utter disbelief on the ground and a complete lack of experience and training with multiple hijackings; nothing of this scope had ever been carried out in the United States and there was no thought given to alerting existing flights about the potential risk. Amid the confusion, conflicting information, and escalating reality that a multiple hijacking was underway, one effort to warn existing flights is noteworthy. A lone United Airlines flight dispatcher took the initiative to send a warning message to 16 existing transcontinental flights about the crash at the World Trade Center. That message was received by flight 93 at 9:24 a.m. The hijacking began at 9:28 a.m.

The Cleveland air traffic control center was responsible for flight 93 as it crossed this part of the country. Air traffic controllers heard calls of "Mayday" accompanied by sounds of a physical struggle. Once in control of the cockpit, one of the hijackers, probably the pilot Jarrah, broadcast to the passengers there was a bomb onboard. The passengers made several calls to family and friends who advised them of the events that unfolded over the last hour, including the crash into the World Trade Center. They too relayed that some passengers had been stabbed and that a bomb was onboard. Amid the commotion aboard the aircraft, it seems certain that the hijackers knew the passengers were aware of their intentions and that they knew of the previous hijackings. The pilot began to roll the plane from side to side to throw the passengers off balance as they rushed forward toward the cockpit. The passengers were determined to avert a similar tragedy and decided to try and reclaim the aircraft.

The sounds of a physical struggle were apparent from the cockpit voice recorder. The passengers kept their fortitude and continued to try and gain access to the cockpit. The pilot then dipped the plane's nose up and down to disrupt them. As the passengers' assault intensified, the hijackers realized their plan had been foiled and they would not reach their intended target. Instead, they decided to intentionally ground the airplane. They rolled the plane on to its back and slammed into the ground in Shanksville, Pennsylvania, killing everyone onboard (9/11 Commission Report, 2002, pp. 10–14.).

Overview of the Law Enforcement Response and Analysis

The Law Enforcement Response

The immediate reaction from federal, state, and local authorities was varied and uncoordinated; the 9/11 Commission Report (2002, p. 315) characterized the response effort as "necessarily improvised." For a short time, while the incident was unfolding, the federal government's response was stymied; extensive delays caused by bureaucracy, poor asset coordination, and little or no decision-making authority resulted in conflicting information and widely confused employees who were ultimately rendered impotent—the question of who was in charge never seemed definitive. The immediate military response was insufficient because the military's mission, training, and preparation was to surveil airspace and borders for *incoming* hostile threats from intercontinental missiles, border penetration, or a water-borne invasion, not from threats inside the country. At best, after the appropriate notifications were made, the military had about 9 min to respond to the threat, which they did (National Commission on Terrorist Attacks Upon the United States, 2002 g, p. 6). What's more, the events of September 11 were not a military failure; they were a law enforcement failure (Borch, 2003).

The World Trade Center.[29] In New York, officials found themselves at the center of perhaps the largest public safety response in US history and certainly in the city's history (McKinsey Report, 2002a, 2002b). The NYPD, the FDNY, the Office of Emergency Management (OEM), and the Port Authority Police of New York and New Jersey (PAPD) were the primary response elements, each autonomous and operationally independent. Members of the FDNY were in Manhattan that morning, filming for a French documentary. The film crew captured the first plane striking the north Tower of the World Trade Center at 8:46 a.m. Immediately, the FDNY transmitted the alarm and responded to the scene. Within minutes, New York City's

---

[29]The material for this section was drawn from National Commission on Terrorist Attacks Upon the United States. (2002a). Emergency preparedness and response. Staff Statement No. 13, pp. 2–3. Retrieved on December 23, 2008 from http://govinfo.library.unt.edu/911/staff_statements/staff_statement_13.pdf

9-1-1 system was overwhelmed with calls from eyewitnesses describing what they saw and identifying the location.

As police officers and firefighters arrived at the scene, they began assembling in the lobby of the north tower awaiting direction. The NYPD ordered a Level 3 mobilization at 8:47 a.m., which brought nearly 1,000 officers from across the city to respond. Officers began clearing emergency routes and evacuation routes as well as staging in different areas; the NYPD ordered a Level 4 mobilization at 9:01 a.m. At 9:03 a.m., the second plane struck the south tower of the World Trade Center. The response effort had just escalated in magnitude and with it came several complications.

The valiant effort by members of the NYPD, the FDNY, the OEM, and the PAPD was made more difficult by firefighting limitations, communication problems, and command and control issues. When the planes struck the towers, they cut through the towers' internal firefighting apparatus including standpipes. There was no water at the site of the crash, thus no way to fight the fire. FDNY commanders quickly made the decision not to fight the fire, but to direct a rescue operation. Years earlier, the PAPD installed a radio "repeater" system for the FDNY that would boost radio transmission signals while operating inside the towers. The system had been activated but a second part of the system that enabled the "master handset" was not activated. When the FDNY tested the system and firefighters did not respond, they mistakenly concluded that it had been disabled by the crash. In fact, firefighters in the south tower were using the system but firefighters in the north tower could not communicate with them. Several responding fire companies responded to the wrong location due to communication problems.

In addition to communication issues, years of rivalry between the FDNY and the NYPD also complicated the response. The incident command system that was underway was not unified (McKinsey Report, 2002a, p. 9). The FDNY rebuffed[30] members of the NYPD's special operations division who checked in at the forward command post and personnel from the city's OEM did not intervene. The FDNY had a forward command post in both the north and south towers for the respective effort at each scene. The overall command post was outside the towers but was moved further away due to falling debris and the general conditions near the scene. At 9:46 a.m., the FDNY ordered a third fifth alarm response, which brought over one-third of the department to the scene.

At this time, the NYPD also had a massive response underway with approximately 2,000 officers on the scene. NYPD rescue teams went to work on their own after being rebuffed by the FDNY and subsequent rescue teams did not check in the FDNY's command post. The fire department, the police department, the OEM, and the PAPD were not communicating each other because of disparate radio systems and lack of a unified plan. The PAPD did not have a standard operating procedure for

---

[30] After September 11, New York City Mayor Michael Bloomberg officially placed the NYPD in charge at the scene of a disaster (Lueck, 2005), which was not well received by the chief of the New York City Fire Department (Gendar, 2005).

a multiagency response and their radios did not work beyond their local geographic area. PAPD commanders responded to the scene and set up an ad hoc response plan. While laudable and necessary, the plan was inherently flawed because there was no way to keep track of the responding officers and their assignments. This was critical because PAPD officers, as well as NYPD and FDNY personnel, were ascending the towers for a rescue/evacuation effort but were unaware of the situation around them.

The communication problems and command control issues complicated situational awareness. The ability to inform personnel inside the towers was severely limited. Conflicting and erroneous information continued to come in to the 9-1-1 center and the information was incorrectly relayed to field units about the condition of the towers and an impending collapse. At 9:59 a.m., the south tower collapsed. Personnel in the north tower were unaware the south tower had collapsed despite radio broadcasts from the NYPD aviation units and the FDNY marine units who relayed the conditions. Some personnel decided to self-evacuate but not with any sense of urgency because someone had notified them. At 10:26 a.m., the north tower collapsed.

The Pentagon. At 9:37 a.m., the Pentagon was struck. An amalgam of federal, state, and local assets responded. By contrast, the response conditions at the Pentagon were not as troubled as they were in New York. The Arlington County fire department, along with the Arlington County police and other assets, had previously worked together and they worked well together. The operational mix of agencies was made easier by activating the incident command system (ICS)—a formal disaster management structure. The ICS in place that day enabled different disciplines (police, fire, EMS) from different jurisdictions (federal, state, county, and local) to work cooperatively among their different roles. The 9/11 Commission Report (2002, p. 314) credits the success of the Pentagon response with (1) "strong professional relationships and trust established among emergency responders; (2) the adoption of the Incident Command System; and (3) the pursuit of a regional approach to response."

For all its credit, the response at the Pentagon did encounter similar difficulties as New York, primarily self-response and communications. Self-responding to the scene without prior approval from the incident commander, while noble, complicates command and control as well as accountability. Communication, as in New York, was the critical obstacle. Disparate radio systems kept agencies from communicating across a common radio frequency, complicating coordination, control, and safety.

Analysis

The task ahead for law enforcement to successfully confront the new structure of terrorism is to create an operating environment where an amalgam of international and domestic agencies from different levels of government can function across common policy boundaries with an operational platform that offers a seamless exchange of voice and data packets to ensure the best possible situational awareness.

Coordination and communication problems. Prior to the September 11 event, the greatest weakness from federal law enforcement authorities was their inability to manage and share intelligence. Although there were significant shortcomings in the government's ability to parse actionable intelligence and dispel the "noise" (Gladwell, 2003), they also did not look for assistance from state and local authorities. There is an array of local services domestic security agencies could have drawn upon to help investigate domestic terror leads or interpret ambiguous information, particularly since local police departments have an intimate knowledge of the community.

On September 11, the greatest weakness among state and local law enforcement agencies was communications, which hampered coordination and postevent mitigation. The problems of communication interoperability[31] were insurmountable on September 11 and police, fire, and emergency medical services were wholly unprepared to work together on such a grand scale for a sustained period of time. While there were many positive results in New York and at the Pentagon, there were also shortcomings that must be addressed.

Law enforcement agencies at the federal, state, and local level have historically had problems integrating well from on-scene control, to communications, to information sharing. The problems result in part from "home-rule" rivalries, interoperability shortfalls, and confrontational attitudes of different agencies because of a generalized lack of trust and understanding between them. This is compounded by differing priorities and missions that lack synthesis. These frictions have caused problems during intelligence briefings and mutual-aid response situations that result in a less-than-ideal partnership for a common response as well as disjointed preemptive operations and information sharing.

In the summer of 2001, domestic intelligence agencies (FBI, CIA, NSA— National Security Agency) were waiting for more definitive evidence that something would launch inside the United States before they disseminated any information to state or local agencies; indeed, they were under a previous directive not to issue any advisories based on daily briefings. As a result they waited for evidence that never came; they never passed along what they already knew to domestic law enforcement and did not warn the public (The 9/11 Commission Report, 2002, p. 265). Indeed, some of the rivalries between agencies were so extensive (e.g., the FBI, the CIA and the NSA) that, although largely concealed from the public, bureaucratic complacency and pervasive conflict between members enveloped a small group of counterterrorism officials to such a degree that preemptive operations were not undertaken, information was slow to move, and personality clashes hindered investigations. When the FBI and other members of the intelligence community failed

---

[31] Interoperability is broadly defined by the US military as: "The ability of systems, units, or forces to provide services to and accept services from other systems, units, or forces, and to use the services so exchanged to enable them to operate effectively together" (Department of Defense, Joint Chiefs of Staff, *DoD Dictionary of Military and Associated Terms,* Washington, DC: Joint Publication 1-02, March 23, 1994, as amended through February 10, 1999).

to act on late leads or to connect the dots by separating the "noise" from useful information (Gladwell, 2003), the clock eventually ran out.

The FBI has primary responsibility for the domestic counterterrorism effort, which includes intelligence collection and criminal investigations. Prior to September 11, there was unenthusiastic commitment from elected leaders to provide the resources necessary to make counterterrorism a national priority. As such, the FBI's law enforcement effort was necessarily reactive. That is, the FBI's operating methodology was a decentralized organizational structure that reflected building criminal cases and gathering after-the-fact evidence to ensure successful prosecutions. Careers at the FBI were built on the agents' ability to create airtight cases that were successfully prosecuted. It stands to reason that there was more emphasis on slow deliberate fact finding where time was on the agent's side. In this model there is no urgency to arrest, which is the first step to disrupting a plot. Urgency gives way to patience, persistence, and a methodical process to ensure legal processes—particularly due process—are adhered to. In this realm the FBI's investigative ability is internationally recognized, such as the successful investigation following the Khobar Towers attack in Africa, despite the massive destruction and wide debris field.

Part of the problem with employing this method as a counterterrorism measure is the inherently reactive nature—disrupting, thus preventing an attack from occurring is not an aspect of this model. In the post-September 11 environment there was a shift in management philosophy from reactive to proactive investigations. Management shifted resources from traditional investigative squads to the counterterrorism effort and aligned counterterrorism with its existing national strategic plan.[32] The future success of this model rests on FBI management's ability to develop the organizational capacity sufficient to support counterterrorism. This includes developing a sophisticated technical infrastructure, hiring personnel with special skills (e.g., analytics, language, accounting, surveillance, and engineering), and developing expertise in incumbent personnel through training.

The FBI must also make proactive use of intelligence that is collected by sharing that information with the thousands of state and local police departments, something they are not accustomed to doing. State and local authorities have long criticized the FBI for hoarding information instead of sharing it with a common purpose. Much of the "mystique" surrounding the FBI's intelligence program is cloaked in language such as "in the interest of national security," "top secret," "classified," "security clearance," or "on a need to know basis." These words elevate the FBI to a superior position over state and local authorities by suggesting that anyone outside the FBI is not trustworthy enough to hear or view certain information. This necessarily excludes several hundred thousand law enforcement personnel at the state and local level who might be in a position to assist the FBI by disrupting a plot or otherwise be vigilant against terrorism. Moreover, the FBI's Joint Terrorism

---

[32] See the FBI's strategic plan at http://www.fbi.gov/publications/strategicplan/strategicplanfull.pdf. Retrieved on January 20, 2009.

Task Force (JTTF), which is composed of officers from state, county, and local law enforcement agencies, does not fully disclose information to task force members outside the FBI. But it is not just state and local authorities that are problematic for the FBI. Prior to September 11 they also did not share information with the CIA or the National Security Council despite repeated requests (Isikoff & Klaidman, 2002; National Commission on Terrorist Attacks Upon the United States, 2002 h, p. 10).

Dilemmas at the local level. The vast majority of municipal law enforcement agencies across America are unable to communicate with their public safety counterparts at the county, state, and federal level. There is a popular misconception that law enforcement agencies within and across jurisdictions are able to respond to emergencies and effectively communicate with each other. Much of the misconception comes from the erroneous belief, popularized by Hollywood and television glitterati, that law enforcement can coordinate their communications and response efforts seamlessly. The truth is that communications between and among agencies and jurisdictions surrounding most municipalities usually occur through individual communications centers; there is heavy reliance on dispatchers and communication operators to transmit messages back and forth via radio or cellular services. Neither method is particularly effective for exchanging critical, timely information.

In the post-September 11 environment, there is a demand from the public that all segments of government—federal, state, county, and local—work cooperatively to ensure a similar situation is mitigated as quickly as possible, without a distinction for who responds (National Task Force on Interoperability, 2003, p. 10). This demand is at the core of the interoperability problem since coordinating communications and assets is *the key* to establishing law enforcement mutual aid. Incompatible equipment and fragmented planning are among the more serious interoperability issues that must be addressed (McKinsey Report, 2002a, 2002b; National Task Force on Interoperability, 2003, p. 15).

Incompatible equipment is the chief evil against which communications interoperability is directed. There is great disparity among communication equipment, particularly radio equipment. Multiple agencies (local, county, state, and federal) and multiple disciplines (police, fire, EMS) responding to the same emergency may find themselves working side by side while still having to relay critical information. This is most likely to occur at large crime scenes or critical incidents (like the World Trade Center, the Pentagon, or the Khobar Towers in Africa) where first responders are literally within visual site of each other but cannot transmit voice communications without their respective dispatcher acting as the relay. This inefficient mode of communications can jeopardize the accuracy of information being transmitted and can ultimately impact the ability to save lives.[33] Even when the relay is timely and accurate, dispatchers may still not reach the intended recipient because of poor

---

[33] See generally, The 9/11 Commission Report (2002), Chapter 9, for a litany of interoperability problems between the NYPD, FDNY, New York City Office of Emergency Management (OEM) and the Port Authority Police.

radio discipline[34] or poor equipment that cannot overcome the physical operating environment (steel and concrete buildings, tunnels or mountainous terrain).

Another cumbersome obstacle to successful joint operations is fragmented planning, which is complicated by "home rule." Home rule is often responsible for poor planning, duplication of effort, and redundant services. Unnecessary repetition wastes time, money, and effort, and the results are typically less than desirable. Local communities supply the majority of law enforcement personnel but they cannot mount a well-coordinated response in a vacuum and must rely on other law enforcement agencies to develop a successful response plan. Once the plan is developed, it must be practiced through live training and tabletop exercises. Preventing and mitigating a future terrorist attack will depend on a counterterrorism plan, where preemption and interoperability are central.

Interoperability as a solution to integration problems. Interoperability is "a measure of the degree to which various organizations or individuals are able to operate together to achieve a common goal" (Hura et al., 2000, p. 7). The concept borrows from the US military that employs this model to enable operations between coalition forces. From the executive level, through middle management, to line-level personnel, interoperability represents a standardized, integrated, and balanced approach to a unified system where public safety disciplines share information seamlessly. Interoperability is not limited to radio communications, which is often the first thought that comes to mind when using the term. A closer look at the integrated fit among law enforcement and other public safety assets reveals four operating levels that comprise interoperability in its totality: strategic, operational, tactical, and technological (Hura et al., 2000, p. 8) (Fig. 7.2).

Strategic Level. At the strategic level, interoperability shapes the policy environment that enables interagency and intergovernmental partnerships. It is here that foreign governments, federal, state, and local policy makers develop positions and allocate resources that guide and constrain decision making to ensure that national security goals are achieved. The strategic level is where law enforcement weaknesses dealing with information sharing, intelligence collection, resources, and preemptive action are resolved. By developing bilateral and multilateral accords among nations and creating domestic intergovernmental partnerships, national security is enhanced because each level is working with unanimity of purpose, acting on the same intelligence, and training together to perfect their craft.

In the post-September 11 environment, preemption is the preferred strategy. The doctrine of preemption is aptly named since it orients domestic and international partners to the prospect of deterrence. The key to prevention is disruption—and disruption is inherently proactive (i.e., offensive). In defining America's new strategy

---

[34]Radio discipline refers to protocols and self-imposed restraint on using the radio while in the field by limiting transmissions to emergencies or other imperative information and refraining from superfluous conversation. Poor radio discipline affects radio traffic and inevitably causes congestion on the channel. See McKinsey Report (2002b, p. 34) for indications of poor radio discipline.

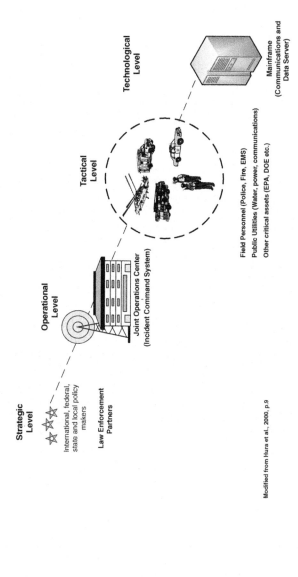

Fig. 7.2 Four levels of interoperability: A law enforcement configuration

to combat terrorism, President Bush, addressing the 2002 graduating class at the West Point Military Academy, made preemption clear:

> [The] new threats also require new thinking. Deterrence—the promise of massive retaliation against nations—means nothing against shadowy terrorist networks with no nation or citizens to defend. Containment is not possible when unbalanced dictators with weapons of mass destruction can deliver those weapons on missiles or secretly provide them to terrorist allies. We cannot defend America and our friends by hoping for the best. We cannot put our faith in the word of tyrants, who solemnly sign non-proliferation treaties, and then systemically break them. If we wait for threats to fully materialize, we will have waited too long.[35]

Domestic and international strategies also help resolve individual contributions by each nation and by each level of local government, so mutual-aid commitment is assured during times of shared interest. This type of cooperation solidifies the willingness and responsibility from each partner to work toward a predefined goal and shape prevention and response protocols. This begins by setting clear priorities for domestic infrastructure protection and allocating resources according to risk.

This is also the point where domestic home-rule rivalries and confrontational attitudes are dissolved in the interest of national security. Confronting the new structure of terrorism requires interdependence and must outweigh organizational pride. Organizations must put aside their differences aside, check their egos at the door, and use training to close the gap between perception and reality. Once this is achieved, the business of intercepting offenders, mitigating crises, and preventing terrorism can thrive. It is not enough to simply resolve these differences on paper. Each level of government must expect to work with their supporting counterparts in nearly all future operations, and increasingly, each agency's policies, procedures, and planning efforts must reflect this reality.

Strategic interoperability is one means of achieving both effective and efficient public safety capability. It represents a rationalized approach that can reduce response time, increase the flexibility of selected assets, and define public safety niches that will be called upon to reduce or eliminate redundancy. Moreover, participation by partnership agencies can increase burden sharing by spreading both the costs and risks across multiple layers of government.

Operational and Tactical Levels. These two levels intersect with strategy and technology to form the basis for a response environment that mitigates a crisis. The strategy that is ultimately developed must be placed into action, within given constraints. Unified operations are carried out from a single location where all the partners are represented and decisions are made, thus eliminating traditional bureaucracy. This is the essence of unified command within the National

---

[35]Retrieved on January 19, 2009 from http://www.whitehouse.gov/news/releases/2002/06/20020601-3.html. The doctrine of preemption has become known as the *Bush Doctrine,* a series various foreign policy principles for dealing with hostile regimes including preventative war and anticipatory military action. The full doctrine appears in *The National Security Strategy of the United States of America,* issued March 16, 2006 (Retrieved on January 19, 2009 from http://www.whitehouse.gov/nsc/nss/2006/nss2006.pdf).

Response Framework.[36] The tactical level represents how various assets behave in the field including their ability to communicate and exchange voice and data with each other directly and how field supervisors intend to respond to the situation.

Planning for and conducting international, interstate, or interagency operations requires a process that can vary from a small local operations (e.g., few mixed agencies for a local response) to a joint division of labor across separate countries, cities, or states. Proactive training is the best measure to counter the inherent problem of "home rule" that so often encumbers operations. Participating in multiagency task forces, serving on steering committees, and conducting practical and tabletop exercises will resolve problems before they occur.

Technological Level. To mount and sustain an effective, coordinated law enforcement response, there must be a comprehensive, cross-functional common services infrastructure. This enables all participating agencies to communicate and share information with others operating in a unified environment. At this level, law enforcement partners and other public safety assets must bridge the current divide between the technical capabilities of disparate systems. The focus here is on communications and information/technology (IT) resources and involves the hardware and software capabilities of systems to accept and receive transmissions from each other in pursuit of the mission.[37]

Identifying critical interoperability shortfalls is a must before different practice groups can assume seamless integration. The most critical of these systems are secure voice and data communications, information dissemination, personnel accountability, and asset tracking. These were the fundamental obstacles to the law enforcement response on September 11. The technology should support high-speed, self-healing, integrated voice, video, data, and geospatial applications among participating agencies. Individual IT components such as radios, laptop and personal computers, and handheld devices should operate across a wireless communications network, where processing power is shared among all devices. Peer-to-peer technology such as this enables every device in the network to act as a router and a repeater for all other devices on the network. This multihopping capability creates a robust network that automatically routes around congestion and line-of-sight obstacles, while improving throughput as user density increases. Because every device serves as a router on the network, a failure of one or multiple devices will not bring the network down. Instead, working devices re-route automatically to functioning devices and allow the data to continue streaming.

---

[36] See Department of Homeland Security, Federal Emergency Management Administration, National Incident Management System (NIMS). Retrieved on January 20, 2009 from http://www.fema.gov/pdf/emergency/nrf/nrf-core.pdf

[37] See National Institute of Standards and Technology (February 1996). Application portability profile (APP): The US government's open system environment profile. Version 3.0. NIST Special Publication 500-230. Gaithersburg, MD.

This type of platform increases efficiency, readiness, and safety of personnel and assets. When the World Trade Center collapsed, the communications system of the PAPD and some cellular services were destroyed, jeopardizing the operation. While operating inside the World Trade Center, police officers and firefighters heard intermittent and unintelligible radio transmissions because the building's physical architecture limited the depth of penetration. In short, there was no communications interoperability (McKinsey Report, 2002a, p. 7, 2002b, p. 25).

Aftermath. On November 27, 2002, President George W. Bush along with Congress established the National Commission on Terrorist Attacks Upon the United States, commonly known as The 9/11 Commission. The Commission's charge was to provide a full accounting of the incident and make recommendations for improvement; the final report was issued on July 22, 2004. While praised for its literary style and comprehensiveness, others criticized it for its partisan politics, lack of specificity, and questionable veracity (DeMott, 2004; Gwertzman, 2004; Henry, 2004; Isikoff, 2003; Ridgeway, 2005). Some of the most important findings include the failure to place suspected terrorists on "watch lists" or to aggressively pursue them once inside the United States; the failure to establish links among hijackers who sought flight training in the United States; the failure to uncover falsifications listed on visa applications or recognize fraudulent documents when proffered; and the failure to expand "no-fly" lists with the names of potential terrorists who were under investigation.

But perhaps the most disturbing finding was the obstructionism by different government agencies. Thomas H. Kean and Lee H. Hamilton, Chairman and Vice Chairman of the 9/11 Commission, respectively, reported that the CIA withheld evidence from the Commission. Kean and Hamilton accused the CIA of failing to disclose reports and video interrogations of detainees when asked and provided "nonspecific replies" to specific questions surrounding the interrogation of suspected terrorists Abu Zubaydah and Abd al Rahim al-Nashiri (Kean & Hamilton, 2008; Mazzetti, 2007; The 9/11 Commission, 2002, p. 146). Dissatisfied with the CIA's answers, Kean and Hamilton went directly to CIA Director George Tenet and asked for permission to interview the detainees themselves. That request was denied. The tapes the CIA said never existed were later destroyed in 2005.

After the CIA, the Pentagon proffered inconsistent and misleading statements to the Commission about the military's response. Various "emails and other evidence" (Eggen, 2006, p. A3) suggested that the Federal Aviation Administration (FAA) made notification to the Department of Defense (DoD) about a hijacked aircraft when, in fact, no such notification had been made and that military officials could not have had United Airlines flight 93 in sight and tracking it at 9:16 a.m. since the flight was not hijacked until 9:28 a.m. Concerns over the inaccuracies were referred to the DoD and the Department of Transportation (DoT) Inspectors General for possible criminal prosecution. On August 31, 2006, Acting DoT Inspector General Todd J. Zinser issued a memorandum concluding that the inaccurate statements made to the 9/11 Commission resulted from "an erroneous timeline entry" and were not deliberate. Administrative action was recommended against two FAA executives and no criminal charges were proffered (Zinser, 2006, p. 1).

Accountability was not easy to come by after September 11. Few were held accountable for the colossal failures and some who uncovered security vulnerabilities at airports before September 11 were silenced by their agency. Bogdan Dzakovic, a former FAA employee, whose job was to purposely uncover security vulnerabilities, was relieved of his position after September 11 when he filed a "whistle-blower" complaint about alleged FAA improprieties (Katovsky, 2006). Dzakovic allegedly uncovered security problems at several US airports and when he made his findings known, his superiors told him not to document the results, not to visit the airports again, and not to follow-up on whether security had improved. On August 16, 2002, DoT Inspector General Kenneth M. Mead issued his investigative findings and recommendations. The report is replete *he said, she said* finger-pointing and *I don't recall* language. On March 18, 2003, Elaine Kaplan, Special Counsel, US Office of Special Counsel, sent a letter to President Bush summarizing Mead's findings. Although she praised Dzakovic for his courageousness for revealing the management problems at FAA, the investigation did not find the problems were deliberate or covered up. Consequently, no further investigative action or recommendations for discipline were made (Kaplan, 2003; Mead, 2002).

The final blow to accountability came on October 6, 2005. Newly appointed CIA Director and former Chairman of the House Intelligence Committee Porter Goss publicly announced that no current or former members of the CIA—including former Director George Tenet—would be disciplined for their actions leading up to September 11 (Linzer & Pincus, 2005, p. A1). Goss alluded to the fact that it would hurt the CIA at a time when it was trying to "rebuild" after September 11 as well as embarrass the President who bestowed the Presidential Medal of Freedom to Director Tenet. The classified findings were not made public but they reportedly fault former Director Tenet, Director of Operations James L. Pavitt, and former head of the counterterrorism center J. Cofer Black along with several other current and former CIA employees. By legislative mandate, The 9/11 Commission closed on August 21, 2004.

There are many policy implications arising from the Commission's final report. Perhaps the most significant change came on March 1, 2003 when the US Department of Homeland Security (DHS) was created, uniting 22 disparate federal agencies. If there is to be a comprehensive and unified domestic effort to counter and respond to terrorism, this appears to be a prudent decision. Since its inception, several smaller initiatives under DHS were begun to upgrade state and local preparedness including the Urban Area Security Initiative, State Homeland Security Program, Metropolitan Medical Response System, and the Citizen Corps Program as well as grants, training, and technical assistance to state and local agencies.

Perhaps the most controversial legislation to be enacted after September 11 was the Uniting and Strengthening America by Providing Appropriate Tools Required to Intercept and Obstruct Terrorism Act of 2001 (Public Law Pub.L. 107-56),[38]

---

[38] Source   http://frwebgate.access.gpo.gov/cgi-bin/getdoc.cgi?dbname=107_cong_public_laws &docid=f:publ056.107. Retrieved on January 22, 2009.

commonly known as the USA PATRIOT Act and various laws relating to the *Bush Doctrine*—the policy of preemption in the post-9/11 world. The PATRIOT Act expanded the power of government and authorized the practice of domestic spying, part of the *Bush Doctrine* of preemption—something that worries many people because of its intrusiveness and potential for Executive Branch abuse (New York Times, 2002; Rosenzweig, 2003). Preemption necessarily involves casting a wider net and collecting and analyzing data to disrupt plots before they are executed. Data collection, data mining, and analysis are the foundation for intelligence-led policing, an emerging police management model based on prevention (McGarrell, Freilich, & Chermak, 2007; Ratcliffe, 2008).[39]

The legacy of domestic spying dating to the Church Committee (1975) and the widespread abuses by the NSA, the IRS, the FBI, and the CIA uncovered by the Committee do not seem so distant nor do they seem impossible.[40] The fundamental precepts of privacy, individualized reasonable suspicion, and no records without a warrant that surfaced 30 years earlier were about to surface once more (Risen & Lichtblau, 2005). FBI Director Robert Mueller was called before Congress in the spring of 2007 to answer for the FBI's use of National Security Letters (NSLs)—FBI-issued administrative subpoenas used to seize records or other information in the absence of a court order—against US citizens. A subsequent court ruling invalidated certain provisions of the PATRIOT Act that allowed the FBI to issue NSLs in the absence of a warrant (Eggen, 2007). NSLs have become a de facto warrantless exception to the Fourth Amendment to be used as a matter of efficiency for law enforcement to act swiftly without the tedious, cumbersome machinations of getting a warrant.

The FBI was not the only federal agency using data mining as a measure of preemption in the war against terror. A General Accounting Office (GAO) investigation found a DoD program known as DARPA—Defense Advanced Research Projects Agency—was the heaviest user of data mining in the fight against terrorism (GAO, 2004; Markoff, 2002). DARPA's Total Information Awareness (TIA) program (Congressional Digest, 2003)[41]—a data and information collection program—was widely criticized by Congress for being too invasive to the privacy interests of American citizens. It is this type of Executive Branch extension—access to data and information—that represents an intimidating and overarching expanding power

---

[39]"Intelligence-led policing is defined as a business model and managerial philosophy where data analysis and crime intelligence are pivotal to an objective, decision-making framework that facilitates crime and problem reduction, disruption and prevention through both strategic management and effective enforcement strategies that target prolific and serious offenders" (Ratcliffe, 2008, p. 89).

[40]See PBS FrontLine, *Spying on the Home Front*, May 15, 2007, retrieved on January 23, 2009 from http://www.pbs.org/wgbh/pages/frontline/homefront/view/. See also Final Report of the Select Committee to Study Governmental Operations with Respect to Intelligence Activities, S. Rep. No. 94-755, 94th Congo 2d Sess. (April 26, 1976); NOVA, February 3, 2009, *The Spy Factory*, retrieved on February 7, 2009 from http://www.pbs.org/wgbh/nova/spyfactory/program.html

[41]See *Congressional Digest* (April 2003, Vol. 82, No. 4, pp. 114–127) for positions favoring and opposing DARPA's Total Information Awareness Program.

base. Because of its "high-value" potential the program was not disbanded; rather, elements of it were moved to other federal agencies incognito (Williams, 2006).

In the post-September 11 environment, the perpetual debate is: How much liberty or privacy should American citizens sacrifice to increase security? This timeless argument finds its way to the forefront of political debate in the Congress, the Senate, state capitols, local city councils, and watchdog groups in varying degrees (German & Stanley, 2007).[42] Privacy protections are embedded in the Fourth Amendment to the US Constitution and law enforcement is adapting to the evolving "electronic" environment. Data and information have become so prevalent in our "knowledge-based society" that facilitating crime through traditional face-to face confrontation is giving way to clandestine meetings over Internet chat rooms where plans are developed and money is transferred. Trolling electronic databases then mining the data is a rich source of telltale behavior. To coordinate intelligence-gathering activities and information dissemination, the law enforcement concept of "fusion centers" is emerging. Fusion centers are defined as organizational structures that combine electronic data and other information on patterns of behavior for the purpose of analyzing, linking, and disseminating intelligence (Allen, 2008; Carter, 2007, 2008). This is the latest law enforcement tool being used to find potentially dangerous people without having to physically confront them to obtain vital information. Fusion centers have a bright future in the post-September 11 intelligence world; how the information is used, stored, and destroyed will be the ultimate test of law enforcement legitimacy in the information age.

Conclusion

Federal, state, and local law enforcement must work cooperatively to prevent future terror attacks, although not everyone agrees with the doctrine of preemption. Striking first by making military or law enforcement decisions on things unseen requires a leap of faith, something democratic governments are not particularly fond of. There is always a "dark figure" that represents the unknown and signals the events in question *might not happen,* that we are *acting on unconfirmed information* or *there may be another explanation for this.* Terrorism is a rallying cry for political purposes and the hype may cause political zeal. In their zeal to protect the populace, government officials desire to act but fear a label that suggests they "over reacted," a sign often interpreted as imperfection, weakness, and panic.

When governments take the initiative to act, there is a presumption that they are acting in good faith based on accurate information. The more they act on their own volition with insufficient or inaccurate information, the more likely they are

---

[42]For an update on this citation, see Mike German and Jay Stanley (July 2008), Fusion center update, American Civil Liberties Union. Retrieved on January 23, 2009 from http://www.aclu.org/pdfs/privacy/fusion_update_20080729.pdf. See also Electronic Privacy Information Center for a list of federal, state, and local legislative actions and a description of fusion centers. Retrieved on January 23, 2009 from http://epic.org/privacy/fusion/

to be publicly castigated and lose legitimacy. This is a difficult and circular situation for law enforcement: If the government acts without enough evidence, then they risk waging unlawful military action, prosecuting innocent people, squandering resources, and losing domestic and international credibility—a dire consequence. If they fail to act, then they might miss a rare opportunity to avert a catastrophe—a dire consequence! If they continually act without bona fide results, then they risk being labeled inept. This too is part of the operating philosophy of terror groups to embarrass and discredit government authorities by showing the masses that the government is chasing a phantom and cannot protect them. Therefore, not only is the government unable to protect its people beforehand, but in the aftermath they cannot find those responsible. The consequence is further slippage into disrepute with its people. And so goes the circle of balancing liberty (not acting) with security (acting).

Belief in things unseen is a difficult proposition for decision makers and many are never convinced, so they wait patiently to develop more information—they wait for the single piece of confirmatory evidence that never comes, thus keeping them from taking action. The Lodi, California case demonstrates the inherent difficulties law enforcement authorities face when trying to uproot a potentially deadly campaign of violence against innocent civilians when the alleged suspects are afforded Constitutional protections and blend seamlessly into the cultural and social landscape, part of the new Al Qaeda's approach. In their zeal the FBI was wrong about their information in Lodi, just as they were wrong in December 2003 when they issued a vague warning that Las Vegas, Nevada, was a target for an impending attack. The initial belief was the New Year's Eve celebration may be the scene. Nothing came of it.

Law enforcement failures that occur from inferences based on small pieces of information will inevitably occur. They are the cost of doing business with an elusive invisible enemy willing to vaporize themselves in pursuit of their cause. "Noise" will exceed actionable intelligence. Innocents will be caught in the same net as the guilty. Consistent mistakes must be dealt with forcefully. But mistakes are just another way of doing business and represent some of the best possible learning experiences. Changing and learning from mistakes as well as how law enforcement treats the public following a mistake is a matter of leadership, something America needs from law enforcement as they uproot insidious terror groups.

References

Agnew, R. (1992). Foundation for a general strain theory of crime and delinquency. *Criminology*, *30*(1), 47–87.

Agnew, R. (1994). The techniques of neutralization and violence. *Criminology*, *32*, 555–580.

Allen, C. E. (July 23, 2008). Information sharing at the federal, state and local levels. Statement before the U.S. senate of under secretary for intelligence and analysis. Washington, DC: Committee on Homeland Security and Governmental Affairs. Retrieved on December 22, 2008, from http://hsgac.senate.gov/public/_files/072308Allen.pdf.

Anderson, E. (1999). *Code of the street: Decency, violence, and the moral life of the inner city.* New York: Norton.

Apple, Jr. R. W. (September 14, 2001). After the attacks: No middle ground. *New York Times*.

Atwan, A. (2006). *The secret history of Al Qaeda*. Berkeley, CA: University of California Press.

Austin, C. J. (2006). *Up against the wall: Violence in the making and unmaking of the black panther party*. Fayetteville, AR: University of Arkansas Press.

Bandura, A., Barbaranelli, C., Capara, G., & Pastorelli, C. (1990). Mechanisms of moral disengagement. In W. Reich (Ed.), *Origins of terrorism: Psychologies, ideologies, theologies, states of mind* (pp. 161–191). Cambridge: Cambridge University Press.

Bandura, A., Barbaranelli, C., Capara, G., & Pastorelli, C. (1996). Mechanisms of moral disengagement in the exercise of moral agency. *Journal of Personality and Social Psychology, 71*(2), 365–374.

Becker, E. (1973). *The denial of death*. New York: Free Press.

Becker, E. (1975). *Escape from evil*. New York: Free Press.

Bergen, P. (2006). *The Osama bin Laden I Know*. New York: Free Press.

Berger, D. (2006). *Outlaws of America: The weather underground and the politics of solidarity*. Oakland, CA: AK Press.

Bindra, S. (September 19, 2001). India identifies terrorist training camps. *CNN.com*. Retrieved on January 29, 2009, from http://archives.cnn.com/2001/WORLD/asiapcf/central/09/19/inv.afghanistan.camp/

Blanchard, C. M. (2007). Al Qaeda: Statements and evolving ideology. Washington, DC: Congressional Research Service. Retrieved on December 21, 2008, from http://fas.org/sgp/crs/terror/RL32759.pdf

Bolz, F., Dudonis, K. J., & Schultz, D. P. (1996). *The counter-terrorism handbook: Tactics, procedures, and techniques*. Boca Raton, FL: CRC Press.

Borch, F. (2003). Comparing Pearl Harbor and "9/11": Intelligence failure? American unpreparedness? Military responsibility? *The Journal of Military History, 67*(3), 845–860.

Borum, R. (2003, July). Understanding the terrorist mindset. *FBI Law Enforcement Bulletin*, pp. 7–10.

Bryan, J. (1975). *This soldier still at war*. New York: Harcourt Brace Jovanovich.

Carter, D. L. (2007). *The intelligence fusion process for state, local and tribal law enforcement*. East Lansing, MI: Michigan State University, Intelligence Program, School of Criminal Justice.

Carter, D. L. (2008). *The intelligence fusion process*. Intelligence Policy Paper Series. East Lansing, MI: Michigan State University, Intelligence Program, School of Criminal Justice.

Chehab, Z. (2006). *Iraq Ablaze: Inside the insurgency*. New York: IB Tauris & Co.

Cloward, R. (1959). Illegitimate means, anomie and deviant behavior. *American Sociological Review, 24*(2), 164–176.

Cloward, R., & Ohlin, L. (1960). *Delinquency and opportunity*. New York: Free Press.

CNN. (September 21, 2001). Bush delivers ultimatum. Retrieved on December 21, 2008, from http://archives.cnn.com/2001/WORLD/asiapcf/central/09/20/ret.afghan.bush/index.html

Coll, S. (February 22, 2004). Legal disputes over hunt paralyzed Clinton's aides. Washingtonpost.com. Retrieved on January 29, 2009, from http://www.washingtonpost.com/ac2/wp-dyn?pagename=article&contentId=A59781-2004Feb21

Congressional Digest. (April 2003). Total information awareness program: Counterterrorism and information technology. *Congressional Digest, 4*, 104–107.

Crenshaw, M. (2001). The psychology of terrorism: An agenda for the 21st century. *Political Psychology, 21*, 405–420.

DeMott, B. (October 2004). Whitewash as public service: How the 9/11 commission report defrauds the nation. *Harper's Magazine*. Retrieved on December 17, 2008, from http://www.harpers.org/archive/2004/10/0080234

Echevarria II, A. J. (2005). Fourth-generation warfare and other myths. Washington, DC: Strategic Policy Studies. Retrieved on December 17, 2008, from http://www.strategicstudiesinstitute.army.mil/pdffiles/pub632.pdf

Eggen, D. (August 2, 2006). 9/11 panel suspected deception by Pentagon. *Washington Post*, p. A3.

Eggen, D. (September 7, 2007). Judge invalidates patriot act provisions. *Washingtonpost.com*. Retrieved on January 20, 2008, from http://www.washingtonpost.com/wp-dyn/content/ article/2007/09/06/AR2007090601438_pf.html

Eldridge, T. R., Ginsburg, S., Hempel II, W. T., Kephart, J. L., Moore, K., & Accolla, J. A. (2004). 9/11 and Terrorist Travel: Staff Report of the national commission on terrorist attacks upon the United States. Retrieved on December 21, 2008, from http://govinfo. library.unt.edu/911/staff_statements/911_TerrTrav_Monograph.pdf

Elliot, M. (August 4, 2002). Could 9/11 have been prevented? *Time*. Retrieved on December 21, 2008, from http://www.time.com/time/nation/printout/0,8816,333835,00.html.

Ezekiel, R. S. (1995). *The Racist Mind*. New York: Penguin.

Fisk, R. (July 10, 1996). Interview with Saudi dissident Bin Laden. The Independent, London.

Gendar, A. (May 10, 2005). City's disaster plan draws fire. FDNY chief calls command system 'bad policy.' *New York Daily News*.

General Accounting Office. (May 2004). Data mining. Washington, DC: U.S. General Accounting Office.

German, M. & Stanley, J. (December 2007). *What's wrong with fusion centers?* Washington, DC: American Civil Liberties Union.

Gibbs, S. (2005). Islam and Islamic extremism: An existential analysis. *Journal of Humanistic Psychology, 45*(2), 156–203.

Gladwell, M. (March 10, 2003). Connecting the dots: The paradox of intelligence reform. *The New Yorker*.

Greig, D. W. (1976). *International law* (2nd ed.). London: Butterworths.

Gunarathna, R. (August 2001). Blowback, a special report on Al-Qaeda, *Jane's Intelligence Review*.

Gunarathna, R. (2002). *Inside Al Qaeda, global network of terror*. New York: Berkley Books.

Gwertzman, B. (August 3, 2004). Cordesman: 9/11 commission report lacks specificity. Interview with Anthony Cordesman, center for international and strategic studies in Washington. *Council on Foreign Relations*. Retrieved on December 12, 2008, from http://www.cfr.org/publication/ 7229/cordesman.html.

Hamm, M. (2005). Crimes committed by terrorist groups: Theory, research, and prevention. Final report to the National Institute of Justice, U.S. Department of Justice, Washington, DC: NCJ# 211203.

Harris, J. C. (2000). Revolutionary black nationalism: The black panther party. *Journal of Negro History, 86*(3), 409–421.

Henry, E. (April 23, 2004). Republicans amplify criticism of 9/11 commission. *CNN.com*. Retrieved on December 17, 2008, from http://www.cnn.com/2004/ALLPOLITICS/04/ 23/commission.senators/index.html

House of Commons Library Report. (2001). 11 September 2001: The response. Research Paper 01/72, International Affairs and Defense Section, House of Commons.

Huntington, S. P. (1996). *The clash of civilizations and the remaking of world order*. New York: Simon and Schuster.

Hura, M., McLeod, G., Larson, E. V., Schneider, J., Gonzales, D., Norton, D. M., et al. (2000). Interoperability: A continuing challenge in coalition air operations. *RAND monograph report*. Santa Monica, CA: RAND.

Isikoff, M. (July 28, 2003). The 9-11 report: Slamming the FBI. *Newsweek, 142*(4), 2–3.

Isikoff, M. & Klaidman, D. (June 4, 2002). The 9/11 terrorists the CIA should have caught. *Newsweek*.

Jehl, D. (December 27, 2001). A nation challenged: Saudi Arabia; Holy war lured Saudis as rulers looked away. *New York Times*.

Johnson, J. T. (June/July 2002). Jihad and just war. *First Things: The Journal of Religion, Culture and Public Life*, pp. 12–14. Retrieved on December 22, 2008, from http://www. firstthings.com/article.php3?id_article=2034

Kaplan, E. (March 18, 2003). Letter to president bush from Elaine Kaplan regarding allegations of mismanagement at the FAA. Retrieved on January 22, 2009, from http://www.osc.gov/documents/cltr3_02.pdf

Katovsky, B. (July 9, 2006). Flying the deadly skies. *San Francisco Chronicle.*

Katzman, K. (2005). Al Qaeda: Profile and threat assessment. Washington, DC: Congressional Research Service. Retrieved on December 21, 2008, from http://fas.org/sgp/crs/ terror/RL33038.pdf

Kean, T. H., & Hamilton, L. H. (January 2, 2008). Stonewalled by the CIA. New York Times.

Kelman, H. C. (1990). Applying a human needs perspective to the practice of conflict resolution: The Israeli-Palestinian case. In J. W. Burton (Ed.), *Conflict: Human needs theory.* New York: St. Martin's.

Lind, W. S., Nightengale, K., Schmitt, J. F., Sutton, J. W., & Wilson, G. I. (October 1989). The changing face of war: Into the fourth generation. *Marine Corps Gazette,* pp. 22–26.

Linzer, D., & Pincus, W. (October 6, 2005). CIA rejects discipline for 9/11 failures. *Washington Post.com.* Retrieved on January 22, 2009, from http://www.washingtonpost.com/wp-dyn/content/article/2005/10/05/AR2005100501503.html

Lueck, T. (September 30, 2005). Mayor's plan puts police commissioner in charge of disaster control. *New York Times.*

Markoff, J. (February 13, 2002). Chief takes over at agency to thwart attacks on U.S. *New York Times.*

Mazzetti, M. (December 22, 2007). 9/11 panel study finds CIA withheld tapes. *New York Times.*

McGarrell, E. F., Freilich, J., & Chermak, S. (2007). Intelligence-led policing as a framework for responding to terrorism. *Journal of Contemporary Criminal Justice, 23*(2), 142–158.

McKinsey Report. (August 19, 2002a). McKinsey report: Increasing FDNY's preparedness. Retrieved on December 22, 2008, from http://www.nyc.gov/html/fdny/html/mck_report/toc.html.

McKinsey Report. (August 19, 2002b). McKinsey report: Improving NYPD emergency preparedness and response. Retrieved on December 22, 2008, from http://www.nyc.gov/html/nypd/pdf/nypdemergency.pdf.

Mead, K. M. (August 16, 2002). Memorandum to Elaine Kaplan from inspector general Kenneth M. Mead on the results of the OIG investigation DI-02-0207. Retrieved on January 22, 2009 from http://www.osc.gov/documents/oscrt6.pdf

Merton, R. (1968). *Social theory and social structure.* New York: Free Press.

Miller, L. (2006). The terrorist mind: A psychological and political analysis. *International Journal of Offender Therapy and Comparative Criminology, 50*(2), 121–138.

National Commission on Terrorist Attacks Upon the United States. (2002a). *The 9/11 commission report.* New York: W. W. Norton.

National Commission on Terrorist Attacks Upon the United States. (2002b). Overview of the enemy. *Staff Statement,* No. 15, p. 2–3. Retrieved on December 23, 2008, from http://govinfo.library.unt.edu/911/staff_statements/staff_statement_15.pdf

National Commission on Terrorist Attacks Upon the United States. (2002c). Outline of the 9/11 plot. *Staff Statement,* No. 16, pp. 3, 6–10. Retrieved on December 23, 2008, from http://govinfo.library.unt.edu/911/staff_statements/staff_statement_16.pdf

National Commission on Terrorist Attacks Upon the United States. (2002d). The aviation security system and the 9/11 attacks. *Staff Statement,* No. 3. Retrieved on December 23, 2008, from http://govinfo.library.unt.edu/911/staff_statements/staff_statement_3.pdf

National Commission on Terrorist Attacks Upon the United States. (2002e). Diplomacy. *Staff Statement,* No. 5. Retrieved on December 23, 2008, from http://govinfo.library.unt.edu/911/staff_statements/staff_statement_5.pdf

National Commission on Terrorist Attacks Upon the United States. (2002f). Threats and responses in 2001. *Staff Statement,* No. 10. Retrieved on December 23, 2008, from http://govinfo.library.unt.edu/ 911/staff_statements/staff_statement_10.pdf

National Commission on Terrorist Attacks Upon the United States. (2002 g). Improvising a home-land defense. *Staff Statement*, No. 17. Retrieved on December 23, 2008, from http://govinfo.library.unt.edu/911/staff_statements/staff_statement_17.pdf

National Commission on Terrorist Attacks Upon the United States. (2002 h). Law enforce-ment, counterterrorism and intelligence collection in the United states prior to 9/11. *Staff Statement*, No. 9. Retrieved on December 23, 2008, from http://govinfo.library.unt.edu/911/staff_statements/staff_statement_9.pdf

National Task Force on Interoperability. (2003). Why can't we talk? Working together to bridge the communications gap to save lives. National Task Force on Interoperability, Washington, DC: NCJ# 204348.

New York Times. (June 23, 2002). Striking first. *New York Times*, p. C12.

Novarro, J. (2005). Hunting terrorists: *A look at the psychopathology of terror.* Springfield, IL: Charles C. Thomas.

PBS FrontLine. (2002). The man who knew. Retrieved on January 8, 2009, from http://www.pbs.org/ wgbh/pages/frontline/shows/knew/

PBS FrontLine. (2006). The insurgency. Retrieved on January 2, 2008, from http://www.pbs.org/wgbh/pages/frontline/insurgency/view/

Perkel, W. (2004). Money laundering and terrorism: Informal value transfer systems. *American Criminal Law Review, 41*, 183–213.

Pillar, P. (2001). *Terrorism and US foreign policy.* Washington, DC: Brookings Institute.

Qutb, S. (1981). *Milestones.* The Mother Mosque Foundation.

Ratcliffe, J. H. (2008). *Intelligence-led policing.* Cullompton: Willan Publishing.

Rhode, D. & Chivers, C. J. (March 17, 2002). A nation challenged; Qaeda's grocery lists and manuals of killing. *New York Times*.

Rhode, D., & Gall, C. (August 28, 2005). In a corner of Pakistan a debate rages: Are terrorist camps still functioning? *New York Times*.

Ridgeway, J. (2005). *The 5 unanswered questions about 9/11.* New York: Seven Stories Press.

Risen, J., & Lichtblau, E. (December 16, 2005). Bush lets U.S. spy on callers without courts. *New York Times,* p. A1.

Rosenbaum, W. A. (1975). *Poiiticai cuiture.* London: Neison.

Rosenzweig, P. (2003). Civil liberty and the response to terrorism. *Duquesne Law Review, 42*, 663–723.

Roth, J., Greenburg, D., & Wille, S. (n.d.). Monograph on terrorist financing. Washington, DC: Staff Report to the National Commission on Terrorist Attacks Upon the United States. Retrieved on December 21, 2008, from http://govinfo.library.unt.edu/911/staff_statements/911_TerrFin_Monograph.pdf

Schultz, R. H., & Vogt, A. (2003). It's war! Fighting post-11 September global terrorism through a doctrine of preemption. *Terrorism and Political Violence, 15*(1), 1–30.

Staub, E. (2003). Notes on cultures of violence, cultures of caring and peace, and the fulfillment of basic human needs. *Political Psychology, 24*(1), 1–21.

Sykes, G., & Matza, D. (1957). Techniques of neutralization: A theory of delinquency. *American Sociological Review. 22*(6), 664–670.

van Creveld, M. (1991). *Transformation of war.* New York: Free Press.

White, J. (2002). *Terrorism:* An introduction (3rd ed.). Belmont, CA: Wadsworth Publishing.

White House Press Release. (September 20, 2001). Address to a Joint Session of Congress and the American People. Retrieved on January 5, 2009, from http://www.whitehouse.gov/news/releases/2001/09/20010920-8.html

Williams, M. (April 26, 2006). The total information awareness project lives on. *Technology Review.*

Wright, L. (2006). *The looming tower: Al-Qaeda and the road to 9/11.* New York: Alfred A. Knopf.

Zinser, T. J. (August 31, 2006). Results of OIG investigation of 9/11 commission staff refer-ral. *Memorandum.* Retrieved on January 22, 2009, from http://www.coherentbabble.com/signingstatements/ExecAgencies/DeptTrans-PIG-08-31-2006.pdf

Chapter 8
Aviation Security in the Face of Tragedy

The FAA has done an inadequate job of insuring that the security network which they require to be in place is performing adequately. Moreover, the FAA seems incapable of keeping abreast of the changing security needs of American airlines. Their history has been to guard against the last attack, not stop the next one (Yeffet from Hearings before the Government Activities and Transportation Committee, 1989, p. 17).

Introduction

As long as people are flying, there will be a need for aviation security. Secure air transportation is an important issue not only domestically, but also internationally. Airlines are seen as national symbols. Airline disasters receive media attention disproportionate to the death toll and, if mass casualties are the goal, an airplane provides hundreds of people at 30,000 feet with no chance of survival. For these reasons, airlines will always be an attractive target for terrorists making aviation security a top priority.

However, security problems are often addressed only after a disaster occurs. Every tragedy leads to cries for reform, such as following the bombing of Pan Am Flight 103 in 1988. For this reason, the Federal Aviation Administration has been referred to as the "tombstone agency" in that change only comes about when people die and even then, in limited quantities (Cobb & Primo, 2003).

The purpose of this chapter is to examine the fallibility of aviation security both past and present by discussing the bombing of Pan Am Flight 103 over Lockerbie, Scotland.

C. Hougham (✉)
John Jay College and the Graduate Center, City University of New York, New York, NY, USA
e-mail: chougham@gc.cuny.edu

M.R. Haberfeld, A. von Hassell (eds.), *A New Understanding of Terrorism*,
DOI 10.1007/978-1-4419-0115-6_8, © Springer Science+Business Media, LLC 2009

Relevant Aviation Security Prior to the Bombing
of Pan Am Flight 103

In 1958, the Federal Aviation Act created the Federal Aviation Agency, which was an independent agency devoted to regulating the airline industry. This independence was short lived when in 1966 the agency was renamed the Federal Aviation Administration (FAA) and came under the control of the Department of Transportation (DOT). The DOT is responsible for all manners of transportation from ground to air to water.

The FAA was given two objectives: overseeing safety concerns and airline regulations and promoting airline businesses (Cobb & Primo, 2003). These two objectives often came into conflict with one another with promotion of airlines often overshadowing the focus on safety. Despite this conflict, it was not until 1996 that the objectives were changed, and the emphasis was placed on safety over promotion.

With numerous Cuban hijackings taking place during the 1960s, the FAA developed a "hijacker profile" and in 1970 created an anti-hijacking program. Part of the program was the introduction of Federal air marshals – a program that had disappeared by the 1990s, but has reappeared.

In early 1972, bombs were discovered on three American airlines. In reaction to these bombs, the FAA made carry-on inspection and passenger scanning mandatory by 1973 (Rumerman, n.d).

The early 1980s witnessed the introduction of improvised explosive devices (IEDs) on airlines. The Yesilkoy incident occurred in 1983. A security procedure at Istanbul's Yesilkoy Airport was in place where baggage being loaded onto the plane was matched with passengers on board. During this procedure, a bag was found that did not match any passenger on board. When the bag was searched, a bomb was found. The flight had been scheduled to connect with a Pan Am flight to the United States (Wallis, 2001).

In 1985, the Kanishka, an Air India jumbo jet exploded after a passenger had a bag with a bomb loaded onto a flight in Vancouver, which would later connect to an Air India flight in Toronto. Air India was the first airline to start bag/passenger matching; however, this did not apply to bags and passengers connecting from other airlines (Wallis, 2001). The passenger checked his bag in Vancouver. He did not have a seat on the Air India flight, which meant he should have had to reclaim his bag in Toronto. After becoming irate with the check-in agent, his bag was checked through to Toronto and then on to Bombay. In Vancouver, the passenger did not show, but his bag was not removed from the luggage hold. Once in Toronto, his bag labeled with a transfer tag was loaded on to the Air India flight with no record of this passenger. The bomb exploded killing all on board and bringing the plane down in the Irish Sea where there was no chance of recovering evidence or finding the perpetrators.

Responding to the Air India bombing, a meeting of the International Air Transportation Association (IATA) was called for airline security chiefs and it was determined that passenger/bag matching should be a mandatory requirement. The only US airline to send a representative was TWA, as the rest of the airlines viewed the Air India problem as "foreign" and irrelevant (Wallis, 2001).

The International Civil Aviation Organization (ICAO) legislated that for international flights, bags and passengers must be identified, and any bags belonging to "no shows" should be unloaded. The ICAO mandated that this be done by December 19, 1987. One-way airlines got around this mandate was if the baggage had been subject to x-ray or other security measures and deemed transportable even if the owner was not present (Wallis, 2001).

The FAA did not take the Air India bombing quite as lightly as the American airlines had. Prior to the ICAO even publishing its legislation, the FAA implemented a requirement of passenger/bag matching for US airlines at "extraordinary risk" airports (Wallis, 2001). If a bag did not match a passenger, the bag was required to be searched and/or left behind.

Unfortunately, this mandate was not received well by the airlines. The opposition came from the fact that the airlines would be responsible for the additional resources needed to match all baggage and the extra time could cause delays. In the airline industry, delays mean angry customers.

Events Leading Up to the Bombing

Political Context

From 1981 to the months prior to the bombing of Pan Am Flight 103, tension in the Middle East was increasing. In 1981, two Libyan fighter aircraft were shot down in the Gulf of Sidra by the US Navy; the sinking of two Libyan radio ships followed this. In January of 1986, Reagan threatened all economic ties with Libya calling the country "a threat to national security and foreign policy of the United States" (Wallis, 2001, p. 14).

In March of 1986 a Libyan Navy patrol boat was sunk. One month later, a West Berlin nightclub, patronized by the US soldiers, was bombed. The CIA intercepted incriminatory messages from Libya allegedly placing them behind the bombing. In retaliation, Reagan deployed a US plane to bomb the Libyan cities of Tripoli and Benghazi. In the US bombing, Colonel Qaddafi's home was destroyed killing his adopted daughter. Colonel Qaddafi offered Libya as a base for Palestinian liberation groups and a training ground for Arab guerillas (Wallis, 2001). Reagan reacted by increasing the military in the Mediterranean, especially off the coast of Libya. The US Navy set one Libyan ship on fire and almost destroyed another. The US aircraft also attacked a missile site. In addition to bombing, the United States imposed sanctions on Libya in 1986 freezing all Libyan assets and prohibiting the US trade. The FAA issued a warning to the US airlines about possible acts of revenge.

The United States was not only having trouble with Libya; in 1988, the US shot down Iran Air Flight 655 – a commercial airline – mistaking it for an F-14 fighter plane. The USS Vincennes fired two missiles bringing down the airline and killing all 290 passengers on board. Iran vowed revenge on the United States for this atrocity. The situation with the Libyans and the Iranians set the stage for retribution from one or both of these countries or any Middle Eastern terrorist group.

Intelligence Reports and Warnings

During the months prior to the Pan Am bombing, Frankfurt authorities had arrested members of the Popular Front for the Liberation of Palestine-General Command (PFLP-GC) founded by Ahmed Jibril, a splinter group of the Palestinian Liberation Organization (PLO). The German police had been conducting surveillance on the group, which they called "Operation Autumn Leaves" (Leppard, 1991). This surveillance eventually led to raids on the apartments of several men. In these raids, the German police confiscated several IEDs made by Marwan Khreesat, including some made out of Toshiba cassette recorders. These IEDs contained Semtex, a plastic explosive, and a dual detonation mechanism utilizing both barometric and timing devices; the inclusion of a barometric detonation mechanism made it clear that these devices were meant bringing down an airliner.

Following this discovery, the FAA issued three bulletins (Leppard, 1991). The first, dated November 11, 1988, was sent to United States and British security offices warning that the German authorities had found a Toshiba radio bomb. The second bulletin dated November 22, 1988, was a "general threat" warning to airlines. Finally, on December 19, 1988, two days before the bombings, the FAA issued the third bulletin in which they gave the full details of the IEDs; thus, it took almost 2 months after the raids before the FAA released full details of the makeshift bomb. Although the FAA recognized that these IEDs were the method of choice, their advice was to "stick rigorously to existing security measures" (Johnston, 1989, p. 171), even though they admitted that devices such as the Toshiba design "would be very difficult to detect by normal x-ray" (Wallis, 2001, p. 42). The existing security measures included bag/passenger matching.

In addition to these FAA warnings, the CIA knew about a meeting of the Libyan Intelligence Service in November of 1988 (Leppard, 1991). They had passed on a warning to Western intelligence, but the warning was ignored.

Lastly, on December 5, 1988, the US Embassy in Helsinki received a phone message in which the caller described a threat of a bomb on a Pan Am flight leaving Frankfurt and heading toward the United States within 2 weeks – this has come to be known as the "Helsinki warning." Pan Am and other agencies were informed of the threat, but it was dismissed as a hoax despite the fact that Frankfurt had many active terrorist cells. Many believed that with the Autumn Leaves raids by the German authorities that the threat was over and all the IEDs in Frankfurt had been discovered, even though intelligence suggested that this was not the case (Leppard, 1991). Thus, the Helsinki warning was never circulated to the Alert Management Systems, the security company for Pan Am at Frankfurt Airport (Johnston, 1989).

The Bombing of Pan Am Flight 103

On December 21, 1988, Pan Am Flight 103, which had originated in Frankfurt, Germany, left Heathrow Airport in London; 38 min into the flight, the plane exploded over Lockerbie, Scotland, scattering debris and destroying houses. All 259 passengers and crew were killed – 189 of the passengers were Americans. Eleven residents were killed on the ground in Lockerbie. It is believed that the explosion was timed to take place over the Atlantic Ocean, thus destroying evidence, but the plane had been delayed in Heathrow. Although devastating, the fact that the plane exploded over land allowed for recovery of evidence, which in 1991 nearly 3 years after the bombing, led police to two Libyan men, Lamen Khalifa Fhimah and Abdel Basset Ali Al-Megrahi, neither of which had actually boarded the plane.

Despite the FAA's advice that airlines "rigorously apply" security, including the requirement of bag/passenger matching at "extraordinary risk" airports, including Frankfurt, the FAA was unaware that Pan Am had discontinued this practice at Frankfurt earlier in the year. Despite the Helsinki warning, or perhaps because it was deemed a hoax, Pan Am failed to reinstate bag/passenger matching in Frankfurt and the FAA failed to monitor whether the airlines were complying with federal regulations. The FAA had made the rule, but the airlines and the airports had the responsibility for passenger and baggage screening (Szyliowicz, 2004).

When Pan Am Flight 103A from Frankfurt landed at Heathrow, luggage was transferred directly on to Pan Am Flight 103 without being counted, weighed, or matched to passengers (Wallis, 2001). In Frankfurt, the bags may have been subject to x-ray screenings, but it is doubtful whether x-rays would have picked up the explosive device hidden in a Toshiba radio. It was also later discovered that despite the warnings, Frankfurt was still using "profile screening" on the day of the bombing. This meant that anyone carrying a UK, US, or West German passport was not considered a threat and only the checked luggage of other passport holders was being x-rayed (Johnston, 1989). Unfortunately, Pan Am relied heavily on x-ray procedures and ignored the FAA mandate to hand search and remove any unaccompanied bag. This reliance on x-rays had continued despite the Helsinki warning.

There is not much published about the planning of the attacks or the men behind them. What we do know is that Fhimah had links to Air Malta airline security and was said to have obtained Air Malta luggage tags for Al-Megrahi. Al-Megrahi was a member of the Jamahirya Security Organization (JSO), the intelligence service of Libya. The JSO was believed to have supplied its operatives with Semtex, detonators, and electric timers, thus making the operation apparently funded and supported by the Qaddafi regime in Libya (Cox & Foster, 1992). Investigators discovered that Al-Megrahi and a Samsonite suitcase containing a bomb were both aboard a flight in Malta. The flight landed in Frankfurt and the bag was transferred to Pan Am Flight 103A; Al-Megrahi did not board that flight. The bag remained on board and was transferred to Pan Am Flight 103 in Heathrow bound for the United States. Despite the various intelligence reports warning of an eminent attack, it still happened. Although communication between intelligence agencies security agencies was not ideal, in the end it was the aviation security that failed.

The Response

The response to the bombing of Pan Am Flight 103 was an enormous undertaking. From the beginning, more than a dozen agencies from several countries were all trying to gain control of the investigation (Leppard, 1991). In fact, this was the first international terrorist investigation where the Federal Bureau of Investigation (FBI) operated overseas (Johnston, 1989). Unfortunately, for many of the agencies involved, the motivation was not a desire to solve the case, but the understanding that the first team to do so would receive the praise (Leppard, 1991). Thus, not only was there a struggle for control, but the various agencies came to resent other agencies being involved leading to a breakdown in communication and a reluctance to share information. In the end, five countries were involved in the disaster, with an absence of international authority (Szyliowicz, 2004).

Fire Department Response

The fire department arrived on the scene shortly after the crash. After surveying the scene, the "major incident plan" was implemented (Leppard, 1991). The major incident plan referred to calling in other, outside organizations. However, any airline crash scenario had only been planned for a small plane; there were no thoughts of a possible jetliner crashing and the massive scale of destruction that would occur including the area that the crash would cover.

Military Response

In the United Kingdom, rescue and investigative work lies in the hands of the area's chief constable, but the United Kingdom allows civilian authorities to request help from the military in a time of crisis (Wallis, 2001). In the case of Lockerbie, the Royal Air Force (RAF) and the army acted before their help was sought. RAF helicopters were used to make aerial surveillance photos of the scene and soldiers were used for search and recovery and all help was needed with 845 square miles to cover (Leppard, 1991).

Police Response

Pan Am Flight 103 crashed in Dumfries and Galloway in Scotland, which had one of the smallest police forces in the country (Leppard, 1991). Chief Constable Boyd remained in charge of the investigation for the first 8 months. This small police force in Scotland was in no way equipped for the type of disaster that had occurred, which slowed the search and recovery process. Chief Constable Boyd was dealing with poor radio communication, which impeded the ability to coordinate his team and others effectively (Leppard, 1991). Due to the presence of so many outside agencies, there was often a repetition of tasks – relatives questioned by as many as three groups of police officers, the same areas searched more than once, etc. (Leppard, 1991). It is unlikely that any police force would have been prepared for such a massive disaster and as such, confusion reigned for several days following the crash.

Boyd called the Strathclyde police force, also in Scotland; the Strathclyde police force was the largest outside of London (Leppard, 1991). Strathclyde sent John Orr and he was made the Senior Investigative Officer.

Despite the second largest police force in the United Kingdom being called in, the British prime minister pushed for London's Metro Police – New Scotland Yard – to take over the investigation. This was not well received by the Scottish Lord Advocate who insisted the Scottish police forces remain in charge. The Scottish police resented the presence of the London Metro Police. Meanwhile the Scottish police and the FBI remained in close contact and communication.

International Investigative Response

The FBI was having its own problems in the investigation. Since this was their first overseas investigation, they were under extreme pressure in the United States. The State Department was telling Washington journalists that the FBI was botching the case; in return, the FBI told reporters at CBS that they knew the exact identity of the bomber and an arrest was imminent (Johnston, 1989). This statement was made in April 1989, about 2 years before the suspects were actually identified.

In addition to the clashes going on between the UK police forces and the US investigative branches, there was also the West German police force (BKA) with which to contend. The Scottish police sent a liaison to West German to gather intelligence on the "Autumn Leaves" group – the group of men from the PFLP-GC who had been arrested as they were considered the prime suspects. The BKA were reluctant to cooperate and the Scottish officer believed information was being kept from him. The BKA refused to see a connection between the PFLP-GC group that they had arrested in Germany and the Pan Am bombing even though the IEDs were remarkably similar to those they had confiscated in the raids. For a year after the bombings, despite evidence to the contrary, the BKA was still claiming that the bomb had been loaded onto the plane in Heathrow rather than Frankfurt as admitting it had originated in Frankfurt would have meant admitting a lapse in intelligence and security.

As further evidence of the clash between agencies, it was not until 3 months into the investigation that all the agencies met for the first time to exchange information. With such a massive investigation, it would seem that a meeting and sharing of ideas between all agencies involved should have taken place sooner. Senior Investigator, Orr, used this meeting to make a connection between the bombing and the German cell of the PFLP-GC. He also used this meeting to express that he believed the BKA had been withholding information and evidence (Leppard, 1991).

Intelligence Response

The Central Intelligence Agency (CIA) was involved in the investigation, which should not come as a surprise given that many of those who died were American citizens. However, according to Johnston (1989), the CIA was there for a different reason. Some of their operatives were on the plane and they had been carrying top-secret documents that needed to be recovered from the debris. According to Johnston, the CIA found the documents they were looking for and took the evidence, breaking the "rules" of the Scottish police for evidence handling. The evidence was returned eventually, but chain of custody had been broken.

While the police, the CIA, and the FBI were conducting their investigation, the Joint Intelligence Group (JIG) was conducting a separate, yet parallel investigation (Leppard, 1991). The JIG was headed by John Armstrong in the United Kingdom. Armstrong was receiving information from both the domestic counter intelligence agency and the agency gathering foreign intelligence. Orr, who was heading the police investigation, was not privy to this intelligence directly – he had to receive all intelligence through John Armstrong (Leppard, 1991). Interestingly, the JIG had no experience in Middle Eastern terrorist groups, yet they were in control of all intelligence.

The Investigation

Regardless of all the confusion and struggles for control, the investigation continued. In order to collect and store the information in a convenient and efficient manner, the Home Office Large Major Enquiry System (HOLMES) was used. This system was designed to collect massive amounts of information relating to a large-scale investigation. Those involved in the investigation could access from the HOLMES outside of Lockerbie (Wallis, 2001).

The Royal Armament Research and Development Establishment (RARDE), which is a group which deals with terrorist incidents using bombs, was called in for their forensic expertise. This group first discovered that Semtex was used in creation of the bomb; they also identified a circuit board found at the crash site by the British Air Accidents Investigations Branch (AAIB) as a Toshiba. This information pointed toward the PFLP-GC group in Germany.

After all the large debris had been cleared, Boyd set up a "productions-search" team to search two wreckage trails that had been identified by the AAIB. The job of this special team was to search meticulously those trails for the smallest bits of evidence. This team discovered pieces of the suitcase that had held the bomb. Based on those pieces, the suitcase was identified as a Samsonite and it was a model that was only sold in the Middle East (Leppard, 1991). By reconstructing the plane's baggage containers, it was determined that this bag had been one of the first on the plane in Heathrow and that it was in a container that held bags that had transferred from the Frankfurt flight. No link was ever discovered between the bag and a passenger on board, pointing to the fact that the bag had boarded without a corresponding passenger.

Although the PFLP-GC was still the prime suspect, a piece of evidence was discovered that started to point the finger away from that terror group and toward the Libyan government. A small piece of a timer was found in the debris. This piece led police to a Swiss communications firm (MEBO) which had only made a limited amount of that particular timer in a special order for the Libyan government. All the timers had been received by the JSO implicating the Qaddafi regime (Cox & Foster, 1992).

With this evidence, the PLFP-GC was ruled out as suspects for the bombing, though it is possible that they shared information with other groups on the construction of the IED. The bomb that exploded on Pan Am Flight 103 had only one detonator, a timing device, unlike those confiscated in the Frankfurt raids, which had both a barometric detonator and a timing device, but the remainder of the apparatus was remarkably similar. One theory is that Jibril, the head of the PFLP-GC in West Germany, went to Qaddafi after his cell had been broken up in the Autumn Leaves raid in order to find someone else who was sympathetic to his cause and would be willing to carry out the bombing (Leppard, 1991).

The Aircraft Accident Investigation Branch presented their findings on August 6, 1990 – a year and a half after the explosion. The investigation uncovered that the bomb had been constructed out of a Toshiba cassette recorder with residue of Semtex, a plastic explosive, with a timing device mechanism as the detonator. The bomb was concealed in the suitcase amidst a variety of objects including men's clothing, child's pajamas, and an umbrella (Wallis, 2001). Through recovered labels, investigators were able to trace the items to Malta where they were manufactured and, ultimately, to the store where they had been sold. The clerk in the store identified Al-Megrahi as the man who had purchased the items. Based on the evidence Lamen Khalifa Fhimah and Abdel Basset Ali Al-Megrahi were charged with the explosion in 1991. The Libyan government refused to hand over the suspects, as they had no extradition laws with the United States or any other country.

Diplomatic Response

In an effort to force the Libyan government to hand over the suspects, in 1992 the United Nations imposed an arms and air embargo, froze Libyan funds, and prohibited sale of oil-related equipment. The United States went a step further and increased the sanction they already had in place by prohibiting military and other exports and cutting off commercial air traffic.

In 1999, Qaddafi finally handed the two suspects over to authorities, although they still claimed they were not behind the bombing. The men were tried in a "neutral" environment, the Netherlands, since no one country had jurisdiction. Fhimah was found not guilty, but Al-Megrahi was given a life sentence with a recommendation that he serve at least 20 years. His first appeal was denied in 2002.

In May of 2002, the United Nations told Libya that the sanctions against the country would be lifted if the government accepted responsibility for the bombing of Pan Am Flight 103 and denounced terrorism. Libya agreed, although they never admitted guilt; they agreed to the terms for economical reasons, it appears, and not out of remorse or regret. Libya offered $2.7 billion to the victim's families, but would only fully release the funds when three conditions had been met: if UN sanctions were cancelled, the US trade sanctions lifted, and if Libya was removed from the list of states sponsoring terrorism. In October of 2008, 20 years after the bombing, Libya paid the final installment after then President George W. Bush signed an order that gives Libya immunity from terror-related lawsuits and dismisses any pending US compensation cases.

This case does not seem to be over. On April 27, 2009, Al-Megrahi was allowed to start a second appeal based on new information. First, the shopkeeper who identified Al-Megrahi in Malta was allegedly offered a "huge payment" from the CIA for identifying Al-Megrahi (Carrell, 2007). Second, the head of MEBO was purportedly offered $4 million from the FBI to testify that the timer found at the Lockerbie site had been delivered to Libya, though he refused the offer (International Progress Organization, BBC Interview, 2007). Finally, a former MEBO employee claims to have stolen one of the prototype timers and given it to an investigator in the Lockerbie case; he has also admitted to lying at the trial about whether this was the same type of timer delivered to the Libyan government (Smith, 2007). This new information casts doubts on the key witnesses for the prosecution and suggests the intelligence agencies investigating may have been a little overzealous to obtain a conviction.

Although the appeal process has started, the Libyan government has applied to the Scottish government for a prisoner transfer agreement to allow Al-Megrahi to finish his sentence in Libya. In order for the Scottish government to approve the agreement, Al-Megrahi will have to drop his appeal (Johnson, 2009). Last year Al-Megrahi was diagnosed with prostate cancer and his health is failing; dropping the appeal and accepting the prisoner transfer agreement would allow him to return to his home country and be closer to his family while serving the rest of his sentence (Johnson, 2009). The Scottish government has said the decision could take more than 90 days; as of this writing, there has been no ruling.

Analysis

Every disaster brings with it the cries for reform; however, what other reforms and policies could have prevented the Lockerbie tragedy? It can be said that something went seriously wrong on that fateful day in December including a breakdown of communication between security agencies and a disregard for the policy (passenger/bag matching) that had been in place for 2 years and that could have prevented the disaster. The problem fell with the FAA's inability to monitor compliance to rules and regulations. It is one thing to make a rule, but there should be methods in place to ensure the rule is being followed – especially in light of specific information. However, it would be close to impossible for the FAA to be able to monitor every US airline at every destination around the world; there must be some trust that the airline is doing what it is supposed to do to ensure the safety of its passengers.

After the Helsinki warning, the FAA could have required a discontinuation of allowing passengers to travel with any electronic device. Not only would passengers be irate, but also the time and effort required to institute such a policy would be immense. One European airline did attempt to place a ban on all battery-powered articles resulting in thousands of items being confiscated and chaos in the airport (Wallis, 2001). Obviously, this was not the solution.

The following are a list of possible policy implementations to improve aviation security:

- Bag/passenger matching
- Working screening devices supplemented with manual searches
- More training and employee incentives
- International cooperation
- Improved ability to monitor airline compliance with regulation
- Independent nongovernment agency to create standards and impose them
- Improved psychological profiling of passengers
- Enforced restricted access to secure areas
- Subject cargo to decompression chamber prior to loading
- Federal manpower supplemented with private security firms

Although every item on this list is practical and logical, they are not all feasible in the face of a large and complex airline industry.

Following Lockerbie, in 1989, a House bill requested $279 billion in order to tighten security and purchase new bomb detection machines (Cobb & Primo, 2003). This bill was denied in the Senate.

The reason reform is so difficult is threefold. First, new security measures are expensive, but it is difficult to determine their effectiveness. Despite the occasional tragedy, air travel remains the safest mode of travel. One can never know how much of that safety is due to new security measures.

Second, security technology is expensive and it is still developing. Airlines that are already in debt do not have the money to spend on machines that will be obsolete in 1–2 years. Finally, the domestic airline system is much more complicated than in other countries, making security and reform issues that much more complex.

The tragedy at Lockerbie led to the 1990 Aviation Security Act. This Act was comprised of 64 recommendations for reform in four major areas. The first area was the implementation of explosive detection devices. The FAA required that these be developed and in place by November 1993. By that date, only one system was in place (Cobb & Primo, 2003). In a recent publication by the United States General Accounting Office, these machines – explosive detection systems (EDS) and explosive trace detection (ETD) equipment – were unstaffed or in disrepair and thus, not being used. The reliance on this technology should be limited and supplemented with manual checks; yet, this would be a timely process, so staff must be trained to identify suspicious items and then search manually. However, if the machines are not working, it is doubtful that all bags are being searched.

The second area for improvement was background checks for the previous 10 years on all airline employees. This was implemented in 1996 and only required that the previous 5 years be checked. Background checks can be misleading. Just because an employee has no criminal record does not make him any less subject to employee misconduct. The check-in agent in Vancouver could have prevented the Air India bombing if she had not given in to the demands of an irate customer. A background check does not guard against employee incompetence or nonchalance. In addition, 5 years is not a very comprehensive background check. A sleeper agent could easily lay low and infiltrate an airline. A background check, while useful for eliminating some prospective employees, is not a safeguard against all possible employee problems.

The third area was increased training for screeners. The FAA, in 1993, imposed 8 h of classroom training and 4 h hands-on. This training time was increased following September 11, but the effectiveness is questionable. Regardless of hours spent training, if an employee is not motivated to do his job effectively through competitive salary rates, rewards, or possibilities for advancement, then training will be rendered useless.

The fourth area was passenger/bag matching – the same policy that had been put into effect in 1986. In 1995, the FAA recommended bag/passenger matching on domestic flights. After the decision in 1986 that this was an invaluable procedure, it is a wonder that it took the FAA another 9 years to recommend it domestically. Bag/passenger matching is not always the solution; some items are carried on to the plane by someone who is unaware of what is contained in the item. The bag and passenger would be a match and would not raise suspicion.

To counter this, airlines are supposed to ask six questions when a passenger is checking in, including "Has anyone asked you to carry anything?" and "Have your bags been in your possession at all times?" This author, prior to 2004 had been asked these mandatory questions about half of the time and only these two questions with no mention of the other four. Since 2004, this author has not been asked these questions at any US airport whether flying domestically or internationally. One way the airlines have gotten around this rule has been to post the questions, which complies with FAA rules.

Other countries appear to be taking this line of security more seriously. For example, security in both the Manchester airport in the United Kingdom and Charles de Gaulle International in Paris stop all customers in the check-in line, take their passport, and scan it into the computer. Customers are then asked a pretty intense line of questioning regarding where and when bags were packed, the number of electronics in your bags, whether they have been repaired or loaned out recently, when you purchased them, etc. It is enough to make even an innocent passenger feel unnerved.

On El Al Airlines, similar questions are asked in addition to "When did you purchase the ticket?" and "How did you pay for the ticket?" This line of questioning allows the security guard, not the check-in agent, time to examine the person's demeanor and identify suspicious behavior. Passengers may be subject to questioning by up to three different screeners (Shuman, 2001). Questions posted on a countertop do little in the way of eliciting an evasive or suspicious response. Had the 9/11 hijackers been asked these routine questions, red flags would have gone up immediately and disaster might have been prevented. The men had paid an enormous amount of money in cash for their tickets, the tickets were one way and purchased the day before the flight, and they had no luggage – all indicators that something was not quite right. One simple policy that barely takes any time or effort could have prevented catastrophe.

Furthermore, bag/passenger matching will not work on a terrorist who is willing to die for his cause. Such was the case in the 2004 Russian plane bombings. The women suspected of the act boarded the plane along with their luggage. They had initially been questioned for suspicious behavior, but after scalping a ticket and bribing an airline agent, they were allowed on the planes. Bag/passenger matching is not a match for employee misconduct.

Overall, the airlines resisted, opposing measures that would take time and money. Due to this opposition and lobbying by the airlines, few of the 64 recommendations were implemented. This begs the question, was the FAA the appropriate agency to regulate the airlines if it was so quick to back down in the face of opposition? Surprisingly, the FAA's objectives were still safety and promotion of airlines as late as 1996 when Congress changed the focus to safety alone. It is no wonder opposition to reform was met with concessions from an agency that was mainly interested in promoting the business side while the safety issue fell to second priority. There should not be conflict between the regulatory agency and the industry it is regulating where the industry is allowed, like a whiny child, to prevail in the end.

Post 9/11, President Bush established a Transportation Security Administration (TSA) within the DOT responsible for security for all modes of transportation. Perhaps with domestic air service being so complicated, the agency designated to overseeing aviation security should be specific to air travel and not responsible for all modes of transportation. As was the case with the FAA, the TSA will not be able to monitor compliance with new security measures, leaving the door open for airlines to continue to do as they please.

Under the Aviation and Transportation Act, the Federal government has been given the responsibility of all passenger and baggage screening doing so with 60,000 federal workers. There is no evidence that federal screeners will perform any better than screeners from a private firm. In fact, the evidence in the report from the General Accounting Office is that the new screening responsibilities are cognitively taxing and they are difficult for personnel. The training required is difficult to complete due to staffing shortages; thus, training is often not completed (Berrick, 2004).

The new government mandate requires that 100% of checked baggage be screened. In order to accomplish this, airlines were setting up giant screening machines in the ticketing area and the TSA agreed to these makeshift arrangements to meet the deadline, but the airline will have to spend additional monies to have the machines installed permanently (Szyliowicz, 2004). Not only are these machines an eyesore, but passengers are required to walk luggage over and drop it off. Anyone is able to walk up and drop off luggage without showing so much as a ticket or identification. As of 2009, passengers at several airports, including one major New York airport, are still being made to drop their checked baggage off at the screening machine. The screeners do not ask for a boarding pass; they just take the baggage.

Even if the bags are screened, there is no guarantee that they will be screened properly or that the type of device like that employed in Lockerbie would be detected, especially if the explosive detection machines are not functioning properly. Every electronic device can be checked against the manufacturer's diagram to find any unexplained wires inside (Wain, 1998). One can hardly imagine an underpaid, overworked government employee taking the time to check for additional wires in an electronic device. At a major airport, a screener asked this author about the electronic contents he had seen in the carry-on luggage after he screened it twice. When the reply was "an iPod," (this was before iPod became the household name that it is today) he looked puzzled and then cleared the bag without once looking inside. An appropriately trained screener should at least know to look, but this author did not fit a profile.

Additionally, even if the machines are working, it requires the vigilance of the screener to detect that something is wrong. This author, while waiting on a rather long check-in line, watched the checked bag screeners get up from their seat in front of the monitor several times while bags were coming through and still mark the bag with the TSA sticker indicating that it had been screened. Technically, it had gone through the screening machine, but if no one is watching what is screened, does it matter?

The media is no help in aviation security. Since 9/11, there have been numerous reports about investigators sneaking explosives and weapons past screeners. A *USA Today* article (9/23/2004) reported that it had done this at 15 airports nationwide ("Airport screeners missed weapons", 2004). They also reported that the airports had not installed equipment to check for explosives on all passengers and carry-on luggage. This type of report does nothing except to point out flaws giving ideas to those who are looking to carry out attacks against the aviation system.

Even the airing of the presidential debates in 2004 contained telling information that could be regarded as potentially dangerous. Presidential candidate John Kerry repeatedly pointed out that items put into the cargo hold on commercial airliners were not subject to screening. The Israeli airline, El Al, subjects all items in the cargo hold to a decompression chamber that reproduces the barometric pressure of the airplane in flight (Shuman, 2001). By doing this, any potential bomb with a barometric detonation device will explode on the ground and cause less damage. This would not have stopped the bomb on Pan Am Flight 103, as that had a timing device, but this concept still has merit and is worth examining further.

A further suggestion following the bombing of Pan Am Flight 103 was to make the cargo hold more bomb resistant by increasing the thickness of walls in the plane. This was immediately dismissed by the airlines as too expensive.

The intelligence network is getting better and communication between jurisdictions is improving, even the TSA is reacting faster by implementing security measures in the face of a threat, but that is still the problem – they are reacting rather than anticipating. In 2001, Richard Reid failed in an attempt to ignite a bomb he had hidden in his shoe; passengers are now required to remove their shoes at most of the major US airports and up until 2007 were not allowed to bring matches on the plane.

In 2006, police in the United Kingdom uncovered a plot to bring liquid explosives concealed in sports drink bottles onto several US-bound flights. Immediately the TSA banned all liquid from being brought on a flight, causing chaos in the airports. This ban was then relaxed to a "3-1-1" system where a passenger is allowed to bring 3 ounces of liquid in a 1-quart zip-top bag. More than 80 countries have adopted this policy (TSA website). However, the reason behind relaxing the rules is cause for concern. Limited quantities of liquid are now allowed because "multiple people working together to mix volatile explosives beyond the checkpoint" was not determined to be a viable scenario (TSA website). Unfortunately, that naïve mentality leads to vulnerability and the need to react rather than anticipate and prevent. History has shown (i.e., September 11) that well-motivated groups and individuals *are* willing to work together to inspire fear and wreak havoc on the populace.

Although it seems counter-productive to create a rule and then relax it, the TSA is under intense pressure from the airlines to improve efficiency, mostly in the face of security standards. Passengers do not want to wait in long security lines, they want to be able to carry what they want on the plane and complaints fall on the airline, not the TSA.

The TSA is also not to blame for the policy of reactance; it would be impossible to anticipate every possible action. Therefore, the real pressure lies in international intelligence agencies to discover a threat before it turns into a reality. This is what makes what happened on Pan Am Flight 103 so disconcerting – the intelligence was there and warnings were put out, but they went largely ignored.

Finally, nothing can be accomplished without international security standards, not only for American airlines, but for international airlines as well. The ICAO has 184 member states, but provides only minimal security standards (Szyliowicz, 2004). Certain member states are unwilling or incapable of providing the necessary levels of security to prevent terrorist activity. The ICAO can set the standards, but has no authority to ensure the standards are being enacted making it a rather useless organization.

Conclusions

Aviation security has consequences domestically and internationally. The bombing of Pan Am Flight 103 was the result of a breakdown in the required implementation of an FAA policy, specifically bag/passenger matching. A few simple checks and disaster could have been averted. The incident points out one of the major flaws in the aviation security system, which despite all the calls for reform, still remains the major problem – the inability of the regulatory government agency, both domestically and internationally, to monitor compliance with its rules and regulations. This aspect should be one of the major focuses of any reform movement.

Many disasters were the result of simple human error or reliance on technology that is not 100% accurate. Airlines and agencies need to understand the human and technological fallibilities and have ways of imposing double-checks. In order to do this, the security staff must have full manpower, accurate training, and a reason to do their job properly. The federal screening system put in place by President Bush cannot accomplish, nor afford, these goals. Federal manpower should be supplemented by private security firms held to the same, or higher, standards as the Federal workers and airlines should be held accountable when they breach protocol.

The FAA was a reactive agency and the TSA will be as well, because no agency, especially in this country, is prepared for every possible threat. Could an incident like what happened at Lockerbie happen again? Maybe. The system is certainly fallible, through both human error and technological error. Nevertheless, if we have learned anything from the Lockerbie tragedy, it is that airlines and government agencies need to learn from previous tragedies rather than dismiss them as foreign or irrelevant.

References

Airport screeners missed weapons. (2004, September 23). *USA Today*, p. 1.

Berrick, C. (2004). *Aviation security: Challenges exist in stabilizing and enhancing passenger and baggage screening operations.* United States General Accounting Office. Retrieved October 13, 2004, from www.gao.gov/new.items/d04440t.pdf

Carrell, S. (2007, October 3). Fresh doubts on Lockerbie conviction. *The Guardian*, p. 17.

Cobb, R. W., & Primo, D. M. (2003). *The plane truth: Airline crashes, the media, & transportation policy.* Washington, DC: Brookings Institution Press.

Cox, M., & Foster, T. (1992). *Their darkest day.* New York: Grove Weidenfeld.

Hearings before the government Activities and Transportation Subcomittee of the Committee on Government Operations. (1989). *The bombing of Pan Am flight 103: A critical look at American aviation security.* Washington, DC: U.S. Government Printing Office.

International Progress Organization. (2007). *Lockerbie trial: An intelligence operation? BBC interview of Dr. Hans Kochler.* Retrieved February 14, 2009, from http://i-p-o.org/IPO-nr-Lockerbie-5Oct07.htm

Johnston, D. (1989). *Lockerbie: The tragedy of flight 103.* London: Bloomsbury Publishing.

Johnson, S. (2009, May 06). *Libyans ask for return of Lockerbie bomber Abdelbasel Ali Mohmed al-Megrahi.* Retrieved June 12, 2009, from http://www.telegraph.co.uk/news/newstopics/politics/scotland/5284462/Libyans-ask-for-return-of-Lockerbie-bomber-Abdelbaset-Ali-Mohmed-al-Megrahi.html

Leppard, D. (1991). *On the trail of terror: The inside story of the Lockerbie investigation.* London: Jonathon Cape.

Rumerman, J. (n.d). *Aviation security.* Retrieved October 23, 2004, from http://www.centennialofflight.gov/essay/Government_Role/security/POL18.htm

Shuman, E. (2001). *El Al's legendary security measures set industry standards.* Retrieved October 16, 2004, from http://www.israelinsider.com/channels/security/articles/sec_0108.htm

Smith, A. D. (2007, September 2). Vital Lockerbie evidence 'was tampered with.' *The Observer*, p. 37.

Szyliowicz, J. (2004). Aviation security: Promise or reality? *Terrorism, 27*, 47–64.

Transportation Security Administration. *Why? The reasons behind TSA security.* Retrieved February 1, 2009, from http://www.tsa.gov/travelers/why.shtm

Wain, C. (1998, December 21). *Lessons from Lockerbie.* Retrieved October 19, 2004, from http://news.bbc.co.uk/1/hi/special_report/1998/12/98/lockerbie/235632.stm

Wallis, R. (2001). *Lockerbie: The story and the lessons.* Conecticut: Praeger Publishers.

Chapter 9
Maritime Security: Case Studies in Terrorism

Brian A. Maule

Introduction

At approximately 11:22 a.m. on October 12, 2000, a small explosive-rigged boat drew alongside the US Navy destroyer *USS Cole* in the seaport of Aden, Yemen.[1] After offering friendly gestures, two suicide bombers Hassan Awadh al-Khamri also known as Hasan al-Ta-Efi ("Hasan") and Ibrahim al-Thawar also known as "Nibrass" detonated their explosives ripping a hole 40 ft in diameter in the ship's port side, killing 17 American servicemen and injuring 39 others.[2] Within hours, three different groups, the Aden-Abyan Islamic Army and two of its off-shoots, the Army of Mohammed and the Islamic Deterrence Forces, claimed responsibility for the attack. However, though US sources suspected the hydra itself, al-Qaeda, believing that the attack was far too sophisticated for the Islamic Army, its claim appeared more credible than the other two because of its past terrorist activity and a common genesis of known members and members of al-Qaeda to the much-romanticized Afghanistan war against the former Soviet Union.[3] Moreover, unlike the Army of Mohammed and the Islamic Deterrence Forces, who were unknown to Yemeni officials, the Islamic Army had released a series of communiqués in 1998 calling for the overthrow of the government of Yemen while expressing support for Osama bin Laden. Also in December 1998, the Islamic Army had kidnapped 16 tourists near Mudiyah, South Yemen. The Islamic Army also claimed responsibility for the

B.A. Maule (✉)
John Jay College of Criminal Justice, New York, NY, USA
e-mail: bmaule@law.nyc.gov

[1] Named for Marine Sgt. Darrell S. Cole killed on Iwo Jima on February 19, 1945, the *USS Cole* is a US$1B guided missile destroyer built in 1995 and at the time of the attack was part of the battle group of the carrier *USS George Washington*.

[2] Indictment S12 Cr. 1023 (KTD) U.S.A. v. AL-BADAWI and AL-QUSO.

[3] Yemen bombers hit UK embassy. *The Guardian*, October 14, 2000. The 9/11 Commission later concluded that the suicide attack on the USS Cole was a "full-fledged operation, supervised directly by bin Laden." 9/11/Commission Report, p. 190.

M.R. Haberfeld, A. von Hassell (eds.), *A New Understanding of Terrorism*,
DOI 10.1007/978-1-4419-0115-6_9, © Springer Science+Business Media, LLC 2009

bombing of the British Embassy in Sana'a, Yemen, which occurred the day after the USS Cole attack.[4]

This chapter will overview and analyze issues related to port security as an emerging threat to the free world's major modes of transportation.

The Attack on *USS Cole*

Whether or not it was the fear of US military reprisals (after all Yemen was a known refuge for al-Qaeda operatives), or comity with Washington, in the beginning the Yemeni response to the Cole attack was swift, if not precise. Several days after the attack, over 70 persons were detained for questioning. Information obtained from a 12-year-old boy led to the recovery of the Nissan four-wheel drive vehicle and boat trailer used in the attack and to an apartment near the harbor used by the two men fitting the 12-year-old boy's description.[5] According to Yemeni President Ali Abdullah Saleh in an interview on Qatar's Al Jazeera Television, the 12-year-old boy was given some money by one of the two men as payment for watching the vehicle until their return. The two men, whose descriptions were corroborated by neighbors, had arrived in Yemen days prior to the attack, had built a corrugated fence at the rented apartment near the harbor to conceal their activities, and had not been seen since the suicide attack on the USS Cole.[6] Based on the descriptions of the two men given by the 12-year-old boy, by neighbors of the apartment near the harbor, and by fishermen in the Port of Aden who had given the men information on the movement of ships in the port, composite sketches of the two suicide bombers were made and sent to Egypt and Saudi Arabia to be compared with photographs of known Arab veterans from the anti-Soviet Afghan war.[7] A search of the apartment on October 16, 2000, discovered bomb-making equipment and residue of military C-4 ,which the Prime Minister of Yemen, Abdul Karim al-Aryani, confirmed was the explosive used in the attack. The use of C-4, al-Aryani opined, indicated "an Afghan connection,"[8] hinting that the attack was beyond the capability of the local Islamic Army. The search of the vehicle and eight "safe houses" used by the suspects also recovered documents that were issued in the Yemeni governorate of Lahij or Hadramawt, the ancestral home of both the suicide bombers and Osama bin Laden. One of the documents, a driver's license, was issued to Abdallah Ahmad Khalid

---

[4]Four of the British tourists were killed during a botched rescue operation by Yemeni forces and the leader of the kidnapping, Abu al-Hassan al-Mihdar, was later executed for the crime. *The Guardian*, October 14, 2000.

[5]Yemeni president calls USS Cole attack "very well-planned." CNN.com, October 18, 2000.

[6]USS Cole probe seeks evidence of conspiracy. CNN.com. October 20, 2000.

[7]Cole Suspect Sketches Created. *Associated Press Online*. October 28, 2000.

[8]C-4 Explosive was used in USS Cole attack. CNN.com. November 1, 2000.

al-MUSSawa,[9] whose photograph was published by the Yemeni government soon after its discovery.[10]

A few weeks later Yemeni sources revealed that one of the composite sketches appeared to match a man suspected in the 1998 bombings of the US embassies in Kenya and Tanzania.[11] The match was of Hassan Awadh al-Khamri a.k.a. al-Ta-Efi, the same man in the published photograph to whom the driver's license was issued. DNA samples from the vehicle and apartment together with blood samples from relatives and "confetti-sized" pieces of flesh recovered from the bomb site would confirm the identity of al-Ta-Efi as one of the suicide bombers and as the same person wanted by the United States for questioning in the suicide bombing of the US Embassy in Nairobi, Kenya. [12] Yemeni officials also disclosed that 17 months prior to the Cole attack, al-Ta-Efi had been released from a Yemeni prison after serving a short time for plotting a terrorist attack in Yemen in 1999.[13]

By November 8, 2000, Yemeni security officials had narrowed their focus to nine detainees but no formal arrest or charges were made.[14] One day later, US officials disclosed that one of the suspects detained by the Yemeni security forces gave an account of an earlier suicide bomb attempt on another US naval ship some 10 months before the *USS Cole* attack.[15] Just as the first bombing of the World Trade Center in 1993 was a prelude to the more devastating 9/11 attacks, the attack on the USS Cole was preceded by an unsuccessful attack on *USS The Sullivans*. According to Yemeni officials, on January 3, 2000, a boat overladen with explosives sank before it could make contact with USS The Sullivans, while the destroyer was participating in training exercises and boarding operations in the Port of Aden.[16]

On November 26, 2000, Yemeni security forces announced the formal arrest of six men for the attack, while three others thought to have fled Yemen shortly after the attack were being sought.[17] What is of particular interest about these arrests is that although Yemeni officials had continually denied accusations that Yemeni government officials might have been involved in the suicide attack, on December 13, 2000, they disclosed that two of the suspects, Walid al-Sourouri and Fatha

---

[9]Burns, John F. Investigators Discouraging Speculation in Cole Attack. *The New York Times*, October 23, 2000: Sec. A; p. 6; Col. 1.

[10]USS Cole plot began after embassy attacks, investigator says. CNN.com. December 20, 2000.

[11]Sketch in Cole attack resembles Africa bomb suspect. *Florida Times-Union*. November 24, 2000.

[12]Whitaker, Brian. Piecing together the terrorist jigsaw. Guardian Unlimited. October 15, 2001. Yemen identifies Cole attackers, prime minister says. *United Press International*. November 17, 2000. Remains of 1 Cole bomber found, US official say. CNN.com, November 17, 2000.

[13]Risen, James and Raymond Bonner. A Nation Challenged: Fatal Attack; Officials Say Bomber Was in Yemeni Custody Earlier. *The New York Times*, December 7, 2001.

[14]Nine people questioned says sources. *Yemen Times*. November 13, 2000.

[15]Cole attack was terrorists' second try, US officials say. CNN.Com November 9, 2000.

[16]Al-Haj, Ahmad. Yemen arrests three suspects in USS Cole bombing. *The Associated Press*, April 7, 2001.

[17]At least 6 arrested in Cole investigation, Yemen official says. CNN.com. November 26, 2000.

Abdul Rahman, were police officials from the town of Lahij and were arrested on allegations of providing false documents to the suicide bombers.[18]

Also, despite the fact that an estimated 100 FBI personnel were in Yemen aiding in the investigation, to this point none were permitted to question any of the detainees or the arrested suspects.[19] According to President Saleh, not only was questioning of Yemen citizens by a foreign law enforcement official forbidden by Yemeni law but extradition of Yemeni citizens to a foreign country was not permitted under Yemen's constitution.[20] FBI agents were also forbidden from questioning neighbors of the eight safe houses used by the suicide bombers and were only allowed to visit the houses after Yemeni security forces had searched them.[21] This caginess appears to be in direct opposition to Yemen's pledge of cooperation; for whereas there should be no questions regarding the overall jurisdiction of Yemen's security forces, a case can be made for shared jurisdiction of the investigation. For just as in a US seaport, such as New York, where the lack of a single, comprehensive authority for security, such as that which exists for the seaports of most other industrialized countries, means that security either to prevent or respond to a terrorist event is multijurisdictional, it is a forgone conclusion that even though the investigative response to an event of the magnitude of the Cole attack in a US seaport will be led and controlled by the FBI, other agencies such as the NYPD will actively participate in the investigation. The failure or diffidence of Yemeni government officials to accept the FBI as having, at the very least, an equal interest in solving the crime and Yemeni reaction to the FBI amounted to a relegation of its agents to third world investigation status, which certainly fueled the allegations of complicity by high-ranking government officials in the bombing. Rather than transparency through full-fledged cooperation, several events helped to fuel these allegations. For example, Yemen's response to US full-page announcements in Yemeni newspapers offering a $5 million reward for information leading to the arrest and conviction of those responsible for the Cole attack. Twice within the same month, the Yemen Telecommunications Ministry changed the US Embassy's telephone numbers that were given in the announcement so that anyone willing to disclose this information was unable to contact the US Embassy to do so.[22] In fact 2 weeks into the investigation, the frustration at what was either gross incompetence of Yemeni investigators

---

[18] Yemen names 6 suspects in USS Cole bombing. CNN.com, December 13, 2000.

[19] One year later, *The New York Times* reported on the charge by one Yemeni official who spoke on condition of anonymity stated that his government was not forthcoming in sharing all of the collected evidence with the FBI. The unnamed official claimed that a letter from bin Laden was found in one of the eight apartments searched but neither the letter nor its existence was disclosed to the FBI. A Nation Challenged: Fatal Attack; Officials Say Bomber of the Cole Was in Yemeni Custody Earlier. *The New York Times*. December 7, 2001. Sec. A; p. 1; Col. 5.

[20] Yemen's President, Naming Names. *The Washington Post*. December 10, 2000.

[21] Risen, James and Raymond Bonner. A Nation Challenged: Fatal Attack; Officials Say Bomber Was in Yemeni Custody Earlier. *The New York Times*, December 7, 2001.

[22] Burns, John F. F.B.I.'s Inquiry In Cole Attack Is Nearing Halt. *The New York Times*, August 21, 2001: Sec. A; Col. 5; P. 1.

or a general effort to obscure evidence came to a head when a videotape from a harbor police surveillance camera delivered to the FBI appeared to have been edited to delete the actual bombing and the preceding minutes that would have showed the small boat approaching the USS Cole.[23] The videotape, whether edited or erased inadvertently, seems to further support allegations of official complicity if not in aiding the terrorists by having advanced knowledge and doing nothing to prevent it. This was evident, according to one US official, because on the day of the suicide attack on the Cole, a "significant number of people" behaved as though they were aware that a major event involving the Cole was imminent because compared to previous refueling visits, on October 12, 2000, there were an unusual number of people in the port who appeared to be on hand to witness the event.[24] In addition, it was reported that the harbor pilot who steered the Cole to the refueling station appeared "really nervous" and "anxious to get off of the ship."[25]

As if to put such allegations to rest, particularly the dubious link between advanced notice and official involvement in the attack, President Saleh reportedly stated that the US Navy had made a mistake by arriving and not asking his government to provide protection for the Cole.[26]This inapt statement is in direct contrast to that of General Anthony Zinni, Centcom commander, who stated in his 2000 congressional testimony that advance notice is usually given to the host country approximately 2 weeks in advance of a ship's arrival in a foreign port of call.[27] Furthermore, given the logistics involved in refueling an 8,400-ton US Navy destroyer, including seeking permission to enter the port, the availability of the fuel itself, and of a harbor pilot, it seems unrealistic that the Cole could have "arrived" without advance notice to Yemen.[28] As such the only questions seems to be if notice of the USS Cole's arrival was leaked to the attackers and if it was, were those Yemeni officials members of or sympathizers of al-Qaeda?

Amidst this uncertainty as to Yemeni complicity or general reticence, trouble was brewing between the US Department of State and the FBI. According to *The New York Times*, John O'Neill, the senior FBI agent leading the investigation in Yemen, was demanding that Washington apply all available pressure on the Yemeni government to follow through on the Yemeni president's announced commitment of full cooperation, which to FBI officials stationed in Yemen was not the case.[29]

---

[23]Burns, John. US Aides Say the Yemenis Seem to Hinder Cole Inquiry. *The New York Times*. November 1, 2000: Sec. A; p. 16; Col. 1.

[24]Burns, John F. and Steven Lee Myers. US Says Yemen has found "Leads" in bombing. *The New York Times*, October 18, 2000.

[25]Ibid.

[26]*Yemen Times*. November 20–26, 2000.

[27]US Senate Armed Services Committee holds a Hearing on the recent attack in Yemen on the USS Cole. October 19, 2000: available at http://www.fas.org/man/congress/2000/zinni_testimony.htm

[28] Prior to the Cole attack, 27 US Navy ships had refueled in Yemen. Gen. Anthony Zinni Testifies before Senate Armed Services Committee on USS Cole Disaster. CNN.com. October 19, 2000.

[29]Burns, John. US Aides Say the Yemenis Seem to Hinder Cole Inquiry. *The New York Times*. November 1, 2000: Sec. A; p. 16; Col. 1.

Severe restrictions including the need to seek express permission to move about the Port of Aden were considered encumbrances by FBI agents. This was the cause of much friction between the FBI and the Department of State in the person of the US ambassador to Yemen, Barbara Bodine, who, to FBI officials, appeared to be more concerned with the broader US–Yemeni relations than with the Cole investigation.[30] In fact, the tension between the FBI's need to "solve" the crime and the State Department's broader mission of diplomacy started at the very onset of the FBI arrival in Yemen when the US ambassador successfully negotiated a deal with Yemeni officials to allow FBI agents in Yemen to carry small arms rather than the rifles, shotguns, and automatic weapons that they wanted to carry.[31]

According to FBI officials, a call from President Clinton to President Saleh initially made matters worse, but soon after, negotiations on easing the tension, specifically on the need for FBI agents to participate in all interrogations involving the USS Cole bombing, resulted in a Memorandum of Understanding signed on November 29, 2000, by the United States and Yemen.[32] Under the terms of the agreement, FBI agents were permitted to be present during all future interrogations but could not question the suspect directly and could only pass written notes and follow-up questions that they wanted answered to the Yemeni official conducting the interrogation.[33]

On interrogation, one of the six arrested, Jamal al-Badawi, informed the police that he received instructions for the bombing of the USS Cole via a telephone call from the United Arab Emirates from Mohammad Omar al-Harazi, a Saudi citizen of Yemen ancestry, whom he had met briefly in Afghanistan during the anti-Soviet war but had not seen since.[34] According to Badawi, al-Harazi, also known as Abd al-Rahim al-Nashiri, did not state directly that the order, or money, for the USS Cole attack came directly from Osama bin Laden, but al-Harazi's demeanor led Badawi to believe that this was indeed the case.[35] The identification of al-Harazi as the point man who had provided the money for the apartment rentals, explosives, and instructions for the bombing sparked an international manhunt for al-Harazi, who was also suspected of orchestrating the 1998 bombing of the American Embassy in Nairobi, Kenya; he was the cousin of Gihad Ali, known as "Azzam," one of the suicide bombers. [36] Moreover, al-Harazi was suspected of several foiled plots including the 1992 plot to kill American soldiers in an Aden hotel, a plot to bomb the US 5th Fleet Headquarters in Bahrain, and a "USS Cole-type" plot to bomb US and

---

[30]Sisk, Richard. State Dept., FBI Eyed in Yemen Feud. *Daily News*, July 7, 2001.

[31]9/11 Commission Report, p. 192.

[32]US State Department Briefing. November 29, 2000: Available at http://www.fas.org/man/dod-101/sys/ship/docs/man-sh-ddg51-001130.htm

[33]US, Yemen and US finalizing agreement on Cole investigation sources say. CNN.com. October 31, 2000.

[34]Yemen names 6 suspects in USS Cole bombing. CNN.com. December 13, 2000.

[35]Yemen names 6 suspects in USS Cole bombing. CNN.com. December 13, 2000.

[36]Yemeni on Delicate Path in bin Laden Hunt. *The New York Times*. December 15, 2000: Sec. A; p. 22; Col. 4.

British warships crossing the Strait of Gibraltar.[37] As a known al-Qaeda operative, al-Harazi was now considered the definitive source for determining whether or not the suicide attack on the USS Cole was an al-Qaeda operation under direct order from Osama bin Laden or an expansion of terrorist operations by the local Islamic Army.

Several months after the *USS Cole attack*, al-Harazi employed a similar *modus operandi* – making all the arrangements and fleeing the country days before the date of the attack – in organizing a failed plot to blow up the US Embassy in India. [38] Almost 2 years to the day of the Cole attack, on October 6, 2002, another explosive-rigged boat attack, this time on the French-flagged super oil tanker Limburg, occurred near the Yemeni city of Al-Mukalla, killing one crew member and releasing 90,000 barrels of Saudi crude oil into the sea.[39]

In November 2002, al-Harazi was finally apprehended in the UAE and handed over to the United States[40] Reportedly, al-Harazi had left Yemen for Afghanistan days before the Cole bombing, fled Afghanistan for Pakistan because of the US invasion and finally fled to the UAE, notably the same location from which he had telephoned his Cole attack instructions to Jamal Badawi.[41]

Badawi also disclosed to Yemeni interrogators that he was to have filmed the attack, but because he had to travel, he instructed Fahd al-Quso to do so instead.[42] al-Quso apparently fell asleep and did not arrive in time to film the attack.[43] A member of a prominent Yemeni family, al-Quso was later arrested at the insistence of the FBI based on corroborating physical evidence taken from one of the searches.[44]

During the interrogation, al-Quso admitted to Yemeni officials that he had traveled to Bangkok, Thailand, with Nibrass (one of the suicide bombers) and gave money, reportedly $36,000 to a one-legged man he called Khallad.[45] From al-Quso's

---

[37]Chakravarty, Sayantan. Terrorism: Target America. *India Today*. p. 50. John J. Lumpkin. US says it has al-Qaida's Persian Gulf operations chief in custody. *The Associated Press*. November 21, 2002. Jerry Seper. Senior al Qaeda chief in custody of US; Leader of Gulf operations offers data. *The Washington Times*, November 22, 2002, P. 1, pg. A01.

[38]Whitaker, Brian. Piecing together the terrorist jigsaw. Guardian Unlimited. October 15, 2001. Karl Vick. Sudan, Newly Helpful, Remains Wary of US: Officials Share Files but Deny Ties to Foiled Attack. *The Washington Post*. December 10, 2001. Sec. A; Pg. A15.

[39]Ships as terrorist Attacks, American Shipper, Nov. 2002, p. 59. Also available at www.al-bab.com. Yemen Gateway. Middle East International. October 25, 2002.

[40]9/11 Commission Report, p. 153.

[41]Seper, Jerry. Senior al Qaeda chief in custody of US; Leader of Gulf operations offers data. *The Washington Times*. November 22, 2002: p. A01.

[42]9/11 Commission Report. p. 507.

[43]Mac Farquhar, Neil and David Johnston. Death Sentences in Attack on Cole. *The New York Times*, September 30, 2004: Sec. A; Col. 5; p. 1

[44]What if. . . by Jim Gilmore. PBS Frontline.

[45]US indicts 2 Yemeni men for allegedly aiding on USS Cole. *The Dallas Morning News*, May 16, 2003. See also Indictment S12 Cr. 1023. US v Al-Badawi and Al-Quso. Days after the 9/11 attacks, al-Quso admitted to FBI interrogators that he was a financier for al-Qaeda operations and would identify Khalid al-Hazmi and Nawaf al-Midhar, two of the hijackers of American Airlines Flight

description, Yemeni officials suspected that Khallad was in fact Tawfiq bin Attash Khallad, whom they had previously arrested on a case of mistaken identity and released on Osama bin Laden's intervention.[46] By fingering Khallad, al-Quso provided a tenuous link between the suicide bombers and al-Qaeda for it was known to US intelligence officials that Khallad, considered by some al-Qaeda members to be bin Laden's "run boy," was suspected of being connected to the 1998 embassy bombings in Africa.[47] Tawfiq bin Attash Khallad a.k.a. "Khallad" was captured in Pakistan in 2003 and handed over to the United States.[48]

Even though by late December 2000 it was evident to US officials that the attack on the USS Cole was an al-Qaeda and not an Islamic Army operation as claimed, there was still no conclusive evidence that it was bin Laden ordered and not the work of a rogue cell or high-ranking al-Qaeda operative. What was known is that the planning for an attack on a US warship was in the works since 1999 (given the failed attempt on USS The Sullivans) and its preparation began months before October 12, 2000. Moreover, the order for such an attack might have been given in 1997 by bin Laden in a letter transported out of Afghanistan by Khallad and subsequently discovered by Yemeni police in one of their raids of the safe houses following the Cole attack.[49] Although the existence of the letter has never been confirmed or denied by the FBI, it is purported to give general instructions for an attack on American ships off the coast of Yemen. Nevertheless, some evidence of the prolonged existence of a plan of attack was provided by Khallad himself during his military hearing at Guantánamo Bay, Cuba, when he accepted responsibility for putting "together the plan for the operation a year and a half prior to the operation."[50]

While Khallad's admission of guilt may be a questionable attempt to absolve his leader, bin Laden himself, of ultimate responsibility (after all, Khalid Sheik Mohamed had done the same thing early in March 2007 when accepting responsibility for the Sept 11, 2007, attacks), it is useful in providing a timeline of one and one-half years for the actual planning to the day of the event.

Despite this admission, it is still uncertain if the actual attack on the Cole had proceeded as planned or if it was catalyzed by a videotape of bin Laden and al-Zawahiri released 3 weeks before the Cole attack calling for "action against this iniquitous and faithless force which had spread its troops through Egypt, Yemen and Saudi Arabia."[51] While this kind of release, which almost always precedes a major

---

77 which flew into the Pentagon, whom he had met days after the Malaysian terrorist summit. What if... by Jim Gilmore. PBS Frontline.

[46]9/11 Commission Report; p. 155.

[47]9/11 Commission Report; p. 192.

[48]Pakistan Captures USS Cole Suspect. *Birmingham Post* (UK), May 1, 2003, Sec.: News; p. 9

[49]*The New York Times*, 8 December 2001.

[50]White, Josh. Al-Qaeda Suspect Says He Planned Cole Attack. *The Washington Post*, March 20, 2007. Sec. A; Pg. A01.

[51]USS Cole probe seeks evidence of conspiracy. CNN.com. October 20, 2000.

al-Qaeda attack, is believed by analysts to be either a broadcasted order to proceed as planned or a terror signal to the world of the imminent event, and although the flow of events culminating in the Cole attack follows this pattern, the ambiguity surrounding the protocol of advanced notice of the Cole's Aden refueling visit clouds the debate regarding ultimate responsibility for the attack. For even if two weeks notice of the Cole's visit was given to Yemen and subsequently leaked to the terrorists, this puts the attack past the release date of the al-Qaeda videotape. Adding to the uncertainty is the conflicting information obtained from interrogated suspects. One account indicated that shortly before the attack there was a dispute over al-Harazi's choice of Hassan and Nibrass as the suicide bombers and that al-Harazi ordered the attack to preempt bin Laden from overridding his choice.[52] The other account was that on al-Harazi's departure to Afghanistan to meet bin Laden to resolve the dispute of his choice of suicide bombers, Hassan and Nibrass, on their own initiative, seized an opportunity and attacked the Cole.[53] Arguably, neither of these accounts appears credible. It seems inconceivable that al-Harazi, though a high-ranking operative in the multicelled but hierarchal al-Qaeda, would deliberately circumvent a dispute knowing that Sheikh Osama bin Laden was against his choice. The second account is even more unconvincing than the first. It appears even more incredible, at least from outside of al-Qaeda, that two disposable, low-ranking operatives would undertake such a major enterprise on their own accord. For even if some suicide bombers are opportunists, the time, planning, and costs invested by al-Qaeda in the Cole attack seem to preclude any notion of capriciousness in its execution. What must be accepted is that the attack on the USS Cole was a well-coordinated and orchestrated plan of action by al-Qaeda as part of a long-term effort to kill Americans and garner support in the Muslim world for such efforts. Furthermore, the devout reverence for bin Laden and his jihad displayed by al-Qaeda members in their suicide attacks both before and after the Cole bombing discredits any suggestion that dissension could have precipitated the attack. Perhaps the clearest statement of this singular allegiance to bin Laden and his cause would come a few years later in the perverse rationale of Fawaz al-Rabe'ie, who on being sentenced to death for the Limburg bombing told the court that "God is great... America is the enemy of God [and] we had given our pledge to Sheikh Osama to kill Americans."[54]

This confluence of suicidal commitment and ideology premised on the unifying belief that "America is the enemy of God" forces us to question if physical access to any of America's 361 seaports to execute a "Cole-type" of attack could be as easy as it was in the Port of Aden, Yemen.

---

[52] 9/11 Commission Report, p. 191.

[53] Verbatim Transcript of Combatant Status Review Tribunal Hearing for ISN 10015 (Abd al-Rahim al Nashiri). Available at http://www.globalsecurity.org/security/library/report/2007/al-nashiri_csrt-hearing070314.htm

[54] Yemen court sentences Limburg bomb leader to death. ABC News Online. February 5, 2005.

Legal Steps for Law Enforcement Cooperation

An amendment to the 1936 Merchant Marine Act, unanimously approved by the US Senate Commerce Committee on August 2, 2001, was aimed primarily at addressing the security issues raised by the 1999 Interagency Commission on Crime and Security, a body comprised of representatives from 18 federal agencies, the Customs Service, and the Department of Justice. The bill, known as the Maritime Transportation Security Act 2002 ("MTSA"), was expanded, following 9/11, to include provisions to secure the nation's seaports against terrorism and signed into law by President Bush on November 25, 2002.[55] In compliance with MTSA, the Department of Homeland Security in a press release dated June 13, 2003 outlined a comprehensive layered defense plan for enhancing the security of US seaports by managing potential threats and coordinating our response to such threats. One layer aimed at securing our seaports from "homegrown" terrorists, or cells that may exist within the United States, is the requirement that all individuals, including port employees, longshoremen and truckers, present approved identification for access to all US seaport facilities and harbor areas. Much like the Coast Guard's mandate of security threat assessment for seaports and ships, under 49 U.S.C. § 144, the Transportation Security Administration, an agency within DHS, is required to assess the threat posed by individuals with access to US seaports and implement an identification credential for preventing any threat posed by unauthorized access. Although generally accepted identification such as driver's license, union cards, and other forms of personal identifications are now acceptable, DHS projects that when fully implemented, the Transportation Worker Identification Credential ("TWIC") will "culminate with the issuance of a credential to confirm that the appropriate background checks have been completed and the individual was found to present no security threat."[56]

The need for such a credential was evident in a January 7, 2007, event that caused quite a scare at many of the nation's seaports and other critical points of infrastructure. According to published reports, the incident began when a cargo container truck with three men, two Iraqis and a Lebanese, was detained at the Port of Miami because the driver could not produce the appropriate documentation requested during the routine inspection. Further suspicion was aroused because the driver somehow indicated that he was alone although the two other men were discovered crouching in the cab. Hours after it began, and only after X-rays showed that the cargo was in fact automotive parts as presented on the cargo manifest, the Port of Miami was reopened and normal operations resumed. However, during the hours of

---

[55]MTSA also incorporates some of the recommendations of the 1988 Maritime Transport System task force commissioned by Congress to "access the adequacy of the Nation's maritime transportation system... to operate in a safe, efficient, secure, and environmentally sound manner." Marine Transportation System Task Force, An Assessment of the US Marine Transportation System: A Report to Congress, Washington, DC, September 1999.

[56]US Coast Guard Transportation Security Administration available at www.uscg.mil/hg/gm/mp/pdf/Part125GuidanceFinal.pdf

uncertainty, cities across the nation responded to the incident with beefed-up security and terrorist response teams.[57] In New York the police department dispatched security personnel and emergency response vehicles to passenger ship terminals, bridges, tunnels, and other critical points of the city's infrastructure as a precaution against any impending acts of terrorism that might occur in concert with the event in Miami.[58] In the end the incident was labeled the result of miscommunication and improper identification, not terrorism. Whether or not a fully implemented TWIC will prevent terrorists from gaining easy access to US seaports is debatable, but at the very least, the Port of Miami incident lends optimism in that it may have signaled our new nationwide preparedness to quickly and adequately respond to a terrorist attack at one of our seaports, especially given that the attack on the Cole has emboldened al-Qaeda members and "galvanized al-Qaeda's recruitment efforts."[59]

The Cole attack also resulted in much discourse in the intelligence community over the community's failure to connect the dots in its assessment of threats in the Gulf region. Of particular concern was whether or not, if given the "proper level of consideration," the assessment by Kie Fallis, a mid-level analyst in the US Department of Defense, could have played a predictive role in preventing the Cole attack.[60] According to then US Senator John Warner, a June 2000 intelligence assessment of threats in the Gulf, authored by Fallis, who subsequently resigned 2 days after the Cole attack, was not given appropriate consideration and was not included in the "final intelligence report provided to military commanders in the Gulf."[61] General Tommy Franks, Commander-in-Chief of US forces in the Persian Gulf at the time, in testimony before the Armed Services Committee, stated that not only had US commanders in the gulf not received any specific threat information for Yemen or the Port of Aden but moreover "had such a warning been received, action would have been taken by the operating forces in response."[62]

Arguably, another significant failure to connect the dots involved the assessment and nondisclosure to the FBI of CIA surveillance photographs of al-Qaeda operatives taken at a series of meetings in Kuala Lumpur, Malaysia, in January 2000. Captured in photographs were Ramzi bin al-Shibh, Mohammed Atta's roommate; Khalid al-Mihdhar and Nawaf al-Hazmi, hijackers of American Airlines Flight 77, which hit the Pentagon; and Tawfiq bin Attash, the one-legged "Khallad," referred

---

[57]CNN.com-Breaking News, Sunday, January 7, 2007.

[58]Grace, Melissa. Miami Scare puts NYPD on Alert. *New York Daily News*, Monday, January 8, 2007.

[59]9/11 Commission Report; p. 191

[60]Scarborough, Rowan. Pentagon Analyst Resigns Over Ignored Warnings. *The Washington Times*, October 26, 2000: A1.

[61]Defense official resigned after Cole attack, says warnings were ignored. October 25, 2000. CNN.com.

[62]Defense official resigned after Cole attack, says warnings were ignored. October 25, 2000. CNN.com.

to by al-Qaeda members as bin Laden's "run boy."[63] Even though at the bare minimum, Khallad's connection to bin Laden was known, it appears that no one in the CIA questioned the significance of the Kuala Lumpur meetings or the identities of the other attendees of the meetings.

By December 2000, some 2 months after the Cole attack, Yemeni officials were ready to wrap-up the investigation and begin the swift and certain process, that is, Yemeni justice. Over the objections of the FBI, the Yemeni court trial was at first slated to begin in January 2001 following the end of the Islamic holy month of Ramadan.[64] However, the publication in Yemeni newspapers of a $5 million US government reward, implying that, contrary to the official Yemeni position, the Cole investigation was incomplete, may have led Yemeni officials to postpone the trial.[65] This sequence of events would reoccur several times during the next 2 years until on June 6, 2004, the trial actually began. Six were accused of carrying out the attack on the USS Cole, belonging to the al-Qaeda network and undermining Yemen's national interest.[66]

Three months after the trial began, all six were found guilty and received varying sentences. Sentenced to death were Jamal al-Badawi and Nashiri (in absentia).[67] Jamal al-Badawi's death sentence was reduced to a 15-year sentence by a Yemeni appeals court.[68] Along with other convicted al-Qaeda operatives, Fahd al-Quso and Jamal al-Badawi would escape from a Yemen prison in April 2003 and al-Badawi again in Feb 2006. On October 25, 2007, after serving less than 7 years of a 15-year sentence, Yemen released Jamal al-Badawi, the mastermind of al-Qaeda's attack on the USS Cole. With al-Badawi's release, several questions loom large. First it must be assumed that in the eyes of Yemeni authorities, al-Badawi had paid his debt to Yemeni society, but what of that to the US? Is less than 5 years of incarceration just punishment for 17 American lives and $250 million of damage to American property? More importantly knowing that he was under indictment in the United States why wasn't he handed over to the United States on being released from a Yemen prison? And why isn't the US government pressuring Yemen to hand him over? If indeed it is a violation of the Yemeni Constitution to extradite a Yemeni to another country as mentioned earlier, then this is the obvious answer, but then assuming that at sometime al-Badawi will more than likely venture out of Yemen

---

[63] What if... by Jim Gilmore. PBS Frontline.

[64] Vise, David A. Yemeni Citizens face Trial in Cole Bombing; Prime Minister Says at Least Three Are Accused of Helping to Organize Attack. *The Washington Post*, December 7, 2000: Sec. A; p. A28.

[65] Burns, John F. The Cole Investigation Proves Frustrating. *The New York Times*, February 1, 2001: Sec. A; Col. 1; p. 6.

[66] Six charged for USS Cole bombing. Aljazeera.net. July 9, 2004

[67] Mac Farquhar, Neil and David Johnston. Death Sentences in Attack on Cole. *The New York Times*, September 29, 2004.

[68] Court Upholds death sentence in USS Cole bombing. February 28, 2005. CNN.com

to frequent his mid-east jaunts, will any of these governments hand him over to the United States?

The answers to these questions as well as the events that led to them do not bode well for US seaports, where by most accounts, security remains inadequate at best. For although this type of terrorism has not occurred in a US seaport, the attack on the USS Cole and Limburg, as well as the attempt on the USS The Sullivans, provides useful opportunities to document our continued vulnerability to these types of attacks and reviews the measures taken to eliminate them.

The Evolving Threat

As international borders handling almost 99% of US trade with noncontiguous countries, including 11.3 million cargo containers in 2005[69] and some 8,100 ships of foreign registry, US seaports and waterways move more than $1.3 billion of US goods daily[70] and contribute $743 billion to the US Gross Domestic Product.[71] They are envisioned by most security experts as potential targets on any list of likely US targets for terrorism. However, because terrorists seek maximum media coverage to display their cause, seaport security experts are most concerned with one specific on-the-surface threat: the hijacking and deliberate explosion of a Liquefied Natural Gas tanker or its use (or that of a fuel-laden cruise ship) as a bomb to damage other ships or any of the military or many industrial installations that line the coast of most of our seaports.

The destruction and potential loss of life that would occur from this type of attack in a US seaport is not unlike that envisioned by Adm. James M. Loy, Under Secretary of the Transportation Security Agency in the US Department of Homeland Security ("DHS"), whose recurring nightmare during his 42-year tenure at the US Coast Guard was of a burning cruise ship that could not be reached by enough rescue helicopters and ships.[72] While his nightmare has remained just that, it is not hard to imagine post-USS Cole attack. In fact 15 years before Cole, it was one of the distinct possibilities posed by the 1985 hijacking of the Italian cruise ship Achille Lauro.[73]

---

[69]Testimony of Assistant Customs Commissioner at US Senate Hearing of the Permanent Subcommittee on Homeland Security and Governmental Affairs, March 28, 2006. Retrieved on January 14, 2008, from http://www.scribd.com/doc/219062/US-Congressional-Record-Daily-Digest

[70]America's Ports Today, The American Association of Ports. Available at www.aapa-ports.org

[71]Remarks of US Secretary of Transportation, Norman Y. Mineta to The American Association of Port Authorities. March 20, 2001. http://www.dot.gov/affairs/032001sp.htm

[72]Marques, Christopher. Threats and Responses: Transportation Security; Safety Chief Tries to Make Travel Easy, Too, The New York Times, December 25, 2002: Sec. A; Col. 1.

[73]Miller, Judith. Hijackers Yield Ship in Egypt: Passenger Slain, 400 are Safe; US Assails Deal with Captors, The New York Times. October 10, 1985: Sec. A; p. 1; Col. 6.

On October 7, 1985, four heavily armed Palestinian terrorists hijacked the Italian cruise ship Achille Lauro with 80 passengers and 320 crew on board.[74] Although, as later disclosed, their intended objective was not the ship itself but installations in Israel, the hijacking that resulted in 2 days of terror and the murder of wheelchair-bound Jewish passenger Leon Klinghoffer could have been more catastrophic.[75]

Furthermore, the possibility of a fuel-laden ship used as a bomb was certainly considered by the Baltimore Port Authority when they closed their port to Liquefied Natural Gas carriers on September 12, 2001, the very next day after the terrorist attacks on the United States. Even though the port was reopened shortly thereafter, and no such attack has occurred in any of our 361 seaports, the possibility of such an attack remains likely and is one of three distinct types of terrorist threats that seaport security officials must anticipate and plan for.[76]

In addition to a Cole-type attack posed by the deliberate explosion of a liquefied gas carrier or its hijacking and use as a bomb to damage a larger ship, especially a cruise liner, or the facilities of the port itself, seaport security must also anticipate and plan for underwater threats to ships and to the port's infrastructure such as that posed by the use of limpet mines or scuba divers committed to terrorism and equipped with explosive devices.[77]

The 1984 CIA mining of the Nicaraguan harbors of Puerto Sandino, Puerto Corinto, and El Bluff shows the potency of such an attack and the imaginable destruction that would result if it was to occur in a US seaport. On March 20, 1984, the Soviet tanker Lugansk, carrying 250,000 barrels of crude oil, struck a sea mine in the Nicaraguan harbor of Puerto Sandino. Nineteen days earlier on March 1, 1984, the Dutch dredge Geopotes VI had also struck a mine in another Nicaraguan port.[78] By March 30, 1984, a total of 10 ships, 5 of foreign registry, were damaged. In addition to damage to ships, injuries to crewmen, and the death of two Nicaraguan fishermen,

---

[74]Over 700 passengers had disembarked to visit Cairo and the pyramids with plans to rejoin the ship 1 day later in Port Said. Judith Miller, Hijackers Yield Ship in Egypt: Passenger Slain, 400 are Safe; US Assails Deal with Captors, *The New York Times*, October 10, 1985, Sec. A; P. 1, Col. 6.

[75]According to news reports the hijackers plan to attack installations in Israel after the ship docked in Port Alshood was in retaliation for Israel's air raid on the PLO's headquarters in Tunisia, the week before during which more than 70 people were killed. Judith Miller, Hijackers Yield Ship in Egypt.

[76]Because some threats posed to our seaports may not include the use of a ship, this analysis is much broader than the one used by Campbell and Gunaratna, who identified the threats to maritime trade as vessel as a means; vessel as a weapon; vessel as a bomb; vessel as a disruption tool, and vessel as a target. Tanner Campbell and Rohan Gunaratna, "Maritime Terrorism, Piracy and Crime," pp. 77–80.

[77]An on-the-surface threat not covered here is the deliberate sinking of a large ship in one of our seaports. While this is quite possible and would be minimally disruptive, it would not garner the media attention as if carried out in one of the world's maritime choke points such as the Straits of Malacca, or the Panama or Suez Canals.

[78]Phillip Taubman, President's "Secret War" in Nicaragua Backfires, *The New York Times*, Apr. 15, 1984, § 4, p. 1; Col. 1.

the mining also resulted in a halt to shipping in the mined ports and the near collapse of the Nicaraguan fishing industry.[79] Although much controversy existed and debate continues as to how to label the event, the incident helps to focus our attention to the horrors that such a threat poses.

However, the most ominous of all the threats we face is the threat posed by the lack of sufficient screening of the 11.3 million cargo containers unloaded at our seaports every year. The lack of sufficient screening could allow terrorists or weapons of mass destruction or disruption ("WMDs") to reach our shores via maritime commerce. Recent accounts of stowaways reaching our shores serve to warn us of just how likely the possibility is that terrorists hiding in a cargo container could gain entry and trigger a catastrophic event in any of the many built-up urban areas that are adjacent to, and part of, most of our nation's seaports. For example, the *Associated Press* reported that 32 Chinese stowaways were found in 2 containers in the seaport of Los Angeles on January 15, 2005.[80] The 28 adults and 4 teenagers were discovered by the Los Angeles Port Police after a crane operator spotted 3 men climbing out of a hole in one container. Each of the two containers concealing the stowaways were equipped with a battery-operated fan, ventilation holes, sleeping bags, and an ample supply of food and water for the journey from the Port of Shekou, China, to Los Angeles. The ship NYK Athena is owned by a Cyprus-based company, is of Panamanian registry, was part of the Japanese fleet of NYK, and had an International Ship Security Certificate.[81] According to Lt. Titus Smith of the Los Angeles Port Police, because "most of the times, we get a couple of people here and there," the number of stowaways discovered in this incident, 32, is significant.[82] Therefore, in view of the facts that, 1 year earlier, 19 Chinese immigrants were also discovered in a container in the same seaport and more recently on October 31, 2006, 3 Panamanians were rescued and 1 died after they jumped from a cargo container ship docked in a New York seaport,[83] it is pertinent to ask what if, instead of stowaways seeking a better economic life, this mode of illegal entry was used by terrorists armed with biological or chemical contraband that could be weaponized and later released into one of our communities? This possibility was somewhat confirmed in October 2001 with the discovery of a stowaway hiding in a cargo container in the Italian seaport of Gioia Tauro.[84] In addition to amenities of comfort, the stowaway was armed with phones, a laptop computer, airport security passes, and an airline mechanic's certificate valid for O'Hare, L.A. International, and New York's JFK airports. While some may be comforted in the knowledge that the stowaways in each of these known events were apprehended, we must be aware that their discovery and arrests were

---

[79] Freddy Cuevas, CIA-Backed Rebels Claim Port Mining is Justified, *Associated Press*, April 11, 1984, Wednesday, AM cycle.

[80] *Associated Press*. Sunday, January 16, 2005.

[81] 32 Stowaways Found on Ship, *Los Angeles Times*, January 16, 2005.

[82] Ibid.

[83] WABC News N.Y., November 1, 2006.

[84] *The Times* (UK), October 25, 2001.

due to chance sightings and not because of any protocol having to do with seaport security post-USS Cole and -9/11.

Even more challenging than the threat posed by terrorists concealed in a container is that posed by the "dirty" container that conceals a WMD, aimed at the port and the established populations of its surrounding areas. With only 8.1% of all cargo containers arriving in US seaports every year inspected,[85] and because a container can easily conceal terrorists, a biological, a chemical, or a nuclear weapon, cargo container shipping has been called the "soft underbelly" of our nation's homeland defense against terrorism.[86] Despite improvements in the monitoring of container cargo, both at home and abroad, because of the rapid growth in containerized shipping throughout the world, it appears as though our vulnerability to this type of threat has outpaced our security against it.

The Adequate (Inadequate?) Response

In 2002 and again in 2003, ABC News conducted a test of our defense against a container-concealed WMD.[87] Using approximately 15 pounds of depleted uranium packed in a lead-lined steel pipe, which was then placed in a teak trunk, the 2003 test started in Jakarta, Indonesia, by placing the teak trunk in a container of furniture bound for the US seaport of Los Angeles. According to the ABC News broadcast, which aired on October 6, 2003, the container was never inspected at its port of origin, Jakarta, Indonesia, and although it was screened at its port of entry by US Customs in Los Angeles, the screening failed to detect the depleted uranium, which has a similar radiation signature to enriched uranium used to make nuclear weapons. What's more, according to Tom Cochran, a nuclear physicist contacted by ABC News, not only should US Customs inspectors have recognized the depleted uranium, but more importantly, their failure to do so means that more than likely they would not have, or cannot, detect enriched uranium. One year later, the DHS' Inspector General Office confirmed that the department's "protocols and procedures... were not adequate to detect the depleted uranium."[88]

---

[85] DHS Performance Report for 2005. Based on the use of Non-Intrusive Inspection technology. Critics contend that the number of screened containers is much lower. See, for example, Sen. Schumer's remarks to the US Senate in support of his amendment to the Port Security Improvement Act 2006.

[86] US Senator Diane Feinstein, *ABC News*, October 6, 2003.

[87] Brian Ross, How Safe are US Borders? Customs Fail to Detect Depleted Uranium – Again, *ABC News*, October 6, 2003.

[88] Effectiveness of Customs and Border Protection's Procedures to Detect Uranium in Two Smuggling Incidents, Department of Homeland Security Office of Inspector General, September 2004. p. 3.

At the same time of ABC's 2003 test of our nation's preparedness against a containerized WMD, and as an integral part of the DHS' multilayered security regime, the US Department of Energy announced its Megaports Initiative designed to detect and prevent a nuclear device from entering the world's commercial stream. In collaboration with DHS, the Megaports Initiative complements C-TPAT and the US Coast Guard's IPSP by installing radiation detection devices at all of the world's megaports. To date, the radiation portals have been installed at 19 locations in 10 foreign countries. In January 2009, Japan's Minami Honmuku Terminal of the Port of Yokohama became the 20th location to install the portals.[89] Currently, the US Department of Energy has partnered with 20 other countries for installations and projects, which when completed, radiation detection portals will be operational in all of the world's 75 megaports.

Whether when completed, radiation detection portals at the world's 75 megaports will prevent WMDs from entering the global commerce stream, the clear message underlying the ABC News simulation seems to echo the September 11 commission's warning that "the greatest danger of another catastrophic attack on the United States will materialize if the world's most dangerous terrorists acquire the world's most dangerous weapons."[90] This warning is even more poignant in light of the contemporaneous details surrounding the ABC News simulation.

Right after the 9/11 attacks, the International Maritime Organization (IMO) agreed upon a regulatory framework to address maritime security. The primary concerns identified were the need to address the security of vessels and ports, the need to track vessels, the need to ensure the integrity of containerized cargo, and the need to verify and authenticate the identity of seafarers.[91] Security measures aimed at addressing these concerns were adopted and later ratified by 108 signatories and made effective on July 1, 2004. In addition to changes to the Safety of Life at Sea (SOLAS) convention, the new international measures include the International Ship and Port Facility Security Code ("ISPS"), which complements the US Maritime Transportation Security Act ("MTSA") by establishing a multilateral security regime containing security-related requirements for member governments together with a series of guidelines on how to meet those requirements.[92] Specifically, under the ISPS, member governments are required to have an approved Port Facility Security Plan (PFSP) for each of its seaports and an International Ship Certificate ("ISC")

---

[89]Hisane Masaki. Japan plans to launch US-backed port security program. Available at www.joc.com/articles/news

[90]Report of The National Commission on Terrorist Attacks Upon the United States. p. 380. The US Department of Energy's Proliferation Security Initiative and its Global Initiative to Combat Nuclear Terrorism aim to prevent the spread of nuclear weapons and weapon-making knowledge, and the chance that WMDs could land in the hands of terrorists.

[91]The International Chamber of Commerce. London, September 22, 2004.

[92]Available at www.imo.org/About/mainframe.asp?topic_id=583&doc_id=2689

for ships[93] registered under their flag.[94] Approved status for ships or seaport facilities shows compliance with the security regime by indicating that risks assessment have been made, and proposed corrective measures have been accepted and certified by the member government.[95]

This is particularly significant not only because ISPS is an international response to perceived global threats made more likely post the three Yemen incidents and 9/11, but also because it governs more than 90% of the world's trade that is transported in more than 230 million cargo containers yearly.[96] As such, it is particularly disheartening to learn that Indonesia, the country of origin for the ABC News "dirty container" simulation, is one of the 108 signatories to the ISPS, and Jakarta, the seaport of entry for the test, is one of the more than 8,000 port facilities worldwide declared in compliance with ISPS by having an approved PFSP.[97] Furthermore, given the perspective of our current political security environment, as the country with the largest Muslim population, the world's largest exporter of liquid natural gas, and exporter of over 2.7 million containers per year,[98] the failure of Indonesian port security officials to detect the depleted uranium and expose ABC's simulation gives much cause for alarm. Even more troubling is the fact that just weeks prior to ABC's test, in the same port of Los Angeles, the then Secretary of the DHS Tom Ridge, in an effort to assure a group of port officials of the Bush administration's commitment to preventing terrorism on US shores, had outlined a number of measures undertaken by the US government to better secure our seaports from a containerized threat such as that simulated by ABC News.[99] Thus, in view of the ABC News simulation, which highlights our continued vulnerability years after the USS Cole and 9/11 attacks, the concern that remains is what has been done on the national level by those responsible for our security to prevent a dirty container from reaching one of our seaports?[100]

For containerized cargo, DHS has implemented a three-layered system based on the view that containerized commerce is best secured if a suspicious container

---

[93] The ISPS Code applies only to ships of more than 500 tons engaged in international voyages and the seaports that service these ships. Information available at www2.imo.org\ISPSCode\ISPSInformation.aspx

[94] The code is even more relevant because it is common in maritime trade for ships to be registered under the flag of one country, owned by citizens of another, and manned by crews from many countries.

[95] Organization for Economic Co-operation and Development estimates initial ISPS compliance costs to ship operators at more than $1,279 million and a similar amount to seaports and their facilities.

[96] OECD Maritime Transport Committee, Security in Maritime Transport, p. 7.

[97] Jakarta International Container Terminal's Port Facility Plan was approved by the IMO on June 23, 2004. See http://gisis.imo.org/Public/ISPS/

[98] Available http://www.oocl.com/trade_news/20030715.htm

[99] John M. Broder, At Nation's Ports, Cargo Backlog Raises Question of Security, New York Times Co., July 27, 2004 Sec. A: Col. 1

[100] Campbell and Gunaratna suggest that there are many indications of planned attacks on maritime targets post-9/11. Campbell and Gunaratna, "Maritime Terrorism, Piracy and Crime," pp. 77–80.

is screened at its port of entry rather than at its port of unloading, thus preventing it from entering the global shipping stream. The Container Security Initiative ("CSI"), a set of bilateral, reciprocal agreements with at present 44 foreign seaports,[101] allows US inspectors to be placed overseas at the world's top seaports where they are able to screen and assess the potential risk of individual containers and, if determined suspicious, either request that it not be loaded onto the ship or labeled for further inspection on arrival in the United States. According to DHS, by moving the loci of container inspections to the ports of origin, CSI extends our zone of security and should not only prevent a "dirty" container from entering the global trade stream but once fully implemented, should screen an estimated 80% of all cargo containers bound for the United States.[102] Securing containerized cargo also means establishing a chain of custody that insures that the cargo is packed in a secure environment and is secured from being tampered with up to the point of it being loaded onto a ship. Under the Customs Trade Partnership Against Terrorism ("C-TPAT") agreement, commercial importers in most countries, in exchange for preferential shipping treatment, have agreed to accept and implement DHS' suggested precautions to improve the safety of their supply lines.[103] As an agreement between international shippers and US Customs, C-TPAT moves the loci of cargo container integrity to the shipping bay of the factory where the container is loaded. Additionally, DHS' 24-Hour Rule mandates that the manifest for all cargo bound for US seaports must be transmitted to the US Coast Guard 24 hours before being loaded onto the ship. This allows DHS to analyze the cargo information for potential risks and, if necessary, stop the container from being loaded onto the ship or target it for further screening at the US seaport of unloading, depending on the type and severity of the potential threat. Further, all ships bound for US seaports are required to provide, in addition to the manifest, detailed and complete information pertaining to their voyage history, cargo, passengers and crew 96 hours prior to arrival at a US seaport. This requirement allows DHS to conduct, if needed, random and strategic boarding of ships within the 12-mile US territorial coastline. Fortunately, should these preventive measures fail and a "dirty" cargo container goes undetected and arrives at a US seaport, special radiation detection portals installed at key seaports are in place to screen designated containers for biological, chemical,

---

[101]Government Accountability Office (GAO), Container Security: Flexible Staffing Model and Minimum Equipment Requirements Would Improve Overseas Targeting and Inspection Efforts, April 2005, GAO-05-557. Customs and Border Protection briefing materials for Republican staff, June 23, 2006 (available upon request). CBP, Performance and Accountability Report, FY2005, p. 25.

[102]US Bureau of Customs and Border Protection: Container Security Initiative. Available at http://www.cbp.gov/xp/cgov/newsroom/fact_sheets/trade_security/csi.xml

[103]Securing the Global Supply Chain: Customs-Trade Partnership against Terrorism. (C-TPAT) Strategic Plan. Available at http://www.cbp.gov/linkhandler/cgov/trade/cargo_security/ ctpat/what_ctpat/ctpat_strategicplan.ctt/ctpat_strategicplan.pdf. As of November 2004, C-TPAT had 7,400 enrolled partners with 86 of the top 100 US importers by containerized cargo volume. DHS Performance Report, 2004. Available at www.CBP.gov

or radiation-emitting contaminants.[104] All the same, according to officials of the Port Authority of New York and New Jersey ("PANYNJ"), the nation's third largest seaport, as of June 2005, only 45% of all arriving cargo containers were scanned for radiation[105] and the most remarkable result of this scanning was the approximately 150 false alarms recorded daily by the 22 radiation detection portals.[106] Nationwide it was estimated that in 2004 there were more than 10,000 recorded false alarms.[107]

However, it should be noted that radiation scanning at US seaports is considered the last layer of DHS' multilayered security regime and as such is geared toward complementing and not replacing the other initiatives. Nevertheless, at a Congressional hearing on the Integrated Deepwater System, a US Coast Guard program to upgrade and/or replace their aging fleet of ships and aircrafts, Representative Marion Barry told the Commandant of the Coast Guard, "Admiral with all due respect to you,... I sincerely hope that you know more about what you're doing than I think you do. I have never seen such a conglomeration of mumbo jumbo in all my days, and you scare me to death."[108]

Another outspoken critic, while applauding the measures taken so far to secure our seaports, claims that the DHS' multilayered security regime is a mere "house of cards." [109] Specifically, even if it is accepted that the underlying basis for the establishment of an end-to-end custody enterprise under C-TPAT is to prevent the opening of every single container, Stephen Flynn, Former Coast Guard Commander, charges that the C-TPAT program is particularly porous for "all a terrorist organization needs to do is find a single weak link within a trusted shipper's complex supply chain."[110] Flynn further claims that C-TPAT "standards are so nominal" that it more

---

[104]In keeping with his commitment to provide security against terrorism as outlined in his 2003 State of the Union's address, President Bush on July 21, 2004, authorized the use of $5.6 billion for pharmaceutical and biochemical research over the next 10 years. The Project Bioshield Act provides funding for the development of bioterrorism countermeasures such as vaccines, antidotes, and other treatments against a possible terrorist attack.

[105]Veronique de Rugy, Is Port Security Spending Making us Safer? Available at www.aei.org/doc.lib/2005_PortSecuritySpending

[106]Another "false alarm" occurred in July 2004 and resulted in the detention of the container ship the CASV Rio Puelo. An anonymous e-mail warning of lemons contaminated with a harmful biological substance led to a 1-week quarantine of the ship and its highly perishable cargo at a loss of $318,000 to its Chilean shipping company. Anthony Ramirez, Sour Surprise for Officers Who raided Container Ship, *The New York Times*, August 7, 2004. Sec. B; Co. 1.

[107]Testimony of Customs and Border Protection Commissioner Bonner before the US House of Representatives Appropriations Committee, Subcommittee on Homeland Security, March 15, 2005. Retrieved on January 14, 2008 from http://www.scribd.com/doc/219218/US-Congressional-Record-Daily-Digest

[108]Federal News Service, Inc., Hearing of the Homeland Security Subcommittee of the House Appropriations Committee; Subject: The Coast Guard Deepwater Program, Washington, D.C., June 22, 2005.

[109]Stephen Flynn, Council on Foreign Relations, "Port Security is Still a House of Cards," *Far Eastern Economic Review*, 169:1 January/February 2006.
[110]Ibid.

or less works "on an honor system."[111] In fact in a May 2005 report, the General Accounting Office ("GAO") criticized the C-TPAT validation process in stating that it is "not rigorous enough to ensure that the security procedures outlined in members' security profiles are reliable, accurate, and effective."[112] The report states that as a result, C-TPAT suppliers were benefiting from the program in receiving reduced scrutiny even before their enhanced security measures were validated by Bureau of Customs and Border Protection. Even worse is the GAO's finding that some containers targeted for inspection in overseas seaports were not being inspected by the overseas authorities in charge of those seaports.[113]

Altogether, these charges and findings paint a grim picture of a multilayered security regime that is not just porous but packed with gaping holes large enough to permit a 40-ft "dirty" cargo container access to one of our seaports and the urban population adjacent to it.[114] Called our modern day "Trojan horse," the cargo container is the foundation of global trade[115] and even though it has contributed much efficiency to maritime trade, for some it is one of the more likely sources of the next terrorist attack on American shores, a fact, they argue, that necessitates the total screening of every cargo container unloaded at a US seaport at a nominal cost estimated to be anywhere from $8 to $100 per container.[116]

Assessing the Proper Response

Opponents of 100% screening claim that despite the "nuke-in-box" scenario being "one of the least likely forms of terrorist attacks… it is used to hamstring global commerce while costing billions of dollars."[117] Further evidence of this divide on the need and cost to screen all cargo containers at our seaports was part of the recent

---

[111] Testimony of Stephen Flynn, March 28, 2006. Retrieved on January 14, 2008, from http://www.cfr.org/publication/7314/ongoing_neglect_of_maritime_transportation_security.html

[112] Homeland Security: Key Cargo Security Program Can Be Improved, GAO, May 2005. Available at www.gao/new.items/d05466t.pdf

[113] GAO report.

[114] According to one expert, "the port itself is rarely the target; it is simply a way to get the WMD into the country." Dennis Michael Egan of System Planning Corp., a container tracking technology provider in a pilot program with DHS. Lisa Harrington, Maritime Security: Open to Risk, Available at www.inboundlogistics.com/articles/features/1004_feature02.shtml

[115] Council on Foreign Relations speech, New York City, Jan. 11, 2005.

[116] Schumer's remarks to the US Senate in support of his amendment to the Port Security Improvement Act 2006. Testimony of Stephen Flynn, March 28, 2006a.

[117] Lara L. Sowinski, A Turning Tide for US Seaports, World Trade Magazine, December 1, 2004. Available at www.worldtrademagazine.com; Alane Kochems, Taking a Global Approach to Maritime Security. The Heritage Foundation; Executive Memorandum #980. September 22, 2005; Admiral James M. Loy and Captain Robert G. Ross, Global Trade, America's Achilles Heel, Defense Horizons, Feb. 2009. RILA Testimony to House Ways and Means Subcommittee on Trade, June 17, 2004.

defeat of US Senator Schumer's proposed amendment to the Port Security Act of 2006. Billed as No. 4930, Schumer's amendment would have required integrated screening, by 2008, of all cargo containers using an advanced nuclear detection system similar to that now in use in Hong Kong, Singapore.[118] While there are many opinions for the amendment's defeat, the consensus seems to be that 100% screening as mandated by Schumer's amendment would not have provided the balance between commercial velocity, costs, and the security measures required to address the weaknesses and vulnerabilities of America's seaports.[119] Ideally, the combined efforts of the public and private sectors should result in such a balance, but according to Republican Duncan Hunter, Chairman of the US House Armed Services Committee, in deciding not to screen all containers arriving at our seaports we have allowed our commercial interest to get ahead of our concerns on seaport security.[120] Similarly, in a special report to the US Congress, the AFL-CIO accused Wal-Mart and the Retail Industry Leaders Association of "having systematically undermined our security by working to defeat and water down rules designed to make America's seaports... safe from terrorist attacks."[121] Other critics of our security regime point the finger not at the private sector but at the federal government contending that a disproportionate amount of the nation's transportation security resources has been allocated to airport security, resulting in a lack of financial appropriation from Washington for the improvements in seaport security mandated by law.[122]

According to Stephen Flynn, federal spending post-9/11 amounts to only 10% of the US Coast Guard's estimated costs required to comply with federal mandates for seaport security enhancement for the next 10 years.[123] The resulting deficit between what the federal government provides and what the Coast Guard has assessed as required is at the very center of much debate and contention regarding our post-9/11 security.[124] Specifically, compared to the more than $18 billion spent on airport security post-9/11, the federal government has spent only $630 million on seaport

---

[118] At the seaport of Hong Kong, every container passes through a three-layered nonintrusive scanning portal. The Image and Scanner Interface Specification ("ISIS") uses image and density scanning to display the contents of every container and detect the presence of a substantial quantity of lead, which may be used to encase and hide a nuclear device. The portal also tags the container with a barcode that can be read and tracked at any time and any point during the journey to its destination. See portal information available at www.SAIC.com/products/security/at-900s

[119] Comments of U.S. senators on the amendment available at http://www.govtrack.us/congress/record.xpd?id=109-s20060914-15

[120] Interview on Fox News. Sunday, March 12, 2006.

[121] Unchecked: How Wal-Mart Uses Its Might to Block Port Security, AFL-CIO, April 2006.

[122] Interview with Bernard S. Groseclose, Jr., President for South Carolina States Ports Authority. Lara L. Sowinski, A Turning Tide for US Seaports.

[123] Testimony of Stephen Flynn before a hearing of the Subcommittee on Coast Guard and Maritime Transportation Committee on Transportation and Infrastructure United States House of Representative. August 25, 2004.

[124] Under MTSA, federal grants only fund 75% of any approved security project.

security,[125] despite the fact that security post-9/11 has become the "the fastest growing and least controllable cost" [126] for the maritime industry.[127] Moreover, as new legislation and regulations covering the full infrastructure of security are enacted together with advances in technology that would make these mandates feasible, port officials are concerned not only with how to pay for the enhanced security costs but also with how to do so while continuing to cover the regular maintenance and improvement costs necessary for the day-to-day operation of their ports. For although there is little or no disagreement among port officials and security experts that the federal mandates are crucial and tantamount to our security infrastructure, the unsettled and widely debated issue is how to pay for them since it appears that "we don't have enough public money to do everything that needs to be done,"[128] despite the fact that "ports more than ever need a greater federal partnership in their efforts to harden their facilities against terrorism."[129]

One of the suggested ways to make up for the deficit is an across the board implementation of user fees.[130] For example, Bernard S. Groseclose of the Port of Charleston, South Carolina, contends that because his port receives no subsidies from the state, it is forced to pass the additional cost for improved security onto the users of his port.[131] Other suggestions include funds provided by state or local governments, the maritime industry or a combination of all sources, in addition to the funds provided by the federal government.[132] Some have even suggested that in view of our finite resources and because the federal money provided to our seaports to enhance security does not necessarily bolster maritime security, it should instead be spent on the coast guard, which is our earliest defense against dangerous cargo.[133] It is submitted that we cannot trade one for the other. Americans are more concerned with security itself rather than with whether or not it is funded by the

---

[125] Security Gaps Already Plague Ports: Proposed DP World Deal Sheds Light on Problems That Continues to Be Vexing, *Wall Street Journal*, Feb. 23, 2006.

[126] Lara L. Sowinski, A Turning Tide for US Seaports.

[127] It is estimated that the implementation of the ISPS Code has cost ship operators $1,279 billion. OECD Maritime Transport Committee, "Security in Maritime Transport," p. 56.

[128] Statement of Former Secretary of DHS Tom Ridge. John McLaughlin, Lloyd's List, April 13, 2004.

[129] Statement of Kurt Nagle, AAPA Applauds Congress For Passing Port Security Bill But Ports "Troubled" That Recent Appropriations Don't Match Congressionally Recommended Funding, Press Release: American Association of Port Authorities, Sep. 30, 2006.

[130] Although different as to how it would be administered, both Senator Fritz Hollings and Representative Dana Rohrabacher have sponsored amendments to various legislations, proposing the use of a per-container fee to fund seaport security. See Rohrabacher's amendment to H.R. 2557 and Hollings amendment to the MTSA.

[131] In July 2003, the Port of Charleston implemented a security surcharge of $1 per foot of the length of the ship per port visit. Lara L. Sowinski, A Turning Tide for US Seaports.

[132] A 2001 survey shows that most American seaports break even or are barely profitable. US DOT, Maritime Administration, Public Port Finance Survey for FY1999, Jan. 2001.

[133] James Jay Carafano, Countdown to 9/11: Five Fixes For Homeland Security by the Fifth Anniversary of the Attacks, The Heritage Foundation. WebMemo #963. January 23, 2006.

federal government, absorbed by the manufacturer, or passed on to the consumer. This is not to say that Americans are unconcerned with costs, but the more important question concerning costs should not be whether or not we can afford such measures, it is whether or not we can afford not to have them.

Conclusions

One indication of the costs that can result from a failure to balance security with the need to maintain maritime velocity can be gleaned from the delays incurred during the implementation of the enhanced security measures, which doubled the unloading time of a ship from 3–4 days to 6–7 days at the port of Los Angeles/Long Beach during the peak of the 2004 shipping period. Even though a labor action differs significantly from a terrorist attack, especially in terms of notice, reference can also be drawn from the 2002 closure of seaports in Southern California due to the IWLU 10-day lockout. While estimates vary, one credible source puts the costs at $466.9 million,[134] which appears nominal relative to the economic catastrophe that would result from a security breach by a single cargo container. In its Terrorist War game, the consulting firm of Booz Allen Hamilton put together a panel of 85 government and industry representatives to test their responses to terrorist attacks using a cargo container to smuggle and detonate both radiological and conventional bombs in a US seaport. The 2-day game estimated that such an attack would do some $58 billion worth of damage to the US economy.[135] Another estimate of a single cargo container breach puts the costs to companies upward of $1 trillion in addition to the costs of response and recovery.[136]

In addition to questions pertaining to the costs of enhanced security, other critics of our lack of progress since 9/11 question our "response and emergency management-business continuity" preparedness to quickly recover and resume normal operations if the next terrorist attack occurs in one of our seaports.[137]

According to Flynn, there is no national incident management scheme in place and "no planning or exercise done for how to restore the system should our preventive efforts fail."[138] Bethann Rooney, Director of Security for PANYNJ, agrees. According to Rooney, although a terrorist event will result in "massive disruption [and] a complete shutdown" of the seaport affected, "we don't yet have clear

---

[134]Organization for Economic Co-operation and Development: Security in Maritime Transport: Risk Factors and Economic Impact, July 2003.

[135]Port Security War Game: Implications for US Supply Chains, Available at http://www. boozallen.com/publications/article/1440496

[136]Michael E. O'Hanlon et al., Protecting the American Homeland: One Year On, *Brookings Institution Press*, Washington, DC, 2003.

[137]Lara L. Sowinski, A Turning Tide for US Seaports.

[138]Ibid.

protocols and procedures to deal with those types of emergencies" as required by Sec 70104, MTSA.[139]

Our lack of clear protocols and procedures to recover from an emergency caused by a terrorist attack on one of our seaports was much politicized and publicly debated in late February 2006 when concerns about the vulnerability of our seaports echoed across the nation on disclosure that the operation and control of six US seaports were slated for transfer to Dubai Ports World ("DPW"), a company based in Dubai, the United Arab Emirates. The deal estimated to be worth in excess of $6.8 billion would have turned over the day-to-day operation and control of the ports of New York, New Jersey, Philadelphia, Baltimore, Miami, and New Orleans from a British company, Peninsula Oriental Steamship Navigation Company, to DPW, a company owned by the United Arab Emirates, home of Fayez Banihammad and Marwan al-Shehhi, two of the 9/11 hijackers.[140] According to critics of the deal, which was sanctioned by the Bush administration, "Dubai, which owns and controls the acquiring company... has been named as a key transfer point for shipments of nuclear components... to Iran, North Korea and Libya."[141] Reacting to snowballing criticism from all sides of the political spectrum, the Bush administration attempted to assure the nation that "nothing in the acquisition has anything to do with the responsibility for security in American ports."[142] Even the president himself tried to put a positive spin on the deal in questioning "why it's OK for a British company to operate our ports but not a company from the Middle East when we [the Bush administration] have already determined that security is not an issue."[143] All the same, the deal that was to take effect on March 2, 2006, was first put on hold and by March 15, 2006, was effectively dead.[144] On December 11, 2006, Dubai Ports World sold its interest in the six ports to American International Group ("AIG") for an undisclosed amount reported to be approximately $750 million.[145] What is particularly important of the "Dubai port" ordeal within the context of this chapter is that it is quite apparent that our seaports continue to be "our most vulnerable targets

---

[139] Statement of Bethann Rooney, Manager of the Port Authority of NY & NJ before the Committee on Transport and Infrastructure Subcommittee on Coast Guard and Maritime Transportation. June 3, 2003. The SAFE Port Act of 2006 appears to correct this deficiency, although it only calls for the development of such a plan for every seaport and, as of November 2006, no such plan was in place.

[140] Bipartisan letter to secretary John W. Snow, Department of Treasury. Available at http://schumer.senate.gov/new_website/record.cfm?id=259436&

[141] Bipartisan letter to secretary John W. Snow, Department of Treasury. Available at www.sente.gov/~schumer/SchumerWebsite/pressroom/press_releases/2006/PR66.UAE.021606

[142] Comments attributed to US State Department spokesman Adam Ereli. February 22, 2006c. CNN.com

[143] Comments attributed to President Bush aboard Air Force One. February 22, 2006b. CNN.com.

[144] According to Rep. Peter King, Chairman of the House Homeland Security Committee, "my office has received more phone calls on this than on any issue in the 14 years I've been in the United States Congress." February 22, 2006a. CNN.com.

[145] Heather Timmons, Dubai Port Company Sells Its US Holdings to A.I.G., *New York Times*, December 12, 2006. Late Edition, Sec. C, Col. 1.

for terrorist attacks" and more importantly, it is accepted that "a single terrorist incident could shut down our system of container transportation, affecting our entire economy, as well as facilities relied on by the Department of Defense as military load-out ports."[146] The ordeal also shows that in stark contrast, our pre-9/11 failure may have been "one of imagination";[147] Americans can not only imagine another attack but are very realistic about the possibility that it may be at one of the nation's 361 seaports.

Therefore, in light of the chilling originality used to facilitate recent acts of terror around the world, our realism about future terrorist attacks on the United States, and the vulnerability of our seaports to such possibilities, it is fair to ask: are we there yet? That is, are we at the point where our seaports are secured from terrorists committed to killing a large number of Americans, crippling our economy, even if temporarily, while garnering worldwide media attention in doing so? More importantly and as inevitable as it seems, if the next terrorist attack occurs at one of our seaports, are we prepared to avoid a recovery fiasco far worse than the one that followed 9/11? By most accounts we are not as prepared as we should be to avoid or recover from it, but we have made significant steps toward securing our seaports in what may well be a never ending war on terrorism.

References

32 Stowaways found on ship. (January 16, 2005). *Los Angeles Times*. Retrieved on January 14, 2008, from http://articles.latimes.com/2005/jan/16/local/me-stowaways16.

A nation challenged: Fatal attack; officials say bomber of the Cole was in Yemeni custody earlier. (December 7, 2001). *New York Times*, Sec. A; p. 1; Col. 5.

ABCNews Online. (February 5, 2005). *Yemen court sentences Limburg bomb leader to death.* Retrieved on January 14, 2008, from www.abc.net.au/news/stories/2005/02/05/1296753.htm

Ahmad, A. (April 7, 2001). *Yemen arrests three suspects in USS Cole bombing.* Associated Press. Retrieved on January 14, 2008, from www.cjonline.com/stories/040801/new_natworld08.shtml

America's Ports Today. (February 2006). The American Association of Ports. Retrieved on January 14, 2008, from www.aapa-ports.org

At least 6 arrested in Cole investigation, Yemen official says. (November 26, 2000). *CNN* Retrieved on January 14, 2008, from archives.cnn.com/2000/US/12/11/cole.family.connection

Broder, J. M. (July 27, 2004). At nation's ports, cargo backlog raises question of security. *New York Times*. Retrieved on January 14, 2008, from query.nytimes.com/gst/fullpage.html?res=9500EFD8153DF934A15754C0A9629C8B63

Burns, J. (November 1, 2000). U.S. Aides say the Yemenis seem to hinder Cole inquiry. *New York Times*. Retrieved on January 14, 2008, from query.nytimes.com/gst/fullpage.html?res=9900E6DD1030F932A35752C1A9669C8B63&n

Burns, J. F. (October 23, 2000). Investigators discouraging speculation in Cole attack. *New York Times*. Sec. A; p. 6; Col. 1. Retrieved on January 14, 2008, from query.nytimes.com/gst/fullpage.html?res=9C01E0DC1631F930A15753C1A9669C8B63

---

[146]Bipartisan letter to Secretary John W. Snow, Department of Treasury. Available at http://schumer.senate.gov/new_website/record.cfm?id=259436&

[147]Depart Office Department Memo, Wolfowitz to Rumsfeld, "Were We Asleep?" September 18, 2001. Report of The National Commission on Terrorist Attacks Upon the United States. p. 577.

Burns, J. F. (August 21, 2001). F.B.I.'s inquiry in Cole attack is nearing halt. *New York Times*, Sec. A; p. 1; Col. 5.

Burns, J. F., & Myers, S. L. (October 18, 2000). U.S. says Yemen has found 'Leads' in bombing. *The New York Times*. Retrieved on January 14, 2008, from query.nytimes.com/gst/fullpage.html?res=9C07EFDD143EF93BA25753C1A9669C8B63

C-4 Explosive was used in USS Cole attack. (November 1, 2000). *CNN*. Retrieved on January 14, 2008, from archives.cnn.com/2000/US/11/03/c-4.cole/

Campbell, T., & Gunaratna, R. (2003). Maritime terrorism, piracy and crime. In R. Gunaratna (Ed.), *Terrorism in the Asia-Pacific: Threat and response*. Singapore: Eastern University Press.

Carafano, J. J. (May 25, 2006). Countdown to 9–11: Five fixes for homeland security by the fifth anniversary of the attacks. The Heritage Foundation. WebMemo #963. Retrieved on January 14, 2008, from www.heritage.org/about/staff/jamescarafanopapers.cfm

Chakravarty, S. (July 2, 2001). Terrorism: Target America. *India Today*. Retrieved on January 14, 2008, from www.india-today.com/itoday/20010702/crime.shtml

CNN. (February 22, 2006a). According to Rep. Peter King, Chairman of the House Homeland Security Committee, "my office has received more phone calls on this than on any issue in the 14 years I've been in the United States Congress." Retrieved on January 14, 2008, from transcripts.cnn.com/TRANSCRIPTS/ 0602/21/ldt.01.html

CNN. (February 22, 2006b). Comments attributed to President Bush aboard Air Force One. Retrieved on January 14, 2008, from transcripts.cnn.com/TRANSCRIPTS/0602/21/ldt.01.html

CNN. (February 22, 2006c). Comments attributed to U.S. State Department spokesman Adam Ereli. Retrieved on January 14, 2008, from transcripts.cnn.com/TRANSCRIPTS/ 0602/21/ldt.01.html

Cole attack was terrorists' second try, U.S. officials say. (November 9, 2000). *CNN* Retrieved on January 14, 2008, from www.cnn.com/2000/WORLD/meast/11/24/yemen.cole/index.html

Cole suspect sketches created. (October 28, 2000). *Associated Press*. Retrieved on January 14, 2008, from http://www.al-bab.com/yemen/cole5.htm

Court upholds death sentence in USS Cole bombing. (February 28, 2005). *CNN*. Retrieved on January 14, 2008, from www.cnn.com/2005/WORLD/meast/02/26/yemen.cole/index.html

Cuevas, F. (April 11, 1984). CIA-Backed rebels claim port mining is justified. *Associated Press*. AM cycle.

De Rugy, V. (September 7, 2005). Is port security spending making us safer? Retrieved on January 14, 2008, from www.aei.org/doc.lib/2005_PortSecuritySpending

Defense official resigned after Cole attack, says warnings were ignored. (October 25, 2000). *CNN*. Retrieved on January 14, 2008, from archives.cnn.com/2000/ALLPOLITICS/ stories/10/25/congress.aid.reut/index.html

Federal News Service, Inc. (June 22, 2005). Hearing of the Homeland Security Subcommittee of the House Appropriations Committee; Subject: The Coast Guard Deepwater Program. Washington, DC. *News Service*. Retrieved on January 14, 2008, from http:// commerce.senate.gov/public/index.cfm?Fuseaction=Search.Search&searchtext=servi

Flynn, S. (January/February 2006). Port security is still a house of cards. *Far Eastern Economic Review, 169:1*. Retrieved on January 14, 2008, from http://info.hktdc.com/ econforum/dj/feer060201.htm

Gen. Anthony zinni testifies before senate armed services committee on uss cole disaster. (October 19, 2000). *CNN*. Retrieved on January 14, 2008, from transcripts.cnn.com/transcripts/ 0010/19/se.03.htm

Gerencser, M., Weinberg, J., & Vincent, D. (n.d.) Port security war game: Implications for U.S. supply chains. Booz & Allen & Hamilton. Retrieved on January 14, 2008, from http://www.boozallen.com/media/file/128648.pdf

Gilmore, J. What if... *PBS Frontline*. Retrieved on January 14, 2008, from http://www.pbs.org/ wgbh/pages/frontline/shows/knew/could

Government Accountability Office (GAO). (April 2005). Container security: Flexible staffing model and minimum equipment requirements would improve overseas targeting and inspection efforts. Customs and Border Protection briefing materials for Republican staff. GAO-05-557 FY2005. Retrieved on January 14, 2008, from rpc.senate.gov/public/_files/Oct506HR4954SafePortActLB.pdf

Harrington, L. (2004). Maritime security: Open to risk. Retrieved on January 14, 2008, from www.inboundlogistics.com/articles/features/1004_feature02.shtml

Homeland security: Key cargo security program can be improved. (May 2005). GAO. Retrieved on January 14, 2008, from www.gao/new.items/d05466t.pdf

IMB says security threats remain despite new safety measures. (September 22, 2004). The International Chamber of Commerce. London. Retrieved on January 14, 2008, from http://www.icc-ccs.org/index.

Kochems, A. (September 22, 2005). Taking a global approach to maritime security. The Heritage Foundation; Executive Memorandum #980. Retrieved on January 14, 2008, from http://www.heritage.org/Research/HomelandSecurity/em980.cfm

Loy, J. M., & Ross, R. G. (February 23, 2009). *Global trade, America's Achilles heel*. Defense Horizons. Vol. 7.

Lumpkin, J. J. (November 21, 2002). U.S. Says it has al-Qaida's Persian Gulf operations chief in custody. *The Associated Press*. Retrieved on January 14, 2008, from www.highbeam.com/doc/1G1-94670273.html

Mac Farquhar, N., & Johnston, D. (September 30, 2004). Death sentences in attack on Cole. *New York Times*, Sec. A; Col. 5; p. 1.

Marine Transportation System Task Force. (September 1999). An assessment of the U.S. Marine Transportation System: A report to Congress. Washington, DC. Retrieved on January 14, 2008, from fdsys.gpo.gov/fdsys/pkg/FR-1999-09-09/pdf/99-23392.pdf

Marques, C. (December 25, 2002). Threats and responses: Transportation security; safety chief tries to make travel easy, too. *New York Times*. Retrieved on January 14, 2008, from query.nytimes.com/gst/fullpage.html?res=9C02E6DB133CF936A15751C1A9649C8B63

McLaughlin, J. (April 13, 2004). Statement of former Secretary of DHS Tom Ridge. *Lloyd's List*. Retrieved on January 14, 2008, from www.nti.org/d_newswire/issues/2004_4_13.html

Melissa, G. (January 8, 2007). Miami scare puts NYPD on alert. *New York Daily News*. Retrieved on January 14, 2008, from http://www.nydailynews.com/news/us_world/2007/07/16/2007-07-16_bomb_scare_at_miami_airport.html

Miller, J. (October 10, 1985). Hijackers yield ship in Egypt: Passenger slain, 400 are safe; U.S. assails deal with captors. *New York Times*. Sec. A; P. 1; Col. 6.

Nagle, K. (September 30, 2006). AAPA applauds Congress for passing port security bill but ports 'troubled' that recent appropriations don't match congressionally recommended funding. *Press Release*. American Association of Port Authorities. Retrieved on January 14, 2008, from www.aapa-ports.org/Press/PRDetail.cfm?ItemNumber=1288

National Commission on Terrorist attacks upon the United States. (2002). The 9/11 Commission Report. New York: W.W. Norton.

Nine people questioned say sources. (November 13, 2000). *CNN*. Retrieved on January 14, 2008, from edition1.cnn.com/2000/US/11/07/uss.cole.02/

O'Hanlon, M. E., Orsag, P. R., Daalder, I. H., Drestler, I. M., Gunter, D. L., Linsay, J., et al. (2003). *Protecting the American homeland: One year on*. Washington, DC: Brookings Institution Press.

Pakistan captures USS Cole suspect. (May 1, 2003). *Birmingham Post (UK)*. Retrieved on January 14, 2008, from http://www.highbeam.com/doc/1P2-9887449.html

Ramirez, A. (August 7, 2004). Sour surprise for officers who raided container ship. *The New York Times*. Retrieved on January 14, 2008, from query.nytimes.com/gst/fullpage.html?res=9904E0DF103CF934A3575BC0A9629C8B63

Remains of 1 Cole bomber found, U.S. official say. (November 17, 2000). CNN. Retrieved on January 14, 2008, from archives.cnn.com/2000/US/12/11/cole.family.connection

Risen, J., & Bonner, R. (December 7, 2001). A nation challenged: Fatal attack; officials say bomber was in Yemeni custody earlier. *The New York Times*. Retrieved on January 14, 2008, from query.nytimes.com/gst/fullpage.html?res=9C0CE5D7133CF934A35751C1A9679C8B63

Ross, B. (October 6, 2003). How safe are U.S. borders? Customs fail to detect depleted Uranium – Again. *ABC News*. Retrieved on January 14, 2008, from http://media.abcnews.com/WNT/story?id=129321&page=1

Scarborough, R. (October 26, 2000). Pentagon analyst resigns over ignored warnings. *Washington Times*. Page A1. Retrieved on January 14, 2008, from www.mail-archive.com/ctrl@listserv.aol.com/msg53650.html

Schumer, C. (2006a) Remarks to the U.S. Senate in support of his amendment to the Port Security Improvement Act 2006. Retrieved on January 14, 2008, from http://www.state.gov/s/d/rm/rls/perfplan/2005/html/29302.htm

Schumer, C. (2006b). Bipartisan letter to Secretary John W. Snow, Department of Treasury. Retrieved on January 14, 2008, from www.sente.gov/~schumer/SchumerWebsite/pressroom/press_releases/2006/PR66.UAE.021606

Security gaps already plague ports: Proposed DP World deal sheds light on problems that continues to be vexing. (February 23, 2006). *Wall Street Journal*. Retrieved on January 14, 2008, from https://www.wallstreetjournal.com.

Seper, J. (November 22, 2002). Senior al Qaeda chief in custody of U.S.; Leader of Gulf operations offers data. *The Washington Times*. P. 1, pg. A01. Retrieved on January 14, 2008, from www.washingtontimes.com

Ships as terrorist attacks. (October 25, 2002). American Shipper. Yemen Gateway. *Middle East International*. Retrieved on January 14, 2008, from www.al-bab.com

Sisk, R. (July 7, 2001). State Dept., FBI eyed in Yemen feud. *NY Daily News*. Retrieved on January 14, 2008, from www.nydailynews.com/archives/news/2001/07/07/2001-07-07_state_dept___fbi_eyed_in_yem.htm

Six charged for USS Cole bombing. (July 9, 2004). *Aljazeera.net*. Retrieved on January 14, 2008, from english.aljazeera.net/archive/2004/07/2008410151842952130.html

Sketch in Cole attack resembles Africa bomb suspect. (November 24, 2000). *Florida Times-Union*. Retrieved on January 14, 2008, from www.jacksonville.com

Sowinski, L. L. (December 1, 2004). A turning tide for U.S. seaports. *World Trade Magazine*. Retrieved on January 14, 2008, from http://www.worldtrademag.com/CDA/Articles/ASIP_general/653d1e36d9af7010VgnVCM100000f932a8c0

Taubman, P. (April 15, 1984). President's 'Secret War' in Nicaragua backfires. *New York Times*, Sec. 4; p. 1; Col. 1.

Timmons, H. (December 12, 2006). Dubai port company sells its U.S. holdings to A.I.G. *New York Times*, Late Edition, Sec. C; Col. 1.

Unchecked: How Wal-Mart uses its might to block port security. (April 2006). AFL-CIO. Retrieved on January 14, 2008, from www.aflcio.org/corporatewatch/walmart/upload/walmart_unchecked_0406.pdf

U.S. Department of Homeland Security Office of Inspector General. (September 2004). Effectiveness of Customs and Border Protection's procedures to detect uranium in two smuggling incidents. Retrieved on January 14, 2008, from www.dhs.gov/xoig/assets/mgmtrpts/OIG-04-40.pdf

U.S. Department of Homeland Security. Performance Report, 2004. Retrieved on January 14, 2008, from http://www.dhs.gov/xlibrary/assets/CFO_DHSPerformanceandAccountabilityReport_2004.pdf

U.S. Department of Homeland Security. Performance Report, 2005. Retrieved on January 14, 2008, from http://www.dhs.gov/xlibrary/assets/CFO_PerformanceAccountabilityReport_2005.pdf

U.S. Senate Armed Services Committee. (October 19, 2000). Hearing on the recent attack in Yemen on the USS Cole. Retrieved on January 14, 2008, from http://www.fas.org/man/congress/2000/zinni_testimony.htm

U.S. State Department Briefing. (November 29, 2000) Retrieved on January 14, 2008, from http://www.fas.org/man/dod-101/sys/ship/docs/man-sh-ddg51-001130.htm

USS Cole plot began after embassy attacks, investigator says. (December 20, 2000). *CNN*. Retrieved on January 14, 2008, from archives.cnn.com/2000/US/12/20/terrorism.threat.02/.

USS Cole probe seeks evidence of conspiracy. (October 20, 2000). *CNN*. Retrieved on January 14, 2008, from archives.cnn.com/2000/US/10/20/cole.evidence/

Verbatim Transcript of Combatant Status Review Tribunal Hearing for ISN 10015 (Abd al-Rahim al Nashiri). Retrieved on January 14, 2008, from http://www.globalsecurity.org/security/library/report/2007/al-nashiri_csrt-hearing070314.htm

Vick, K. (December 10, 2001). Sudan, newly helpful, remains wary of U.S.: Officials share files but deny ties to foiled attack. *The Washington Post*, Sec. A; Pg. A15. Retrieved on January 14, 2008, from www.washingtonpost.com/ac2/wp-dyn/A17882-2001Dec9

Vise, D. A. (December 7, 2000). Yemeni citizens face trial in Cole Bombing; Prime Minister says at least three are accused of helping to organize attack. *The Washington Post*, Sec. A; Pg. A28.

Whitaker, B. (October 15, 2001). Piecing together the terrorist jigsaw. *Guardian Unlimited*. Retrieved on January 14, 2008, from www.guardian.co.uk/Archive/Article/0,4273,4277367,00.html

White, J. (March 20, 2007). Al-Qaeda suspect says he planned Cole attack. *The Washington Post*, A01. Sec. A; Pg. A01.

Wolfowitz, P. (September 18, 2001). Were we asleep? Depart Office Department Memorandum, Wolfowitz to Rumsfeld, in Report of The National Commission on Terrorist Attacks Upon the United States.

Yemen and U.S. finalizing agreement on Cole investigation sources say. (October 31, 2000) *CNN*. Retrieved on January 14, 2008, from edition.cnn.com/2000/US/10/31/uss.cole.01/

Yemen identifies Cole attackers, Prime Minister says. (November 17, 2000). *UPI*. Retrieved on January 14, 2008, from www.highbeam.com/doc/1P1-68820754.html

Yemen names 6 suspects in USS Cole bombing. (December 13, 2000). *CNN*. Retrieved on January 14, 2008, from http://topics.cnn.com/topics/uss_cole

Yemeni on delicate path in bin Laden Hunt. (December 15, 2000). *New York Times*, Sec. A; p. 22; Col. 4.

Yemeni president calls USS Cole attack 'very well-planned.' (October 18, 2000). *CNN*. Retrieved on January 14, 2008, from archives.cnn.com/2000/US/10/18/cole.investigation/index.html

Yemen's president, naming names. (December 10, 2000). *The Washington Post*. Retrieved on January 14, 2008, from washingtonpost.com

Chapter 10
Rail Transport Security

Charles A. Lieberman and Rebecca Bucht

Introduction

Recent events provide evidence that railway targets continue to be extremely vulnerable to terrorist attacks. The high concentration of individuals in a relatively limited area provides an opportunity for high casualties, a goal among some terrorist organizations – especially among many Islamic fundamentalist groups, such as Al-Qaeda. While utilizing explosive devices has been the most frequently employed tactic employed in attacks against railway targets,[1] there are numerous other means that may be employed in the future, including the use of weapons of mass destruction (WMD). As trains tend to enter densely populated areas, the use of a WMD has the potential to result in catastrophic damage. In comparison to airline security, the limited measures utilized in maintaining security for railway targets provides an opportunity for terrorists to maximize the impact of an attack while minimizing the risk of achieving operational goals.

There have been numerous significant terrorist attacks against rail targets, including the following: the August 10, 2001, attack in Angola that killed over 250; the March 11, 2004, attack in Madrid, Spain, that killed over 190; the July 7, 2005, attacks in London, that killed over 50; the July 11, 2006, attack in Mumbai, India, that killed over 180; and the February 17, 2007, attack on the Samjhauta Express, a train traveling from India to Pakistan, that killed over 60.[2] The victims of these terrorist attacks were comprised of primarily civilians, including women, children, and the elderly. This chapter will focus on the Angola and Spain bombings, including an overview of the events, the actors responsible for the attacks, the response by

---

C.A. Lieberman (✉)
Department of Law, Police Science and Criminal Justice Administration, John Jay College of Criminal Justice, New York, NY, USA
e-mail: clieberman@jjay.cuny.edu

[1] Rand Worldwide Terrorism Incident Database. http://www.rand.org/ise/projects/terrorismdatabase/

[2] BBC News: *Angola train toll rises*, 2001, August 12; *Madrid attacks timeline*, 2004, March 12; *Dozens dead in India train blasts*, 2007, February 19; and *Scores dead in Mumbai train bombs*, 2006, July 11.

M.R. Haberfeld, A. von Hassell (eds.), *A New Understanding of Terrorism*,
DOI 10.1007/978-1-4419-0115-6_10, © Springer Science+Business Media, LLC 2009

the government's representatives and agencies, and an overview and analysis of rail security.

Overview of March 11, 2004, Madrid Railway Attack

On Thursday, March 11, 2004, 10 backpacks packed with explosives detonated in and around Madrid. Two days later, authorities had detained the first suspects, and within 3 weeks had identified much of the network responsible for organizing and planning the attacks. Suspects detonated an explosive device in an apartment, killing the seven suspects and one police officer, rather than surrender to the police forces closing in. Authorities believe that at least five members eluded capture and exited the country. One of the suspected escapees, Mohamed Afallah, died as the result of a May 2005 suicide operation in Iraq.[3]

The Attack

An Islamic fundamentalist group, allegedly associated with Al-Qaeda, employed a devastating attack against the rail system in Madrid, Spain, leading to the deaths of 191 persons and injuring approximately 1,800; the terrorist attack causing the greatest loss of life in Europe since the 1988 bombing of an airliner over Lockerbie, Scotland. The subsequent investigation led authorities to conclude that the terrorist attack involved perpetrators placing 10 backpacks with explosive devices on four commuter trains with the intent to detonate all the devices simultaneously in order to destroy the station and maximize casualties. This Islamic fundamentalist group allegedly targeted Spain due to the presence of its military forces in Iraq and was the first major attack in Europe since the 9/11 attacks in the United States. The March 11, 2004, attacks took place approximately 911 days after the September 11, 2001, attacks in the United States.

Starting at 7:39 a.m., ten near simultaneous explosions, occurring within a few minutes of each other, caused significant damage to the train cars and injury or death to those individuals traveling within. An additional three explosive devices were subsequently located and disarmed by explosives experts working with law enforcement.

> At 07:39 on 11 March 2004, 10 terrorist bomb explosions occurred almost simultaneously in four commuter trains in Madrid, Spain, killing 177 people instantly and injuring more than 2000. There were 14 subsequent in-hospital deaths, bringing the ultimate death toll to 191.[4]

---

[3] Jordán, 2006

[4] Gutiérrez de Ceballos, Turégano-Fuentes, Perez-Diaz, Sanz-Sánchez, Martin-Llorente & Guerrero-Sanz, 2004.

According to a BBC report,[5] investigators conclude that four trains, C2/ 17305CA, C1/21431, C1/21435, and C7/21713, were boarded by terrorists at Alcala de Henares station and loaded with backpacks that each contained approximately 10 kg (22 lb) of explosives. The trains subsequently departed Alcala de Henares station within 15 min of each other, between 7:00 a.m. and 7:15 a.m. It is believed the terrorists exited the trains before they left the station.

At 7:39 a.m., as the first train came to a stop in Madrid's Atocha station, three explosive devices were detonated. The devices were located in the third, fourth, and sixth carriages of the train. Almost simultaneously, four explosive devices were detonated in the first, fourth, and sixth carriages of the second train, which was about 500 m from the station because it was running 2 min behind schedule. Investigators believe that the terrorists planned to detonate the devices while both trains were in Atocha station to cause structural damage to the station and maximize casualties.

At 7:41 a.m., two explosive devices were detonated in the fourth and fifth carriages of the third train as it passed through El Pozo station. At 7:42 a.m., one explosive device was detonated in the fourth carriage of the fourth train. As a result of the four train attacks, all trains into Madrid were stopped. Based on forensic evidence from the four trains attacked in conjunction with the undetonated devices that were discovered, the devices were believed to have been detonated by mobile phone.

The Investigation of the March 11 Attacks

On March 11, at 10:50 a.m., as a result of witness statements, Spanish security forces identified and secured an abandoned van near the Alcala de Henares railway station in Madrid. Following standard operating procedures, the van was subsequently transported to central police facilities, arriving at approximately 3:00 p.m., and a search was conducted. As a result of this search, police found an audiotape with passages from the Koran in Arabic and seven fuses for explosives, with traces of dynamite (Goma 2-ECO); later determine to have been manufactured in Spain.[6]

On March 12, an Arabic-speaking man with a Moroccan accent led Madrid TV to a videotape found in a trashcan outside Madrid's largest mosque. The Interior Ministry released a small portion of the tape, with the following excerpts:

> We declare our responsibility for what happened in Madrid exactly two-and-a-half years after the attacks on New York and Washington. It is a response to your collaboration with the criminals Bush and his allies. This is a response to the crimes that you have caused in the world, and specifically in Iraq and Afghanistan, and there will be more, if God wills it. You love life and we love death, which gives an example of what the Prophet Muhammad said. If you don't stop your injustices, more and more blood will flow and these attacks will seem very small compared to what can occur in what you call terrorism.[7]

---

[5]BBC News, (2004b).

[6]Olmeda, 2005.

[7]Daly, 2005.

On April 3, 2004, as police were closing in, seven of the key suspects and one police officer died as the result of an explosion at an apartment in Madrid. The individuals suspected of being involved in the March 11 attacks that died included the following: Serhane ben Abdelmajid Fakhet (AKA El Tunecino), a Tunisian suspected of being the leader of the group; Jamal Ahmidan (AKA "El Chino" or "Mowgli"), a Moroccan also suspected of being a leader of the group; Allekema Lamari, an Algerian described as the "emir" of the train bombings by the Spanish authorities, who was charged in 1997 with belonging to an Algerian extremist group and sentenced to 14 years in prison, but who was released in 2002 after receiving a reduced sentence; Mohammed Oulad Akcha and Rachid Oulad Akcha, Moroccan brothers that are suspected of placing bombs on the trains; and Abdennabi Kounjaa (AKA "Abdallah"), a Morrocan also suspected of placing bombs on the trains.

Subsequent to the trial of the 28 people charged in connection with the March 11, 2004, Madrid train bombings, 21 were found guilty; however, a ruling by Spain's Supreme Court on July 17, 2008, acquitted four of those convicted, while convicting one suspect that had been cleared of supplying explosives for the attack. The courts decisions led to the conviction of 18 of the 28 persons charged with the attack. The following is a brief description of the individuals involved in the trial and their dispositions.[8]

Jamal Zougam, a Moroccan, was found guilty of 191 counts of murder and sentenced to 30 years for each charge, in addition to the 1,856 counts of attempted murder, for which he was sentenced to 20 years for each charge. Zougam, who ran a mobile phone shop in Madrid, was arrested 2 days after the attack. He was reported to have been under surveillance by Spanish authorities since the 2003 bombings in Casablanca, which killed 45 people. Three witnesses observed Zougam leave a backpack on one of the bombed trains.

Otman El Ghanoui, a Morrocan, was found guilty of 191 counts of murder and sentenced to 30 years for each charge, in addition to the 1,856 counts of attempted murder, for which he was sentenced to 20 years for each charge. In addition, he was sentenced to four counts of "terrorist carnage," at 15 years each and 12 years for belonging to a terrorist group.

Jose Emilio Suarez Trashorras, a Spaniard who had worked as a miner, was sentenced to 25 years for each of the 192 deaths (191 deaths as a result of the 3/11 attack and one additional count for the April 3 explosion that led to the death of police officer Francisco Javier Torronteras during the police raid attempting to arrest seven other suspects). Trashorras was detained on March 18, 2004.

Abdelmajid Bouchar, a Moroccan, was sentenced to 18 years for his involvement in the 3/11 attacks. Bouchar, who stated he was an Iraqi immigrant worker, was arrested in June 2005 at a railway station in Belgrade, Serbia, after being questioned by Serbian authorities. Youssef Belhadj, a Moroccan, was arrested on February 1, 2005 in Belgium and later extradited to Spain, where he was found guilty of belonging to a terrorist group and sentenced to 12 years. Spanish authorities

---

[8]BBC News, 2008a; BBC News, 2005.

believe Belhadj is also Aby Dujanah, Al-Qaeda's spokesman who claimed responsibility for the attacks. He is also believed to have been linked to the Casablanca bombing. Hasan El Haski, a Moroccan, was detained in the Canary Islands on December 11, 2004, charged with the 191 murders and 1,755 attempted murders, but only convicted of belonging to a terrorist group and sentenced to 15 years.

Basel Ghalyoun, a Syrian, was sentenced to 12 years for his involvement in the 3/11 attacks, but his conviction was overturned by Spain's Supreme Court. Ghalyoun owned an apartment in Madrid where members of an Islamist cell were alleged to have met. In addition, it was alleged that he visited mosques in Madrid with the purpose of recruiting members for the cell. Ghalyoun was initially identified as having been on one of the trains that were bombed, but witnesses later retracted. The prosecution suggested the retraction was due to the changed appearance of Ghalyoun, who was alleged to have cut his hair and gained weight.

In December 2004, Rabei Osman Sayed Ahmed (AKA "Mohammed the Egyptian") was extradited to Spain after being arrested on June 8, 2004, in a joint operation between Italy, Spain, France, and Belgium in Milan, Italy. Subsequent to the trial in Spain (he was found not guilty in relation to the 3/11 attacks), he was returned to Italy in 2005, where he was put on trial, convicted of having links to terror cells in Europe and Iraq, and sentenced to 10 years.

Islam and Spain

In the early part of the 8th century, Islamic armies crossed the Strait of Gibraltar and conquered much of Spain, maintaining control until the end of the 15th century, when the Granada, the last stronghold of the Islamic empire on the Iberian Peninsula, fell to the forces of Ferdinand and Isabella in 1492.

> In 711 A.D., Arab armies under Tariq ibn Ziyad crossed the Straits of Gibraltar, conquering Spain and sweeping northwards into France. The Madrid bombings seem to indicate that Muslim fundamentalists are well aware of their history and are using Spain's proximity to North Africa as a conduit to carry their struggle into the heart of Western Europe.[9]

Subsequent to the Catholic conquest of Muslim held lands in Spain, the freedom of religion promised to Muslims was rescinded and Muslims were subjected to the Inquisition, as many Jews had been, as a result of the 1,478 decision of Pope Sixtus IV and the influence of the First Grand Inquisitor, Tomas de Torquemada. Many of the great mosques on the Iberian Peninsula, such as the ones in Granada and Cordoba, were converted into Catholic churches. Haahr (2006) provides an analysis of the terrorist threat from Spain's Moroccan communities:

> Spanish security officials continue to worry that members of al-Qaeda will take advantage of the clandestine immigration pipeline route by inserting terrorists to make their way to either the enclaves or to the Spanish mainland.[10]

---

[9]Daly, 2005.
[10]Haahr, 2006.

Response to March 11 Attack in Madrid

Subsequent to the March 11, 2004, attacks on the Madrid transit system, the focus shifted from separatist or nationalist acts of violence, specifically those related to ETA, to the threat from Islamic fundamentalists. Although a purported spokesperson for Al-Qaeda claimed responsibility in a videotape that was recovered 3 days after the incident, the extent of coordination and cooperation among the individuals involved remains uncertain.[11] Governmental agencies in Spain continue to investigate the presence and influence of Al-Qaeda in Spain, specifically in the areas where the majority of Muslims reside, which is primarily in southern Spain.

According to Haahr (2006)[12], Spanish security officials continue to be concerned with the threat posed by Al Qaeda and its affiliated networks, in their continued utilization of the existing clandestine immigration pipeline to bring terrorists into the country. In response, the Director General of the National police had attempted to increase counter-terrorism personal in areas with high levels of Muslim population and immigration, such as Granada, Malaga, Alicante, Melilla, and Cueta. In addition, the commission investigating the 3/11 attacks concluded the following:

The Commission investigating the March 11, 2004 terrorist attacks in Madrid recently concluded that since the late 1990s, foreign radical Islamists have been using Spain for jihadist activities in support of al-Qaeda's terrorist operations, particularly al-Zarqawi's anti-Coalition attacks in Iraq. On-going counter-terrorism investigations reveal that Salafist Islamists traveled to Spain in the late 1990s to early 2000s to organize a network of cells for recruiting suicide bombers for operations in Iraq, Bosnia, and elsewhere and, for terrorist training in al-Qaeda camps in Afghanistan and Indonesia. These foreign jihadists played a significant role in creating and organizing the cells that were involved in 9/11, conducted the Madrid attacks (11-M), and planned to bomb the National High Court. Moreover, the National Center of Intelligence (NCI) has identified numerous Muslim immigrants who have recently left Spain to join the insurgency in Iraq.[13]

Political Ramifications of the March 11 Attacks

As a result of these bombings, 3 days prior to the general election in Spain, the incumbent was not re-elected. There has been much speculation as to the political impact of the March 11 bombings, but there is no significant empirical evidence that the terrorist attack led to the regime change in Spain. Lago and Montero (2006) concluded that the March 11 attacks "did not change the voting preferences of Spaniards; rather, voting choices were influenced by negative views of the government's support for the invasion of Iraq and government manipulation when informing the public about the responsibility for the attacks before the elections".[14]

---

[11] BBC News, 2004b

[12] Haahr, 2006.

[13] ibid.

[14] Lago & Montero, 2006.

Although there is no empirical data on the effects of the attack itself and the political crisis management, it is reasonable to suspect, that the latter was more important in influencing the vote. Other political context had also an influence, meaning that similar electoral outcomes in any other context are hardly repeatable. Spanish bipolar party system with small differences among the two biggest parties together with a unique situation of wide discontent in the electorate on the Government's policy in the question of Iraq created a unique window of opportunity for the terrorists in causing indirectly a small but sufficient commotion against the government. And even though this is a hindsight assessment, it is possible, that the ruling Government could have been able to manage the crisis better if they had legitimized the participation in the war in Iraq better, and even if they had not, the mere unbiased information and an approach that would have emphasised the sympathy for the victims and the society more than the distant strategy they had, could have been enough in maintaining their lead in the elections.[15]

Overview of August 10, 2001, Angola Railway Attack

One of the deadliest terrorist attack on railways occurred along one of Angola's few functional railway routes on Friday, August 10, 2001.[16] The railway line, an economic necessity for the provinces it serves, connects Luanda, the capital, with Dondo, a town 180 km southeast of the capital, and, with service three times a week, provided for the much needed transport of goods and people to and from the capital. The day of the attack, the train was filled with people returning home for the weekend. The train hit and detonated an anti-tank mine that was placed on the tracks 150 km from Luanda, igniting the train's fuel tank. Men armed with automatic weapons stood on both sides of the tracks, firing at people fleeing the burning train.

Of the trains estimated 500 passengers 252 died and 165 were injured. The train was carrying primarily civilians, with the exception of a few guards that accompanied all trains for security; however, the organization responsible for the attack, UNITA, claimed that the train was a military target. The high number of casualties was partially due to the delay in medical and military response to the incident. Angola, heavily reliant on foreign aid in face of a huge humanitarian crisis brought on by over 20 years of civil unrest was ill-equipped to deal with the casualties of the attack. It took a while for word of the attack to reach the authorities, and further delays before the response teams reached the site of the attack. The local provincial hospitals did not have the supplies or capacity to treat all the victims. Several of the more severely injured had to be transported to Luanda for proper care.

Despite military personnel aboard the train to protect the passengers from rebel attacks and robbers, little could be done to prevent the threat posed by a mine laid on the tracks or to protect the passengers from the vast automatic weapon fire that followed. In addition, people who managed to flee to the relative safety of the bush lands did not find their way into care due to injuries sustained during the incident

---

[15]Sinkkonen, 2008.
[16]Riley, 2004.

and due to fears that the UNITA militants who were shooting at them may not have dispersed. According to reports from BBC Africa, hundreds of people were still missing on the Sunday after the attack.[17]

A week prior to the attacks, the president's advisory council had listed conditions for holding elections in 2002. One of the conditions was "the free movement of people and goods".[18] Besides directly attacking infrastructure used to provide said free movement, the attack also coincided with a visit of a US delegation to assess whether or not conditions in Angola were stable enough for a general election to be held.

History of the Angolan Conflict

Angola is a former Portuguese colony on the southeast coast of Africa. Its capital, Luanda, was founded by the Portuguese in 1567 and functioned as a trading arena for slaves throughout the 17th and 18th centuries. Nationalist movements developed with the formation of the MPLA, Movimento Popular da Libertação de Angola (Popular Movement for the Liberation of Angola), in 1956. Both FNLA, Frente Nacional para a Libertação de Angola (National Front for the Liberation of Angola), formed in 1962 and UNITA, União Nacional para a Independência Total de Angola (National Union for the Total Independence of Angola), were founded in 1966 as a result of a split within the FNLA. Support for the three groups followed local ethnic group divisions, with the Kimbundo people of the richer coastal trading regions supporting the MPLA, UNITA enjoying support of the largest ethnic group, the Ovimundo tribe, and FNLA being backed by the north-west Bakongo nationalists.

UNITA's founder and leader, Jonas Savimbi, resigned from his post as foreign minister and main representative of the Ovimundo within the FNLA in 1964. He traveled to China in 1965 where he received military training and found Maoism. Upon his return in 1996, he turned down an invitation to join the MPLA and focused on leading UNITA, which he claimed as the representative of black peasants. In accordance with Maoist principles, Savimbi concentrated on raising the level of political consciousness and education of the peasants. The UNITA constitution proclaimed to strive for a government proportionally representative of the population.

Savimbi, described both as brilliant and brutal, psychopathic and precociously intelligent by everyone from foreign diplomats to family members, remained the undisputed leader of UNITA until his assassination in 2002. Labeled as "evil in a red beret" in his obituary in the *Economist*, he once said, "those with force will be respected, those with force make history." His followers continue to describe him as the "father of the nation" and the "father of the revolution." After the 1974 revolution in Portugal, the Angolan people were granted independence in 1975.

---

[17]BBC News, 2001c.

[18]Economist (2001, August 16).

Following negotiations in Portugal, MPLA, UNITA, and FNLA agreed to establish a transitional government in January 1975. Within 2 months, fighting ensued between the three and civil war broke out. By 1976, over 90% of the white settlers had left Angola, deliberately destroying the countries infrastructure rather than handing factories and transportation over to the native Angolans.

The cold war powers were drawn into the conflict, with the Soviet Union and Cuba supporting the Marxist MPLA and the United States supporting UNITA and FNLA. In addition, South Africa backed UNITA in order to weaken the South West African People's Organization (SWAPO) which was fighting for the independence of its colony Namibia from bases in southern Angola. South African troops pulled out in 1988, with the Cubans following shortly after. The United States continued to fund UNITA efforts, with a record $50 million in 1989.

Short cease fires between MPLA and UNITA were brokered in 74, 89, 91, and 94. Following MPLA dropping Marxist ideals for social democratic ones in April 1991 and the Bicesse accord in May 1991, the United Nations monitored elections were held in 1992. MPLA won 54% of votes and UNITA 34%. UNITA rejected the results and resumed civil war. UN sanctions were imposed on UNITA for the first time in 1993.

American policy shifted away from UNITA and in favor of MPLA in the mid- to late 1990s. Large deep offshore deposits of oil were discovered, which renewed in particular the British and American interests in the nation. UNITA continued to control many of the diamond mining regions, and was able to collect significant funds from the sale of diamonds, despite international efforts to curb the unregulated diamond trade and UN freezing of bank accounts used by UNITA.

A second peace deal, the Lusaka Protocol, was signed in 1994. The first 7,000 UN peacekeepers arrived in 1995 as the government and Savimbi confirmed their commitment to peace. An agreement to form a unity army was reached in 1996, and plans for forming a unified government continued. However, Savimbi did not attend the inauguration of the unified government in April 1997. The situation deteriorated rapidly and full scale fighting resumed by 1998. The UN peacekeeping mission was ended in 1999.

Following the breakdown of the Lusaka Protocol, UNITA's operations moved more toward those of a guerilla movement of terrorist nature and away from the conventional army tactics it had employed previously.[19] The attacks were high profile including attacks on purely civilian targets and firing of missiles at NGO airplanes such as WFP aid flights. It is thought that the aims of these attacks was to show that despite suffering large losses at the hands of the government army, UNITA remained a force to be reckoned with and to convince the government to resume negotiations.

---

[19]BBC News, 2001b, July 3, Analysis: Unita's changing tactics.

Reactions to the Angola Attack

On August 13, UNITA's top general, Abreu Kamorteiro, admitted that UNITA attacked the train, but claimed that it was escorted by a battalion of FAA [the Angolan army] and was carrying fuel and military equipment. According to UNITA, 26 soldiers and 11 police officers were killed. UNITA denies that many civilians were killed.[20]

On August 14, 2001, Kofi Annan officially condemned the attack "in which a very high number of civilians were killed" and noted that UNITA "bears the responsibility for this indefensible loss of life".[21] On the same date, the Southern African Development Community issued a communiqué in which it listed specific actions the region intended to take against UNITA, in accordance with UN-mandated sanctions. On August 15, 2001, Angola's churches "ordered" a month-long religious fast in the name of peace and called on the rebels to stop fighting and negotiate with the government. The churches maintained a larger base of support that any other organization in the country and campaigned actively for peace.[22] On August 16, 2001, the UN Security Council issued a statement strongly condemning the terrorist attack on the Angolan train near the town of Maria Teresa.

> As in previous attacks, such as Caxito, UNITA personnel deliberately targeted civilians... Members of the Security Council reiterated their support for all existing sanctions against the UNITA faction headed by Jonas Savimbi pending the organization's full implementation of its Lusaka Protocol obligations... Members of the Council reiterate their support for the preparations under way for holding elections in 2002 in Angola and state that such actions by UNITA should not be allowed to stymie those efforts.[23]

On August 18, 2001, thousands of Angolans demonstrated in Luanda against the train attack in a rally organized by the government. The demonstrators marched to the UN headquarters, where Minister for Women and Family, Candida Celeste, handed over a letter calling for tougher action against UNITA. The president of the European Union issued the following statement on August 21, 2001:

> The EU is appalled by the brutal attack perpetrated on Friday 10 August by UNITA on civilians traveling on the regular train between Luanda and Dondo (Cuanza Norte Province), which caused around 250 casualties and 165 injured. This terrorist act against innocent men, women and children, cannot but be strongly condemned by the EU. The EU believes that the continuation of such a course of action does not contribute to create the necessary confidence building measures towards a serious and effective dialogue that can lead to peace and national reconciliation in Angola. The EU urges UNITA to immediately cease these kinds of actions against civilians that inflict terrible distress to the Angolans, to comply with the provisions and spirit of the Lusaka Protocol and to engage seriously in the search for peace through concrete actions that confirm its declared willingness to dialogue.[24]

---

[20] Angola Peace Monitor (2001, September 5), Issue 12, vol. 7.

[21] Angola Peace Monitor (2001, September 5), Issue 12, vol. 7.

[22] Economist *A third force* May 11th 2000 | LUANDA From The Economist print edition http://www.economist.com/displaystory.cfm?story_id=S%26%29%28%2C%2BRQ%5B%2B%0A.

[23] Angola Peace Monitor (2001, September 5), Issue 12, vol. 7.

[24] Angola Peace Monitor, Issue 12, vol. 7, 5th September 2001. http://www.actsa.org/Angola/apm/apm0712.html.

On August 22, 2001, President Jose Eduardo dos Santos announces that he did not intend on running in the next elections, which, at the time were scheduled to be held no later than 2003. No elections have been held since 1992, while, at the time, the next elections had been tentatively scheduled for 2006. On August 23, 2001, UNITA submitted a document "Proposals for the solution of the Angolan conflict" sent to the UN Security Council and the US Government. In the document they call for recognition of Savimbi as leader of the entirety of UNITA, repulsion of all laws passed against the rebel leadership, as well as demand that UNITA and the government be regarded as equal parties in the conflict.

Impact on the Angola Conflict

The demise of the Lusaka Protocol saw UNITA refusing to cooperate in an initiative that seemed to correspond to the goal of "government proportionally representative of the population" proclaimed by its constitution in the 1960s. UNITA had lost significant amounts of both international and local support. International attention was being paid to the conflict both due to the immense humanitarian crisis evolving the size of the oil deposits discovered and the perceived threat to the stability of the region that the conflict posed. While remaining undeniably corrupt to this date, the MPLA was enjoying vast international support. All these factors put pressure on UNITA, who responded with attacks aiming more at undermining the order maintained by the government than raising and maintaining popular support.

Some blame for the increase in violence and high-profile attacks by UNITA can be placed on the governing MPLA's refusal to heed to UNITA's negotiating wishes. It can be argued that UNITA may have been ready to settle with the MPLA in face of losing popular support, but few who knew Savimbi believe he would have settled for shared governance with the MPLA. UNITA shifted from a nationalist group fighting for democracy that, upon killing a Swedish NGO worker during a kidnapping event sent an official delegation to Stockholm to apologize, into a terrorist organization that blew up a local passenger train and proceeded to gun down fleeing civilians with machine guns.

The train attack was one of a series of attacks on civil and NGO targets which led to increased popular sentiment against UNITA. Although the turning point in the resolution of the conflict was undoubtedly the assassination of Savimbi in February 2002, the deterioration of popular support heavily influenced UNITA's decision to disarm and work toward forming an official democratic opposition party as opposed to continuing armed battle following the demise of their founder and leader. To date, UNITA is one of the few terrorist groups who have successfully been integrated into local government.

In a civil war situation, when the international and public favor shifts from one party to another – do some specific precautions need to be taken? What could the MPLA and international forces have done differently? As Savimbi declared in a BBC interview June 2001, it is not possible to "say 'capture the bastards and hang them' [when] at the same time you're talking about negotiations for peace. It does not work that way".[25]

Nearly 8 years after the attack, UNITA still has popular support in Angola; however, the 2008 elections in Angola led to the political defeat of UNITA, who received only slightly more than 10% of the vote, in contrast to the 82% for the ruling MPLA.[26] This election was the first in Angola in more than 16 years, which led to the 1992 political rift between UNITA and MPLA, in addition to the years of subsequent violence. UNITA leader, Isaias Samakuva, despite earlier allegations of voting irregularities and legal challenges, stated that he accepts the election results and hopes that the MPLA will govern in the interest of all Angolans.[27]

Overview and Analysis of Rail Security

Based on the experience of the United Kingdom, specifically in regards to preventive measures necessitated by the bombing campaign conducted by the IRA, Riley (2004) provides a list of security measures that could be easily employed to diminish the threat of terrorism directed toward railway targets.

- Repairing gaps in fencing to provide more control around the perimeter of rail facilities.
- Improving lighting, both to deter terrorists and to improve facility observation.
- Installing blast resistant trash containers to reduce the utility of placing bombs in trash containers while ensuring that passengers had a place to dispose of trash (and that bombers would be less able to hide explosives among accumulated trash).
- Installing close-circuit television to provide stationmasters and security personnel with better visibility throughout the facilities.
- Installing signage to increase awareness about the danger of unattended packages and to improve the ability to evacuate facilities during emergencies.
- Training of personnel and passengers to have a role in security by reporting suspicious behavior, identifying suspicious (especially unattended) packages and luggage, and improving readiness for evacuation and emergency actions.[28]

Wilson, Jackson, Eisman, Steinberg, Riley (2007) provide an analysis of passenger rail systems. While most terrorist attacks against railway targets minimal casualties, recent events (such as Madrid in 2004, London in 2005, and Mumbai in 2006) have illustrated the devastating potential of strategic strikes designed to inflict

---

[25] BBC News, 2001a. Savimbi told to respect accords.

[26] Angola Peace Monitor, Issue 11, vol. 14, Sept 2008.

[27] BBC News, 2008b.

[28] Riley, 2004, p. 8.

mass casualties. Therefore, if security measures could act as a deterrent for large-scale attacks, the casualties associated with terrorist attacks against railway targets could be significantly reduced.[29]

The variety of targets among railway systems includes the railway tracks, the station, train platforms, and infrastructure associated with the rail system. Rail stations, tracks, and infrastructure security depend on many factors, including their location; the three primary typologies found among railway systems are underground or subterranean, ground level, and above ground or elevated. Tracks for railway systems, whether passenger or cargo, tend to have limited security, if any. Additional factors that determine the vulnerability of rail systems include the visibility, velocity, and braking capability of the train, in addition to the level of security for the tracks and infrastructure.

Visibility will depend on lighting, cameras, and other electronic devices to monitor the path of the train. Velocity of the train, combined with the braking system, will determine the stopping distance of the train, which could impact the ability to minimize damage and casualties. In addition, faster moving trains will likely be subjected to greater damage if terrorist employ a device to derail the train. While the damage caused by a derailment of higher speed trains may be greater, many new trains feature enhanced safety measures, which mitigate the potential threat. The security of the rail system will depend on measures employed to deter individuals from interfering with the system, such as motion sensitive cameras or CCTV, fences to prevent individuals from accessing secure areas or tracks, and regular patrol or maintenance of tracks and other elements integral to the infrastructure.

Rural railway tracks are relatively effort intensive targets if the purpose of the attack is to do more than inconvenience transportation infrastructure. The more vulnerable structural points such as switches, bridges, and tunnels are kept under surveillance and there are procedures in place to monitor for tampering with the remaining stretches of the rail networks. The critical mass of explosives necessary to cause significant damage to trains from the outside is such that it is often discovered. Even when trains are derailed, casualties and injuries are rare unless there are other compounding issues such as the train impacting densely populated areas or the fleeing passengers being ambushed by gunfire.[30]

Aside from the episode in Angola, the most casualties in attacks on rural trains have involved explosives placed inside of the trains. One such incident is that of the Samjhauta Express in India, where explosives coupled with petrol tanks set two carriages on fire causing 65 fatalities.[31] Many fatalities could have been avoided had the passengers been able to evacuate the carriages more efficiently. This incident also demonstrates the resiliency of trains to such attacks. Even though the two

---

[29] Wilson et al., 2007, p. 16.

[30] Besides the Angola incident described in this chapter, see also the 27March05 incident in Thailand. MIPT Terrorism Knowledgebase entry http://tkb.org/Incident.jsp?incID=22667

[31] BBC News. (2007, February 19). Dozens dead in India train blasts.

carriages and their passengers were significantly damaged; the rest of the train, carrying the remaining passengers, was able to continue on its journey after the affected carriages were removed.

There have been other attempts and successful attacks involving explosives left in luggage on trains. Luggage screening and inspections of the trains for unaccompanied luggage and unaccounted for artifacts could be improved on in order to minimize the threat of these types of attacks.

Law Enforcement and Emergency Response

With regard to outside attacks on trains and tracks in rural areas, intelligence gathering and analysis have the greatest defense and protection potential. Where the frequency of attacks does not justify the costs of securing the vast areas that rail systems cover, timely intelligence can narrow down the time and location of a particular threat to proportions where localized increased surveillance and protection is both possible and beneficial. As was the case in Angola and India, the outcomes of the attacks were as severe as they were due to the rural areas not having the emergency transportation and medical capacity to deal with events of the magnitude that occurred. Well coordinated emergency response teams, medical, and tactical, could mitigate the human consequences of attacks on railway targets.[32]

Conclusion

Recent events provide evidence that railway targets continue to be extremely vulnerable to terrorist attacks. While utilizing explosive devices has been the most frequently employed tactic employed in attacks against railway targets, there are numerous other means that may be employed in the future, including the use of weapons of mass destruction. In comparison to airline security, the limited measures utilized in maintaining security for railway targets provides an opportunity for terrorists to maximize the impact of an attack while minimizing the risk of achieving operational goals.

The impact of attacks on railway targets is mitigated by the frequency of use by civilian passengers. The expectation of passenger safety could be undermined, which can have significant economic impact. Terrorist attacks may have political ramifications. The UNITA attacks in Angola did not result in increased support for the organization and may have contributed to their political defeat in the 2008 elections. However, the Al-Qaeda inspired attacks in Spain may have shifted the perspective of the population to elect a new leader, which led to foreign policy changes, including the withdrawal of troops from Iraq. While there is no empirical evidence that the attacks impacted the elections, the timing of the attacks and the result in the

---

[32]Gutierrez de Ceballos et al., 2005; Riely, 2004; Wilson et al., 2007.

elections provide the appearance of success on the part of the terrorists, which can be viewed as being equally significant to having any verifiable result.

References

ACTSA (2001, September). *Angola Peace Monitor, issue 12, vol. 7*. Angola Peace Monitor. http://www.actsa.org/Angola/apm/apm0712.html

ACTSA (2008, September). *Angola Peace Monitor, issue 11, vol. 14*. Retrieved January 18th, 2009 from http://www.actsa.org/Pictures/UpImages/Angola/APM_September_2008.pdf

BBC News. (2001a, June 14). Savimbi told to respect accords. Retrieved December 24th, 2008 from http://news.bbc.co.uk/2/hi/africa/1388796.stm

BBC News. (2001b, July 3). Analysis: Unita's changing tactics. Retrieved January 18th, 2009. http://news.bbc.co.uk/2/hi/africa/1420102.stm

BBC News. (2001c, August 12): *Hundreds missing in Angola train attack*. http://news.bbc.co.uk/1/hi/worls/africa/1487368.stm

BBC News. (2004a, March 12). Madrid attacks timeline. Retrieved January 18th, 2009 from http://news.bbc.co.uk/1/hi/world/europe/3504912.stm

BBC News. (2004b, April 28). Timeline: Madrid investigation. Retrieved January 18th, 2009 from http://news.bbc.co.uk/2/hi/europe/3597885.stm

BBC News. (2005, March 10). Madrid bombing suspects. Retrieved January 18th, 2009 from http://news.bbc.co.uk/2/hi/europe/3560603.stm

BBC News. (2006, July 11). Scores dead in Mumbai train bombs. Retrieved December 24th, 2008 from http://news.bbc.co.uk/2/hi/south_asia/5169332.stm

BBC News. (2007, February 19). Dozens dead in India train blasts. Retrieved December 24th, 2008 from http://news.bbc.co.uk/2/hi/south_asia/6374377.stm

BBC News. (2008a, July 17). Madrid bombings: Defendants. Retrieved January 18th, 2009 from http://news.bbc.co.uk/2/hi/europe/4899544.stm

BBC News. (2008b, September 9) Angolan ex-rebels accept defeat. Retrieved January 18th, 2009 http://news.bbc.co.uk/2/hi/africa/7605454.stm

Daly, J. C. K. (2005, May 25). The Madrid Bombings: Spain as a "Jihad" Highway to Western Europe. *Spotlight on Terror, 2(4)*. Retrieved February 2nd, 2009 from http://www.jamestown.org/

Economist (2000, May 11). *A third force*. Retrieved February 2nd, 2009 from http://www.economist.com/

Economist (2001, August 16): *UNITA – down but not out*. http://www.economist.com/displayStory.cfm?Story_ID=E1_SPJGRP

Gutierrez de Ceballos, J. P., Turégano-Fuentes, F., Perez-Diaz, D., Sanz-Sanchez, M., Martin-Llorente, C and Guerrero-Sanz, J. E. (2005, February). 11 March 2004: The Terrorist Bomb Explosions in Madrid, Spain – An Analysis of the Logistics, Injuries Sustained and Clinical Management of Casualties Treated at the Closest Hospital. *Critical Care, 9(1)*. Retrieved February 2nd, 2009 from http://ccforum.com/content/pdf/cc2995.pdf

Haahr, K. (2006, May 4). Emerging Terrorist Trends in Spain's Moroccan Communities. *Terrorism Monitor, 4(9)*. Retrieved February 2nd, 2009 from http://www.jamestown.org/

Jordan, J. (2006, March 9). The Madrid Attacks: Results of Investigations Two Years Later. *Terrorism Monitor, 4(5)*. Retrieved February 2nd, 2009 from http://www.jamestown.org/

Lago, I. and Montero, J. R. (2006). The 2004 Election in Spain: Terrorism, Accountability, and Voting. *Taiwan Journal of Democracy, 2(1)*, 13–36.

Olmeda, J. A. (2005). Fear or Falsehood: Framing the 3/11Terrorist Attacks in Madrid and Electoral Accountability. Real Institute Elcano. Retrieved February 2nd, 2009 from http://www.realinstitutoelcano.org/documentos/195/Olmeda195.pdf

Riley, J. (2004, March). *Terrorism and Rail Security*. Santa Monica, CA: Rand. Retrieved December 24th, 2008 from http://www.rand.org/pubs/testimonies/2005/RAND_CT224.pdf

Sinkkonen, T. (2008, July, 11) The Aftermath of Madrid Terrorist Attack: Psychological factors behind political behavior. *Paper presented at the annual meeting of the ISPP 31st Annual Scientific Meeting, Sciences Po.* Retrieved January 22nd, 2009 from http://www.allacademic.com/meta/p255696_index

Wilson, J. M., Jackson, B. A., Eisman, M., Steinberg, P., and Riley, J. (2007). *Securing America's Passenger-Rail Systems.* Santa Monica, CA: Rand. Retrieved January 22nd, 2009 from http://www.rand.org/pubs/monographs/2007/RAND_MG705.pdf

Chapter 11
Securing the Gold: Olympic Security from a Counter-Terrorist Perspective

Albert Gamarra

Introduction

The Olympic Games are set up to promote the principles of humanity, understanding, and cooperation among the people of the world. The Olympics symbolize the ideals of unity and peace (Czula, 1978; US Olympic committee, 1996). Thousands of athletes from hundreds of countries compete and depict sportsmanship, and all is broadcast to a worldwide audience.

Hatred and conflict among groups and nations are supposedly forgotten in the name of the Olympic spirit. With its large audience, the Olympics are considered one of the greatest media events in the world. The popularity of the Olympics is hoped to promote positive ideologies such as those of sportsmanship and goodwill to wide audiences. Yet the games have also been used to promote negative ideologies such as those of hate, as Hitler did in the 1936 Berlin games (Hoberman, 1986). Through television the Olympics have been able to reach an audience of billions around the world that would not be reached otherwise. The 2008 Chinese Olympics were designed to show off a modern albeit totalitarian nation with the aggressive cruelty of the state barely hidden behind the many layers of censorship and intimidation.

The large television audience and general international attention the Olympics receive creates a genuine threat of exploitation. In 1972, Palestinian terrorists exploited the publicity and wide audience available through the Olympics kidnapping and murdering Israeli athletes as the situation was broadcast live to millions of homes around the world (Reeve, 2000). The Olympic Games continue to be a target for groups that wish to have their ideological messages broadcast to a large audience.

The security of the Olympics is important to ensure that groups that promote hate and who wish to spread terror do not tarnish the message of the Olympics. The purpose of this chapter is to present some data on Olympic security threats

A. Gamarra (✉)
John Jay College and the Graduate Center, The City University of New York, New York, NY, USA
e-mail: tito1183@hotmail.com

M.R. Haberfeld, A. von Hassell (eds.), *A New Understanding of Terrorism*,
DOI 10.1007/978-1-4419-0115-6_11, © Springer Science+Business Media, LLC 2009

and measures that have and could be implemented to combat terrorism. These measures could provide assistance in securing the Olympics and can also be applied to security at other large sporting and non-sporting events. Although many sources have discussed security threats and counter-terror measures deployed during the Olympic Games, they have done so in a general and cursory fashion. No source has comprehensively studied the games through a risk assessment and counter-terrorism view.

Attacking During the Olympic Games

In the history of the modern Olympic Games there have been two successful attacks. On September 5, 1972, the first successful attack occurred at the Munich Olympic Games as Palestinian terrorist took hostage and later killed a contingent of Israeli athletes. The second successful Olympic attack occurred on July 27, 1996, at the Atlanta Olympic Games, as accused bomber Eric Rudolph set off a pipe bomb in Centennial Olympic Park that killed one person and injured over a hundred. These attacks differed in the ideology of the person or group who perpetrated the act, yet were similar as the attacks garnered worldwide attention.

On September 5, 1972, at the Munich Olympic Games, a group of eight Palestinians broke into the living quarters of the Israeli Olympic team killing two immediately and taking nine hostages (Reeve, 2000; Sonneborn, 2003). The kidnappers claimed to be part of the "Black September" faction and demanded the release of over 200 Palestinian prisoners held in Israeli jails (Reeve, 2000). The group sought to bring the plight of the Palestinian Liberation Organization to a global audience of 900 million (Reeve, 2000). The event ended tragically with all the Israeli hostages and five of the Palestinian hostage takers being killed (Wolff & Yaeger, 2002). But, "while tactically it did not advance their cause, it showed better than any speech at the UN" the despair and severity of the Palestinian people and their want of a homeland (Bowman, 2003, p. 8).

The Munich Olympic tragedy was the result of the Black September group learning from the mistakes of others who had previously sought to use the Olympics as a publicity tool for their cause and the failure of German Olympic officials to implement proper security measures. In 1968 thousands of Mexicans marched against the Olympics because of the perceived gratuitous use of money by government officials to procure the Olympic Games. These Mexicans citizens felt that the government would have better been served using the civil funds to help curb the widespread poverty in the country (Czula, 1978). The government responded to these protest by murdering over 300 protesters. However, this event was not widely publicized since the protest occurred prior to the official start of the Olympic Games (Czula, 1978). This event could have had a dramatic impact on the Black September terrorist as they prepared for the attack on the 1972 Olympic Games. The group could have realized that only a violent attack perpetrated during the games would garner the worldwide attention that they sought for their cause (Czula, 1978).

Failures on the part of the German authorities were also to blame for the Munich Olympic Game attacks. German officials failed to take into account that the

Olympics could be targeted to bring worldwide attention to a cause, as the Mexican protestors had attempted to do prior to the 1968 Mexico games. In addition, German officials craved a positive atmosphere during the games and believed that any type of excessive security would detract from the atmosphere of the games (Wolff & Yaeger, 2002; Sonneborn, 2003). Prior to the games, officials hired a police psychologist, Dr. Georg Sieber, to create threat assessment scenarios for the games (Wolff & Yaeger, 2002). Sieber presented a number of scenarios to German Olympic officials, including one that was eerily similar to the Munich tragedy (Wolff & Yaeger, 2002). His threat assessments were deemed incompatible with the image authorities wished to present, and he was told to scale them back (Wolff & Yaeger, 2002). German officials never implemented his recommended security measures which called for more security personnel and more secure living quarters. This type of attitude was prevalent throughout the Munich games.

German Olympic officials were very careful in their presentation of the games because of the 1936 Berlin games. The 1936 Berlin games were awarded to Germany as a way of showing the world that the country was once again a part of the global community (Vercamer & Pipes, 1996). The games, which had been awarded prior to Hitler's ascension to power, would be overrun with German propaganda. Although there was no visible racist or religious discriminatory propaganda, the country still had a racist undertone that made many visiting athletes uncomfortable. The atmosphere of racism and propaganda of German superiority was rampant at the 1936 Berlin games (Vercamer & Pipes, 1996). This was the atmosphere that German officials wished to avoid at the 1972 Munich games. Security at the 1972 Munich games was an afterthought as "The Games of Peace and Joy" took place (Reeve, 2000).

In the summer of 1972, a number of members of the Black September group were chosen for a secret operation. The chosen members were ordered to spend a month training in Libya (Sonneborn, 2003). In September they were ordered to Munich for their secret mission. After a number of days at the games they would receive the information for their mission. This is when they finally learned that they would be attacking the living quarters for the Israeli athletes at the games.

The "Black September" terror group was an offshoot of Yasser Arafat's Fatah organization. "Black September" claimed to be an independent organization that had no decision-making or financial ties to Fatah (Reeve, 2000). The group took its name from the failed September resistance in Jordan by Palestinians that later resulted in their eviction from the country (Reeve, 2000). The group had previously been responsible for a number of assassinations and hijacking in Jordan. Among those assassinated by the group was the prime minister of Jordan, Wasfi Tell, on November 28, 1971.

During the early days at the Munich games the Black September members conducted surveillance at the Olympic facilities. The terrorists were able to discern that spectators were able to access restricted areas as security at gates was lacking or non-existent (Wolff & Yaeger, 2002). In addition, it was rather obvious that only a six-foot-high fence protected the Olympic village and athletes' living quarters with few to no security guards patrolling the area (Sonneborn, 2003). It was also noticeable that the fence was small enough that athletes would regularly climb the fence to avoid the walk to the official entrance while officials ignored this fault in security (Reeve, 2000; Wolff & Yaeger, 2002). This failure proved pivotal to the "Black September" terrorist, as this fence allowed them access to the athletes' living quarters. Once over the fence, the terrorist knew where to find the quarters of the Israeli athletes, as fellow terrorists had taken jobs at the Olympic village in preparation for the attack (Reeve, 2000). The terrorists had no resistance from security as they broke into the Israeli athletes' quarters and took them as hostages.

The Failed Response

As Olympic security officials received reports of the commotion, they responded by sending an unarmed guard (Wolff & Yaeger, 2002). The terrorists ignored the guard, deeming him non-consequential to their plan, like most of the security measures implemented by German officials. The terrorist demanded that 234 Palestinian terrorist held in Israeli prisons and 2 from German prisons be released (Reeve, 2000). Olympic officials attempted to negotiate with the terrorist in vain knowing that the terrorist demands were unrealistic. Although the terrorist continually delayed the deadline for their demands, they would not alter them.

The lack of preparation for an attack at the games meant that officials were also unprepared to attempt an assault to rescue the hostages. Israeli officials offered to assist the Germans by sending in a Special Forces team. The Germans did not have any Special Forces unit but still rejected the Israeli offer. The Germans did not want any assistance on the matter from other countries. The Israeli unit, which had been prepared to leave as soon as German officials asked for assistance, would never leave Israel (Reeve, 2000).

German officials were more concerned with handling the matter quickly and quietly as they sought to not detract from the games. Furthermore, the Germans even went so far as to stubbornly not cancel the following mornings' events (Sonneborn, 2003). Once they realized that the hostage situation would not end quickly, officials finally canceled the rest of the days events. At this point all attention would turn to the hostage situation (Sonneborn, 2003). Major news agencies and spectators of the Olympic events would gather around the location of the hostage situation hoping to gain a view of the situation. The lack of a media blackout and secure perimeter around the hostage location would prevent any rescue of the hostages from the Olympic village (Sonneborn, 2003). The first attempt at rescue was canceled after the terrorists were alerted by spectators who were pointing and yelling instructions at the rescue team (Sonneborn, 2003). A second attempt at rescue which involved attacking the terrorists as they moved through the parking lot of the Olympic village was thwarted when one of the terrorist noticed police officers preparing for the assault (Sonneborn, 2003). This response provides an insight into the inexperience and lack of preparation that led to the Munich Olympic tragedy.

After extensive negotiations there was an agreement to move the site of the negotiations from the Olympic village to Furstenfeldbruck airport (Wolff & Yaeger,

2002). As the Palestinians left the Olympic village, German officials were surprised to find out that there were eight terrorists involved. The German officials, conducting the negotiation, had misinformed security officials that there were only five terrorist (Sonneborn, 2003). Officials had prepared to mount an assault at Furstenfeldbruck airport, but were unprepared and had provided only five sharpshooters to subdue the eight terrorists (Wolff & Yaeger, 2002). Even after officials discovered that there were eight terrorists, they failed to notify the snipers of this fact.

The snipers were not the only part of the counter-terrorism plan. There was to be a 16-person assault team that would pose as a "fake" airplane crew (Reeve, 2000). This crew would kill any of the terrorists who boarded the plane leaving the reminder for the snipers to kill. The assault team had reservations about this counter-terrorism plan that would lead to them aborting the mission. The team felt that it was a suicide mission as some were not properly dressed, others felt the plane did not offer adequate protection and some believed if that a terrorist pulled a grenade it would take out the entire assault team (Reeve, 2000; Sonneborn, 2003).

The counter-terrorism plan was left in the hands of only the snipers who also experienced mission problem. The snipers did not have any walkie-talkies and could not communicate. Some of the snipers were in each other's line of fire (Reeve, 2000). After the shooting began there was no assault or Special Forces unit to provide support to the snipers (Wolff & Yaeger, 2002). The snipers were not prepped prior to the operation and thus were unable to differentiate between the terrorists, hostages, and other individuals present during the operation (e.g. pilots, negotiators) (Sonneborn, 2003). The assault unit did not arrive at the scene until an hour after the shooting began. They arrived about a mile from where the incident was taking place. It took the assault team another half-hour to get to the battle zone as the gun battle neared its end. The lack of preparedness and communication by officials led to the massacre at the airport that left five terrorist dead, one police officer dead, and all of the hostages dead (Reeve, 2000).

In the aftermath of the Munich Olympic Games the Israeli government would covertly enact "Operation Wrath of God". This operation would include a number of targeted assassinations aimed at members of the Black September group and others who were involved in the Munich tragedies preparation and operation (Reeve, 2000). The assassinations were widely publicized and received negative reactions from the international community especially among Arabs (Reeve, 2000). Despite the perceived success at capturing most, if not all those responsible for the Munich incident the operation was not deemed a complete success. It led to retaliatory terrorist attacks and did not prevent further violence in the region.

Securing the Games Post the Munich Attack

The Munich massacre led to changes in security at the games. Olympic villages were the focus of security measures, as officials in future Olympic cities wished to avoid a repeat of Munich (Wolff & Yaeger, 2002). Other security measures implemented in the aftermath of Munich included the X-raying of luggage at airports, remote-controlled robots to inspect suspicious objects, and the deployment of large amounts of armed security personnel (Wolff & Yaeger, 2002). Security as one of the major priorities of the games was lasting legacy of the Munich tragedy.

On the early morning of July 27, 1996, the 10th day of the Centennial Olympic in Atlanta, Georgia, a concert was being held at the Olympic Park (Johnston, 1996). A little after midnight, a security guard Richard Jewel located an unattended green knapsack underneath a bench (Noe, 2004). The security guard alerted senior officials to the suspicious package. After examining the bag, officials determined that it was deemed a credible threat and ordered an evacuation (Noe, 2004). An anonymous bomb threat to 911 increased the belief that the bag contained a bomb (CNN, 1996–2004). The bomb threat was delayed for over 10 min as 911 officials had difficulty in locating the address of the Olympic Park (CNN, 1996–2004). Once alerted to the phoned bomb threat officials increased efforts to evacuate the park without causing pandemonium that could result in injuries or casualties (CNN, 1996–2004). As officials continued the orderly evacuation of the crowd, the bomb exploded at about 1:25 a.m. (Shinbun, 1996). The bomb left one person dead and over a 100 people injured in its aftermath (Shinbun, 1996).

The Atlanta Olympic Games security measures were "the most stringent ever during peacetime in the nation" (Wilson, 1996). The measures included over $227 million in security spending, the deployment of over 30,000 public and private security personnel, and the use of high-tech security equipment (Wilson, 1996). Yet these measures were unable to detect and prevent the bomb from entering and exploding in Centennial Olympic Park. The Olympic Park was a public place; as such it had no security checks for the thousands that entered each day (Shinbun, 1996). The lack of security made the park a prime target for attack. The emergency 911 system received a call reporting a bomb threat at the Olympic Park but, unable to locate its address, the operator was delayed in relaying the message to authorities at the park (CNN, 1996). This probably delayed the evacuation of the park (CNN, 1996). Had authorities not discovered the bomb prior to the call to the 911 system the delay could have led to an increased number of casualties and injuries.

The perpetrator of the attack at the Atlanta Olympic Games was Eric Rudolph (Campo-Flores, Skipp, & Burger, 2003). Rudolph is a suspected survivalist, anti-government militant, and religious extremist (Campo-Flores et al., 2003). He is also suspected of being involved in a number of bombings and attacks at both abortion clinics and gay nightclubs (Fonda, et al., 2003). The motive behind Eric Rudolph attack on the park was his ideological views. He felt that the games represented the international cooperation that his right wing militant ideology opposed. His attack on the games could have been a way to present his protest against the international presence of the Olympics and its host, the United States, which he viewed as an enemy.

In the aftermath of the attack (on Centennial Olympic Park) authorities increased police presence, installed more surveillance equipment, and started searching visitors' belongings randomly (CNN, 1996). After the games in Atlanta, the International Olympic Committee formed a "transfer of knowledge program" (Wolff &

Yaeger, 2002). The programs aim was to provide future Olympic organizers with the knowledge of past security measures implemented at the games. The program would help them in organizing security for their games and provide them with assistance from past security officials to help in understanding and implementing security.

Analyzing the Olympic Games Threat

Organized athletic activity was prevalent in ancient civilized societies such as Egypt, China, and even among Native Americans (US Olympic Committee, 1996). The earliest record of an ancient Olympic Games taking place indicates that it took place in 776 B.C. The ancient Olympic Games combined the ideals of worship and athleticism. This made hard work, preservation, and self-reliance important parts of a successful life (US Olympic Committee, 1996). During the Olympic Games, all fighting between Greek city-states would stop as a sign of respect for the spirituality of the games. After nearly a thousand years of the Olympics, the conquer of Greece by the Roman Empire signified the end of the ancient games.

In the 19th century, French aristocrat Baron Pierre de Coubertin worked to bring about the rebirth of the modern Olympics. His interest in the ancient Greek Olympiad along with his belief in the importance of physical fitness led him to champion for the establishment of a modern Olympiad (US Olympic Committee, 1996). Coubertin believed that the poor physical conditioning of the French led to their defeat in the Franco-Prussian War in 1871. He admired the British school system that advocated both education and athletics. He believed it was this multi-tiered school system that was the foundation of the British Empire both politically and militarily.

In 1894 Coubertin staged a presentation involving poetry, music, and songs to motivate international officials to approve the restoration of the Olympic Games. He succeeded in convincing 79 delegates from 12 countries to vote in approval of the establishment of a modern Olympic Games (US Olympic Committee, 1996). Coubertin believed that the Olympic Games would serve as an important international event promoting world peace (US Olympic Committee, 1996). The games would be re-launched in the spring of 1886 in Athens, Greece.

The establishment of the modern Olympics with its ideals for international cooperation and world peace was not championed by all nations. Some groups, such as the fascists and marxists opposed the ideals of the games. The fascist critique was based on "fascist ideology, which extols the cult of the nation, the glorification of war, and the doctrine of race" (Hoberman, 1986, pp. 88–89). The fascist ideology did not believe in the IOC's dream of tolerance and diversity in the world. Despite their ideological differences both Fascism and Olympic spirit shared the ideological view of the importance of physical fitness as it pertains to a "symbol of force" (Hoberman, 1986, p. 90). Hitler overlooked the fascist critique of the Olympics as he sought to use the games as a tool of propaganda. He believed the 1936 Berlin games represented an opportunity to depict the political, military, and athletic superiority of the German nation to a global audience (Hoberman, 1986).

The neo-marxist critique of the Olympics argued that the games were a means of promoting imperialism and diverting attention away from the class struggle (Hoberman, 1986). Neo-marxist believed that sports were a means of social control and that they were associated with anti-intellectual tendencies (Hoberman, 1986). Soviet participation in the Olympics in 1952 supported the belief of world peace and coexistence between conflicting ideologies (Hoberman, 1986). The Olympics represented a rare but great opportunity to bring about a policy of "peaceful coexistence" between the nations of the world (Hoberman, 1986, p. 106). It can be argued that Stalin's motives were not so altruistic and that perhaps he desired to apply for Olympic membership, viewing it as a means of promoting Soviet athletic superiority similar to what Hitler had done at the 1932 Berlin games.

The Olympic Games changed with the advent of television. The viewing audience has grown from originally being broadcast to millions of homes to presently being broadcast to billions of homes. Over 170 countries are currently involved in the Olympics compared to the 13 originally involved in 1896 (US Olympic Committee, 1996). Host nations must procure a large number of venues to support and house the athletes and games, while at the same time providing security for the venues and athletes. The need for funding has forced the host nations to sell excessive advertising spots at the Olympics. In 1996 Atlanta was "criticized by members of the IOC as well as the press for the city's efforts to raise money from the Olympics by leasing public areas to small vendors and selling advertising" (Andranovich, Burbank, & Heying, 2001, p. 11).

There are few events comparable to the Olympics that can allow an advertiser to sell their product to such a large and diverse audience. Many advertisers wish to have their products associated with the games and its ideal of excellence (Martin, 2000). Commercialism threatens the Olympic ideals of unity and peace, as those ideals may be replaced with the ideals of the capitalism and greed. This is exemplified by big corporate sponsors' expenditures of $40–$50 million to advertise at the 2004 Athens games, with the majority of these sponsors being American (www.livingroom. org, 2004).

Actions of the International Olympic Committee (IOC) have assisted in promoting the view of the games being a capitalist venture. The IOC members profit from the games by selling television right, trademarks to Olympic symbols, and bidding rights to host nations (Martin, 2000). The corrupt bidding process of the 2002 Salt Lake City Winter Games symbolized the changing capitalistic nature of the Olympics (Barney, Wenn, & Martyn, 2002). Commercialism has made the Olympics a target for groups with anti-capitalistic and anti-Western ideologies. These groups may be encouraged to attack the games as they view it as a legitimate target of their cause.

Numerous terror groups threaten the security of the Olympics. These groups or individuals view the Olympics as an opportunity to showcase their ideological message to a large viewing audience. Right wing groups have long viewed involvement in international affairs as the enemy of their militia ideology (Simonsen & Spindlove, 2004). These groups target the Olympics because they showcase the international cooperation that the groups oppose. Many domestic terror groups are anti-government and may wish to portray (to the global community) instability within their government by attacking the Olympics before a worldwide audience. In 1996, authorities arrested members of a Georgia militia group accusing them of preparing a bomb plot (Rice, 1996). The close proximity of where these individuals were arrested to the Atlanta Games may signify that they were preparing to attack the games (Rice, 1996).

The geographical location of host nations is a factor that affects security (of the Olympics). Land and maritime borders and proximity to hostile nations or regions can provide security threats. The 2004 Olympic Games in Athens, Greece, best demonstrated the additional risk of geographic factors. Greece, with its long borders both along the land and sea makes its easily susceptible to intrusion from hostile groups or individuals from neighboring countries (Brownstein, 2004). Greece is also in close proximity to Middle Eastern nations that are currently the focus of the "War on Terrorism" (Brownstein, 2004). This sparked increase in security measures taken by Greece and elevated the costs of providing these measures among all these fronts (Brownstein, 2004).

Olympic organizers wish to present the games without an omnipresent security force. In 1972 a leading police psychologist presented terror scenarios to organizers of the Munich games. These were ignored because the security measures recommended for implementation were not consistent with the way the organizers wished to present the games (Wolff & Yaeger, 2002). Organizers wanted the police psychologist to scale down security measures to better fit the atmosphere of the games. This type of thinking was prevalent during the 1972 Munich games and led to the massacre of Israeli athletes by Palestinian terrorist (Wolff & Yaeger, 2002). The lack of consistency in providing security, while at the same time presenting a carefree image of the games are factors that affect the ability to protect the Olympics.

Many counter-terrorism experts believe that international terrorists pose the biggest threat to the Olympics (Smith, 1996). These terrorists range from Islamic fundamentalist to South American paramilitary groups that may target the Olympics to promote their ideology in the global terror community. An attack on the games could help boost morale in such terror groups and provide them with a vehicle for recruitment. These groups are very resourceful and may have the means to attain unconventional weapons such as nuclear, biological, or chemical agents making them a volatile threat to the Olympics. The attack on the games would symbolize strength and could be used to intimidate governments that do not wish to be attacked by such a resourceful organization.

The threat from international state sponsored agents comes from hostile nations that seek to tarnish the image of enemy states. North Korea sought to do this when South Korea hosted the Olympics in 1988. The North Koreans accused the United States and Japan of creating a "wicked and treacherous plot to use the sacred Olympic movement for impure political and military purpose" (Anderson, Waller, & Sandza, 1988, p. 2). The United States and South Korea believed that North Korea was attempting to attack the Olympics. This concern was heightened when a captured North Korean agent stated to authorities that she was in training for a mission to attack the games (Anderson et al., 1988). North Korea did not attack the Seoul Olympics but its actions depict how hostility between nations can lead to an attack at the games.

Counter Measures

The threats to the Olympics come from both domestic and international terror groups and rogue states. Intelligence gathering for the games should be based on an international effort to gather information on threats and methods to prevent them. Host nations may be best prepared to deal with threats from domestic terror groups. Their knowledge and expertise of such groups makes them best prepared to handle domestic terror groups. Assistance from other nations would help the gathering of information of threats from international terror groups. The cooperation in intelligence gathering would help secure the games and ensure that it is done efficiently.

In understanding the security needs of the Olympics, it is helpful to understand why the Olympics are a target for attack and who poses a threat to them. Terrorism expert Robert M. Blitzer and special Olympic counsel member J. Gilmore Childers believed counter-terrorism operations at the Olympics should be centered on three areas of security (US Senate hearing, 1996). These three areas of security were divided among different US agencies at the Salt Lake City Olympic Games. These areas are "Intelligence; Tactical–Investigative; and Explosive Devices Detection and Response" (US Senate hearing, 1996). These areas are each individually important to counter terrorism at the Olympics. It is only through the establishment of a network system by which each of these operates symbiotically that they are most efficient at countering terrorism. The efficiency of one area affects not only its ability to provide security, but also the ability of the other two to provide security.

The tactical–investigative aspect of security at the games involves law enforcement and the tools utilized to prevent terrorism at the games. The deployment of law enforcement has traditionally been in the hands of the host nation for most of the history of the modern Olympics Games (Vistica, 2003). Host nations, at times, have provided this security by solely deploying their own officers, while other host nations have deployed both their officers and military personnel to provide security. During the 2004 Olympics, the Greek government initially did not want to accept assistance from other nations for security at the games. They changed their view after being heavily criticized by many nations for their inadequate security measures. The Israeli government threatened to boycott the games unless Israeli agents were allowed to provide security for their athletes (Vistica, 2003).

The Olympics are an international event and should be protected by an international security force. The tradition of security solely handled by the host nation is a substantial security flaw. Many host nations do not have the resources for the growing security need at the Olympics (Shipley, 2003). The rising costs of providing security at the games have led to widespread commercialism of Olympic venues as host nations seek to secure additional funds. If these costs were reduced through the cooperation of multiple nations providing resources to assist in security, the large commercial presence at the games could be reduced. An international force specifically created for the games would have the advantage of understanding how to implement security without affecting the atmosphere of the games. This would ensure that proper security measures are implemented and are not ignored by organizers who fear that security would adversely affect the presentation of the games.

An international security force would be prepared with the resources and expertise necessary to secure the tools needed to communicate and detect threats to the games. These tools would include quick efficient databases to detect identities of possible terrorists. Such a unit would be prepared and knowledgeable in deploying surveillance equipment. This equipment would include cameras in place at both the Olympic venue itself and in helicopters and blimps (Simpkins, 2003).

The explosive devices detection and response would operate to detect explosives and respond to any attack at the games. This would include the use of nuclear, biological, and chemical weapons detectors, X-ray machines, metal detectors, and bomb dogs to assist in preventing entry of weapons or suspicious packages to Olympic and non-Olympic venues. Anti-terror measures such as the "missile umbrella" were used in the 2004 Athens Olympic Games. The "missile umbrella" included ground to air and air-to-air missiles to protect against possible ballistic missile attacks at the games (Unknown author, 2004a).

The response deployment includes rapid deployment of personnel to areas based on the need for security. An international force would have the experience of having dealt with security at the Olympics and would be efficient at such activities. This could help in preventing a lack of preparedness that could hinder response to an attack at the games. The response deployment force would not only include the international security force but also emergency management teams and medical personnel. These units would work together to capture those responsible for attacks and to protect the innocents who may be injured in an attack at the games.

Counter terrorism at the Olympics could encompass other measures that cannot be categorized into any of these three areas. This includes the selection process for Olympic cities. Security has become a pivotal part of the Olympics. It has been speculated that the cost of the security may one day equal the cost of the Olympics (Johnston & O'Driscoll, 2004). There must be a security assessment of host cities not only during the initial selection process but also during the years leading to the games themselves. This process must include factors such as the current political climate of the perspective host city, volatility of the region around the prospective host city, and the geographic border of the nation. These factors could lead to increased threats and costs to providing security at the Olympics. Changing world events can cause certain regions of the world to become more volatile. Future host nations in such regions should be reassessed to ensure that they are still safe enough for the Olympics to take place.

Conclusion

The Olympic Games were created with the principles of humanity and international cooperation. The games have over time become a tempting target to groups that wish to promote their ideological messages to a large audience. This has led to two successful attacks on the games and numerous attempted attacks on the games. Stringent security measures are necessary to ensure that integrity of the Olympics ideology is not tarnished.

The threats to the games come from both domestic and international terror groups. These groups attack the Olympics because they portray the unity and international cooperation many of these groups' adamantly oppose. These groups have anti-government and racist ideologies that conflict with the Olympic ideology. The games' large viewing audience attracts groups who seek to promote their own ideological causes. The increased commercialism at the games has led to increased corruption and may encourage attack from groups that are anti-capitalism or anti-Western.

There are counter-terrorism lessons to be learned from the previous attacks at the Olympic Games. The Munich incident was the result of a lack of international cooperation and lack of security preparation. Security officials at the Munich games were aware of the possible threats posed yet chose to be ignorant because of the overriding need to shed only a positive light on the games. The lack of awareness for possible threats and lack of preparation resulted in an inability to properly react to the hostage situation. The Atlanta incident, on the other hand, was not the result of a lack of security preparation. The attack had more to do with the inability for first respondents to react to the threat once it was perceived. The failure of respondents once the threat was perceived led to the higher-than-necessary injury total. Olympic security is a multi-tiered process that involved preparation, operation, and response to the incident. As future games take place, host nations must be willing to take all these factors into account.

The introduction of an international security force at the Olympics is pivotal toward providing adequate security at the games. The international security force would provide consistency in resources and experience to combat threats to the Olympics. The advantages of such a force would increase security in the three areas of counter-terrorism "Intelligence; Tactical–Investigative; and Explosive Devices Detection and Response" (US Senate hearing, 1996). The creation of such a force would also reduce costs and commercialism at the games and the threats associated with it. The force would have expertise in understanding the delicate balance of security implementation and the concerns of preserving the image and presentation of the games. As the most recent Olympic Games in China ended without any terrorism-related incident, it is not advisable to treat this most recent Olympics as a template for future Olympic Games security as it is doubtful that any future host nation will be able to mobilize the level of security parallel or comparable to the Chinese government's effort in 2008. An investment of close to 300 million dollars in the security measures would probably remain an unprecedented expense in the history of the Olympic Games (http://securitysolutions.com/news/olympic-games-security/).

References

Anderson, H., Waller, D., & Sandza, R. (1988). A threat to the Olympics. *Newsweek*, July 4, 1988, pp. 1–3.

Andranovich, G., Burbank, M., & Heying, C. (2001). Olympic cities: Lessons learned from mega-event politics. *Journal of Urban Affairs, 23*(2), 1–20.

Anonymous (2007). China reveals Security Strategy for 2008 Olympic Games. Retrieved from http://securitysolutions.com/news/olympic-games-security/

Barney, R., Wenn, S., & Martyn, S. (2002). *Selling the five rings: The International Olympic Committee and the rise of Olympic commercialism.* Salt Lake City: University of Utah Press.

Bowman, E. (2003). Sartre on Munich. *Sartre Studies International, 9*(2), 5–8.

Brownstein, R. (2004). Securing the games. *Electronic Design, 52*(17), 45–50.

Campo-Flores, A., Skipp, C., & Burger, F. (2003). How he stayed hidden. *Newsweek, 141*(24), 36.

Czula, R. (1978). The Munich Olympic assassinations: A second look. *Journal of Sport and Social Issues, 2,* 19–23.

Fonda, D., Cuadros, P., Fulton, G., Land, G., Richards, C., & Sikora, F. (2003). *Time, 161*(23), 8.

Hoberman, J. (1986). *The Olympic crisis: Sport, politics and the moral order.* New York: Aristide D. Caratzas Publishing.

Johnston, D. (1996). Justice department split over handling of suspect in Atlanta bombing. *New York Times,* October 10, 1996, p. A. 31.

Johnson, K., & O' Driscoll, P. (2004). Security issues, fears fade as games roll smoothly to close. *USA Today*, August 30, 2004, p. D. 04.

Martin, B. (2000). Design flaws of the Olympics. *Social Alternatives, 19*(2), 1–6.

Noe, D. (2004). *The Olympics Bombed.* Retrieved from world wide web http://www.crimelibrary.com/terrorist_spies/terrorists/eric_rudolph/1.html

Reeve, S. (2000). *One day in september: The full story of the 1972 Munich Olympic massacre and the Israeli revenge operation "Wrath of God".* New York: Arcade Publishing.

Rice, M. (1996). Arrests cast spotlight on games' security. *Florida Times Union*, April 27, 1996. p. A. 5.

Shinbun, Y. (1996). Blast Rocks atlanta; 2 dead, 110 injured as games will go on. *The Daily Yomiuri*, July 28, 1996. p. 1.

Shipley, A. (2003). Greece playing it safe with Olympics; up to $1 billion to be spent on security at '04 summer games. *The Washington Post*, January 4, 2003, p. A. 01.

Simonsen, C., & Spindlove, J. (2004). *Terrorism today: The past, the present, the future.* New Jersey: Prentice Hall.

Simpkins, E. (2003). Blimp takes on the terrorists. *The Sunday Telegraph*, June 8, 2003, p. 8.

Smith, J. (1996). Counter-terrorism to be Olympic event for U.S. *The Washington Post*, April 23, 1996, p. A. 09.

Sonneborn, L. (2003) *Murder at the 1972 Olympics in Munich.* New York: Rosen Publishing Group, Inc.

United States Olympic Committee (1996). *Olympism: A basic guide to history, ideals and sports of the Olympic movement.* California: Griffin Publishing.

U.S. Senate Hearing (1996). *Olympics and the threat of terrorism.* Retrieved from the world wide web http://www.fas.org/irp/congress/1996_hr/s960611b.html

Unknown author. (2004a). Missile umbrella underway during Athens 2004 Olympic games. *Xinhua News Agency,* March 16, 2004, p. 1.

Unknown author. (2004b). *Olympic Sponsorship Opportunities.* Retrieved from world wide web http://www.livingrooom.org.au/olympics/archives/olympics/archives/olympic_sponsorship_opportunities.php

Unknown author. (2004c). *Olympic Park Reopens.* Retrieved from world wide web http://www.cnn.com/US/9607/30/park.reopen/index.html

Vercamer, A., & Pipes, J. (1996). *The 1936 Olympic Games in Germany.* Retrieved from the world wide web www.feldgrau.com/1936olymp.html

Vistica, G. (2003). Trials for Athens Olympics show Greek security remains flabby. *Wall Street Journal,* September 29, 2003, p. A. 3.

Wilson, S. (1996). Security efforts tough, pervasive but not failsafe. *The Oregonian,* July 28, 1996. p. A. 12.

Wolff, A., & Yaeger, D. (2002). When the terror began. *Time Europe, 160*(10), 1–1.

Chapter 12
1995 Tokyo Subway Attack: The Aum Shinrikyo Case

Ji Hyon Kang

Introduction

The 1995 Tokyo subway attack is an important event in the study of terrorism. It was one of the most famous attacks by a religious terrorist group. The Aum Shinrikyo cult had an apocalyptic doctrine, and their perception was that they could save people through their terrorist attacks. This attack was also based on the millennial vision, and it can be coined as a bioterror attack by a non-state agency. This attack implies that biological weapons became a new threat against countries, even in domestic terrorism. Indeed, the fact that the Aum Shinrikyo made unsuccessful attempts of attack before the 1995 Tokyo event shows the importance of prevention and the use of surveillance doctrines against potential domestic terrorist groups. Due to ineffective surveillance, the Aum Shinrikyo was able to finally succeed.

One of the major concerns aroused by the Tokyo attack was that subways became realistic targets of terrorists. Even before this incident, the subway was mentioned as a favorable target of terrorists; actually, the 1995 Tokyo attack shows the danger and the possibility of subway attacks using a biological weapon, sarin gas. In this chapter, the focus will be on the prevention of subway attacks and protection of the subway system and its riders. Since the Tokyo attack, the risk of subway attacks has become a practical issue, and it is urgent to clarify the ways to protect or minimize the risk of subway terrorism, specifically against biological weapons. In order to fully understand the specific terrorism issue, the details of the 1995 attack will be provided as well as Tokyo's law enforcement agencies' response. Additionally, in order to protect the citizens, further policy changes are deemed necessary.

J.H. Kang (✉)
John Jay College/Graduate Center, The City University of New York, New York, NY, USA
e-mail: jihyonkang@yahoo.com

M.R. Haberfeld, A. von Hassell (eds.), *A New Understanding of Terrorism*,
DOI 10.1007/978-1-4419-0115-6_12, © Springer Science+Business Media, LLC 2009

Description of the Attack

Description of the 1995 Tokyo Subway Attack

Twelve persons died, and more than 5,000 people were injured in the Tokyo subway attack in 1995. In terms of its operational angle, the attack was perfectly planned and executed. Packets of a poisonous gas, sarin, were punctured on five subway trains, and each of these identical packets contained 900 ml of the gas. These were concealed in lunch boxes and soft drink containers and placed on the subway floor. Terrorists put on gauze surgical masks – the kind often worn by Japanese citizens to protect them from germs – and then boarded the subway cars. Each one of the sarin bag was hidden with newspaper, and it was dropped near their feet. As the members of Aum Shinrikyo prepared to leave the train, they punctured the sarin bags with the tips of their umbrellas, and they quickly exited the train. All but two of the eleven sarin packets were punctured on five subway trains, releasing toxic gas into the restricted space of subway cars and the underground stations. The bags leaked a concentrated liquid containing sarin without any scent or noise. Subway riders did not realize that there was poison gas, even though many of them started suffering from the effects immediately.

As the trains continued on their routes, passengers complained of illness. Several riders were rushed to hospitals. However, the issue of a possible terrorist attack was not apparent to those involved. The train finally stopped and was evacuated more than 1 h after the attack. The Hibiya line, for instance, continued to Sinjuku Station after the attack, and it was sent back in the other direction as usual. An hour and 40 min later, the train finally stopped.

This was the most significant terror attack in Japan's modern history. The Aum Shinrikyo cult, under the leadership of Shoko Asahara, was responsible for the attack. They planned the attack and rehearsed it. Masami Tsuchiya, Aum's chief chemist, made the sarin gas that he had learned about in Russia and succeeded in manufacturing his first usable gas in 1993 (Lifton, 2001; Muir, 1999).

The Characteristics of the Attack

First, the targets were subways and its riders. The Tokyo attack generated the real threat of subway attacks. Attacks on the subway created a panic in the public and in law enforcement agencies. The 1995 subway attack raised significant concerns regarding the public transit, especially subways. Second, the Tokyo attack was intended to generate casualties, while prior terrorists focused on creating fear (Cameron, 1999). If they were interested in generating of fear only, the attack with the deadly gas in the dense trains was not necessary. A small release of this chemical substance has the potential to cause a great number of casualties. The subway was dense with people, and the sarin gas was spread quickly by the movement of the trains. The plan was to release the sarin during Monday morning rush hour, between 8:09 a.m. and 8:13 a.m. At that time, most riders were just arriving at their destinations to begin their workday. The three subway lines attacked were the most crowded lines during rush hour, so the terrorists intended to cause the most harmful result with their attack. Third, the 1995 attack was conducted by domestic terrorists. The attack implied a new threat of domestic terrorism, especially by religious groups. It raised the importance of utilizing surveillance and control oversight mechanisms over radical religious groups.

Finally, the Tokyo attack raised the need for a practical, operational, policy to handle terrorist attacks appropriately, especially on subways. Improper response can cause a great number of casualties in dense subway. Indeed, deaths and injuries on public transit can generate panic among citizens. Biological attacks differed from other traditional attacks because in under these circumstances, quick involvement can significantly reduce the deaths and injuries. Compared to an explosion, such as the one on September 11 in the United States, it is possible to save lives and prevent the spread of disease or exposure to poisonous substances with proper sanitization and rapid prophylaxis (Pangi, 2002). However, in the Tokyo case, the identification of the problem occurred too late, and the handling of situation was inappropriate and inadequate. This caused more damage and fear than the original attack did.

Aum Shinrikyo's Rationalization Regarding the Attack

There were two major purposes for the attack. First, the attack was planned to cause confusion in central Tokyo and to halt a police raid toward the Aum cult. Asahara became aware that the police were about to investigate the cult on March 18, 1995 – 2 days before the attack. The attack was planned hastily, and the cult had little time to make pure sarin for the attack (Reader, 2002). Consequently, this decreased the number of causalities. Second, the attack was based on the millennium vision (Cameron, 1999; Maekawa, 2001; Whitsel, 2000). Based on this vision, the Aum cult believed that they are ones who are selected for the new world, and the terrorists thought they could save society through their attack.

In the viewpoint of Asahara, the 1995 attack was his solution against inner and outer opposition. After the failure of election, the cult was exposed to society, and the majority of the public saw the cult as a strange form of a religious belief (Cameron, 1999; Reader, 2002). The rituals of the cult were eccentric. They strongly emphasized devotion to their leader; they drank the blood of Asahara for enlightenment. They also wore headgear to obtain salvation and isolation from the society (Lifton, 2001; Pangi, 2002). As the cult became larger and its membership grew, its eccentric rituals produced protests inside itself. To combat this inner and outer opposition, Asahara chose the path of violence.

The Background of the Terrorists and Their Leader

The Aum Shinrikyo

Aum means the supreme, Shinri means the truth, and Kyo means the religion. The Aum Shinrikyo (The Supreme Truth Religion) was founded in 1987 by Shoko Asahara, and the doctrine of the cult was a mixture of various religions: Buddhism, Shinto, Hindu, and new age doctrines. The Aum Shinrikyo was based on an apocalyptic doctrine regarding the new millennium, and the Shoko Asahara was believed to be a messianic figure (Cameron, 1999). The cult grew quickly and became a large group with 10,000–60,000 members with a $300 million–$1 billion budget. The Aum Shinrikyo also became popular in other countries: Russia, Australia, the United States, Germany, Taiwan, and the former Yugoslavia.

The Aum Shinrikyo was distinct from other religions in many perspectives. First, its doctrine rejected the world and emphasized harsh physical and ascetic practices (Poolos, 2003; Lifton, 2000). It demanded an absolute devotion to its leader and secession from the rest of the world (Reader, 2002). These dissocializing and introverted ways of life came from the ideology of "authenticity," and they were part of the new age religions' characteristics (Maekawa, 2001). With their charismatic leader, Shoko Asahara, the cult members believed that they would become the leaders and survivors of the Armageddon (Cameron, 1999). In terms of organization, the Aum cult differed from traditional religious groups. Its structure was unified and extremely hierarchical, and it was organized into ministries derived from the Japanese government system (Cameron, 1999). This illustrated the ambition of the cult leader and his dominant viewpoint over the country.

The recruitment methods of the Aum Shinrikyo were unique. Recruits were drawn from the universities, and the cult members were active in attempting to recruit persons in the areas of medicine, biology, chemistry, physics, and electronic engineering (Cameron, 1999; Pangi, 2002; Poolos, 2003; Rosenau, 2001). Once becoming a member of the cult, it was extremely difficult to leave the group. The cult used various methods for controlling the cult members including the use of drugs, sleep deprivation, poor nutrition, and some extraordinary methods such as small electric shocks to the head (Cameron, 1999; Lifton, 2001; Poolos, 2003).

Shoko Asahara – His Personality and Leadership

Shoko Asahara was born in 1955 at Kyushu, and he was sightless in one eye and partially blind in the other at birth. He attended a school for the blind, where he took advantage of his partial sight to dominate other students and commit fraud (Poolos, 2003). After graduation, Asahara tried to open a pharmacy and failed. However, in 1984, he successfully founded a yoga school. This time, his dream of salvation was refined, and he enjoyed the reputation of a famous yoga teacher.

Asahara was a brief member of the Kofuku no Kagaku, one of non-traditional religions in Tokyo. After leaving the Kofuku no Kagaku, he developed a bitter rivalry with its leader, Okawa Ryuho (Reader, 2002). Asahara stayed in a Himalayan retreat in an attempt to achieve self-enlightenment. Triggered by his first success at self-levitation, he found the Aum Shinrikyo in 1987 and called himself "today's Christ" and "the savior of this century" (Poolos, 2003, p. 12). He grew more eccentric as the cult spread. He made every follower sit one level below him and kiss his toe in greeting. The cult was also isolated from the rest of the world (Lifton, 2000; Poolos, 2003). He claimed that Armageddon would arrive from the United States, and it would happen in either 1997, 1999, or 2000 (Poolos, 2003; Reader, 2002).

The Path to Become a Terrorists Group

At first, the Aum cult was not violent even though they were isolated from society. It was the Asahara's failure to win an election that catalyzed the violence of the Aum Shinrikyo (Cameron, 2002; Olson, 1999; Pangi, 2002). According to Cameron (1999), the cult has complex motivations of violence, namely "to punish the world it ultimately hoped to save; to speed Armageddon, necessary before salvation; to protect Asahara' visionary status by ensuring that his prophesies came to fruition; and to satisfy Asahara's fascination with such weapons" (p. 279). The cult members from various areas, especially from the fields of scientific fields, were helpful in initiating the search for the ultimate biological weapon.

Asahara declared that the Aum Shinrikyo would require the most powerful weapons to fight against the coming struggle: Armageddon (Rosenau, 2001). In addition, the cult ran a biological warfare program (Schwan, 2004). Asahara established a laboratory in Kamikuishiki headquarters at the base of Mount Fuji, and he ordered his followers to produce a usable, harmful biological agent. Endo, the Aum's ministry of health, first acquired *Clostridium botulinum* where a microorganism that produces botulinum toxin which is considered to be one of the most poisonous substances on earth. In April 1990, Endo selected three places to test the toxin on human beings: the area around the Japanese Parliament, Yokosuka Naval Base – the headquarters of the US Navy's seventh fleet, and the area near the Narita International Airport. However, none of these attacks succeed in generating deaths. In 1992, the cult attempted to obtain the Ebola virus and experimented with poisonous mushrooms and Q fever. In a test on the cult members, one person died from eating food containing harmful microorganisms. In June 1993, the second attack with botulinum toxin failed to kill the Japanese royal family during the wedding of Prince Naruhito. Thereafter, Aum's interest moved to *Bacillus anthracis*. The cult members pumped the material into a sprayer and disseminated it into the air; however, again, no casualties resulted.

Finally, their interest shifted to the botulinum toxin and was tested in the crowded Kasumigaseki Station. This attack failed because of the conscience of a terrorist rather than ineffective technique or poison. This failure is important in understanding the 1995 Tokyo subway attack because it led Asahara to decide to use sarin, a more effective agent, in March 20, 1995, subway attack.

Analysis of the Law Enforcement Response

The Response to the Attack and Its Problems

After the Tokyo incident, several agencies and persons were blamed for their response to the terror attack. First, the subway authority and employees were blamed. They did not recognize the problem and its reason: the poisonous gas. Immediately after the release of the sarin gas, passengers suffered from its impact, but the trains continued as scheduled. In the Chiyoda line, especially, passengers indicated that they saw an unknown fluid leaking onto the floor of a train car. Train employees responded by cleaning it up with newspapers and their bare hands, and they did not suspect or inquire as to what it was. The train went on as scheduled, and two passengers died later from the exposure to sarin. Identification of the agent was not discovered until 9:27 a.m. while the sarin gas was released shortly before 8:00 a.m., and the Marunouchi line continued to run until the gas' discovery. This delay of the identification of the problem brought more destructive results (Reader, 2000).

Police agencies and other emergency agencies such as the fire authority and ambulances in Tokyo also did not identify the problem and respond appropriately to the tragedy. Although there were calls to the metropolitan police shortly after the attack, the decision to stop trains was not made until one and a half hours later. The contaminated trains ran and disseminated the poisonous gas. No response or decision was made until 30 min later when the National Police Agency (NPA) determined that there had been a major incident. Police and military authorities did not reveal the agent as sarin gas until almost 2 h after the attack. They did not share the information with other emergency organizations for another hour, and this was even more detrimental. The information about the agent and the dispersal methods were not provided to the victims and emergency responders until several hours after the attack (Pangi, 2002).

The medical specialists and the media were blamed for their inappropriate response, also. Many hospitals refused to take victims, and one hospital refused service to a victim for about 1 h (Murakami, 2001). There was not much information about sarin at that time, and many hospitals had little or no experience with it. Some media persons were also blamed for the severity of the disaster because they did not do anything to help. They were present at the subway entrance and filmed the victims, but they hesitated to take the victims to hospitals (Murakami, 2001). These problems were due to the lack of knowledge. It was the first bioterror case in Japan, so the possibility of domestic bioterror in subways had not been imagined there. This strongly implied that there is a need for a policy to prevent further attacks and to respond appropriately to similar terror attacks if and when they do occur.

Arrest of the Terrorists and the Compensation of the Victims

Shortly after the attack, the responsible terrorists, including Shoko Asahara, were arrested. Asahara was sentenced to death, and he later appealed that court decision. As of July 2004, eight terrorists have received the death penalty including Asahara. However, the Diet of Japan (Japan's legislature) rejected the request from government officials to outlaw the Aum cult. The reason for rejecting that was that the officials could not prove that Aum posed a "threat to society," and this denial of a threatening nature of the Aum cult angered the public (Fukuda, 1999; Murakami, 2001). The Aum Shinrikyo changed its name as Aleph and still exists as a recognized and legal entity.

Victims of the 1995 subway attack encouraged the Japanese government to employ a rapid and comprehensive action of compensation since the compensation issues remained unresolved 9 years after the attack (Kyodo news, 10/06/04). In 2004, over 1,000 victims were in the process of suing the Aum's assets, but only 30% of them have received any money. The remainder of these victims received help from a workers' accident compensation organization. Even though Aum has made a public apology and stated their willingness to pay compensation, many victims question their sincerity.

Lessons Learned from the Tokyo and Other Subway Attacks

The Tokyo subway attack raised significant issues concerning the understanding of what can be referred to as "new terrorism." It showed that a biological weapon can be obtained or manufactured without much difficulty. The Aum cult obtained the raw materials for biological weapons from the domestic market in Japan. The purchase was made through its front companies without any restraint. It was made possible because Japan did not control or inspect biological materials which were purchased by legitimate research firms or companies (Cameron, 2002). Also, it implied that such an attack can happen anywhere in the world. Japan was considered as a safer country, with regard to potential terrorist attacks, safer than the United States or middle-east countries. The target, subway trains and stations, raised an additional important issue. Suddenly, subways became one of the most popular places for terrorists to consider an attack on due to its symbolic effect and potential to cause massive amounts of causalities.

The Tokyo case suggested that there is a greater need to control certain types of structures and radical religious groups (Reader, 2002). The Aum Shinrikyo showed how a cult can easily transform into a violent terrorist group. The hostile attitude toward society was developed. In the process toward violence, the law enforcement agencies missed the clues and their criminal activities. Especially, 2 years before the subway attack, the cult released anthrax in Tokyo. Public heath officials collected air samples for analysis. They were suspicious that the cult might cook bodies down for disposal, and the air samples were tested for only body proteins (Milius, 2003). No body proteins were found, and the officials failed to detect this earlier use of biological weapon: anthrax. The group was also linked to a 1994 sarin gassing in a residential neighborhood in Matsumoto, Japan. It killed seven people, but it was not revealed until the investigation of the 1995 subway attack. If the law enforcement agencies were suspicious of the cult's interests in biological weaponry, the 1995 sarin gas attack may never have happened.

The Tokyo attack showed that the delay of the response caused more deaths and injuries than the attack itself. There were several reasons for the delay. The biological attack was unprecedented. It was difficult to make a quick, proper decision regarding response for most of the government agencies as well as the subway employees. The contingency and response plan against biological weapon attacks was absent in most of the government agencies except the military. Many people did not know how to respond to the attack. At first, there was no information about the simultaneous attacks on five trains, and each incident was regarded as a separate attack. The bureaucracy of Japan was also an obstacle regarding instant response and cooperation. The government agents were highly independent, and this fact deterred a rapid response to the attack (Pangi, 2002).

In the understanding of the terrorist attacks, it is important to identify the group's motivation, and religiously motivated terrorist groups are expected to be the most prone to use mass destruction (Post, 2002). Based on the different characteristics of terrorist groups, states should handle them differently, and few previous scholars attempted to analyze different policy orientations accordingly for different groups. Miller (2007) analyzed successful state policies depending on different group motivations, and he classified five categories of a state's policy options: do nothing, conciliation, legal reform, restriction, and violence. Miller (2007) insists that his categorization is much more superior to analyze state polices compared to the traditional dichotomous classification of state policy – coercion vs. conciliation.

In the analysis of policy success of religious terrorism groups, the 1995 sarin gas attack on the Tokyo subway is considered a failed policy of Tokyo's government because of its lack of involvement and conciliation (Miller, 2007). This subway attack also points to the difficulties of the state to deal with religious groups. The Japanese government allowed legal status of Aum Shinrikyo, as a religious entity in 1989, and this reflects the general approach of Japanese government of conciliating response to terrorists during the 1970s and 1980s (Angel, 1990). The 1995 subway attack was not the first attempt of Aum Shinrikyo, and there were two previous attempts in 1994 to use gas. In addition, after the 1995 subway attack, an assassination against the head of the National Police Agency was attempted (Reader, 2000). From March to September 1995, the Japanese government arrested almost 400 members of Aum Shinrikyo including the leader of Shoko Ashara, but the government did not outlaw the group. Under the Anti-subversive Activity Law of Japan, it was decided that the Aum did not have a political objective (Marshall, 1999). Instead, the law passed in 1999 to monitor potentially dangerous religious groups, and this plays a role in restricting the group's activities.

Aum Shinrikyo continues their activities to recruit and acquire property, but it claims to have discontinued its violent history. Since changing its name to Aleph in January 2000, it must provide the membership list and financial report annually to the government of Japan (Miller, 2007). The Aleph is currently under the surveillance and restriction. Even with the importance of legal restriction, legal reform cannot bring the effective control over the terrorist religiously motivated groups alone. Other types of restriction and surveillance are required to monitor the religious terrorist groups, and this is especially important while considering the willingness of its members to die for their purpose (Miller, 2007).

The Development of the "Subway Attack Protection/ Response Policy"

The Need for a Contingency Plan Against Subway Attacks

Considering that the purpose of a terror attack is generation of fear, the transit system is a perfect target. However, not all public transit branches are attractive to terrorists. Compared to subways, buses are not favored by terrorists (Begley & Sharon, 2001). Buses are open to the air, and it is easy to escape from them. Subways are underground, more crowded, enclosed, easy to reach, less secure, and hard to escape from. Especially with biological agents, it is possible to kill or injure people on the trains, in the stations, and on the street outside. The fast movement of trains accelerates the spread of biological agents.

The subway system is more favorable when terrorists are using biological weapons. The biological agents are inexpensive compared to a nuclear weapon, for instance, easy to carry, and hard to detect as they are tasteless and odorless. They can also cause a large amount of panic within the public. Diseases can be transmitted from person to person, and the aftermath of the biological agent will last for a long time (Schwan, 2004). The result of attacks using biological agents is more serious in the dense and blocked trains and stations. In the Tokyo case, if a pure and strong biological agent had been used, the effect would have been even more dangerous and disastrous.

Terror on the subways is difficult to prevent and respond to appropriately. Public transit has crowded areas and detecting terrorists before attacks is difficult. Indeed, after the attack, as shown in the Tokyo case, identifying the problem and coping with it was hard. Other attacks in subways have shown the difficulties encountered when dealing with the aftermath. For instance, 220 people were killed or injured in a fire on a subway train in the South Korean city of Daegu, on February 18, 2003. A man ignited a milk container containing flammable liquid on a train. It was a case of arson, and not a biological weapon attack. However, it showed how easy it is to cause huge casualties on subways. Several passengers tried to stop the attacker when he tried to use a cigarette lighter, but it was impossible. Indeed, the appropriate response was not enacted because the subway system had no protective devices, and the employees were untrained.

For an action plan regarding bioterrorist attacks against subways, three themes should be considered: protect subways and stations from the attack, set up a policy for the emergency response, and instruct subway riders and citizens quickly and effectively. In addition, the 1995 subway attack aroused an issue of control over dangerous religious groups.

Recommendation for the Future

Protection Physical Subways and Stations from the Attack

To protect subways and its riders from biological attack, several technological devices will be helpful. Detection of the dissemination of biological agent as soon as possible, chemical sensors, and CCTV could be helpful. Chemical sensors will inform the dispersion of biological agent, and CCTV will be useful to find the exact location of the attack. The PROTECT (Program for Response Options and Technology Enhancements for Chemical/Biological Terrorism) program, under the National Nuclear Security Administration's Chemical and Biological National Security Program (CBNP), is providing the model of response system. According to the PROTECT program, Washington, D.C., and Boston initiated the use of chemical sensor alarming devices against the biological weapons since 1998 (NNSA – PROTECT program). It emphasized the importance of CCTV and chemical sensors to detect the problem earlier. The PROTECT program also recommend that the location of center room should be far enough from potential targets to avoid the effect from the agent (Policastro & Gordon, 1999).

Other devices, such as luminous tiles and nonflammable walls are also useful. After the explosion in subway in South Korea, the Daegu subway lines established a plan to use luminous tiles on the ground of the stations against attacks and accidents. The walls in subway stations should be covered with noninflammable materials. Every station should have fire alarming sensors and CCTV also.

Recommendation for Law Enforcement Agencies and First Responders

The train workers, police officers, emergency medical professionals, firefighters, and physicians would be the first responders in any biological weapon attack against a subway. They should understand their roles in the bioterror attacks and the training that is required. As Policastro and Gordon pointed out, the response time is critical, and a rapid response will be possible with the training of the first responders, including train workers and police officers.

The only agency, which has a plan against biological attacks, is the military. To use the military training program will be helpful in saving money and time for initiation for the training program inside the transit system or police agencies. As a matter of fact, the Bay Area Rapid Transit System (BART) in San Francisco sent a team of police officers to the army's chemical weapons facility in Fort McClellan, Alabama, for training against bioterrorism in the year after the Tokyo subway attack (Begley & Sharon, 2001). In Seoul, the capital of South Korea, the subway system initiated emergency escape trainings and first-aid exercises against attacks in subways. The Korean subway system also has performed trainings against explosion.

Subway Passengers and Citizens

The role of the subway riders is critical in an emergency in subways to decrease the damages. The posters in subway trains and stations will be helpful to instruct the right response in case of an emergency. Also, the guidebook for the response will be useful. The Korean National Intelligence Service distributes "the guidebook for the emergency escape in case of biological terror and explosion in the public transit." The guidebook is provided in the subway stations and bus terminals. In the manual, the information to distinguish the terrorists from public and to detect the biological agent or ignite materials is included. It also emphasizes to report to the authorities in case of emergency or suspicious situations. In case of an emergency, the way to prevent more deaths and injuries should be specified, and the symptoms of chemical and biological terror should be explained to detect the problem as soon as possible. This will be very helpful in decreasing the number of deaths and injuries.

The Oversight over the Dangerous Religious Groups

One of the lessons from the Tokyo subway attack was the need of surveillance and control over dangerous religious groups. It is difficult, even impossible, to differentiate the dangerous religious groups from others before the groups engage in actual terrorist attacks. Also, to control religious groups is further difficult because of the freedom of religion, and it is impossible to supervise every religious group in the nation. The realistic way is to detect the problem of the cult as soon as possible. For instance, if there is clue/evidence about their terror attack or plan, the appropriate response should be enacted as soon as possible. In case of the Aum Shinrikyo, the cult committed illegal crimes before the attack, and some of its rituals were inhumane. The Aum Shinrikyo tried several attacks before the Tokyo subway attack, and its strong emphasis on devotion ignited some illegal actions such as forfeit of the cult member's asset and even homicide of formal members.

However, there was no investigation conducted into these events. Especially, the Japanese legal system did not have appropriate laws enacted to handle these terrorists and to control religious groups. After the attack, various laws were passed to apply retroactively to the Aum Shinrikyo case (Pangi, 2002). This suggests the importance of the proactive response of the legal system against the violent religious groups. Reader (2002) also indicated the importance of the Aum case in "political considerations regarding new religious movements and to issues of the legitimacy of police intervention in the working of religious groups" (p. 151). Some European countries, especially France and Belgium, decided to start some form of surveillance and control over the "dangerous sects," and the 1995 Tokyo attack was the motivation of these movements (Fautre, 1999).

The Tokyo attack raised other issues such as the regulation of chemical materials in the domestic market and international cooperation for anti-terrorism. As pointed out, the raw materials for biological weapons were received from the domestic market in Japan with its phantom company, but there was no legal regulation to prevent it from happening. Also, even though it failed, the Aum cult tried to acquire nuclear weapons from Russia (Cameron, 1999).

Conclusion

Schwan (2004) explained the four areas in which deterring the prevention of biological weapon attack could take place: "obtaining the agents, growing or producing agents, weaponizing the agents, and dispersing the agents" (2004, p. 231). The 1995 Tokyo subway attack was a case in point to show that all of these four factors are important. The Japanese government and emergency responders could not prevent the attack in any of the stages of these four factors.

The possibility and fear of terror attacks against subways becomes higher, but the preparation and prevention policies against them are insufficient. The best way is to prevent the attack before it happens, but it is not always possible. The next best way to handle the subway attacks is to decrease the damages from the attacks. To decrease the damages and casualties, a quick response is critical. For this, the use of technology is strongly recommended. To handle the crisis appropriately the emergency responders are in need of training. The cooperation of the public is also critical, so the guidebook for the public will be helpful.

The development of technological devices, training programs, and the guidebook for the emergency response will be the first step to deter subway bioterrorism. More studies about the issues concerning decrease of the risk are required.

References

Angel, R. (1990). Japanese terrorists and Japanese countermeasures. In R. Barry (Ed.), *The politics of counterterrorism: The ordeal of democratic status*. Washington DC: Foreign Policy Institute.

Begley & Sharon. (2001). Study the lessons of Aum Shinrikyo. *Newsweek* (cover story), 11/05/2001.

Cameron, G. (1999). Multi-track Micro-proliferation: Lessons from Aum Shinrikyo and Al Quaida. *Studies in Conflict & Terrorism, 22*, 277–309.

Fautre, W. (1999). Belgium's anti-sect war. *Social Justice Research, 12*(4), 377–392.

Fukuda, M. (1999). The de-nationalization of Aum followers: Its hidden political purpose. *Tsukuru*, November 1999.

Lifton, R. J. (2001). *Destroying the world to save it: Aum Shinrikyo, apocalyptic violence, and the new global terrorism*. New York: Henry Holt and Company.

Maekawa, M. (2001). The dilemma of authentic self ideology in contemporary Japan. *International Journal of Japan Sociology, 10*, 16–28.

Marshall, A. (1999). It gassed the Tokyo subway, microwaved its enemies and tortured its members, so why is the Aum cult thriving? *The Guardian*, July 15.

Milius, S. (2003). Cult anthrax. *Science News*, 2/22/2003.

Miller, G. D. (2007). Confronting terrorisms: Group motivation and successful state policies. *Terrorism and Political Violence, 19*, 331–350.

Muir, A. M. (1999). Terrorism and weapons of mass destruction: The case of Aum Shinrikyo. *Studies in Conflict & Terrorism, 22*, 79–91.

Murakami, H. (2001). *Underground The Tokyo Gas Attack and the Japanese Psyche*. New York: Vintage International.

NNSA (2004). (National Nuclear Security Administration) Chemical and Biological National Security Program. PROTECT (Program for Response Options and Technology Enhancements for Chemical/Biological Terrorism). Available from transit-safety.volpe.dot.gov/security/pdf/PROTECT_factsheet.pdf

Olson, K. B. (1999). Aum Shinrikyo: Once and future threat? *Emerging Infectious Diseases, 5*(4), 513–516.

Pangi, R. (2002). Consequence management in the 1995 sarin attacks on the Japanese subway system. *Studies in Conflict & Terrorism, 25*, 421–448.

Policastro, A. J., & Gordon, S. P. (1999). The use of technology in preparing subway systems for chemical/biological terrorism. *APTA 1999 Rapid Transit Conference Proceedings Paper.* Available from http://www.apta.com/research/info/briefings/documents/policastro.pdf

Poolos, J. (2003). *The nerve gas attack on the Tokyo subway.* New York: The Rosen Publishing Group, Inc.

Post, J. (2002). Differentiating the threats of chemical and biological weapons: Motivations and constraints. *Peace and Conflict, 8*(3), September 2002.

Reader, I. (2000). *Religious violence in contemporary Japan: The case of Aum Shinrikyo.* Honolulu, HI: University of Hawaii Press.

Reader, I. (2002). Spectres and shadows: Aum Shinrikyo and the road to megiddo. *Terrorism and Political Violence, 14*(1), 145–186.

Rosenau, W. (2001). Aum Shinrikyo's biological weapon program: Why did it fail? *Studies in Conflict & Terrorism, 24*, 289–3301.

Schwan, W. (2004). Bio-terrorism: Should I be worried?, In A. A. Nyatype-Coo & D. Zeisler-Vralsted (Eds.), *Understanding terrorism – threats in an uncertain world.* Upper Saddle River: Pearson Prentice Hall.

Whitsel, B. C. (2000). Catastrophic new age groups and public order. *Studies in Conflict & Terrorism, 23*, 21–36.

Chapter 13
2005 London Bombings

Charles A. Lieberman and Serguei Cheloukhine

Introduction

On Thursday July 7, 2005 (the 7/7 attacks), a series of explosions, three on the London Underground and one on the upper deck of a bus, led to 52 deaths and more than 700 persons injured. (BBC News (2005, July 7); BBC News (2005, July 12); BBC News (2005, July 17)) The perpetrators of the 7/7 attacks were later identified as Mohammed Sidique Khan, Hasib Hussein, Shazad Tanweer, and Jermaine Lindsay. Two weeks later, on July 21, 2005 (the 7/21 attacks), there was an attempt to replicate the 7/7 attacks, but only the detonators on four bombs exploded, while a fifth device containing explosives was discovered 2 days later, on July 23. The perpetrators of the 7/21 attacks were later identified as Ibrahim Muktar Said (also known as Muktar Mohammed Said), Yassin Hassan Omar, Ramzi Mohamed, Hussein Osman, and Manfo Kwaku Asiedu. Subsequent to preliminary investigations, both attacks were believed to have been perpetrated by Islamic fundamentalists. On July 22, the day after the second train attack in London within a 2-week period, police, based on inaccurate intelligence that he was one of the individuals involved with the July 21 terrorist attacks, responded to Stockwell station in London and fatally shot Jean Charles de Menezes.[1]

Islamic fundamentalism and its associated violence has become an increasing problem in recent decades throughout the world. This religious violence, sometimes referred to as *jihad*,[2] has been accentuated as a result of numerous attacks in western Europe, such as the murder of Theo Van Gogh[3] in the Netherlands, the March 11,

---

C.A. Lieberman (✉)
Department of Law, Police Science and Criminal Justice Administration, John Jay College of Criminal Justice, New York, NY, USA
e-mail: clieberman@jjay.cuny.edu

[1] Cascinani, 2008; Independent Police Complaints Commission, 2007a, 2007b; BBC News (2007, November 1): *What happened: The death of Jean Charles de Menezes.*

[2] "Jihad against Jews and Crusaders," the February 23, 1998, statement by the World Islamic Front, is credited with being the first 'fatwa' against the West.

[3] BBC News (2004, November 2): *Gunman kills Dutch film director.*

M.R. Haberfeld, A. von Hassell (eds.), *A New Understanding of Terrorism,*
DOI 10.1007/978-1-4419-0115-6_13, © Springer Science+Business Media, LLC 2009

2003, train bombings in Madrid,[4] and the July 7 and 21, 2005, attacks on London public transit. This chapter provides an overview of the time line of the events, the individuals involved in the planning and execution, and the law enforcement response and analysis for both the July 7 and the July 21 attacks.

> In compliance with Allah's order, we issues the following fatwa to all Muslims: The ruling to kill Americans and their allies – civilians and military – is an individual duty for every Muslim who can do it in any country in which it is possible to do it, in order to liberate the al-Aqsa Mosque and the holy mosque [Mecca] from their grip, and in order for their armies to move out of all the lands of Islam, defeated and unable to threaten any Muslim. This is in accordance with the words of Almighty Allah, "and fight the pagans all together as they fight you all together," and "fight them until there is no more tumult or oppression, and there prevail justice and faith in Allah."[5]

Overview of the Threat

The Threat from Islamic Fundamentalism and Al-Qaeda

Prior to the 7/7 attacks, some experts, such as Bamford (2004) and Katzman (2005), proposed that Islamic fundamentalists, such as Al Qaeda and its associated networks, pose the most significant threat to western nations, specifically western European nations, in the twenty-first century.[6] Hoffman (2006) describes the four levels of the new Al-Qaeda: Al-Qaeda Central; Al-Qaeda Affiliates and Associates; Al-Qaeda Locals; and Al-Qaeda Network. Al-Qaeda Central is comprised of the remnants of the pre-9/11 Al-Qaeda, centered in or around the Afghanistan and Pakistan borders and continues to exert coordination, if not some command and control commissioning attacks, surveillance, and planning and executing operations.

Al-Qaeda Affiliates and Associates are comprised of formally established insurgent or terrorist groups that have prior relationships with pre-9/11 Al-Qaeda, including groups in groups and insurgent forces in Uzbekistan and Indonesia, Morocco and the Philippines, Bosnia and Kashmir. Hoffman (2006) proposes that the goal is to co-opt these groups into the greater global jihad, forming a critical mass from these geographically scattered movements, thereby creating a single group. Until this goal is met, Al-Qaeda fosters relationships with these groups and provides essential local, logistical, and other support to facilitate strikes against common enemies. Hoffman (2006) posits that Al-Qaeda's continued influence and vitality is evident by its relationships with the following geographically diverse groups:

> al-Ittihad al-Islami (AIAI), the late Abu Musab Zarqawi's al Qaeda in Mesopotamia (formerly *Jamaat al Tawhid wa'l Jihad*), Asbat al-Ansar, Ansar al Islam, Islamic Army of Aden,

---

[4]BBC News (2004, April 28): *Timeline: Madrid Investigation.*

[5]"Jihad against Jews and Crusaders"

[6]Bamford, 2004, p. 739; Katzman, 2005, p. 5.

Islamic Movement of Uzbekistan (IMU), Jemaah Islamiya (JI), Libyan Islamic Fighting Group (LIFG), Moro Islamic Liberation Front (MILF), Salafist Group for Call and Combat (GSPC), and the various Kashmiri Islamic groups based in Pakistan – e.g., Harakat ul Mujahidin (HuM), Jaish-e-Mohammed (JeM), Laskar-e-Tayyiba (LeT), and Laskar i Jhangvi (LiJ).[7]

Al-Qaeda Network are home-grown Islamic radicals from geographically diverse areas, such as North Africa, South and Southeast Asia, and recent converts in Europe, that have no direct connection to Al-Qaeda or any other identifiable terrorist group, but share the radical jihad ideology of Al-Qaeda and are prepared to carry out attacks against the common enemy. Al-Qaeda Network are motivated by "a shared sense of enmity and grievance felt toward the United States and West in general and their host nations in particular".[8] An example of this category is the Hofstad Group in the Netherlands, from which a member, Mohammed Bouyeri, murdered Dutch filmmaker Theo Van Gogh in Amsterdam in November 2004.[9]

Al-Qaeda Locals consists of dispersed cells of Al-Qaeda adherents who have or had some direct connection with Al-Qaeda and is comprised of two subcategories. The first category includes persons who have had some prior experience and involvement in terrorist attacks, such as having taken part in jihad in Algeria, the Balkans, Chechnya, or Iraq and may have trained at an Al-Qaeda facility pre-9/11. The second category, which includes the individuals involved in the 7/7 attacks, includes persons recruited locally, brought to Pakistan for training and then returned to their homeland with the skills and knowledge necessary to successfully implement in a terrorist attack. There is no evidence that any of the 7/7 bombers were involved in any of the foreign conflicts discussed above; however, at least two of the 7/7 bombers, Tanweer and Khan were recruited locally and went to Pakistan prior to executing the attacks.[10]

Sageman (2008) describes how Islamist fundamentalism has evolved, from the organized hierarchical structure associated with early jihadi groups, such as Al-Qaeda prior to the 9/11 attacks, to the modern fluid, independent, and unpredictable loosely affiliated networks responsible for many of the recent attacks around the world. While Al-Qaeda may not have its pre-9/11 operational influence, leadership is regrouping and consolidating in the border region between Afghanistan and Pakistan. Reports of new training camps in Waziristan, Pakistan, provide evidence to support this analysis.[11]

---

[7] Hoffman, 2006, p. 4.

[8] Hoffman, 2006, p. 6.

[9] BBC News. (2004, November 2). *Gunman kills Dutch film director.*

[10] Laville, Gillan & Aslam, 2005.

[11] Sageman, 2008, p. 127; Leapman, 2008.

Vulnerability of Railway Targets

According to a March 2004 report by RAND, between 1998 and 2003 there were over 180 attacks on trains and related rail targets, such as depots, ticket stations, and rail bridges worldwide (estimates taken from the RAND-MIPT Terrorism Incident Database). Explosive devices, such as bombs and mines, have been the most frequent weapon utilized in attacks on rail targets, although firearms and arson have also been employed. The logistical complexities of rail targets are vastly smaller than for attacks against airlines. Due to the expectation by passengers that travel remains fast and inexpensive, in conjunction with the practicality involved in employing certain measures, such as passenger screening, metal detectors, or armed guards, the security at local and national railway sites is minimal in comparison to the security for air travel, particularly after the 9/11 attacks.

> Rail transportation has several unique features making it inherently vulnerable to attack. Rail passenger facilities in particular rely on open architecture and the rapid and easy movement of patrons in and out of facilities and on and off trains. In addition, both freight and passenger rail networks traverse dense urban landscapes that may offer multiple attack points and easy escape as well as vast rural stretches that are difficult to patrol and secure. Passenger rail facilities present potentially inviting targets for terrorists for a variety of reasons. They are easily penetrated and may have high concentrations of people. The logistics of a passenger rail attack are comparatively simple. For example, given the typical passenger density in a passenger rail station, substantial casualties can be inflicted with a *backpack-sized bomb.*[12]

Overview of the Events on July 7, 2005

On Thursday, July 7, 2005, four Islamic fundamentalist suicide bombers detonated explosive devices hidden in backpacks on the public transportation system in London, UK. Three of the suicide bombers nearly simultaneously detonated their devices on the London subway system known as the Underground, while the fourth suicide bomber detonated his device on the upper deck of a bus. As a result of these attacks, 52 persons were killed, including the 4 suicide bombers, and over 700 persons suffered injuries. These attacks were the most significant attacks in London, in terms of deaths and injuries, since the bombings of London during World War II.[13]

The perpetrators of these attacks were later identified as Mohammed Sidique Khan, Hasib Hussein, Shazad Tanweer, and Jermaine Lindsay. These events represented the "deadliest bombings in London since World War II and the first suicide attacks in modern Western Europe." However, the United Kingdom is no stranger to terrorism, including threats from Islamic fundamentalists. The year prior to the 7/7 attacks, police and security services arrested five Islamic fundamentalists that were plotting to target locations in the United Kingdom for the detonation of home-made

---

[12]Riley, 2004, p. 2.

[13]Strom and Eyerman, 2008, p. 8.

explosive devices using more than 1,300 pounds of fertilizer kept in a storage unit, which could have led to hundreds of deaths. According to a Security Service report, there were links between the 7/7 bombers and the fertilizer explosives plotters.[14]

Five men have been convicted and given life sentences for a bomb plot that could have killed hundreds in Britain. Jurors in the Old Bailey trial heard of plans to target a shopping centre, nightclub and the gas network with a fertilizer bomb. The plot was smashed by police in 2004 and today, after a year-long trial, five men have been convicted and given life sentences. Omar Khan, 25, from Crawley, West Sussex, was found guilty of conspiring to cause explosions likely to endanger life between January 1 2003 and March 31 2004.[15]

Timeline of the Events

On July 6, 2005, London was awarded the privilege to host the 2012 Olympic Games. Although this may have been a factor with the timing of the attack, it is likely that the attack had been planned well in advance, supported by the precision with which it was carried out. Subsequent to the 7/7 attacks, police and Security Services (MI5) were able to piece together the events involving the individuals suspected of conducting the attack from witnesses, forensics, and closed circuit television cameras (CCTV). The following is the time line provided by official sources[16] of the events leading up to the attack.

At 3:58 a.m., a light blue vehicle, hired by Shazad Tanweer and believed to be occupied by Tanweer, Mohammad Sidique Khan and Hasib Hussein, was caught on CCTV in Leeds. At 4:54 a.m., the vehicle stops for fuel and Tanweer looks directly at the CCTV and leaves. At 5:07 a.m., a red vehicle, occupied by Jermaine Lindsay, arrives at Luton station car park. Approximately 90 min later, the blue vehicle arrives and parks next to the red vehicle. The four men exit the vehicles and remove and put on backpacks (rucksacks), which appear to be full. Later examination of the vehicles found explosives and a 9 mm handgun among the items recovered from the vehicles.

At 7:15 a.m., the four men enter Luton station and, 6 min later, are caught on CCTV headed for the platform for the King's Cross Thameslink train, which leaves the station at 7:40 a.m. At 8:23 a.m., the train arrives at King's Cross and the four are caught on CCTV a few minutes later heading in the direction of the London Underground. At approximately 8:30 a.m., four men fitting their description are seen hugging, appearing happy or euphoric. Based on the evidence, Khan must have gone to board a westbound Circle Line train, Lindsay a southbound Piccadilly Line train, Hussein a Piccadilly Line train, and Tanweer an eastbound Circle Line train.

---

[14]Security Service MI5: *Links between the 7 July bombers and the fertilizer plotters.* http://www.mi5.gov.uk/output/links-between-the-7-july-bombers-and-the-fertiliser-plotters.html

[15]UK Home Office: Five convicted of UK bomb plot (April 30, 2007). http://www.homeoffice.gov.uk/about-us/news/five-convicted-uk-bomb-plot

[16]House of Commons, 2006; Intelligence and Security Committee, 2006.

At 8:50 a.m., the Circle Line train number 204, traveling from the Liverpool Street to Aldgate station, pulled out of the station. Seconds later, smoke billowed out of the tunnel as a result of the detonation of an explosive device by Tanweer, killing 8 and injuring 171. Forensic evidence suggests that Tanweer was sitting toward the back of the second carriage from the front of the train. Nearly simultaneously at Edgware Road, also sitting in the second carriage from the front of the train, Khan, detonated his explosive device, killing 7 and injuring 163. The third near simultaneous attack occurred at approximately 8:50 a.m. on Piccadilly Line train number 311 traveling from King's Cross to Russell Square, Lindsay, sitting in the first carriage on the train, detonated his explosive device, killing 27 and injuring over 340. The total for these three simultaneous attacks on the London Underground included 42 deaths, including the three suicide bombers, and nearly 680 injured.

The last of the bombers, Hussein, was seen exiting the King's Cross station onto Euston Street at 8:55a.m., at which time he unsuccessfully attempted to call, using his mobile phone, the other three bombers, who were already dead as a result of their suicide attacks. At 9:00 a.m., Hussein goes back into King's Cross station and purchases a 9 V battery, which led investigators to speculate that perhaps Hussein did not detonate his explosive device because he needed to replace a faulty battery. At 9:19 a.m., Hussein was seen on Grays Inn Road. Around the same time, a man fitting the description of Hussein was seen on the number 91 bus traveling from King's Cross to Euston Station. The man was described as looking nervous and pushing past people. It is believed that Hussein switched for the number 30 bus toward Marble Arch. At 9:47, almost an hour after the Underground attacks, Hussein detonated his explosive device on the top level of double-decker bus number 30, near Tavistock Square, killing 13 people, including Hussein.

Overview of the Events on July 21, 2005

On Thursday, July 21, 2005, five Islamic fundamentalist actors attempted to replicate the 7/7 attacks, but only the detonators on four bombs exploded, while a fifth actor abandoned the attack, dumping the device without attempting to detonate the explosives. The perpetrators of the 7/21 attacks were later identified as Islamic fundamentalist actors Ibrahim Muktar Said (AKA Muktar Mohammed Said), Yassin Hassan Omar, Ramzi Mohamed, Hussein Osman, and Manfo Kwaku Asiedu. Subsequent to a trial, Ibrahim Muktar Ibrahim, Yassin Hassan Omar, Ramzi Mohamed, and Hussein Osman were found guilty earlier this week. No verdict was reached for Adel Yahya, 24 and Manfo Kwaku Asiedu, 34, two other men accused of taking part in the 7/21 attacks. Yahya and Asiedu both now face a retrial.[17]

---

[17]Summers & Cascinani, 2007; BBC News (2007b, July 11): 21 July: Attacks, escapes and arrests; BBC News (2007a, July 11): In pictures: 21 July investigation; BBC News (2007, March 30): Police hunted suspect before 21/7; BBC News (2007, March 9): Teabags in 21/7 bomb – jury told.

On July 21, 2005, at 12:25 p.m., Said was seen at the London Underground Stockwell station walking toward the platforms which are the interchange for the Northern and Victoria train lines. At approximately 12:53 p.m., Said, who was carrying a backpack or rucksack, is believed to have boarded a Number 26 bus, which runs from Waterloo to Hackney Wick. While he sat on a seat toward the rear of the bus, he apparently attempted, unsuccessfully, to detonate the explosive device in the backpack. At 1:06 p.m., he was recorded on the CCTV of the bus exiting the bus on Hackney Road, East London, near the junction with Columbia Road. The bus driver reported hearing the explosion and smelling smoke, which, upon investigation, was discovered to be Said's backpack. The explosion from the detonator of the device blew out the windows at the front of the top deck of the double-decker bus. On July 29, 2005, police arrested Ibrahim Muktar Said, 27, at a flat in North Kensington, London.

On July 21, 2005, at approximately 12:25 p.m., Yassin Hassan Omar was also seen at the London Underground Stockwell station, carrying a small purple backpack. Omar boarded a Victoria Line train and attempted, unsuccessfully, to detonate the explosive device between Oxford Circus and Warren Street stations. He was seen without the backpack in Warren Street station at 12:40 p.m., where he ran toward the exit and jumped over the ticket barrier. Witnesses described hearing an explosion at the front of the northbound train as it entered the station. On July 27, 2005, Omar was arrested at a house in Small Heath, Birmingham.

On July 21, 2005, at approximately 12:25 p.m., a third man, Ramzi Mohamed, was seen at the London Underground Stockwell station. Mohamed boarded a northbound Northern Line train and attempted, unsuccessfully, to detonate the explosive device between Stockwell and Oval stations. Witnesses reported hearing an explosion and seeing smoke. At 12:34 p.m., he was caught on CCTV on the passenger concourse prior to leaving the Oval Street station. Mohamed was chased by members of the public, but escaped on Brixton Road, heading toward Brixton. He was last seen at about 12:45 p.m. on Tindell Street. On July 29, 2005, Mohamed was arrested by police in North Kensington.

On July 21, 2005, at approximately 12:20 p.m., Hussein Osman was seen entering the London Underground Westbourne Park station and was caught on CCTV at 12:21 p.m. at Westbourne Park station carrying a small red backpack. Osman boarded a train heading toward Shepard's Bush on the Hammersmith and City Line. At approximately 12:25 p.m., he attempted, unsuccessfully, to detonate the explosive device. Witnesses reported hearing an explosion and seeing a passenger lying on the floor on top of a smoking backpack. Osman exited the train at Shepard's Bush station, possibly through a window at the end of the carriage, and climbed down from the tracks, as this part of the line was above ground. He was last seen running toward the A40 and boarded a number 220 bus south toward Wandsworth. At approximately 1:20 p.m., Osman was caught on the bus on CCTV. Police believe he exited the bus at approximately 2:07 p.m. near Mapleton Road, Wandsworth. On July 29, 2005, Osman was arrest by police in Rome.

A fifth bomb was discovered in an open area at Little Wormwood Scrubs Park in West London, which is north of Shepard's Bush, on July 23, 2005, 2 days after these attacks. Police believe that there may have been a fifth bomber, who abandoned the plan for an unknown reason[18]. Manfo Kwaku Asiedu of Finsbury Park,[19] north London, was charged in relation to the discovery of the unexploded device. Asiedu asserted that he only went along with the plot because he feared being killed by the others.

Overview of the Law Enforcement Response and Analysis

Through the utilization of modern investigative techniques, including, but not limited to, interviews, forensics, and review of closed circuit television cameras (CCTV), the police and security services were able to piece together the events prior to the attacks and identify the individuals involved in these terrorist attacks (7/7 and 7/21).

Investigation of the 7/7 Attacks

A massive police and intelligence effort was initiated immediately after the attacks to identify the responsible parties and prevent further attacks. By the end of the first day, police have information regarding Khan and Tanweer. On July 9, police uncovered more evidence linking Khan and Tanweer to the sites of the attacks. A review of records determined that Khan had been peripherally involved with a prior investigation. Within a week, the investigation provided evidence that Khan, Tanweer, Hussein, and Lindsay employed suicide attacks using explosive devices hidden in backpacks.

There was initially a great deal of confused information from police sources as to the origin, method, and even timings of the explosions. The same day police stated that all three explosions in the Underground system between the Aldgate and Liverpool Street stations, between the Russell Square and the King's Cross stations, and at Edware road occurred simultaneously. It was also reported that the explosion on the Number 30 double-decker bus was left in the bus and not set off by a suicide bomber. Forensic examiners had initially thought that military grade plastic explosives were used, and, as the blasts were thought to have been simultaneous, that synchronized timed detonators were employed. This all changed as further information became available. Post-incident forensic analysis provided evidence that the explosive devices were comprised of home-made organic peroxide-based materials, which were then packaged in backpacks. Organic peroxide explosive is unstable, but

---

[18] Carter, 2005.

[19] BBC News. (2006, February 7). *Abu Hamza jailed for seven years*. Finsbury Park Mosque is known for Egyptian born, anti-Western cleric Abu Hamza al Masri, who was convicted of inciting murder and race hate and sentenced to 7 years.

does not require great expertise to manufacture and can be produced using readily available materials and equipment.[20]

Investigators examined about 2,500 items of CCTV[21] footage and forensic evidence from the scenes of the attacks. The bombs were probably placed on the floors of the trains and bus. It has been reported that the intention was to have four explosions on the Underground forming a cross of fire with arms in the four cardinal directions, possibly centered symbolically at King's Cross. It was said that one bomber was turned away from the Underground as the explosions had already started, and took a bus instead. It is also possible that the fourth bomber meant to take the Northern Line, which was suspended that day due to technical difficulties.

The bombs exploded underground, when trains were crossing, thus affecting two trains with each explosion. This is one of the features which led rapidly to the suspicion of a terrorist attack by suicide bombers as the cause of the explosions. The four explosions were widely reported as suicide bombings, but at the time the police would only confirm that they believed the bombers died in the bombings. However, in the aftermath of the subsequent July 21, 2005, London bombings and the shooting of Jean Charles de Menezes,[22] Sir Ian Blair publicly confirmed that they did believe they were dealing with suicide bombers.[23]

It is not clear why the bombers carried identifying items, which led to the discovery of the bomb factory in Leeds. The bombers may have carried identifying items in order to be credited with carrying out the attacks and viewed as martyrs by others that identify with the Al-Qaeda ideology. The bomb factory appears to have been intended for future use and a number of other explosive devices are said to have been found in the bombers' car at Luton station. In addition, the bombers bought return tickets to London from Luton, implying that they may have meant to return. This has led to speculation that the bombers may have expected to survive the attacks, perhaps having been misled about the time that they had to escape or the nature of the devices that they were carrying.

---

[20]Intelligence and Security Committee (May 2006). Report into the London Terrorist Attacks on July 7, 2005, p. 11.

[21]Closed-circuit television (CCTV), as a collection surveillance cameras doing video surveillance.

[22]Independent Police Complaints Commission, 2007a, 2007b; Holmwood, L. ITV to screen de Menezes drama. *guardian.co.uk,* December 19, 2008. Accessed February 19, 2009. http://www.guardian.co.uk/uk/2008/dec/19/de-menezes-shooting-itv. *Jean Charles de Menezes was a Brazilian national living in the Tulse Hill area of south London. de Menezes was shot dead at Stockwell Tube Station on the London Underground by unnamed Metropolitan Police officers. Initially witnesses claimed incorrectly that he was wearing bulky clothing and that he had vaulted the ticket barriers running from police. A police spokesman said on the day that, "his clothing and behavior added to their suspicions," and that he ran onto the train after police had issued warnings. It soon became clear that de Menezes did not vault and run from the police, but police did not alter their statement until the correct information was leaked to the press. They later issued an apology, saying that they had mistaken him for a suspect in the previous day's failed bombings and acknowledging that de Menezes in fact had no explosives and was unconnected with the attempted bombings.*

[23]BBC News (2007c, July 11): Sir Ian Blair's statement in full.

The first three bombs exploded within 50 s of each other, suggesting that a timing device or remote activation was used. It is believed that mobile phones were used to remotely detonate the Madrid train bombs, either by using the phones' alarm function or by calling the phone. The former method would work in the London Underground, but the bombs could not have been detonated by calling the phones as mobile phone signals are not available. As of July 19, 2005, no forensic evidence of either of these mechanisms had been made public, making a manual detonation likely. The 2004 Madrid train bombings (also known as 11-M, 3/11, 11/3, and M-11) were a series of coordinated bombings against the commuter train system of Madrid, Spain on the morning of March 11, 2004, which killed 191 people and wounded over 1,700.

On July 12, 2005, a Metropolitan Police press conference provided further details on the progress of the investigation.[24] Investigators focused on a group of four men, three of whom were from Leeds, West Yorkshire, and were originally reported as being primarily "cleanskins," meaning previously unknown to authorities. On July 12, 2005, the BBC reported that Deputy Assistant Commissioner Peter Clarke, Metropolitan Police Counter-Terrorism Chief, stated the property of one of the bombers had been found at both the Aldgate and Edgware Road blasts. Police subsequently raided six properties in the Leeds area that same day, including two houses in Beeston, two houses in Thornhill, one house in Holbeck, and one house in 18 Alexandra Grove, Hyde Park. One man was arrested. According to West Yorkshire police, a significant amount of explosive material was found in the raids in Leeds and a controlled explosion was carried out at one of the properties. The explosives found in the vehicle associated with one of the suspects at Luton railway station was subjected to controlled explosions.[25]

The Security Service, also known as MI5, are responsible for protecting the United Kingdom against covertly organized threats to national security, including terrorism, espionage, and the proliferation of weapons of mass destruction. In addition, MI5 provides security advice to other governmental organizations to assist in reducing vulnerability to threats.[26] The Metropolitan Police Services is one of the largest law enforcement agencies in the world, employing "31,000 officers, 14,000 police staff, 414 traffic wardens, and 4,000 Police Community Support Officers (PCSOs) as well as being supported by over 2,500 volunteer police officers in the Metropolitan Special Constabulary (MSC) and its Employer Supported Policing (ESP) programme. The Metropolitan Police Services covers an area of 620 square miles and a population of 7.2 million."[27]

---

[24] Metropolitan Police. Press conference (July 12, 2005): Assistant Commissioner Specialist Operations, Andy Hayman. http://www.met.police.uk/

[25] Lawrence, 2005

[26] http://www.mi5.gov.uk/output/about-us.html

[27] http://www.met.police.uk/about/

Overview of 7/7 Bombers

Jermaine Lindsay conducted the suicide bombing on Piccadilly Line train number 311 traveling from King's Cross to Russell Square, killing 27 and injuring over 340. Lindsay was alleged to have been a violent drug dealer in Huddersfield prior to his conversion to Islam.[28] Friends say that after his conversion, Lindsay rejected old friends and old habits and completely embraced an extremist, anti-Western, fundamentalist Islam, reminiscent of Al-Qaeda rhetoric. Lindsay's mother recalls their shock at the 9/11 attacks and wondered how Muslims could have done something like that. His wife, Lewthwaite, now 22 (who has since unofficially taken the Muslim name Sherafiyah) denied Lindsay's involvement until authorities produced forensic evidence to confirm his identity.[29] Lindsay was influenced greatly by the extremist and discredited preacher Abdullah el-Faisal (who was opposed vehemently in London by mosques such as Brixton Mosque) and Lindsay also had many of el-Faisal's taped lectures.

Hasib Mir Hussein conducted the suicide bombing on the Number 30 bus that exploded in Tavistock Square, detonating an explosive device and killing 13 persons. Investigators found his remains and personal effects on the bus. At 18 years old, he was the youngest of the group of four. Hussein, a British national of Pakistani origin who was born and raised in the United Kingdom, had become a devout Muslim after visiting Pakistan in 2003, after which he began wearing traditional Muslim dress and growing a beard, and made the Muslim pilgrimage to Mecca, the hajj. Around this time, he began associating with Shazad Tanweer and Mohammad Sidique Khan, two other suspected bombers. The three frequented the Stratford Street mosque in Beeston, and were also intimately associated with the Hamara Youth Access Point, a drop-in center for teens. Hussein had minimal interaction with law enforcement, but was cautioned by police for shoplifting in 2004.

Shazad Tanweer conducted the suicide bombing on the Circle Line train Number 204, traveling from the Liverpool Street to Aldgate station, killing 8 and injuring 171. He was a British national of Pakistani origin who was born and raised in the United Kingdom.

Mohammad Sidique Khan conducted the suicide bombing on the Edgware Road train, killing 7 and injuring 163. He was a British national of Pakistani origin who was born and raised in the United Kingdom. On September 1, 2005, a video of a pre-recorded statement by Khan was aired on Al Jazeera:

> I and thousands like me are forsaking everything for what we believe. Our driving motivation doesn't come from tangible commodities that this world has to offer. Our religion is Islam – obedience to the one true God, Allah, and following the footsteps of the final prophet and messenger Muhammad... Your democratically elected governments continuously perpetuate atrocities against my people all over the world. And your support of them makes you directly responsible, just as I am directly responsible for protecting and avenging my Muslim brothers and sisters. Until we feel security, you will be our targets. And until

---

[28] Bradley, 2005
[29] Alvarez, 2005

you stop the bombing, gassing, imprisonment and torture of my people we will not stop this fight. We are at war and I am a soldier.[30]

Investigation of 7/21 Attacks

Muktar Ibrahim, Yassin Omar, Ramzi Mohammed, and Hussein Osman were found guilty of the July 21, 2005, bomb plot have been jailed for life and were sentenced to serve a minimum 40 years before they can apply for parole. The following is a statement presented by Deputy Assistant Commissioner Peter Clarke, head of the Metropolitan Police Service's Counter-Terrorism Command and National Coordinator of Terrorist Investigations:

> These men obviously set out to replicate the horrors that had been inflicted on Londoners on 7 July 2005. But this was no spur of the moment plan – it had been hatched over several months. They failed to set off their bombs – not through want of trying. But no-one will forget the impact or the consequences of what they did – coming just two weeks after 52 innocent people had been murdered by other terrorists. Despite the carnage of 7 July, on 21 the public responded courageously, and without thought for their own safety. We can all salute the incredible courage of Angus Campbell as he confronted Ramzi Mohammed when he tried to set off his bomb. And we can reflect on the selfless actions of other members of the public as they tried to restrain or chase the terrorists. The convictions show that the jury rejected the blatant, indeed ridiculous lies told by these defendants in a futile attempt to escape justice. These men are dedicated terrorists who no longer pose a danger to the public, but recent events have shown that the threat from terrorism is, at the moment, ever present.[31]

The extent of Al-Qaeda involvement in or prior knowledge of the 7/7 attacks remains unclear. [32] There has been speculation regarding links between the bombers and another alleged Al-Qaeda cell in Luton, which was broken up in August 2004. That group was uncovered after Al-Qaeda operative Muhammad Naeem Noor Khan was arrested in Lahore, Pakistan. His laptop computer was said to contain plans for tube attacks in London, as well as attacks on financial buildings in New York and Washington.[33] The group was placed under surveillance, but in August 2, 2004, the *New York Times* published his name, citing Pakistani sources. The leak caused police in Britain and Canada to make arrests before their investigations were complete. The US government later said they had given the name to some journalists as background, for which Tom Ridge, the US Homeland Security Secretary at the time, later apologized.

---

[30] Intelligence and Security Committee, 2006, p. 12.

[31] Metropolitan Police Service News Article (2007, July 21): Bomb Plotters Jailed. http://cms.met.police.uk/news/convictions/bomb_plotters_jailed

[32] MSNBC Staff, 2005.

[33] Chossudovsky, 2005.

When the Luton cell was broken up, one of the London bombers, Mohammad Sidique Khan was briefly scrutinized by MI5 who determined that he was not a likely threat and he was not put under surveillance.[34]

In addition to MI5 hierarchically organizing investigative targets according to whether they are "essential," "desirable," or "other," the Joint Terrorism Analysis Centre (JTAC) also introduced an analogous three-tier, hierarchical model in early 2005 regarding the degrees of connection between targets and Al-Qaeda leadership:

- *Tier 1* described individuals or networks thought to have direct links to Al-Qaeda.
- *Tier 2* described individuals or networks loosely affiliated with Al-Qaeda.
- *Tier 3* described individuals or networks inspired by Al-Qaeda ideology.[35]

In May 2005, JTAC considered the majority of its focus on individuals and groups from Tiers 2 and 3 only loosely affiliated to Al-Qaeda or entirely separate (albeit with shared ideological beliefs). The JTAC considered the group responsible for the Madrid bombings in 2004, a Tier 3 group. The agencies used tiered designations, described above, to prioritize resource expenditure, but none of these hierarchies took into account the relevance of unknown factors. If investigators had kept in mind a network conception of Al-Qaeda, rather than directing activities through hierarchical assessments driven by what was "known," different decisions might have led them to discover the plans of Khan and Tanweer.

The Intelligence and Security Committee (ISC) report reaches the same conclusion in a more indirect way: The chances of identifying attack planning and of preventing the 7/7 attacks might have been greater had different investigative decisions been taken prior to the attacks. The ISC report concludes that in light of the other priority investigations being conducted and the limitations on Security Service resources, the decision not to give greater investigative priority to these two individuals were understandable.[36] While the ISC and government reports agree that scarcity of resources, rather than mistaken decisions about risk, was the main reason MI5 did not investigate the two men, investigative decisions made during the crucial time period between 2003 and 2005 could have impacted the outcome.[37] MI5 allocated resources to investigate Khan and Tanweer late in 2004 due to their associations with individuals arrested during Operation Crevice. However, MI5 soon diverted the funding to investigations considered higher priority. Yet, a number of experts question whether the ISC report's focus on resources was adequate to develop an understanding of how MI5 decision making went wrong. [38]

---

[34]Leppard, 2005

[35]Intelligence and Security Committee, 2006, p. 27; Irons, 2008

[36]Irons, 2008.

[37]HM Government, 2006; Home Office, 2006; London regional Resilience Forum, 2006.

[38]McGrory, 2006; McGrory & Hussein, 2005

Conclusion

Though it is possible that the 7/7 terrorists could have been neutralized prior to conducting the attacks had security or police services followed up on links among the individuals involved in the fertilizer plot and the individuals involved in the 7/7 attacks, all law enforcement, whether in the United Kingdom or elsewhere in the world, have limited resources and cannot follow up on every lead and must prioritize based on limited information; therefore, law enforcement will inevitably miss opportunities to detect and prevent crime, including terrorist attacks.[39] Khan and Tanweer, though peripheral to the fertilizer bomb plot, were key leaders in the 7/7 terrorist attack. However, MI5's failure to share information about Khan and Tanweer to local police contributed to this tragedy. Those previously identified individuals could have been monitored more closely and local law enforcement could have provided the resources necessary to conduct an investigation of possible threats to national security. Key features of the impact were that management tiers were more affected than operational tiers, and that communication between agencies was inadequate, especially outside the emergency services and among senior colleagues at a strategic level.

Inter-agency and intra-agency cooperation and communication, specifically intelligence sharing, continue to be problematic within law enforcement communities. Many agencies are loathe to share information for a variety of reasons including the following: fear of compromising sources, stealing resources, other agencies taking credit for investigation and/or arrest of perpetrators, and other agencies ruining an investigation. The authors propose that an investigation conducted by local police, who may not have the expertise or training commensurate with national agencies, are far superior to the alternative presented during the review of these incidents – no investigation. Law enforcement and other governmental investigative agencies, in this case the Metropolitan Police Service and MI5, must improve cooperation and communication to prevent future terror attacks. Key to this is learning lessons from the tragic experiences of other countries (for example 9/11, Bali, Madrid, and Moscow), no less than from the United Kingdom its own, and acting to ensure that gaps are filled, and the ability to respond continually improves.

References

Alverez, L. (2005, July 19). New Muslim at 15, a bombing suspect at 19. *International Herald Tribune.* Retrieved December 24th, 2008 from   http://iht.com/articles/2005/07/18/news/bomber.php

BBC News. (2004, April 28). *Timeline: Madrid investigation.* Retrieved January 11th, 2009 from http://news.bbc.co.uk/2/hi/europe/3597885.stm

BBC News. (2004, November 2). *Gunman kills Dutch film director.* Retrieved January 11th, 2009 from http://news.bbc.co.uk/2/hi/europe/3974179.stm

---

[39] Haberfeld, King & Lieberman, 2008.

BBC News. (2005, July 7). *London blasts: At a glance*. Retrieved January 11th, 2009 from http://news.bbc.co.uk/2/hi/uk_news/4659331.stm

BBC News. (2005, July 12). *Tube log shows initial confusion*. Retrieved January 11th, 2009 from http://news.bbc.co.uk/2/hi/uk_news/england/london/4674469.stm

BBC News. (2005, July 17). *Image of bombers' deadly journey*. Retrieved January 11th, 2009 from http://news.bbc.co.uk/2/hi/uk_news/politics/4689739.stm

BBC News. (2006, February 7). *Abu Hamza jailed for seven years*. Retrieved January 22, 2009 from http://news.bbc.co.uk/2/hi/uk_news/4690224.stm

BBC News. (2007, March 9). *Teabags in 21/7 bomb – jury told*. Retrieved January 11th, 2009 from http://news.bbc.co.uk/2/hi/uk_news/6435195.stm

BBC News. (2007, March 30). *Police hunted suspect before 21/7*. Retrieved January 11th, 2009 from http://news.bbc.co.uk/2/hi/uk_news/6511137.stm

BBC News. (2007a, July 11). *In pictures: 21 July investigation*. Retrieved January 11th, 2009 from http://news.bbc.co.uk/2/hi/in_pictures/6237594.stm

BBC News. (2007b, July 11). *21 July: Attacks, escapes and arrests*. Retrieved January 11th, 2009 from http://news.bbc.co.uk/2/hi/uk_news/6752991.stm

BBC News. (2007c, July 11). *Sir Ian Blair's statement in full*. Retrieved January 11th, 2009 from http://news.bbc.co.uk/2/hi/uk_news/7073662.stm

Bradley, A. (2005, August 8). Bomber was Huddersfield drug dealer. *The Huddersfield Daily Examiner*. Retrieved February 17, 2009 from http://www.examiner.co.uk/news/tm_objectid=15866918&method=full&siteid=50060-name_page.html

Bamford, B. W. C. (2004). The United Kingdom's 'War Against Terrorism'. *Terrorism and Political Violence, 16*(4), 737–756.

Carter, H. (2005, July 25). Police fear fifth bomber at large. *The Guardian*. Retrieved January 22, 2009 from http://www.guardian.co.uk/uk/2005/jul/25/july7.uksecurity1

Cascinani, D. (2008, December 12). The grey area of Menezes' killing. *BBC News*. Retrieved January 11th, 2009 from http://news.bbc.co.uk/2/hi/uk_news/7767449.stm

Chossudovsky, M. (2005, July 20). The Pakistani connection: The London bombers and "Al Qaeda's Webmaster" where are the maps of the London underground? *Global Research*. Retrieved January 22, 2009 from http://www.globalresearch.ca/index.php?context=va&aid=712

Haberfeld, M., King, J., & Lieberman, C. (2008). *Terrorism within a Comparative International Context: The Counter-Terrorism Response and Preparedness*. NIJ Grant #2004-DB-BX-1010.

HM Government. (2006, July). *Countering international terrorism: The United Kingdom's strategy*. Retrieved December 24th, 2008 from http://www.mi5.gov.uk/upload/ct_strategy.pdf

Hoffman, B. (2006, July). Islam and the west: Searching for common ground. *Testimony presented to the senate foreign relations committee on July 18th, 2006*. Retrieved January 11th, 2009 from http://foreign.senate.gov/testimony/2006/HoffmanTestimony060718.pdf

Home Office. (2006, September). *Addressing Lessons from the emergency response to the 7 July 2005 London bombings*. Norwich, UK: HMSO. Retrieved January 22nd, 2009 from http://security.homeoffice.gov.uk/news-publications/publication-search/general/lessons-learned?view=Binary

House of Commons. (2006). *Report of the official account of the bombings in London on 7th July 2005*. London, UK: The Stationary Office. Retrieved February 2nd, 2009 from http://news.bbc.co.uk/2/shared/bsp/hi/pdfs/11_05_06_narrative.pdf

Independent Police Complaints Commission. (2007a, November 8). Stockwell one: Investigation into the shooting of Jean Charles de Menezes at Stockwell underground station on 22 July, 2005. IPCC. Retrieved January 22nd, 2009 from http://www.ipcc.gov.uk/stockwell_one.pdf

Independent Police Complaints Commission. (2007b). Stockwell two: An investigation into the complaints about the Metropolitan police Service's handling of public statements following the shooting of Jean Charles de Menezes on 22 July 2005. *IPCC*. Retrieved January 22nd, 2009 from http://www.ipcc.gov.uk/ipcc_stockwell_2.pdf

Intelligence and Security Committee. (2006, May). *Report into the London terrorist attacks on 7 July 2005*. London, UK: The Stationary Office. Retrieved January 22nd, 2009 from http://www.official-documents.gov.uk/document/cm67/6785/6785.pdf

Irons, L. R. (2008). Recent patterns of terrorism prevention in the United Kingdom. *Homeland Security Affairs, 4*(1). Retrieved January 22nd, 2009 from http://www.hsaj.org/

Katzman, K. (2005). Al Qaeda: Profile and threat assessment. *Congressional Research Service*. Retrieved January 22nd, 2009 from http://www.law.umaryland.edu/marshall/crsreports/crsdocuments/RS220492102005.pdf

Laville, S., Gillan, A., & Aslam, D. (2005). Father figure inspired young bombers. *The Guardian*. Retrieved January 22nd, 2009 from http://www.guardian.co.uk/uk/2005/jul/15/july7.uksecurity6

Lawrence, D. (2005). US stocks rise, erasing losses on London bombings; gap rises. *Bloomberg*. Retrieved January 22nd, 2009 from http://www.bloomberg.com/apps/news?pid=10000103&sid=aflPCIrU37Ns&refer=news_index

Leapman, B. (2008). 400 in UK trained at terror camps. *Telegraph*. Retrieved January 22nd, 2009 from http://www.telegraph.co.uk/news/uknews/1557505/4000-in-UK-trained-at-terror-camps.html

Leppard, D. (2005). MI5 judged bomber 'no threat'. *Times Online*. Retrieved January 22nd, 2009 from http://www.timesonline.co.uk/tol/news/uk/article545011.ece

London Regional Resilience Forum. (2006, September). *Looking back moving forward: Lessons identified and progress since the terrorist events of 7 July 2005*. London, UK: Government Office for London. Retrieved December 24th, 2008 from http://www.londonprepared.gov.uk/downloads/lookingbackmovingforward.pdf

McGrory, D. (2006, June 19). US 'issued alert' on 7/7 bomber in 2003. *Times*. Retrieved February 2nd, 2009 from http://www.timesonline.co.uk/tol/news/uk/crime/article676305.ece

McGrory, D., & Hussein, Z. (2005, July 22). Cousin listened to boasts about suicide mission. *Times*. Retrieved February 2nd, 2009 from http://www.timesonline.co.uk/tol/news/uk/article546817.ece

MSNBC Staff. (2005, July 7). Islamic group claims London attack. *MSNBC News*. Retrieved February 2nd, 2009 from http://www.msnbc.msn.com/id/8496293

Riley, J. (2004, March). *Terrorism and rail security*. Santa Monica, CA: Rand. Retrieved December 24th, 2008 from http://www.rand.org/pubs/testimonies/2005/RAND_CT224.pdf

Sageman, M. (2008). *Leaderless Jihad: Terror networks in the twenty-first century*. Philadelphia, PA: University of Pennsylvania Press.

Strom, K. J., & Eyerman, J. (2008). Interagency coordination: A case study of the 2005 London train bombings. *National Institute of Justice, 260*, 8–12. Retrieved February 2nd, 2009 from http://www.ncjrs.gov/pdffiles1/nij/222899.pdf

Summers, C., & Cascinani, D. (2007, July 9). Bomb would have been 'devastating'. *BBC News*. Retrieved January 11th, 2009 from http://news.bbc.co.uk/2/hi/uk_news/6687311.stm

Chapter 14
Reforming Power Structures: Russian Counter-Terrorism Response to Beslan

Serguei Cheloukhine and Charles A. Lieberman

Introduction – The Beslan Incident

On the morning of September 1, 2004, over one thousand hostages, primarily children enrolled at the school and their family members, were taken at a local school in a small Russian town in the Republic of North Ossetia. The Beslan attack was conducted by a group of approximately thirty terrorists that had arrived from a neighboring village, Psedah – located in the Republic of Ingushetia. Official reports attribute infamous Chechen warlord Shamil Basayev[1] with being the mastermind responsible for the Beslan attack. Basayev was killed in 2006, reportedly by Russian Special Forces; however, Chechen rebels assert that Basayev was killed by a mine.

The hostages were forced into the school gym, the assembly hall, and other areas of the school. The terrorists set up explosive devices, prepared defenses, and executed adult male hostages, throwing their corpses out of a window. Government representatives received Basayev's letter addressed to President Putin demanding the withdrawal of all military forces out of the Chechen Republic and a videotape of the hostages. Early official reports stated that terrorists captured 354 hostages, though the total number of hostages was 1,187.

The next day, when the outside temperature was nearly 100°F, hostages were deprived of water and food. None of the government officials requested by the terrorists for negotiations responded, including the President of the Republic of North Ossetia A. Dzasokhov, who refused to go inside. The President of the Republic of Ingushetia M. Zyazikov was prevented from participating in negotiation by the Kremlin. The response by the former President of Ingushetia Ruslan Aushev led to the release of 26 women and children. Although V. Andreev, the Chief of the

S. Cheloukhine (✉)
Department of Law, Police Science and Criminal Justice Administration, John Jay College of Criminal Justice, New York, NY, USA
e-mail: scheloukhine@jjay.cuny.edu; sergueic@jjay.cuny.edu

[1] The Russian Security Service unit eliminated terrorist Basayev in 2006. According to the Russian Federation Law "The War on Terrorism," clause 16.1 burial of terrorists, killed in counter-terrorism operation carried out by the designed governmental agencies of Russian Federation. In doing so, their bodies are not given out to relatives and places are not disclosed.

M.R. Haberfeld, A. von Hassell (eds.), *A New Understanding of Terrorism*,
DOI 10.1007/978-1-4419-0115-6_14, © Springer Science+Business Media, LLC 2009

regional FSB, was the chief of counter-terrorist operations for attacks in the region, there was limited communication and cooperation among the governmental forces assigned to Andreev, which included other senior officials from the FSB, the MVD and the military.

Two days after the seizure, President Putin's advisor Mr. Aslakhanov arrived to the North Caucuses for negotiations. The time the leader of the Chechen separatists Aslan Maskhadov condemned the attack on the Internet, Mr. Aushev suggested contacting Maskhadov through Zakayev to assist in negotiating the release of the hostages. However, before negotiations were able to yield results, reports of explosions in the school led to an assault on the school by government forces. There were more than 120 explosives devices positioned throughout the school and the detonation of some of these devices caused the roof of the gym, where the majority of the hostages were held, to collapse, contributing to hundreds of deaths. The evacuation of the hostages was spontaneous and unorganized. Terrorists grabbed[2] some hostages and retreated into other areas in the school. The fighting, which continued until the evening, involved governmental forces employing heavy weapons such as grenade launchers, thermo-baric ammunition, and tanks. Because of this incident, 332 people were killed, including 319 hostages, 186 children among them. N. Kulaev, the only terrorist captured, was tried, convicted, and sentenced, in May 2006, to life in prison.

The Beslan incident represents the fourth largest hostage-taking terrorist act in Russia over the past 12 years. In June 1995, Basayev's terrorist group held more than 1,500 hostages in the Budyonnovsk city's hospital (Stavropol region). In January 1996, S. Raduev's terrorist group seized a hospital in Kizlyar (the Republic of Dagestan).[3] Moreover, in October 2002, M. Baraev's group seized more than thousand people in the theater on Dubrovka in Moscow.[4] However, the Beslan incident stands apart due to the targeting of children and the number of victims killed. The school seizure symbolizes a multifaceted event that uncovered major failures in response to the Beslan incident due to the mismanagement of intelligence. Moreover, it offers insight into the consequence that previous actions have on decisions made throughout terrorist attacks, during the "fog of war" that affects decision making in counter-terrorism operations. It proved the "failure of effective incident command that resulted in mismanaged objectives, ineffective transfer and chain of command, and errors in the dissemination of public information and intelligence."[5] No other terrorist act in Russia drove so much public attention toward the investigation of both the attack and the government response.

---

[2]Newsru.com. November 25, 2004.

[3]Investigation of the terrorist attack in Budyonnovsk was put on hold several times. Only years later, either one or several terrorists at once were tried in court. Raduev, who masterminded the attack in Kizlyar, was charged with the terrorism only 5 years later.

[4]During the storm of the theater in Moscow, all terrorists were killed and there was simply nobody to be charged.

[5]Forster, P. Beslan: Counter-terrorism Incident Command: Lessons Learned *Homeland Security Affairs*. http://www.hsaj.org, accessed October 1, 2008.

This chapter focuses on the following questions:

- What administrative, police, and military structures were in charge for national security before and after the Beslan incident?
- How did power structure,[6] especially Army reforms, affect decision making in counter-terrorism operations?
- Why did the second Chechen war, referred to as a counter-terrorism operation, result in the formation of the powerful armed militants and the terrorist underground?
- What lessons have the Russian government and law enforcement learned?

The Law Enforcement Response to Counter Terrorist Activities

Reforming of special security services is an inevitable consequence of a terrorist attack. For example, the September 11, 2001, attacks in New York and Washington, DC, led to major reform of the United States (US) intelligence services. The March 14, 2004, transit attack in Madrid led to a reorganization of the Spanish law enforcement. The July 5, 2005, transit attacks in London led to the reorganization of Special Branch of Scotland Yard.[7] These reforms generally take the following components of counter-terrorism into consideration:

- Exchange and dissemination of terrorism-related intelligence;
- Coordination among governmental agencies engaged in counter-terrorism;
- Terrorism prosecution
- Elimination of terrorism-financing sources and weapons traffickers

Militants[8] breaking into Ingushetia in June 2004[9] and the Beslan incident coincided with reforms in both the MVD and the FSB, which were a part of the administrative reorganization of the Russian government. President Putin's decree

---

[6] Russian power structures include FSB, MVD, and Defense Department with its Army, Air Force, and Navy, as well as Secret Services.

[7] The Counter Terrorism Command (SO15), which combined the Special Branch (SO12) and Anti-Terrorism Branch (SO13), was formed on October 2, 2006 (http://www.met.police.uk/so/counter_terrorism.htm).

[8] Chechnya declared independence when the Soviet Union broke apart in 1991. President Yeltsin responded immediately with military force, which had little impact. In 1994, the conflict between Russia and militant Chechen separatists grew into a war. After 9/11, Russia eagerly proclaimed that its efforts against Chechen fighters were part of the war on terrorism. Toward Chechen militants, Russian government and law enforcement officials synonymously used terminology "illegal armed formations" and "terrorists."

[9] About 1,000 militants who took part in the attacks Monday night, June 22, 2004 in the Russian republic of Ingushetia near the border of war-ravaged Chechnya killed 92 people and wounded 125. Among the dead were 67 members of law enforcement agencies.

"Urgent measures on increase of efficiency to fight terrorism"[10] recommended considering the Beslan incident as an example for needed reforms. Accordingly, the government and the law enforcement were to develop proposals on creation of a new system of mutual interaction to help prevent future human catastrophe in the Russian Federation.

The MVD and the FSB counter-terrorist structural reforms, which had been enacted in spring 2005, included the following:

- Operation management in North Caucasus.
- The system of law enforcement management.
- The statute in obtaining and analyzing the intelligence data on militant and terrorist leaders in North Caucasus.
- Special unit's status and tactics in the region.

The System Prior to the Beslan Incident

According to the 1998 law "The War on Terrorism," the governmental organizations that are directly engaged in the war on terrorism in Russia are the FSB, the MVD, the Counter-Intelligence Services, and the Defense Department.[11] In actuality, until 2003, the FSB was the primary organization engaged in counter-terrorism activities. The FSB antiterrorism unit was formed out of the Department of Fight Against Terrorism,[12] which had been subordinated to the FSB Fifth Department of Analysis, Forecast and Strategic Planning.[13] The department's management was created within the Federal Service of Counter-Intelligence (*Upravlenie po borbe s terorismom*, UBT – Department to Combat Terrorism, which continued to exist as a part of FSB). After Budyonnovsk seizure[14] (June 1995), the FSB Chief M. Barsukov authorized the creation of the FSB counter-terrorism center based on the Department to Combat Terrorism. The war on terrorism became one of the main tasks of the Perspective Program Department in FSB, created in 1996. In 1997, rooted in the counter-terrorist center, the Department to Fight Against Terrorism (DFAT) was eventually formed. At the FSB regional levels, the Departments for Protection of Constitutional Structure and Fight Against Terrorism (DPCSFAT) were also established.

---

[10]http://www.inpravo.ru/data/base874/text874v176i193.htm

[11]"Sobranie zakonodatelstva RF," 03.08.98, N 31, clause 3808, Rossiskaya gazeta, 146. 04.08.98.

[12]Upravlenie po bor'be s terrorismom, UBT.

[13]Service for operative information and international relation (*Sluzhba operativnoi informatsii I mezhdunarodnykh svyazei* (former) *Sluzhba analiza, prognoza I strategicheskogo planirovaniya*).

[14]Poole, S. (2006). Unspeak. How Words Become Weapons, How Weapons become a Message, and How That Message become Reality. Grove Press.

In North Caucasus, in July 2003, the Directorate of the Regional Operative Head-quarters (ROSH)[15] for carrying out counter-terrorist operations in North Caucasus was reassigned from FSB to MVD. On a federal level, in August 2003, the antiterror-ist Center T, surrounded by the Main Department for Combating Organized Crime (GUBOP), was created within MVD. The center also generated regional divisions that began to engage in arrests of terrorist suspects on a large scale. For example, in December 2004, MVD carried out numerous operations against the terrorist group Hizb ut-Takhrir[16] in Dagestan.

Consequently, the tasks of the MVD and FSB counter-terrorist divisions began to cross over because there was no coordinating center where those departments could exchange the information about terrorist activities. "The War on Terrorism" law stated that the President and the Russian government could create antiterror-ist committees at the federal and regional levels to coordinate counter-terrorism tasks.[17] The Federal Antiterrorist Committee (FAC), at federal and regional levels, was created a decade ago in 1998. However, in the Chechen Republic, the regional committee was formed in July 2004. The FAC, which, according to the Regulations of the Committee, is required to meet at least once every 3 months, was not capable of providing daily information exchange, and has limited utility in the fight against terrorism. Several federal and regional departments collect intelligence data on mili-tants in North Caucasus, despite the fact that the same tasks are in the jurisdiction of MVD and Main Intelligence Directorate (*GRU*). However, there was no information exchange among these departments either.

By the summer 2004, despite the numerous Kremlin claims regarding interna-tional terrorism in the Chechen Republic, the system of data exchange with other countries was still at a developmental stage. While the antiterrorist center was created under FSB management in 2000, the center had limited functionality. Con-sequently, by September 1, 2004, the Russian terrorist attack prevention system had been operating without a coordination center, had an ineffective system of intelli-gence, and did not have a mechanism for data dissemination among the Russian power structures and special services of other countries.[18]

---

[15] Regional'nyi operativnyi shtab po upravleniyu kontr-terroristicheskoi operatsiei na Severnom Kavkaze, ROSH.

[16] Russia's Federal Security Service (FSB) has long accused Hizb ut-Tahrir links with sepa-ratist fighters and alleged Arab mercenaries combating Russian troops in the breakaway Chechen Republic. It claims members of the Islamic Movement of Uzbekistan (IMU), a radical Central Asian-based Islamic organization, recently joined the group. The IMU is linked to the Taliban reli-gious militsia and was also routed during the US-led military campaign in Afghanistan. In February 2003, the Russian Supreme Court put Hizb ut-Tahrir and 14 other groups on a list of banned ter-rorist organizations. A month before, Hizb ut-Tahrir was outlawed in Germany on anti-Semitism and anti-Israeli propaganda charges.

[17] Federal Law "The War on Terrorism" 06.03.2006 N 35. Collection of Laws of the Russian Federation, March 13, 2006, N 11, Clause 1146.

[18] The decree of the Government Councils, 2000.

Changes in the System of Interdepartmental Coordination and Information Exchange

The following changes took place in the counter-terrorism departments of the MVD and the FSB in 2004.

MVD: Main Department for Combating Organized Crime (*GUBOP*) was renewed into the Department of Fight against Organized Crime and Terrorism (*DBOPIT*). At the same time, the Department of Analysis and Strategy Development in the field of counter-terrorism was created. Besides, the Center "T," the Center "C" of special maintenance and the special purpose *militsia* group "Lynx" fell under the jurisdiction of the Department of Fight against Organized Crime and Terrorism. The MVD Operative Management Center was reassigned the functions to maintain the headquarters' activity in managing the counter-terrorism operations in the North Caucasus region.[19]

FSB: The Department for the Constitutional Protection and Combating Terrorism was renamed the Service for the Constitutional Protection and Combating Terrorism and Mr. A. Bragin was appointed as its new director.[20] Prior to that, in June 2003, Bragin had been appointed to the FSB central administration as deputy chief of the Department to Combat Terrorism. The renaming of FSB and MVD departments was superficial and had no impact on counter-terrorism or level of coordination among agencies.

Meanwhile, each country that had gone through high-scale terrorist attacks, such as the United States, Israel, and Spain, faced problems coordinating, collecting, and analyzing data regarding future attacks. Intelligence data should not only be accessible to all counter-terrorist centers but also forwarded to the governmental agencies tasked with responding to an incident involving terrorism.

In some countries, for example, newly created special services unite previously independent structures, such as with the creation of the Department of Homeland Security in the United States. In addition, special coordinating structures, such as centers for obtaining and assessing the information on terrorist threats, are also generated. Examples of these structures include the Joint Terrorism Analysis Center in the United Kingdom, the Terrorist Threat Integration Center in the United States (which was recently replaced by the National Counter-Terrorism Center), and the *Centro Nacional de Coordinacion Antiterrorista* (National Center of Anti-Terrorist Coordination) in Spain. These departments, where one can find representatives of all power structures in the country combating terrorism, are responsible for data gathering and dissemination. They prepare forecasts of a potential terrorist threat. In addition, the same centers are responsible for information exchange with law enforcement services of other countries.

---

[19]Boragan, I., Soldatov, A., Zakhvaty i kontrzakhvaty. Rossiiskie spetssluzhby posle Beslana. *Political Journal*, October, 2005.

[20]Sluzhba po zashchite konstitutsionnogo ctroya b borbe s terrorismom FSB. http://www. agentura.ru/dossier/russia/fsb/structure/terror/

In contrast, the Russian Security Services system does not have such a structure. In October 2004, the FSB Chief N. Patrushev acknowledged that a full-time operating center in charge for action coordination of all departments fighting terrorism must be created.[21] However, such a center does not yet exist. Therefore, the problem associated with coordination and information dissemination among the FSB, the MVD, the Service of Counter-Intelligence, and the Defense Department (the primary participants according to the "War on Terrorism" law) has not been solved.

Information Exchange with Other Countries' Special Services

After the FSB structural reforms in the Department for Protection of Constitutional Structure and Combating Terrorism, a new division, the Directorate to Combat International Terrorism (*UBMT FSB*), was created. Soon after Beslan, President Putin stated that this management should direct counter-operations against foreign militants outside of Russia. In addition, in October 2004, former FSB Deputy Director A. Safonov was appointed as the Russian Federation special representative for the international cooperation to combat terrorism and transnational organized crime.

Creation of the UBMT FSB is a positive step, but it is not enough to solve a problem of daily exchange of intelligence with the secret services of other countries.[22] The special representative has authority to apply diplomatic pressure on countries that are not extraditing terrorist suspects (for example, the United Kingdom and Mr. Zakayev[23]). The UBMT FSB has contacts with secret services in other countries (within the limits of the signed memorandum with FBI[24] as well), but there is no coordination or information sharing with MVD.

Coordination Center and Information Exchange in North Caucasus

At present time, in North Caucasus region, there are two coordination centers to combat terrorists and illegal militants: the Regional Operative Headquarters to carry out the counter-terrorist operation in North Caucasus (*ROSH*) and the Unified Group of Army (troops) in North Caucasus (*OGV*), which is subordinate to ROSH. The purpose of ROSH, created in January 2001, was to supervise all Special Forces

---

[21] *Zaversheno formirovanie voiskovoi gruppirovki na Severnom Kavkaze* http://www.agentura.ru/timeline/2007/gruppirovka/. *Accessed November 4, 2008.*

[22] The decree of the President of the Russian Federation, 2004.

[23] Braithwaite, R. A crisis so serious we've forgotten how it started. *The Independent* 20 January 2008.

[24] Russian News. Glavy FSB i FBR podpisali memorandum o sotrudnichestve v bor'be s mezhdunarodnym terrorismom. December 6, 2004. http://palm.newsru.com/russia/06dec2004/fsb_fbi.html. Accessed November 21, 2008.

and other units tasked to detect and suppress terrorist organizations, their leaders, and supporters in the North Caucasus region. Originally, ROSH was managed by the FSB's deputy director, the chief of the Department on Protection of Constitutional Structure and Combating Terrorism. However, in July 2003, management responsibility of ROSH was transferred to MVD, but ROSH has remained under FSB control.

There are numerous examples of the shift of management. Rear Admiral Yu. Maltsev, who had supervised the FSB's Operative Management on Coordination of Counter-Terrorist Operations, was appointed as MVD deputy minister and the chief of ROSH. Ten days after the school seizure in Beslan, FSB general A. Edelev was appointed as the new ROSH chief, in charge for all FSB coordination management in North Caucasus. However, prior to the appointment he had been transferred to MVD where he received the rank of militsia general-lieutenant and the position of deputy minister. Thus, the responsibility for ROSH activities remains the MVD priority and this principle was not changed after Beslan.

In November 2004, 3 months after Beslan, the Southern Federal District Governor D. Kozak at the Commission on Coordination of Federal Enforcement authorities in North Caucasus stated, "In the past two years, the Regional Operative Headquarters functions were not regulated, at present days, it eventually has been reformed."[25] This statement reflected a positive assessment of the reforms subsequent to the Beslan incident.

Defense Department's Army Reassignments

The United Group of Army (OGV) in North Caucasus was formed by the Defense Department at the end of September 1999. The OGV core task was to liberate the territory of the Chechen Republic from illegal militant separatist groups. In March 2000, an OGV operation involved the elimination of R. Gelaev's terrorist group in Komsomolskaya village, after which militants continued to conduct attacks using terrorist methods.[26]

From the very beginning, army generals V. Kazantsev, V. Moltenskoy, S. Makarov, and V. Baranov were appointed to the OGV commander positions. In September 2003, V. Baranov was appointed as the commander of OVG, while simultaneously serving as the deputy commander-in-chief of the MVD Internal Troops. In July 2005, the deputy commander-in-chief of the MVD Internal Troops E. Lazebin was appointed as the new commander of the OVG, which placed yet another structure designed to combat terrorism under MVD management.[27]

---

[25]RIA News 11.30.2004.

[26]Trenin, D. Russia and Anti-Terrorism. *Carnegie Endowment.* http://www.carnegie.ru/en/pubs/media/72290.htm

[27]Obedinennaya gruppirovka voisk (sil) na Severnom Kavkaze. http://www.agentura.ru/dossier/russia/mvd/ogv/

Reassigning the counter-terrorism accountability to the MVD and army divisions was a positive step to combat illegal militants but not terrorists. The tactics of using MVD Internal Troops and heavy weapons could not destruct terrorist groups that are in constant hiding and preparing attacks on other regions. For this purpose the MVD Internal Troops possess neither corresponding experience (the task to combat terrorism was actually given to MVD only in 2003) nor the opportunities to conduct secret-service operation. Counter-Intelligence Service subdivisions of the Internal Troops operate only in the importance of tactical investigation and are not able to fulfill the goal of secret-service infiltration into terrorist groups.

For example, UK authorities in Northern Ireland had been using a similar strategy for decades. Until the end of the 1970s, in addition to the local police, the Royal Ulster Constabulary (RUC), both the military and the security services (MI5) were tasked with addressing the phenomenon of terrorism. MI5's Counter-Intelligence[28] group rarely operated in the region and employed a single officer for communication in Northern Ireland. The number of terrorist acts in the United Kingdom began to decrease only after MI5 was reassigned to the main department combating terrorism in 1992.[29]

Coordination in Case of Hostage Captures and Subversive Terrorist Attack

Prior to August 2004, it was assumed by Russian authorities that in a case involving a hostage situation or a counter-terrorist response, the chief of the regional FSB Management was to be the chief of the Main Department of Internal Affairs (or the chief of the local militias department). In practice, this principle never worked.

During the hostage situation in Budyonnovsk (June 1995), the operative head-quarters was headed by the Minister of Interior General V. Erin. The FSB Director S. Stepashin performed the task of the deputy chief, and later on, the MVD Deputy Minister General M. Egorov supervised headquarters. In addition, the Deputy Prime Minister of the Russian Federation N. Egorov and the assistant of the General Prosecutor O. Gaydanov took part in the meetings held in the vicinity of the terrorist attack.

During the hostage capture in the Dagestan's Kizlyar and Pervomaisk (January 1996), the MVD Deputy Minister General P. Golubets supervised the actions of the operative headquarters. Throughout the hostage situation in Lazarevskoe village, next to Sochi (September 2000), the operative headquarters was headed by the FSB deputy chief, the Chief of the Department Combating Terrorism N. Ugryumov, and by the MVD Deputy Minister V. Kozlov.

During the hostage situation in Dubrovka theater (October 2002), V. Pronichev, the FSB Deputy Director (the MVD Deputy Minister V. Vasilev was the Deputy

---

[28] http://www.mi5.gov.uk/output/Page2.html

[29] Walker, C. Clamping Down on Terrorism in the United Kingdom. *Journal of International Criminal Justice.* Advance Access published online on November 18, 2006.

Chief of headquarters), headed the operative headquarters. Thus, in all cases the officials in the position of a deputy chief of the federal departments were in charge.[30]

After the militant's intrusion into Ingushetia in June 2004, this principle was changed. In August 2004, 12 MVD Internal Troop colonels headed new divisions – the Group of the Operative Management that was created in every region of the Southern district. The Group of the Operative Management is the operating special body intended to manage the united forces and means given to suppress subversive terrorist acts and eliminate their consequences. They include divisions of operative and special function of the MVD Internal Troops, Special-Purpose Militsia Squad (*OMON*), Special Detachment of Quick Reaction (*SOBR*), and Defense Department (*DD*). The chief of Group of the Operative Management received status of the deputy chief of the republican antiterrorist commission, thus becoming the second-in-command after the governor. In case of hostage situation or militants' intrusion, the Group of the Operative Management commander automatically becomes the top chief officer of the operative headquarters and makes decision without the coordination with Moscow. Therefore, the names of Group of the Operative Management commanders are kept secret.

In fact, during the Beslan event, the Chief Officer of the North Ossetia-Alaniya Group of the Operative Management had already been appointed. However, his role in the operative headquarters actions was minimal. In Beslan, the Chief of the local FSB Management V. Andreev supervised the operative headquarters. At the same time, two FSB Deputy Directors – Anisimov and Pronichev – and the chief of the MVD "Center T" Demidov were at headquarters. Thus, for the first time in Russian hostage crises, the accountability was shifted to the regional power structures.

After Beslan incident, the principle of Group of the Operative Management domination (not designated during the crisis) was strengthened. Numerous counter-terrorism exercises in North Ossetia and in other regions of the Southern federal district were carried out. Only in 2004, the Group of Operative Management carried out 12 special tactics exercises. By the end of 2004, there were approximately 19,000 Russian military from various departments incorporated into the group structures.[31]

In February 2005, the Southern Federal District Governor D. Kozak criticized the Group of the Operative Management system. Due to the perception that the current policies and responses to terrorism were inefficient, Mr. Kozak drafted a decree reassigning the management of headquarters combating terrorism to the regional FSB chief management. However, this decree has not been adopted by the State Duma. Delegation of responsibility to local authorities and local power structures (to Governors and Group of the Operative Management commanders) has no equivalent in Western countries.

---

[30]Chechen rebels' hostage history. September 1st, 2004. BBC News: http://news.bbc.co.uk/2/hi/europe/2357109.stm

[31]*Operativnyi shtab Chechenskoi Respubliki po provedeniyu Contr-terroristicheskoi operatsii.* http://www.agentura.ru/dossier/russia/regions/rosh/

For example, in the United States, sectors of responsibility are distributed as follows: the local police are responsible for crime within their jurisdiction. The FBI Hostage Rescue Team (HRT)[32] is responsible for terrorist crisis resolution and the ranking member of HRT present becomes the chief of the operative headquarters. Thus, the federal authorities have the responsibility to deal with terrorist attacks in all cases. In the United Kingdom, the commissioner of Scotland Yard becomes the chief of the operative headquarters. The prime minister makes decision about the counter-attack after the meeting with COBRA (Cabinet Office Briefing Room A) group that consists of chiefs of special services; after that, the chief of Scotland Yard writes out the combating order to special SAS troops. That is, in the United Kingdom, the counter-terrorism responsibility also remains in central structures and not in local authorities.[33]

Accordingly, the use of the Group of the Operative Management as the center of decision making during crises similar to Beslan, when the tactics are not clear, will actually lead to shifting of responsibility (in case of failure S.C.) from the federal authorities to a local government and power structures.

Changes in the System of Obtaining Intelligence on Terrorist Acts

In June 2005, the Chief of the FSB Department of Fight against the International Terrorism Y. Sapunov acknowledged that in the first quarter of 2005, FSB had prevented more than 70 terrorist attacks. Mr. Sapunov also informed that in the previous year, in 50 Russian regions, terrorist organizations such as "Brothers Moslems," "Khizb-ut-Takhir," and "Islamic movement of Uzbekistan" were identified.[34] However, as there is no more substantial information on the prevented terrorist acts, it is impossible to confirm this information. Meanwhile, the FSB divisions combating terrorism, accountable for obtaining the information on acts of terrorism, structurally, were not changed during the last year. These reforms have covered only the North Caucasus region.

By the summer of 2004, some FSB divisions in charge for gathering intelligence on terrorist groups have operated in North Caucasus.[35] Executives of two ROSH structures lead counter-terrorist operations: the FSB Operative Headquarters and the FSB Operative-coordination Management in North Caucasus (*OKU*).

---

[32]http://www.fbi.gov/hq/isd/cirg/tact.htm

[33]Its purpose is to enable the prime minister, senior ministers, key government officials, and other persons (Metropolitan Police Commissioner, Mayor of London, Director of the SAS and Intelligence Officials) to obtain vital information about an incident and to secure lines of communication to the police and other emergency services, army, hospitals, and all relevant branches of government.

[34]Anti-terror. *Bor'ba s terorismom nashe obshchee delo.* http://www.guardantiterror.ru/?st=298&rub=25. Accessed November 9, 2008.

[35]Murphy, 2004.

The FSB Operative Headquarters are tasked with carrying out counter-terrorist operations and the forces of Chechen President R. Kadyrov[36] are subordinate to this agency. The FSB Operative-coordination Management in North Caucasus (*OKU*) has created the Temporary Operative Group (*VOG*) of the FSB Management in military counter-espionage. The primary goals of the Temporary Operative Groups include refugee screening, counter-intelligence, prevention of terrorism, and responding to hostage crises. Subsequent to the terrorist attack in Beslan, this system was subject to essential changes. On November 25, 2004, the State Duma Deputy V. Dyatlenko, the member of the parliamentary commission investigating the school seizure in Beslan, stated: "Inside the counter-terrorist structure, the special intelligence service which unites the efforts of all matters of operative-search activity, the FSB, MVD, and the military intelligence service, is now functioning."[37] The focus of the Temporary Operative Group is tactical intelligence data that would allow the location of militants involved in terrorism, not on proactive preventive intelligence regarding future plans by the militants. However, proactive preventive intelligence is a function of military intelligence, which was confirmed by the appointment of a United Forces Group deputy commander as the commander-in-chief of a new intelligence group.

Tactics of the Special Division After the Beslan Incident

By the summer of 2004, all North Caucasus power structures employed sending small (4–6 officers) autonomous groups, composed of members of FSB, MVD and GRU, into the Chechen Republic to eliminate terrorists. The commanders of the federal power structures would decide whether to engage in a laborious and complex covert operation or to execute swift attacks on the militant terrorists. The preference in favor of the latter was made at the beginning of the second Chechen war in 1999, which was a compulsory choice. It is difficult to determine the inception of the tactic to eliminate militants by small (3–5 officers) groups, which were composed of law enforcement from the central power structures. These groups take order from Moscow only and by all possible means had to act at their own risk to prevent information leakage. As a result, the Temporary Specialized Operative Group (*VSOG*) appeared. They included a driver and three senior officers. Six similar groups were created: five for actions in the regions of the Chechen Republic and one for Ingushetia. When VSOG arrives at the place of operation, they do not take orders from ROSH. Temporary regional police departments (*OVD*) provide them with ammunition, transport, and housing, while they do not supervise their activity

---

[36]Megan K. Stack, The brutal biography of Chechnya's Ramzan Kadyrov. *Los Angeles Times,* June 17, 2008. http://www.latimes.com/news/nationworld/world/la-fg-kadyrov17-2008jun17,0,1103942.story

[37]Beslan Commission. http://www.council.gov.ru/inf_ps/chronicle/2004/12/item2632.html. Accessed on November 9, 2008.

in any way. Groups are engaged in direct terrorist elimination. Originally, the operation lasts 1 month but usually extend until terrorists are killed. The final reports are sent in Polaroid photos to make sure that there are neither documents nor traces.

Covert operations in the Chechen Republic were rarely conducted, as operatives encountered significant difficulty recruiting Chechen agents, which was also a problem during the Soviet regime. However, the main problem was information leakage in relation to counter-terrorist operations. After R. Kadyrov, a former leader of Chechen militants, obtained access to ROSH meetings for his battalion commanders, the fear of information leakage relating to counter-terrorist operations in Khankala to anti-Russian Chechen militants increased substantially.

There are significant trust issues between Russian forces and former anti-Russian militants, who are now working with the Russian forces. The system of Temporary Militsia and FSB Departments (*VOVD* and *VO FSB*) continues to operate, working with the former anti-Russian Chechen militants. However, law enforcement from central regions of Russia, who lack understanding of local customs in Chechnya, is focused on physical security rather than the enforcement of the law. As a result, the activity of the Russian special services in the Chechen Republic, including the FSB, MVD, and GRU, is reduced to security checkpoints.

Main Intelligence Directorate (GRU)

At the beginning of the second Chechen campaign,[38] the main Intelligence Service of the General Staff authorized the creation of two special troops: "East" and "West." Originally, they were the special group of the military commandant's office of the Chechen Republic, later they received the status of battalions. The official name is the Battalions of Special Purpose of the 42nd Motor-Shooting Division of the Defense Department, a mountain group.

The base of the group "East," whose commander is Captain S. Yamadaev,[39] the former commander of the national guards of the Chechen Republic (an anti-Russian militant group), is in Gudermes. The base of the group "West," whose commander is major Said-Magomed Kakiev[40] (who received the reward of the Hero of Russia), is in Grozny. Both battalions recruit ethnic Chechens, many of whom have blood enemies among the militants, which provides greater fidelity and loyalty to Russia. Both battalions have engaged in militant identification and elimination, primarily in the North Caucasus mountain region of the Chechen Republic. The activity of

---

[38]The second Chechen war, in a later phase better known as the War in the North Caucasus, was launched by the Russian Federation starting August 26, 1999, in which Russian federal forces largely retook control of the separatist region of Chechnya.

[39]Battalion "Vostok" was formed in 1999; more precisely, it arose on the base of those passed to the federal forces side under the general command of the Yamadaev brothers, who opposed Wahhabism in the Chechen Republic.

[40]Battalion MO "West". *Global Challenge Research*. http://www.axisglobe-ru.com/article. asp?article=346. Accessed November 9, 2008.

these divisions is greatly appreciated in Moscow. The battalion "East" eliminated 38 militants preparing an attack in Dagestan shortly after the Beslan incident.

The FSB, from its part, uses two groups. The first is the Consolidated Special Group (*SSG*) of the regional operative headquarters of the FSB operative management. Groups include officers from the FSB regional management and Special Purpose Groups of the MVD Internal Troops (until the fall of 2002, SOBR fighters performed their tasks). Such 10 groups were created in April 2002 to perform special operations in Shalinskiy, Vedenskiy, Nozhay-Yurtovskiy, and Kurchatovskiy regions of the Chechen Republic. These groups operate independently of the local counter-espionage bodies and take orders from the Temporary Unified Group, which in its turn submit to ROSH. These groups are also engaged in militant elimination. Besides Special Purpose Group, FSB sends to the Chechen Republic the "Alpha" divisions, the so-called "heavy faces" group. They are engaged in elimination too and take orders from FSB in the Chechen Republic.[41]

However, all these means appear to be insufficient. The battalions "East" and "West," Temporary Specialized Operative Group, Temporary Militsia Department, and FSB Temporary Departments are obviously not enough to destroy militants in such quantities so that they would not be able to organize high-scale terrorist attacks. The problem is not in the fact that the Chechen Republic is a very specific area with the diverse terrain and special national character of the local population, etc. The "death squads" have never been the effective weapon against terrorists and the guerrilla fighters. In Algeria, for example, the activity of French "death squad," which were eliminating the leaders of the Popular Front, ended in failure.[42] In Spain, the activity of the group "antiterrorist group of liberation" (Grupo Antiterrorista de Liberacion – GAL[43]), which was terrifying Basque villages in the middle 1980s, ended with resignation of several ministers. In Northern Ireland, the spot-checks of SAS[44] and special subdivisions of the police (Metropolitan Police Special Branch – MPSB[45]) ended with no result.

In May 2004, the special service group of the Chechen Republic (the so-called "Kadyrov's guards"[46]) was reassigned to the republican MVD. In June 2004, the

---

[41] Heavy Faces and Others, 2004.

[42] Harry de Quetteville, French general in court over Algeria torture. August 26, 2001. http://www.telegraph.co.uk/news/worldnews/africaandindianocean/algeria/1363625/French-general-in-court-over-Algeria-torture.html; accessed on November 20, 2008.

[43] World: Europe Spain's state-sponsored death squads. http://news.bbc.co.uk/2/hi/europe/141720.stm

[44] The SAS in Northern Ireland. *Elite UK Forces.* http://www.eliteukforces.info/special-air-service/history/northern-ireland/, accessed November 20, 2001.

[45] Specialist Operations is part of the Metropolitan Police Service (MPS) and is divided into three sections known as commands. The three commands are: Counter Terrorism Command, Specialist Protection, and Royalty Protection.

[46] Smirnov, A. Yamadaev vs. Kadyrov: The Kremlin's Quandary with Chechnya. *North Caucasus Weekly,* Volume 9, Issue 15. April 17, 2008.

formation of a special purpose division, which included the former officers of Kady-rov's guards, began in the MVD of the Chechen Republic. The commander of the President A. Kadyrov's security service and assistant to the Gudermes military commandant A. Yasaev became the head of the division.[47]

After the Ingushetia incident (June 2004), the wide-ranging tactics to use military forces was strengthened. Besides, the decision was made to apply this tactics onto all territories of the North Caucasus. The MVD Special Purpose Groups actively confront extremists outside the Chechen Republic and take part in operations to eliminate terrorists in any Russian region. The Chechen special troops can be involved in the events similar to the ones in Ingushetia. Actually, it was the first time that the federal authorities authorized the use of the Chechen troops in other republics of North Caucasus.

Tactics Involving Capture of Terrorists' Relatives Tactics

Provisionally, after Beslan incident, the new tactic, such as capture of terrorists' rel-atives, was assumed. On October 29, 2004, the capture of terrorist's relatives was discussed publicly for the first time in State Duma. Attorney General V. Ustinov stated the following: "There should be a simplified practice of legal procedures, counter-capture of hostages, protection of witnesses and agents planted into terror-ist groups. As for counter-capture: if people commit a terrorist act, if we can call them "people," then the detention of terrorists' relatives and showing to the terror-ists what can occur to these relatives, can save our people."[48] At a legislative level this idea was not approved, however, it was accepted at the executive level. The first use of this tactic occurred in Spring 2004 when more than 40 relatives of Field Commander M. Khambiev were detained.[49] As a result, Khambiev has surrendered to the federal authorities. The second detain occurred during the attack in Beslan. In September 2004, in Nadterechny region of the Chechen Republic, the relatives of Aslan Maskhadov's wife including her elderly father were detained. In Decem-ber 2004, there were several reports on the detention of additional relatives of A. Maskhadov. Another example of this tactic being employed was in Urus-Martan in August 2005 when N. Humadova, the sister of the Field Commander D. Umarov, was detained.[50]

The practice of counter-capture not only contradicts the Russian legislation, but also is useless, both, for the prevention of terrorist attacks and for actions during crises. It is unknown what the power structures will do with relatives in case of an

---

[47] Kadyrov's interview to strana.ru, 2005.

[48] http://www.duma.gov.ru/index.jsp?t=pressa_ru/1013.html

[49] *"Voluntary Surrender" of Magomed Khambiev.* Human Rights Center "Memorial", October 3, 2004. http://www.memo.ru/eng/memhrc/texts/01new404.shtml

[50] *"In December 2004 Maskhadov' eight relatives have been abducted in the Chechen Republic."* Human Rights Center "Memorial". *December 1, 2005.*

unsuccessful storm similar to Beslan. The tactic of detention of terrorists' relatives is designated to intimidate both the terrorists and their relatives, but if the terrorists do not capitulate and surrender, the tactic's effectiveness would be nullified. The detention of relatives as an effort to trap field commanders has been employed as a tactic in countering guerrilla warfare. Examples include Germany during World War II and France during the Algerian campaign.[51] Although tactical success was achieved, the use of this method led to strategic failure. Numerous deaths occurred during the detention of the terrorists' relatives, possibly due to the conditions in the detention centers, as well as some of the interrogation tactics employed.

The Main Intelligence Directorate, the MVD, and the FSB special groups are, in reality, the instruments of revenge but are not effective in counter-terrorism actions directed at the militants. Meanwhile, counter-terrorism operations outside the Chechen Republic now occur in residential areas in city, including storming of militants' dwellings in Dagestan, Karachaevo-Cherkessia, and Ingushetia. For this reason, the use of special groups in other territories of North Caucasus will not decrease either the impact or the prevalence of militants' raids in the region; instead, it will increase tensions. It has already occurred in Dagestan, where in April 2005, the attempt of Kadyrov's group, which were alleged to have used excessive force, led to an ethnic conflict. Thus, the only positive result of the reform was the creation of a Regional Division of the Special Purpose FSB Center in Southern federal district.

Establishment of New Divisions

The MVD Internal Troops

In the fall of 2004, the MVD began deploying the Internal Troops (*VV*) personnel in North Caucasus. This meant to expand the personnel of the 49th Operative Purpose Brigade that was established in 2002. In June 2005, the MVD Internal Troops Commander-in-Chief General–Colonel N. Rogozhkin declared that by 2006 the management of counter-terrorist operation in the Chechen Republic will be transferred to the Internal Troops. Instead, by the beginning of 2006, the Internal Troops brigade-battalions were switched back to the previously existed battalion–regiment structure. At the locations where the battalion of 600 people had been deployed, a regiment of two thousand people was now located. In Sochi and Nalchik based on separate battalions, two additional regiments were created.

Additional forces of the Internal Troops were relocated to Krasnodar, Dagestan, Karachaevo-Cherkessia, Kabardino-Balkariya, and Kalmykia regions. In these regions, Groups of Operative Management are formed as well. Besides, all military commandants' offices of the Defense Department operating in mountain areas, Vedenskiy, Nozhay-Yurtovskiy, Itum-Kalinskiy, and Shatoyskiy, are subordinated to the General Headquarters Management of the MVD Internal Troops.

---

[51] http://www-rohan.sdsu.edu/faculty/rwinslow/africa/algeria.html

The principle of Internal Troops command has also been changed. In June 2005, President Putin signed decree that approved the operative-territorial association of MVD Internal Troops. Particularly, there are three operative-territorial associations: district, regional command, and regional management. These distinctions are based on volume, scale, and importance of problems, in addition to the number of personnel. The management for MVD Internal Troops was used as a framework for the first command of the Internal Troops in all regions of North Caucasus, whose task is to carry out counter-terrorist operations without using the Defense Department divisions. In other regions, the structure stays the same.[52]

The armies of the Defense Department in the North Caucasus region also increased in numbers. The special troops and tactical groups of the Defense Department 42nd Motor-Shooting Division operate in *Bamut, Vedeno*, and *Shatoy*. In 2006, in *Botlikha*, at the border between the Chechen Republic and Georgia, the Mountain-Shooting Brigade similar to the brigade in Karachaevo-Cherkessia was created.

By the end of 2007, the number of military men in the North Caucasus military district reached 45,701 people, which are four divisions of full personnel.[53] Among those are the Marines in Dagestan (Kaspiysk), several groups of 19th Motor-Shooting Division (Vladikavkaz), and 135th Motor-Shooting Division (Prokhladny, Kabardino-Balkariya). Besides, in March 2005, the State Duma approved the amendments to the law "On Defense," which, for the first time, allows the government to employ military forces in Russia (against terrorists) with all available weapons.[54]

Federal Security Service

In July 2004, the Border Guard service switched from a linear principle of state border protection to zonal. Ten regional boarder guard managements were cut down to seven within federal districts. As a part of this reform, in August 2004, the Regional Border Guard Directorate of Southern Federal District (*RPU FSB* of the Russian Federation in Southern federal district) was created with the headquarters in Rostov-on-Don. Commenting on the Internal Troops reforms, the commander-in-Chief General N. Rogozhkin acknowledged that former organizational changes had forced to reject the heavy combat operation that was not always justified. Thus, the use of tanks at storming building in city areas, as it occurred in the winter of 2004–2006, will, probably, continue.

Having authorized using force against terrorists, the State Duma followed the Spanish model. For example, 4 days after the attacks in Madrid (March 14, 2004), the Spanish parliament approved a new law on national defense that for the first time

---

[52]To Strengthen Borders, 2005.

[53]Russian Domestic Policy: A Chronology. July–September 2005. http://www.da.mod.uk/colleges/arag/document-listings/russian-chronologies/csrc

[54]The Federal Law on Counteracting Terrorism. March 6, 2005. http://www.memo.ru/2008/09/04/040908 1eng/part11.htm, accessed Nov. 22, 2008.

mentioned the use of armed forces to fight terrorism.[55] However, in Spain, the army can be involved only in case to support actions of the federal security, in particular for the protection of the transport system and major events. The Russian army, in contrast, has much more active function. The regional (territorial) management of FSB in Southern federal district has the secondary division in a new system fighting terrorism. However, it is the only division in power structures that conducts secret-service tasks in the region.

Conclusion

The Beslan attack has only locally affected the reforms in law enforcement and power structures of Russian Federation. The tragic event of September 2004 coincided with the structural reforms in FSB and MVD; however, they did not change the direction of the reforms.

Despite its proposed reform in 2004, the Uniformed Coordinating Center to Combat Terrorism has not been created. Thus, the problem of coordination and information exchange between FSB, MVD, International Counter-Intelligence Service, and Defense Department has not been resolved. Information exchange with special services of other countries continues to be problematic as well. The accepted measures have either partially been carried out (only in FSB the Directorate on Fight against the International Terrorism was created) or have been implemented merely at a diplomatic level.

In North Caucasus, coordination centers for counter-terrorist operations were transferred to the MVD and its army divisions. However, MVD Internal Troops do possess either equivalent experience or the necessary subdivisions of secret-service investigation for effective detection of terrorists. Creation of Operative Management Groups for actions during hostage situations and response to terrorist attacks, when tactics are not clear, shifted responsibility to the local government and power departments in case of possible failure.

At the federal level, the departments responsible for acquiring the information on terrorist acts were not significantly changed. In North Caucasus, the unified intelligence service of Unified Group of Army, which was created after the school seizure in Beslan, is only capable of solving the tactical intelligence problems, i.e., obtaining the information about the militants location and attacking them, etc. Thus, there were no significant changes in this important area.

Subsequent to the Beslan attack, the practice of detaining relatives of militants was endorsed by the Russian government. However, this not only contradicts Russian legislation, but also is unproductive in preventing and responding to terrorist attacks. This method is ineffective, as the threat addressed against relatives a priori cannot be carried out, even though the counter-capture is considered the action of intimidation. Capture of hostages for trapping field commanders has been

---

[55]Miguel Ángel Ballesteros. NATO's Role in the Fight Against International Terrorism. January 12, 2005. *Department of Strategy, Escuela Superior de las Fuerzas Armadas (CESEDEN).*

used before; however, if tactically those attempts were successful, they resulted in comprehensive failure.

For example, the detention of relatives as an effort to trap field commanders has been employed as a tactic in countering guerrilla warfare in Germany during World War II and France during the Algerian campaign. Numerous deaths occurred during the detention of the terrorists' relatives, possibly due to the conditions in the detention centers, as well as some of the interrogation tactics employed. Therefore, the use of this method led to strategic failure.

The scale of Main Intelligence Directorate, MVD, and FSB actions has been expanded into all North Caucasus Republics. However, these groups are used to attack but not for intelligence gathering or proactive operations to prevent future terrorist attacks. Currently, outside the Chechen Republic, major counter-terrorist operations occur in residential areas in Russian cities. Consequently, the use of these special divisions outside the Chechen Republic will not affect intelligence gathering or proactive operations to prevent future terrorist attacks; rather it will increase tensions. The only positive result of this reform is the creation of the first regional division of the special purpose FSB Center in Dagestan that is accountable for the Southern federal district. In the long term, there is a plan to form tactical rapid response units, such as an equivalent of special weapons and tactics (SWAT) teams.

Currently, the divisions of MVD, Internal Troops, and FSB Border Services expand in the region. Moreover, while planning a new system to combat terrorism, the republican (territorial) FSB directorates in Southern district were given the secondary role. Meanwhile, these are the only divisions in power structures that are able to conduct secret-service operations in regard to the terrorists' attacks.

Traditionally, there were three major directions of the agencies' activity: revealing, prevention, and suppression of crime. It is necessary to recognize that shifting the responsibility from FSB to MVD in North Caucasus has reflected in low activity of FSB as a whole and fight terrorism in particular. In the past years, there were no positive changes in these directions.

At present, it is difficult to see the efficiency of actions in eliminating the channels financing terrorists. One of the first responses by the United States after the September 11, 2001 attacks were to seize the accounts of those suspected of financing terrorists. However, in Russia, the concept of national strategy against legalization of criminal proceeds and terrorism financing, which developed by the Federal Service on financial monitoring, has not yet been adopted. The Russian law "Counteraction to terrorism," which is being discussed and considered for adoption, in the State Duma, is also unlikely to significantly change the situation. The basic innovations of this project do not include the mechanism to prevent the attacks, but actions of authorities and Special Forces *subsequent to an attack*. These structural reforms changed reactive counter-terrorism management but not the proactive measures needed to prevent future attacks.

Appendix: MI5 organization chart[56]

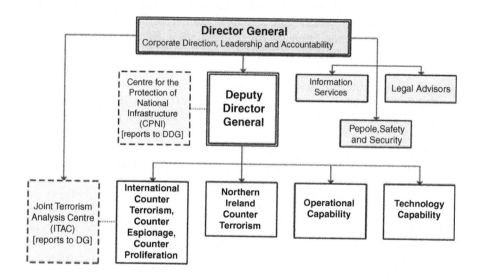

[56]http://www.mi5.gov.uk/output/Page62.html

References

Anti-terror. (2008). *Bor'ba s terorismom nashe obshchee delo*. Accessed November 9, 2008 from http://www.guardantiterror.ru/?st=298&rub=25

Ballesteros, M. (2005). NATO's role in the fight against international terrorism. January 12, 2005. *Department of Strategy, Escuela Superior de las Fuerzas Armadas (CESEDEN)*.

Battalion, MO. (2008). West. *Global Challenge Research*. Accessed November 9, 2008 from http://www.axisglobe-ru.com/article.asp?article=346

BBC News. (2006, July 10). Obituary: Shamil Basayev. BBC News. Accessed November 10, 2008, from http://news.bbc.co.uk/2/hi/europe/4727935.stm.

Beslan Commission. (2008). Accessed November 19, 2008 from http://www.council. gov.ru/inf_ps/chronicle/2004/12/item2632.html

Boragan, I., & Soldatov, A. (2005, October) Zakhvaty i kontrzakhvaty. Rossiiskie spetssluzhby posle Beslana. *Political Journal*.

Braithwaite, R. (2008, January 20). A crisis so serious we have forgotten how it started. *The Independent*.

Chechen Rebels' Hostage History. (2004, September 1). *BBC News* Accessed January 9, 2009 from http://news.bbc.co.uk/2/hi/europe/2357109.stm

De Quetteville, H. (2001, August 26). French general in court over Algeria torture. Accessed November 20, 2008 from http://www.telegraph.co.uk/news/worldnews/africaandindianocean/algeria/1363625/French-general-in-court-over-Algeria-torture.html

De Waal, T. (1999, September 30). Shamil Basayev: Chechen warlord. BBC News. Accessed November 10, 2008, from http://news.bbc.co.uk/2/hi/europe/460594.stm.

Dunlop, J. (1999). Russia: The Islamic threat. *Hoover Institution*, (4). Accessed February 9, 2008 from http://www.hoover.org/publications/digest/3533581.html.

Europe Spain's State-Sponsored Death Squads. (2008). Accessed November 9, 2008 from http://news.bbc.co.uk/2/hi/europe/141720.stm

Forster, P. (2008). Beslan: Counter-terrorism incident command: Lessons learned *Homeland Security Affairs*. Accessed October 1, 2008 from http://www.hsaj.org

FSB Puts Ahead. (2005, February 24). *The Businessman*.

Heavy Faces and Others. (2004, September 17). *The Moscow News*, 35.

"In December 2004 Maskhadov' eight relatives have been abducted in the Chechen Republic." *(2005, December 1)*. Human Rights Center "Memorial".

Maskhadov and Basayev will be caught by the special intelligence groups of FSB, MVD, and GRU. *Newsru.com*. November 25, 2004

Murphy, P. (2004). *The wolves of Islam: Russian and the faces of Chechen terror*. Washington: Brassey's Inc.

Obedinennaya gruppirovka voisk (sil) na Severnom Kavkaze. (2008). Accessed November 9, 2008 from http://www.agentura.ru/dossier/russia/mvd/ogv/

Operativnyi shtab Chechenskoi Respubliki po provedeniyu Contr-terroristicheskoi operatsii. (2008). Accessed November 9, 2008 from http://www.agentura.ru/dossier/russia/regions/rosh/

Poole, S. (2006). *Unspeak. How words become weapons, how weapons become a message, and how that message become reality*. New York: Grove Press.

Ramzan Kadyrov's interview to strana.ru. (2005, March 13).

Roth, J., Greenberg, D., & Wille, S. (2004). National Commission on Terrorist Attacks Upon the United States: Monograph on Terrorist Financing. Staff Report to the Commission. Accessed November 10, 2008, from http://govinfo.library.unt.edu/911/staff_statements/911_TerrFin_Monograph.pdf

Russian News. (2004, December 6). *Glavy FSB i FBR podpisali memorandum o sotrudnichestve vbor'be s mezhdunarodnym terrorismom*. Accessed November 21, 2008 from http://palm. newsru.com/russia/06dec2004/fsb_fbi.html

(2005, July–September). *Russian domestic policy*: A chronology. Accessed November 9, 2008 from http://www.da.mod.uk/colleges/arag/document-listings/russian-chronologies/csrc

Sluzhba po zashchite konstitutsionnogo ctroya b borbe s terrorismom FSB. (2008). Accessed November 9, 2008 from http://www.agentura.ru/dossier/russia/fsb/structure/terror/

Smirnov, A. (2008, April 17). Yamadaev vs. Kadyrov: The kremlin's quandary with Chechnya. *North Caucasus Weekly, 9*(15).

Sobranie zakonodatelstva RF. 31, *Rossiskaya gazeta,* 146. 04.08.98

Soldatov, A., & Borogan, I. (2007). *The Caucasus front line: The strategy of other's mistakes.* www.agentira.ru.

Stack, M. (2008, June 17). The brutal biography of Chechnya's Ramzan Kadyrov. Los *Angeles Times*, http://www.latimes.com/news/nationworld/world/la-fg-kadyrov17-2008jun17, 0,1103942.story

Trenin, D. (2008). Russia and anti-terrorism. *Carnegie Endowment*. Accessed November 9, 2008 from http://www.carnegie.ru/en/pubs/media/72290.html

The SAS in Northern Ireland. (2001). *Elite UK Forces*. Accessed November 20, 2001 from http://www.eliteukforces.info/special-air-service/history/northern-ireland/

The Federal Law on Counteracting Terrorism. (2005, March 6). Accessed November 22, 2008 from http://www.memo.ru/2008/09/04/040908 1eng/part11.html

The Federal Law. (2006, March 13). "The War on Terrorism" 06.03.2006 N 35. Collection of Laws of the Russian Federation, N 11, Clause 1146.

The decree of the President of the Russian Federation № No1167 "About urgent measures on the increase of efficiency combating terrorism" September 13, 2004.

The decree of the Government Councils of the CIS states on the Antiterrorist Center of the states-participants of the Commonwealth of Independent States. Minsk, December, 2000.

The decree of the President of the Russian Federation №1293 "About the special representative of the President of the Russian Federation in the International Cooperation combating terrorism and the transnational organized crime" November 10, 2004.

To Strengthen Borders. (2005, July 21). *The Shield and Sword*.

Walker, C. (2006). Clamping down on terrorism in the United Kingdom. *Journal of International Criminal Justice*. Advance Access published online on November 18, 2006.

Winslow, R. A Comparative Criminology Tour of the World. Accessed May 10, 2009.

Voluntary Surrender of Magomed Khambiev. (2004, October 3). *Human Rights Center "Memorial"*. Accessed November 9, 2008 from http://www.memo.ru/eng/memhrc/texts/01new404.shtml

Chapter 15
Beirut 1983: Have We Learned This Lesson?

Agostino von Hassell

Introduction

The facts are stark. Very early at 06:22 a.m. on October 23, 1983, a lone suicide bomber drove a Mercedes truck – packed with the equivalent of 12,000 lbs of TNT – into the building housing many of the Marines of the 24th Marine Amphibious Unit (24th MAU), killing 241 Marines and members of other US Services. Most of the Headquarters and Services Company of Battalion Landing Team, 1st Battalion, 8th Marines (BLT 1/8) was wiped out. At the same time, another suicide bomber drove a van into the barracks housing the French Foreign Legion, killing several dozen Legionnaires. Reading and watching the news coverage now of the efforts by the Marine Corps and the Army to keep the peace in Iraq brings back many memories of peacekeeping in Beirut in 1982–1984. Beirut also comes to mind when talking to veterans who tried to keep peace in Somalia.

Only time will tell if we have learned the bloody lessons of Beirut. This chapter does not recount the specific events. Exhaustive detail can be found in US Marines in Lebanon (1982–1984), published by the History and Museums Division, Headquarters Marine Corps, 1987, and in the seminal investigative report of the Long Commission.[1] The main purpose of this chapter is to analyze the response to these terrorist attacks and ascertain if and what lessons have been learned, and how these lessons could be implemented in the future.

Lessons Learned or to Be Learned?

The five-member Department of Defense Commission on the Beirut International Airport Terrorist Act, October 23, 1983, was established by then –

A. von Hassell (✉)
399 Park Ave. 26th Floor, New York, NY 10022, The Repton Group LLC., USA
e-mail: avonhassell@thereptongroup.com

Parts reprinted by permission from the Marines Corp Gazette

[1] Numerous books have been published about the Beirut deployment. Most useful are *Peacekeepers at War: A Marine's Account of the Beirut Catastrophe* by Michael Petit, Faber & Faber, Boston, 1986 and *The Root* by Eric Hammel, Harcourt Brace Jovanovich, New York. 1985.

M.R. Haberfeld, A. von Hassell (eds.), *A New Understanding of Terrorism*,
DOI 10.1007/978-1-4419-0115-6_15, © Springer Science+Business Media, LLC 2009

Secretary of Defense Casper W. Weinberger on November 7, 1983. It was chaired by ADM Robert L.K. Long, USN (Ret), who had retired in July 1983 after 40 years of service.[2] Details of this scathing report may be found in the official report. (http://www.ibiblio.org/hyperwar/AMH/XX/MidEast/Lebanon-1982-1984/DOD-Report/index.html) (see p. 44). The official policy and posture of the USMNF constituted tacit approval of the security measures and procedures in force at the BLT Headquarters building on October 23, 1983.

With the benefit of hindsight, it has become apparent that the Beirut bombing was a failure of intelligence, a clear failure of command and control, a failure of effective rules of engagement (ROE), a failure of clear-cut mission orders, and a failure in Washington to understand the Middle East – and, more specifically, Lebanon, which at that time was among its most complicated and incendiary components, if not the most complicated and incendiary component.

It was not, again with 20 years of hindsight, a failure of the 24th MAU and its commander, Col Timothy J. Geraghty. His only fault may have been to bunch too many Marines into one building, creating an attractive target for terrorists. This mistake, though, has to be admitted and shouldered as well at the highest levels of the US military and even of the US government, because their assumptions about the environment into which they had inserted the peacekeeping Marines were false, especially after the environment deteriorated around the Marines as Lebanon grew more volatile over the 13 months of the peacekeeping mission up to that fateful Sunday in October. Military headquarters and the upper echelons of the US government assumed a much more secure environment for those fated Marines than in fact existed by autumn of 1983. When the peacekeeping Marines arrived they were cheered; 13 months later they were deeply resented. The administrators in charge, both military and civilian, did not adjust properly to these rapidly changed conditions and did not implement security measures commensurate with safeguarding the lives of these well-intentioned and noble Marines.

This writer jotted down a sign at Echo Company, BLT 2/8: *They sent us to Beirut, to be targets who could not shoot. Friends will die into an early grave, was there any reasons for what they gave?*[3]

Certainly a gallows humor ditty like this scrawled on a sign indicated how the peacekeeping Marines felt. The increasing enmity toward the US forces was palpable. Indeed, this hostility extended to the French, the Italian, and the British forces stationed there as members of the multinational peacekeeping force. However, geopolitics then being what they were – and have continued to be up to today – the Americans were the number one target for terrorists wishing to make a global statement, and making global statements and blackmailing legitimate governments with wholesale and pointless bloodletting is what terrorists most want to do. This is

---

[2] The other four members of this commission were Robert J. Murray, a former Under Secret of the Navy and former Deputy Assistant Secretary of Defense (International Security Affairs); LTG Joseph T. Palastra, Jr., USA, then on active duty: Lt Gen Lawrence F. Snowden, USMC(Ret); and Lt Gen Eugene F. Tighe, USAF(Ret).

[3] BLT 2/8 replaced 1/8 in Beirut right after the bombing.

true to such an extent that "bloodmail" sums up their political aims as accurately as the term "greenmail" describes a hostile takeover attempt in business.

That bittersweet ditty scrawled on a sign at Echo Company BLT 2/8 was not too far from the cynicism underlying the despised situation summed up by Marines as "Can't Shoot Back Saloon."[4] In short, "Can't Shoot Back Saloon" describes the situation faced by Marines when their hands are tied behind their backs and no retaliatory action is permissible no matter the offensive and even lethal aggression perpetrated against them. The Marines of the AMU and the BLT knew how vulnerable they were that autumn of 1983 in Beirut. Any further doubt of the parlous conditions faced by this peacekeeping force can be eradicated by a quick takeout from *The Root Scoop* – the six-page newspaper of the 24th MAU. On September 22, 1983, one month and one day before the bombing, *The Root Scoop* published a cartoon showing a Marine in a foxhole with incoming artillery from all directions. The Marine, on the radio, asks, "Yes Sir, it's hard to tell if we're the target. Do I draw?"

That Marine in the cartoon, and every other Marine then on duty station in Beirut, knew that he or she was an attractive target to terrorists. Below, and very shortly, this writer will offer firsthand proof that some of those Marines were targeted on a daily basis by a well-placed sniper in a minaret, who, blessedly, was no sharpshooter. Otherwise he would have caused a daily casualty or two. Thank the stars this terrorist sniper was not a Marine-trained sharpshooter.

Overall, many lessons have been learned since the Beirut catastrophe. The four most important are as follows:

1. *Intelligence*: The need for superior intelligence, including and especially human intelligence (HUMINT). The intelligence analysis capabilities of a present-day Marine expeditionary unit (special operations capable) [MEU(SOC)][5] vastly surpass the capabilities organic to the MAU in Beirut back in October of 1983. Such an expanded intelligence capability is a direct result of the inept intelligence that failed to prevent the October 23, bombing, both of the US Marines and of the French Legionnaires. This new capability is of the utmost importance, especially so since every postmortem on the October 23, 1983, bombing noted inefficient and insufficient HUMINT (human intelligence) as a major contributing factor to the effectiveness of the element of surprise the terrorists were able to bring to bear that day.

2. *Rules of Engagement*: Realistic rules of engagement are now applied. This is crucial and addresses the problem of the cynicism and fatalism that congeal to undermine troop morale when gallows humor stemming from "Can't Shoot Back Saloon" conditions prevails. Adjusted and updated rules of engagement (ROE)

---

[4]Late in the mission that sign was changed to the "Can Shoot Back Saloon."

[5]Gen Alfred M. Gray was the Commanding General, 2d Marine Division at the time of the Beirut bombing. He absorbed many of the lessons of that tragedy. When he, as Commandant, evolved the innovative concept of the highly capable MEU(SOC) units, he incorporated many of the lessons learned.

are more in line today with the actual threat faced by our forces. The trouble with asymmetrical warfare is identifying the enemy. This difficulty first manifested itself concertedly for American forces in Vietnam, where such ruses as children soliciting candy approached American combatants, all the while wired with lethal explosives. These sacrificial decoys presaged the latter day nightmare of the suicide bombers, both the individual type on foot used so frequently and to such devastating effectiveness in Israel, as well as those suicide bombers, like the two driving the explosive trucks against the BLT barracks and the Legionnaires station in Beirut on October 23, 1983 – not to fail to include the suicidal terrorist pilots and crews used in the crashed and fuel-laden airplanes on 9/11.

3. *Chains of Command*: Chains of command have been realigned, streamlined, and rendered better informed and more flexibly and quickly responsive. This is crucial because the people in charge that Sunday in October were too many, too remote, too out of touch with the situation faced by the Marines on the ground, and too systematically handicapped. This adverse condition led first to administrative complacency, then to a false sense of security for the deployed Marines, and then, when the catastrophe occurred, to a too slow and too encumbered command response. Today's chain of command is leaner, better informed, and far more responsive.

4. *Cultural Training*: Heavy-duty cultural training is now standard and mandatory prior to on-site deployment of all Marines. Such training and orientation to local conditions and customs is now common and as necessary as boot camp. This means the deployed Marines are not inserted as strangers in a strange land. They are not merely briefed but educated about the conditions that will prevail in their new venue, both in terms of overall environment and underlying ambiance.

All four of these vital changes were confirmed by the former Commandant, Gen James L. Jones. They have been in place now for years and are subject to continual assessment, updating, and improvement. At the highest echelons of Marine command the realities of modern, limited warfare, of guerrilla warfare, and now, especially of terrorist warfare, are grasped and the risks and vulnerabilities of deployed troops are assessed and evaluated so that countermeasures are constantly evolving, from command and control enlightenments down to basic troop training. The Beirut tragedy impelled much of this updated management thinking and troop training application (Von Hassell, 2008, Personal communication).

The Failure of Intelligence

On April 18, 1983, the US Embassy in Beirut was destroyed by a massive car bomb that took the lives of 17 US citizens and over 40 others. What has never been formally acknowledged, yet is widely known, is that at that time many senior station chiefs of the Central Intelligence Agency (CIA) were holding a meeting in the Embassy. Eight of the killed in action were employees of the CIA, including chief

Middle East analyst Robert C. Ames and station chief Kenneth Haas. This meeting was also confirmed by Robert Oakley in 1987. He was a former US State Department coordinator for counterterrorism during the 1980s. Oakley has also served as US Ambassador to Pakistan, Zaire, and Somalia (von Hassell, field notes, 1983).

These intelligence officers were stationed all over the Middle East. Many were killed. With one stroke most of the human intelligence network in the Middle East was wiped out. Sure, agents and sources were still in place, but they had lost their handlers, and many intelligence networks withered away. This loss of human intelligence was also directly confirmed to this writer by Robert "Bud" McFarlane, who served as national security adviser to President Ronald Reagan from 1983 to 1985 (von Hassell, field notes, 2008).

The loss of effective human agent networks would be felt for years and, retired CIA officers now acknowledge, seriously degraded Washington's ability to collect solid information on the Middle East. Both Oakley and McFarlane confirmed this view.

It takes years to re-establish intelligence networks. At the same time, Washington had already decided to redirect intelligence gathering from agents in place to electronic and signals analysis. Note that after September 11, 2001, demands were made on the CIA to rapidly re-establish an effective global agent network – a task that takes years.[6]

The S-2 sector (intelligence) for the MAU was ill-equipped to analyze a steady stream of intelligence about militia groups. In 1989, aboard the USS Nassau (LHA 4), a Marine intelligence officer who had served with the 24th MAU recalled, "We got no guidance from Washington or any of the higher headquarters. We had no training in analyzing this type of intelligence." He recalls that the intelligence section received a steady stream of reports warning of attacks. "The volume [of these reports] was very high, and we had no prior training on how to properly review this information." This assessment of MAU intelligence operations and the improvements under the then-Commandant, Alfred M. Gray, were the subjects of lengthy discussions between this writer and the then-Lt Col Matthew E. Broderick who was the CO of the BLT assigned to 26th MAU in 1989.[7]

It was worse than that. Officers trained in battlefield intelligence suddenly had to learn how to understand the incomprehensible politics of Lebanon and try to sort out who the players were. The need for this understanding was urgent because Marines – after having initially been received with cheers – incrementally got dragged into more and more confrontations and firefights resulting in casualties.[8]

The intelligence officer aboard the Nassau recalls that the G-2 office had tracked 57 separate militias. These included assorted factions of the Druze, the Maronite,

---

[6]The effort required to establish an effective intelligence network was substantiated in a discussion 2 years ago with the former CIA Director, Richard Helms. This writer interviewed Mr. Helms in connection with an upcoming book on Office of Strategic Services operations in World War II.

[7]Broderick retired as a brigadier general. He also commanded a MEU deployed to Somalia.

[8]Based in part on verbal discussions in 1989 with Lt Col Matt Broderick. Similar comments were made to this writer in late September 1983 by Maj Andrew Davis who was killed in the bombing.

and various other Islamic fundamentalist factions such as the Amal and Hezbollah. Another major factor was the Syrian Army, actively engaged in combat in the Shouf Mountains above Beirut and specifically in the once fancy resort area of Souk el Ghar.[9] One group of dissident combatants there was nicknamed the "Pink Panthers." They had stolen a truckload of camouflage uniforms that turned pinkish after a first wash. Who were they? Nobody knew.[10]

Without any tangible guidance from higher headquarters, the intelligence section was in no position to properly give the MAU commander guidance on what was a real threat and what was not.[11] Similarly, an officer of the Italian troops in the multinational peacekeeping force, Capitano de Fregata Pier Luigi Sambo, later stated: "We never had a clue who was who."[12] He was the commander of the San Marco Battalion, Italy's tiny Marine Corps, that occupied the sector just north of the Marine Corps sector around the Beirut International Airport. Yet even without intelligence support, the Italians managed to serve superb dinners accompanied by choice Italian wines.

About this precarious intelligence dearth, the Long Commission grimly stated: "There was an awareness of the existing dangerous situation at every level, but no one had specific information on how, where and when the threat would be carried out. Throughout the period of the USMNF [United States Multinational Force] presence in Lebanon, intelligence sources were unable to provide proven, accurate, definitive information on terrorist tactics against our forces. This shortcoming held to be the case on 23 October 1983."

The Rules of Engagement

Until October 23, the MAU virtually operated on ROE that limited the right to shoot back unless the hostile force could be clearly identified.[13] Even as the climate in Beirut changed, starting in April 1983, and Marines became the subject of ever more frequent attacks, including heavy shelling by what was assumed to be Syrian artillery – 122 mm mortars, RPG-7s (rocket propelled grenades) from various militia groups, and snipers – it was up to the combined amphibious task force commander to formally authorize return fire – hence the "Can't Shoot Back Saloon".[14]

The actual language of the ROE was exceptionally complex. The reality in the field was, "Don't shoot back unless you know at whom you are shooting." Some

---

[9]These statements are substantiated by comments in the Long Commission report.

[10]This theft was confirmed to this writer by WO Charles W. Rowe, Jr., who served with the MEU public affairs office (PAO) staff in 1983. It was also confirmed by the then-SSgt Randy L. Gaddo, who served with the 24th MAU.

[11]See the Long Commission report.

[12]This rank is equivalent to a commander, US Navy.

[13]See detailed discussion in the Long Commission report that includes copies of all ROE.

[14]This writer saw with his own eyes the frequent attacks on Marine forces ashore.

days this was truly bizarre. Near the Beirut University library that inept sniper operated from a minaret, taking occasional shots at the Marines of Weapons Company,
1/8, who used the roof of the library as an observation post. This went on for weeks.

No casualties were taken, and the Marines never shot back. Why? Under the ROE
they were not allowed to shoot – the enemy was not clearly identified. Around 1600
each day the sniper would climb down, exit the minaret tower, give a casual salute
to the Marines, and go home after a long day's work.

Until October 23, 1983, the ROE specifically stated that

- When on post or on mobile or foot patrol, keep a loaded magazine in the
  weapon. Weapons will be on safe, with no rounds in the chamber.
- Do not chamber a round unless instructed to do so by a commissioned officer unless you must act in immediate self-defense where deadly force is
  authorized.
- Keep ammunition for crew-served weapons readily available but not loaded in
  the weapon. Weapons will be on safe at all times.

The perimeter guards at the BLT building on the morning of October 23, were in
full compliance with these rules and were unable to shoot fast enough to disable or
stop the bomber.

The Long Commission report concluded that these restrictive rules of engagement, in effect until October 24, seriously degraded the Marines' mission and ability
to defend themselves. Washington and the many higher headquarters in a complex
chain of command did not accept that the peacekeeping mission that started in 1982
had evolved into a small war.[15] The Marine Corps ignored the most basic rule first
formulated in the 1980s in the *Small Wars Manual*, "Delay in the use of force...
will always be interpreted as weakness." Perception of weakness leads to disaster.
It especially enables terrorists intent on "bloodmail": the advancement of geopolitical objectives through the maiming and killing of noncombatants or of combatants
handicapped by overly restrictive ROE. The troubled history of the Middle East has
shown this perception to be accurate over and over again.

Some limited but ineffective retaliatory force was applied in the months, weeks,
and days before the bombing. It included a combination of naval gunfire, close
air support (CAS), and Marine 155 mm artillery. But this force was applied with
massive delays and often not with clear objectives. This writer recalls how Marine
positions around the Beirut International Airport were the targets of presumably
Syrian-shelling, and it would be hours before any counter-battery fire was permitted. These delays were caused in part by a misperception of how the mission had
evolved and a chain of command almost absurd in its complexity.

What also contributed to the tenuous position of the Marines was that much of
the force applied was not in support of the Marines ashore but in direct support of
the Lebanese Armed Forces (LAF), engaged in pitched battles with Syrian units and

---

[15]Discussion with Bud McFarlane in 1988.

their proxies. Yet this distinction is crucial: By the spring and summer of 1983, in the perception of the locals, the United States was no longer neutral but an active player in the conflict, though one with its hands often tied.[16] The disastrous consequences of being placed in such a precarious position obtained again for the US forces, very notably a decade later in 1993 in Somalia and in the Khobar Towers bombing incident in Saudi Arabia in 1996.

The Chain of Command

The chain of command in Beirut in October 1983 was unnecessarily complex and hideously slow and unwieldy. On average it would take 4 h or more in wasted response time for approval on a request by the MAU commander for naval gunfire, CAS, or permission to use organic artillery.[17] Why? That is the baffling question that galvanized support for today's streamlining in the chain of command.

Until October 23, 1983, the chain of command was as follows[18]: President to the Secretary of Defense, through the Joint Chiefs of Staff to Commander in Chief (the term Commander in Chief now refers only to the president of the United States.), US Forces Europe (USCinCEur). In the theater, operational command ran from USCinCEur to Commander in Chief, US Naval Forces Europe (CinCUSNavEur), and from CinCUSNavEur to Commander, Sixth Fleet (ComSixthFlt). Operational command flowed from ComSixthFlt to Commander, Task Force 61 (CTF-61), who was designated Commander, US Forces Lebanon. The MAU commander was Commander, US Forces Ashore Lebanon.

Requests to return fire had to work their way through most of this chain of command, causing extensive delays. The Long Commission summed it up thus: "The Commission concludes, however, USCinCEur, CinCUSNavEur, ComSixthFlt and CTF-61 did not initiate actions to effectively ensure the security of the USMNF in light of the deteriorating political/military situation in Lebanon."

In short, the Commission found a lack of effective command supervision of the USMNF prior to October 23, 1983. The Commission concluded that the failure of the USCinCEur operational chain of command to inspect and supervise the defensive installations, and especially to secure the perimeter, directly contributed to the catastrophe that ensued.

The Commission attributed direct responsibility for the catastrophe to the unwise relaxation of security rules and procedures on-site by both the commander of the MAU and the commander of the BLT. The stricter security rules and procedures had

---

[16]These assertions are backed by the detailed analysis in the Long Commission report as well as a letter to this writer written in late 1983 by Capitano de Fregata Pier Luigi Sambo.

[17]This writer saw the lengthy fire support request process first hand on several occasions in September and early October 1983. The MAU PAO officer, Maj Bob Jordan, also confirmed the time it took to process fire support requests to the writer at the time.

[18]This chain of command is based on the details contained in the Long Commission report.

been put in place by upper-echelon command. This on-site relaxation of security rules and procedures by the in situ commanders was a major mistake.

A Changed Mission

With the benefit of hindsight it is almost haunting to read and see how the mission of the Marines changed rapidly from friendly peacekeeping to besieged self-defense, but how the perception in Washington that it was purely a peacekeeping mission never changed.

Again, the Long Commission encapsulated accurately how the mission had changed but command and control strategy had not: "The Commission concludes that US decisions as regard[ing] Lebanon taken over the past 15 months have been, to a large degree, characterized by an emphasis on military options and the expansion of the US military role, notwithstanding the fact that the conditions upon which the security of the USMNF were based continued to deteriorate as progress toward a diplomatic solution slowed. The Commission further concludes that these decisions may have been taken without clear recognition that these initial conditions had dramatically changed and that the expansion of our military involvement in Lebanon greatly increased the risk to, and adversely impacted upon the security of, the USMNF."

This writer recalls a colonel with the LAF who, in September 1983, remarked that, "Lebanon is like a bingo game that doesn't end. Once you are in it, you cannot pull out."

From the earliest days of the mission in Lebanon, the Marines, the French, the Italians, and a tiny contingent of the British were slowly dragged into this bingo game. Their mission was to "keep the peace." Yet, what made them something other than peacekeepers was their overt support for the LAF as well as for the formal Government of Lebanon.

The reality that both the LAF and the government were in a precarious state did not enter the chain of command approach to strategize the changed mission. The LAF and the legitimate government were essentially just one of many factions fighting against each other, yet this stark reality did not have sufficient impact on the changing nature of the mission. As the Long Commission concluded: "By the end of September 1983, the situation in Lebanon had changed to the extent that not one of the initial conditions upon which the mission statement was premised was still valid."

But it was even more complicated than that. The Marines had, by October 1983, come to be perceived as an active force in the raging civil war.[19] The Marines, along

---

[19]There are several contemporary sources for these statements. The most exhaustive, that also analyzes the "guilt factor," was a very detailed article published in the Sunday magazine of the *New York Times* by Thomas L. Friedman on April 8, 1984. Another source is the *Nouveau Magazine*, published in Beirut on September 24, 1983. A third source is *Monday Morning* published in Beirut

with the balance of the multinational peacekeeping force had entered Lebanon with an impossible mission and loaded down with a heavy dose of guilt.

Keeping the peace and stabilizing the Lebanese Government was the formal mission statement. The reality of Lebanon was distinctly different – an effective and stable government had been fiction for most of the civil war that started in 1975.

US Marines first landed in the Port of Beirut on August 25, 1982 at the direct request of Palestine Liberation Organization (PLO) chairman, Yasser Arafat. He had been promised by the US negotiators that the Marines would cover the evacuation of about 18,000 PLO fighters. He was also assured that the various Palestinian refugee camps would remain "safe," even though specifics for that mission were never spelled out.

This initial deployment was to last 30 days, but the Marines pulled out on September 10, 1982. As soon as they left all hell broke loose in Lebanon. The popular President-elect, Bashir Gemayel, was assassinated, and Israeli troops invaded West Beirut. Christian Phalangists entered the Palestinian refugee camps of Sabra and Shatila and massacred hundreds of Palestinians. During this slaughter the Israelis merely stood by.

This meltdown in legitimate government, and in civilized law and order, in Lebanon forced the return of the multinational peacekeepers, spearheaded by the US Marines. On paper, the MNF mission was to keep the peace. "But we were actually driven by collective guilt," said Capitano de Fregata Pier Luigi Sambo of the San Marco Battalion. "We had left early and the killings took place. We didn't have a real mission." The Italians were charged with patrolling the main Palestinian refugee camps of Sabra and Shatila.

In the end the US Marines spent over 550 days in Beirut and essentially accomplished nothing – the same way their French, Italian, and British counterparts in the MNF accomplished nothing.

Conclusions

The Beirut catastrophe of 1983 is clearly a lesson learned, but one difficult and challenging in the extreme to apply. Some of the recent experience of the United States suggests that critical lessons have indeed been learned and improvements pioneered and applied, notably in the four areas detailed above: intelligence, ROE, chain of command, and cultural training. This writer believes that the US military needs to evolve new doctrine for operations like those in Lebanon in 1983, in Somalia 10 years later, and in the Khobar Towers tragedy 3 years later still. All three of these operations involve civil warfare, guerrilla warfare, limited warfare, asymmetrical warfare, or some combination or permutation of all four types of complex modern warfare, whether purely military or paramilitary in the nature of the conflict.

---

on October 2, 1983. Starting on page 6, that magazine carried a lengthy interview by Lydia Georgi with Col Timothy Geraghty.

All four of these types of complex modern warfare come replete with psychological challenges not present in classic warfare where there are clear linear lines of battle, a well-defined and easily recognizable adversary, and traditional ROE. Not only was Lebanon in 1983 like a bingo game that amounted to a trap: once in, in, forever; but it was as complex psychologically as the difference between a world-class chess match between dedicated grandmasters and a simple front porch game of checkers between two dilettantish amateurs. All four types of limited modern warfare entail deep psychological challenges for both commanders and their troops.

These kinds of limited conflict are like being trapped in a fun house that is both no fun and, worse, potentially deadly. Both friend and foe typically look exactly alike, a constant, confusing, and almost inevitable condition of almost all civil warfare. ROE are not fixed but flexible, and often evolve and change, sometimes even on a daily basis. And, most disconcertingly, battle lines are circular, not linear. This means the "enemy lines" extend concentrically from whatever position the troops occupy. This in turn means the troops are always at the eye of the storm, with the isotropic circles of potential adversaries whirling around the eye, as on a weather map. Or, still worse, the troops may occupy the dangerous bull's eye on a circular battle map resembling a target featuring concentric lines of potential adversaries. This predicament undermines morale and fighting spirit, especially if "Can't Shoot Back Saloon" conditions apply.

Such new psychological realities call for new doctrine. Commanders must avoid the mistake made in Beirut, of putting the Marines essentially at the center of a spider web woven by hostiles, sealing their doom. And the troops must be oriented and trained to cope with the difficult reality of a non-distinct enemy operating on a concentrically circular battlefield on which the troops occupy the dangerous center. Add to that the horror of diplomatic breakdowns and sovereign hegemony and the challenges escalate exponentially. Diplomatic and political solutions disappeared amid the chaos of Lebanon in 1983 and of Somalia 10 years later.

Then came the sovereign hegemony issues represented in the Khobar Towers incident, where a foreign government, in the interests both of territoriality and diplomatic legerdemain, played a double game. That double game involved such delicate issues as non-extradition of criminals and the placating of bellicose and threatening neighbor states guilty of sponsoring, albeit surreptitiously, terrorist activities on foreign soil, even against their neighboring states. In the case of the Khobar Towers incident this meant that Saudi Arabia feared and placated Iran.

Diplomatic and political solutions, as well as issues of sovereign hegemony, further complicate the psychological challenges and ambiguities of modern complex warfare. On a larger scale, these three factors sometimes replicate the difficult choices and limited options available in hostage negotiations. Make one choice, you are damned for it; make the opposite choice, you are damned for that. Dissident combatants in guerrilla warfare, and especially perpetrators of terrorism, know one thing: They are in a win–win situation. Draw an outsized retaliatory military response, especially one costing the lives of innocent noncombatants, and they prove their more powerful adversary heartless. Draw an inappropriately mild or neutral response from this same more powerful adversary, and the terrorists prove this adversary to be weak, as essentially happened in Beirut.

In view of these harsh psychological realities of modern limited warfare, the new doctrine we need should draw strict distinctions between peacekeeping and peace-making operations. Peacekeeping essentially means an operation in a more or less pacific environment, while peacemaking would apply to operations requiring the application of force in a hostile environment. Essentially, the current operations in such hostile environments as those in Iraq and in Afghanistan should be consid-ered peacemaking. In confronting the challenges they represent we must keep in mind, and implement, the lessons of Beirut, of Somalia, and of the Khobar Towers incident.

References

Anderson, T. (1995). *Den of lions: Memoirs of seven years*. New York: Crown Publishers.

Friedman, T. L. ((1989) *From Beirut to Jerusalem*. New York: Doubleday.

Hammel, E. (1985) *The Root*. Kansas City, MO: Pacifica Press.

Hourani, A., & Shehadi, N. (Eds.). (1991). *The Lebanese in the World*. London: Centre for Lebanese Studies.

Mackey, S. (1989). *Lebanon: Death of a nation*. Chicago: Congdon and Weed.

Petit, M. (1986). *Peacekeepers at war:* Boston: Faber & Faber, Inc.

Pintak, L. (1988). *Beirut outtakes: A TV correspondent's portrait of America's encounter with terror*. Lexington, MA: Lexington Books.

Rabinovich, I. (1984). *The war for Lebanon, 1970–1983*. Ithaca, NY: Cornell University Press.

Salhani, C. (1998). *Black september to desert storm: A journalist in the middle east*. Columbia, MO: University of Missouri Press.

Sutherland, T. (1996). *At your own risk*. Golden, CO: Fulcrum Publishing.

U.S. Marines In Lebanon. (1982–1984). Benis M. Frank, History and Museums Division, HQ, USMC Report of the DoD Commission on Beirut International Airport Terrorist Act, October 23, 1983, 20 December 1983.

Von Hassell (1983). Field notes.

von Hassell (2008). Field notes.

http://www.ibiblio.org/hyperwar/AMH/XX/MidEast/Lebanon-1982-1984/DOD-Report/index.html

Chapter 16
Lost in Transition: Khobar Towers and the Ambiguities of Terrorism in the 1990s

Staci Strobl and Jon R. Lindsay

Introduction

On June 25, 1996, a fuel truck packed with explosives detonated on the perimeter of Khobar Towers, a residential complex housing US Air Force personnel operating out of King Abdul Aziz Air Base in Dhahran, Saudi Arabia. Nineteen American airmen were killed and over 500 other Americans, Saudis, and Bangladeshis were injured. This was the deadliest terrorist attack on the US military personnel since the 1983 bombing of the Beirut barracks which killed 241 Marines, presaging even worse mass-casualty attacks to come. The bombing as well as the official investigations in its wake prompted the military services to adopt more robust force protection measures, yet the strategic threat of Islamist terrorism remained less appreciated for several years to come.

The Khobar Towers attack occurred in the middle of a decade of considerable uncertainty and drift in American security policy. From the end of the Cold War in 1991 until the terrorist attacks of September 11, 2001, there was no broad consensus about America's strategic priorities in the world, notwithstanding its heightened level of global military activity. The decisive US-led victory in the first Gulf War was followed by far less decisive patrolling of Iraqi skies in order to enforce "no-fly" zones and conduct occasional punitive strikes aimed at indefinitely containing Saddam Hussein. Deployments to Muslim countries added fuel to smoldering local anti-American sentiment and at the same time presented targets to terrorist actors. The Khobar Towers bombing, in particular, has been primarily attributed to Iranian-backed Hezbollah, a formidable enemy to the United States even as military efforts were focused on Iraq. All the while, the US military and civilian policy makers failed to appreciate the scope and determination of irregular, non-state Muslim extremist groups whose attacks would define military engagement and foreign policy in the next decade.

S. Strobl (✉)
Department of Law, Police Science, and Criminal Justice, John Jay College of Criminal Justice, Cornell University, New York, NY, USA
e-mail: strobl@jjay.cuny.edu

M.R. Haberfeld, A. von Hassell (eds.), *A New Understanding of Terrorism*,
DOI 10.1007/978-1-4419-0115-6_16, © Springer Science+Business Media, LLC 2009

The 19th century Prussian officer Carl von Clausewitz (1976) observed, "The first, the supreme, the most far-reaching act of judgment that the statesman and commander have to make is to establish ... the kind of war on which they are embarking; neither mistaking it for, nor trying to turn it into, something that is alien to its nature" (pp. 88–89). The bombing of Khobar Towers was a tragic and shocking event, and while certainly seen at the time as symptomatic of the growing problem of Islamist terrorism, the origins of the attack were nonetheless treated at best as an important collateral concern to other more primary military objectives. Terrorism was seen as a dangerous risk factor for the US political and military missions; countering it was not yet a major mission in its own right. Contrast this to the primary emphasis that terrorism and counter-terrorism received after 9/11. With the benefit of several years of hindsight and many more mass-casualty attacks, Khobar Towers appears to be a far more ominous harbinger of things to come than was recognized at the time.

This chapter proceeds in four parts. First, we discuss the emerging terrorist threat in the 1990s, focusing in particular on Hezbollah in Saudi Arabia but also other groups possibly associated with the bombing. Second, we discuss the details of the bombing plot as revealed in the 2001 federal case against 14 of the suspects (which remains open as of this writing), culminating in an account of the bombing itself. Third, we review the various official investigations of the bombing and the broader counter-terrorism policy measures pursued by the US government in response. Fourth, we conclude with a discussion of how and why an ambiguous emerging threat was met with an inadequate policy response. Many painful and valuable force protection lessons were learned through Khobar Towers, but the tragedy is further amplified by the lessons in counter-terrorism which were not learned for several more years.

Islamist Extremism in Saudi Arabia

There is lingering ambiguity over the identity of the perpetrators of the Khobar Towers attack. The Federal Bureau of Investigation (FBI) theory of the case, which resulted in a 2001 indictment, fingered members of the Saudi Arabian branch of Hezbollah, which has operated in the kingdom since 1987 and had as many as 1,000 members (Cordesman & Burke, 2001). Known as Hezbollah Al-Hijaz and acting with Iranian assistance, their main goal was almost certainly to force a retreat of the US military presence in Saudi Arabia, which was viewed by many Muslims as offensive to Islam, and by Iran as a significant security threat. In addition, the connection to and support from Hezbollah and Iran was also a convenient means of countering more localized Shi'ite grievances against the Saudi government. Historically, the approximate 2 million Shi'a[1] in Saudi Arabia, who were concentrated in the eastern part of the country, have experienced systematic discrimination. They

---

[1] Shi'ism is a sect of Islam that broke away from the dominant group (Sunni) during a dispute in the seventh century over the legitimate heir to the prophet Muhammad and the suitable ruler of Muslims (*caliph*). Shi'a turned to the prophet's son-in-law and cousin 'Ali as caliph, but he was

are barred from government jobs, exposed to an anti-Shi'ite public education curriculum and until recently, prohibited from celebrating Shi'ite holidays in public. Shi'a in Saudi Arabia are also known to be economically depressed relative to their Sunni counterparts (International Crisis Group, 2005). Sunni clerics in Saudi Arabia regularly refer to Shi'a as infidels and have even made calls for ethnic cleansing (Jones, 2005). This discriminatory environment was a factor in creating a push toward Hezbollah-related extremism among Saudi Shi'a in the 1990s, particular after the government's 1993 promise of addressing their concerns was not forthcoming.

The Khobar Towers bombing represented the last major instance of state-sponsored terrorism against US interests, the form of terrorism traditionally recognized as most dangerous. At the same time, however, a new non-state form of terrorism was emerging, exemplified by Osama bin Laden's Sunni extremist Al-Qaeda network, manifesting in several deadly attacks against Americans in the late 1990s and into the next decade. In recent years speculation has grown, based on reports uncovered by the 9/11 Commission, that Al-Qaeda may have also been responsible, or even the sole perpetrator, of the Khobar Towers attacks. Contradictory evidence, however, suggests that this theory has been merely an unsubstantiated rumor circulating within the Saudi Shi'ite community, perhaps to deflect Shi'ite responsibility. Notably, the rise in Sunni-based extremist groups like Al-Qaeda, propelled Shi'a in Saudi Arabia to seek a more moderate relationship to the government in the late 1990s as ". . . the focal point of Shiite activism. . . was essentially communalistic, devoted above all to defending community interests vis-à-vis other sectarian groups and the state." (International Crisis Group, 2005, p. 5).

The Khobar Towers bombing represented the culmination of state-sponsored Hezbollah terrorism, the type of threat more familiar to US officials, but it also occurred amid a new looming non-state sponsored terrorist threat. Notably, a state-sponsored Shi'ite group (Hezbollah Al-Hijaz) and a non-state Sunni group (Al-Qaeda) vary considerably in terms of strategic motives and thus in options for the US counter-terrorism response. The persisting ambiguity regarding the affiliation of the bombers thus precludes any definitive historical interpretation of the planning, as well as helps to explain the difficulties contemporaries had in fully appreciating and responding to the terrorist threat in this particular case.

Despite the significant ambiguity as to those responsible, the 2001 indictment points to Hezbollah Al-Hijaz (a.k.a. Saudi Hezbollah). According to the narrative in the indictment, in 1996, the leader of Hezbollah Al-Hijaz was Abdel Karim Al-Nasser, whose military wing was commanded by Ahmad Al-Mughassil, reportedly the overseer of all terrorist attacks against Americans in Saudi Arabia. Saudi Hezbollah acted as a branch of mainline Hezbollah, meaning "Party of God" in Arabic, a Lebanese Shi'ite organization originally formed as a counter to Israel. Born from pro-Syrian Lebanese seeking the ouster of Israel from Lebanon in the early

---

murdered by political opponents. Later, his grand-son Hussein led an insurrection against the Shi-a-perceived illegitimate Umayyad caliphate and was massacred in Karbala, Iraq. This massacred is commemorated by Shi'a as the ultimate spiritual sacrifice during 'Ashura celebrations (Lewis, 1995).

1980s, the group was inspired by the Ayatollah Ruhollah Khomeini and his successful Islamic revolution in Iran (Esposito, 2002). Many early Hezbollah militants trained with the Iranian Revolutionary Guard, led by Fazlollah Mahallati, who was sent to Lebanon by Iranian clerics. The organization receives financial backing by Iran at a rate of $100–$200 million per year (Levitt, 2005).

Locally, Saudi Hezbollah is known by the name *Daneshjuyan-e Khat-e Emam*, which in Farsi means Followers of the Line of the Imam, referring to Khomeini. In the 1990s, they also looked to the charismatic Lebanese clerics Ayatollah Muhammad Hussayn Fadlallah and Hassan Nasrallah for spiritual guidance (Nasr, 2006; Levitt, 2005), upholding the religious requirement of the faithful to practice *Shī'á marjá al-taqlīd*, or the obligation to seek guidance from leading clergy on all matters, a principle Khomeini referred to as *vilayat-e-faqih* (International Crisis Group, 2005). From the pulpit, Fadlallah has regularly called for armed struggle against the enemies of Islam. Given the aforementioned principle, such a call for armed struggle (*jihad*) becomes a requirement for the faithful. Fadlallah's book, *Al-Islam wa montiq al-quwwa* ("Islam and the Logic of Power," 1981), explains his revolutionary ideology and was thus adopted by Hezbollah. According to Fadlallah, Muslims are embroiled in a post-colonial struggle against former colonial powers, the British and the French, as well as neo-imperialist Americans, to which they contribute the greatest responsibility for many more general ills. As critics of capitalism, Hezbollah clerics believe that western powers have caused the poverty, pollution, and corruption in Southern Lebanon and Muslim environs and that the "modern materialism" practiced by these countries merely enslaves the poor and oppressed.

Hezbollah's justification for the use of violence stems from notions of *jihad* in Islamic thought, revived in modern times after being relatively dormant since the tenth century (Noorani, 2002). The word itself means struggle, but also denotes a holy war against infidels in defense of the *ummah* (Muslim community). Although clerics make many caveats as to when violent jihad is appropriate, according to one Hezbollah cleric, when corruption reaches levels that can be fought in no other way, violence is justified. Such a state of affairs occurs when there is an "insufferable and draconian form of oppression" (Saad-Ghorayeb, 2002, p. 25). In principle, most Islamic doctrine states that jihad must be defensive; however, Shi'a clerics have constructed jihad as defensive by definition and therefore have created a broader sense of its legitimate use (Esposito, 2002).

To further its political and ideological aims, Hezbollah has used terrorist tactics against western powers, in particular the United States. Until 9/11, Hezbollah was considered responsible for the most American terrorist-related deaths over any other group (Levitt, 2005). Imad Fayez Al-Mugniyeh has been named by many sources as the overall mastermind behind Hezbollah terrorist operations in his role as the head of the organization's security section in the 1980s and 1990s (Ranstorp, 1997).

Hezbollah is known to have kidnapped 87 mostly western foreigners since its inception although it has never formally admitted responsibility. And, it most likely was responsible for the April 1983 car bombing at the American Embassy in Beirut which killed 17 Americans and 40 others.[2] In October of the same year, a Hezbollah suicide driver crashed an explosives-laden truck into the Marine barracks in Beirut, killing 231 servicemen participating in a US peacekeeping mission (Ziegler, 1998, pp. 3–5). The United States withdrew from Lebanon in early 1984, sending a message to Hezbollah that terrorism could be an effective coercive tool against great powers. These attacks, as well as Hezbollah-sponsored car bombs on Israeli targets in Argentina in the early 1990s, also demonstrated the group's penchant for vehicle-borne explosive attacks and mass casualties, again exhibited in the Khobar Towers attack. Hezbollah thus learned strategic and tactical lessons through these bombings that it would attempt to repeat against the United States in 1996.

The Khobar Towers Plot

According to the indictment against the perpetrators of the Khobar Towers attack *(US v. Al-Mughassil,* 2001), the plot dates back to 1993 when the group convened regular meeting at the Sayyeda Zainab shrine in Damascus. Despite being outlawed in Saudi Arabia, Hezbollah Al-Hijaz managed to hold regular meetings in Lebanon, Syria, and Iran throughout the early 1990s, pursuant to the Khobar Towers attack. The group's members at this time were primarily drawn from the Shi'ite minority in the Eastern Province of Saudi Arabia which contains the city of Dhahran, the center of oil production in the Saudi kingdom, headquarters of its national oil company Aramco and site of the Khobar Towers (Shenon, 1996). Young men were recruited for the Saudi Hezbollah during religious pilgrimages to Sayyeda Zainab shrine from the Eastern Province after their loyalty to clergy in Iran and their dissatisfaction with the Saudi government was confirmed. Those who wished to join were then sent to Lebanon or Iran for military and ideological training.

Between 1993 and the time of the attack, Ahmad Al-Mughassil (a.k.a. Abu Omran) led various members of the organization in tracking the routines of the 30,000 Americans working in Saudi Arabia. These surveillance teams were often kept unaware of each others' activities, which were coordinated by Al-Mughassil. Reports of the surveillance activities were provided to Al-Mughassil, who spent most of his time in Beirut, Saudi Hezbollah chief Al-Nasser, and intelligence or military officers in Iran with whom Al-Mughassil primarily was in contact. The group identified and confirmed Khobar Towers, a large residential complex in Dhahran that housed the US personnel deployed to Saudi Arabia, as an important American military target by late 1994, although they did not settle on the target until mid-1995 after also considering other American targets on the Red Sea, in Riyadh, and elsewhere in the Eastern Province.

Al-Mughassil coordinated preparations from Beirut, summoning conspirators to visit him with surveillance reports and asking him to verify the accuracy of maps. He

---

[2]Most attribute this attack to Islamic Jihad, often considered merely a front for Hezbollah (Howard & Sawyer, 2004).

visited Saudi Arabia in late 1995 or early 1996 to arrange for explosive hiding sites around Qatif, 20 miles north of Khobar. During this visit Al-Mughassil reportedly said that he would need enough explosives to destroy a row of buildings. This is important because, as discussed below, American security improvements for Khobar Towers only commenced in early 1996; these focused on preventing a perimeter penetration like the Beirut barracks attack, but Al-Mughassil was clearly already focusing on procuring a much bigger bomb that would even be effective in a standoff attack at (rather than within) the perimeter. There was speculation after the attack that American security measures may have deterred a penetration attack and driven perpetrators to a standoff; on the contrary, it appears that the group was planning for a spectacular high-explosive attack well before.

Returning to Beirut, Al-Mughassil then coordinated several transfers of explosives from Beirut, burying them in 50 kg bags and paint cans in the Qatif sites. Hezbollah's pawns in these preparations were kept unaware of more than their small contribution. Thus when Saudi border guards interdicted a March 1996 shipment of 38 kg of plastic explosives and arrested three Hezbollah operatives, the plot was able to continue unchecked. Al-Mughassil returned personally to Saudi Arabia to replace these footsoldiers (providing the new conspirators with forged Iranian passports), hide the timing device and take charge of the final phase of the operation. Al-Mughassil arrived under the pretense of being on a Hajj pilgrimage, which was in April and May in 1996, recognized by American intelligence officers as a period of heightened potential threat (Creamer & Seat, 1998, pp. 14, 18).

In June 1996, the conspirators purchased a 4,000 gal Mercedes-Benz fuel or sewage tanker truck from a Saudi dealership using stolen identification. Over the next 2 weeks Al-Mughassil and several of his deputies transformed the tanker into a truck bomb, using a mixture of explosives and gasoline. The construction of the bomb and timer assembly occurred at a farm outside Qatif, during which time Al-Mughassil reportedly also discussed plans to bomb the US consulate in Dhahran. Also that month, key members of the plot and high-ranking Saudi Hezbollah leaders (including Chief Al-Nasser) attended meetings at the shrine in Damascus where plans were finalized and Al-Mughassil recognized as the attack leader.

On June 25, 1996, the plan was executed. Shortly before 10:00 p.m., Hezbollah Al-Hijaz members drove a scout car and a getaway car into a public parking lot adjacent to the complex and 80 ft from building 131 of the residential towers, parking in a dark area of the lot where the overhead lights were out. The scout car signaled by blinking its headlights that the coast was clear for Al-Mughassil and underling Ali Al-Houri driving the truck bomb to proceed. They entered the parking lot, driving parallel to the fence, then turned away, stopped, and backed the truck up to the fence to best position the blast effects. They exited the truck, ran to the getaway car, and then both cars sped out of the parking lot (Jamieson, 2008, p. 10). They immediately fled Saudi Arabia using a variety of false passports.

Air Force sentries posted on the roof of building 131 observed this suspicious activity with increasing alarm. They reported the threat to Central Security Control and initiated an evacuation of the building by personally knocking on doors and orally alerting residents. In the 4 minutes before the explosion, they were able to clear only the top three floors of the eight-floor building, but many personnel were doubtlessly saved by being in the concrete stairwells rather than in rooms in the front of the building, which bore the brunt of the blast (Cohen, 1997). The truck bomb sheared off the face of building 131 and blew out windows from several adjacent buildings, killing 19 and injuring 372 Americans as well as over a hundred Saudis and Bangladeshis, many by flying shards of glass. The explosion left an impact crater that was 35 ft deep and 85 ft wide and could be felt as far away as Bahrain (Cordesman & Burke, 2001). It left charred vehicles and flipped over Humvees in its wake (Wright, 2006). Estimates of the size of the bomb varied significantly at first, but technical analysis eventually converged on an estimate of 20,000 lb TNT equivalent (Cohen, 1997). It was larger than any truck bomb the FBI had ever seen previously (Benjamin & Simon, 2003, p. 224) and two orders of magnitude larger than anything security personnel had planned to defend against.

Americans were alert to the increasing terrorist threat in the months prior to the bombing, although they lacked any indication of the exact timing, target, and means of attack. Although Saudi Arabia had been seen as a relatively safe deployment location in the early 1990s, this perception was shattered on November 13, 1995, when a 250 lb car bomb exploded in Riyadh at the Office of the Program Manager Saudi Arabian National Guard (OPM-SANG), killing five Americans and two Indians. The Saudis arrested four individuals who, in a televised confession, attacked the regime for not adhering to *sharia* (Muslim law), stated that the US presence in the Kingdom demanded *jihad* and cited radical Islamists who influenced them, naming Osama bin Laden in particular (Benjamin & Simon, 2003, p. 132). Most ominously, intelligence gathered indicated that Muslim extremist groups, including Hezbollah, had cautioned that they would target American military centers if those responsible for the Riyadh bombing were beheaded (Shenon, 1996), which is exactly what the Saudis did on May 31, 1996 (Downing, 1996).

After this event the Americans initiated a host of force protection improvements to military facilities. The Air Force conducted two thorough vulnerability assessments on Khobar Towers, which they identified as a vulnerable target, and implemented well over a hundred new security measures around Khobar Towers to deter a penetration-type attack, such as additional checkpoints and sentries, reinforced jersey barriers and fence improvements. Attack scenarios envisioned a bomb of at most a few hundred pounds like the OPM-SANG attack, which was thought to be large at the time. Although the north perimeter of the facility, just 80 ft from a residential building, was recognized as a vulnerability because it was under Saudi and not American control, it was thought to be manageable given the expected magnitude of the threat.

Intelligence provided vague warnings of potential plots brewing, but nothing specifically actionable. Sentries observed several instances of potential surveillance. It is not known if any of these were Al-Mughassil's men. Saudi police wrote off some of these as instances of curious Saudi citizens trying to get a look at Westerners. In one case, however, a car backed into a Jersey barrier, which was viewed as a potential penetration probe. In the months after the OPM-SANG attack there was a spate of small (10–15 lb) bombings in Bahrain which caused some injuries and in one case eight fatalities. Building 131, the primary target of the June 25 attack, was evacuated on May 5 due to a suspicious package which turned out to be a toolbox; there were no other evacuation drills held for this building (Creamer & Seat, 1998) although it contributed to the heightened sense of urgency of the threat to American Forces.

Hezbollah Al-Hijaz achieved tactical surprise with its attack on Khobar Towers. The timing, size, and mode of delivery of the truck bomb were all quite unexpected. While it is unclear what if any tactical intelligence as to these matters existed (the detailed discussions of intelligence in the various investigations remain classified), there was certainly strategic warning as to the risk from various terrorist groups known to be operating in Saudi Arabia and with the motive and capability to inflict harm on American interests. Whether the US forces were prepared to deal with this warning is a different matter, to which we now turn.

Investigations and Responses

The Khobar Towers bombing occurred on the eve of a G-7 plus Russia summit in Lyons, France. President Clinton took the opportunity to make terrorism a major topic of discussion, exhorting allies to adopt measures to thwart terrorist financing, communications, and cross-border movement. He ordered an immediate FBI investigation as well as a Department of Defense (DoD) commission on military force protection postures (Clinton, 1996a, 1996b).

This section reviews these in turn, first discussing the botched attempt at bringing the perpetrators to justice in the US criminal justice system, and second the ways in which the DoD investigations and responses almost exclusively emphasized defensive force protection and command accountability measures. Lost in the shuffle was any sort of coordinated national counter-terrorism response; given the international and domestic political conditions of the late 1990s, that seems to have been a bridge too far.

The FBI Investigation: A "Byzantine Case"

For many concerned with terrorism, the criminal justice system remains a viable avenue of response as a source of "soft power" which can bring justice in a normative, legal structure (Wedgewood, 2001) despite the transnational context.[3] Such a response does not preclude military reprisal, contrary to the dualistic thinking that the criminal justice versus military response discourse sometimes engenders. The criminal justice approach is distinct from military responses in that it assumes terrorists are violating a criminal code and therefore subject to judicial procedural norms. It also focuses efforts on the perpetrators rather than the broader theater of

---

[3] Blanche (2001) aptly described the case as such.

a particular government, territory, sub-state, or non-state organization which characterize military responses (LaFree & Hendrickson, 2007). Although conceptions of war have shifted significantly since the Cold War in response to the threat of non-state terrorist actors, particularly with US willingness to employ unilateral military force absent of legal findings, in the 1990s, however, this transition was still in its early stages, and the US military was still operating from a paradigm of industrial and technological superiority in conventional warfare (Cohen, 2007). In the absence of declaring a war on terror (which would happen after 9/11, even if legal implications remained unclear) or seeking military redress with Iran, holding the perpetrators criminally responsible appeared desirable. Sageman (2008) argues that criminal prosecutions have the express benefit over other responses because they treat the terrorists as no different from ordinary murderers and money launderers, thus depriving them of the political attention they crave in expressing their particular ideological message. By contrast, a grand military response from the United States or other great powers is often exactly what terrorists desire in order to demonstrate ex post facto the alleged nefarious nature of their enemies and the righteousness of their cause. Although some have criticized an excessive law-enforcement bias in counter-terrorism prior to 9/11, this was motivated in part by a desire to delegitimize the political standing of terrorists (Kraft, 2008).

Problems of jurisdiction naturally flow from criminal cases involving American service personnel in a foreign nation. Khobar Towers occurred before the creation of the International Criminal Court (ICC), a transnational court which hypothetically could bring terrorists to justice outside the political milieus of the relevant state parties and individuals. However, the United States and Saudi Arabia have thus far declined to become a party to such a court for fear of being subject themselves to ICC criminal complaints. In any case, the relevant choice after Khobar Towers was between the Saudi or the US criminal justice systems, an important decision to make in a clear fashion in order to structure relationships and garner resources effectively. Unfortunately, the convoluted machinations of Saudi–US relations, as well as the lack of coordinated action on the part of US agencies involved in the investigation, created a confused criminal justice response. Ultimately, the United States brought a federal indictment, impelled only by the statute of limitations, which did not lead to trial proceedings.

According to international law, the United States has the right to indict for an attack that took place on Saudi soil because it falls under the purview of "passive personality" in which the individuals were targeted for national identity reasons (Wedgewood, 2001). At the time of this writing, all 14 defendants in the indictment (13 Saudis and one Lebanese) remain untried. Several of the defendants are in Saudi custody to this day while three, including ringleader Al-Mughassil, are at large and believed to be in Iran.

The lack of commitment by the Saudi government to a thorough and transparent process formed the primary obstacle to the investigation. Despite lip service to a joint endeavor, the Saudi government never provided substantive assistance to the investigation and at times appeared to have been engaged in actively thwarting it. The Saudis initially disallowed the FBI access to suspects that the Saudis had detained from Hezbollah Al-Hijaz, and refused them the opportunity to investigate the get away car used in the attacks (International Policy Institute for Counterterrorism, 1999). The site of the attacks was being bulldozed by Saudi authorities the day after, before thorough evidence collection could be accomplished (Jamieson, 2008). Saudi authorities, however, resented the reported attempts by the American to take over the case and sideline the Saudis. They were equally unimpressed by the FBI agents assigned to the case, who spoke very limited Arabic and had little knowledge of the region (Cordesman & Burke, 2001). The tensions amounted to a culture clash between the investigation teams with the Saudis responding by withholding case details and leads.

The United States was ineffective in pressuring the Saudis to cooperate with the investigation, even at the highest levels of negotiations (Schwartz, 2002). According to Unger (2004), President Clinton met with Saudi Prince Abdullah in 1998 and specifically expressed his disappointment in the stalled investigation. Many counter-terrorism officials in Washington had received promises for cooperation from Prince Bandar bin Sultan bin Abdul Aziz Al Saud, the Saudi Arabian ambassador to the United States, to no avail. Meanwhile, Louis Freeh, Director of the Federal Bureau of Investigation (FBI), frustrated at the Clinton Administration's ineffective attempts to jump start the joint investigation, pursued his own means of pressuring the Saudis by enlisting former President George H. W. Bush to place a phone call to Prince Abdullah urging the Saudis to engage in a joint, transparent investigation. Such an end run around the current president placed considerable strain on the working relationship between Freeh's FBI and the Clinton Administration.

The disparate efforts to coax Saudi cooperation failed, and ultimately the FBI conducted a stunted investigation, reportedly permitted to interview only six of the defendants in Saudi custody who were ultimately listed on the subsequent federal indictment (Freeh, 2003). Interestingly, the Saudis indicated their displeasure at the release of the 2001 indictment, and also intimated that they had already held a trial for those responsible, but provided no details about the process, or documents to back up the claim (Schwartz, 2002). The Saudis, though agreeing that the US-indicted defendants were responsible for the attacks, denied that they were connected to mainline Hezbollah and Iran, saying they were merely Saudi dissidents. In 1998, the Saudi Interior Minister Prince Nayef Bin Abdul-Aziz was quoted by Kuwaiti newspaper *Al-Rai Al-Aam* (2004) as saying "The bombing took place at Saudi hands and no foreign party had any role in it" (May 24, 1998, p. 1). Most attribute this denial to Saudi Arabian unwillingness to acknowledge internal opposition within their kingdom (Hegghammer, 2008; Wright, 2006), or perhaps more significantly, fear of the consequences that implicating Iran would have on their own national security (Jamieson, 2008).

International political constraints precluded any sort of clear American action against the most likely culprit of the bombing, Iran. American officials suspected Iranian involvement almost immediately after the bombing, and early intelligence returns, as well as what could be gleaned from Saudi interaction, pointed to Hezbollah involvement. However, the Saudis had long been engaged in a regional balancing act between Iran and Iraq, and they worried that American retribution against Iran would cause unacceptable blowback for the kingdom. America for its part needed Saudi Arabia to provide basing for its operations to contain Iraq and to stabilize global oil supplies. American desires to punish Iran ultimately were a lower priority than maintaining relations with the Saudis and operations in Iraq, and knowing this the Saudis could afford to slow-roll the criminal investigation. In fact, Unger (2004) reports that in actuality the Saudis never pressed charges against those allegedly responsible who were in their custody. The failed coordination between the Saudi and the US government has furthermore been attributed to an extension of George H.W. Bush's policy in which Saudis were not questioned on matters considered internal issues to their country. Yet, as the 1990s marched on, managing the internal security environment of Saudi Arabia became a key national security issue for the United States, a lesson Clinton was beginning to learn during his presidency when he began to significantly increase funding for counter-terrorism (Benjamin & Simon, 2003).

In addition, a subsequent civil suit against Iran by victims' families of the attack also was unsuccessful. Dismissed on June 6, 2006, in federal district court in Washington, D.C., the judge indicated in her opinion that the plaintiffs provided no evidence of involvement by Iranian officials in the bombing. She found testimony provided by Freeh, that the attacks were planned and funded by senior leaders in Iran, to be unsupported.[4] And, in yet another bizarre twist, the US State Department filed an amicus curiae brief which sided with the Iranian government by arguing that the evidence against Iran was not compelling. Lawyers for the plaintiffs speculated that the dismissal was motivated by political considerations, coming at a time when the United States was trying to improve relations with Iran (Timmerman, 2006).

Unfortunately, the lack of punishment and accountability sent Hezbollah and Iran the message that, as in Beirut 13 years earlier, it could strike the United States with impunity. Hezbollah stepped up operations in the following year, assassinating Iranian dissidents abroad and attempting to smuggle weapons into Europe (Benjamin & Simon, 2003, pp. 224–225). On Clinton's direction Richard Clarke at the National Security Council developed a secret plan for retaliatory air strikes against Iran, yet military options short of regime change appeared inadequate to the challenge. Such drastic action would have been impossible to sell politically, and there was a slight hope that the new Iranian president Mohammad Khatami might bring forth a more moderate Iran. The administration thus opted to step up covert pressure on Hezbollah operatives abroad to make sure they knew they were being scrutinized, resulting in an eventual decrease in Hezbollah and Iranian intelligence activity (Naftali, 2005, pp. 249–251).

While intelligence agencies took some limp action to manage the Hezbollah and Iranian threat, mismanagement of the criminal case continued in the years after the

---

[4]Interestingly, FBI investigators in 1999 revealed that they had corroborated evidence of at least indirect involvement of Iran based on Saudi sources (Cordesman & Burke, 2001).

attack. In particular, the handling of suspect Hani Al-Sayegh, arrested by Canadian authorities under suspicion of being involved in the Khobar Towers attack and extradited to the United States in 1997, represents a mystifying twist in the case. Attorney General Janet Reno had permitted him into the United States solely for the prosecution. Once in the United States, Al-Sayegh reneged on promises to act as the primary informant against the other alleged Hezbollah perpetrators, claiming he knew nothing about the attacks and was not in Saudi Arabia when they occurred. He was deported in 1999 to Saudi Arabia at their request and denied his own political asylum appeal to remain in the United States. One reason for the deportation was reportedly that there was not enough evidence to try Al-Sayegh or his alleged co-conspirators. (Benjamin & Simon, 2003; Schwartz, 2002; US Deports, 1999). Another explanation suggests that the rift between the Clinton administration and Freeh had grown so vast that Reno had lost control over Freeh and, therefore, the investigation. Meanwhile, Freeh had lost faith in her to "make the hard decision to indict Iranian officials for the Khobar bombing" (Benjamin & Simon, 2003, p. 331). In light of the indictment released 2 years later against Al-Sayegh and the Khobar perpetrators under Attorney General John Ashcroft, the deportation appears to be a wasted opportunity. It is also not clear why a deportation of a prime suspect to Saudi Arabia makes sense given the strained cooperation on the investigation. Access to this suspect later became problematic in launching grand jury proceedings for the eventual indictment.

Al-Sayegh fell through the evidentiary cracks of the pre-9/11 criminal justice system. The standard of proof for a criminal prosecution, beyond a reasonable doubt, is a higher evidentiary bar to meet than would be required in intelligence gathering to formulate military or foreign policy response or in terrorism cases after 9/11. In the post-9/11 legal environment, Al-Sayegh could have been held in US custody as a material witness, despite the reported lack of evidence of his own role in the attacks and his lack of cooperation, providing that grand jury proceedings were underway (US v. Abdullah, 2nd Cir., 2003).

And finally, complicating any assessment of the criminal justice response is the outstanding uncertainty about the true identity of the group responsible. The FBI under Louis Freeh, Saudi Interior Minister Prince Nayef and others worked under the theory that Hezbollah was responsible, while still others have since differed, including the 9/11 commission, and pointed to bin Laden. If the true perpetrators were bin Laden and Al-Qaeda, the criminal justice response to the Khobar bombing was not only mismanaged, but off target as well. Benjamin and Simon (2003) imply that Freeh's obsession with Khobar Towers and Hezbollah may have overshadowed any serious investigations as to involvement by Sunni extremist groups, an attitude that may have stemmed from his reported vulnerability to Saudi manipulation. If so, he may have disregarded intelligence obtained shortly after the bombing which pointed to bin Laden and allegedly documented bin Laden's attempt to facilitate explosive shipments into Saudi Arabia in the months before the attack (Eggen, 2004). According to the 9/11 Commission Report (2006), DIA and Central Intelligence Agency (CIA) analysts had uncovered "some signs," unspecified, that Al-Qaeda aided Saudi Hezbollah in accomplishing the attack on Khobar

Towers (p. 60). Other sources point to cooperation between Hezbollah and bin Laden in putting the Khobar Towers plot in motion. Hezbollah terrorist mastermind Imad Mugniyeh has been reported to have attended training sessions for the Khobar Towers attacks in Lebanon by invitation of bin Laden (Harik, 2004). Still other sources indicate that Al-Qaeda and Hezbollah have engaged in adhoc cross-training and tactical information sharing with a plethora of other terrorist groups. They have also allegedly worked together laundering money in support of their terrorist activities, specifically from locations in Lebanon's Beka'a Valley (Levitt, 2005). On the other hand, an important cadre of scholars, who have scrutinized the publicly available sources related to the Khobar Towers attack, maintain that it was the work of Hezbollah Al-Hijaz (Hegghammer, 2008; Wright, 2006; Burke, 2004; Benjamin & Simon, 2003). At the very least, bin Laden released a statement of praise for the Khobar Towers attacks saying, "I have great respect for the people who did this. What they did is a big honor that I missed participating in" (as quoted in Bergen, 2002, p. 88). Ironically, the bin Laden family construction company later had the honor of receiving the contract to rebuild Khobar towers (Hegghammer, 2008).

More general problems with a criminal justice response to terrorism are also evident in the Khobar Towers case as well. Defining who within an overall terrorist network is legally culpable remains a judgment call with no bright line rule and subject to political manipulation, thus undermining the legitimacy of criminal law. Wedgewood (2001) points out that Brigadier General Ahmad Sharifi was not indicted though he is the alleged Iranian handler for the Hezbollah Al-Hijaz defendants, unless indictment of him was sealed from the public. This suggests the additional problem of information disclosure in a criminal case which may open a Pandora's box of discovery from a variety of sensitive agencies, compromising sources and methods. The relatively slow movement of judicial procedures can also make a criminal justice response less satisfactory (Wedgewood, 2001). In the case of Khobar Towers, 5 years elapsed between the attack and the indictment, which merely marks the beginning of any criminal case making its way through the courts.

Of related legal interest, Khobar Towers also prompted the United States to initiate negotiation in the United Nations regarding the *International Convention for the Suppression of Terrorist Bombings*, which the General Assembly adopted on December 15, 1997. Like previous international conventions which focused on very specific acts such as crimes against diplomats, civil aviation, maritime safety, and hostage taking in order to sidestep definitional controversy over the "terrorist or freedom-fighter" question, the convention requires parties to criminalize some specific conduct, in this case bombing public places, in order to improve international law enforcement cooperation (Witten, 1998).[5] Implementing such laws remains orders of magnitude more difficult than passing them.

---

[5]The first exception to this trend which finally defined terrorism was the 1999 *International Convention for the Suppression of the Financing of Terrorism* (Kraft, 2008).

Investigating Force Protection: Organizational Learning or Witch-hunt?

In addition to the FBI investigation there were four other inquiries. The House National Security Committee conducted a preliminary assessment, releasing a public report on August 14. Secretary William J. Perry appointed retired General Wayne A. Downing to lead an investigatory task force for the Department of Defense. Downing, who as a former commander of US Special Operations Command and part of Joint Special Operations Command was a recognized authority on combating terrorism, delivered a report to Perry on August 30, that was critical of Air Force and US Central Command chains of command. In reaction, the Air Force conducted an independent review into possible dereliction of duty, led by Lieutenant General James F. Record with General Court Martial Convening Authority. The Record Report found no basis for criminal proceedings, and further investigation by the Air Force Inspector General and Judge Advocate General found no basis either for administrative sanctions. A summary report in July 1997 by Secretary of Defense William S. Cohen (who relieved Perry for Clinton's second term) demurred, however, holding the wing commander Brigadier General Terry J. Schwalier accountable for lapses in force protection and removing his name from the Major General promotion list, effectively ending his career. (US House, 1996; Downing, 1996; Record, 1996; Swope & Hawley, 1997; Cohen, 1997).

Apart from the issue of personal accountability, which will be explored later, there was broad consensus on the findings of the various investigations, and the Defense Department moved to implement most of the recommendations. The findings fall into three broad categories: the general circumstances of the Air Force deployment in Saudi Arabia, deficiencies in intelligence, and specific tactical force protection measures and preparedness.

The 4404th Wing (Provisional) and its higher headquarters, Joint Task Force Southwest Asia, stood up in response to United Nations Security Council Resolutions 687 and 688 to contain potential Iraqi aggression following the end of the Gulf War in 1991. Initially intended as a short-term operation, this evolved into an indefinite mandate to enforce UN sanctions and the "no-fly zone" in Iraq south of the 32nd parallel as the air component of Operation Southern Watch. Five years later, the 4404th was still operating as a temporary organization with inadequate personnel continuity and resources. Almost all personnel were on short 90 day tours, with 10% of the entire command turning over each week (Schwalier was the first wing commander assigned a year-long tour, in July 1995). This situation was especially hard on security and intelligence personnel, where the former lacked the time and manpower to develop teamwork for responses to complex attacks and the latter were unable to develop a mastery of the local intelligence picture or the close interpersonal relationships with Saudi counterparts needed for effective counter-intelligence and counter-terrorism. More broadly, there was no policy standardization of vulnerability assessment requirements or force protection measures across DoD units, no prioritization of force protection funding, and several ambiguities about who had ultimate responsibility for force protection among military echelons and between US agencies like DoD and State, leaving each local commander to rely on their own judgment.

The intelligence posture of the 4404th was inadequate. In late 1994 general threat reporting began to take a more ominous tone, and intelligence personnel suspected state-sponsored groups were targeting US facilities and Khobar Towers in particular. The 1995 OPM-SANG bomb in Riyadh and surveillance incidents throughout 1996 lent credibility and urgency to a growing body of reporting that the terrorist threat was on the rise; however, there was no tactical information as to the precise timing, target, and means of attack on June 23. The size of the truck bomb in particular, 20,000 lb TNT equivalent, was a complete surprise as intelligence and security personnel expected something on the order of magnitude of the 250 lb car bomb in Riyadh. Within the US intelligence community as a whole, there was insufficient analytical effort dedicated to the analysis of long-term terrorist trends and intentions to better characterize the emerging threat, and there was likewise no analyzed intelligence product tailored to the needs of force protection in Dhahran. At the tactical level, the base Security Police had no organic intelligence capability (The Downing report noted that "the Security Police commander essentially served as his own intelligence officer") and support from the Air Force Office of Special Investigations (AFOSI) detachment was severely limited by 90 day tours, manning shortages, a lack of counter-intelligence training, and almost no Arabic language skills (the House investigation points out the entire 4404th had only one linguist). Adequate understanding and warning of terrorist activity is almost impossible without a strong human intelligence (HUMINT) program, and while discussions of HUMINT are classified in the investigation reports, it is clear that it was severely lacking (Ziegler, 1998). This left personnel dependent on Saudi cooperation, hampered by rapid personnel turnover and subject to politicization by Saudis concerned about how the Kingdom might be perceived or what Americans might do with the information.

Khobar Towers was an inherently vulnerable target, located in an urban area with an uncontrolled public parking lot on its north perimeter. The Saudis had provided the US forces with the facility, convenient to the airfield, at no cost, and Saudi Arabia was perceived as relatively safe before 1995, so the risk-reward balance was perceived as acceptable. After the 1995 OPM-SANG bombing, there were many force protection upgrades to Khobar Towers. A vulnerability assessment in January 1996 made 39 recommendations for improvement, 36 of which were implemented immediately. Not implemented was the installation of shatter-resistant mylar film for the windows, an expensive and difficult construction project that would require Saudi cooperation, and was thus postponed for later in Schwalier's 5-year improvement plan. Also, fire alarms were not installed in the building because it was assessed to be built of non-flammable materials, and personnel were not dispersed to other locations due to the unreasonable impact on operations. The improvements that were implemented, such as more austere entry controls, barriers and sentries, provided a robust defense against any attack attempting to penetrate the perimeter. As the AFOSI detachment commander observed prophetically in an April 1996 message to AFOSI headquarters in Washington, "Security measures here are outstanding, which in my view would lead a would-be terrorist to attempt an attack from a position outside the perimeter." (Downing, 1996) Such a "standoff" attack was less well defended against, but it was thought to be manageable given an expected yield of only a few hundred pounds of explosives. Officers asked Saudi counterparts to move the perimeter out and to clear brush to improve visibility, but they received resistance to both, the latter ostensibly because the sight of Western behavior within the compound, such as jogging in shorts and uncovered women, would be offensive to Saudi culture.

The only substantive point of disagreement in the investigations was the personal accountability of the 4404th commander, Brigadier General Schwalier. While the two Air Force investigations found that he did the best job he could in the circumstances he found himself, taking security very seriously while still accomplishing the Operation Southern Watch mission, Defense Secretary Cohen nonetheless denied his promotion. Cohen argued that the threat of a "standoff" attack was foreseeable in advance and that Schwalier could have done more to mitigate it by installing mylar windows, as many personnel were killed or severely injured by flying glass, and by developing and exercising more robust contingency plans for building evacuation, including using the buildings loud speaker during an attack (He pointed out that the Sergeant who initiated the evacuation of the top floor by knocking on doors and doubtlessly saving lives was, while commendably resourceful, unaware of other procedures or resources like the "Giant Voice" loud speaker system.) While this appeased public and congressional calls for accountability, it was widely perceived as a witch-hunt by military officers, who felt the judgment ignored the real constraints of command and promoted a dangerous "zero defects" mentality and risk aversion among commanders in forward areas. Air Force Chief of Staff General Ronald R. Fogleman submitted his request for retirement prior to Cohen's announcement. While careful to insist that it was not a resignation in protest, Fogleman also later admitted that he completely agreed with the critical interpretation of an article in the *Weekly Standard* entitled "The Scapegoat: How the Secretary of Defense Ended the Career of an Exemplary Air Force General" (Kohn, 2001; LaBash, 1997). Air Force Secretary Sheila Widnall reflected that Schwalier had been the victim of Congressional political posturing and Cohen's own-troubled relationship with the Air Force (Sheila Widnall, personal communication, Feburary 6, 2009). Schwalier maintained he had done everything that could have been reasonably expected to protect Khobar Towers; over a decade later the Air Force Board for the Correction of Military Records agreed and moved to reinstate his second star (Holmes, 2008a). The Pentagon again disagreed with the Air Force, accusing the service of exceeding its authority, blocking Schwalier's promotion in March 2008 (Holmes, 2008b).

Shortly after the bombing, Secretary of Defense Perry said that "the Khobar Towers attack should be seen as a watershed event pointing the way to a radically new mindset and dramatic changes in the way we protect our forces deployed overseas from this growing threat." (as quoted in Murrey, 1999, p. 1). The Air Force stood down the 4404th Wing and relocated approximately 3600 personnel from Riyadh and Dhahran and 100 aircraft to Prince Sultan Air Base, a remote and sprawling facility 50 mile south of Riyadh. Military dependents were sent back to the United States and personnel confined to the base (except on official business), which was surrounded with 20 ft high berms.[6] The Air Force also restructured its Security Police and created a new Force Protection Agency consolidating AFOSI, intelligence and security staff to standardize guidance, education, and direct support to the field (Widnall, 1997). The Chairman of the Joint Chiefs of Staff reported a year after the bombing that all but 2 of the 81 recommendations in the Downing Report had been implemented, establishing an office for combating terrorism in the Joint Staff, increasing funding for force protection measures and developing more robust guidance, policy, and force-wide training programs.[7] By 2000, over $80 million of the Joint Staff Combating Terrorism Readiness Initiatives Fund had been allocated to military installations, a Memoranda of Understanding signed with the State Department and force protection was far more institutionalized throughout the services, although many specific installations still had room for improvement (US GAO, 2000). Until the 2001 attack on the Pentagon, there were no additional attacks on US military installations, although the warship *USS. Cole* was attacked by Al-Qaeda during a port call in Yemen in October 2000, killing 17 sailors.

Conclusions: Khobar Towers in Context

Countering terrorism is very difficult because it involves so many difficult collective action problems. Intelligence organizations must share information and coordinate analytical effort. Government agencies must coordinate all the various diplomatic, informational, economic, and military instruments of national power, all within a sound legal framework. Federal, state, and local organizations must collaborate in law-enforcement and consequence management efforts. Most challengingly of all, sovereign states, each of which has all of these same internal coordination challenges, must cooperate in all these dimensions. All of these entities must consistently persevere with this coordination over time, even though terrorist events themselves will be extremely episodic. In the absence of clearly articulated common interests and effort to reorient resources toward these challenging collective problems, individual agencies and states have much stronger incentives to pursue their own interests. In the 1990s, US officials were unable to adequately articulate the threat or muster the political consensus to address these problems and craft a robust counter-terrorism program.

---

[6] In 2003, following the invasion of Iraq, the Air Force shifted its forces to Qatar and returned control of PSAB to the Saudis.

[7] The US General Accounting Office (1997) also noted that DoD was still having troubles establishing consistency in proscriptive physical security measures, vulnerability assessment requirements, and central force protection accountability. This is understandable given the magnitude of the changes.

It was a decade of profound strategic drift in American Foreign Policy. The end of the Cold War did not provide a peace dividend as anticipated. Instead it ended a long period of strategic consensus and ushered in a motley host of new challenges. The United States embarked on various state-building adventures in Haiti, Somalia, Colombia, Bosnia, and Kosovo, with results ranging from mediocre to disastrous. This prompted some observers to foresee non-state political and criminal actors as major emerging forces shaping the security environment; at the same time the heady growth of the Internet economy and globalization also prompted enthusiastic visions of a high-tech "Revolution in Military Affairs." Military weapons procurement remained largely consistent with Cold War priorities focused on deterring or conducting high-intensity combat against a peer competitor, presumably China or Russia. American grand strategy was muddled, even as the American military was active around the globe.

Terrorism was evolving from something of a vexing criminal problem to a novel tactical and strategic manifestation of warfare, and the Khobar Towers bombing was but one of several high-profile incidents marking this shift. In the previous year, the Tokyo subway was attacked with sarin gas by the millenarian group Aum Shinrikyo, domestic terrorists struck fatally in Oklahoma City, and the threat of Sunni transnational terror led by Osama bin Laden was starting to be registered by counter-terrorism officials; all of these attacks introduced new layers of complexity atop the known problem of state-sponsored terrorism. New technologies of communication and movement and easier access to more potent weapons provided improved capabilities for new kinds of actors whose motivation, organization, and affiliation were still not well understood.

The Clinton administration had issued Presidential Decision Directive 39, "US Policy on Terrorism," in June 1995. It was the first attempt to centralize counter-terrorism policy in the Executive Branch, addressing the problem of "asymmetric warfare" directly and assigning responsibilities to all the various bureaucratic organs for combating terrorism and consequence management (Benjamin & Simon 2003, p. 230). Following Khobar Towers, the United States spent at least $6.7 billion in fiscal year 1997 (classified spending is likely higher) growing to over $10 billion in fiscal year 2000, an increase notable in an era during which the administration was trying to trim federal spending in an attempt to balance the budget (US GAO, 1999a,1999b). Budget officials noted, however, that there seemed to be a disconnect between the increased spending and any articulation of the methods, goals, and objectives in combating terrorism (US GAO, 1999a). With all of the other international and domestic crises of the 1990s, the administration was unable to muster the focus or political capital to develop a consistent and coordinated response. As Ambassador Michael Sheehan observed:

> Those of us who devoted our careers to counterterrorism watched in frustration as the institutional focus of the US government locked onto terrorism in the weeks and months following an attack, but inevitably faded as time passed….[In] the pre-9/11 world…terrorism occasionally emerged as a foreign policy headache but would reliably return to the back burner, second to the more traditional challenges posed by the Soviet Union or China (Alexander & Kraft 2008, p. xvi).

In Saudi Arabia, in particular, the United States did not adequately understand the threat it was up against. Many extremist groups, Shi'ite and Sunni, state sponsored or autonomous, had the motivation to attack US forces which were based in Saudi Arabia, the location of some of Islam's holiest places, engaged in military operations against an Arab country. Some clearly had the capability to do it in spectacular style.

In particular, sectarian cleavages in Saudi Arabia were notably underappreciated. Shi'ite social networks became sites through which various ideologies around the meaning of US military deployment in Saudi Arabia were produced and maintained. Without understanding Shi'ite grievances in its context, US officials were unable to foresee the determination of a group of Saudi Hezbollah to attack Americans. Extremist anti-US and anti-government attitudes were played close to the chest by Saudi Shi'a and yet, within intimate circles, they were a point of pride. Coined "cultural intimacy" by Herzfeld (1997, 2001), such attitudes can serve the internal function of providing cohesion among group members. Saudi Hezbollah's growth within the overall more moderate Shi'ite landscape of the 1990s occurred within a cultural context in which anti-US sentiment was seen as part and parcel to other more conventional Saudi Shi'ite grievances (Jones, 2006). Shoring up identity through radicalization became all the more palatable to some Shi'a during a decade in which identity politics ramped up to explosive levels as popular Sunni clerics published and distributed treatises calling Shi'a *rawafid*, a pejorative label meaning "rejectionists," and Gulf governments, including Saudi Arabia, were reacting, often brutally, to an overblown moral panic about insurrectionary pan-Shi'a aspirations. US officials, in aligning themselves so closely with the Saudi government, fell victim to its sanitized version of internal threats. This, coupled with an insular cultural context, led to the failure in fully understanding that Hezbollah, operating in an everyday social context, could be well enough organized, financed and ideologically motivated to effectively strike the most advanced military in the world – a situation that could only have been remedied through an increased commitment by US HUMINT capabilities.

Yet, complex groups like Hezbollah and Al-Qaeda are difficult to unravel even in the best of intelligence circumstances. Such groups are non-hierarchical, fluid, evolving, and enmeshed in their social context in ways difficult to detect from the outside. Social bonds among conspirators are based on their purpose, whether to facilitate financing or logistical support, but are also embedded within social cliques and friendships (Sageman, 2004). Further complicating matters is the "ingrained cultural reticence" evident in Saudi society which is a major obstacle in learning about Saudi social and political life (Wright, 2006, p. 27) and also in effecting any influence from outside. Given the lamentable HUMINT posture in Saudi Arabia at the time, there was little hope of achieving this. Intelligence positions were manned on short 90 day rotations, completely insufficient to develop the situational awareness and relationships (with both sources and Saudi partners) needed to conduct effective HUMINT operations. AFOSI was chronically short staffed, charged with both counter-intelligence and internal affairs investigations. The entire wing had only one Arabic linguist, rendering intelligence almost completely dependent on what Saudi partners may or may not like to share, along with whatever political spin they might add. Even if there had been a more robust collection effort, there was no focused analytical capability to do the difficult multi-source analysis necessary to piece together the identity and operations of subversive networks.

In many historical cases of intelligence failure, as with Pearl Harbor and 9/11, all of the necessary information was in the system, but it was never brought together or recognized as important by decision makers; in Roberta Wohlstetter's (1962) famous formulation of the problem, the signal was lost in the noise. In this case, however, there simply was not a wide enough HUMINT net cast to even draw actionable information into the system, much less have a chance of putting the pieces together. There was, however, enough warning of the generally heightening threat, especially following the OPM-SANG bombings, and lost opportunities to follow up on surveillance and interdictions of explosives bound for Al-Mughassil's group. HUMINT networks cannot be grown overnight, but why wasn't there more urgency put on them? While Saudi intransigence, including hasty execution of the OPM-SANG suspects, is certainly a factor, it is clear the United States did not emphasize intelligence collection and analysis.

One likely reason for intelligence underinvestment is rooted in organizational behavior: organizations emphasize their essential missions, and military organizations, in particular emphasize offensive missions (Allison & Zelikow, 1999; Halperin, 1974; Snyder, 1989). For the 4404th Wing, this meant patrolling the Iraqi no-fly zone, and the intelligence needed to support that mission is almost completely derived from technical imagery and signals intelligence (IMINT and SIGINT). HUMINT, by contrast, supported a secondary, defensive mission, which is why it was outsourced to a service support organization, AFOSI, which was under resourced and, as a law enforcement organization focused on internal affairs, somewhat out of its depth. For the Air Force as for the rest of the US Government, countering terrorism was not a strategic focus (Sheila Widnall, personal communication, Feburary 6, 2009). Only in the post 9/11 environment (or among esoteric counter-terrorism units) would HUMINT be appreciated as a critical enabler for offensive operations against a primary strategic adversary.

Organizational interests again trumped strategic concerns in the investigatory emphasis on force protection. The investigations focused heavily on the personal accountability of officers in the prelude to the attack. The Air Force at the time was reeling from several accountability crises, including the accidental shoot down of two Army Blackhawk helicopters in Iraq, a B-52 crashed by a pilot with a questionable record, and the fraternization scandal involving Lieutenant Kelly Flinn (Kohn, 2001), thus the question of whether any officers were derelict in their duty took on an inflated importance. Secretary Cohen's censure of Brigadier General Schwalier turned on particular details, like the failure to install mylar window coatings or activate the "Giant Voice" loudspeaker, measures that may not in fact have had much effect mitigating consequences (Creamer & Seat, 1998) and certainly would not have prevented the attack. After the attack the military undertook much needed reforms in force protection measures, most dramatically in the relocation of forces into the remote interior of the kingdom. The defensive nature of force protection measures must be emphasized; they were treated as the equivalent of designing buildings to survive in an area subject to earthquakes or bad weather, rather than a strategic interaction with a lethal adversary. They did not include the proactive, offensive aspects of counter-terrorism which require so much legal, intelligence, and international coordination. All things being equal, organizations seek autonomy, and force protection is something a military organization can do on its own. While not to downplay the difficulty of organizational reform in such a complex organization (Murrey, 1999), or the importance of defensive measures in any counter-terror program, hardening facilities is clearly more organizationally autonomous than deploying a robust HUMINT-based, interagency and international counter-terrorism capability. Force protection is the relatively easier problem, because the military organization owns it. Thus it became a focal point for the investigations and for reform.

In fairness to the military, an additional reason it focused exclusively on force protection was that it was unclear what else could be scrutinized. While Iranian involvement was suspected early on, action was politically infeasible. The plot itself and its perpetrators remain shrouded in uncertainty to this day. The shenanigans on the criminal justice front and a strange brew of incompetence and international political constraint served to reinforce the ambiguity of the threat and the discombobulating effect of the response. Internal disagreements between the FBI and the Clinton Administration created an incoherent approach to the investigation and a divided, ineffective front in dealing with Saudi reluctance to cooperate. Although the responsibility for counter-terrorism in the executive branch is diffused and agencies compete to impose their own preferences (Crenshaw, 2002), the aftermath of the Khobar Tower bombing underscores the importance of mutual coordination among agencies in managing investigative cooperation from foreign governments. The post-9/11 efforts to provide more centralized leadership and coordination of counter-terrorism efforts may hold some promise in this regard.

In addition, by deporting Al-Sayegh to an uncooperative Saudi Arabia because of a reported lack of evidence, the United States lost its only suspect ever in its custody, effectively crippling its ability to bring anyone to trial. Although the post-9/11 material witness laws were not yet in effect, creative approaches should have been taken to keep Al-Sayegh in custody, so that he would have been on hand for the subsequent indictment in which he is named. Canadian authorities conducted their own investigation into Al-Sayegh and concurred with US suspicions, an important third-party check on the allegations. It would seem that because military reprisal was off the table due to a Middle Eastern political balancing act, the criminal justice response should have been given top organization billing with clear leadership, coordination, and resources. The failure to achieve justice in the federal case once again sent a message to terrorist perpetrators that they could act without punishment. And perhaps more importantly, because none of the perpetrators have been brought to justice by US authorities, many victims' families have expressed anger at the United States for dropping the ball on the criminal investigation and even feel that their loved ones were forgotten by the country to which they gave their lives. One political blogger lamented that there has "...still been no justice achieved for the families. . ." in a moving online tribute to the victims on the tenth anniversary of the bombing (Malkin, 2006).

It is always easier in hindsight to identify problems (Fischhoff, 1975). We have touched on several issues here that may have made a difference in June 1996 if they had been addressed. However, the tragedy of Khobar Towers goes beyond the 19 lives lost and hundreds injured. The real tragedy is the uncomfortable air of inevitability around the Khobar Towers bombing. The various intelligence, force protection or law enforcement measures that might have been improved in Dhahran seem paltry next to the general unpreparedness of the US government to deal with large-scale Islamist terrorism, and that unpreparedness, furthermore, seems itself almost unavoidable given all the ambiguity, diverse commitments and political constraints of the 1990s.

The overarching lesson, thus, is the importance of understanding what sort of war one is in. If it is recognized that a state and its security apparatus is fighting a long-term war with a dangerous strategic actor like Hezbollah or Al-Qaeda, then setbacks caused by a wily adversary must be expected. Terrorism does not just happen like earthquakes; it is deliberately inflicted for some definite purpose. One can and should attempt to deter and defend against attacks, but against a creative and determined adversary that will never be sufficient. In the post-9/11 campaigns in Iraq and Afghanistan, US forces are regularly, unfortunately, subject to mass-casualty terrorist bombings. While each is investigated and commanders should be relieved in the event of gross negligence, nevertheless, these are recognized as the wages of war. US forces take their hits, but then also take their fight to the enemy. In 1996, however, there was a totally different mindset. The United States was not at war. Unfortunately, someone was at war with the United States.

References

9/11 Commission Report (2006). 9/11 Commission, chaired by T. H. Kean. New York: Barnes & Noble.

Alexander, Y., & Kraft, M. B. (Eds.). (2008). *Evolution of U.S. counterterrorism policy.* Westport, CT: Praeger Security International.

Allison, G. T., & Zelikow, P. (1999). *Essence of decision: Explaining the cuban missile crisis.* New York: Addison Wesley Longman.

Al-Rai Al-Aam ("Public Opinion") (2004, May 31). Kuwait. Retrieved From January 29, 2009 from www.alraimedia.com

Benjamin, D., & Simon, S. (2003). *The age of sacred terror: Radical Islam's war against America.* New York: Random House.

Bergen, P. L. (2002). *Holy war inc.: Inside the secret world of Osama bin Laden.* New York: Free Press.

Blanche, E. (2001, May). Al Khobar: The search continues. *Middle East, 312,* 15.

Burke, J. (2004). *Al-Qaeda. The true story of radical Islam.* New York: I.B. Tauris.

Clausewitz, Carl von. (1976). *On War.* (M. Howard & P. Paret, Ed. & Trans.). Princeton, NJ: Princeton University Press.

Clinton, W. J. (1996a, June 29). Radio Address on terrorism from G-7 summit meeting. In Y. Alexander, & M. B. Kraft (Eds.), *Evolution of counterterrorism policy (2008)* (Vol. I, pp. 74–75). Westport, CT: Praeger.

Clinton, W. J. (1996b, August 5). American security in a changing world. In Y. Alexander, & M. B. Kraft (Eds.), *Evolution of counterterrorism policy (2008)* (Vol. I, pp. 76–79). Westport, CT: Praeger.

Cohen, A. (2007). Knowing thy enemy. *Policy Review, 145,* 41–53.

Cohen, W. S. (1997, July 31). *Report: Personal accountability and force protection at Khobar Towers. United States Air Force.* Retrieved December 18, 2008 from http://www.au. af.mil/au/awc/awcgate/khobar/report.htm

Cordesman, A. H., & Burke, A. A. (2001, June). *Islamic extremism in Saudi Arabia and the attack on Al Khobar.* Washington, DC: Center for Strategic and International Studies.

Creamer, R. L., & Seat, J. C. (1998, April). *Khobar towers: The aftermath and implications for commanders.* Research report, Air Command and Staff College, Maxwell Air Force Base.

Crenshaw, M. (2002). Counterterrorism policy and the political process. In R. Howard & R. Sawyer (Eds.), *Terrorism and counterterrorism: Understanding the new security environment* (pp. 450–458). New York: McGraw Hill.

Downing, W. A. (1996, July 31). *Force protection assessment of US CENTCOM AOR and Khobar Towers, report of the downing task force.* Washington DC: Department of Defense. Retrieved December 18, 2008 from http://www.fas.org/irp/threat/downing/unclf913.html

Eggen, D. (2004). 9/11 panel links Al Qaeda, Iran. *The Washington Post,* A12.

Esposito, J. L. (2002). *Unholy war: Terror in the name of Islam.* Oxford: Oxford University Press.

Fadlallah, M. H. (1981). *Al-Islam wa montiq al-quwwa.* Beirut: Al-mu-assasa al-jamiyya lil-dirasat wal-nashr.

Fischhoff, B. (1975). Hindsight does not equal foresight: The effect of outcome knowledge on judgment under uncertainty. *Journal of Experimental Psychology: Human Perception and Performance, 1*(3), 288–299.

Freeh, L. (2003, May 20). American justice for our Khobar heroes, *Wall Street Journal,* p. 18.

Halperin, M. H. (1974). *Bureaucratic politics and foreign policy.* Washington, DC: Brookings Institution Press.

Harik, J. P. (2004). *Hezbollah: The changing face of terrorism.* London: I.B. Taurus.

Hegghammer, T. (2008, February). Deconstructing the myth about al-Qa'ida and Khobar. *CTC Sentinel, 1*(3), 20–22.

Herzfeld, M. (1997). *Cultural intimacy: Social poetics in the nation-state.* New York: Routledge.

Herzfeld, M. (2001). Performing comparison: Ethnography, globetrotting and the spaces of social knowledge. *Journal of Anthropological Research, 57*(3), 259–276.

Holmes, E. (2008a, January 16). Khobar Towers general gets second star. *Air Force Times.* Retrieved February 7, 2009 from http://www.airforcetimes.com/news/2008/01/airforce_schwalier_080113w

Holmes, E. (2008b, April 8). Pentagon blocks promotion of Khobar Towers CO. *Air Force Times.* Retrieved February 7, 2009 from http://www.airforcetimes.com/news/2008/04/airforce_schwalier_040408w

Howard, R. D., & Sawyer, R. L. (Eds.). (2004). *Terrorism and counterterrorism: Understanding the new security environment.* New York: McGraw-Hill.

International Crisis Group (2005, September 19). *The Shiite Question in Saudi Arabia.* Brussels: International Crisis Group. (Middle East Report No. 45)

International Policy Institute for Counterterrorism (1999, October 6). *Khobar suspect to be deported from U.S.* Retrieved January 19, 2008 from http://212.150.54.123/spotlight/det.cfm?id=337

Jamieson, P. D. (2008). *Khobar Towers: Tragedy and response: Tragedy and response.* Washington, DC: U.S. Air Force History and Museums Program.

Jones, T. C. (2005). The clerics, the Sahwa and the Saudi state. *Strategic Insights, 4.* Retrieved January 26, 2008 from http://www.ccc.nps.navy.mil/si/2005/Mar/jonesMar05.pdf

Jones, T. C. (2006, March/April). Shifting sands. *Foreign Affairs.* Retrieved January 26, 2008 from http://www.foreignaffairs.org/20060301fareviewessay85213b/tojones/shifting-sands.html

Kohn, R. H. (Ed.). (2001, Spring). The early retirement of Gen Ronald R. Fogleman, chief of staff, United States Air Force. *Aerospace Power Journal, 15*(1), 6–23.

Kraft, M. B. (2008). Evolution of U.S. counterterrorism laws, policies, and programs. In Y. Alexander, & M. B. Kraft (Eds.), *Evolution of U.S. counterterrorism policy* (Vol. 1, pp. 1–44) Westport, CT: Praeger Security International.

Labash, M. (1997). The scapegoat: How the secretary of defense ended the career of an exemplary air force general. *The Weekly Standard, 3*(11), 20–29.

LaFree, G., & Hendrickson, J. (2007). Build a criminal justice response to terrorism. *Criminology & Public Policy, 7*(1), 781–790.

Levitt, M. A. (2005, February 16). Iranian state sponsorship of terror: Threatening U.S. security, global stability and regional peace. *Congressional testimony*. Washington, DC: The Washington Institute for Near East Policy.

Lewis, B. (1995). *The middle east*. New York: Touchstone.

Malkin, M. (2006, June 25). Khobar Towers: Ten years later. *Michelle Malkin* [blog]. Retrieved February 7, 2009 from http://michellemalkin.com/2006/06/25/khobar-towers-10-years-later/

Murrey, T. W., Jr. (1999, October). Khobar Towers' progeny: The development of force protection. *Army Lawyer*. U.S. Army, 1–18.

Naftali, T. J. (2005). *Blind spot: The secret history of american counterterrorism*. New York: Basic Books.

Nasr, V. (2006). *The Shia revival: How conflicts within Islam will shape the future*. New York: W.W. Norton & Co.

Noorani, A. G. (2002). *Islam & jihad: Prejudice versus reality*. London: Zed Books.

Ranstorp, M. (1997). *Hizb'allah in Lebanon: The politics of the western hostage crisis*. London: Macmillan Press.

Record, J. F. (1996, October 31). *Independent review of the Khobar Towers bombing*. Washington, DC: U.S. Air Force.

Saad-Ghorayeb, A. (2002). *Hizb'ullah: Politics and religion*. London: Pluto Press.

Sageman, M. (2004). *Understanding terrorism networks*. Philadelphia: University of Pennsylvania Press.

Sageman, M. (2008). *Leaderless jihad*. Philadelphia: University of Pennsylvania Press.

Schwartz, S. (2002). *The two faces of Islam: Saudi fundamentalism and its role in terrorism*. New York: Anchor Books.

Shenon, P. (1996, June 26). 23 U.S. troops die in truck bombing in Saudi base. *The New York Times*. Retrieved January 4, 9009 from http://partners.nytimes.com/library/world/africa/062696binladen.html?scp=1&sq=khobar%20towers&st=cse

Snyder, J. L. (1989). *The Ideology of the offensive: Military decision making and the disasters of 1914*. Ithaca, NY: Cornell University Press.

Swope, R. T., & Hawley, B. G. (1997, April). *Report of investigation concerning the Khobar Towers bombing*. Washington, DC: U.S. Air Force Inspector General and Judge Advocate General.

Timmerman, K. R. (2006, June 6). Judge dismissed Khobar Towers suit against Iran. *Newsmax*. Retrieved February 7, 2009 from http://archive.newsmax.com/archives/articles/2006/6/8/213400.shtml

U.S. Deports Saudi in Airmen's Bombing Deaths. (1999, November 12). *New York Times*. Retrieved January 16, 2009 from http://query.nytimes.com/gst/fullpage.html?res=9F05E1DD1730F931A25753C1A96F958260

U.S. General Accounting Office (U.S. GAO). (1997, July). *Combating terrorism: Status of DOD efforts to protect its forces overseas*. Washington, DC: Author.

U.S. General Accounting Office (U.S. GAO) (1999a, March 11) *Combating terrorism: Observations on federal spending to combat terrorism*. Washington, DC: Author.

U.S. General Accounting Office (U.S. GAO) (1999b, July 9). *Combating terrorism: Observations on growth in federal programs*. Washington, DC: Author.

U.S. General Accounting Office (U.S. GAO) (2000, July). *Combating terrorism: Action taken but considerable risks remain for forces overseas.* Washington, DC: Author.

U.S. House National Security Committee (1996, August 14), *The Khobar towers bombing incident.* Washington, DC: U.S. Congress.

U.S. v. Al-Mughassil, et al. [indictment] (2001). Retrieved January 4, 2009 from http://www.fbi.gov/pressrel/pressrel01/khobar.pdf

Unger, C. (2004). *House of bush. House of saud.* New York: Scribner.

Wedgewood, R. (2001, July 6). *Special policy forum report: Khobar Towers five years later—evaluating the criminal justice approach to counterterrorism.* Policy Watch #544. Washington, DC: The Washington Institute for Near East Policy.

Widnall, S. (1997, July 31). *Statement of the secretary of the air force.* Washington, DC: U.S. Air Force.

Witten, S. M. (1998). The international convention for the suppression of terrorist bombings. *The American Journal of International Law, 92*(4), 774–781.

Wohlstetter, R. (1962). *Pearl harbor: Warning and decision.* Stanford, CA: Stanford University Press.

Wright, L. (2006). *The looming tower: Al-Qaeda and the road to 9/11.* New York: Random House.

Ziegler, J. J. (1998, April). *From Beirut to Khobar Towers: Improving the combating terrorism program.* Research report, Air Command and Staff College, Maxwell Air Force Base.

Chapter 17
The Siege in Mumbai: A Conventional Terrorist Attack Aided by Modern Technology

William LaRaia and Michael C. Walker

Introduction

In this chapter, the authors attempt to explain the recent (November 2008) terrorist attacks in Mumbai, India, which led to the death of almost 175 people and injury to an additional 300. This attack differed from most due to its focus on multiple targets in a large metropolitan area; the rather small number of actual operatives who took part in the attack; how the attackers were broken into small, two-man teams; how the attackers used a variety of munitions to conduct their operations; and finally the very high level of technological sophistication used by the Mumbai attackers.

Before we discuss the actual attacks, however, it is important for the reader to develop an understanding of several, very important issues which, ultimately, led to the attack on Mumbai. These issues can be better explained through an understanding of the history of South Asia including its religious background; the colonial antecedents of modern India, Pakistan, and Kashmir; the independence movement of 1947; and how the borders of India and Pakistan, and who would inhabit each country, became established.

Finally, it is important to observe how terrorism has developed in the region from first being a part of the struggle for an independent Kashmir, to young men traveling to Afghanistan to fight a jihad against the Soviet invaders, to those same jihadists returning to Pakistan and India to take up arms against those countries in the war for an Islamist nation. In this regard it is also important to investigate how much aid, comfort, training, and financing has been provided to these aspiring jihadists by the governments of the countries in the region in order to undermine the stability of other governments in South Asia.

W. LaRaia (✉)
Department of Law, Police Science, and Criminal Justice, John Jay College of Criminal Justice, New York, NY, USA
e-mail: wlaria@jjay.cuny.edu

M.R. Haberfeld, A. von Hassell (eds.), *A New Understanding of Terrorism*,
DOI 10.1007/978-1-4419-0115-6_17, © Springer Science+Business Media, LLC 2009

Colonial Influences in South Asia

The subcontinent of India was subject to Islamic influences during the past 1,000 years. In the tenth and eleventh centuries, Turks and Afghans invaded India and settled the area around Delhi (Simonsen & Spindlove, 2006). During this period, according to Simonsen and Spindlove (2006), there were two major cultural and religious systems – those of the Hindus and Muslims. The cultures shared trade and had a lasting influence on each other. The British appeared on the subcontinent in 1619 and, by the middle of the 1800s, controlled most of present-day India, Pakistan, and Bangladesh. In 1857, a bloody rebellion in North India, led by mutinous Indian soldiers, resulted in the transfer of all political power to the British Crown (Simonsen & Spindlove, 2006, p. 391).

It is important to view India, and later Pakistan, Bangladesh, and Jammu and Kashmir, from the perspective of their colonial history. The colonization process, according to Blackwell (2003, p. 394), "involved in no small measure the use of military power to advance and defend the economic interests of the colonizing power securing cheap raw materials and subsequently, opportunities for investment and markets for manufactured goods." Although this may be seen by many as a good thing to happen to a "backward" country, the colonizers failed to provide for the growth of institutions such as trade unions, political parties, and a free press (Blackwell, 2003). When the colonizers finally withdrew, the country was left lacking the political and social infrastructure, which is the hallmark of a democracy. Further, upon their withdrawal, the colonizers sought to maintain their relationships with those who they had placed in positions of power. To summarize, those groups upon whom the colonial power looked favorably became the dominant group upon the withdrawal of the colonizers. The only thing that changed was the flag under which the country operated.

The only exception to the above was the traditional group identities to tribes, clans, and other groups that, according to Blackwell (2003), cut across national boundaries established by the colonizers. Another important identity that most colonial occupiers were unable to change was a region's religious beliefs. This is especially true of Islam which Blackwell (2003) identifies as:

> one of the belief systems which has been allowed to remain intact in the colonial and post-colonial world. It provides an institutional form, a set of cultural practices, a way of life, and perhaps most importantly a source of faith and hope.... Autocratic rulers have used their own versions of it to justify their rule. The west has been happy with such rulers and with religious belief systems that can be so easily mobilised against atheist ideologies of communism and socialism (pp. 396–397).

The Formation of India, Pakistan, and Jammu and Kashmir

By the end of the 19th century, India had taken the first steps to gain independence. The Indian leader Mahatma Gandhi had used the Indian National Congress political party as a tool to achieve self-government. According to Simonsen and Spindlove (2006)

Following Gandhi's concepts of nonviolent resistance, the party used both parliamentary means and non-cooperation to compel the British to award India its independence. In 1947, India was awarded Commonwealth status and Jawaharlal Nehru became the first Prime Minister. A period of continuing and escalating bloody conflicts between the Hindus and Muslims finally led to the British partition of India (p. 391).

The subcontinent of India was divided along religious lines, for the most part, with the Muslim population moved into East Pakistan (now Bangladesh) and West Pakistan (which are separated by a distance of over 1,000 miles) where they had a majority and the Hindu population moving into India proper where Hindus were the majority. The forced movement of populations based upon their religion caused anger and animosity which continue to this day (Simonsen & Spindlove, 2006).

One of the major glitches brought about by this partitioning of the subcontinent occurred, in August 1947, in the case of the State of Jammu and Kashmir (J&K). The first Prime Minister of India, Jawaharlal Nehru, did not want to part with the state despite its majority Muslim population (77% according to the British census of 1941 (Bose, 2003)). Nehru was joined by Lord Mountbatten, the departing British administrator of India, in convincing the Hindu Raja of Kashmir to accede his state to India (Simonsen & Spindlove, 2006). In October of that year, several thousand Pashtun tribesmen from Pakistan invaded Jammu and Kashmir, and the Raja sent a request to India for military support to repulse the invaders. In January 1948, the United Nations Security Council established a Commission to mediate the issues in Kashmir. Later, the United Nations directed "the government of Pakistan to 'use its best endeavors' to 'secure from the State of Jammu and Kashmir of tribesmen and Pakistani nationals... who have entered the state for the purpose of fighting' " and the Government of India to put together a plan to withdraw its forces from Jammu and Kashmir and to conduct a plebiscite (election) to decide whether Jammu and Kashmir will join India or Pakistan" (Bose, 2003, p. 38). According to Bose (2003), "That the plebiscite was never held is regarded by Pakistanis... as proof of Indian perfidy.

> The typical Indian rejoinder is that since Pakistani forces never vacated the areas of J&K under their control, the first condition specified by the United Nations for holding the plebiscite was not fulfilled, and the blame lies with Pakistan. (p. 40)

A truce was declared in January 1949, which left a Line of Control (LOC) dividing the State of Jammu and Kashmir between India and Pakistan. According to Bose (2003):

> The ceasefire line left the Indians with the bulk of Jammu and Kashmir's territory (139,000 of 223,000 square kilometers, approximately 63 percent) and population. The Indians gained the prize piece of real estate, the Kashmir Valley, and they also controlled most of the Jammu and Ladakh regions. These areas became Indian Jammu and Kashmir (IJK) (p. 41).

A stalemate, briefly broken by invasions into the territory by Pakistani forces in 1965 and 1999, has existed since the truce. Bose (2003) states that:

The Kashmir conflict is driven by a complex of multiple, intersecting sources, and the Kashmir problem is, consequently, defined by multiple, interlocking dimensions. Nevertheless, the ruptured relationship between the IJK's people – especially its Kashmiri-speaking Muslim population – and the Indian Union is the core of the contemporary problem. ...the gap between democratic aspirations and a repressive reality remain wide in India's Kashmir (p. 51).

It is estimated that India presently has 400,000 troops stationed in IJK, a force that is two-thirds the size of Pakistan's entire army. According to Stern (2000):

The Pakistani government thus supports . . . irregulars [in IJK] as a relatively cheap way to keep Indian forces tied down. . . . [The support] includes, at minimum, assisting the militants' passage into Indian-held Kashmir. That much Pakistani officials will admit, at least privately. The US government believes that Pakistan also funds, trains, and equips the irregulars. Meanwhile, the Indian government claims that Pakistan uses them as an unofficial guerilla force to carry out "dirty tricks", murders, and terrorism in India (p. 116).

According to Maley (2003), "Kashmir has become a symbolic issue in the domestic politics of both India and Pakistan, and in neither country have political leaders shown much disposition to embrace imaginative approaches to the problem, lest they be accused of betraying fundamental national interests" (p. 210).

A History of Terrorism in Pakistan and India

Terrorism differs radically when one compares Pakistan's experience with India's. Pakistan has been rather unscathed by attacks inside the country from terrorist groups, while India has suffered greatly at the hands of terrorists who come into the country to engage in acts of terrorism. Although terrorist attacks have had an effect on India, they have not undermined the country's government or its capacity to be the region's financial leader.

In Pakistan, however, terrorist forces have undermined the government. As Maley (2003) stated:

The problem of terrorism in Pakistan has a paradoxical character, since its manifestations spring from two seemingly contradictory features of the political system. On the one hand, the weakness of the state has permitted sectarian terrorism to flourish in recent years. On the other hand, the staff of agencies of the state and most notably the Inter-Services Intelligence (ISI) directorate of the Pakistan Armed Forces, have played a role in nurturing terrorist groups committed to advancing Pakistan's geopolitical interests with respect to its eastern neighbour India and its western neighbour Afghanistan. As a result, the problem of terrorism in Pakistan is intimately related to the debilitating problems that afflict the country more generally (p. 207).

According to Maley (2003), "One of the most striking contrasts between India and Pakistan is that whereas [India] was largely successful in building on the legacy of . . . [institutions] inherited from British colonialism, Pakistan almost from its origin was faced with severe challenges in its search for appropriate political forms" (p. 207) for doing so. Further, the government of Pakistan has supported or sponsored terrorist groups, notably the Taliban and Al-Qaeda, who conduct their activities in neighboring countries (Maley, 2003).

Both sides of the conflict in Kashmir – the Indian Army and the Pakistani "mujahideen" – are targeting and killing thousands of civilians (Stern, 2000). According to Stern (2000):

> Pakistan has two reasons to support the so-called mujahideen. First, the Pakistani military is determined to pay India back for allegedly fomenting separatism in what was once East Pakistan and in 1971 became Bangladesh. Second, India dwarfs Pakistan in population, economic strength, and military might. In 1998 India spent about two percent of its $469 billion GDP [Gross Domestic Product] on defense, including an active armed force of more than 1.1 million personnel. In the same year, Pakistan spent about five percent of its GDP on defense, yielding an active armed force only half the size of India's (p. 115).

While the secular freedom fighters have taken a back seat in the fighting in Kashmir, Pakistan-based Islamist groups, partly funded by Pakistan, are now much more dominant (Stern, 2000)). According to Stern (2000):

> Whatever their exact numbers, these Pakistani militant groups – among them, Lashkar-i-Taiba and Harkat-ul-Mujahideen – pose a long-term danger to international security, regional stability, and especially Pakistan itself. Although the current agenda is limited to "liberating" Kashmir, which they believe was annexed by India illegally, their next objective is to turn Pakistan into a truly Islamic state. Islamabad supports these volunteers as a cheap way to keep India off balance (p. 118).

Additionally, the government of Pakistan allows religious education in the form of "madrasahs" to flourish in the place of a state-sponsored education program. Since education is not mandatory and it is believed that only 40% of Pakistanis are literate, madrasahs fill the gap. Most of these schools instruct only religious theory, failing to instruct on secular topics that can lead to viable employment opportunities (Stern, 2000). Some of the madrasahs instruct students the importance of Jihad (holy war) against nonbelievers. As Stern (2000) points out:

> Even worse, some extremist madrasahs preach jihad without understanding the concept: They equate jihad – which most Islamic scholars interpret as the striving for justice (and principally an inner striving to purify the self) – with guerrilla warfare. These schools encourage their graduates, who often cannot find work because of their lack of practical education, to fulfill their "spiritual obligations" by fighting against Hindus in Kashmir or against Muslims of other sects in Pakistan. Pakistani officials estimate that 10 to 15 percent of the country's tens of thousands of madrasahs espouse such extreme ideologies (p. 119).

It has been estimated that there are over 6000 madrasahs, with over 600,000 students, in Pakistan. The students who attend these schools are mostly from families who cannot afford to feed, clothe, or house them, so the parents dedicate the children to Allah. Of the 6000 madrasahs, almost 80% are located far away from the cities and away from prying eyes. It is in these schools where military training takes place (Qadir, 2001).

Lashkar-e-Taiba

According to most intelligence sources to date, Lashkar-e-Taiba (LeT) (the army of the pure) has been responsible for many attacks both in Jammu and Kashmir and in India itself, including the Siege of November 26, 2008. Lashkar-e-Taiba, the terrorist army of Markaz Dawa-Wal-Irshad (Center for Islamic Invitation and Guidance), is a Pakistan-based group composed of religious radicals which seeks to drive out Indian forces from Jammu and Kashmir, seeks the destruction of India, and has pledged to plant the 'flag of Islam' in Washington, Tel Aviv, and New Delhi (Stern, 2000). Based until 2002 near Lahore in Pakistan's Punjab Province, LeT carries out its attacks with two-man teams. Although nearly none of the attackers survive the attacks, LeT refuses to refer to their attacks as "suicide missions" since suicide is forbidden by their ultra-orthodox form of Sunni Islam; rather it refers to the missions as "daredevil" actions. LeT refers to the members of the group who engage in such missions as fedayeen (those who dare their lives) (Bose, 2003). The aim of the attackers is to penetrate the target and kill as many as possible, thereby inflicting a large psychological impact on its victims, without regard for their own lives.

According to Spindlove and Simonsen (2009), "LeT has 2,200 officers across the country and an estimated two dozen launching camps along the Line of Control. . . . Two LeT training camps are located in Muzaffarabad, the capital of Pakistan-held Kashmir" (p. 350).

Lashkar-e-Taiba has a rigorous training program for its officers. The training for future fedayeen consists of 2 months of instruction in the handling of AK-type rifles, light machine guns, pistols, rocket launchers, and hand grenades. In addition, LeT provides a 21-day program of instruction, called Duara Aam (basic phase), where the students "are motivated to internalize jihad as an exclusive, life-long mission, mainly through extensive exposure to semi-mythical stories glorifying the lives and exploits of Islam's historical martyrs" (Spindlove & Simonsen, 2009, p. 350). During Daura Khaas, the 3-month-long second phase, the students are given further weapons training as well as training in survival and ambush techniques (Spindlove & Simonsen, 2009).

Lashkar-e-Taiba has few problems raising money to finance its operations, despite being declared a banned Terrorist Organization in Pakistan. According to Stern (2000), "Lashkar-i-Taiba . . . raises funds on the Internet. Lashkar and its parent organization . . . have raised so much money that they are reportedly planning to open their own bank" (p. 120). In addition, Lashkar raises money to reward the families of the fedayeen killed in attacks which, according to Stern (2000), helps perpetuate the cycle of violence. Further, Lashkar-e-Taiba is also supported, financially and logistically, by Pakistan's Directorate of Inter-Services Intelligence Services (ISI). According to Spindlove and Simonsen (2009), "LeT has also become a focus for the Pakistani ISI to use in its campaign against India . . . the LeT is used to pit Muslims against Hindus, and placing bombs and targeting either of the religious groups they hope to succeed in their objective" (p. 343).

Attacks by Lashkar-e-Taiba Prior to November 2008

Prior to its attack on the various targets in Mumbai on November 26, Lashkar-e-Taiba has a very bloody history, both in Jammu and Kashmir and in India proper. The following is a list, by no means all inclusive, of attacks that LeT has taken credit for or which have been credibly linked to the group:

1999 – 2002	At least 55 fedayeen attacks were targeted against police, army, and government installations in Indian Jammu and Kashmir (IJK) (Bose, 2003).
December 13, 2001	Five armed attackers struck the Indian Parliament building, killing 14 guards and officials but no political leaders (Maley, 2003).
July, 2002	Attackers struck on the outskirts of Jammu in a slum district, killing 29 Hindus (Bose, 2003).
September 24, 2002	Raid on Akshardam Temple in Gujarat killed 28 Hindu worshippers (Anti-Defamation League, n.d.).
August 25, 2003	Double bombing in Mumbai killed 52 and wounded 175 (Anti-Defamation League, n.d.).
October 29, 2005	Three coordinated suicide bombs in New Delhi during Hindu festival of Diwali killed at least 63 and wounded over 200 (Anti-Defamation League, n.d.).
July 11, 2006	Bombs fashioned in pressure cookers exploded in seven commuter trains in an 11-minute period in Mumbai killing 209 and wounding 714 people (CNN.com, 2006).

Pakistan's Directorate of Inter-Services Intelligence (ISI)

Most non-Pakistanis acknowledge, but the Pakistan government generally denies, that its Directorate of Inter-Services Intelligence (ISI) of the Pakistani Armed Forces has played a significant role in supporting terrorist groups committed to furthering Pakistan's interests in relation to Kashmir, India, and Afghanistan (Maley, 2003). Lloyd (2002) states that:

> If the military has been the stabilizing element in Pakistani governance, it is safe to say that the Inter-Services Intelligence (ISI) has been the central destabilizing element. . . . Although its primary task is the collection of domestic and foreign intelligence, the ISI is also responsible for watching over foreigners, diplomats, the Pakistani media, and politically active segments of Pakistani society. The ISI's reach, however, also extends beyond Pakistan's borders
>
> The directorate's importance derives from the fact that the agency is charged with managing covert operations outside of Pakistan – whether in Afghanistan, Kashmir, or farther afield.

The ISI supplies weapons, training, advice and planning assistance to terrorists in Punjab and Kashmir, as well as the separatist movements in the Northeast frontier areas of India.[1] (p. 278)

The ISI had acquired vast resources and autonomy during the military regime of General Zia-ukl Haq during the 1980s and, along with the Central Intelligence Agency (CIA) of the United States, had a primary role in the war against Soviet occupation of Afghanistan (Bose, 2003). After the Soviets abandoned their quest to conquer Afghanistan, the ISI quickly turned its attention to a more important task, supporting the country's national cause to take back Kashmir. As Bose (2003) puts it:

In an unexpected windfall, for the ISI, sizeable numbers of youth from Indian Kashmir were, for the first time since 1947, prepared to take up arms against Indian rule. Between 1988 and 1990 ISI operatives assisted the JKLF [Jammu Kashmir Liberation Front], which saw Pakistan as a vital strategic ally, in launching the insurrection. …As the armed revolt rapidly acquired a popular character owing to the severe and indiscriminate nature of Indian repression during 1990, thousands of Valley youths started to cross the LOC [Line of Control] in search of weapons and training. The Kashmir *jihad* was on (p. 125–126).

Further, the arms caches that the United States has supplied in the fight against Soviet occupation of Afghanistan have been made available to insurgents. According to Simonsen and Spindlove (2006, p. 396), "The ISI made the city of Darra, Pakistan the primary source of weapons for the Sikh, Tamil, and Kashmiri liberation movements. …The availability of weapons … turned the major cities of Pakistan into shopping centers for international weapons dealing."

Simonsen and Spindlove (2006) further describes the crucial activities of the ISI in dealing with its long-range goal of sponsoring separatism and terrorism in Kashmir as follows:

- Religious radicalism was propagated in small, but lethal, doses to promote separatism and communal outlook.
- Training and indoctrination of selected leaders from the Kashmir Valley was arranged to create militant cadres.
- A large number of youths from the Kashmir Valley and Poonch sector were given extensive training in the use of automatic weapons, sabotage, and attacks on security forces.
- Automatic weapons and explosives were issued to these people.
- Special teams were trained to organize disruption and engineer incidents to damage the myth of a democratic and secular image for India and Kashmir (Simonsen & Spindlove, 2006, 396–397).

---

[1] Federation of American Scientists, 'Directorate for Inter-Services Intelligence', 27 November 2001, www.fas.org/irp/world/pakistan/isi

The Mumbai Massacre

On November 26, 2008, Mumbai City suffered an attack of terrorism that has caused a paradigm shift as to how emergency response can prevent and react to such events. As you can see from the history of the region described earlier in this chapter, long-standing hatred, attacks, and the counterattacks were planned and calculated over extended periods of time.

In order to adequately describe the Mumbai Massacre, it is necessary to work from the beginning or preparation stages that have been uncovered by investigators. The evidence that has been obtained during investigations of the routes toward the targets will be explored. The use of technology prior to and during the attack is revealed, and how the technology used affected the outcome. A time line of the events during the attack is measurable from the standpoint of surveillance cameras and media coverage. Included in the time line is the law enforcement response. The response will be analyzed and comparisons to differing response disciplines made. The lessons learned from the Mumbai Massacre should certainly jump start the training and retraining of law enforcement.

The 10 terrorists that arrived in Mumbai were trained to accomplish a mission. The mission on November 26, 2008 was to attack predetermined locations in Mumbai and kill as many as possible. Over an 18-month period, 500 commandos were trained to standards near the level of the elite US Navy SEALS. The training, done in three phases, was completed in two separate camps in Pakistan. The initial phase of training was basic physical fitness and firearms. The second phase comprised of marine navigation and swimming, and the third phase involved training to sabotage underwater installations. During the attack, all but one terrorist was killed. The surviving terrorist, Mohammad Ajmal Aamer Kasab, revealed that he received additional training in marine commando skills by a Lashkar-e-Taiba (LeT) instructor named Abu Yusuf. Yusuf, also known as Muzamil, has been named by Indian officials as one of the Pakistan-based LeT leaders that planned the attacks (Henderson & Nelson, 2008).

Several months prior to the Mumbai attack, police in India foiled a terrorist plot to attack a police camp in northern India and arrested five suspects. The suspects were arrested with AK-47 rifles, pistols, grenades, and ammunition, the same type of weapons carried by the 10 men who attacked Mumbai. One of the suspects had hand-drawn sketches of 8–10 Mumbai landmarks (Worth & Kumar, 2008). This information, along with messages intercepted by various intelligence agencies, prompted warnings to the government of Mumbai that future attacks would come by way of the sea. The warnings were then passed along to the businesses that may be potential targets. It has also been reported that some of the attackers may have been previously employed by the locations that were attacked. According to media reports, the terrorist captured in the November attacks told authorities that some members of the group checked into the Taj Mahal Hotel for 4 days sometime before the attack. There are reports that during the siege, when confronted by military forces, the terrorists were able to use doorways and paths hidden to ordinary guests. This prior reconnaissance allowed for ease of movement in the nonpublic portions of the structures (Gandossy, 2008). During the reconnaissance, security vulnerabilities would be noted and then exploited during the attack. Kasab told investigators that some of the attackers had stayed at the hotel and stockpiled weapons and explosives (Bradsher, 2008).

The Mumbai attack was not the first time that small arms and grenades were used. However, this attack does confirm the extensive use of modern technology. The new technology used can be traced to the preplanning stage of the attack. Information obtained during interviews and interrogation of the surviving assailant revealed that Google Earth images of the Mumbai targets were memorized by the attackers. Satellite telephones were also used as evidenced by their recovery after the events. Global positioning system (GPS) receivers were used to navigate to the targets as the attackers approached Mumbai by boat; additionally, in accordance with their fedayeen (daredevil rather than suicide attacker) beliefs, coordinates were also plugged into the GPS devices so that they could navigate an escape, should they survive. The use of cell phones to coordinate and communicate during the attacks gave the terrorists an advantage during the siege with the unwitting help of the local media. Industry competition creates the need for the media to broadcast live action video, thus allowing for instructions to be given to the terrorists from remote locations to evade and counter law enforcement and military efforts to contain and control the movements of the attackers.

There are a number of instances where terrorist plots and attacks have shown the intent to disrupt large cities. One such plot has a very eerie similarity to the events in Mumbai. A little more than 15 years before the Mumbai attacks, a plot was foiled in New York City that targeted specific locations, using similar weaponry and traveling to the locations using watercraft.

> The planned attack, which came to be known as the "Landmark" plot, called for several tactical teams to raid sites such as the Waldorf-Astoria, St. Regis, UN Plaza hotels, The Lincoln and Holland tunnels, and a midtown Manhattan waterfront heliport servicing business executives and VIPs traveling from lower Manhattan to various New York-area airports. The militants carried out extensive surveillance both inside and outside the target hotels using human probes, hand-drawn maps, and video surveillance. Detailed notes were taken on the layout and design of the buildings, with stairwells, ballrooms, security cameras, and personnel all reconnoitered (Burton & West, 2008, p. 1).

A Global Security & Intelligence Report produced by STRATFOR, a Strategic Forecasting Company, makes the following comparisons:

> The first relates to the target set. Both New York and Mumbai are the respective financial centers of their countries and home to their nations' major stock exchanges. In both cities, the planners had picked out high-profile soft targets – sites that have less security personnel and countermeasures than, say, a military installation or key government building. Softer security means gaining access to strategic assets and people is easier. Stratfor has long stressed the importance of maintaining vigilance at soft targets like hotels that cater to international guests, as these are likely targets for militant Islamists. Both plans also involved infiltrating hotel staff and booking rooms in the hotels to gain inside information and store supplies.

> The second similarity involves how both plans included peripheral targets to cause confusion and chaos and thus create a diversion from the main targets. In Mumbai, transportation

infrastructure like the city's main railway station was attacked, and militants detonated explosive devices in taxis and next to gasoline pumps. Meanwhile, roving gunmen attacked other sites around the city. In a country where coordination among first responders is already weak, the way the attackers fanned out across the city caused massive chaos and distracted security forces from the main prize: the hotels. Attacking Cama Hospital also sowed chaos, as the injured from one scene of attack became the targets of another while being rescued.

A third similarity exists in the geography of the two cities. In both plots, the use of watercraft is a distinctive tactical similarity. Watercraft gave militants access at unconventional locations where security would be more lax. Both Mumbai (a peninsula) and Manhattan (an island) offer plenty of points where militants can mount assaults from watercraft. Such an attack would not have worked in New Delhi or Bangalore; these are landlocked cities where militants would have had to enter by road, a route much more likely to encounter police patrols. Being centers of trade and surrounded by water, both Mumbai and New York have high levels of maritime traffic. This means infiltrating the area from the water would raise minimal suspicions, especially if the craft were registered locally (as was the case in the Mumbai attack). Such out-of-the box tactics take advantage of security services, which often tend to focus on established threats.

A fourth similarity lies in transportation. In addition to using watercraft, both plots involved the use of deceptive vehicles to maneuver around the city undetected. The Landmark plotters used taxis to conduct surveillance and planned on using a delivery van to approach the hotels. In Mumbai, the attackers planted bombs in taxis, and at least one group of militants hijacked a police van and used it to carry out attacks across the city. Using familiar vehicles like taxis, delivery vans, or police vans to carry out surveillance or attacks reduces suspicion and increases the element of surprise, allowing militants to stay under cover until the moment of attack (Burton & West, 2008, p. 3–4).

The Operation

The time line that follows has been determined by investigators based on their interrogations of Kasab and evidence recovered by investigators.

"The journey starts in a small boat that leaves Karachi, Pakistan at 0800 h on the morning of Saturday, November 22, 2008" (Ministry of External Affairs India, 2009, p. 4). On Sunday November 23, two days prior to the attacks, 10 terrorists and 7 crew members left Karachi, Pakistan, aboard the *al-Husseini*. Investigators later learned that the *al-Husseini* is owned by LeT commander Zaki-ur-Rehman-Lakhvi (Ranga, 2008). The vessel sailed unchecked by the Pakistan Coast Guard. It sailed in the Arabian Sea toward India for a nearly 500 nautical mile trip.

On Monday November 24, 2008, they hijacked a fishing trawler by luring its captain to the *al-Husseini* by hoisting a SOS flag, a distress signal that other mariners are required to answer. That trawler, named *Kuber*, was based in Porbandar, India, and had blown off course (CNN-IBN (2008)). The *Kuber's* captain and four crew members were murdered and the hijackers assumed their identities; the terrorists then spent the next 2 days sailing toward Mumbai.

On Wednesday November 26, 2008, the attackers boarded two inflatable rubber dinghies for the last five miles of their trip. The dinghies separated and landed at two different locations in Mumbai. One group landed at Badhwar Park near Cuffe Parade, an area of extreme poverty. As the men, all described as being in their early twenties, came to shore, they stripped off the orange windbreakers they were wearing. Now dressed in T-shirts and blue jeans they began offloading large heavy backpacks, each taking care to claim the pack assigned to him. The second dinghy came ashore at Sassoon Docks (Bradsher, 2008).

Upon arrival on shore, the 10 terrorists broke into five teams with the surviving terrorist, Mohammad Ajmal Amir Kasab, paired with the group leader, Ismail Khan. The teams then took taxis to their destinations. The terrorists placed IEDs in two of the taxis, killing the drivers (Ministry of External Affairs India, 2009, p. 5).

The terrorists identified by the Mumbai Police (Ministry of External Affairs India, 2009, pp. 1–3) are as follows:

Name	Age	Resident of	Name	Age	Resident of
Ismail Khan	25	NWFP, Pakistan	Mohammad Ajmal Amir Kasab	25	Punjab, Pakistan
Hafiz Arshad	23	Multan, Pakistan	Naser	23	Faisalabad, Pakistan
Shoaib	21	Sialkoat, Pakistan	Javed	22	Okara, Pakistan
Abdul Rehman	21	Arifwala, Pakistan	Fahadullah	23	Okara, Pakistan
Babar Imran	25	Multan, Pakistan	Nazir	28	Faisalabad, Pakistan

First Group

One group (Ismail Khan and Mohammad Ajmal Amir Kasab) arrived at the Chhatrapati Shivaji Terminus (CST). This train station is headquarters of Central Railways and more than 3.5 million passengers pass through the station daily. At about 21:20 h, the two terrorists entered the station and started firing indiscriminately (Ministry of External Affairs India, 2009, p. 5).

> They carried AK-56 assault rifles, a Chinese manufactured copy of the Russian AK-47. It holds a 30-round magazine with a firing rate of 600 to 650 rounds per minute. In addition, the terrorists each carried a duffel bag loaded with extra ammunition, an average of 300 to 400 rounds contained in as many as 12 magazines, along with half a dozen grenades, and one plastic explosive, or I.E.D. [Improvised Explosive Device].

> The attackers displayed a sophisticated level of training, coordination, and stamina. They fired in controlled, disciplined bursts. When [the NYPD representatives days later] toured the hotels and railway stations, they saw evidence that shots were fired in groups of three aimed at head level. With less experienced shooters, you'd see bullet holes in the ceiling and floor. This group had extensive practice. And the number of casualties shows it (Kelly, 2009, pp. 1–2).

These terrorists were challenged by a small number of policemen at the station. Some of the only security video footage released after the attacks show pictures of the two assailants walking through the train station. Police were viewed as they took cover, engaged targets, and retreated during the attempt to stop the gunmen (Telegraph.co.uk, 2008). A photographer from the Mumbai Mirror tabloid was working across the street when the attack at the station unfolded. He followed the sound of the gunfire and reported that "They were firing from their hips. Very professional. Very cool." For more than 45 minutes he followed as they moved from platform to platform shooting and throwing grenades (Associated Press, 2008).

Soon after they met resistance from railway police, the duo walked out of the station and entered Cama Hospital from the rear entrance. There they encountered resistance from police and a gun battle ensued. The information that was obtained during the interview and interrogation of Kasab in regard to the Cama attack indicated that the attackers were instructed by their Pakistani handlers to avoid Muslim casualties, so when they saw several burka-clad women and children at the hospital, they decided to leave. At Cama Hospital, a group of policemen engaged the two terrorists, who were on the terrace, for 45 min. Finally, the duo threw hand grenades, which killed two policemen and injured several others. After leaving Cama Hospital, the duo hid behind bushes and opened fire on a police van (Ali, 2009).

The police van, which was responding to the report of gunfire, carried three senior counterterrorism officers and four police officers was ambushed. Five of the officers were killed. The assailants pulled the bodies of three officers from the van and hijacked the police vehicle (Ministry of External Affairs India, 2009, p. 6). The surviving police officers inside the van were believed dead by the attackers. One of those officers, a constable, overheard the terrorists as they scoffed when they saw that the police officers they had killed had been wearing bulletproof vests, "One of them laughed and said, 'Look, they're wearing jackets.'" The constable was in the backseat along with an officer who was unconscious and both were thought dead. The constable had been hit by three bullets, two of which left his hands nearly paralyzed. At one point, a cell phone rang from the pocket of the unconscious officer. The gunman in the front seat turned around and fired. "He didn't even look back properly, he just fired," the constable said. "I think my colleague had been still alive. He died with those bullets." The journey inside the van took about 10 min. One of the men drove the van, while the other pointed his rifle out of the window and fired on a crowd milling outside a theater (Kakade, 2008). The Metrobig Cinema can be described as a large multiplex movie theater. Reports state that as many as 10 people were shot and killed outside the theater. When one of the van's tires went flat, they abandoned the vehicle. The terrorists hijacked another car and drove away. The constable inside the van made his way to the radio and transmitted the location and vehicle description to his colleagues. Police set up barricades and waited for the car to arrive. On seeing the police barricade, the militants tried (m)aking a U-turn and began to fire on police. Police, now ready for them, countered the attack with more fire. During the effort, one officer was killed and one was injured. One of the two terrorists was killed and the only terrorist to survive the day was injured and taken into custody (Ahmed, 2008). Inside the hijacked vehicle, police recovered two Kalashnikov rifles, eight magazines, two pistols, ammunition, empty cases, and five hand grenades from the two terrorists (Ministry of External Affairs India, 2009, p. 6).

Second Group

While the first squad was attacking the train station, Cama Hospital, and the cinema, another team (Hafiz Arshad and Naser) attacked the Leopold Café and Bar. The café, a fixture in Mumbai for 130 years, is commonly known as "Leo's" and is a famous tourist restaurant, which is popular to foreigners as well as Indians. Two terrorists threw one hand grenade and fired their assault rifles into the crowd (Ministry of External Affairs India, 2009, p. 5). Eyewitness accounts from patrons inside the café reiterate the point that the terrorists picked targets that would give them a maximum body count. The café was crowded and patrons were located on two levels. One witness recalls, "The place was packed at the time. I closed the doors behind us," he said. "It was obvious after a couple of magazine changes that these guys weren't going to leave; they were walking through the restaurant and indiscriminately shooting at the bodies. I realized just after I came out of the cupboard and had a look that they were shooting the bodies that were actually on the floor over and over again." He said the men continued to spray bullets from their rifles for around eight and a half minutes more (Simpson, 2008). Investigators determined that 10 people died and many were injured inside this location (Ministry of External Affairs India, 2009, p. 6).

Leaving the Leopold Café and Bar at about 21:40 h, the terrorists then ran to the Taj Mahal Hotel, located about a half of a kilometer away, where they joined a second team (Shoaib and Javed). The web site for the hotel provides the following description:

> Since it opened in 1903, the Taj Mahal Palace & Tower has created its own unique history. From Maharajas and Princes to various Kings, Presidents, CEOs and entertainers, the Taj has played the perfect host, supportive of their every need. The hotel is an architectural marvel and brings together Moorish, Oriental and Florentine styles and offers panoramic views of the Arabian Sea and the Gateway of India, the hotel is a gracious landmark of the city of Mumbai, showcasing contemporary Indian influences along with beautiful vaulted alabaster ceilings, onyx columns, graceful archways, hand-woven silk carpets, crystal chandeliers, a magnificent art collection, an eclectic collection of furniture, and a dramatic cantilevered stairway. The hotel has 565 rooms including 46 suites along with twelve ballrooms with a capacity ranging from 25 to 500 persons auditorium style or 18 to 2000 persons for cocktails or receptions (www.tajhotels.com).

The Taj Mahal was attacked by the pair of terrorists. The first pair entered the main lobby at 21:38 h and opened fire, killing 20 people in the first few minutes. The second pair entered the hotel from the North Court entrance at 21:43 h and fired indiscriminately and hurled grenades (Ministry of External Affairs India, 2009, p. 7). One eyewitness told the BBC that he had seen a gunman opening fire in the Taj Mahal's lobby. "We all moved through the lobby in the opposite direction and another gunman then appeared towards where we were moving and he started firing immediately in our direction" (BBC News, 2008). Guests and staff from the hotel were herded into different sections or areas of various sizes. One group of about fifty near the pool retreated to the second floor of a restaurant and hid under tables (Associated Press, 2008). A manager, who runs the company that owns the Taj Mahal, said the terrorists appeared to have scouted their targets in advance. "They seem to know their way around the back office, the kitchen. There has been a considerable amount of planning," he told a news conference (Badam, 2008). The four terrorists moved to the Heritage Wing and set fire to that portion of the hotel, gutting the first, fifth, and sixth floors (Ministry of External Affairs India, 2009, p. 7). The Taj attack turned into a hostage situation since many guests locked themselves in their rooms and others were sequestered in different parts of the hotel. The operation lasted over 50 hours until it was brought to an end the morning of November 29. Although the terrorists killed 32 persons including hotel guests and staff, nearly 450 guests were rescued. The four terrorists were killed during this operation and police recovered four Kalashnikov assault rifles, eight magazines, three pistols and magazines, a number of unexploded grenades, live and empty cases of ammunition, mobile telephones, and one GPS instrument (Ministry of External Affairs India, 2009, p. 8).

The terrorists continued to use technology as a tool in their attack at the hotel. During the attacks the terrorists were in touch with their controllers in Pakistan via telephone. They received a stream of instructions and it was apparent that the controllers were monitoring Indian television channels (Ministry of External Affairs India, 2009, p. 8).

The following consists of transcripts and translations of selected intercepted conversations between the terrorist group at the Taj and their handlers:

November 27, 2008 at 01:08 h:

Handler:	How many hostages do you have?
Terrorist:	We have one from Belgium. We have killed him. There was one chap from Bangalore. He could be controlled only with a lot of effort.
Handler:	I hope three [sic] is no Muslim amongst them?
Terrorist:	No, none (Ministry of External Affairs India, 2009, p. 54).

November 27, 2008 at 01: 37 h:

Handler:	The ATS [Anti-Terrorism Squad] Chief has been killed. Your work is very important. Allah is helping you. The "Vazir" [Minister] should not escape. Try to set the place on fire.
Terrorist:	We have set fire in four rooms.
Handler:	People shall run helter skelter when they see the flames. Keep throwing a grenade every 15 min or so. It will terrorize. Here, talk to "Baba."
Handler (2):	A lot of policemen and Navy personnel have covered the entire area. Be brave! (Ministry of External Affairs India, 2009, p. 53–54)

November 27, 2008 at 03:10 h:

Terrorist:	Greetings!
Handler:	Greetings! There are three Ministers and one Secretary of the Cabinet in your hotel. We don't know in which room.
Terrorist:	Oh! That is good news! It is the icing on the cake.
Handler:	Find those 3–4 persons and get whatever you want from India.
Terrorist:	Pray that we find them.
Handler:	Do one thing. Throw one or two grenades on the Navy and police teams, which are outside.
Terrorist:	Sorry. I simply can't make out where they are (Ministry of External Affairs India, 2009, p. 51).

It was not until 05:55 h on November 28 that the police asked the media to stop live telecast of the happenings at the Taj (zeenews.com, 2008).

Following the assault, the police recovered four Kalashnikov assault rifles, eight magazines, three pistols and magazines, a number of unexploded grenades, live and empty cases of ammunition, mobile telephones, and one GPS instrument (Ministry of External Affairs India, 2009, p. 8).

Third Group

While the first group was attacking the train station, the Cama Hospital, and the cinema and the second group was attacking the Leopold Café and the Taj Mahal Hotel, at 22:00 h, the third group, consisting of two terrorists (Abdul Rehman and Fahadullah), entered the Oberoi–Trident Hotel complex. The Oberoi Hotel is located in Nariman Point, the main financial district of Mumbai, and according to its web site the hotel:

> offers impeccable service, understated luxury and excellent facilities. The Oberoi has 333 guestrooms and contains the Kandahar Restaurant. The Trident claims to have 'The best view of Mumbai' and the hotel, according to its website, delivers a memorable experience for guests – from excellent amenities to warm and friendly service. Apart from the 547 well-appointed rooms, the hotel features multiple restaurants, a bar, and modern fitness facilities (www.tridenthotels.com).

According to the hotel company's chairman, P.R.S. Oberoi, "two gunmen, slender and in their mid-20s, ran up the circular driveway at the entrance to the Trident. They shot the security guard and two bellhops. The hotel had metal detectors, but none of its security personnel carried weapons because of the difficulties in obtaining gun permits from the Indian government" (Anand, Pokharel, Rosenberg, Trofimov, & Wonacott, 2008). Oberoi continued to describe that "the gunmen raced through the marble-floored lobby, past the grand piano into the adjoining Verandah restaurant, firing at the guests and shattering the windows. At the end of the lobby, they burst into a bar called the Opium Den, shooting dead a hotel staff member" (Anand et al., 2008). The attackers preyed on a group of guests, running after, and shooting them, killing most but not all of them. Reporters of the Wall Street Journal were able to interview one of the guests that survived the shooting and the dialog between the hotel guests and the terrorists indicate that retaliation was one of the purposes for the attacks.

> The gunmen returned to the Verandah, climbed a staircase, dashed down a corridor lined with jewelry and clothes shops, and stopped in front of the glass doors of Tiffin Restaurant, a swanky restaurant with a sushi bar in the Oberoi hotel. There they killed four of six friends who live in south Mumbai and had just settled down at a table near the front door. One member of the group, a mother of two, threw herself to the ground and shut her eyes, pretending to be dead. The men circled the restaurant, firing at point blank range into anyone who moved before rushing upstairs to an Indian restaurant called Kandahar.

> At the Kandahar, workers ushered those guests closest to the kitchen inside it. The assailants jumped in front of another group that tried to run out the door, shouting "Stop" in Hindi. They corralled 16 diners and led them into a stairwell and up to the 20th floor. One man in the group dialed his wife in London and told her he'd been taken hostage but was OK. Everybody drop your phones," one of the assailants shouted, apparently overhearing. Phones clattered to the floor as the three women and 13 men dug through their purses and pockets and obeyed.

> On the 20th floor, the gunmen shoved the group out of the stairwell. They lined up the 13 men and three women and lifted their weapons. "Why are you doing this to us?" a man called out. "We haven't done anything to you." "Remember Babri Masjid?" one of the gunmen shouted, referring to a 16th-century mosque built by India's first Mughal Muslim emperor and destroyed by Hindu radicals in 1992. "Remember Godhra?" the second attacker asked, a reference to the town in the Indian state of Gujarat where religious rioting that evolved into an anti-Muslim program began in 2002.

> "We are Turkish. We are Muslim," someone in the group screamed. One of the gunmen motioned for two Turks in the group to step aside. Then they pointed their weapons at the rest and squeezed the triggers. A few minutes later they walked upstairs to the terrace. Unbeknownst to the terrorists, four of the men were still alive. The terrorists holed up on the 16th and 18th floors where they kept many guests hostage (Anand et al., 2008).

The following consists of transcripts and translations of selected intercepted conversations between the terrorist team at the Oberoi–Trident complex and their handlers:

November 27, 2008 at 03:53 h:

Handler:	Brother Abdul. The media is comparing your action to 9/11. One senior police officer has been killed.
Abdul Rehman:	We are on the 10th/11th floor. We have five hostages.
Handler (2):	Everything is being recorded by the media. Inflict maximum damage. Keep fighting. Don't be taken alive.

Handler:	Kill all hostages, except the two Muslims. Keep your phone switched on so that we can hear the gunfire.
Fahadullah:	We have three foreigners including women. From Singapore and China.
Handler:	Kill them.

(Voices of Fahadullah and Abdul Rehman directing hostages to stand in a line, and telling two Muslims to stand aside. Sound of gunfire. Cheering voices in background. Kafa hands phone to Zarar)

| Zarar: | Fahad, find the way to go downstairs (Dossier, 2009, pp. 52–53). |

National Security Guard (NSG) Commandos took charge of the operations on the morning of November 27, 2008. The operations were concluded after 42 hours on the afternoon of November 28, 2008. The two terrorists were finally killed but, during the attack of the Oberoi–Trident Hotel complex, a total of 32 persons were killed, 10 of which were hotel staff. Police recovered two Kalashnikov rifles, six magazines of which two were loaded, a number of empty cases, and hand grenades (Dossier, 2009, p. 9).

Fourth Group

While the first team was attacking the train station, hospital, and cinema; the second team attacked the Leopold and the Taj hotel; and the third team was conducting its operations at the Trident–Oberoi hotel complex, the last two-man team (Babar Imran and Nazir) attacked a five-story building named the Chabad House. The Chabad House is one of eight synagogues in Mumbai and has been described as the epicenter of the Jewish community in the city. The facility, located near the Leopold Café, had an educational center, a synagogue, a hostel and offered drug prevention services.

During the attack, the terrorists took advantage of the fact that local security forces were operating in several locations throughout the city, some nearby. The building was attacked and six of its occupants, including Rabbi Gavriel Noach Holtzberg and his wife, Rivka, who was 5-months pregnant, were killed. Their two-year-old son Moshe survived the attack after being rescued by his Indian nanny. During the siege, a US Chabad official Rabbi Levi Shemtov talked with one of the terrorists, calling on Holtzberg's cell phone. The Federal Bureau of Investigation (FBI) and other negotiation experts helped guide him through the process which included around five phone calls. Having to find an Urdu speaker to speak with him, they were unable to directly speak to any of the hostages, but Shemtov did say he heard the voice of one woman screaming in English, "please help immediately" (Kalman, Weichselbaum, & Boyle, 2008).

Shortly before dawn on Friday, November 28, Indian security forces began an attack on the Chabad House which would not end until sundown that evening. Television footage showed troops rappelling from a helicopter into the building, and soldiers on the ground closing in. Throughout this operation, the terrorists, like the other teams, received instructions over the telephone from their controllers. The controllers warned the terrorists about the use of helicopters and about the landing of commandos on the terrace of the building.

The following is a transcript of conversations between the terrorists at the Chabad House and their handlers:

November 27, 2008 at 19:45 h:

Terrorist: Greetings. What did the Major General say?
Handler: Greetings. The Major General directed us to do what we like. We should not worry. The operation has to be concluded by tomorrow morning. Pray to God. Keep two magazines and three grenades aside, and expend the rest of your ammunition (Ministry of External Affairs India, 2009, p. 51).

At the same date and time, the following was recorded:

Handler: Keep in mind that the hostages are of use only as long as you do not come under fire because of their safety. If you are still threatened, then don't saddle yourself with the burden of the hostages, immediately kill them.
Terrorist: Yes, we shall do accordingly, God willing.
Handler: The Army claims to have done the work without any hostage being harmed. Another thing; Israel has made a request through diplomatic channels to save the hostages. If the hostages are killed, it will spoil relations between India and Israel.
Terrorist: So be it, God willing.
Handler: Stay alert (Ministry of External Affairs India, 2009, p. 54).

November 27, 2008 at 22:26 h:

Handler: Brother, you have to fight. This is a matter of prestige of Islam. Fight on so that your fight becomes a shining example. Be strong in the name of Allah. You may feet [sic] or sleepy but the Commandos of Islam have left everything behind. Their mothers, their fathers. Their homes. Brother, you have to fight for the victory of Islam. Be strong.
Terrorist: Amen! (Ministry of External Affairs India, 2009, p. 52)

Following the siege, police recovered 2 Kalashnikov rifles, 4 magazines, 3 pistols, about 250 rounds of ammunition, 4 mobile phones, and 1 GPS instrument (Ministry of External Affairs India, 2009, p. 9).

The Aftermath

Once the authorities gained control of the locations that were attacked the investigations began. The evidence left behind has been analyzed and Mumbai Police have revealed what they know about the explosive devices. The Sakaal Times (2009) reports the findings as:

> The group of ten terrorists that carried out the attacks was provided with ten Improvised Explosive Devices (IEDs) from their Pakistani masters and handlers. All of the bombs used during the Mumbai terror attacks were of similar nature and all were RDX-based, investigations by Mumbai Police and intelligence agencies have revealed. Seven of these bombs had been detonated and three were recovered later. "The three devices are similar and bear the unmistakable signature of having been made by the same individual or same team at the same time," the investigators disclosed. Each IED weighed approximately eight kilograms and each contained four to five kilograms of tightly packed black, greasy RDX. Each had a black colored programmable electronic timer switch with five wires numbered one to five. Wires number one and four were found connected in all the devices while numbers two, three and five were left unconnected. Each device had two detonators and steel ball bearings of four to six mm diameter, which were embedded and placed around the charge. The power source was two 9-volt batteries. The timer bore instructions in Urdu [the official language of Pakistan] for setting the time (Sakaal Times, 2009).

Information in the Dossier provides tangible evidence and its relationship to the terrorists and their suspected controllers and handlers. The pistols recovered from the scenes were "Diamond Nedi Frontier Arms Company, Peshawar" (Peshawar is in Pakistan). The hand grenades that were recovered were made by Arges, an Austrian company. Arges had given a franchise to manufacture hand grenades to a Pakistan Ordinance Factory near Rawalpindi. The satellite phone recovered from the fishing trawler, *Kuber*, was used to call telephone numbers that have linkages with the LeT. A GPS set was recovered that reveals that the route was set from about 150 NM south east of Karachi, Pakistan, to Mumbai. These and other items for personal use contained unmistakable signs of having been manufactured in Pakistan (Ministry of External Affairs India, 2009, pp. 10–11).

Shortly after the attack on the Taj Mahal Hotel, Indian agencies were able to intercept mobile telephone calls made from and to the hotel. The controllers/handlers used the virtual number to contact a mobile telephone which was with one of the terrorists. This conversation was intercepted and, thereafter, all calls made through the virtual number were also intercepted and recorded. The transcripts of the conversations show that the terrorists were being instructed and guided by their controllers/handlers. It is interesting to note that the virtual number of the terrorist's phone has been traced back to the country code (1) for the United States and the area code (201) for Northern New Jersey (Ministry of External Affairs India, 2009, p. 12).

Attacks Used Conventional Weapons but Modern Technology

Terrorists certainly rely on new technology. The terrorists who struck Mumbai stunned authorities not only with their use of sophisticated weaponry but also with their comfort with modern technology.

The terrorists navigated across the Arabian Sea to Mumbai from Karachi, Pakistan, with the help of a global positioning system handset. While under way, they communicated using a satellite phone with those in Pakistan who are believed to have coordinated the attacks. They recognized their targets and knew the most direct routes to reach them in part because they had studied satellite photos from Google Earth.

Finally and, perhaps, most significantly, throughout the 3-day siege at two luxury hotels and a Jewish center, the Pakistani-based handlers communicated with the attackers using Internet phones that complicated efforts to trace and intercept calls.

Those handlers who were apparently watching the attacks unfold live on television were able to inform the attackers of the movement of security forces from news accounts and provide the gunmen with instructions and encouragement, authorities said.

Hasan Gafoor, Mumbai's police commissioner, said that as once complicated technologies – including global positioning systems and satellite phones – have become simpler to operate, terrorists, like everyone else, have become adept at using them. "Well, whether terrorists or common criminals, they do try to be a step ahead in terms of technology," he said (Kahn, 2008).

Indian security forces surrounding the buildings were able to monitor the terrorists' outgoing calls by intercepting their cell phone signals, but Indian police officials said those directing the attacks, who are believed to be from Lashkar-e-Taiba (LeT), a militant group based in Pakistan, were using a 'Voice over Internet Protocol' (VoIP) phone service, which has complicated efforts to determine their whereabouts and identities.

VoIP services, in which conversations are carried over the Internet as opposed to conventional phone lines or cell phone towers, are increasingly popular with people looking to save money on long distance and international calls, but the same services are also increasingly popular with criminals and terrorists, a trend that worries some law enforcement and intelligence agencies. "It's a concern," said one Indian security official, who spoke anonymously because the investigation was continuing. "It's not something we have seen before" (Kahn, 2008).

In Mumbai, authorities have declined to disclose the names of the VoIP companies whose services the Lashkar-e-Taiba (LeT) handlers used, but reports in Indian news media have said the calls have been traced to companies in New Jersey and Austria. Yet investigators have said they are convinced that the handlers who directed the attacks were actually sitting somewhere in Pakistan during the calls. One senior Lashkar-e-Taiba (LeT) leader who American officials believe may have played a key role in planning the Mumbai attacks is Zarrar Shah. Mr. Shah, known to be a specialist in communications technology, may have been aware of the difficulties in tracing VoIP (Kahn, 2008).

Target Selection

During testimony before the US Senate Committee on Homeland Security and Governmental Affairs on January 28, 2009, Brian Michael Jenkins of the RAND Corporation, a nonprofit research organization, elaborated on how terrorists continue to focus on "soft targets" that offer high body counts and that have iconic value. Jenkins stated:

> Nationally and internationally recognized venues that offer ease of access, certainty of tactical success, and the opportunity to kill in quantity will guide target selection. Public spaces are inherently hard to protect. Major investments in target hardening make sense for government only when these provide a net benefit, that is, when they do not merely displace the risk to another equally lucrative and accessible target (Jenkins, 2009, p. 2).

Warnings issued by the government necessitate that security managers assess the risk based upon the likelihood that they will be a target and then conduct a cost/benefit analysis of possible responses to the risk. There is also the opportunity to lose patience waiting and wondering if the warning is credible. The bottom line is, how long do we keep up this level of security.

The Chairman of the company that owns the Taj Mahal Hotel in Mumbai, Mr. Ratan Tata, stated to a CNN reporter. "It's ironic that we did have such a warning and we did have some measures," Tata said. "People couldn't park their cars in the portico where you had to go through a metal detector,' he said, explaining one of the measures. "But if I look at what we had – which all of us complained about – it could not have stopped what took place. They didn't come through that entrance," he said, referring to the entrance that had a metal detector. He did not identify which entrance had the security device. "They came from somewhere in the back. They planned everything," he said of the attackers. "I believe the first thing they did, they shot a sniffer dog and his handler. They went through the kitchen, they knew what they were doing." He did not elaborate on the hotel's warning or when the security measures were enacted (Gandossy, 2008).

Law enforcement officers need to be aware that the terrorists do not function with the mindset that they are accustomed to seeing in ordinary criminals. The terrorist commandos were mentally and operationally prepared for dramatic encounters with the law enforcement and military personnel who responded. This point was underscored by the hasty ambush of a responding police vehicle, resulting in the death of police officers, "Rather than remaining hidden and let the police vehicle pass by safely, running its lights and siren furiously, the terrorists chose the brazen tactic of assaulting the police directly" (Trindal, 2009, p. 7).

There were in fact a number of heroic events that occurred during the attacks and two such events occurred within a short time of one another. The first such event has been outlined previously when the officer left for dead inside the hijacked police van was, despite being wounded, able to radio his colleagues and tell them the direction and type of vehicle in which the terrorists were travelling, thus preventing them from reaching another target location and saving an unknown number of lives. Additionally, the information permitted the Mumbai Police officials to know the direction of travel of the terrorists and set up a roadblock.

> That hasty roadblock, in fact captured the only terrorist to be taken alive. When one of the terrorists' stolen sedans turned onto Marine Drive en route to the next target, the driver realized that they were facing a police roadblock. During the attempt to turn around, a vicious firefight ensued between police and the terrorists. In an uncoordinated albeit heroic effort to stop the terrorist team, officers assaulted the vehicle – however, as is customary

in India, not all of the police officers were armed with firearms. But they fought with what they had. [Assistant] Sub-Inspector Tukaram Omble, despite being unarmed, clutched the barrel of an AK rifle held by terrorist [Mohammad] Ajmal Amir Kasab; he absorbed six fatal shots, but other police officers clubbed Kasab into submission. Abu Ismail Khan, the other member of that terrorist team, was killed during the police counterattack (Trindal, 2009, p. 6).

Mumbai Police Response

Part of the success of the terrorists comes from the response of the Mumbai Police and part of their failure may be attributed to police training and equipment. A review of the events surrounding the attacks was published in a Global Security & Intelligence Report produced by STRATFOR. The report states:

> Among the most troubling aspects of the Mumbai attack were accounts by journalists of Indian police shooting at the attackers and missing them. Some journalists have said this failure can be explained by the fact that many Indian police officers are armed with anti-quated revolvers and Lee-Enfield rifles. The Lee-Enfield is an accurate and reliable battle rifle that shoots a powerful cartridge, the .303 British. Like the 30–06 Springfield and the .308 Winchester, the .303 British is a man stopper and is deadly out to long ranges. The kinetic energy produced by such cartridges will penetrate body armor up to the heavy Type III level, and the amount of kinetic energy they impart will often even cause considerable shock trauma damage to people wearing heavy body armor.

> The .303 British is a formidable round that has killed a lot of people and big game over the past century. Afghan sharpshooters used the Lee-Enfield with great success against the Soviets, and the Taliban are still using it against coalition forces in Afghanistan. There is also nothing wrong with a .38 revolver in capable hands. The problem, then, lies in the hands – more specifically, in the training – of the officers so armed. If a police officer does not have the marksmanship to kill (or even hit) a suspect at 20 or 30 meters with aimed fire from a battle rifle, there is little chance he can control the automatic fire from an assault rifle or submachine gun effectively. In the end, the attackers outclassed the Indian police with their marksmanship far more than they outclassed them with their armaments (Burton & Stewart, 2009).

The lack of a specialized police response unit hampered efforts to thwart the attack in Mumbai. Dr. Neil C. Livingstone (2009), an expert in terrorism and counterterrorism, found that:

> The city of Mumbai has no rapid-response anti-terrorism or SWAT (Special Weapons and Tactics) unit, so – after much hand-wringing and bureaucratic bickering – a federal unit, the Marine Commando Force (MCF), was activated. But the MCF is based in India's capital, New Delhi, which is 3 h away from Mumbai by air, and some reports suggest that the Indian Navy wanted a written request from the government before it would release the commandos for the operation.

> A further complication was that the MCF has no dedicated aviation resources of its own, or even the authority to requisition a commercial aircraft, and was forced to wait for a military transport to be dispatched from another location. Moreover, once the MCF reached Mumbai, the local transport it was provided was in the form of buses rather than helicopters. The bottom line is that it took 9 h for the government commandos to reach the scene, and it is not unfair to suggest that each hour's delay clearly resulted in more casualties.

The local police who initially responded to the attacks – and for hours were the only security forces on the scene – were hampered by inadequate communications. In addition, they possessed only limited body armor (which was improperly strapped on), substandard weapons, few, if any, scopes for their rifles, and no night-vision equipment. It goes without saying that they also lacked flash-bang grenades, pin-hole cameras, robots that could be used to search for and detonate explosives, and equipment that reads the heat signatures of bodies; all of these and other high-tech equipment items are now standard issue for Western SWAT and elite anti-terrorism units.

The local police also were not trained in room-clearing operations and/or hostage negotiations. Some individual Indian police officers demonstrated commendable bravery, but many of their actions were uncoordinated and even, in some situations, counterproductive. In several locations, the Mumbai police even failed to set up adequate perimeters around the attack sites (Livingstone, 2009, p. 9).

Questions were also raised as to why it took so long for the commandos to arrive on scene. According to the *Times of India* (2008), the Mumbai Chief Minister, Vilasrao Deshmukh, is briefed on the attack at 21:30 h but he waits until 23:00 h to request NSG commandos from the Indian Union Home Minister, Shivraj Patil. Patil then directs 200 commandos be dispatched to Mumbai. By the time that the commandos are prepared for action and a transport plane has been located and fueled, four and a half hours have passed. It takes the plane three and one half hours to fly to Mumbai and another 90 min for the commandos to be in place – nine and one half hours had elapsed after the start of the attacks (The Times of India, 2008).

It is extremely important to point out that there are very few countermeasures that could have been taken that would have stopped or even helped curtail the assaults. Metal detectors at the entrances, jersey-type barriers, photo ID checks, and the like would not stop an attacker from walking onto or into the properties and opening fire killing and wounding innocent people as they go.

Lessons Learned

The lesson learned from the attack should be addressed at the national (or federal) level, the state level, the local (or municipal) level, and lastly by the public sector.

This is an excerpt from Chief Intelligence Officer Donald Van Duyn of the Federal Bureau of Investigation (FBI) when he appeared before the US Senate Committee on Homeland Security and Governmental Affairs on January 8, 2009:

The principal lesson from the Mumbai attacks reinforces the notion that a small number of trained and determined attackers with relatively unsophisticated weapons can do a great deal of damage. Other terrorist groups, to include al-Qa'ida and its affiliates, will no doubt take note of the Mumbai attacks and attempt to emulate them. What this means for the FBI is that we must continue to maintain a high level of vigilance for all indications of developing terrorist activity. The planning for the Mumbai attacks probably unfolded over a fairly long period with careful surveillance of the target sites and transportation routes. The FBI must continue to work closely with its state, local, and tribal law enforcement partners, especially in our Joint Terrorism Task Forces, to follow up on indications of suspicious activity that could potentially be related to terrorism. Similarly, we must carefully monitor travel to participate in terrorist activities or fighting overseas, such as that recently reported by ethnic Somalis traveling to fight in Somalia. As the experience of the United Kingdom indicates, individuals who receive terrorist training or experience overseas clearly represent a threat. In addition, we need to continue to heighten the public's awareness to the continued threat of terrorist attacks and the need to report suspicious incidents.

As an example of how we have already begun implementing these lessons learned, the FBI worked immediately after the attacks to identify any US links to the planners and attackers. Whenever possible, all information was shared with the Indian government to aid in its investigation. The FBI disseminated more than 15 intelligence reports to the USIC [United States Intelligence Community] based on information collected in Mumbai from both interviews and physical evidence. These classified reports are available to cleared state, local and tribal law enforcement personnel in Joint Terrorism Task Forces and in State and Local Fusion Centers. In addition, the FBI and the Department of Homeland Security (DHS) jointly issued an unclassified alert about the attacks to state, local, and tribal officials on November 27, 2008. The FBI and DHS also issued an Intelligence Bulletin on December 3, 2008, to building owners and operators, as well as the US law enforcement community, to alert them to preliminary findings regarding the techniques and tactics used by terrorists in the Mumbai attacks. The bulletin indicated that the FBI and DHS had no credible or specific information that terrorists were planning similar operations against similar buildings in the United States, but urged local authorities and building owners and operators to be aware of potential attack tactics.

Another lesson learned from the Mumbai attacks is that terrorist groups that appear to be primarily a threat to their surrounding localities can sometimes have broader aspirations. Although (LeT) has historically focused its attacks against Indian forces in the Kashmir region, the Mumbai attacks reinforce the reality that (LeT) has the capability to operate outside its home base. The group did so in 2001 with an attack on the Indian Parliament building in New Delhi and is suspected of having been involved in the 2006 Mumbai train bombings. These actions highlight the need to examine other groups that appear to be active only locally and determine whether they have the operational capability and strategic intention to undertake a more regional or global agenda.

A great deal of work by federal, state, and local governments has contributed to preventing another attack in the US Homeland since 9/11, but the threat, while somewhat lessened as a result of the successes in the global war on terror, remains(Van Duyn, 2009, p. 4).

The United States has taken measures to implement a plan to deal with events like the Mumbai attack that can easily overwhelm one single community. The events of September 11, 2001 and subsequent natural disasters solidified the need for emergency response to be coordinated through training and planning.

On February 28, 2003, the President (George W. Bush) issued Homeland Security Presidential Directive 5 (HSPD–5), "Management of Domestic Incidents," which directed the Secretary of Homeland Security to develop and administer a *National Incident Management System* (NIMS). This system provides a consistent nationwide template to enable Federal, State, tribal, and local governments, nongovernmental organizations (NGOs), and the private sector to work together to prevent, protect against, respond to, recover from, and mitigate the effects of incidents, regardless of cause, size, location, or complexity. This consistency provides the foundation for utilization of NIMS for all incidents, ranging from daily occurrences to incidents requiring a coordinated Federal response.

NIMS is based on the premise that utilization of a common incident management framework will give emergency management/response personnel a flexible but standardized system for emergency management and incident response activities. NIMS is flexible because the system components can be utilized to develop plans, processes, procedures, agreements, and roles for all types of incidents; it is applicable to any incident regardless of cause, size, location, or complexity. Additionally, NIMS provides an organized set of standardized operational structures, which is critical in allowing disparate organizations and agencies to work together in a predictable, coordinated manner (Federal Emergency Management Agency – National Incident Management System, 2003).

Fred Burton and Scott Stewart analyze and report on mitigating armed assaults for Stratfor. Based on their research, the factors that would help mitigate the impact of armed assaults are:

Reviewing the long history of armed assaults in modern terrorism shows that the tactic has forced many countries to develop specialized and highly trained forces to combat it. For example, it was the failed rescue attempt of the Israeli athletes in Munich that motivated the German government to create the elite Grenzschutzgruppe 9 (GSG 9), which would become one of the best counterterrorism forces in the world. The activities of the Provisional Irish Republican Army likewise helped shape the British Special Air Service into its role as an elite counterterrorism force.

When we view the entire spectrum of counterterrorism capabilities, however, the greatest gap in capability between Indian and European or Indian and American forces is not the gap between elite counterterrorism forces, but the gap at the level of the "cop on the street." This is significant because street cops are a critical line of defense against terrorists. The importance of street cops pertains not only to preventing attacks by collecting critical intelligence, noticing surveillance or other preoperational planning activity and questioning or arresting suspects, it also applies to the tactical response to armed attackers.

In the United States, local police would be aided during such a confrontation by the widespread adoption of "active shooter" training programs. Following a series of attacks including the highly publicized 1999 Columbine school shooting; it became apparent that the standard police tactic of surrounding an attacker and waiting for the SWAT team to go in and engage the shooter was not effective when the attacker was actively shooting people. As police officers waited outside for backup, additional victims were being killed. To remedy this, many police departments have instituted active shooter programs.

While the details of active shooter tactical programs may vary somewhat from department to department, the main idea behind them is that the active shooter must be engaged and neutralized as quickly as possible, not allowed to continue on a killing spree unopposed. Depending on the location and situation, this engagement sometimes is accomplished by a single officer or pair of officers with shoulder weapons. Other times, it is accomplished by a group of four or more officers trained to quickly organize and rapidly react as a team to locations where the assailant is firing.

Active shooter programs have proven effective in limiting the damage done by shooters. In several cases, including the March 2005 shooting at a high school in Red Lake, Minn. Today, many police departments not only have a policy of confronting active shooters, they also have provided their officers with training courses teaching them how to do so effectively. Such training could make a world of difference in a Mumbai-type attack, where there may not be sufficient time or resources for a specialized tactical team to respond.

Armed off-duty cops and civilians also can make a difference in armed attacks. In February 2007, for example, a heavily armed gunman who had killed five victims in the Trolley Square Mall in Salt Lake City was confronted by an off-duty police officer, who cornered the shooter and kept him pinned down until other officers could arrive and kill the shooter. This off-duty officer's actions plainly saved many lives that evening.

One other factor where European and American law enforcement officers have an edge over their Indian counterparts is in command, control and communications. Certainly, an armed assault is very chaotic no matter where it happens, but law enforcement agencies in the United States have a lot of experience in dealing with communications during complex situations. One such example is the February 1997 shootout in North Hollywood, where two heavily armed suspects wearing body armor engaged officers from the Los Angeles Police Department in a lengthy shootout. Following that incident, in which the responding officers' handguns and shotguns proved incapable of penetrating the suspects' heavy body armor, many police departments began to arm at least some of their units with AR-15s and other high-powered rifles. Ironically, the LAPD officers almost certainly would have welcomed a couple of old battle rifles like the Lee-Enfield in the gunfight that day (Burton & Stewart, 2009, p. 4).

Consistent with previous attacks around the world were some of the features of the target city: the country's financial capital, a densely populated, multicultural metropolis, and a hub for the media and entertainment industries. Obviously, these are also descriptions of New York City (Kelly, 2009).

The New York City Police Department (NYPD), which deployed a team of its officers to Mumbai after the attacks, has analyzed their findings and put forth initiatives to combat situations in order to mitigate an attack like the one in Mumbai. Recognizing how everyday technology, such as a cell phone, can play a very important part in a terrorist attack, they are examining ways to shut down cell phone calls in and around future hostage-taking scenarios without shutting down the communication devices of the police.

NYPD Commissioner Raymond W. Kelly told the Senate Committee on Homeland Security & Government Affairs that:

> We [the NYPD] raised the possibility that we might have to deploy our Emergency Service officers too thinly in the event of multiple simultaneous attacks such as those in Mumbai. We also recognized that if the attacks continued over many hours, we would need to relieve our special units with rested officers. In response to both challenges, we have decided to provide heavy weapons training to experienced officers in the Organized Crime Control Bureau. They will be able to play a supplementary role in an emergency. Similarly, we decided to use the instructors in our Firearms and Tactics Unit as another reserve force. Combined, these officers will be prepared to support our Emergency Service Unit in the event of a Mumbai-style attack (Kelly, 2009, p. 5).

The NYPD also discussed the complications of media coverage that could disclose law enforcement tactics in real time. This phenomenon is not new. In the past, police were able to defeat any advantage it might give hostage takers by cutting off power to the location they were in. However, the proliferation of handheld devices would appear to trump that solution. When lives are at stake, law enforcement needs to find ways to disrupt cell phones and other communications in a pinpointed way against terrorists who are using them (Kelly, 2009).

Leaders in the private sector have, at the very least, watched in horror as events like the Mumbai attacks cripple the industry they try to make successful. The hotel industry, in particular, has begun to meet in order to coordinate and cooperate with each other on issues of security.

In July 2008, security directors representing eight major hotel companies met for the first time in Washington and they discussed the chances that an attack against any hotel in a major city will have a deleterious effect on the city. It may have an even wider effect on the entire hotel industry. The objective of this summit "was to create a networking capability, share best practices, impart intelligence and ascertain how new technology can be used for physical security". In November 2008, together with the Department of Homeland Security (DHS) and the Alcohol Tobacco and Firearms Bureau, the group met again and explored ideas related to technology and physical barriers.

Marriott International Lodging studied the tactics that were employed before and during the hotel attacks in Mumbai. There were several lessons learned that are applicable to high-risk facilities:

(1) It was widely reported that the terrorists had been in the hotel for several months, at times posing as guests. Taking photographs and learning the layout of the hotel. *Awareness training should be conducted for employees to understand what may be suspicious and should be reported. We recently developed discipline specific posters to be placed in nonpublic areas of hotels, outlining suspicious activities to increase awareness. The housekeeper cleaning a room who finds diagrams of the hotel should report it. Where feasible, a covert surveillance detection team should be employed that is specifically trained to identify individuals conducting hostile surveillance.*

(2) It was also widely reported that when the police responded, they were not familiar with the building layout and plans provided to them were outdated and did not indicate where recent renovations had taken place. *Hotel management should develop a relationship with local authorities and conduct joint training exercises. Current Building plans with detailed photographs and video, where available, should be provided to authorities.*

(3) The Taj Hotel management reported that they had lowered the hotel's security measures due to information provided by intelligence agents. *Hotels should consider the feasibility of obtaining independent intelligence analysis capabilities. Security professionals should interpret intelligence and determine mitigation measures. Hotel managers in most cases are not trained in intelligence analysis and do not understand countermeasures necessary to deter or mitigate an attack.*

(4) The hotel lacked physical security measures which would have made it more difficult for the attackers. This included multiple entrances, lack of a sprinkler system, and open stairways. *Hotel design should consider security features early in the architectural planning stage* (Orlob, 2009, p. 4).

The general public can actually be the first line of defense when it comes to thwarting a terrorist attack. One of the organizations that cater to the public is a group called CAT Eyes or Community Anti-Terrorism Eyes. This organization is a worldwide program designed to "eliminate racism and terrorism through educating and empowering the average citizen," to "increase the awareness of the public through a passive Anti-terrorism program," and to educate every person on the "indicators of terrorism that they may encounter through daily activities". The goal of CAT Eyes is to train citizens nationwide to observe and report possible terrorist activities and their slogan is "Protecting America with Pride, Not Prejudice."

The CAT Eyes Program is an initiative to educate citizens in the civilian community to be effective in detecting potential terrorist activities. CAT Eyes gives US citizens a program that will empower them to fight back against terrorism. CAT Eyes specializes in industry-specific anti-terrorism training, web-based training programs, and anti-terrorism security assessments (http://cateyes.us).

Conclusion

In the end, a very small group of determined individuals with rifles, pistols, grenades, and improvised explosive devices were able to attack a few heavily populated locations in a city with a population exceeding 13 million people and bring that community to a standstill as they killed nearly 175 people and wounded almost 300.

It is important for the general public to regain a sense of normalcy as they recover from the attacks of terrorists. Less than one month after the attacks, the Taj Mahal and the Oberoi-Trident reopened their doors to guests. Some people question whether or not celebrations should be scaled down for New Year's Eve. Most celebrated life and remembered the victims. Amid tight security, the Mumbai Annual Marathon took place in January with nearly 35,000 people registered to participate. Thousands of runners, many with messages for peace scrawled on their T-shirts, participated in the marathon, Mumbai's first international sporting event and the biggest public gathering since the attacks in November (Chandran, 2009).

In the aftermath, heightened security in Mumbai has become the norm. The United States has taken steps to review and analyze the attacks in an effort to prevent the same situation from happening here. The lessons learned from the Mumbai attacks are used to anticipate how, when, and why the attacks of the future may occur, and whether or not they can be stopped or prevented. If and when the attacks do occur, these same lessons will be used to defeat the unrest by mounting overwhelming odds in the favor of law enforcement at every level.

As this chapter is being finalized, it has been a little over 3 months since the devastating attacks in Mumbai. Until very recently, as late as January 2009, the Pakistani government had denied any link to the Mumbai attacks and even denied the fact that the attackers were of Pakistani origins, despite overwhelming evidence to the contrary. In fact, on January 7, 2009, Pakistan's National Security Advisor Mahmud Ali Durrani confirmed that the surviving gunman, Muhammad Ajmal Kasab, is a Pakistani citizen. However, according to *The New York Times* article on the matter, "Hours later Mr. Durrani, a respected retired army general and former ambassador to the United States, was fired by the Pakistani prime minister for 'irresponsible behavior'" (i.e., acknowledging the fact that Kasab was Pakistani) (Oppel, 2009). The Times points out that this shows

how deeply the aftermath of the Mumbai siege has riven the country's fragile government as it comes to grips with what American officials have said is clear evidence that Pakistani nationals plotted the attack. ...Even as officials in Islamabad asserted that the country's premier spy agency, the Directorate for Inter-Services Intelligence, was trying to shed long-standing sympathies and ties to Islamist militants, evidence continued to grow that it was a militant group established by the agency two decades ago [Lashkar-e- Taiba] that carried out the Mumbai attacks (Oppel, 2009).

Finally, on February 12, 2009, Pakistan Interior Minister Rehman Malik acknowledged that "parts of the murderous Mumbai terror attacks were planned on its soil" and stated that six suspects were being held including someone who Malik referred to as a "main operator." (IBNLive.com) Although many have suggested a link between the terrorists, Lashkar-e-Taiba, and the Pakistan Inter-Services Intelligence (ISI) directorate, Malik stressed that the Pakistan state had nothing to do with the killings. Malik said, "This was an individual act, act of individuals or non-state actors. Their purpose was to create terror for their own motives. These motives need to be determined. Both India and Pakistan need to work it out" (IBNLive.com, 2009).

"There are nine bodies – all of them young men – that have been lying in a Mumbai hospital morgue since Nov. 29", Thomas L. Friedman (2009) writes in an Op-Ed piece in *The New York Times*, "They may be stranded there for a while because no local Muslim charity is willing to bury them in their cemetery. This is good news." The bodies are those of the nine terrorists killed in the Siege of Mumbai. Freidman goes on to explain that, although India has the second largest Muslim population in the world next to Indonesia, "the leadership of India's Muslim community has called them by their real name – 'murderers' not 'martyrs' – and is refusing to allow them to be buried in the main Muslim cemetery of Mumbai." Explaining this decision, Friedman writes:

"Indian Muslims are proud of being both Indian and Muslim, and the Mumbai terrorism was a war against both India and Islam," explained M.J. Akbar, the Indian-Muslim editor of Covert, an Indian investigative journal. "Terrorism has no place in Islamic doctrine. The Koranic term for the killing of innocents is 'fasad.' Terrorists are fasadis, not jihadis. In a beautiful verse, the Koran says that the killing of an innocent is akin to slaying the whole community. Since the ... terrorists were neither Indian nor true Muslims, they had no right to an Islamic burial in an Indian Muslim cemetery" (Friedman, 2009).

References

Addison, T., & Murshed, M. (2005). Transnational terrorism as a spillover of domestic disputes in other countries. *Defence and Peace Economics, 16*(2), 69–82.

Ahmed, S. (2008, December 3). *Painful recall: How Mumbai police nabbed terrorist.* Retrieved February 8, 2009, from ibnlive.in.com/news/painful-recall-how-mumbai-police-nabbed-terrorist/79642-3-1.html

Ali, S. A. (2009, January 9). *Cama Hospital attack plan dropped to avoid Muslim casualties.* Retrieved February 5, 2009, from www.timesofindia.indiatimes.com/articleshow/msid-3775003.cms

Anand, G., Pokharel, K., Rosenberg, M., Trofimov, Y., & Wonacott, P. (2008, December 1). *India Security Faulted as Survivors Tell of Terror.* Retrieved February 5, 2009, from online.wsj.com/article.SB122809281744967855.html

Anti-Defamation League. (n.d.). *Lashkar-e-Taiba: Terrorism and violence.* Retrieved February 23, 2009, from http://www.adl.org/main_Terrorism/Lashkar-e-Taiba.htm?Multi_page_sections=sHeading_3

Associated Press. (2008, November 29). *AP: Timeline of Mumbai terrorist attacks.* Retrieved February 5, 2009, from http://www.editorandpublisher.com/eandp/news/article_display.jsp?vnu_content_id=1003917726

BBC News. (2008, November 27). *BBC NEWS | South Asia | Mumbai rocked by deadly attacks.* Retrieved February 10, 2009, from http://news.bbc.co.uk/2/hi/south_asia/7751160.stm

Badam, R. T. (2008, November 27). *Mayhem in Mumbai: Terrorists besiege hotels, kill 119 in two days.* Retrieved January 7, 2009, from http://www.policeone.com/terrorism/articles/1760761-mayhem-in-Mumbai-terrorists-besiege-hotels-kill-119-in-two-days/

Blackwell, D. (2003). Colonial history and post-colonial context: the matrix of war and terrorism. *Psychodynamic Practice, 9*(3), 392–400.

Bose, S. (2003). *Kashmir: roots of conflict, paths to peace.* Cambridge, MA: Harvard University Press.

Bradsher, K. (2008, November 28). *Armed teams sowed chaos with precision – NYTimes.com.* Retrieved February 5, 2009, from http://www.nytimes.com/2008/11/29/world/asia/29tock.html

Burton, F., & West, B. (2008, December 3). *From the New York landmarks plot to the Mumbai attack | Stratfor.* Retrieved February 7, 2009, from http://www.stratfor.com/weekly/20081203_new_york_landmarks_plot_mumbai_attack

Burton, F., & Stewart, S. (2009, January 14). *Mitigating Mumbai | Stratfor.* Retrieved February 3, 2009, from http://www.stratfor.com/weekly/20090114_mitigating_mumbai

CNN.com. (2006, October 1). *India police: Pakistan spy agency behind Mumbai bombings.* Retrieved February 23, 2009, from http://www.cnn.com/2006/WORLD/asiapcf/09/30/india.bombs/

CNN-IBN. (2008, December 7). *Blunder at sea made Mumbai attack possible.* Retrieved February 5, 2009, from http://ibnlive.in.com/news/blunder-at-sea-made-mumbai-attack-possible/79910-3.html

Chandran, R. (2009, January 18). *Mumbai runs marathon for peace, in memory of victims.* Retrieved January 26, 2009, from www.reuters.com/article/lifestylemolt/idustre50homm2009118

FEMA–National Incident Management System. (2003, February 28). Retrieved February 2, 2009, from www.fema.gov/pdf/emergency/nims/NIMS_core.pdf

Friedman, T. L. (2009, February 18). *No Way, No How, Not Here.* Retrieved February 23, 2009, from //http://www.nytimes.com/2009/02/18/opinion/18friedman.html

Gandossy, T. (2008, November 30). *Taj Mahal hotel chairman: We had warning – CNN.com.* Retrieved February 10, 2009, from http://www.cnn.com/2008/WORLD/asiapcf/11/30/india.taj.warning/index.html

Henderson, B., & Nelson, D. (2008, December 7). *Gunmen had elite training 'from Pakistan'.* Retrieved December 26, 2008, from www.timesonline.co.uk/tol/news/world/asia/article5298993.ece

IBNlive. (2009, February 12). *26/11 dossier: Pakistan accepts India's blame.* Retrieved February 23, 2009, from ibnlive.in.com/news/2611-dossier-pakistan-accepts-indias-blame/85145-2.html

Jenkins, B. M. (2009, January 28). Testimony. *Terrorists can think strategically, senate homeland security & governmental affairs.* Retrieved February 10, 2009 from http://hsgac.senate.gov/public/_files/012809Jenkins.pdf

Kahn, J. (2008, December 9). *Mumbai terrorists relied on new technology for attacks – NYTimes.com.* Retrieved February 3, 2009, from http://www.nytimes.com/2008/12/09/world/asia/09mumbai.html

Kakade, R. (2008, November 30). *Mumbai officer, left for dead, rides with Mumbai gunmen.* PoliceOne.com. Retrieved January 7, 2009, from http://www.policeone.com/terrorism/articles/1761296-Mumbai-officer-left-for-dead-rides-with-Mumbai-gunmen/

Kalman, M., Weichselbaum, S., & Boyle, C. (2008, December 1). *Rabbi's pal heard voice of evil on phone during Mumbai massacre.* Retrieved December 29, 2008, from http://www.nydailynews.com/news/us_world/2008/11/30/2008-11-30_rabbis_pal_heard_voice_of_evil_on_phone_.html

Kelly, R. W. (2009, January 8). Hearing. *Lessons from the Mumbai terrorist attacks, senate committee on homeland security & governmental affairs.* Retrieved January 26, 2009 from http://hsgac.senate.gov/public/_files/010809Kelly.pdf

Livingstone, N. C. (2009). Mumbai: The lessons learned. What not to do-implications for the west. *DomPrep Journal, V*(1), 9.

Lloyd, J., & Nankivell, N. (2002). India, Pakistan, and the legacy of September 11th. *Cambridge Review of International Affairs, 15*(2), 269–287.

Maley, W. (2003). The 'War against terrorism' in South Asia. *Contemporary South Asia, 12*(2), 203–217.

Ministry of External Affairs India. (2009, January). *Dossier.* Retrieved January 15, 2009, from The Hindu: http://www.hindu.com/nic/dossier.htm

Oppel, R. A., & Masood, S. (2009). *Gunman in Mumbai siege a Pakistani, official says – NYTimes.com.* Retrieved February 23, 2009, from http://www.nytimes.com/2009/01/08/world/asia/08pstan.html

Orlob, A. (2009, January 28). Hearing. *Lessons from the Mumbai terrorists attacks, Part II, senate committee on homeland security & governmental affairs.* Retrieved February 10, 2009 from http://hsgac.senate.gov/public/_files/012809Orlob.pdf

Qadir, S. (2001). The concept of international terrorism: An interim study of South Asia. *The Round Table, 360,* 333–343.

Ranga, K. (2008, December 12). *LeT Commander Own al-Husseini.* Retrieved February 5, 2009, from www.mid-day.com/news/2008/dec/121208-Mumbai-terror-attack-Zaki-ur-Rehman-Lakhvi-Lashkar-e-Taiba-Mohammad-Ajmal-Amir-Qasab-POV.htm

Sakaal Times. (2009, January 9). *Mumbai Terror probe: IEDs made at same time by same person.* Retrieved February 4, 2009, from www.sakaaltimes.com/2009/01/09222201/Mumbai-terror-probe-IEDs-made.html

Simonsen, C. E., & Spindlove, J. R. (2006). *Terrorism today: The past, the players, the future (3rd ed.).* Alexandria, VA: Prentice Hall.

Simpson, A. (2008, December 1). *Mumbai attacks: Australian at Cafe Leopold 'held off attackers singlehandedly'.* Retrieved February 8, 2009, from http://www.telegraph.co.uk/news/worldnews/asia/india/3539024/Mumbai-attacks-Australian-at-Cafe-Leopold-held-off-attackers-singlehandedly.html

Spindlove, J. R., & Simonsen, C. E. (2009). *Terrorism today: The past, the players, the future* (4th ed.). Alexandria, VA: Prentice Hall.

Stern, J. (2000). Pakistan's Jihad culture. *Foreign Affairs, 79*(6), 115–127.

Telegraph.co.uk. (2008, November 26). *Video of CST terrorist attack.* Retrieved January 7, 2009, from link.brightcove.com/services/link/bcpid1137883380/bctid3706221001

The Hindu. Mumbai Terror attacks – Dossier of evidence. (n.d.). Retrieved January 15, 2009, from http://www.hindu.com/nic/dossier.htm

Times of India. (2008, November 30). *Why did NSG take 9 hrs to get there?.* Retrieved February 11, 2009, from timesofindia.indiatimes.com/articleshow/msid-3775003.cms

Trindal, J. W. (2009). The Mumbai attacks-lessons for the Western World. *DomPrep Journal, V*(1), 6.

Duyn, D. V. (2009, January 8). www.senate.gov. Hearing. *Senate Committee on Homeland Security & Governmental Affairs.* Retrieved February 5, 2009, from http://hsgac.senate.gov/public/files/010809VanDuyn.pdf

Worth, R. F., & Kumar, H. (2008, December 5). *Police foiled earlier plot against Mumbai – NYTimes.com.* Retrieved February 5, 2009, from http://www.nytimes.com/2008/12/06/world/asia/06mumbai.html

Zeenews.com. (2008, November 30). *Mumbai terror attack: A timeline.* Retrieved January 5, 2009, from http://www.zeenews.com/nation/2008-11-27/486894news.html

Chapter 18
Conclusions – A New Understanding of Counter-Terrorist/ism Response

M.R. Haberfeld

Introduction

This chapter's aim is to provide some templates for an effective counter-terrorism/t response for the multitude of agencies that deal with the terrorist threat and the phenomenon of terrorism on a daily basis or at minimum are charged with such responsibilities. As we provided a rather amorphous definition of terrorism in the introductory chapter of this book, we would like to translate the amorphous into practical by building on the lessons learned from the analysis of various terrorist events depicted in the chapters and also building upon this author's personal experience in the field of countering terrorist activities in urban environments.

As much can and should be learned from analyzing the past events and the responses, correct or incorrect, of the various responsible agencies, there is also much of a need to create some generic templates that would fit most if not all of the cases depicted in the chapters. Although much more should be learned from the information presented to the reader, we chose to emphasize three very basic and necessary areas, from which lessons must be learned. The three areas are risk management, creation of an intelligence file, and creation of contingency plans. These areas are not the only one that need to be addressed, but they appear as a common thread or theme that was missing in the response of all the agencies – prior, during, and in the aftermath of the various terrorist attacks. The order of presentation of these areas, from risk management through creation of the intel file to contingency planning, reflects the time line of terrorist activities that can and should be disrupted at the stage of planning and prior to the execution but if not possible we should be, at minimum, prepared to respond to the aftermath and not serve as yet another force multiplier for the Have Nots through the inaction or misguided actions of the Haves.

M.R. Haberfeld (✉)
Department of Law, Police Science and Criminal Justice Administration, John Jay College of Criminal Justice, New York, NY, USA
e-mail: mhaberfeld@jjay.cuny.edu

M.R. Haberfeld, A. von Hassell (eds.), *A New Understanding of Terrorism*,
DOI 10.1007/978-1-4419-0115-6_18, © Springer Science+Business Media, LLC 2009

Risk Management

According to Bodish (2002), risk management is a systematic and analytical process that considers the likelihood of various threats to assets of various nature: individuals, utilities, communications, and emergency services. The following goals should be taken into consideration while creating the risk management plan:

Identify actions that will reduce the risk.
Prepare to mitigate the consequences of the attack.

In order to achieve the above goals, one needs to take into consideration the following principles:

While risk generally cannot be eliminated, it can be reduced by enhancing protection from validated and credible threats.

Although many threats are possible, some are more likely to occur than others.

All assets are not equally critical.

It is upon each and every law enforcement and/or military organization to determine what are the critical structures and or individuals that need to be protected and prepare the risk management plan accordingly. In order to do so, one needs an effective risk management program that needs to be composed of three elements:

Threat assessment – which identifies and evaluates threats based upon various factors, including the following:

- Terrorists' capability
- Terrorists' intentions
- The likelihood of a potential attack
- Lethality and potential impact of a terrorist attack

Vulnerability assessment – which is composed of a process that identifies weaknesses that might be exploited and suggests options to eliminate or mitigate those weaknesses.

Criticality assessment – which provides a basis for prioritizing through a systematic identification and evaluation of organization's assets based upon a variety of factors, which are the following:

- The importance of its mission
- The importance of its function
- Whether people are at risk
- The significance of a structure or a system

The most critical exercise in creating an effective risk management plan will be based on a thorough analysis of the probability levels of an undesired event. Here we can learn much from the US Department of Defense (DOD) that provides us with the following template:

Probability levels of an undesired event	
Probability level	Specific event
A. Frequent	Likely to occur frequently
B. Probable	Will occur several times
C. Occasional	Likely to occur sometimes
D. Remote	Unlikely, but possible
E. Improbable	Very likely

No matter what kind of terrorist event a given agency is trying to prepare for, based on its thoroughly gathered and maintained intelligence, the above template could guide the customized response like a perfectly functioning barometer.

Building an Intelligence File

One of the recommendations that appear to repeat itself in many chapters is a thorough and well-organized intelligence gathering capability, which is a goal that can be achieved basically by any organization if they are willing to follow the following steps, as outlined below, based on this author's own experience in creating intelligence files as well as the knowledge attained from visiting numerous police forces, some of which excel in the art of intelligence gathering.

Step I

The consideration prior to creating an intel file is to decide the pros and cons of using a hard copy – paper file versus a computerized version. The considerations will include

- Security considerations
- access – portability
- sharing capabilities – interoperability
- technical problems
- archiving
- tampering

Security considerations will include decisions with regard to

- open access
- need to know basis
- misplacement
- access verification

- disaster vulnerability
- replication options

Access – portability will include the decisions with regard to

- volume – size
- links
- applications
- stand alone

Sharing capabilities will include decisions with regard to

- open access
- need to know basis
- misplacement
- access verification
- disaster vulnerability
- replication options

Technical problems will include decisions with regard to

- matching systems
- security considerations
- man-made disasters
- natural disasters

Archiving will include decisions with regard to

- power loss
- interoperability in place but not utilized
- interoperability in place locally but not internationally (Interpol, Europol)
- technical problems overseas due to man-made or natural disasters

Tampering will include decisions with regard to

- space
- access
- security
- liability
- links

After resolving and/or adjusting to the above problems, the agency can move the next step, which will include the actual creation of the intelligence file.

Step II. Creating an Intel File

The creation of the intel file is a complicated process that is easily compromised if one does not follow the principles outlined below. There should be no shortcuts in this area as one omission will render the other efforts incomplete, irrelevant, and worst than anything – misleading.

Information to be included or to be gathered include

- name(s), a.k.a
- d.o.b. – including all the fake ones
- nationality – including all the citizenships (real and forged ones)
- physical descriptions – including past, present, disguised, and projections
- affiliations – past, current, projected
- associations (professional) – including past, present, projected
- associations (personal) – including past, present, projected
- associations (peripheral) – including past, present, projected
- family members – including past (through divorce or death) current, and future (including not formalized)
- all the other Intel gathered through informants, surveillance, wire tapes, reports, financial info, etc.
- criminal record – including past, present, projected
- finger prints, DNA samples, photographs, samples of handwriting
- educational background
- hobbies
- list of special skills and expertise
- ideological affiliation/orientation
- religious affiliation
- contact addresses – including past, present, and projected
- travel patterns – including past, present, and projected
- media related info from web sites, newspapers, books, TV appearances, etc.
- any and all other info available re: the suspect

Create Links (A)

- Duplicate all the info available from other files re: the suspect.
- Create duplicates of all the info that makes references to other suspects and if needed create new files.
- Create a linkage system that will refer the investigator to the other/relevant files.

Create a Backup System

- E-system.
- Paper system.
- Store additional set in another location, both for the electronic and the paper systems.

Create Security Access System

- Need to know the basis – design levels of security clearance system (for local international access)
- Design accountability system
- Design identification/signature system
- Design a secure handling of the info system

Create Links (B)

- Identify other sources of info that should be consulted, periodically, for the updating purposes (within your organization – i.e., Organized Crime Bureau, Narcotics).
- Identify list of organizations, web sites, and other entities that could/should be contacted periodically for updating and other relevant assistance (i.e., Homeland Security – specific offices, Interpol, Europol – specific offices).

Develop Personal Relationship

- With the relevant personnel in your organization
- With the relevant personnel in other organizations at a local, state, federal, and international level
- With CIs (Confidential Informants) – past, current, potential

Crisis Preparation

Another important lesson we can learn from the chapters' analysis is the need to create a contingency plan while preparing for the next crisis – crisis preparation approaches are still in dire need of revisions. Regardless of the size of the responding agency, each one can customize and prepare accordingly to its resources (Homeland Security, 2008). Although the NIMS or the National Incident Management System was created in the United States and customized (at least in theory through the creation of CIMS – City Incident Management Systems) by various city agencies, one cannot ignore the very basic principles that need not to be overlooked just because a standardized training is being offered, a training that fails to take into consideration the various bureaucratic and logistical aspects that plague police agencies around the country and the world.

Volumes have been written about the proper emergency response planning by experts in the field like Erickson (1999) and Maniscalco and Christen (2002) but they are precisely what they are, voluminous in content, although excellent, too hard to digest for an average law enforcement agency and even for the military, just too many details that entail too many resources. Maybe the real key to the new understanding of the phenomenon of terrorism and the counter-terrorist response is simplicity, a few simple and customized approaches that will require much personal dedication and awareness but not necessarily that many expensive resources.

Use of the following, generic, template can supplement the ideas already in place in some agencies and maybe provide yet another insight into how things need to be implemented, with the realistically grounded disclaimer that all contingency plans should be created based on the projected severity levels of the undesired events and these considerations are frequently politically induced and not operationally sound:

Step I. Immediate reaction to a terrorist attack

- Protect the public
- Save lives
- Prevent additional attacks
- Preserve the crime scene
- Identify the perpetrators

Step II. Requirements to follow Step I

- Expeditious and comprehensive departmental response.
- Head of the department or other high-ranking officer must assume responsibility for the operation.
- Command center has to be established – away from potential targets.

Step III. Creation of contingency plans (CPs)

- The most basic form of crisis preparation but very realistically driven and outlined to the smallest detail.
- Outlines how a department intends to respond to a crisis situation – based on various scenarios.
- Explains the roles of agency employees.
- Identifies the chain of command – in case of declining availability of ranking officers.
- If a number of CPs exist – for different events – they must be similar in structure and same roles and tasks assigned to people involved in each CP.
- Each employees must review the CP.
- Employees must be encouraged to give their input about the plan.
- Review the CP with other agencies that experienced similar events and/or are preparing similar CPs.

Step IV. Dealing with the problems

- CPs become dated quickly.
- Employees retire, resign, are reassigned.
- Availability of the equipment and command center and other work sites can change.
- CPs do not provide an adequate and relevant solution – re: magnitude of the possible terrorist incidents (like the Mumbai attack in 2008).

Step V. Creating solutions to the problems

1. Someone in a ranking position is designated as the CRISIS COORDINATOR who will

   - review the CP on a regular basis
   - at least every 6 months
   - be aware of all personnel movements
   - visit all the locations mentioned in the plan
   - be aware of major equipment purchases

2. Responsibility linked to a position rather than an individual.
3. Place the CP into the agency's computer network – for access of all the employees.
4. Mutual-aid agreements – joint Command Center.

Step VI. Training for the preparedness

The tabletop exercise
   - Pros and cons – which need to be identified by each and every agency
Full-field training exercise
   - Pros and cons – which need to be identified by each and every agency

Step VII. Evacuation plans

   - Review the evacuation plans on a regular basis.
   - At least every 6 months.
   - Be aware of all structural/ construction changes.
   - Visit all the locations mentioned in the plan.
   - At least every 6 months.
   - Coordinate with other agencies – inside and outside your city's jurisdiction.

Whether we manage the possible risk from a lone wolf or a well-organized terrorist group, the processes in place or the ones that should be in place are the same, from risk assessment and analysis through the composition of the intel file to the creation of the contingency plans. Although the scope and intensity of the consequences of the various terrorist attacks perpetrated by Timothy McVeigh or the terrorists in Mumbai may have varied, the principles of preparing for such attacks, ahead of time, cannot be overemphasized nor can we afford to be in an ad hoc response mode based on some miscalculated or ignored risks. Learning about the response of various agencies around the country and the world should provide the reader with more specific ideas that may be utilized in specific circumstances or customized to the local realities. One principle should always guide the responders or the ones who outline the policies for the responding agencies – there is always something to be learned – from the past, the present, and the future, and we should never be complacent with what we know on any given day – it is never sufficient.

The last words concluding this volume will represent yet another lesson learned by this author from what others have said and done:

It Is Our Duty to Be Prepared –

"All forms of terrorism have been spreading because everyone is ready to capitulate before them. But as soon as some firmness is shown, terrorism can be smashed".

Aleksander Solzhenitsyn

References

Bodisch, R. J. (2002, February). Combating terrorism: The importance of risk Management. *Crime & Justice International, 18*(59), 5–6; 22–23.

Erickson, P. A. (1999). *Emergency Response Planning for Corporate and Municipal Manager*. San Diego: Academic Press.

Homeland Security. (2008, December). National incident management system. Retrieved January 23rd, 2009 from http://www.fema.gov/pdf/emergency/nims/NIMS_core.pdf

Maniscalso, P. M., & Christen, H. T. (2002). *Understanding Terrorism and Managing the Consequences*. Upper Saddle River, NJ: Prentice Hall.

http://www.defenselink.mil/policy/sections/policy_offices/hd/assets/downloads/dcip/Studies/Other/CIAOCriticalInfrastructureVulnerabilityOct98.pdf

Index

Note: The letters f, n and t following the locators refer to figures, notes and tables respectively

CPSIA information can be obtained
at www.ICGtesting.com
Printed in the USA
BVOW09s1033180318
510886BV00008B/232/P